Wissenschaftliche Untersuchungen
zum Neuen Testament · 2. Reihe

Herausgeber / Editor
Jörg Frey (Zürich)

Mitherausgeber / Associate Editors
Friedrich Avemarie (Marburg)
Markus Bockmuehl (Oxford)
Hans-Josef Klauck (Chicago, IL)

296

Moral Language
in the New Testament

The Interrelatedness of Language and Ethics
in Early Christian Writings

Kontexte und Normen neutestamentlicher Ethik/
Contexts and Norms of New Testament Ethics

Volume II

Edited by
Ruben Zimmermann and
Jan G. van der Watt

in Cooperation with
Susanne Luther

Mohr Siebeck

Ruben Zimmermann is Professor for New Testament Studies at the Johannes Gutenberg-University of Mainz.

Jan G. van der Watt is Professor for New Testament Studies at the Radboud-University of Nijmegen/NL.

Susanne Luther is currently research assistent (wissenschaftliche Mitarbeiterin) at the Chair of New Testament Studies of Professor Zimmermann at the Johannes Gutenberg-University of Mainz.

ISBN 978-3-16-150354-2

ISSN 0340-9570 (Wissenschaftliche Untersuchungen zum Neuen Testament, 2. Reihe)

Die Deutsche Nationalbibliothek lists this publication in the Deutsche Nationalbibliographie; detailed bibliographic data are available on the Internet at *http://dnb.d-nb.de*.

The book was printed by Laupp & Göbel in Nehren on non-aging paper and bound by Buchbinderei Nädele in Nehren.

Printed in Germany.

Foreword

This volume is the result of a "Humboldt-Kolleg" conference that was held at the University of Pretoria (South Africa) in September 2008 and was supported by the Alexander von Humboldt-Foundation (Germany). It was part of the joint research project of Jan van der Watt and Ruben Zimmermann on Ethics in the New Testament, which was undertaken in 2008 and supported by a Feodor Lynen-Fellowship of the Alexander von Humboldt-Foundation.

This project is to be seen in the context of other research projects by the editors on Ethics in the Ancient World at the Universities of Mainz (Center for Ethics in Antiquity and Christianity) and Nijmegen. It represents the second volume in the series "Context and Norms of New Testament Ethics".

Among the various aspects of an "implicit ethics" in Early Christian writings the important role of language has often been underestimated. This volume specifically focuses on the relationship between language and ethical expression. The participants were asked to consider at least three aspects related to moral language: the intratextual level, the intertextual level and the extratextual level.

We would like to extend our gratitude to the Alexander von Humboldt-Foundation for their support and the University of Pretoria for providing the facilities.

We would also like to thank Elise Henning for practical arrangements during the conference. Jutta Nennstiel and Susanne Luther were responsible for the editing of this volume and deserve our sincere gratitude. Thanks also to Almuth Peiper and Charlotte Seiwerth, who helped with the indices.

Jan G. D. van der Watt
Ruben Zimmermann

Mainz, July 2010

Table of Contents

III. Pauline Literature

IV. Later New Testament and Early Christian Writings

V. Hermeneutical Questions

Moral Language in the New Testament

An Introduction

RUBEN ZIMMERMANN / SUSANNE LUTHER

Morality requires language. Language carries ethical meaning.

These two basic statements probably find general consensus, but questions arise as soon as the interrelatedness of language and morality is specified. This volume proposes to address this problem and shed more light upon morality and language in the New Testament. In more concrete terms the following questions may be addressed: How do Ethics and Language belong together? Indeed, do they belong together at all? Does language have a special ethical value – or is morality related solely to particular contents without being influenced by means of the linguistic medium in which it is communicated? Is there a certain form or genre of "moral language" – is, for instance, the imperative grammatical form the only way to express an ethical statement? Or can any grammatical form, or any form of language be used to communicate a sense of ought, or moral obligation?

1. Ethics and Language – Interactions

1.1 Ethics and Language – Two Contradictory Statements

Putting the introductory questions into two contradictory statements, the subject of this volume may be defined with sharper clarity: 1.There is no language of ethics! 2. Language has always been ethical!

"There is no language of ethics!" This first statement is based on a distinction between language and ethics. "It is clear that ethics cannot be put into words. Ethics is transcendental." By using such formulations in his *Tractatus logico-philosophicus*,[1] the early Wittgenstein expresses his conviction that statements must be logical and verifiable in order to satisfy scientific requirements. Ethical statements require no such logic or verifiability. Instead, they are based on non-rational value systems. Wittgenstein said, "In the world everything is as it is, and everything happens as it does

---

[1] See Ludwig Wittgenstein, *Tractatus Logico-philosophicus* (Suhrkamp-Edition 12; Frankfurt am Main: Suhrkamp, 1963); cf. idem, *Tractatus Logico-Philosophicus* (trans. David F. Pears and Brian F. McGuinness; London: Routledge, 1971), 6.421, 147.

happen: in it no value exists – and if it did exist, it would have no value. If there is any value that does have value, it must lie outside the whole sphere of what happens and is the case." (6.41) "Hence also there can be no ethical propositions. Propositions cannot express anything higher." (6.42)

Questions related to values must be differentiated from propositions. Thus, in the end, language is immaterial for ethics – such are the conclusions of linguistic philosophy.

Having a brief look at various works on "The Ethics of the New Testament," one might get the impression that this assessment also largely reflects the opinions of the exegetes. Schrage speaks of Jesus' "eschatological" ethics or "The Christological ethics of Paul;"[2] in *The Moral World*, Meeks speaks of "social setting" and "Christian communities;"[3] Marxsen searches for the origins of so-called "Christian ethics" among the various "ethics of the New Testament."[4] And these are only a few prominent representatives. The language and the linguistic form of ethics is not considered on its own because ethics relate completely to particular contents of individual writings, to one sociologically-definable community situation or to statements of faith or a theological concept in its entirety.

"Language has always been ethical!" This second statement advocates the identification of language and ethics. This is clearly supported by the theme of this volume (and the corresponding conference), *Moral Language in the New Testament,* though not yet endorsed entirely. This title is an allusion to an epoch-changing work on meta-ethics – namely, Richard Mervyn Hare's book, first published in 1952, *The Language of Morals,*[5] in which he intends to prove, in the context of analytical-philosophical issues, that moral statements do indeed possess logic – or in other words – that there are ethical statements. Ethics makes use of particular statements that should be analysed with regard to their logic and structure.

However, our second statement goes far beyond Hare. Ethics do not simply make use of linguistic statements; ethics occur in and through language. We act simply by speaking – this is an approximation of Austin's

---

[2] See Wolfgang Schrage, *The Ethics of the New Testament* (trans. David E. Green; Minneapolis, Minn.: Fortress, 1988). In a similar way also Eduard Lohse, *Theologische Ethik des Neuen Testaments* (Stuttgart: Kohlhammer, 1988) including an analysis of the traditional background.

[3] See Wayne A. Meeks, *The Moral World of the First Christians* (LEC 6; Philadelphia: Westminster Press, 1986), here chapter 1: "The Social Setting" (19-39); chapter 4: "The Christian Communities" (97-123).

[4] See Willi Marxsen, *"Christliche" und christliche Ethik im Neuen Testament* (Gütersloh: Gütersloher Verlag, 1989).

[5] See Richard M. Hare, *The Language of morals* (Oxford: Oxford University Press, 1964).

well-known statement, "how to do things with words"[6]. Thus, completely independent of particular contents, structures and faith statements, language has always had an ethical dimension, related as it is to human action, to human action; language itself is a part of ethics.

1.2 A Linguistic Turn in New Testament Ethics?

The purpose of this volume is to find a pathway between these two extremes: the strict separation between language and ethics on the one hand, and their identification on the other. We would like to formulate a middle position that reflects the fundamental conviction providing the initial motivation for the Humboldt-Kolleg – that *the ethics of the New Testament is linguistically constituted; it occurs in and through language.* When we think about actions and their motives in the New Testament, and then want to communicate about this, we need language. To be precise, we are concerned here with meta-ethics – reflection upon ethics. However, we are not concerned only with the "language of morals," or more precisely, with the meta-ethical question of the meaning of language in an "ethics of the New Testament" approach; instead, we are concerned with "moral language" in an extended sense, with linguistic statements in the New Testament that possess an ethical dimension in both context and effect.

Regardless of whether we are talking about the New Testament and its moral claims in present-day ethical discourse, or whether we ourselves turn to the statements of the New Testament that fulfil an ethical dimension on the level of a narrative or a letter, we are always dealing with language. The ethical dimension is accessible to us only by means of language – or more precisely – by means of the text. Thus, we have no other option: if we turn to the New Testament with ethical questions, then we turn to texts. Even if we concentrate our ethical reflection on such main ideas as "love" and "justice," on the factual or fictional communicative situation, or on the sociological question of the "lived ethos," we must always begin with texts and must involve them in ethical reflection.

1.3 Three Dimensions of the Interrelatedness

Apart from many interesting insights from the field of meta-ethics, we will not narrow our subject to a certain question of moral philosophy. Investigating moral language in the New Testament must serve to foster a better understanding of ethics in the New Testament in general. According to our point of view, three overlapping aspects can be distinguished, which may be helpful for the interpretation of concrete New Testament texts: an intra-

---

[6] John L. Austin, *How to do Things with Words* (Cambridge, Mass.: Harvard University Press, 1962).

textual level (linguistic and analytic philosophical methods: syntactical form, style and logic), a textual and intertextual level (form criticism, discourse analysis) and an extra-textual level (speech-act analysis; rhetorical criticism; reader-response criticism).

a) Intra-textual level (linguistic and analytic philosophical methods)
On a first level, we can ask which aspects of syntactical form, style and logic are used in ethical statements. As Hare has pointed out, there are several forms of imperatives; but imperatives are not the only form of moral language. There are implicit imperatives; there is the complex difference between "is-" and "ought to/should-"sentences and between prescriptive and descriptive moral language; there are narrative, metaphoric, ironic texts, etc., which convey morality within their specific style.

Why do we consider a certain text "ethical"? Where does the ethical quality of a statement come from? Which linguistic devices are used to express ethics in the New Testament writings? All of these questions surface in an intra-textual reading.

b) Textual and intertextual level (form criticism, discourse analysis)
The form of a certain text unit (on a macro- and micro-level) influences its meaning and moral quality. We can find a variety of genres in the New Testament, and each of them creates ethics in a certain way (e.g. parable, virtue list, hardship catalogue, household-code). According to genre theory, a form can only be found by comparison with other texts; moral texts are part of an intertextual system. However, intertextuality cannot be tied solely to genre. Ethical texts are – as any other texts – built within the tension of reception and production, and include "tradition" as well as "innovation."

In which way does the genre of the text influence its ethical meaning? Which pretexts and intertexts are part of the ethical statements, and in which way does the text refer to them (e.g. the law)?

c) Extra-textual level (but still in relation to the text – speech act analysis, rhetorical criticism, reader-response criticism)
Texts are part of communication. As already Bühler and later Searle and Austin have pointed out, we do things with words. Texts are part of practical ethics and play a formative role in the ethos of a community.

What ethical impact did texts have, and currently do texts have, on their readers? Which linguistic and rhetorical style is used to connect with the addressees? Why do we consider a text powerful or polemical? Can we speak of an implicit ethical subject within the text?

Of course the separation of these sections is primarily a heuristic effort, and the overlapping of various aspects is evident in interpreting concrete texts. However, all contributions refer to at least one of these aspects; while some concentrate on one, others try to deal with two or three aspects.

2. The Contributions

The first three contributions deal with methodological and conceptional aspects. In "Ethics in the New Testament and Language: Basic Explorations and Eph 5:21–33 as Test Case," *Ruben Zimmermann* maps the field of language and ethics. He expounds on the distinction between "ethos/morals" and "ethics" and focuses on two aspects of New Testament ethics in particular: on "ethos remembered" (the ethos of a group rooted in the behaviours and rituals, put down in texts of certain genres, which allow the communication and reflection in order to exert an identity-building function) and on "implicit ethics" (as opposed to ethics as a systematic-theoretical examination of the lived ethos). Investigating the "implicit ethics" of the New Testament Scriptures is argued to involve the examination of the norms and maxims for action mentioned in the text, their traditional and contemporary context, the logic (i.e. the hierarchy) of values, the ethical argument and structure of the motives, the carrier of ethical judgements or moral agent, the concrete ethos corresponding to or contradicting the ethical argument and the field of application. First, however, it involves the analysis of the linguistic forms in which ethical statements are presented. As New Testament ethics are set down in textual form, the examination must focus on textuality. Taking up the three levels of interrelatedness between ethics and language (i.e. intra-textual, intertextual and extra-textual level) Zimmermann offers some examples for the different forms of ethical language in the New Testament: the imperative mood and the internal structure or logic of the ethical statement are discussed on the intra-textual level, form and genre on the inter-textual level, and speech-act analysis of language on the extra-textual level. Finally, the house-hold table of Eph 5:21–33 is taken as a test case on which the merit of the language based approach on ethics is demonstrated, and the statement that ethics is based on language is corroborated from the analysis of the text.

Etienne de Villiers, in "Defining Morality in Christian Ethics and the Study of New Testament Ethics," makes a case against a one-sided and exclusive reliance on analytical moral philosophy. In defining morality in both the study of the moral language of the New Testament and Christian ethics, he advocates taking as the starting point a comprehensive account of the New Testament on the nature and shape of the original conceptions of Christian morality in the early Christian church. Based on the observation that New Testament scholars tend to turn to analytical moral philosophy in order to attain value-free, objective, universally valid concepts and distinctions as analytical tools for the study of the moral language or morality of Christians, De Villiers provides an overview of the meta-ethical discussion in English analytical philosophy on the nature and definition of moral language. He thus refers especially to C. L. Stevenson, R. M. Hare and G. E. Moore and their quest for a purely formal definition of morality, as well as to opposed approaches of G. J. Warnock, W. K. Frankena and especially K. Bayertz, who denies the feasibility of providing a universally valid, objective definition, but regards the endeavor as historically and culturally multifaceted, variable and never neutral. In conclusion, De Villiers states that the diversity and divergence in defining morality in analytical moral philosophy should advise New Testament scholars and Christian ethicists against attempting to formulate a neutrally descriptive definition of morality, which is then applied to Christian morality or the moral language in the New Testament. His suggested approach finds its point of departure in the New Testament texts, which apart from providing guidelines for action, include a comprehensive vision of the Christian life.

Sean Freyne's essay, "In Search of Identity: Narrativity, Discipleship and Moral Agency," investigates the significance of the relationship between agency and action for moral discourse and concentrates on an intertextual reading of Mark and John, focusing on their treatment of Jesus' disciples from the perspective of the prescriptive and descriptive role of narrative in the development of human self-identity. Freyne's methodology is based on the approach of Paul Ricœur's model of selfhood with the tension between *Idem* and *Ipse*, permanence and change, self and the other. Freyne suggests that the acquired character traits of the disciples as Galilean fishermen contributed to their failure to understand and appreciate the possibilities and challenges for a new selfhood that Jesus was offering them. The Johannine notion of "being true to one's word" converges with Ricœur's model of permanence over time once the *Ipse* has been freed from the constraints of the *Idem* and implies the role of the other in forming moral identity. The contrast between the Markan and Johannine representation of the disciples that emerges in their narratives, despite their conformity concerning the *imitatio Christi,* is dependent on differences in their perception of the main character, Jesus. Freyne argues that in order for this narrative approach to identity-formation to lead to a narrative approach to Christian ethics, the stress of New Testament ethics must be put on the agent, rather than the content, in order to discern how a Christian self-identity is constructed and maintained. The consideration of the *Idem-Ipse* tension is presented as a fruitful way to explore this issue, with the interesting result that Christian moral agency is formed in different ways and with different consequences.

The next section of the volume focuses on moral language in the Jesus tradition and the Gospels. As the title promises, *Karl-Wilhelm Niebuhr*'s contribution, "Jesus' 'Conception of Man' as an Expression of his 'Ethics,'" explores the relation between Jesus' anthropology and the expression of his "ethics" as manifested in his ministry. By way of interpreting the contours of the ministry and the person of Jesus, i.e. by understanding the narrative complexes as an expression of an ethical intention, Jesus' ethical orientation is determined. Niebuhr identifies three contexts of Jesus' ministry, which are definitive for his conception of man: the scope of creation (God as Creator and Father), the scope of Israel (the promises of the restoration; the 12 disciples as representing the tribes of Israel) and the scope of the Eschaton (impending judgement). From these bases his ethics develop, which are generally based upon the assumption of God's beneficial will for his people and the modelling of their attitude of love founded upon God's example. The fulfilment of God's will is even represented in the final judgement, which constitutes the primary loving objective of ethical admonition and warning. Jesus' ministry addresses first of all those marginalized from society with the effect of giving them life, which centres in the gift of eschatological communion with God and is characterized by the essential aspect of its surrender to the kingdom of God. This is regarded a main principle of Jesus' ethics: the story of his life of austerity and deprivation, and his death on the cross, tell of the surrender of his life for others. Through his example, the principle of surrendering one's life was instilled into Christian ethics – an ethics of mimesis. Thus the narrated ministry of Jesus text-pragmatically has the function of an implicit impulse for action, forms a "role model ethics," which is theologically loaded through the narrative structures of the Jesus story.

Matthias Konradt's main thesis in his contribution, "'Whoever humbles himself like this child …': The Ethical Instruction in Matthew's Community Discourse (Matt 18) and Its Narrative Setting," is that the ethics of the Gospel of Matthew cannot be sufficiently comprehended by just considering the passages which explicitly convey ethical teaching and instruction. Matthew rather conveys his ethics by constructing a narrative world, through which the foundations of his worldview are articulated, within which his ethical convictions are embedded and from which they gain their plausibility. This is illustrated by an analysis of Matt 18, read within the wider context of the communication process that encompasses the entire gospel. The analysis demonstrates that the ethical instruction – Jesus impresses an ethos of humility or lowliness on his disciples – is closely linked to the narrative context, as the thematic focus of the Christological story constitutes the basis for, substantiates and informs the ethical statements in this chapter. Matt 18:1–5 is presented as an example for conveying strong ethical imperatives by means of descriptive language, thus establishing the ethical guideline of the following discourse. This strategy in turn corroborates the proposition through illustrative metaphorical and parabolic language, which allows the reader to interact in reaction to rhetorical questions or through identification with the *personae dramatis*, thus conveying ethical guidance. Konradt demonstrates the importance of relating Matthew's ethical admonitions with the Gospel story: the evangelist's ethical convictions form an integral part of his worldview, which in turn is unfolded in the narration of a story. This is why the Christological perspective, his notion of God and Jesus (as merciful shepherd) and his anthropological presupposition that human beings are dependent on God's mercy constitute the foundation of his ethical argumentation.

Jan G. van der Watt, in "Ethics through the Power of Language: Some Explorations in the Gospel according to John," examines the influence of language on the dynamics of ethics and the way the author of John's Gospel uses language to attain his ethical goals. The ethical system of John is characterized as primarily relational and grounded in Christology; i.e. actions are embedded in identity, and ethics are inextricably linked with accepting the faith in Jesus. Hence, ethical material is even to be found in the performative text, John 20:30–31, which formulates a central purpose of the Gospel: to lead the readers to faith in Jesus or to strengthen their faith through the words of the Gospel. John 8 serves as the basic text for an analysis of the ethical function of language in John. Among the linguistic techniques employed, the use of ethical topics or particular words and combinations of words (phrases and propositions) with ethical meanings are mentioned. Likewise, the ethical implications of literary features such as irony and contextual-semantic influences upon the meaning of a word, of breaks in the structure of the argument (open spaces, discontinuous and conflicting dialogue), of proverbial statements and of characterization, vilification of characters, forensic language and imagery are explored. It becomes clear that a large variety of not specifically ethical linguistic devices are employed to support ethical argumentation in giving the text an informative and simultaneously performative nature, serving to advance the Gospel's communicative goal(s). Thus, although the close connection between form and content is evident, it is the content (conveyed through the vocabulary used), not the linguistic or rhetorical strategy, which functions as the decisive element informing the ethical dimension of a text. However, in order to identify ethical language, the pertinent "language codes" are to be taken into consideration, as communication is itself based upon social conventions.

In his essay, "As the Father has sent me, I send you: Towards a missional-incarnational Ethos in John 4," *Kobus Kok* demonstrates that Jesus embodied a missional-incarnational ethos, which is conveyed through the inclusive moral language of the Johannine narratives, and which implicitly formulates the imperative ethical paradigm for his followers to imitate: Jesus' unconditional love-ethics in their continued mission. Kok employs the narrative of Jesus and the Samaritan woman (John 4) to illustrate how ethics and the motivation of a particular conduct (ethos) is conveyed through narrative. Through the construction of a virtual reality, the actual world, replete with conventional perceptions and norms, can be changed by constructing a new worldview and thus establishing a new basis of understanding and motivation. In John soteriology implies re-socialization and partaking in a new social reality; the new common identity of the followers of Jesus becomes now the new basis for their conduct, their ethos. In linking John 4 to the Johannine sending motif and the imperative of the missional ethos of Jesus' followers (John 20:21), Kok integrates the micro-narrative of the Samaritan woman within the ethical dimension of the macro-narrative of the Gospel, thus arguing that John 4 implies the imperative of the embodiment of a Christ-like ethos, which is based on the understanding of God's loving mission in the world, and that Jesus' mission is by implication the mission of his followers, who are to imitate Jesus' love-ethics in their continuing mission. This ethical dimension of mission is explained as a reaction to the linguistic statement of John 20:21 and is characterized as an 'MRI-ethos:' missional, relational and incarnational. Kok presents the missional-incarnational ethos conveyed through the narrative in John 4 as an imperative for the church's self-understanding, as a missional-incarnational spirituality and ethos results in a dynamic missional movement.

As the Pauline Letters are concerned with concrete problems in the life of the congregations the linguistic devices Paul uses to appeal to his audience are of special interest. The following section wants to address the Pauline Writings, the first two essays in a more general way, the following by focussing on one special metaphor ("putting on Christ"), on one particular writing (Philemon), and on one specific text (2 Cor 3).

Hermut Löhr, in "The Exposition of Moral Rules and Principles in Pauline Letters: Preliminary Observations on Moral Language in Earliest Christianity," analyses the language of the Pauline letters with a view to its linguistic and rhetorical means of conveying moral instruction. The description of the moral language, the exposition of arguments, the terms and categories employed and the rhetorical techniques applied, e.g. of the manner of linguistic presentation of ethical statements, are presented as essential for understanding the relation between theology and ethics in

Pauline thought. Repetition and extension, generalization, the argumentative application of general and abstract (elementary and conventional) norms and virtues or theological concepts are identified as rhetorical means that serve the purpose of conveying basic moral rules and principles. The use of general and abstract terminology in Paul's moral language has its counterweight in the use of personification, where the ethical discourse is transferred from the level of authoritative instruction and obedience to set norms to the level of recommendation and self-responsibility and personal commitment resulting from personal choice. The reference to his apostolic authority and presentation of himself or Christ as an ethical example is an important strategy of Pauline argumentative persuasion. Moreover, the introduction of gradations of the general rules discussed, as well as the recognition of a concept of moral progress in Pauline literature, counters any oversimplification evoked through generalization. Löhr's contribution illustrates that an analysis of the moral language used in the letters of Paul can help identify basic moral rules and lead to an understanding of their implicit ethics, although there is no systematic ethical reflection or general theory, nor even a fixed set of values, to be found. Pauline ethics can be characterized as implied ethics, oscillating between authoritative ethics based on specific or general rules and ethics relying on responsible reflection and choice of the individual.

Jeremy Punt's contribution on "'Unethical' Language in the Pauline letters?: Stereotyping, Vilification and Identity Matters" locates the use of stereotype and vilifying language of the New Testament within the rhetorical conventions of antiquity, ascribing to "unethical" language the intention of negotiating identity, of marking out identity of self and others, of defining the self through others. Since the identity in Christ constituted the new ethos, Paul was deeply concerned with negotiating this identity – both through ethical considerations and admonition and through his use of the language of stereotyping. Focusing on Galatians, Punt describes Paul's use of stereotype and vilifying language and discusses its purpose, strategies and consequences. Owing to the situational context of insider-outsider conflicts, Paul intends to deride his opponents by explicit and implicit vilification, through which he seeks to persuade his audience to accept and affirm their views against those of their opponents. The pragmatic purpose of the invocation of racial and ethnic categories, of stereotyped "othering," curse rhetoric and stereotypical sexual slander is the negotiation (invention and maintenance) of categories of social identity, accompanied by Paul's attempts at re-establishing his position in and his (social) control over the community. Punt situates these intentions within the context of imperial ideology and hegemony, and the latter's influence on early Christian discourse, and he concludes that the dominated are forced to use the language of the dominators, despite the danger of implicating themselves. Thus, vili-fying and stereotyping language is not opposed to identity, community and morality; rather, it controls the construction and negotiation of all three.

Starting from Rudolf Bultmann's distinction between indicative and imperative, *Friedrich Wilhelm Horn*, in "Putting on Christ: On the Rela-tion of Sacramental and Ethical Language in the Pauline Epistles," elabo-rates on imagery encountered twice in the Pauline epistles that speaks of "putting on the Lord Jesus Christ" (Rom 13:14) and "putting on Christ" (Gal 3:27) – the first statement being situated in an ethical context and the second in a sacramental one. While Gal 3:26–28 denotes baptism as a place where the separation into different religious, social, and gender groups is abolished, and unity among the baptized is generated by the new garment – Christ, the ethical-eschatological admonition of Rom 13:11–14 calls the addressees to cast off the works of darkness and to "put on" the Lord Jesus Christ. In contrast to Gal 3:27, putting on Christ is regarded as an action to be performed consistently, not only once in the context of baptism. Whereas secondary literatures has so far assigned both statements to the imperative and indicative mood, respectively, Horn postulates that the ethical use of the metaphor cannot be explained by the indicative-imperative model. As both the argumentation of Rom 13:11–14 and the context of Gal 3:27 lack any reference to a preceding indicative, Horn ex-plains the usage of the metaphor through the notion of a participatory Christology: "putting on Christ" implies embracing the reality of Christ and also the continuation of life in the presence of the elevated Christ. The distinctively Pauline use of the metaphor is characterized by the underly-ing conception of a participatory Christology, which encompasses the en-tire Christian life. Thus the metaphor must be regarded as an essential component of Pauline ethical argumentation and as the fundamental basis of all ethics.

In "Moral Language in the New Testament: Language and Ethics in 2 Cor 3," *François S. Malan* sets out to detect an ethical dimension directed towards the addressees of 2 Corinthians in Paul's defence of his ministry. Although the text is not characterized by imperatives, prohibitions and prescriptions, an analysis of the rhetorical devices used by the apostle and the different levels of speech-act theory allow the detection of the implied moral impact of 2 Cor 3. Among the rhetorical devices used, Malan cites the repeated use of the *pluralis sociativus*, which bears on the motivation and direction of beliefs and behaviour. Initiating the discourse with two rhetorical questions (vv. 1–2), which engage the readers, the metaphorical depiction of the congregation as letter of Christ (v. 3) sensitizes them to live up to their responsibility. Paul's defence of his adequacy as an apostle (vv. 4–6) implies the responsibility of the addressees to live according to their status as God's covenant partners in opposition to the Israelites (vv. 12–18). Vv. 7–11 state the empowerment of the congregation through the Spirit and challenge them to adapt their way of life to the example of Christ. Malan concludes that while 2 Cor 3 viewed from its context is an apologia for Paul's ministry, its subtext is an appeal to the Corinthians to live up to their new identity. Paul directs them through such rhetorical methods as the conventional logical argument of "from the lesser to the greater," the devices of antithesis and repetition or the climactic structure of the argumentation, by appealing to their responsibility towards God and the world, and through indirect warnings. The transformation of the addressees' hearts and minds is described as the progressive maturation of the believer – becoming more and more like Christ.

In his contribution on "Moral Language in Philemon," *Pieter G. R. de Villiers* argues that the letter to Philemon is not only a personal letter addressing the specific problem of reconciling Philemon with his slave, Onesimus, but a letter written to a house church, which has a collective moral impact with moral implications for a number of people within the Pauline missionary team and the house churches. Philemon's behavior affected the ethos of the community of believers in challenging established relationships between members who shared a social system, thus motivating moral reflection. The letter provides insights in the identity and ethos of early Christianity, especially the Pauline tradition, and it can be read in the light of the relation between individual and social ethics. It does not provide a systematic-theoretical reflection on the ethos of the community, but practical advice, expressed in metaphorical and implicit moral language. Apart from referring to ethical matters and binding norms and values explicitly (Phlm 8, 9, 14), the norms of fellowship, faith and love must be extracted from implicit references (e.g. in Phlm 4–7). By means of descriptive language Paul stresses the significance of certain norms and values and presents them as exemplary, thus hoping to stabilize the ethos of the churches and implicitly providing moral guidance. The ethical arguments Paul employs are not only deontological, but they also show a teleological focus. De Villiers also focuses on the motif of mission, stating that at the centre of Paul's missionary work and preaching were reconciliation and salvation; this leads to the conclusion that the inclusive nature of Paul's missionary work also functioned as an ethical norm. The ethical communication in Philemon therefore goes beyond situational ethics, reflecting universally valid norms and values that were based on the inclusive nature of the gospel and its implications for conduct in interpersonal relationships.

The following passage groups several essays that look at various aspects of the interrelatedness between language and ethics in the later New Testament and Early Christian writings. *Jörg Frey's* contribution, "Disparagement as Argument: The Polemical Use of Moral Language in Second Peter," demonstrates that the introduction of the so-called "false teachers" in 2 Peter 2:1–22 with polemical language and rhetorical standard charges serves the purpose of vilifying his opponents' and disparaging their conduct and character. Although the predominant issues between the author of 2 Peter and his opponents are addressed in the light of eschatological expectation, the hope for the parousia and the reliability of the prophetic word, the opponents are accused of immoral behavior within an extensive polemic. They are described as people of not only dangerous and erroneous teaching but also morally corrupt conduct and an animal-like, evil nature, whose eschatological condemnation is already certain. Frey interprets the rhetorical technique in 2 Peter 2 as used primarily for vilification and disparagement in preparation for the theological argument in 2 Pet 3:1–13, as a literary construct which might represent the author's own views and interests more than the actual conduct and nature of the real-life opponents. Thus, the disparagement of the opponents serves as an additional "argument" in the theological struggle for the "true" apostolic teaching. The essay considers such an "argument" as questionable, historically, theologically and also morally. While polemical vilification of opponents was a customary rhetorical device in antiquity, 2 Peter 2 cannot merely be explained as an example of an ancient polemical convention, for "moral language" and high moral claims are used for rather immoral purposes – dehumanizing polemics always convey an inhuman and destructive force.

Gert J. Steyn bases his contribution, "Some Possible Intertextual Influences from the Jewish Scriptures on the (Moral) Language of Hebrews," on the assumption that – as in Judaism and Christianity religion and morality were closely associated – the Jewish Scriptures and their interpretation are of essential importance as intertexts for the composition of moral texts in the New Testament. Focusing on Hebrews, Steyn first engages with possible intertextual influences on the language and theology of Hebrews from the moral language of the Decalogue and other laws, and can demonstrate that traces of the moral language are adopted, but reinterpreted in the light of the Christ-event. Second, narrative intertexts, which represent a commemoration of the exemplary behaviour of characters from Jewish history, are investigated and their possible influence of the *commemoratio* of Heb 10–12 is described as serving as a general model for the readers concerning their faith and perseverance despite their present difficult situation. Third, two of the maxim-like ethical formulas of Heb 13 (vv. 2, 5, the maxim-like formulas on entertaining strangers and against avarice), are compared with Jewish festival traditions. Just as Ps 118(117) was connected with the Passover, and Deut 31 with the Sabbatical Year and with the Feast of Tents, Hebrews might have been influenced by these Scriptural intertexts linked with Jewish festival traditions. Steyn's analysis of the moral language of Hebrews illustrates that the Jewish Scriptures wielded an important intertextual influence during the compilation of the letter, as did also other early Christian documents on different levels: unintentional or subconscious influence (implicit reference) with regard to law texts, intentional and conscious influence (explicit influence) as far as narrative intertexts and liturgical traditions in connection with the Jewish festival traditions are concerned.

Susanne Luther, in "Protreptic Ethics in the Letter of James: The Potential of Figurative Language in Character Formation," focuses on the extent to which, and in which forms, the linguistic and psychological potential of metaphoric and generally figurative language was used in early Christianity and which function and significance are assigned to figurative language, illumined by the argumentative context of the "post-conversional discourse" in enhancing ethical admonition and teaching. With a focus on the Letter of James, two distinctive dimensions are developed: first, it is claimed that the ethical instruction conveyed is not paraenetic but protreptic, i.e. the letter does not primarily communicate specific explicit rules for concrete actions but rather advice on character formation. Second, James is not intent on conveying ethical standards by imposing prescriptive instruction via cognitive discernment but aims at a radical and lasting amelioration of character through the formal conveyance of ethics by means of figurative language. An exemplary range of Jacobean passages is presented to provide an overview of the form and function of figurative devices used, such as metaphors, moral agents, macarisms, parables and an *ekphrasis*. Moreover, the congruence of form, content and pragmatic purport characteristic of the author's ethical teaching is demonstrated. The argumentation proceeds on a meta-level and is corroborated by figurative language, which both cooperate in advancing ethical instruction with a focus on character formation and intend to prepare within the recipients the foundation, the ethical grounding, for subsequent concrete admonitions and instructions. It is the formation of character which is aimed at – on the figurative level as well as through the kind of ethics conveyed within the entire argumentative text – as the main stress concerning ethical instruction in the Letter of James is on protreptic ethics.

In "The 'Ethics' of Badmouthing the Other: Vilification as Persuasive Speech Act in First Clement" *Lambert D. Jacobs* sets out to show by reference to examples from 1 Clem in what ways the author used invective, vilifying language as a pragmatic rhetorical device in order to harm his opponents and to warn and direct his addressees to act in the right way. Considering the vilification within speech-act perspective, Jacobs asks how the language in 1 Clem achieved its goals of badmouthing and derogating its opponents. Accusations of hypocrisy and deceit, means of belittling the strength and appearance of the opponents by describing them as few, young and of no repute, accusations of arrogance and boastfulness, the charge of blasphemy, the adversaries' portrayal as dark, shadowy characters with the intent of deliberately blurring their personalities, the accusation of their evil influence through sorcery, alleging their moral depravity in sexual or financial or moral conduct and their intention of leading the addressees astray and their association with dubious historical characters are presented as rhetorical means of vilifying the opponents and discouraging the audience from being associated with such people as those described. Apart from the vilification through ridiculing the opponents as persons, 1 Clem disparages their thinking and teaching, which is presented as ludicrous, limited and foolish. The argumentation of the letter is examined and found corroborated with Scripture citations and warnings in the light of the impending Eschaton and the judgement of God, which both serve as admonitions to the addressees. Jacobs elucidates the rhetorical skill of the author of 1 Clem by highlighting his vilifying techniques, such as continuously showing the offenders in a bad light and caricaturing them as dubious figures, with the intention of warning his own community of addressees against the opponents and against conduct that models the conduct of the opponents, seeking by contrast to define the correct conduct. The means employed to this intent are speech acts that serve the strategy of vilification.

The last section includes two contributions that demonstrate the possible impact of New Testament moral language on current ethical problems in South Africa, where the corresponding conference took place. *Richard A. Burridge's* contribution on "Ethics and Genre: The Narrative Setting of Moral Language in the New Testament" pursues a twofold quest: it sets out to analyse which means of reading the ethical demands of the New Testament led to the distinctive use of the Bible by the Dutch Reformed Church during apartheid in South Africa, as well as which role it played in the struggle for liberation, as a test case for how the New Testament is applied to ethics today. Burridge applies his biographical approach to Jesus and the gospels to ethical debates in stressing that in order to live up to the ethical demand of the gospel, Jesus' ethical teaching must be grounded in his practical example, and his words must be considered, as well as his deeds, in the reconstruction of New Testament ethics. Based upon his analysis of the biographical genre of the gospels, he pleads for an ethics of imitating Jesus' words and deeds thus hearing the biblical teachings within the context of an open and inclusive community, which includes the experiences of those marginalized from society (black and coloured people, women, homosexuals etc.) and is open to "voices of protest."

Elijah Mahlangu, in "The Familial Metaphorical Language of Inclusion in the New Testament and HIV/AIDS Destigmatization in Africa," suggests that the immense social problems of stigmatization and discrimination in connection with the AIDS pandemic in Africa should be addressed from a theological point of view with recourse to the familial metaphorical language used in the New Testament to describe the church, the family of God. By exploring five major perspectives of the use of familial language in the New Testament (Mark, Luke-Acts, Matthew, John and Paul), Mahlangu demonstrates that those living with HIV and AIDS can be affirmed by the ethical and moral language encountered in the New Testament to address the stigma associated with the disease. The stigma, which is described as a social construction relating to a deviation from an ideal or expectation, leads to discrimination, rejection and exclusion. The New Testament familial language of inclusion, however, can provide an interpretative paradigm that might help to deconstruct the stigma and include people living with HIV/AIDS as part of God's family: PLWHA can identify with those ostracized in the Gospels or find a new community in the ecclesiology expressed in metaphors like God as Father, Jesus as healer, God's family etc. The metaphors of kinship language reveal an ethic of inclusion, which communicates the gospel's message and conveys ethical instruction on how Christians should treat each other: as members of God's family. Mahlangu stresses the practicability of this approach in indicating parallels between the ethics of God's family in the New Testament and traditional African family ethics.

I. Ethics and Language

Ethics in the New Testament and Language:

Basic Explorations and Eph 5:21–33 as Test Case[1]

Ruben Zimmermann

The New Testament is a collection of texts. Thus we cannot speak about ethics in the New Testament without taking the textual medium into account. Due to the dependence on texts, ethical discourse is called on to take a special look at the linguistic nature of the ethics of the New Testament. However, such study is astonishingly infrequent within the literature on ethics of the New Testament.[2]

After a few remarks on the basic terms in the ethical discourse I will, first, demonstrate the role of language within other ethical aspects, which build a grid of "implicit ethics." Taking up the three levels of interrelatedness between ethics and language (i.e. intratextual, intertextual and extratextual level), I will secondly offer some examples for the different forms of ethical language in the New Testament. Finally, and thirdly, the house-hold table of Eph 5:21–33 is taken as a test case, on which the merit of the language based approach on ethics can be demonstrated.

1. Terminological and Methodological Approach

The issue "moral language" requires clarity on the meaning of the term "moral." More general all of the terms used within ethical discourse like "ethics," "ethos," and "morals" have to be defined, even more, because they are often used without providing a more precise definition. What do we mean when we speak of "ethics" or "morality" etc.? In which way does "language" play a role in this?

Even though many of the contributors use the terms "ethics" and "ethos" precisely and reflectively, I think that it is valuable to begin a vol-

---

[1] This paper is based on the introductory paper of the Humboldt-Kolleg-Conference in September 2008 in Pretoria/SA. The oral style of the paper has been kept in this article.

[2] See the survey on most recent ethics by Richard B. Hays, "Mapping the Field: Approaches to New Testament Ethics," in *Identity, Ethics, and Ethos in the New Testament* (ed. Jan van der Watt; BZNW 141; Berlin/New York: de Gruyter, 2006), 3–19.

ume like that, with a working definition that can serve as the basis for further discussion. At this time I would like to deal with the well-known difference between "ethos/morals" and "ethics" and have a more precise look at two aspects of this by speaking about an "ethos remembered" and an "implicit ethics."[3]

1.1 "Ethos remembered"

In the past years, Michael Wolter has worked increasingly on a definition of ethos. He understands "ethos" as a "canon of institutionalized actions that are valid within a social system."[4] Ethos is thus based on the customs and conventions of actions in a concrete community. This can also be seen in the etymology of the term "morals" which derives from the Latin "mos, mores" (= customs) and which is considered to be synonymous to ethos. Based on the constitutive relatedness of ethos to a social system, Thomas Schmeller uses the consistent definition "Actually every ethos is a group ethos."[5]

Jan van der Watt used a wider definition in his volume *Identity, Ethics and Ethos in the New Testament*. According to him, "ethos is understood not only as the specific, unique, and repetitive actions of a particular group or community, ... but it is also used as a broader description of the behaviour as it is presented in the different books of the New Testament."[6]

However, ethos also means the morals, present in the books of the New Testament, of the early Christians – it is concerned with "historical ethos." This ethos, like the issues discussed intensively in the problem of the "historical Jesus," is, however, not directly accessible to us. It is a construct that we can put together only out of the New Testament texts and that is accordingly burdened by ideology.

---

[3]   See for instance Annemarie Pieper, *Einführung in die Ethik* (UTB.W 1637; 4th ed.; Tübingen/Basel: Francke, 2000), 24–30.

[4]   According to the definition of Michael Wolter, "Die ethische Identität christlicher Gemeinden in neutestamentlicher Zeit," in *Woran orientiert sich Ethik?* (ed. Wilfried Härle et al.; MThSt 67; Marburg: Elwert, 2001), 61–90; idem, "Ethos und Identität in paulinischen Gemeinden," *NTS* 43 (1997): 430–444, here 430–431; also idem, "'Let no one seek his own, but each one the other's' (1Corinthians 10:24): Pauline ethics according to 1 Corinthians," in *Identity, Ethics, and Ethos in the New Testament* (n. 2), 199–217, here 200: "the term ethos designates a canon of institutionalised practices, which a given group regards as liable."

[5]   See Thomas Schmeller, "Neutestamentliches Gruppenethos," in *Der neue Mensch in Christus. Hellenistische Anthropologie und Ethik im Neuen Testament* (ed. Johannes Beutler; QD 190; Freiburg i. Br.: Herder, 2001), 120–134, hier 120: "Eigentlich ist jedes Ethos Gruppenethos"; see earlier already Leander E. Keck, "On the Ethos of Early Christians," *JAAR* 42 (1974): 435–452, here 120.

[6]   Van der Watt, "Preface," in: *Identity, Ethics and Ethos in the New Testament* (n. 2), iv–ix, here vii.

Instead of speaking of an "historical ethos," we should rather speak of an "ethos remembered"[7] due to the following reason: the ethos of a group roots itself in the behaviours and rituals. It must however also be communicated and reflected within the group in order to have an identity-building function. Ethos is itself tied to language in so far as a community establishes for itself its morality through language. Collective identity always requires an entrenchment in media, and language, especially conventionalized forms of language as they are found in genres, is the singled-out media of this self-reflexivity.[8] I will come back to this point later. Prime examples of linguistic forms of ethos are commands, community rules or house rules. They are the morals of a particular group, put down in text. The New Testament texts contain lots of texts containing such a 'remembered ethos.'

1.2 Ethics and Implicit Ethics

In contrast, "ethics" is the critical examination, the questioning of the motive of the morals. It was Aristotle who referred in this way to the "ethical theory" (ἠθικὴ θεωρία, *An. Post.* I,33 = 89b 9). For him, ethics questioned the foundation of the life of the polis composed in custom and habit (Aristotle, *Eth. Nic.* 1180b 3). In this tradition, ethics can be defined as the systematic-theoretical examination of the lived ethos. "Ethics" is concerned with a rational analysis of morals. According to Annemarie Pieper, it is the "science of moral action" that examines "human practice in regards to the conditions of its morality."[9] "Theological ethics" is then correspondingly the reflexivity on the moral judgements and actions of people in the scope of Christian belief.[10]

---

[7] This phrase is built in allusion to James D. G. Dunn, *Christianity in the Making I: Jesus Remembered* (Grand Rapids: Eerdmans, 2003). See more general on the "memory" paradigm the instructive collection of *Memory, Tradition, and Text. Uses of the Past in Early Christianity* (ed. Alan Kirk and Tom Thatcher; Semeia Studies 52; Atlanta, Ga.: SBL Press, 2005).

[8] See more general on that issue Ruben Zimmermann, "Memory and Form Criticism: The Typicality of Memory as a Bridge between Orality and Literality in the Early Christian Remembering Process," in *The Interface of Orality and Writing: Speaking, Seeing, Writing in the Shaping of New Genres* (ed. Annette Weissenrieder and Robert B. Coote; WUNT 260; Tübingen: Mohr Siebeck, 2010), 130–143.

[9] See Pieper, *Einführung* (n. 3), 27–28.

[10] See the definition in Gerfried Hunold, Thomas Laubach and Andreas Greis, "Annäherungen. Zum Selbstverständnis theologischer Ethik," in *Theologische Ethik. Ein Werkbuch* (ed. Gerfried Hunold, Thomas Laubach and Andreas Greis; Tübingen/Basel: Francke, 2000), 1–9, here 3: "Theologische Ethik ist die wissenschaftliche Reflexion auf das moralisch-sittliche Urteilen und Handeln des Menschen im Horizont des christlichen Glaubens."

However, this definition would remain incomplete if it were not supplemented with the thought that this reflexivity takes place within the perspective of value judgements. Thus it is concerned with the question of
whether and why an action is "right" or "good" or, in the scope of a value
hierarchy, if it is "better" or "worse" than another.

The New Testament undoubtedly contains texts that reflect actions and
thus make value judgements. After telling the parable of the Good Samaritan, Jesus asks which of the three acted "correctly" – according to the Torah commandments that had been previously discussed: "Which of these
three, do you think, proved neighbor to the man who fell among the rob-
bers?" (Luke 10:36). After the parable of the two sons and the father, Jesus
asks: "Which of the two did the will of his father?" (Matt 21:31) – or in
other words – which one acted "correctly" according to his father's
wishes? Matthew also puts "justice" as a main ethical norm in a comparative context by speaking of a "better justice" (see Matt 5:20 among others:
ἡ δικαιοσύνη πλεῖον τῶν γραμματέων καὶ Φαρισαίων). In the Pauline
letters, ethics are also carried out in the scope of evaluations of "good" and
"evil" (see Rom 7:13–21: τὸ καλόν – τὸ κακόν). Actions should undergo
an evaluation of values and legal interests in order to choose the good:
πάντα δὲ δοκιμάζετε, τὸ καλὸν κατέχετε (test all things; hold fast what is
good, 1 Thess 5:21). Many more examples could be given.

The question is, however, can one therefore speak of "ethics" or an
"ethical theory" in the New Testament? Even if no systematic synopsis of
these meta-reflections on norms for actions are to be found in the New
Testament writings, implicit and sometimes explicit reasons as well as the
argumentative recourse to certain ethical maxims and norms underlie the
individual paraenesis.[11] For example, Paul was not only a situational ethicist, interested in the clarification of concrete cases. Instead he formulated
rules of behaviour and value standards that could claim, in the middle of
all the diversity, more than individual or perhaps even universal validity
and could explicitly call on reason, as is shown clearly in Rom 12:1–2.[12]

---

[11] See Friedrich Wilhelm Horn, "Ethik. NT," *RGG⁴* 2 (1999): 1608–1609: "Obwohl
es sich oft um Situationse. handelt …, zeigt dieser Rahmen doch einen über die Situation
hinaus führenden Begründungszusammenhang der E.;" Wayne A. Meeks, "The poly-
phonic ethics of the apostle Paul," in *In search of the early Christians. Selected essays*
(ed. Allen R. Hilton and H. Gregory Snyder; New Haven, Conn.: Yale University Press,
2002), 196–209.

[12] See on reason in ethics Stanley K. Stowers, "Paul on the Use and Abuse of Reason," in *Greeks, Romans, and Christians: Essays in honor of Abraham J. Malherbe* (ed.
David L. Balch et al.; Minneapolis, Minn.: Fortress Press, 1990), 253–286; Ian W. Scott,
Implicit Epistemology in the Letters of Paul. Story, experience and the spirit (WUNT
2/205; Tübingen: Mohr Siebeck, 2006), here 53: "Paul's ethical teaching is often supported by reasoned argument." Also Hans Dieter Betz, "Das Problem der Grundlagen der

Therefore it is justifiable to speak of a motive for action in the sense of "ethics" or better of "implicit ethics" – and not only of the ethos of Early Christian communities.[13] This "ethics" should be called implicit because the New Testament authors themselves render no systematic account for norms of action and contexts of reason – similar perhaps to the ethics of Aristotle.[14] We, however, can retrospectively derive, from individual motives, an "ethical superstructure" underlying them and at the same time put the mosaic stones together into a complete picture. The term "implicit" (which has been borrowed from the literature of reader-response criticism[15]) takes orientation here primarily from the writings themselves and less from the postulated authors of the works. It is thus more precise to speak of "implicit ethics" of a New Testament scripture.

I have posed the question elsewhere of the elements of such "implicit ethics" in a wider scope that should lead us out of the narrowness of the Bultmannian differentiation between "indicative and imperative."[16] At a conference in 2007 in Mainz, we considered this question more intensively and discussed an entire set of motive contexts of New Testament ethics. As our current conference takes up this issue again and can be seen as a continuation of this work, I would like to repeat the set of perspectives here.

---

paulinischen Ethik (Röm 12,1–2)," in *Paulinische Studien. Gesammelte Aufsätze III* (ed. Hans Dieter Betz; Tübingen: Mohr Siebeck, 1994), 184–205, here 199.

[13] See David G. Horrell, "Approaches to Pauline Ethics. From Bultmann to Boyarin," in *Solidarity and Difference. A Contemporary Reading of Paul's Ethics* (ed. David G. Horrell; London: T&T Clark, 2005), 98: "Paul's letters do not, however, only imply a particular kind of shaping of the community and its ethos, they also contain explicit and self-conscious argumentation on questions of conduct and attempts to articulate ways to resolve conflict and disagreement." See also Hermut Löhr, "Ethik und Tugendlehre," in *Neues Testament und Antike Kultur: Weltauffassung, Kult, Ethos* (vol. 3 of *Neues Testament und Antike Kultur*; ed. Kurt Erlemann et al.; Neukirchen-Vluyn: Neukirchener, 2005), 151–180, here 151.

[14] See Aristoteles, *Eudemische Ethik* (trans. Franz Dirlmeier; 4th ed.; Berlin: Akademie, 1984); idem, *Nikomachische Ethik* (trans. Franz Dirlmeier; Stuttgart: Reclam, 2001); Sarah Broadie, *Ethics with Aristotle* (New York: Oxford University Press, 1991); Otfried Höffe (ed.), *Aristoteles. Die Nikomachische Ethik* (Berlin: Akademie, 1995); David Bostock, *Aristotle's Ethics* (Oxford: Oxford University Press, 2001); Ursula Wolf, *Aristoteles' Nikomachische Ethik* (Darmstadt: WBG, 2002).

[15] See Wolfgang Iser, *Der „implizite Leser"* (Stuttgart: Fink, 1994).

[16] See Ruben Zimmermann, "Jenseits von Indikativ und Imperativ. Entwurf einer ‚impliziten Ethik' des Paulus am Beispiel des 1. Korintherbriefes," *ThLZ* 132 (2007): 259–284; the following outline refers to the German version p. 274–276; see again with new aspects Ruben Zimmermann, "The 'Implicit Ethics' of New Testament Writings. A Draft on a New Methodology in Analysing New Testament's ethics," *Neot* 43/2 (2009): 398–422.

1.3 The Search for an "implicit ethics of the New Testament" (basic grid)

If we want to investigate the "implicit ethics" of a New Testament scripture, we should include the following aspects:

2. Norms and Maxims for Action:
Which leading norms and maxims of action are mentioned?

Under the heading "norm" or "maxims for action," we should designate here – in connection to the wide definition of Maximilian Forschner[17] – a basic principle that puts a normative obligation on the behaviour of the individual or the group. Thus, for example in Paul, general *moral instances* such as "nature" or "custom/habit" and institutionalized *moral codices* (e.g. the Torah) can be differentiated. Even individual *people* can obtain moral status if they enjoy authority within a peer group, such as Jesus or the presbyter of the letters of John. Finally, a norm can identify a goal that goes beyond the factual validity of rules. The differentiation between *formal-ethical* principles (e.g. golden rules) and individual *material-ethical* goods (e.g. ἐλευθερία, ἀγάπη), that can be introduced as the instances of motive can also be useful.

3. History of Traditions of Individual Norms/Moral Instances:
In which traditional and contemporary context do these norms exist?

Norms have a dimension of time. They can be classified in tradition and religious history. In this process it can be helpful heuristically to differentiate ideal-typically between Jewish and Greek ethics. Nevertheless, Hellenistic Judaism, or perhaps the role of law in non-Jewish discourse,[18] demonstrates that one-sided determinations do not do justice to Early Christianity. Instead of monocausal derivations, the goal of this methodological step should be no more but also no less than to develop potentials of meaning and scopes of understanding.

---

[17] See Maximilian Forschner, "Norm," in *Lexikon der Ethik* (ed. Otfried Höffe; Munich: Beck, 1992): 200–201.

[18] See already Aristoteles, *Nic. Eth.* 1134a; Holger Sonntag, ΝΟΜΟΣ ΣΩΤΗΡ. Zur politischen Theologie des Gesetzes bei Paulus und im antiken Kontext (TANZ 34; Tübingen: Francke, 2000); Klaus Haacker, "Der ‚Antinomismus' des Paulus im Kontext antiker Gesetzestheorie," in *Versöhnung mit Israel. Exegetische Beiträge* (ed. Klaus Haacker; Neukirchen-Vluyn: Neukirchener, 2002), 171–188.

4. Logic of Values:
Which inner context of different norms is produced?
Which emphasis of norms, which hierarchy of values can be recognized?

The various norms are not individually positioned as equal to each other. They are evaluated and are put into relation to each other within a hierarchy of values. Only in this way can the independent profile of the respective reflexivity of action be recognized. If one wishes to analyse the use of norms in New Testament texts in this regard, it is helpful, in connection to a moral-philosophical discussion, to differentiate between a "classificatory" and a "comparative" value concept.[19] An example: the Pauline admonition in 1 Thess 5:21 (test all things; hold fast what is good [τὸ καλόν]) assumes a classificatory valuation that differentiates between good and evil, between "valuable" and "valueless." In contrast, in 1 Cor 7:38 we see the comparative logic of values: "Thus he who marries his partner does well (καλῶς ποιεῖ), and he who does not will do better (κρεῖσσον ποιήσει)."

5. Ethical Argumentation/Structure of Motives:
According to which internal structure of motives, according to which ethical argumentation does the ethical judgement take place?

Ethics searches for the internal structure of motives according to which a norm or an action is judged to be 'good' or 'right.' Ethics is thus more than the rhetorical description of the argumentational pattern, even if this can be very useful in the perception of the ethical method of argumentation. The differentiation within ethical theory, which has been common since Charles D. Broad[20], between "deontological" and "teleological" argumentation is instructive for the analysis of the ethical structure of motives. The ethical argumentation is called *deontological* when the customarily correct action is deducted from a prescribed norm (τὸ δέον – the obligation, the duty) (Imperative: Do the prescribed good for its own sake.) The motive is *teleological* or consequential when the value of an action is measured by the aims of the action (τὸ τέλος) or the consequences (Imperative: Do so, so that a desired goal is reached). Annemarie Pieper differentiated seven

---

[19] See Franz von Kutschera, *Einführung in die Logik der Normen, Werte und Entscheidungen* (Freiburg i. Br./Munich: Alber, 1973), 85–87. The "metrical" concept of value as employed in analytical moral philosophy has no relevance for Pauline ethics.

[20] See Charles D. Broad, *Five Types of Ethical Theory* (ILPP; London: Routledge, 1930), 206–207; this can be found – with different terminology – in Henry Sidgwick, *The Methods of Ethics* (London: MacMillan, 1874), 200, further Friedrich Paulsen, *System der Ethik. Mit einem Umriß der Staats- und Gesellschaftslehre* (Berlin: Hertz, 1889), 221–250.

more ethical structures of motives, such as the discursive, the dialectic, or the analogous methods[21] that can serve as heuristic instruments.

6. The Carrier of Ethical Judgements:
Who is the ethical subject/the carrier of ethical judgements?
Which factors constitute the ethical subject?

In order to make an ethical judgement, it is necessary to have an ethical subject[22] in the sense of a personal arbitration. Very different factors determine the ethical subject in its judgement-making. In this process, the question arises as to the importance of reason (see Rom 12:1; Phil 4:8), the emotions (see 1 Cor 9:16; Rom 7:15) or conscience. Has the decision been made 'autonomously' or 'heteronomously?' Which order of preferences is being followed? What is the relationship between the carrier of ethical judgements and other people or higher authorities or powers (see Rom 7:18–19)? How do individual ethics and social ethics relate to each other, can the subject also be of a collective dimension?

7. The Resulting Ethos as Lived:
Which concrete ethos corresponds to or contradicts the ethical argumentation?

As helpful as it is heuristically to differentiate the investigation of norms and the motive of actions from their actual implementation, it is equally impossible to separate them. Ethics is, in the end, the reflection of a lived ethos and thus reciprocally interwoven with it. Therefore, the aspects that can socio-historically be raised to an ethos of the community can and must be brought into the ethical system as a whole. The separation between ethos and ethics does, however, make it possible to keep the contra-factual function of ethical reflection in view, as difficult as this is to name in each case, when the text does not do it itself.

8. Field of Application:
Which field of application of a norm is mentioned?

The New Testament texts exist in concrete communication contexts. Paul often deals with the concrete ethical questions of his community. In doing this he differentiates between norms of action that are valid for him, for his

---

[21] See on the methods of ethical arguing the list of Pieper, *Einführung* (n. 3), 200–232.
[22] See Michael Wolter, "Ethisches Subjekt und ethisches Gegenüber. Aspekte aus neutestamentlicher Perspektive," in *Diakonie in der Stadt. Reflexionen – Modelle – Konventionen* (ed. Heinz Schmidt and Renate Zitt; Diakoniewissenschaft 8; Stuttgart: Kohlhammer, 2003), 44–50.

assistants, for individual community members or for the community as a whole. Beyond this, he makes general-anthropological value judgements that go far beyond the concrete situation. Or for example, he addresses the Philemon letter not only to the master of the house but rather, consciously, to all members of the house in order to give the problem an importance greater than the individual.

Finally, the canon as the location of tradition de-contextualizes concrete individual decisions and gives them a universal claim that must be reflected hermeneutically. Thus the question is asked here as to the differing scopes and fields of application of the ethical judgements – we are concerned with the relationship of particularism and universalism.

1. Linguistic Form

8. Addessee/Field of
application

2. Norms and Values
for Action

7. The resulting
ethos as lived

The
‚implicit ethics‘

3. History of
Traditions of
Individual Norms

6. The Moral agent

4. Priorities of
Values

5. Ethical ‚Logic‘/Structure
of Motives

Perspectives in analysing the „implicit ethics “ of New Testament Writings

Those who are familiar with my outline will have noticed that I have skipped over the first point. I would like to address it here at the end because it will be the central focus of this conference.

1. Linguistic Form:
Which linguistic form does the ethical statement take?

Origin and destination is the concrete existing text in its linguisticality. Clearly, language also plays a role in the other areas of the "implicit ethics," be it in that the individual norms can be made concrete within the perspective of "historical semantics," the tradition history as "linguistic convention and inter-textuality" or the form of argument as "linguistic rhetoric."

Thus it becomes clear that the above differences fulfil a heuristic function. Individual points should not be considered as self-excluding aspects but rather demonstrate overlaps with other perspectives. Nevertheless, it is worth looking with greater precision at each individual aspect for itself. We want to do this in this volume with regard to the linguistic dependency of "implicit ethics" but must always keep in the backs of our minds that this dimension remains linked to other aspects. Instead of as a comprehensive "linguistic turn" of New Testament ethics, we understand this viewpoint as a conscious limiting of the object. The conference does not claim to be able to cover all aspects of New Testament ethics. Rather the attempt will be made to discuss the question of New Testament ethics within a special focus, namely the relationship of language and ethics.

2. Forms of Ethical Language with New Testament Examples

Language carries ethical meaning. Ethics require language. If then we can answer the question of the linguisticality of ethics positively, the further question arises as to the forms and levels on which this linguisticality of ethics enters our consciousness.

In the introduction we set out a suggestion for differentiation that I would like, in the following, to take up again, to look at more precisely and to explain using examples from the New Testament. When we speak of "language" with regard to our focus on the New Testament we mean written language. Language can thus be concentrated on "textuality," so that I would in the following like to speak of the dependence of ethics on text. We can differentiate among three levels of textuality: intra-textuality, inter-textuality and extra-textuality of ethics.

2.1 On the intra-textual Level

On this first level, we could ask which syntactical forms, stylistic features, and structural logic are used in presenting ethical statements. There are several forms of imperatives. There is the complex difference between "is" and "ought to/should" sentences, between prescriptive and descriptive moral language. There are narrative, metaphoric, ironic texts etc. that transport morality through their specific style.

I cannot give a comprehensive overview here of all the linguistic options for making ethical statements. Instead I would like to begin with the fundamental and elementary question: what constitutes the ethical quality of a linguistic statement? Or even more fundamentally – why are sentences ethical at all? What makes an ethical sentence different from a non-ethical one? Cannot every statement be interpreted ethically? Is the valuation system or the context of action thus not always determined externally to the text, for example through psychology or the communication system and hermeneutics?

While, among moral philosophers, naturalists or intuitionalists may challenge the idea that one can at all analyse ethical sentences logically[23], I would like to follow the argumentation of Hare, who studied the ethical quality of linguistic statements. Hare writes: "Ethics, as I conceive it, is the logical study of the language of morals"[24] and *Freedom and Reason* begins with the sentence: "The function of moral philosophy – or at any rate of the hope with which I study it – is that of helping us to think better about moral questions by exposing the logical structure of the language in which this thought is expressed."[25] His question was, "what are the logical rules for talking ethically?"[26] Which linguistic and logical characteristics must be fulfilled in order for us to perceive a sentence as "ethical" or to speak of an ethical judgement?

Here is not the place to depict or evaluate Hare's theory.[27] It doubtless has its limits and problems. I would like to use his work only to the effect that he demonstrated that 1) there are sentences that are not ethical and that 2) ethical language does indeed exhibit a rationally describable and partially logical structure.

According to Hare there are three forms of speech – statements, commands and question, whereby the questions can be related back to one of the other two forms. Thus, according to Hare, we can differentiate only two fundamental forms of speech – the indicative and the imperative.[28] "An indicative sentence is used for telling someone that something is the

---

[23] See Rudolf Carnap, *Philosophy and Logical Syntax* (London: Routledge, 1971), 23; Charles Stevenson, *Ethics and Language* (New Haven, Conn.: Yale University Press, 1965), 20–36.

[24] Richard M. Hare, *The Language of Morals* (Oxford: Oxford University Press, 1964), III.

[25] Richard M. Hare, *Freedom and Reason* (Oxford: Clarendon Press, 1963), V.

[26] See Richard M. Hare, "Imperative Sentences," *Mind* 58 (1949): 21–39, 23.

[27] See for instance John L. Mackie, *Ethics. Inventing right and wrong* (Hardmondsworth: Penguin, 1977), 92–93; *Seminar: Sprache und Ethik. Zur Entwicklung der Metaethik* (eds. Günther Grewendorf/Georg Meggle; Frankfurt: Suhrkamp, 1974).

[28] See Hare, "Imperative Sentences" (n. 26), 24–25: "In general, a question can be translated into a command, either to put values to the variables in a sentential function, or to assert one of the component sentences of a disjunction. ... We are left, according to the traditional division, with indicatives and imperatives."

case; an imperative is not – it is used for telling someone to make something the case."[29]

The imperative requires there to be a choice between alternative actions. Hare "... presupposes that there is a choice between alternatives facts, i.e., between alternative courses of action."[30] The affirmation of an indicative statement involves the recognition of a fact, while the affirmation of an imperative lies in the doing of that which was demanded. "The rule that an imperative cannot appear in the conclusion of a valid inference, unless there is at least one imperative in the premise, (may be confirmed by an appeal to general logical considerations)."[31]

The New Testament exegesis is thus urged to describe, as exactly as possible, the linguistic form and inner logic – let us say the "grammar" – of ethical statements in the New Testament and to study them in regards to their inner structure. If we follow Hare's basic differentiation between indicative and imperative statements, we must look particularly at imperative statements.

a) The Imperative Mood

However, this is not as easy as it seems. While a grammarian can decide formalistically which sentences or verb forms are categorized as "imperative," for the ethicist it depends more on the mood, on the inner logic that makes a statement appear imperative or indicative. What I mean here can be seen clearly by looking at the Koine Greek of the New Testament. Here there are grammatical imperatives that are not imperatives at all and, vice-versa, the function of the imperative is expressed by non-imperative verb forms.

Grammatical imperatives can also express a request or a concessive utterance. In John 2:19, λύσατε τὸν ναὸν τοῦτον can be the equivalent of the concessive clause ἐὰν καὶ λύσητε.[32] The "imperatives" in The Lord's Prayer (Matt 6:9–15) also are not commands in the ethical context, but rather requests. Accordingly, we read:

– "Give us today our daily bread" (τὸν ἄρτον ἡμῶν τὸν ἐπιούσιον δὸς ἡμῖν σήμερον·) or
– "Hallowed be thy name" (= Let thy name be hallowed, ἁγιασθήτω τὸ ὄνομά σου·)
– "Thy kingdom come" (= Let thy kingdom come, ἐλθέτω ἡ βασιλεία σου·)
– "Thy will be done" (= Let thy will be done, as in heaven, also on earth, γενηθήτω τὸ θέλημά σου).

---

[29] Hare, *Language of Morals* (n. 24), I. 1.3 (p. 5).

[30] Hare, "Imperative Sentences" (n. 26), 25.

[31] Hare, *Language of Morals* (n. 24), I. 3.2 (p. 32).

[32] So Friedrich Blass, Albert Debrunner and Robert W. Funk, *Greek Grammar of the New Testament and Other Early Christian Literature* (Chicago, Ill.: Chicago University Press, 1961), 195; furthermore 2 Cor 12:16: Ἔστω δέ, but granting/be that, ...

In these examples we also notice other particularities of the imperative in Koine Greek in comparison to modern languages.

First, what is most striking to German or English speakers is the fact that Greek has imperative forms for the third person singular and plural as well as for the second person. Second, it is interesting that it is logical in our languages that there are no imperative forms in the past tenses. We do not command things to happen in the past. In Greek, however, there is an "aoristic imperative." This demonstrates once more that the aorist cannot be equated with a past tense in English but this does not explain why the aorist can be used both for the narrative time of the past and for the imperative.

„The present imperative is progressive or durative, referring to an action already in progress, while the aorist is indefinite or 'ingressive,' referring, usually to an action which is to be commenced."[33] Let me give some examples: 1 Cor 14:1: Διώκετε τὴν ἀγάπην, ... pursue love!, means: Keep on pursuing love *or* Keep love as your goal. Or 1 Cor 7:2: ἐχέτω καὶ ἑκάστη τὸν ἴδιον ἄνδρα ἐχέτω. The present imperative means: and let each woman continue to have her own husband. The difference is demonstrated in: 1 Cor 7:11 -ἐὰν δὲ καὶ χωρισθῇ, μενέτω (present imperative) ἄγαμος ἢ τῷ ἀνδρὶ καταλλαγήτω (aorist imperative), can be translated: "let her keep/remain unmarried or let her start reconciling to *her* husband.

Further I would like to indicate the forms that express the imperative mood but grammatically do not use the imperative. Hare speaks in such cases of "crypto-imperatives."[34] Elliptical imperatives possess a certain in-between position, for example in:

Col 3:17 καὶ πᾶν ὅ τι ἐὰν ποιῆτε ἐν λόγῳ ἢ ἐν ἔργῳ, πάντα ἐν ὀνόματι κυρίου Ἰησοῦ, εὐχαριστοῦντες τῷ θεῷ πατρὶ δι' αὐτο
And whatever you do in word or deed, [*do*] all in the name of the Lord Jesus, giving thanks through Him to God the Father.

The *"future indicative"* can also be used imperatively, often in quotations of Old Testament commands, such as in Matt 5:43: Ἠκούσατε ὅτι ἐρρέθη· ἀγαπήσεις (future ind. 2nd pers.) τὸν πλησίον σου καὶ μισήσεις τὸν ἐχθρόν σου which we would translate as: "You shall love your neighbour and hate your enemy."

Subjunctive can also be used in the form of a "hortatory and prohibitive subjunctive" and occurs in the first person singular as well as plural (e.g. Gal 5:25–26, πνεύματι καὶ στοιχῶμεν. μὴ γινώμεθα κενόδοξοι, let us also walk by the Spirit; let us not become conceited, ...; see also John 14:31). We also see the *"infinitive"* in the imperative mood, for example in Rom

---

[33] Eugene van Ness Goetchius, *The Language of the New Testament* (New York, N.Y.: Scribner's, 1965), 262.

[34] Hare, "Imperative Sentences" (n. 26), 24.

12:15: χαίρειν μετὰ χαιρόντων, κλαίειν μετὰ κλαιόντων (Rejoice with those who rejoice, weep with those who weep).[35] Finally, the imperative mood is expressed with *participles*, for example Col 3:13: ἀνεχόμενοι ἀλλήλων καὶ χαριζόμενοι ἑαυτοῖς (forbear one another and forgive each other) or Eph 4:32: χαριζόμενοι ἑαυτοῖς, καθὼς καὶ ὁ θεὸς ἐν Χριστῷ ἐχαρίσατο ὑμῖν (Forgive one another, just as God in Christ forgave you).

This degree of linguistic differentiation in New Testament Greek should be captured as precisely as possible and not be prematurely categorized under the blanket term "imperative." Nonetheless, grammatical or modal analysis is not sufficient for conceptualizing imperative statements.

b) The 'Grammatical Logic' of Ethics
Thus I come to my second sub-point – the internal structure or logic of an ethical statement. How can ethical statements be substantiated or logically comprehended?

Let us look at an example. Why should debtor A, whose debts have been forgiven by creditor B, forgive the debts of debtor C, for whom he himself is creditor?

Or formulated negatively – if debtor A demands a prison sentence for person C for whom debtor A is a creditor, debtor A must in turn accept that his own creditor B will also demand a prison sentence for him. His own interests are thus in opposition to the transference onto another equivalent case.

The ethical logic that is behind this example is that of universalizability. However, you will be astounded – the example corresponds not only to the parable of the unmerciful servant (Matt 18:23–35) but also exactly to the example of the creditor that Richard M. Hare uses in *Freedom and Reason*.[36] Only the assumption of the principle of universalizability – 'anyone who is in my situation should put his debtor into prison if he does not pay his debts' – stands in opposition to the singular prescription that says "I ought to put A into prison because he does not pay what he owes me."

For Hare, universalizability is one of two central criteria of ethical judgments. The other is that of prescriptivity. "When we are trying, in a concrete case, to decide what we ought to do, what we are looking for (as I have already said) is an action to which we can commit ourselves (prescriptivity) but which we are at the same time prepared to accept as exemplifying a principle of action to be prescribed for others in like circumstances (universalizability). If, when we consider some proposed action, we find that, when universalized, it yields prescriptions which we cannot

---

[35] Another examples is Phil 3:16: πλὴν εἰς ὃ ἐφθάσαμεν, τῷ αὐτῷ στοιχεῖν.

[36] Hare is fully aware of the parallel, he writes: "The example is adapted from a well-known parable," Hare, *Freedom and Reason* (n. 25), 90.

accept, we reject this action as a solution to our moral problem – if we cannot universalize the prescription, it cannot become an 'ought'."[37]

Thus, according to Hare, there are four necessary components to a moral argument of this kind: "(1) facts, (2) logic, (3) inclinations"[38] and later he adds the "power of imagination."

The first requirement (of moral argumentation) is that the facts of the case must be given because every moral discussion revolves around a certain number of facts, be they actual or assumed. Second, we possess the logical framework that is provided by the meaning of the word "ought" (i.e. prescriptivity and universalizability, which are both necessary). Because moral judgements must be universalizable, B cannot say that he should put A into prison without obligating himself to the opinion that C, who, as assumed, finds himself in the same position in relation to B, should put him (B) into prison. And because moral judgements are prescriptive, this would in fact mean prescribing that C put him (B) into prison, which he is not willing to do because he has a strong inclination not to go to prison. This inclination delivers us the third necessary component of the argument. If B were a completely apathetic person, who in fact did not care what happened to him or other people, the argument would not affect him.[39]

Hare emphasizes that, in this method of moral argumentation that forces the actors to search for the universalizability of their own singular norm of action, it is not important whether the actors actually must fear ever being on the receiving end of the norm in question. Rather it is important that the actors, in the search for the universalizability of the norm of action to be questioned, must imagine the hypothetic case in which he himself is in the position of the other person and he must then ask himself whether he in that case can accept the norm.

Hare says: "if *C* did not exist, it could be no answer to the argument for *B* to say 'But in my case there is no fear that anybody will ever be in a position to do to me what I am proposing to do to *A*'. For the argument does not rest on any such fear. All that is essential to it is that B should disregard the fact that he plays the particular role in the situation which he does, without disregarding the inclinations which people have in situations of this sort."[40]

Because, in verifying the universalizability of a norm, it is necessary to imagine cases in which one is in the situation of another, Hare names the

---

[37]   Hare, *Freedom and Reason* (n. 25), II. 6.2 (89–90).
[38]   Hare, *Freedom and Reason* (n. 25), 93.
[39]   See Hare, *Freedom and Reason* (n. 25), 92–93.
[40]   See Hare, *Freedom and Reason* (n. 25), 93–94.

"power of imagination" as the fourth necessary component of moral argumentation.[41]

Hare's coupling of prescriptivity and universalizability has since been greatly criticized and does not have to be used as a criterion in our examination. Nonetheless it to Hare's credit that he has demonstrated that moral statements exhibit an inner logic that can be analysed in regards to its structure and plausibility.

This should remain in our consciousness in the course of the analysis of ethical texts from the New Testament. It is wrong for New Testament ethics to be considered across-the-board as "ethics of command" in which an ethical judgement is always deduced from metaphysical premises. Of equally little help is the still popular classification of "indicative and imperative."[42] Often New Testament authors exhibit rational argumentations or even logical deductions with which they justify a demanded action or category of values. Thus we can ask – how does an ethical judgement arise, which strategy of argumentation is employed here?

We are concerned here with the structure of motives, with the logical deduction, with which an ethical judgement is justified. It is not only formal logic as the study of congruence that can be determined in this process to be a linguistic form or syntax.[43] Other patterns of motives can also be described as linguistic structures and categories. In this way premises can be determined that lead to conclusions. In this process there are inductive and deductive conclusions, enthymemes and syllogisms. One can also define so-called "presuppositions" or "implicatures." Presuppositions[44] are understood to be the implicit presumptions of a statement.[45] The term "implicature," which goes back to the linguistic philosopher Paul Grice[46], at-

---

[41] See Hare, *Freedom and Reason* (n. 25), 94.

[42] See my critical reflection in Zimmermann, "Jenseits von Indikativ und Imperativ" (n. 16), 260–265.

[43] So Joseph M. Bochenski, *Grundriß der Logik* (Paderborn: Schöningh, 1973), 11: Logic is "die Lehre von der Folgerichtigkeit. Da für die Folgerichtigkeit nicht die inhaltliche Bedeutung, sondern die syntaktische Form der Ausdrücke entscheidend ist, sprach man auch von formaler Logik."

[44] Janos S. Petöfi and Dorothea Franck (eds.), *Präsuppositionen in Philosophie und Linguistik* (Linguistische Forschungen 7; Frankfurt am Main: Athenäum, 1973); Ruth M. Kempson, *Presupposition and the Delimitation of Semantics* (Cambridge: Cambridge University Press, 1975).

[45] Bertrand Russell's classical example is "The present king of France is bald." This statement includes the presupposition, that there currently is a king in France; for that reason you call it "existence-presupposition." Cf. Heinz Vater, *Referenz-Linguistik* (Munich: Fink, 2005), 32.

[46] H. Paul Grice, "Logic and Conversation," in *Speech acts* (ed. Peter Cole and Jerry Morgan; Syntax and Semantics 3; New York, N.Y.: Academic Press, 1975), 41–58, German translation: "Logik und Konversation," in *Handlung, Kommunikation, Bedeutung*

tempts to capture the phenomenon in which aspects of meaning are alluded to and presupposed in linguistic statements, but are not themselves stated.

Irreconcilable contradictions are revealed demanding a particular judgement, or argumentations are made with analogies or with the figure "a minore ad maius." Beyond "pure logic" also (which can be applied to antiquity only with limitations), a whole series of such structures of motive are used within the New Testament, as they were also described especially for the letters of Paul.[47]

Thus the figure of the postulated consequences of action within the scope of the „act-and-consequence connection" also belongs to the classical repertoire of ethical grammar. In order to attain or avoid certain consequences, a certain action is classified as correct and good. Corresponding sentences are found in document Q:

Luke 6:37:
Καὶ μὴ κρίνετε, καὶ οὐ μὴ κριθῆτε· καὶ μὴ καταδικάζετε, καὶ οὐ μὴ καταδικασθῆτε. ἀπολύετε, καὶ ἀπολυθήσεσθε·
(Judge not, and you will not be judged; condemn not, and you will not be condemned; forgive, and you will be forgiven)

Luke 6:38:
δίδοτε, καὶ δοθήσεται ὑμῖν· μέτρον καλὸν πεπιεσμένον σεσαλευμένον ὑπερεκχυννόμενον δώσουσιν εἰς τὸν κόλπον ὑμῶν· ᾧ γὰρ μέτρῳ μετρεῖτε ἀντιμετρηθήσεται ὑμῖν.
(Give, and it will be given to you; good measure, pressed down, shaken together, running over, will be put into your lap. For the measure you give will be the measure you get back.)

According to the terminology of ethical tradition, one can characterize such a justification as "teleological" because an act is evaluated in terms of a particular goal (τέλος). A "deontological structure of motive," which evaluates actions within the framework of a prescribed norm or duty, must be differentiated from this.

(ed. Georg Meggle; stw 1083; trans. A. Kemmerling; Frankfurt am Main: Suhrkamp, 1993), 243–265. An example for a generalized conversational implicature would be a sentence like "I have four children," which implies that the speaker does not have more than four children, for if the speaker had five or six children, the sentence would also be valid.

[47] See Johan S. Vos, *Die Kunst der Argumentation bei Paulus. Studien zur antiken Rhetorik* (WUNT 149; Tübingen: Mohr Siebeck, 2002). See Werner Wolbert, *Ethische Argumentation und Paränese in 1 Kor 7* (MoThSt.S 8; Düsseldorf: Patmos, 1981), 54–71; Franz Furger, "Ethische Argumentation und neutestamentliche Aussagen," in *Ethik im Neuen Testament* (ed. Karl Kertelge; QD 102; Freiburg i. Br.: Herder, 1984), 13–31 – as the corresponding replique of Rudolf Schnackenburg, "Ethische Argumentationsmethoden und neutestamentlich-ethische Aussagen," in *Ethik im Neuen Testament*, 32–49; most recently see Wolfgang Fenske, *Die Argumentation des Paulus in ethischen Herausforderungen* (Göttingen: Vandenhoeck & Ruprecht, 2004).

We often see mixed figures of thought, as in the passage on the taming of the tongue in James 3:1–13:

My brethren, let not many of you become teachers, knowing that we shall receive a stricter judgment. [2] For we all stumble in many things. If anyone does not stumble in word, he *is* a perfect man, able also to bridle the whole body. [3] Indeed, we put bits in horses' mouths that they may obey us, and we turn their whole body. [4] Look also at ships: although they are so large and are driven by fierce winds, they are turned by a very small rudder wherever the pilot desires. [5] Even so the tongue is a little member and boasts great things. See how great a forest a little fire kindles! [6] And the tongue *is* a fire, a world of iniquity. The tongue is so set among our members that it defiles the whole body, and sets on fire the course of nature; and it is set on fire by hell. [7] For every kind of beast and bird, of reptile and creature of the sea, is tamed and has been tamed by mankind. [8] But no man can tame the tongue. *It is* an unruly evil, full of deadly poison. [9] With it we bless our God and Father, and with it we curse men, who have been made in the similitude of God. [10] Out of the same mouth proceed blessing and cursing. My brethren, these things ought not to be so. [11] Does a spring send forth fresh *water* and bitter from the same opening? [12] Can a fig tree, my brethren, bear olives, or a grapevine bear figs? Thus no spring yields both salt water and fresh. [13] Who *is* wise and understanding among you? Let him show by good conduct *that* his works *are done* in the meekness of wisdom.

First, using examples or miniature parables such as the horse's bit and ship's rudder, analogous conclusions (James 3:5: οὕτως καὶ ἡ γλῶσσα, even so the tongue …) are drawn. In the next step, by means of the example of the fire, the effects of lying and false talk are illustrated. Instead of an analogous conclusion, here there is a metaphoric identification: James 3:6: καὶ ἡ γλῶσσα πῦρ (And the tongue is a fire); there is also a metaphorization in the example of the taming of animals (vv. 7–8) by speaking of "the taming of tongues" (But no man can tame the tongue). Finally, ambiguous speech is ethically devalued by the process of irreconcilable contradictions during which rhetorical questions are employed.

Conclusion: An ethical statement can be studied inter-textually in regards to its linguistic structure, be it that grammatical forms and stylistic instruments are understood descriptively, be it that the argumentation structure that leads to a value judgement is analysed.

3.2 On the inter-textual Level (i.e. Form Criticism)

The nature of a particular unit of text (on the macro- and micro-levels) influences its meaning and moral quality. Since the early phases of form criticism, we have been used to classifying New Testament texts into certain genres.

In this process, the question arises as to whether there are "ethical genres." In the literature one spoke of "paraenesis" or "paraenetical genres." Martin Dibelius, who used the term within his form criticism, described with this term text "der Mahnungen allgemein sittlichen Inhalts aneinanderreiht" (that strings together admonitions with general moral content)[48] and has the character of an (admonitory) sermon. The Pauline paraenesis are "not expansive, religiously or theologically-motivated arguments but rather individual admonitions, often in the form of sayings, that are fastened loosely to each other or stand unconnected next to each other."[49] Due to the very few examples of παραινέω in the New Testament (the verb occurs only twice in Acts 27:9, 22; the noun παραίνεσις does not appear at all) as well as to factual considerations, *Rudolf Hasenstab*[50] had already correctly indicated the limits of the concept of paraenesis and demanded that it be replaced by a paraklesis model.[51] More recently, the conference proceedings published by James M. Starr and Troels Engberg-Pedersen discuss the possibilities and limitations of the "paraenesis concept,"[52] which is however suitable neither as a genre term nor as a comprehensive pattern of motive of New Testament ethics due to the historical semantics and the use of the term in antiquity.[53]

Within so-called "new form criticism," Klaus Berger has identified in his form criticism three fundamental genre forms by drawing on the moods of speech of ancient rhetoric. These forms are 1) symbuleutic genres, 2) epideictic genres, and 3) dicanic genres. According to Berger, especially symbuleutic texts aim at "den Hörer zum Handeln oder Unterlassen zu

---

[48] See Martin Dibelius, *Die Formgeschichte des Evangeliums* (4th ed.; Tübingen: Mohr Siebeck, 1961), 16–17 and 234–265.

[49] Dibelius, *Formgeschichte* (n. 48), 239: "… nicht weit ausholende, religiös oder theologisch begründete Erörterungen, sondern einzelne Mahnungen, oft in Spruchform, lose aneinander gehängt oder unverbunden nebeneinander stehend."

[50] See Rudolf Hasenstab, *Modelle paulinischer Ethik. Beiträge zu einem Autonomie-Modell aus paulinischem Geist* (TTS 11; Mainz: Matthias Grünewald, 1977), 67–94; see before already Heinrich Schlier, "Vom Wesen der apostolischen Ermahnung," in *Die Zeit der Kirche. Exegetische Aufsätze und Vorträge* (ed. Heinrich Schlier; 4th ed.; Freiburg i. Br.: Herder, 1966), 74–89, here 82–83; Anton Grabner-Haider, *Paraklese und Eschatologie bei Paulus. Mensch und Welt im Anspruch der Zukunft Gottes* (NTA 4; Münster: Aschendorff, 1968).

[51] See Hasenstab, *Modelle paulinischer Ethik* (n. 50), 67–94. Similar Rudolf Schnackenburg, "Ethische Argumentationsmethoden und neutestamentlich-ethische Aussagen," in *Ethik im Neuen Testament* (n. 47), 32–49, here 34: "Wir sollten also eher von Paraklese als von Paränese sprechen."

[52] James Starr and Troels Engberg-Pedersen (eds.), *Early Christian Paraenesis in Context* (BZNW 125; Berlin/New York: de Gruyter, 2004); also Wiard Popkes, *Paränese und Neues Testament* (SBS 168; Stuttgart: Katholisches Bibelwerk, 1996).

[53] See here the summery of Wiard Popkes, "Paraenesis in the New Testament. An Exercise in Conceptuality," in Starr/Engberg-Pedersen, *Early Christian paraenesis* (n. 52), 13–46, here 14–15.

bewegen" (motivating the listener to action or to forbearance)[54] as corresponds to the etymology of the Greek συμβυλεύομαι (to advise to do something). Seen like this, symbuleutic genres can be considered to be "ethical
genres" that do not only descriptively exhibit motives of action, but also
prescriptively press for action.

Under the heading "symbuleutic genres," Berger lists more than twenty
different genres that range from the "simple command" to the complex
"symbuleutic argument."[55] We find here individual micro-genres, such as
"words of woe" (§55) as well as the macro-genre "letter" (§61: The New
Testament letter as a symbuleutic genre). Berger also combines texts into
their own, new genre classifications, such as "Postconversionale Mahnrede" (post-conversational admonitory speech, §40) or "protreptische
Mahnrede" (protreptic admonitory speech, §62). These classifications have
also been taken up in more recent discussions, for example by Michael
Wolter.[56] In addition, we meet the classic, well-known moral genres such
as "household-table" (§41) or "virtue and vice catalogue" (§47).

I do not want to discuss the justification for the diversity of genres offered here or the claim to the ancient rhetorical categories, but rather I
want to turn to a more fundamental question: why are these texts identified
as symbuleutic texts or the genres as ethical genres?

In his argumentation, Berger turns out to be a supporter of the so-called
"new form criticism." This is characterized by the fact that individual, usually linguistically form-building elements are linked to a superior form
that, in comparison with similar texts, inductively leads to the description
of a genre.

Thus the virtue and vice catalogues can be characterized as "sequences
of nominal characters in which morally positively- or morally-negatively
evaluated behaviour or its carrier or perhaps only corresponding characteristics are listed."[57] Often these catalogues exhibit strictly dualistic struc-

---

[54] See Klaus Berger, *Formgeschichte des Neuen Testaments* (Heidelberg: Quelle und
Meyer, 1984), 18.

[55] See Berger, *Formgeschichte* (n. 54), C. Symbuleutische Gattungen, § 36–§ 62,
117–220. Die "symbuleutische Argumentation" wird bereits unter der Untergruppe "Argumentation" bei B. Sammelgattungen erwähnt, see § 30, 93–100. The number of para-
graphs differs from the number of sub-genre, because he discusses also more general
topics (for instance § 37: Allgemeine Merkmale von Paränese) or specific questions (§
46: Paränese im Jakobusbrief).

[56] So the structure according to Berger, *Formgeschichte* (n. 54), 217, which Michael
Wolter explored further, cf. Wolter, "Ethische Identität" (n. 4), 63: "Protreptische Mahnungen fordern zur Beibehaltung oder Übernahme einer neuen Existenzorientierung (z.B.
nach Bekehrung), während es den paränetischen Mahnungen um die ,Praxis des neuen
Seins' geht."

[57] Berger, *Formgeschichte* (n. 54), § 47, 148: Tugend- und Lasterkataloge sind "Rei-
hungen nominalen Charakters, in denen moralisch positiv oder moralisch negativ gewer-

tures in which, as in Gal 5:19–21, virtues and vices are contrasted with each other.

Thus we could state that genres are ethical genres when they exhibit particular, form-building elements that transport a moral appeal or a moral judgement by means of grammatical form (e.g. the imperative) or of semantic content (e.g. virtues). In this, the ethical character would be able to be reduced completely to a single linguistic element so that the difference to the intra-textual level can only be determined quantitatively.

According to more recent genre theories, we can regard genre only within limitations as "a system of classification" that is itself prescribed through elements of a text.[58] At other opportunities I have attempted to demonstrate that genres are instead constructs that fulfil specific functions in the communication of communities.[59]

The ethical character of a genre can thus not be completely separated from form-building elements; however, these could be brought into the wider scope of the communication situation. For the communication participants, the individual elements fulfil the function of categorizing individual texts into other, known text types and their specific uses ("seat in life"). They can play a role in ethical discourse only through these connections. In relation to the example of the vice and virtue catalogue, the addressees of these texts are reminded of well-known sequences of value concepts as they commonly occurred for instance in Hellenistic Jewish conversation theology.[60] Only the conventional use of individual text types in ethical discourse allows the ethical character of a genre to emerge. Such a consideration holds two advantages:

---

tetes Verhalten oder dessen Träger oder auch nur entsprechende Eigenschaften aufgezählt werden."

[58] See Rüdiger Zymner, *Gattungstheorie. Probleme und Positionen der Literaturwissenschaft* (Paderborn: mentis, 2003), Kapitel 1: "Probleme der Gattungstheorie" (7–36); David Duff (ed.), *Modern Genre Theory* (Harlow: Longman, 2000); Peter Wenzel, "Gattungstheorie und Gattungspoetik," *Metzler Lexikon Literatur- und Kulturtheorie* (3rd ed.; Stuttgart: Metzler, 2004), 212–214.

[59] So you can distinguish a traditional, communial and identity-making function within a certain community, see on that topic Ruben Zimmermann, "Formen und Gattungen als Medien der Jesus-Erinnerung. Zur Rückgewinnung der Diachronie in der Formgeschichte des Neuen Testaments," in *Die Macht der Erinnerung* (JBTh 22 [2007]; ed. Otmar Fuchs and Bernd Janowski; Neukirchen-Vluyn: Neukirchener, 2008), 131–167; see also the concrete application on the parables-genre in Ruben Zimmermann, Gleichnisse als Medien der Jesuserinnerung. Die Historizität der Jesusparabeln im Horizont der Gedächtnisforschung, in *Hermeneutik der Gleichnisse Jesu* (ed. Ruben Zimmermann; WUNT 231; Tübingen: Mohr Siebeck, 2008), 87–121, here 108–121.

[60] See Stephen C. Mott, "Greek Ethics and Christian Conversion: The Philonic Background of Titus II 10–14 and III 3–7," *NT* 20 (1978): 22–48.

On the one hand, the category of "ethical genre" can be expanded to text types that up to now (according to form criticism) have not been included in the repertoire of ethical texts because, for example, the direct character of address or the classic value concepts are missing. Concretely these are narrative or image texts. Each in their own way, however, they have an appellative and therefore also an ethical character.[61] Especially narrative texts such as the parables or the Gospels can become models of action. At other times I have demonstrated how, for example, parables can be the expression of ethico-poetics or aesthetic ethics.[62]

On the other hand, it is clear that the issue of genre remains tied into a wider scope of inter-textuality. In order to completely understand the ethical dimension, for example, of an admonitory speech, one needs the pre-knowledge of the "prophetic admonitory speech." The tension between "reception and production" is part of the formation of ethical texts; they therefore reflect the presence of "tradition" as well as of "innovation."

We may ask: which pre- and inter-texts form part of the ethical statements? How are they referred to and what is their functionality (e.g. the law)?

In the end, a communication-theoretical consideration of the genres makes it clear that the transition from inter-textuality to extra-textuality is fluid.

Thus, I come to my third focus:

3.3 On the extra-textual Level (e.g. Speech Act Analysis)

The linguisticality of ethics can be considered under a third focus – one that I would like to summarize under the heading "extra-textuality." Texts (in different forms) are an integral part of the communication process. As

---

[61] See for example Ruben Zimmermann, *Geschlechtermetaphorik und Gottesverhältnis. Traditionsgeschichte und Theologie eines Bildfelds in Urchristentum und antiker Umwelt* (WUNT 2/122; Tübingen: Mohr Siebeck, 2001), 300–325 (for 2 Cor 11:1–4); Christine Gerber, *Paulus und seine ‚Kinder'. Studien zur Beziehungsmetaphorik der paulinischen Briefe* (BZNW 136; Berlin/New York: de Gruyter, 2005); Charles A. Wanamaker, "Metaphor and morality. Examples of Paul's moral thinking in 1 Corinthians 1–5," *Neot.* 39 (2005): 409–433.

[62] See Ruben Zimmermann, "The Etho-poietic of the parable of the good Samaritan (Lk 10:25–37). The ethics of seeing in a culture of looking the other way," *Verbum et Ecclesia* 29 (2008): 269–292; idem, "Die Ethico-Ästhetik der Gleichnisse Jesu. Ethik durch literarische Ästhetik am Beispiel der Parabeln im Matthäus-Evangelium," in *Jenseits von Indikativ und Imperativ* (vol. 1 of *Kontexte und Normen neutestamentlicher Ethik / Texts and Contexts of New Testament Ethics*; ed. Friedrich Wilhelm Horn and Ruben Zimmermann; WUNT 238; Tübingen: Mohr Siebeck, 2009), 235–265.

Bühler and later Austin have pointed out[63], we do things with words. It is therefore valid to ask what texts do and not only what texts mean.

This fundamental observation is particularly relevant for ethics. If texts remain ineffective, they are also irrelevant for 'practical ethics.' The reflexivity of action and its motives reach their actual goal only if they play a role in the action. Motives of action must lead to action. Thus this last point is perhaps the most important of all.

Adapted to our topic, the question is: By means of which linguistic instruments do New Testament texts lead to action? How do ethics emerge from the texts and interact in the real life of the community of addressees, of later readers and finally in our own lives? What are the ethical impacts of such texts on their readers? How do the texts (try or aim to) facilitate or manipulate the reader? Which possible influence do the texts have on practical-ethical discourse?

When I speak of the "extra-textual" dimension from this perspective, the text remains the definitive origin and component part of this approach. From the perspective of the text, we shall reflect, in this last point, on the historical and (when applicable the present-day) communication situation and potential impact of the text.

We could take various methodological paths in this process. Ideas of literary hermeneutics could be used; methods of literary aesthetics or reader-response criticism or pragmatics could be applied.

The effect on the reader has even been discussed within analytic ethics. Ayer and Stevenson, as supporters of so-called "emotivists," have interpreted the moral statements as expressions of emotion with which subjective approval or disapproval should be expressed. While for Ayer, a moral statement can be equated one-to-one with an expression of emotion (e.g. It is bad that John stole = John stole, ugh!), for Stevenson the expression of emotion is simultaneously connected to an appeal to a conversation partner: you do the same or do not do the same. Regarded thus, moral statements are appeals to follow one's own convictions. Thus moral sentences have no descriptive or rational dimension. An ethical argumentation "in the end does not serve an appeal to reason but rather a strategy of persuasion through the waking of emotions."[64]

I consider the speech act theory to be particularly useful in this case, in the form that it was set down by John L. Austin in *How to do Things with Words*, which I have mentioned several times, and then was adopted and

---

[63] Karl Bühler, *Sprachtheorie: Die Darstellungsfunktion der Sprache* (Stuttgart: Lucius & Lucius, 1999; reprint of the first edition; Jena: G. Fischer, 1934); John L. Austin, *How to do Things with Words* (Cambridge, Mass.: Harvard University Press, 1962).

[64] See Annemarie Pieper, *Einführung in die Ethik* (6th ed.; Tübingen: Francke, 2007).

expanded by John Searle.[65] One of the basic convictions is that one should appreciate the "indirect speech act" of a linguistic statement that lies outside the content of the statement. Formulated more technically, one should separate the propositional statement clearly from an assertion. (Searle: "a proposition is to be sharply distinguished from an assertion or statement of it").[66] In saying, "Ladies and gentlemen, may I have your attention, please," a speaker is requesting that the audience be quiet.

Searle identifies four speech acts:[67]

1. Utterance acts: production of statements, including Austin's phonetic and phatic acts
2. Propositional acts: referring and predicating (expressing the propositioin)
3. Illocutionary Acts: Stating, questioning, commanding, etc.
4. Perlocutionary acts: persuading, convincing, etc.

While value judgements, in the sense of definitions, can be put into the level of the propositional act ("X is good;" X refers to an object of the world and is characterized as 'good'), the prescriptive dimension is only tangible on the illocutionary level. It is particularly to Searle's credit that he has described the illocutionary act more precisely. Searle has set down the following classification of illocutionary speech acts:[68]

assertives = speech acts that commit a speaker to the truth of the expressed proposition
directives = speech acts that are to cause the hearer to take a particular action, e.g. requests, commands and advice
commissives = speech acts that commit a speaker to some future action, e.g. promises and oaths
expressives = speech acts that express the speaker's attitudes and emotions towards the proposition, e.g. congratulations, excuses and thanks

---

[65] Searles major contributions to the subjects are John R. Searle, *Speech Acts: An Essay in the Philosophy of Language* (Cambridge: Cambridge University Press, 1969); idem (ed.), *The Philosophy of Language* (Oxford: Oxford University Press, 1971); idem, *Intentionality: An Essay in the Philosophy of Mind* (Cambridge: Cambridge University Press, 1983). The term "Speech Act" had also been already used by Karl Bühler in his "Die Axiomatik der Sprachwissenschaften," *Kant-Studien* 38 (1933): 19–90, 43, where he discusses a "Theorie der Sprechhandlungen" and in his book *Sprachtheorie* (Jena: G. Fischer, 1934) where he uses "Sprechhandlung" and "Theorie der Sprechakte."

[66] Searle, *Speech Acts* (n. 65), 29.

[67] See Searle, *Speech Acts* (n. 65), 24–25; also the good summery on Searle in Richard S. Briggs, *Words in Action: Speech Act Theory and Biblical Interpretation* (Edinburgh: T&T Clark, 2001), 43–63.

[68] See John Searle, "A Taxonomy of Illocutionary Acts," in *Expression and Meaning: Studies in the Theory of Speech Acts* (ed. John Searle; Cambridge: Cambridge University Press, 1981), Chapter 1, 1–29, especially 12–20; first in Keith Gunderson (ed.), *Language, Mind, and Knowledge* (Minnesota Studies in the Philosophy of Science 7; Minneapolis, Minn.: Minnesota University Press, 1975).

declarations = speech acts that change the reality in accordance with the proposition of the declaration, e.g. baptisms, pronouncing someone guilty or pronouncing someone husband and wife

Assertive declarations = assertive speech acts with the force of a declaration, e.g. you are guilty as charged

Each of these speech acts contains an ethical dimension. Normative ethical texts, for example, want to express own value judgements (expressives), to lead the listener to their own actions or self-obligations (directives, commissives) and ask question of truth (assertives). Thus it is not surprising that the well-known book *Speech Act* by John Searle explicitly depicts, in the second section, a system of ethics. Searle attempts within his theory to make the connection between linguistics and ethics, which, however, has been disassembled again by most recipients in a detached way of reading.[69] Some recipients who recognize the connection accuse Searle of normatively interpreting the empirical approach of John Austin. However, I would like to take up this connection of linguistics and ethics in a positive way. John Searle attempts to show by means of his speech-act-grammar that to be and ought to be are, in many cases, are closely connected with each other.

The speech act theory has, despite Derrida's[70] protest, been used in the interpretation of texts and for the interpretation of biblical texts.[71] To do this, we must identify various levels and communication situations in which the speech acts take place. Let us take an ethical sentence from John 13:15: "For I gave you an example that you also should do as I did to you." The following communication situations must be considered here:

1. Jesus says this to his disciples, whose feet he has washed (narrative speech act)
2. John tells his community that Jesus said… (historical speech act)
3. Contemporary readers read that John told his community what Jesus said (contemporary speech act)

---

[69] It is mainly linguists and ethicists who refer to Searle's work – linguists refer to the first part of the book, ethicists to the second. Searle himself mocks these separated ways of reading in his last chapter, see Searle, Speech Acts (n. 65), 263.

[70] See Jacques Derrida, "Signature événement contexte," in *Marges de la philosophie* (ed. Jacques Derrida; Paris: Les Editions de Minuit, 1972), 365–393 and the English translation in Jacques Derrida, "Signature Event Context," *Glyph* 1 (1977): 172–197; see also the reply John R. Searle, "Reiterating the Differences: A Reply to Derrida," *Glyph* 1 (1977): 198–208.

[71] See Andreas Wagner, *Sprechakte und Sprechaktanalyse im Alten Testament. Untersuchungen der Nahtstelle zwischen Handlungsebene und Grammatik* (BZAW 253; Berlin/New York: de Gruyter, 1997); with a focus to the New Testament see Briggs, *Words in Action* (n. 67).

Further, we can describe a "directive speech act" on the illocutionary level. Jesus (and/or John) attempts to get his disciples/his audience to do something, but not only to wash, but furthermore to love on another as he loved them.[72] To say it more clearly: the speech act dimension is not about the rational analysis of the structure of motive (as in the intra-textual perspective) but rather about the description of the contextual interaction between the text and the reader/listener.

We can describe this influence on texts with clear ethical claims more exactly. As an example, I would like to refer to a statement from the Sermon on the Mount: Jesus said: "If any one strikes you on the right cheek, turn to him the other also (Matt 5:39) On the propositional level the sentence talks about turning the other cheek. But what is the deeper meaning? What is the audience meant to understand? Or in other words: What is the illocutionary act of the statement?

At a first look, Jesus wants his followers to turn the other cheek as a gesture of submission. Thus we could discover an "expressive illocutionary act," demonstrating the devote state of Christians. But what is literally performed is – according to Searle[73] – only the so-called "secondary illocutionary act." The "primary illocutionary act" is the indirect one. Jesus' statement should not be misunderstood as a command of subordination and passivity. On the contrary, Jesus urges the reader to stay active, to resist playing the role of the victim. In this way, we must understand the statement as a "directive illocutionary act." The following verse confirms this line of interpretation. "If someone takes your coat, let him have your cloak as well; if he makes you go a mile with him, go with him two" (Matt 5:40–41). This behavior does not demonstrate passivity, but rather active non-violent resistance.

We can also describe the ethical dimension of texts that are not primarily, i.e. in the propositional act, classified as ethical texts. This is true, for example, for narrative texts that, in regards to the propositional act, are not ethical texts but do indeed possess an appeal structure. The ethical dimension of Johannine texts can be captured in this way. Parables are also texts that exhibit an implicit appeal structure and therefore can be interpreted as "directive speech acts." Thus the parable of the Prodigal Son does not need a concluding appeal to action from the Evangelist (as, for example, Luke

---

[72] See on this contextual interpretation Richard A. Burridge, *Imitating Jesus. An Inclusive Approach to New Testament Ethics* (Grand Rapids, Mich.: Eerdmans, 2007), 327.

[73] Searle introduced the notions of "primary" and "secondary" illocutionary acts. But in contrary to our expectation the primary illocutionary act is the indirect one, which is not literally formed. The secondary illocutionary act is the direct one, performed in the literal utterance, cf. Searle, *Speech Acts* (n. 65), 178.

10:36–37) but nevertheless fulfils a "directive illocutionary act" to the older son, whose reaction is not included.

Instead of adding further examples, I would like to deal with this topic concretely, using one case study.

4. Ephesians 5:21–33 as a Test Case

One might now ask what the additional benefit of linguistic text analysis is for ethics. In order to bring my more fundamental considerations to a point, I would like to use a final text to demonstrate, in outline form, that it is indeed valuable to capture the ethical language of a biblical text as exactly as possible.

I have chosen Eph 5:21–33 – the first section of the so-called household table of the letter to the Ephesians. The text is usually perceived from two aspects. On the one hand, it is quoted as a classic text with which the subordination of women to men is justified. On the other hand, it is disputed that this is an ethical text at all. The primary interest of the text is – according to those scholars – not the clarification of the man-woman relationship but rather the depiction of a special ecclesiology. Through the appreciation of linguistic aspects there emerges, however, an ethical interpretation of the text with a very different accentuation.

4.1 Intra-textual Observations

Let us begin with several selected linguistic observations on the intra-textual level.[74]

a) Imperative:

The text is filled with imperatives. It is however worth looking closely at the linguistic form of the imperatives. The section begins in Eph 5:21 with a participle (Ὑποτασσόμενοι ἀλλήλοις) that has imperative character ("Be subject to..."). Translators and commentators agree that there follows a clear imperative directed towards wives: "Wives, submit to your own husbands, as to the Lord." However, if we look at the Greek text, we see that this imperative towards wives is missing completely and has to be added from the preceding sentence (v. 22: αἱ γυναῖκες τοῖς ἰδίοις ἀνδράσιν). One could still attribute this omission to a question of style; however, v. 24 removes all doubt that the elliptical form of speech is a pure coincidence. For here the author surprisingly reverses the former used categorization.

---

[74] For a linguistic analysis in detail see Zimmermann, *Geschlechtermetaphorik und Gottesverhältnis* (n. 61), 327–343.

Submission is spoken of here indicatively (ὑποτάσσεται = 3rd person singular indicative present active); explicit is only the subordination of the
church to Christ. The call for wives to submit to their husbands has to be
discovered; it is not directly stated.

Eph 5:24
ἀλλὰ ὡς ἡ ἐκκλησία ὑποτάσσεται τῷ Χριστῷ, οὕτως καὶ αἱ γυναῖκες τοῖς ἀνδράσιν ἐν
παντί.
As the church is subject to Christ, so let wives also (be subject) in everything to their
husbands.

This strange tendency is finally confirmed by means of the summarizing
last sentence (Eph 5:33: πλὴν καὶ ὑμεῖς οἱ καθ᾽ ἕνα, ἕκαστος τὴν ἑαυτοῦ
γυναῖκα οὕτως ἀγαπάτω ὡς ἑαυτόν, ἡ δὲ γυνὴ ἵνα φοβῆται τὸν ἄνδρα).
In both cases, translations have usually used a pure imperative. For
example Luther 1984: "ein jeder habe lieb seine Frau wie sich selbst; die
Frau aber ehre den Mann." In the Revised Standard Version we read:
"however, let each one of you love his wife as himself, and let the wife see
that she respects her husband." If we look at the text exactly, we see that
the demands are formulated in different ways: ἕκαστος ... ἀγαπάτω is a
common imperative directed to the husbands; for the wives, in contrast, the
subjunctive aorist is used: ἡ δὲ γυνὴ ἵνα φοβῆται.

Explicit grammatical imperatives, however, can be found in the section
directed to the husbands: Οἱ ἄνδρες, ἀγαπᾶτε τὰς γυναῖκας (Eph 5:25,
ἀγαπᾶτε = imp. pres. 2nd pers. plur.)

Or the ethical obligation to love is expressed with ὀφείλω (= "should,
ought to;" Eph 5:28: οὕτως ὀφείλουσιν [καὶ] οἱ ἄνδρες ἀγαπᾶν τὰς
ἑαυτῶν γυναῖκας). The indicative future, as explained above, can also be
understood in the imperative (§ 362 Blass-Debrunner-Funk) as in the quote
from Gen 2:24 again with the man as the addressee: ἀντὶ τούτου κατα-
λείψει ἄνθρωπος [τὸν] πατέρα καὶ [τὴν] μητέρα καὶ προσκολληθήσεται
πρὸς τὴν γυναῖκα αὐτοῦ, καὶ ἔσονται οἱ δύο εἰς σάρκα μίαν (Eph 5:31).
The imperative of the subordination of wives to their husbands that has
been asserted throughout the history of the text is not truly expressed any-
where in the text.

b) Ethical Syntax/Basic Structure: Metaphoric Interaction
Let us now look at the argumentative structure, the structural ethical
grammar of the text. The text has a two-part structure in which the husband-wife relationship and the Christ-church relationship can be separated
from one another. On the one hand, the conceptual pair, husband and wife,
are mentioned (six times in vv. 22a; 23a; 24b; 25a; 28a; 33c). On the other
hand, Christ and the church are explicitly named together five times (vv.
23b; 24a; 25b; 29b; 32b) and in other places are related to each other in a

subject-object structure (v. 27a). The two areas, however, do not stand disconnectedly next to each other, but rather are related closely to each other. This connection is created above all by the particles ὡς (5 times), οὕτως (3 times) and καθώς (twice).

The classification of the two elements does not take place one-sidedly. Instead the two levels determine themselves and increase in precision reciprocally. This is imposed on them by the fact that the author continuously jumps back and forth between the two statement areas and on the one hand illuminates the husband-wife relationship by means of the Christ-church relationship (e.g. v. 23ab) while on the other hand the inter-sexual dimension gains precision through the Christ-church connection.[75]

The ethical motivation thus does not take place with a simple analogous conclusion (as ... so), but rather a metaphoric interaction is created between two areas that enables a reciprocal semantic determination. From an ethical perspective, we can determine that everything that is said about the relationship between Christ and the church can and must also be directly related to the relationship between the husband and wife.

4.2 Inter-textual Level: Genre Household-Code

Let us now look at the inter-textual level with a focus on the genre. The text is correctly classified as a household-table text. Beginning with Xenophons *Oikonomikos*, the household-table genre enjoyed great popularity in Greco-Roman antiquity.[76] The texts were meant, in a particular way, to regulate life together in the household, in which there were always hierarchical relationships between husband and wife, parents and children, master and slaves, which were justified naturalistically. The role of the husband toward his wife was traditionally described using semantics of dominance: the husband should rule and the wife should be submissive, even if the relationship during Hellenism could be relativized as caring domi-

---

[75] See the table in J. Paul Sampley, *"And the two shall become one flesh." A study of traditions in Ephesians 5:21–33* (MS.SNTS 16; Cambridge: Cambridge University Press, 1971); Zimmermann, *Geschlechtermetaphorik und Gottesverhältnis* (n. 61), 330; more recently Gerhard Sellin, *Der Brief an die Epheser* (KEK 8; Göttingen: Vandenhoeck & Ruprecht, 2008), 424–457.

[76] See Marlies Gielen, *Tradition und Theologie neutestamentlicher Haustafelethik. Ein Beitrag zur Frage einer christlichen Auseinandersetzung mit gesellschaftlichen Normen* (Frankfurt am Main: Hain, 1990); Johannes Woyke, *Die neutestamentlichen Haustafeln: ein kritischer und konstruktiver Forschungsüberblick* (SBS 184; Stuttgart: Katholisches Bibelwerk, 2000); James P. Hering, *The Colossian and Ephesian Haustafeln in Theological Context: An Analysis of their Origins, Relationship, and Message* (New York, N.Y.: Peter Lang, 2007), for a brief look also Berger, *Formgeschichte* (n. 54), 135–140.

nance[77] or modified as pedagogical primacy.[78] In various places in the New Testament, we see other texts that can be classified into the household-table genre based on form-building elements (e.g. Col 3:18–4:1; Eph 5:21–6:9; 1 Peter 2:18–3:7, Tit 2:1–10).

The synopsis below shows the verses central to our topic:

Col 3:18	Eph 5:21–22	1 Petr 3:1	Tit 2:4–5
Αἱ γυναῖκες, ὑποτάσσεσθε τοῖς ἀνδράσιν ὡς ἀνῆκεν ἐν κυρίῳ.	αἱ γυναῖκες τοῖς ἰδίοις ἀνδράσιν ὡς τῷ κυρίῳ,	Ὁμοίως [αἱ] γυναῖ-κες, ὑποτασσόμεναι τοῖς ἰδίοις ἀνδράσιν,	ἵνα σωφρονίζωσιν τὰς νέας ... ὑποτασσομένας τοῖς ἰδίοις ἀνδράσιν,
Wives, be subject to your husbands, as is fitting in the Lord.	Wives, (*be subject*) to your own husbands, as to the Lord.	Likewise you wives, be submissive to your husbands	and so train the young women ... to be submissive to their husbands

The submission of the wife is established in each case with the verb ὑποτάσσεσθαι. The relationship of the sexes in the marriage is regulated along strict hierarchical lines. It is interesting, however, in which way the author of Ephesians draws on the known genre. Unlike in the New Testament comparative texts, the keyword ὑποτάσσεσθαι is missing in the direct determination of the relationship between husband and wife (s. table). The justification of the roles of the sexes, which in *Oikonomikos* literature was normally naturalistic, is replaced by a Christological justification. In this process, the usual semantics of dominance are expanded and penetrated by the keyword "love." The men should, using Christ as a role model, love their wives as they love their own bodies (v. 28). Instead of reading about the maintenance of patriarchal claims or the cementing of a role of dominance, we read in Eph 5 about a comprehensive call for husbands to love their wives, which, perhaps unusually for us, does not rank in the usual characteristics of ancient marital relationships. One can love friends or children but not wives. The stipulation to love is thus a clear penetration of the usual role norms. The stipulation for wives to submit themselves (vv. 22–24, 33) is linguistically relativized and seems, in the face of this obligation of the husbands, pale and formulaic.

Finally the framing verses show that a critical reception of the household-table genre is important for Eph 5:21–33. At the end it is not submission that is demanded of the wife but the honouring of her husband (v. 33:

---

[77] See e.g. Plutarch, *Conj. praec.* 142e.

[78] See on that change referring to ancient texts Zimmermann, *Geschlechtermetaphorik und Gottesverhältnis* (n. 61), 338–341; also Ines Stahlmann, *Der gefesselte Sexus: weibliche Keuschheit und Askese im Westen des Römischen Reiches* (Berlin: Akademie, 1997), 30–38.

"wife, honor your husband") and the entire section is placed under the heading of reciprocal subordination (v. 21: "Be subject to one another").

On the inter-textual level we can determine a clear reference to the household-table genre. However, the author of Ephesians wants to call up the household-code schema in his addressees in order to finally create a dissenting and critical reception.

4.3 Extra-textual Level (Speech Acts)

But why this way of speaking? What is meant to be said, what should be achieved with the statement? Thus, I have come finally to the extra-textual level.

On the level of the propositional act, the text explains the relationship of husband and wife with reference to the relationship of Christ and the church. But what is the intended effect? Which function should the text have fulfilled in ethical discourse? The consideration of illocutionary acts can help us here.

The text is a direct address to wives (v. 22) as well as husbands (v. 25). As we have seen, however, the forms of speaking vary. While direct imperatives toward the wives are avoided, clear appeals are addressed to the husbands. The husbands are thereby called on to take intensive care of their wives.

Based on the metaphoric interaction, the explanation, directed to the husbands, about the love of Jesus can be understood as an illocutionary, directive speech act towards the husbands. What Christ does with the church forms an indirect set of instructions for action for the husbands. Accordingly the husbands are responsible for the care, beauty and purity of their wives.

Men should not demand beauty and purity from their wives, rather they should provide for it! While the wife is allowed to put up with the good deeds of her husband, the husband should work hard to put his love into action. The pains that the husband takes for his wife demand all his energy, the text even calls this "devotion of life." This difference in emphasis also corresponds to the unequal lengths of the sections addressed to the wives (vv. 22–24: 3 verses) and to the husbands (vv. 25–33a: 8 verses).

The linguistic structure (imperative), the critical reception of the household-table genre, and the speech act analysis come together to a complete uniform ethical interpretation. It may hence be postulated that Eph 5:21–33 is not primarily admonishing women, but rather that men are being instructed on their obligation to love.

We do not know what impact the text had on the historical addressees. Within that patriarchal society, such a challenge to the husbands must have been seen as impertinence. And even for today's male readers the text can be explosive. For contemporary ethical discourse, the text can also develop the catalytic role of breaking apart the patriarchal structures of the societal relationships of the sexes towards equal partnership.

I have arrived at my conclusion. That which I have demonstrated in out-line form using the example of Eph 5:21–33 can be employed for many New Testament ethical texts. Ethics is based on language and is constituted by a linguistic dimension that has been described here in its intra-textual, inter-textual and extra-textual perspectives. The separation of these "lev-els" has primarily a heuristic aim and the overlapping of various aspects is inevitable and will become evident in interpreting concrete texts.

Defining Morality in Christian Ethics and the Study of New Testament Ethics

ETIENNE DE VILLIERS

1. Introduction

Christian ethics and the study of the ethics of the New Testament are for the most part conceived of and operated as two distinctive theological disciplines. On the one hand the sharp distinction and independent operation of these two theological disciplines are justifiable. After all, as Bruce Birch and Larry Rasmussen, among others, have pointed out: Christian ethics and Biblical ethics – and that would include New Testament ethics – are not identical.[1] In trying to provide moral guidance to present day Christians, Christian ethics has to deal with many new moral issues as the result of developments in modern technology, to which no reference in either the Old or New Testament is found. It would just not make sense to try to seek direct moral guidance in the Old or New Testament on typically contemporary moral issues relating to, for example, the utilisation of nuclear energy, global warming, genetic engineering and cloning. Apart from that the moral guidance that is provided in the Old and New Testament is sometimes, mainly as a result of the vast differences between the cultural settings of the Old and New Testaments and our own contemporary cultural setting, inapplicable and even unacceptable to us as Christians today. The Old Testament prohibition of usury (Deut 23:19) and prescriptions regarding the death penalty (e.g. Lev 20; 21:19) and the New Testament injunction that women should keep silent and not take on a leadership role in the congregation (1 Tim 2:11–12) come to mind.

On the other hand, it is also undeniable that Christian ethics and the study of New Testament ethics are dependent on one another and, as a result of that, should cooperate far more closely than is usually the case. After all, the Bible remains the prime source of moral instruction for Christian ethics. The Bible is the classical document in which the foundational story for the church of God's initiatives culminating in Christ's mission is told and in which the original formulation of the moral implications of

---

[1]   Bruce C. Birch and Larry L. Rasmussen, *Bible and ethics in the Christian life* (Minneapolis, Minn.: Augsburg Fortress Press, 1989), 11.

Christ's life and actions for the life and actions of believers is given. And the dedicated effort of many New Testament scholars to accurately trace the moral message of a particular New Testament author in a particular text? I do not believe that the motivation that drives such effort is, in the case of the majority of New Testament scholars, solely to make a scholarly contribution to the advancement of the discipline of New Testament studies that is recognised by their peers. I believe that their deepest motivation is – and should be – to provide contemporary Christians with insights from the moral message of the New Testament that would assist them in living authentic Christian lives today. The theological discipline that has the task to reflect on the shape Christian living should take on today is Christian ethics. Close co-operation between the study of New Testament ethics and, for that matter, also between the study of Old Testament ethics and Christian ethics is therefore indispensable.

Can this interdependence of Christian ethics and the study of New Testament ethics also be demonstrated with regard to the theme of this conference: "moral language in the New Testament"? Or do we have to entirely rely on insights from non-theological human sciences to assist us in the clarification of such more "formal" aspects of the study of New Testament ethics, or for that matter, of Christian ethics? It is conspicuous that in the introductory letter to this conference reference is almost immediately made of the usefulness of "interesting insights from the field of meta-ethics." Specific mention is made of the fact that ethics and language have been a major concern in analytical moral philosophy. The names of C. L. Stevenson and R. M. Hare are highlighted and the opinion is expressed that it would be worthwhile to focus on some of the relevant aspects investigated by these analytical moral philosophers. The impression is given that the natural academic partner for New Testament scholars who want to investigate the moral language of the New Testament more closely is analytical moral philosophy.

It is, however, not only New Testament scholars who tend to immediately draw such a conclusion when analytical tools are needed in the study of the moral language or morality of Christians. Christian ethicists tend to do the same. Allow me to use my own experience as an example. When I worked on my doctoral thesis on the distinctive character of Christian morality in the late seventies of the previous century, I needed a definition of "Christian morality" to assist me in delineating the shape and scope of Christian morality.[2] What did I do? I turned to the extensive debate on the definition of morality in English analytical moral philosophy and devoted a substantial part of a chapter of my dissertation to this de-

---

[2]   Etienne de Villiers, *Die eiesoortigheid van die Christelike moraal* (Amsterdam: Rodopi, 1978).

bate. The definition of "morality" I accepted in the end was for the most part derived from insights gained in this debate.

Why do New Testament scholars and Christian ethicists tend to be dependent on moral philosophy when more formal aspects such as the nature and definition of Christian moral language or Christian morality are investigated? The conspicuous answer is of course that analytical moral philosophy has given much attention to meta-ethical issues over a period of decades and has developed a substantial body of literature on these issues. For theologians not to take cognisance of the views of analytical moral philosophers on meta-ethical issues would be academically irresponsible and even foolhardy. But would that be the only reason? Are we as theologians not also turning first of all to a non-theological discipline such as moral philosophy for academic guidance, because of the assumption that it would provide us with value-free, objective, universally valid concepts and distinctions that would enhance the scientific quality and value of our own investigations? Deliberating now on my own reasons for turning to analytical moral philosophy in my attempt to define "Christian morality" in my doctoral dissertation I have to admit that I was of the opinion at the time that moral philosophy can provide an objective definition of morality that would be applicable to all moralities, whether of a religious or a non-religious nature.

What I would like to do in this paper is to focus on the issue of the definition of morality, which, in my opinion, ought to be addressed in a conference with a theme such as "The moral language of the New Testament." By depicting the language in the New Testament that is the focus of study at this conference as "moral" the assumption is clearly made that there is such a type of language in the New Testament that can and should be distinguished from other language types. The logical question that is immediately raised is: "what is it that distinguishes moral language from other types of language?" "how can moral language be defined?" Or in the words of the introductory letter to this congress: "why should certain texts be considered 'ethical?' Where does the ethical quality of a statement come from ...?" Of course, it does not mean that one cannot study the moral language of the New Testament without first providing an explicit definition of "moral" or "morality." It does, however, mean that as long as no such definition is provided, implicit assumptions are made of what distinguishes moral language from other types of language and that no justification of such implicit assumptions is provided.

I am giving attention in my paper to two questions. The first is: what does moral philosophy have to offer with regard to the definition of morality? And the second is: how should we deal with this offer made by moral philosophy in the study of New Testament ethics and in Christian ethics?

2. What Moral Philosophy has to Offer with Regard to the Definition of Morality

It would not be possible to provide a complete overview of the different efforts in moral philosophy to define morality over say the last century. It should suffice to provide two pictures of the position on the definition of morality in moral philosophy during different periods. The first, more detailed picture, relates to the period that is also covered in the discussion in my doctoral dissertation on the definition of morality, namely the period starting after the Second World War and stretching into the seventies. It was a period during which the intense and very influential meta-ethical discussion in English analytical philosophy on the nature and definition of moral language came off the ground. The second picture is nothing more than a snapshot provided by a prominent contemporary philosopher of two important ways in which morality is understood today.

In my dissertation I started off the discussion on the definition of morality by pointing out that the debate in meta-ethics during the previous decades primarily had been on the question whether moral judgements could be defined in terms of only "formal" criteria without any reference to the "content" or subject of the judgements. I identified R. M. Hare's purely formal definition of morality as one of the most influential. Hare was of the opinion that any attempt to define "moral" by referring to more than just formal features boils down to building a particular normative ethical theory into the definition. In his book *The Language of Morals* he indicated two formal features to which a moral judgement has to comply, namely *prescriptivity* and *universalizability*.[3] The prescriptivity of a moral judgement implies, in Hare's opinion, an imperative. By accepting the moral principle "One ought to do x" I commit myself to the acceptance of the imperative "Let me do x" and to actually doing x in the appropriate circumstances. The universalizability of moral judgements, according to Hare, entails that when I insist that, seen from a moral perspective, I ought to do x, I also have to insist that anyone else ought to do x, except if there are relevant differences between such a person and myself and/or between his or her situation and mine.

In his book *Freedom and Reason* Hare admitted that the word "moral" actually plays a much smaller role in such an analysis than he had been of the opinion earlier. He was at that stage rather of the opinion that it is the

---

[3] Richard M. Hare, *The Language of Morals* (Oxford: Clarendon, 1952). In his book *Freedom and Reason* (Oxford: Clarendon, 1963) Hare summarises his view on moral judgement in *The language of morals* as such: "… moral judgements are a kind of *prescriptive* judgements, and they are distinguished from other judgements of this class by being *universalizable*" (4).

logic of the word "ought" rather than that of the word "moral" that demanded universalizability.[4] Universalizability and prescriptivity should
therefore be regarded as necessary, rather than sufficient conditions for
calling a judgement moral. It is only when, apart from these two formal
features, a judgement also has a third formal feature, that it sufficiently
complies to the conditions to call it a "moral" judgement. Moral principles,
according to Hare, have the added formal characteristic that a person accepts them, in the end, to guide his life by, and therefore they always, in
the case of conflict with other principles, have priority for him or her.[5]

In hindsight the discussion in analytical moral philosophy, starting with
C. L. Stevenson's emotivism and culminating in R. M. Hare's prescriptiv-
ism, in which the goal to formulate a purely formal definition of morality
was dominant, was a very situated philosophical discussion that can only
be fully understood as critical response in Cambridge philosophical circles
to the influential version of ethical intuitionism of the Cambridge philosopher G. E. Moore. Moore's major work *Principia Ethica* was published in
1903 and immediately met with enthusiastic response.[6] One reason for that
was that Moore claimed that after many centuries he solved the problem of
ethics by being the first philosopher to attend with sufficient care to the
precise nature of the questions which it is the task of ethics to answer.
What Moore believed to have discovered by doing this was threefold.
First, that "good" is the name of a simple indefinable property, different
from any natural property. Hence Moore speaks of good as a non-natural
property. Secondly, he takes it that to call an action right is simply to say
that of the available alternative actions it is the one which does or did produce the most good. Thirdly, in the final chapter of *Principia Ethica* he
comes to the conclusion that "personal affections and aesthetic enjoyments
include *all* the greatest, and *by far* the greatest goods we can imagine ..."[7]

The main problem with Moore's view is that it is impossible to prove
that a particular goal one tries to achieve, indeed possesses the non-natural
property "good." One can claim to have experienced through intuition that
such a non-natural property is indeed present. If someone else, however,
disputes the claim the only thing left that one can do, is to assert with as
great a show of certainty as possible that one's preferred end is "good." In
After Virtue Alasdair MacIntyre humouristically relates that many debates
on "good" ends in philosophical circles in Cambridge in the early twen-
tieth century were nothing more than emotive contests of persuasion in
which the sole purpose was to move the opponent by means of all sorts of

---

4   Hare, *Freedom* (n. 3), 37.
5   Hare, *Freedom* (n. 3), 168–169.
6   George E. Moore, *Principia Ethica* (Cambridge: University Press, 1903).
7   Moore, *Principia Ethica* (n. 6), 189.

rhetorical gestures to agree to the ends one prefers. He also comes to the conclusion that emotivism as a philosophical view most probably developed out of such experiences.[8] As it became philosophical consensus that Moore's claim that the meaning of "good" consists in its reference to a non-natural property could not be substantiated, C. L. Stevenson, who was a student of Moore, suggested that the meaning of evaluative terms should rather be found in the use that is made of them.[9] In his opinion they are used to *move* people to accept certain ends or to execute certain actions. R. M. Hare disagreed with him and was of the opinion that moral terms are rather used to *tell* people to execute certain actions. In spite of this difference of opinion Stevenson and Hare, and other analytical moral philosophers who contributed to the discussion on a purely formal definition of morality in the decades after the Second World War, shared the conviction that the meaning of moral terms should not be understood in terms of reference to a particular natural or non-natural object or property, but rather in terms of the distinctive use that is made of such terms.

At the time I was writing my doctoral dissertation there was in analytical moral philosophy growing resistance against a purely formal definition of morality. G. J. Warnock's book *The Object of Morality* provides a prominent example of this turn away from a formal definition.[10] He is of the opinion that a formal definition such as Hare's does not exclude evaluative language that in vernacular would not be called moral, like for example the values a sadist uses to guide his life by. Although he does not deny that moral language is sometimes used to tell somebody what to do, he is also of the opinion that to engage in moral discourse is not necessarily to prescribe. In the end he comes to the conclusion that moral discourse cannot be defined in terms of a distinctive use of language in guiding other persons' actions. "What is it, then, that is distinctive of 'moral discourse?' How is it that we can tell … when we have a specimen or stretch of moral discourse before us? The obvious answer to this question seems to me to be the right one: we go by what that specimen or stretch of discourse is *about*."[11] What Warnock is saying is that in common parlance we do not recognise moral language by its *formal features*, but by its reference to a particular *content*, namely the wellbeing of people. According to him we only call a guideline for action "moral" if we are of the opinion that fol-

---

[8]   Alasdair C. MacIntyre, *After Virtue: A study in moral theory* (Notre Dame, Ind.: University of Notre Dame Press, 1981), 16–18.

[9]   Charles L. Stevenson, *Ethics and Language* (New Haven, Conn.: Yale University Press, 1944). Cf. also idem, *Facts and Values* (New Haven, Conn.: Yale University Press, 1963).

[10]   Geoffrey J. Warnock, *The Object of Morality* (London: Methuen, 1971).

[11]   Warnock, *Morality* (n. 10), 131.

lowing it would in one way or another be *beneficial* and breaching it would in one way or another be *disadvantageous* to human beings.[12]

It is clear from my dissertation that I was convinced by those moral philosophers at the time who asserted that moral discourse refers, one way or another, to the wellbeing of human beings. I was, however, of the opinion that the reference to human wellbeing has to be qualified more precisely. Just to say that moral discourse refers to human wellbeing, is not enough, because a purely *prudential* judgement also refers to human wellbeing, be it that it exclusively refers to what is to the benefit or in the interest of the speaker himself. I was therefore of the opinion that the qualification needs to be added that *moral* judgements are distinguished from other evaluative judgements by its reference to the consideration of the wellbeing of *other* people. To avoid falling into the trap against which Hare warned with regard to definitions of morality in terms of reference to a particular content, of inadvertently introducing elements of normative ethical theory into a descriptive definition of morality, I proposed that any reference to a particular understanding of wellbeing or a particular way in which the wellbeing of other people should be taken into account, should be avoided in the definition of morality.

An example of a definition of morality in which the borderline between descriptive and normative is (inadvertently?) crossed is provided by W. K. Frankena, who wrote an introduction to ethics that was widely used in the seventies: "X has a morality or moral AG (action guide) only if it includes judgements, rules, principles, ideals, etc. which 1) concern the relations of one individual to others, 2) involve or call for a consideration of the effects of his actions on others (not necessarily all others), not from the point of view of his own interests or aesthetic enjoyments, but from their point of view."[13] As D. Little and S. B. Twiss rightly point out such a definition of morality would exclude the possibility of calling the code of conduct of the Navaho Indians in North America "moral" because it is not based on the point of view of the other, but rather on the point of view of the consequences conduct has for one's own wellbeing. However, on account of the general belief of Navaho Indians that the wellbeing of the other members of the tribe is a prerequisite for one's own wellbeing, it would be rather difficult to concur with the conclusion that the Navaho Indians do not have

---

[12] Warnock, *Morality* (n. 10), 55 and 57.

[13] William K. Frankena, "The concept of morality," in *The definition of morality* (ed. Gerald Wallace and Arthur D. McKinnon Walker; London: Methuen, 1970), 156. Cf. idem, *Ethics* (Englewood Cliffs, N.J.: Prentice-Hall, 1973), 113–114.

morality. The reason is that the code of conduct of the Navaho Indians also takes the wellbeing of the other into account, be it in an indirect way.[14]

In an effort to avoid the trap Hare warned against it sufficed in the discussion of the definition of morality in my dissertation to say that the *moral point of view* is one that crystallised in the course of the history of humankind as a result of the unavoidable clash of human interests and the need for the formulation of action guidelines on how the wellbeing or interests of fellow human beings ought to be taken into account. The *morality* of a group of people was defined by me as that part of their values and action guidelines or norms that has reference to the consideration of the wellbeing of others.[15]

My participation in this conference has given me the opportunity, after many years, to again try to get abreast of the newest developments in the meta-ethical discussion on the definition of morality. I have found the book of the German philosopher Kurt Bayertz *Warum überhaupt moralisch sein?*, published in 2004, in this regard very informative.[16] What is especially noteworthy to me is that he, in the chapter he devotes to the definition of morality, does not even try, as the English analytical moral philosophers in the decades after the second world war did, to provide a universally valid, objective descriptive definition of morality. He admits from the start that the phenomenon of morality has historically and culturally been multifaceted, variable and often controversial. A definition of morality can therefore never be neutral. It always reflects a particular normative ethical approach and can as such be criticised.[17]

Bayertz identifies two important uses of the concept of morality. In the first, wider use of the concept "morality" refers to a complex of norms, values or ideals that provides every individual with general guidelines to give shape to his or her life. A morality in this broad sense shows an individual her place in life and tells her what life is about. Such systems of orientation are found in all human societies, so that their existence can be regarded as an anthropological constant. The further one goes back in history the more homogenously they are blended with dominant mythical and religious beliefs. For the most part such systems of orientation find their legitimation in tradition. It is only later in history that such systems are also intently designed by certain individuals and contrasted with tradition. They are presented by these individuals as critically reflected views on the

---

[14] David Little and Sumner B. Twiss, "Basic terms in the study of religious ethics," in *Religion and morality: A collection of essays* (ed. Gene Outka and John P. Reeder, Jr.; Garden City, N.Y.: Doubleday, 1973), 53–58.

[15] De Villiers, *Eiesoortigheid* (n. 2), 60.

[16] Kurt Bayertz, *Warum überhaupt moralisch sein?* (Munich: Beck, 2004).

[17] Bayertz, *Warum* (n. 16), 33.

right understanding of the world and the right way of living one's life. With that the transition to philosophical thinking, to *ethics* as the attempt to provide a systematic exposition and justification of the principles that ought to guide one's life, takes place. In this sense Ludwig Wittgenstein has described ethics as the investigation of what really matters in life. According to Wittgenstein the purpose of ethics is "to find the meaning of life that makes life worthwhile, or to investigate what the right way of living is."[18]

According to Bayertz the difference between *morality in the wider sense* as anthropological constant and *ethics* as individually designed thought system does not lie so much in their content and function, because both formulate general and comprehensive normative guidelines for human conduct and life. The difference lies primarily in the fact that ethics does not rely on the authority of tradition, but tries to provide justification for its guidelines on a theoretical and methodological level.[19]

Bayertz mentions the ethical theories of the philosophers of ancient Greece as early and influential examples of the attempt to provide philosophically reflected life orientation. The question of Socrates: "How ought a man to live?" can be regarded as the key question of the whole of ancient Greek ethics.[20] Whether and how in the difficult conditions of life, in which evil seemingly overcomes the good, *eudaimonia*, that is a good and successful life, is possible, is the leading question. What is also typical of ancient Greek ethics is that the emphasis is not so much on the formulation of guidelines for action in concrete situations, but on the identification of the highest goals individuals should strive to achieve and the ideal type of person they should strive to be in order to live a happy life. As a result of the fact that the Christian religion provides a comprehensive framework of orientation for the whole of human life and conduct, Bayertz is of the opinion that it provides a prominent example of morality in the wider sense.[21]

Morality in a more narrow sense is, in Bayertz's opinion, already present in the Old Testament, although it there still forms an integral part of a comprehensive morality in the wider sense. If one looks more closely at the commands in the second table of the Ten Commandments, it becomes clear that they have certain features that distinguish them from other more purely religious commandments, for example the commands in the first table that relates more to the relationship with God. First of all they express *minimal demands* that everyone can and should comply to. Se-

---

[18] Ludwig Wittgenstein, "Vortrag über Ethik" (1930), in *Vortrag über Ethik und andere kleine Schriften* (ed. Joachim Schulte; Frankfurt am Main: Suhrkamp, 1991), 10–11.

[19] Bayertz, *Warum* (n. 16), 34.

[20] Plato, *Gorg.* 550c; *Resp.* 344e, 352, 618.

[21] Bayertz, *Warum* (n. 16), 35.

condly, they do not provide positive guidelines for action, but rather *negative prohibitions* that lay down certain limits to our actions. Thirdly, their subject matter is the *protection* of the interests of those human beings on whom the actions of an individual can have an impact. They forbid us to inflict particular forms of harm on other persons. When we take these three features together it is clear that we have to do here with a different conception of morality than in the case of the morality in a wider sense we have already discussed. Morality in the wider sense indicates the goals we ought to strive for to lead a good life. It is, in other words, concerned with the wellbeing of the acting subject herself. Morality in the narrower sense is concerned rather with the wellbeing of *other* persons that may be negatively impacted by the acting subject.[22]

Bayertz does not deny that no such distinction between a morality in a wider and a morality in a narrower sense were made in the Old and New Testament and for the greatest part of church history. Not doing harm to fellow human beings has always been regarded in Christianity as an integral part of living a religiously righteous life in the eyes of God. Bayertz also admits that in ancient Greek ethics the theme of respecting and considering the interests of others also got its fair share of attention, especially in discussions on the concept of justice. What he does assert, however, is that in the course of Western history morality in the narrower sense has increasingly been distinguished and eventually even been completely severed from morality in the wider sense. Morality in the narrower sense – one may even say morality as such – is today regarded as a separate social institution that has as *function* the minimising of anthropogenic evil. It works against the spontaneous egoism of individuals and their limited sympathy for other persons and protects the interests of other persons they deal with. With its social function in modern societies the *content* of morality in a narrower sense correlates. Its directives prohibit especially hurting, killing, stealing from and cheating other people and tell us to keep to agreements. As such it consists of a *minimal morality* regarded as necessary for living together in modern societies.[23] It is this minimal morality that has as limited social function to ensure the *survival of others*, which is today referred to in Western societies – if not in most contemporary societies – when the term "morality" is used. Bayertz therefore argues that he is justified in using the term "morality" in his book to only refer to morality in the narrower sense.[24]

The historical process in which this reduced concept of morality originated can be described as a process of *functional differentiation* in which

---

[22] Bayertz, *Warum* (n. 16), 37–39.

[23] Bayertz, *Warum* (n. 16), 39.

[24] Bayertz, *Warum* (n. 16), 41–42.

different types of values guiding human conduct have been severed from one another and have become separate, autonomous social institutions. Today it is possible to sharply distinguish between a moral, a religious, a judicial and an aesthetic evaluation. As a result we find that such evaluations often clash with one another. A particular action can be regarded as morally wrong, but legally permissible, or morally permissible, but religiously prohibited. This raises the difficult and uniquely modern issue of the *priority* of moral over against non-moral or extra-moral evaluation. Do moral duties weigh more than judicial, religious and religious norms in the case of conflict, or not?[25]

3. How to Deal with the Definitions of Morality Moral Philosophy Offers

The overview of the definitions of morality offered by moral philosophy in different periods provided in the previous paragraph is incomplete, but still revealing. In the conclusion of my paper I would like to reflect on this picture and make some remarks on how Christian ethics and the study of New Testament ethics ought to deal with the definitions of morality offered by moral philosophy:

3.1 The Diversity and Divergence of the Offer have to be Taken Seriously

What is clear from our overview is that during the two periods covered no uniform, objective and universally valid descriptive or classifying definition of morality was provided by moral philosophy. The picture that emerged is rather one of a very diverse and even divergent offer of definitions. The purely formal, prescriptivist definition of R. M. Hare was offered by him in opposition to G. E. Moore's view of morality and as a correction of C. L. Stevenson's emotivist understanding of moral language. Definitions or morality in terms of its subject matter of the wellbeing or interests of other persons, were clearly offered as alternative to purely formal definitions, regarded as inadequate. Such definitions in terms of the wellbeing of other people have been confirmed by Bayertz in his own definition of morality in a narrower sense. However, his introduction of the concept of morality in a wider sense must be regarded as a correction of the tendency in modern moral philosophy to suffice with a rather narrow conception of morality. I have little doubt in my mind that Bayertz's willingness to make room for morality in a wider sense, has to be understood against the background of Alasdair MacIntyre's incisive and influential

---

[25] Bayertz, *Warum* (n. 16), 41.

attack in *After virtue* against the dominant, but in his opinion hopelessly inadequate, conception of morality in modern moral philosophy and his plea to re-introduce a contemporary version of a comprehensive virtue ethics in the vein of Aristotle's ethics.[26]

The fact that during different periods in history different and divergent definitions of morality have been offered by moral philosophy has as unavoidable consequence that the theologian who wants to borrow a definition of morality from moral philosophy is pretty much at the mercy of the dominant position taken by moral philosophers at a particular point in time. As a result of the fact that the definition or morality that is regarded as the most adequate in moral philosophy at a particular point in time can within a short period of time be rejected as inadequate, even a few years time can make a huge difference with regard to the definition the theologian will end up with.

One may argue that the definition of morality the theologian departs from, needs not necessarily have drastic and negative consequences for the views he or she develops. That may be the case. The conclusion that borrowing a definition from moral philosophy is always an innocuous affair is however not justified. One's choice of a definition of morality can sometimes have far-reaching consequences. I have personal experience of that. As a result of the fact that in the late seventies of the previous century purely formal definitions of morality were increasingly regarded as inadequate in moral philosophy I adopted in my doctoral dissertation a definition of morality determined by the parameters of the analytical philosophical discussion at the time. This definition played a rather crucial role in the development of my main argument in the dissertation, because I used it as an analytical tool to help me identify the factors determining the distinctive content of moralities in general and Christian morality in particular. In hindsight the definition I used provided me with a rather restricted view of morality – a view of morality strictly in terms of action guidelines or duties – that foreclosed the possibility of identifying certain dimensions of Christian morality that could be depicted as distinctively Christian such as the central role of distinctive virtues in Christian life.

In the light of my own experience I would like to warn fellow Christian ethicists and New Testament scholars not to uncritically borrow a definition of morality from moral philosophy. A New Testament scholar who relies unreservedly on R. M. Hare's formal prescriptivist definition may find in the end that it has prevented him to do justice to elements of New

---

[26] Cf. also Alasdair C. MacIntyre, *Three rival versions of moral enquiry: Encyclopaedia, genealogy, and tradition* (Notre Dame, Ind.: University of Notre Dame Press, 1990).

Testament ethics that fall outside the scope of right actions and the pre-scriptive use of moral language.

3.2 New Testament Studies and Christian Ethics should take One Another seriously

I am of the opinion that Bayertz is right in saying that it is not possible to provide a value-free, objective definition of morality. Rather than trying to first formulate such a neutral descriptive definition of morality, and shaping one's study of say Christian morality or the moral language in the New Testament in accordance with it, insights gained in New Testament studies and Christian ethics on the shape and scope of Christian morality in the early Christian church and today should rather be the departure point for defining Christian morality. This means that when we need a definition of morality or moral language in Christian ethics or in New Testament studies we should, apart from consulting moral philosophers, also take cognisance of relevant developments in both these disciplines, and for that matter, also Old Testament studies.

What is it that New Testament scholars and Christian ethicists could learn from one another? Let us start with the Christian ethicists. Christian ethicists could, with the help of expert New Testament scholars, form a reliable picture of the nature and shape of the original conceptions of Christian morality reflected in the books of the New Testament. I recently had the opportunity to read Richard Hays's *The moral vision of the New Testament*.[27] It struck me that Hays resists any portrayal of the ethics of the authors of the books of the New Testament as reflecting an uncritical assimilation of traditional Hellenistic or Judaic moral codes of conduct. He is, for example, not happy with Martin Dibelius's view that the blocks of moral advice that characteristically occur at the end of Paul's letters, should be understood as *paraenesis,* as general collections of maxims adopted from popular Hellenistic philosophy.[28] It is conspicuous that he deliberately writes of "visions of the moral life in the New Testament," thereby indicating that the ethical teaching of the New Testament authors are, for the most part, based on a coherent set of theological convictions and relate to more dimensions of the moral life than just actions.[29] His exposition of Paul's ethical teaching – to which I restrict myself here – starts with a discussion of three recurrent, interlocking theological motifs that provide, in his opinion, the framework for this teaching: eschatology, the cross, and the new community in Christ. In sum, one can, in his opinion,

---

[27] Richard B. Hays, *The moral vision of the New Testament: A contemporary intro-duction to New Testament ethics* (San Francisco, Calif.: Harper, 1996).

[28] Hays, *Moral Vision* (n. 27), 17.

[29] Hays, *Moral Vision* (n. 27), 14.

say that Paul sees the community of faith being drawn into the story of God's remaking of the world through Jesus Christ. "Thus, to make ethical discernments is, for Paul, simply to recognize our place within the epic story of redemption. There is no meaningful distinction between theology and ethics in Paul's thought, because Paul's theology is fundamentally an account of God's work of transforming his people into the image of Christ … The distinctive shape of obedience to God is disclosed in Jesus Christ's faithful death on the cross for the sake of God's people. That death becomes metaphorically paradigmatic for the obedience of the community: to obey God means to offer our lives unqualifiedly for the sake of others. Thus, the fundamental norm of Pauline ethics is the christomorphic life."[30]

I am of the opinion that the New Testament scholar who wants to come to grips with the meaning of "moral" when he studies the moral language of the New Testament, should at least take cognisance of the significant shift in Christian ethics over the last thirty years away from the conception of Christian morality as merely a set of action guidelines or duties that was dominant in Protestant ethics for so long to a more comprehensive one that also includes moral vision, character and virtues. The most influential representative of the new conception of Christian morality is the American theologian Stanley Hauerwas.

Already in a collection of some of his articles *Vision and virtue,* published in 1974, Hauerwas provides an outline of his view on Christian morality.[31] "Methodologically," he writes, "it is my contention that the current difficulty of Christian ethics stems from the far too narrow conception of moral experience accepted by many philosophical and religious ethicists. When ethics is limited to an analysis of the justification for particular actions, then it is indeed difficult to make sense of Christian ethics. The language of the Gospel includes, but points beyond, judgments about particular actions and practices to the nature of the self and how it is formed for our life project. Once ethics is focused on the nature and moral determination of the self, vision and virtue again become morally significant categories. We are as we come to see and as that seeing becomes enduring in our intentionality. We do not come to see, however, just by looking but by training our vision through the metaphors and symbols that constitute our central convictions. How we come to see therefore is function of how we come to be since our seeing necessarily is determined by how our basic images are embodied by the self – i.e., in our character. Christian ethics is the conceptual discipline that analyzes and imaginatively tests the images most appropriate to score the Christian life in accordance with the central

---

[30] Hays, *Moral Vision* (n. 27), 45–46.

[31] Stanley Hauerwas, *Vision and virtue: Essays in Christian ethical reflection* (Notre Dame, Ind.: University of Notre Dame Press, 1974).

conviction that the world has been redeemed by the work and person of Christ."[32] In his later works Hauerwas lays special emphasis on the indispensable role that the church and its practices of worship and service play as a school for the shaping and developing of Christian character. The church, in turn, is described by him as nothing but a "story-formed community," a socially identifiable community of people with a collective memory of a particular history told in the Bible, culminating in the story of the life of Jesus.[33]

When one compares these influential views on the shape of Christian morality in the early church – reflected in Paul's letters – and the shape of Christian morality today, three conclusions can be drawn:

1. They express a comprehensive conception of Christian morality that resembles Bayertz's morality in a wider sense. Central to this comprehensive conception of morality is a distinctively and holistic Christian vision of how Christians ought to live their lives. Typical of this moral vision is that in it faith in God's actions and words and orientation on the goals Christians should strive to achieve, the persons they ought to become and how they should conduct themselves are integrated in an inseparable way. In fact, faith in the actions and words of God are seen to hold decisive implications for the way Christians ought to live.

2. This conception of Christian morality is also comprehensive in the sense that it does not only refer to right actions, but also to other dimensions of morality, namely preferred goals and virtues and even practices in the church.

3. It is not possible to pick out purely moral language (or precepts), and separate it from purely religious language. Therefore, instead of taking the term "moral" to refer to language that is exclusively and purely such, one should rather take it to refer to the provision of life orientation for Christians that is provided by language, even if it is used primarily to refer to God's actions and words.

From which definition of Christian morality should we then preferably depart in our deliberations on the moral language of the New Testament? I conclude by proposing the following definition: Christian morality is orientation provided to Christians on how they ought to live in a vision of life based on their faith in the actions and words of God. In the vision orientation is more specifically provided on the important goals they should strive for, the sort of persons they ought to become and how they should conduct themselves.

---

[32] Hauerwas, *Vision* (n. 31), 1–2.

[33] Stanley Hauerwas, *A community of character: Toward a constructive Christian social ethic* (Notre Dame, Ind.: University of Notre Dame Press, 1981), 9.

4. Conclusion

In this paper an attempt has been made to provide a case against a one-sided and exclusive reliance on analytical moral philosophy when defining morality in both the study of the moral language of the New Testament and Christian ethics. The diversity and even irreconcilability of the definitions provided in analytical moral philosophy have been demonstrated, as well as its one-sided emphasis on the dimension of action guidelines or duties, at the cost of other dimensions of morality. To depart from a definition of morality provided by analytical moral philosophy in the study of the moral language of the New Testament or in Christian ethics may therefore be not so innocuous. New Testament scholars and Christian ethicists should rather learn from one another that Christian morality has had a comprehensive nature from the start. They should remind one another that apart from guidelines for action Christian morality also includes a comprehensive vision of the Christian life, of the goals Christians should strive to attain and the virtues they should embody.

In Search of Identity:

Narrativity, Discipleship and Moral Agency

SEAN FREYNE

The precise relationship between agency and action is a highly significant aspect of all moral discourse. Aristotle formulated the connection succinctly: the person who acts voluntarily (ἑκών) and with deliberation (βούλευσις) depends on the principle of action (ἀρχή) that one has in oneself (ἐν αὐτῷ), rendering it possible for one to act or not to act. Thus, the question of moral agency points us immediately to a "who" or person who possesses the physical and self-reflective dimensions of personhood that enable them to act responsibly and in conformity with that which is deemed to be "the good life."[1]

Ethical reflection within a Christian frame of reference is based on a different starting point to that of the Nicomachean Ethics, yet here too the issue of agency is central to the discussion. Two different trajectories, which can be loosely identified with the Gospels and the Pauline writings are represented within the New Testament. Both models point to the eschatological horizon of the Christian story as the context and goal of Christian selfhood, thus identifying Christian ethics as teleological rather than deontological. Yet they differ as to how this eschatological goal is achieved in the present. In the case of Paul, his own radical shift of horizons from the centrality of Torah to the centrality of Christ meant that he viewed the goal of Christian moral living as conforming to the death and resurrection of Jesus, understood as the eschatological event. The gospels too focus on the person of Jesus, but while they are all written from a post-Easter perspective, their narrative structure points to the remembered life of Jesus as a model for Christian living. We are thus presented with two varying approaches to the good life from a Christian perspective: "life in Christ" and discipleship or following of Jesus. Each has distinctive, though mutually quite compatible views on Christian moral agency and how it is formed.

---

[1] Paul Ricœur, *Oneself as Another* (Chicago, Ill.: University of Chicago Press, 1992; English trans. of *Soi-méme comme un autre*; Paris: Éditions du Seuil, 1990), 89–90.

The "in Christ" model suggests a quasi-mystical transformation of the self so that one's own ego is replaced by that of Christ: "I live, now not I, but Christ lives in me" (Gal 2:20), or, "Let this mind be in you which was also in Christ Jesus" (Phil 2:5), are typical expressions of this understanding. True, Paul does introduce a biographical dimension into his understanding of the moral life when he points to his own life as a *mimesis* of that of Christ, and therefore, an example to be followed by the Corinthians (1 Cor 11:1). Yet it is clear from his paraenetic instructions that he has in mind the death/resurrection paradigm of the Easter faith, rather than drawing on the Jesus-biography in any substantial way.[2]

By contrast, the discipleship model is based on the memory of a physical accompanying of Jesus as prophet, moral guide and teacher. As we shall see, it involves a radical re-orientation of the self under the direction and inspiration of the master, but without the immediacy of the self-emptying dimension in the Pauline understanding. While discipleship does indeed involve a process of "losing one's life," "taking up one's cross," or "becoming the least of all and the servant of all," there is a more marked temporal dimension to its full actualization that is not as clearly articulated in the Pauline ethical system. Thus, Jesus reminds the disciples that "they are the ones who have endured/persevered through (διαμεμενηκότες) with him in his trials" (Luke 22:28), indicating perseverance, commitment and sharing as important aspects of faithful following. Paul on the other hand envisages a transformation of the self with immediate ethical consequences through the mystical experience of dying and rising with Christ in the baptismal ritual (Rom 6:1–11). In short there is a clear narrative dimension to the discipleship model that is not always present in the Pauline model, where the memory of the historical Jesus is – to put it mildly – muted.

Each of the Synoptists, but also the author of the Fourth Gospel, has his own perspective on discipleship in accordance with the demands and needs of the communities they were addressing. Yet each is anchored in the historical memory that during his public ministry Jesus had a core group that formed a permanent retinue of followers. Mark is closest to that reality, presenting a highly realistic narrative that virtually identifies discipleship with the Twelve whom Jesus chose to be with him and to be sent to carry on his mission of preaching the good news and engaging with evil as it manifested itself (Mark 3:13–15). For Matthew, discipleship has become a

---

[2] Anselm Schulz, *Nachfolgen und Nachahmen: Studien über das Verhältnis der neutestamentlichen Jüngerschaft zur urchristlichen Vorbildethik* (Munich: Kösel, 1962), 332–335, shows that while the earliest layers of the tradition display an independent usage of both conceptions based on their linguistic background, they can both be combined in later developments such as John 13:31–14:4 and 1 Pet 2:21 in describing the Christian life, while retaining elements of their separate religio-cultural origins.

verb rather than a noun: "go, *make disciples* of all the nations" – and this includes observing "all" the instruction that the Matthean Jesus has given throughout the gospel (Matt 28:19–20; cf. 13:51; 27:57). Luke retains the broader Matthean view of discipleship as characteristic of the church universal (Luke 6:17; 19:37; Acts 6:1, 7), even when the term μαθητής has to compete with other designations, such as μάρτυς/witness, to describe what membership of the messianic community entails.[3]

In this paper I have chosen not to follow the differing Synoptic usage of the term disciple as descriptive of the Christian moral agent, but will concentrate rather on an inter-textual reading of Mark and John, focusing on their treatment of the group around Jesus. My choice of these two gospels is based on their differences rather than their similarities, for reasons that I hope will become clear as we progress. In this reading exercise I will be guided by the insights of French phenomenologist, Paul Ricœur, whose collection of essays entitled *Oneself as Another* (1992) is a classic discussion of the role of narrative in the development of human self identity, a role that is, he claims, both prescriptive and descriptive.[4] His approach, therefore, makes the essential move from personal identity to moral agency through the medium of narrative. While Ricœur's discussion is focused on the individual, it can equally apply to community self-awareness, especially when this is based on the messianic ideal, which arose from the biblical notion of corporate personality.[5]

1. Identity, Narrativity and Agency according to Ricœur

According to Ricœur, personal identity is fashioned and maintained between two poles, which he describes as the *Idem,* or "Sameness," and the *Ipse,* or "Selfhood." Selfhood is not identical with Sameness, even when the two overlap and each can pose a threat to the other. Narrative plays a crucial role in mediating between these two poles, on the one hand identifying the points where they overlap, and on the other highlighting how the *Ipse* can to an extent free itself from the controlling influence of the *Idem*, thereby allowing the question "Who am I?" rather than "What am I?" to be explored. This in turn enables change to occur by allowing the Self to explore new and innovative forms of identity. Narrative's role in such a process is to chart how change occurs over time while at the same time

---

[3]   Sean Freyne, *The Twelve: Disciples and Apostles: A Study in the Theology of the First Three Gospels* (London: Sheed & Ward, 1968).

[4]   Ricœur, *Oneself as Another* (n. 1), 114–115.

[5]   Gerd Theissen, "Gruppenmessianismus: Überlegungen zum Ursprung der Kirche im Jüngerkreis Jesu," *JBTh* 7 (1992): 101–123.

affirming continuity. As Ricœur writes: "[t]he weakness of the criterion of similitude or sameness in the case of a great distance in time, suggests that we should appeal to another criterion of identity, namely the uninterrupted continuity between the first and the last stage of the development. That is why the threat to identity is not entirely dissipated unless we can posit as the basis of the uninterrupted continuity, a principle of permanence in time."[6] Without such a sense of continuity and permanence it is difficult to attribute responsibility for past and future actions, since the moral agent is always in a state of flux.

Ricœur identifies two models of permanence over time, which we can recognise as being our own, what he elsewhere calls "mineness." These models, he describes, as "character" and "keeping one's word," but each belongs to the opposing pole of the self already identified. Thus, he claims, character is inscribed in Sameness, its first trait being habit or disposition. While these dispositions are acquired over time, they become identifiers of the self. This is achieved through our identification with "values, norms, models and heroes," *in* which a person recognises their true self, leading eventually to recognising oneself *by* them. Important as such a recognition is, it can lead to what Ricœur calls "the sedimentation" of character, that is, the inability to consider change of any kind, and thereby stifling the possibilities which the self craves for.[7]

Character, understood as permanent disposition or habit that has been internalised, is in danger of emphasising "what" over "who" in the process of self-identification. However, this outcome can be avoided by a recognition that we use "character" as a designation for protagonists in a story, suggesting that it too is capable of change over time, that is, character can have a history. "What sedimentation has contracted, narrative can redeploy" is Ricœur's pithy way of expressing the dynamic of the narrative process as applied to character. And he goes on to describe this redeployment as a "balancing of the immutable traits which lead to the anchoring of the history of a life in a character, with those traits which tend to separate the identity of the self from the sameness of the character."[8]

If character is in danger of stressing Sameness to the point that the potentiality of the self is completely stifled, it is equally possible for this other pole – the *Ipse* – to be cut adrift from the *Idem*. In these instances Ricœur's second model, "being true to one's word" comes into play. This sense of obligation to the truth of one's word is described as self-constancy. Unlike character, this aspect of the self is not based on generalised traits, but is totally dependent on the "Who" or *Ipse* who decides to

---

6   *Oneself as Another* (n. 1), 116.
7   *Oneself as Another* (n. 1), 118–121.
8   *Oneself as Another* (n. 1), 122.

honour its commitment. Thus, he concludes, "the continuity of character is one thing; the constancy of friendship is quite another."[9]

Having established the dialectic that constitutes the process of self-identification and the role of narrative in that process, Ricœur goes on to develop its prescriptive role, irrespective of whether one is speaking of character or of being true to one's word. "In narrativising the aim of the true life, narrative identity gives it the recognisable features of characters loved or respected. Narrative makes the two ends of the chain of personal identity link up with one another: The permanence in time of character and that of self-constancy."[10] Ricœur thus highlights the ethical dimension of achieving authentic selfhood. Irrespective of which end of the spectrum one approaches the matter, the narrative self has "a common boundary" with moral theory, and that shared horizon is essential to all ethical and personal reflection.

Along the way Ricœur engages with other notions of selfhood, especially those which put the very notion of the self into doubt, influenced, he claims, by non-Western philosophical traditions. It is here that the role of the other becomes crucial, a role that is central to narrative plots where characters engage with each other in various ways. For Ricœur the notion of "mineness," that is, the question "Who am I?" is irreducible. It need not lead to self-absorption, but rather to engagement with the other. In situations in which the question "Who am I?" does not lead to any clear answer, the very fact of posing it at all shows how important the notion of identity is, since in such extreme situations it masks the underlying question "What is going to happen to me?" Thus Ricœur concludes: "I do not see how the question "Who" can disappear. For really how can we ask ourselves *what* matters, if we could not ask the question *to whom* does it matter?"[11] Once the self meets the other the space between them becomes an important locus for both moral reflection and self-reflection. Ricœur asks "Is not the moment of self-dispossession essential to authentic selfhood? And must one not, in order to make oneself open, available, belong to oneself in a certain sense? ... If my identity were to lose all importance in every respect, would not the question of others also cease to matter?"[12]

---

[9] *Oneself as Another* (n. 1), 123.
[10] *Oneself as Another* (n. 1), 165–166.
[11] *Oneself as Another* (n. 1), 137–138.
[12] *Oneself as Another* (n. 1), 138–139.

2. Character, Constancy and Moral Agents in Mark and John

It is time to move from these stimulating, but somewhat abstract reflections on narrativity, selfhood and ethics, and turn to the gospel narratives of Mark and John. Ricœur's remark about the "extremely lively debates on the question of moral identity" cited earlier is apposite with regard to the literary turn in New Testament studies over the past two decades. There have been a number of highly illuminating discussions about the disciples in Mark's gospel, exploring their role as characters within the plot as well as their extra-textual referents.[13] None of these studies has explicitly dealt with the disciples as moral agents, however, and Ricœur's model of selfhood's constant tension between *Idem* and *Ipse*, permanence and change, self and the other would appear to provide a fruitful way to explore an important dimension of the Markan narrative and its significance within early Christianity. In the light of the foregoing discussion it would seem feasible to suggest that the acquired character traits of the disciples as Galilean fishermen contributed to their failure to understand and appreciate the possibilities and challenges for a new selfhood that Jesus was offering them.

On the other hand there is a distinctive Johannine ring to some of Ricœur's statements about the other model of permanence over time, namely, "being true to one's word" once the *Ipse* has been freed from the constraints of the *Idem*. In Ricœur's view, this consistency, even in situations where one has changed one's mind, draws its ethical justification from "the obligation to safeguard the institution of language" by respecting and responding to the trust that others have placed in one's word. Here too the role of the other in forming moral identity comes clearly into view. For him this ethical justification has its own temporal implications, namely, a permanence that is named as the self-constancy of the *Ipse*, which stands as the polar opposite to the permanence of character that the *Idem* provides.

The contrast between the Markan and Johannine representation of the disciples that emerges in their respective narratives is surely dependent on the very different pictures of the main character, Jesus, that each paints, since in both the model of following the master continues to operate, even when both do introduce elements of the *imitatio Christi* that would gradually assert itself with later generations of Christian believers. However, at the narrative level, seemingly irreconcilable differences emerge in the descriptions of the originating moment in the Markan call and the Johannine

---

[13] Theodore J. Weeden, *Mark: Traditions in Conflict* (Philadelphia, Pa.: Fortress Press, 1971), 23–51; Elizabeth Struthers Malbon, "Disciples/Crowds/Whoever: Markan Characters and Readers," *NT* 28 (1986): 104–130; Robert Tannehill, "The Disciples in Mark: The Function of a Narrative Role," *JR* 57 (1977): 134–157.

encounter experience. If Martin Hengel recognises the impossibility of any historical mediation between them, perhaps, Ricœur's reflections on character and constancy can provide an alternative avenue towards understanding the contrast, not just in regard to the call accounts, but to the treatment of the permanent group around Jesus throughout both narratives.[14] It is this possibility that I now wish to explore.

(A) The Markan Disciples as Characters

As previously noted, Ricœur emphasises that the common use of the word character to designate *the personae dramatis* in a narrative suggests a temporal dimension to the notion, understood as those stable dispositions of the *Idem* that makes up one pole of human identity. This temporal dimension of the seemingly stable notion of character calls for evaluative judgements as to whether the Markan disciples remain "true to character" or are prepared to embrace new possibilities of selfhood that would call for a radical separation – physical, religious and emotional – from all that they had heretofore taken as given. "Old habits die hard" as they say. What is surprising therefore is the alacrity with which the two pairs of brothers from Bethsaida are depicted as abandoning all to follow Jesus (Mark 1:16–20). Perhaps the image of becoming "fishers of men" was a successful rhetorical ploy by Jesus to lure them into following, without any clear indication of the life changes that were involved.

Certainly, the enormity of the decision was to come home to them later in the narrative when faced with the rich young man's inability to respond to Jesus' challenge of total renunciation involved in discipleship. Jesus' reflection that this was humanly impossible, but achievable with God's help, draws from Peter the rather anxious, or perhaps it is the boastful, reaction: "we have left all to follow you" (Mark 10:28). One recalls Ricœur's comment that behind the "Who" question remains the "What will happen to me" question at moments of self-doubt or anxiety. Jesus' reassurance that they will receive a reward both in this time and in the world to come (v. 30), has baffled the commentators somewhat, since it apparently suggests that the disciples will receive everything back by a hundredfold in the present time, all that they had previously been asked to abandon. Does this mean that nothing of the *Idem* will be lost, once they were prepared to take the plunge in search of a new *Ipse*? However, the promise of a "hundredfold" points to a symbolic rather than a literal meaning (cf. Mark 4:20) – "a richer social and religious fellowship" – as Vincent Taylor puts it, referring to life within the Christian community.[15]

---

[14] Martin Hengel and Anna Maria Schwemer, *Jesus und das Judentum* (Tübingen: Mohr Siebeck, 2007), 237–239 and 360–365.

[15] Vincent Taylor, *The Gospel according to Mark* (London: Macmillan, 1963), 435.

What the Markan story line does not develop but what the first hearers of the gospel would certainly have understood, is that the habits and dispositions of these Galilean fishermen were the polar opposite to that which Jesus was proposing. They were being radically challenged to abandon the stable *Idem* of their lives, based, as we saw, on "values, norms, models and heroes," the adoption and internalising of which had brought them to a satisfactory self understanding. They were being asked to find in Jesus a new hero to emulate, a new set of values that ran counter to the kinship and honour/shame world of their upbringing and self-identification. In terms of Ricœur's model of self-identification they were being told that their former *Ipse* or sense of self, rooted as it undoubtedly was in the Mosaic symbolic world of temple, land and Torah, must now be replaced by alternatives that were by no means clear, and that were cloaked in less familiar, prophetic images that did not immediately conform to their expectations, as can be seen at an early stage in the narrative with their failure to understand even one parable (4:10–13).

As the narrative progresses the disciples are on a journey, one that should lead from sameness to a new selfhood, but each time they are forewarned about what is about to transpire for their hero in Jerusalem, their old value system reasserts itself. This journey does not reach its triumphant goal in Jerusalem in the manner that they surely continued to expect, but ended rather with a reverse journey to Galilee, the very arena where their old selves had been fashioned (Mark 14:27; 16:7). There has been much discussion among the commentators as to the significance of this command to return to Galilee. Many have merely assumed that all was well in the end and that the disciples did indeed return to Galilee, there to encounter Jesus, as Matthew's reading of Mark indicates.[16] Yet in fact the saying of Jesus before his arrest at Mark 14:27, which is alluded to at 16:7, promises neither an appearance nor the parousia, but simply a statement "that I will go before you to Galilee." This statement with its use of the verb προάγω in both instances, echoes the journey up to the holy city, when the disciples followed in shock and fear, Mark tells us, as Jesus was "going ahead of them" (ἦν προάγων αὐτοὺς ὁ Ἰησοῦς, Mark 10:32).[17] There is nothing in Mark's story line that suggests that the return journey to Galilee will be any more successful in terms of discovery of the new identity to which they had been summoned. Indeed the last appearance of Peter is in the courtyard of the high priest where he is heard cursing and swearing that he

---

[16] Robert Fowler, *Let the Reader Understand: Reader-Response Criticism and the Gospel of Mark* (Minneapolis, Minn.: Fortress Press, 1984), 228–260.

[17] Ernst Lohmeyer, *Galiläa und Jerusalem* (FRLANT 34; Göttingen: Vandenhoeck & Ruprecht, 1936), 17–18.

is neither a Galilean nor a follower of Jesus – a rejection of both his past *Idem* and his potentially new *Ipse* – a tragic figure indeed! The mention of his subsequent weeping on recalling Jesus' prediction of his disloyalty softens the picture somewhat but does not totally remove its impact (Mark 14:66–72).

Erich Auerbach in his influential study of representation in western literature was loud in his praises of Mark's narrative realism, especially in the treatment of Peter's character as leader of the Twelve (disciples).[18] Certainly, for whatever reason, Mark does concentrate special care and attention in his representation of the leader of the group.[19] Thus, prior to the name-giving, which Mark combines with his list of the Twelve (3:16a), the name Peter is not used, unlike Matthew's and Luke's indiscriminate usage of both Simon and Peter from the beginning, nor does he ever use the combination Simon Peter. After the name-giving Peter is the constant form of address, except for two highly significant occasions. Firstly, after his Caesarea Philippi declaration about Jesus' messianic identity, Peter seeks to dissuade him from going to Jerusalem, and is rebuked in the strongest possible terms: "get behind me Satan, for you think the thoughts of men, not the thoughts of God" (Mark 8:33). Within the discourse of the story the use of the name Satan for what appears to have been a spontaneous reaction of Peter's, is highly significant, since of all the gospels, Mark's is the most explicit in presenting Jesus' whole ministry as a war on the demonic forces. This rebuke to Peter, therefore, puts his confession of Jesus' messianic status on a par with those of demoniacs earlier (Mark 1:24–25; 5:7), as being empty and meaningless. The second incident is even more telling. As Jesus is going through his Gethsemane experience, the disciples slept even though Jesus had asked for their support. On discovering their lack of concern Jesus reverts to his old name: "Simon do you sleep?" (Mark 14:37). Clearly, from the point of view of the story, Peter has reverted to his old self, and that means that he has not really changed his all too-human perspective on Jesus' identity or his own old self-understanding.

Other named disciples and the group as a whole equally fail to live up to their call. Thus the disciples ignore Jesus' use of a little child as the image of who was the greatest in the kingdom of heaven (Mark 9:37), by preventing the little children to be brought to him (Mark 10:13). Clearly, they have failed to recognise the values' revolution that Jesus had initiated and their own role in it, as the Twelve, the symbolic representatives of the restored and renewed Israel. By preventing an outsider to perform exor-

---

[18] Erich Auerbach, *Mimesis: The Representation of Reality in Western Literature,* (Princeton, N.J.: Princeton University Press, 1953).

[19] Freyne, *The Twelve* (n. 3), 87–88 and note 1.

cisms in Jesus' name, John had failed to appreciate the inclusive nature of Jesus' vision, displaying a separatist and sectarian mentality. His failure to acknowledge the importance of "the other" shows an obsessive concern about his own in-group, something that he and his brother James demonstrate in their request for special places in the messianic kingdom that they obviously expected would shortly arrive in Jerusalem (Mark 9:38–41; 10:35–37). Once it became obvious that this was not going to happen in the manner they had expected, it comes as no surprise to hear that they all abandoned Jesus and left him to his fate (Mark 14:50).

As Elizabeth Struthers Malbon has pointed out, the contrast in the amount of narrative space given to the male disciples and the sudden appearance for the first time in the narrative of the "women who followed him in Galilee and ministered to him" (Mark 15:40–41), can only be intended as a radical shock to the readers.[20] Unlike the male disciples who had abandoned him in his hour of need, the women remained faithful, even if there was nothing they could do to prevent his fate. The fact that the three women who had received the good news of Jesus being risen, may or may not have informed Peter and the disciples as instructed by the young man – Mark seems to leave the matter open deliberately, if one follows the shorter ending (16:1–8) – does raise the question of how we are to understand their role in the outcome of the plot. Certainly, their fear and flight from the tomb are not meant as a criticism or a failure on their part, and perhaps we are better to follow the advice of Mark elsewhere: "let the reader understand" (Mark 13:14)! From the perspective of this analysis it introduces the issue of gender into the discussion of Christian identity. In a Jewish patriarchal society, the role of the male was that of house owner and master of the household including the women folk. The challenge that Jesus posed in terms of the call to discover a new selfhood was more readily availed of by women, precisely because they were not tied to the *Idem* of their own cultural identity, but longed for freedom and the right to self-identification independently of their masters. That the Jesus movement gave them such freedom would seem to be the obvious implications of Mark's noting of their presence at this late point in the story. His open-ended conclusion, suggests that it was not always an easy decision for women then or now.

(B) Disciples in the Fourth Gospel: Being True to One's Word

When one turns to the Fourth Gospel after reading Mark, it is noteworthy how attention on the disciples recedes, with the increased emphasis on the

---

[20] Elizabeth Struthers Malbon, "Fallible Followers: Women and Men in the Gospel of Mark," *Semeia* 27 (1984): 29–84.

person of Jesus as the Logos incarnate. Insofar as it is possible to speak of a plot to this sustained discourse about Jesus' identity, the Johannine disciples are "flat" characters in contrast to Mark's more vivid and varied presentation. While the gospel does continue with the narrative pattern set by the Synoptics, and so fits loosely into the genre of a *Bios* or Ancient Life, the timelessness, or better the invasion of this world's time with that of "the age to come," does attenuate considerably the sequential nature of the plot, and therefore dissipates its narrative potential with regard to character development and change. Past and future are repeatedly collapsed into the present of Jesus' hour. Thus on the one hand he informs the Samaritan woman that "the hour is coming and now is" (John 4:23), while on other occasions in dealing with opponents he can claim that "before Abraham was I am" (John 8:58) and that Isaiah saw his glory (John 12:41). This difference relates to the different Christological and theological starting points of the two works, as mentioned previously. Whereas the Markan Jesus presents genuine human traits, as e.g. in the agony scene (Mark 14:32–42), and is, therefore, a believable model for following and imitation, John's Jesus is such a divine figure, so totally in charge of the situation, even at his arrest and trial, that at first reading at least, he is in the words of Wayne Meeks, "too alien to human weakness to provide a convincing model."[21]

In Ricœur's categories, the main character's *Ipse* is so totally at one with his *Idem*, which in John's gospel is "from above" that he cannot readily function as the kind of human hero in whose values and norms the disciples might discover a totally new set of human dispositions that they could appropriate and internalise. From the very beginning they are said to believe in him, and throughout, belief in Jesus' word is all that is asked of them (John 1:49). In Ricœurian terms this means being true to their word because he is true to his. From the outset of the narrative they are presented as having seen and recognised his glory (John 2:11), and they therefore, are cast as representatives of those of "his own" who have received him, and as such are "born of God" in contrast to the many who did not, as the Prologue announces the outcome (John 1:12–13).

This contrast between the two portrayals is particularly noteworthy in the account of the disciples' first encounter with Jesus in John, and their call narrative in Mark. In John the setting for the encounter is not by the lakeside in the midst of the everyday labours of fishermen, but rather in the Judean desert, where various religious groups are to be found concerned about the identity of Israel's expected redeemer. John the baptiser, already

---

[21] Wayne A. Meeks, "The Ethics of the Fourth Evangelist," in *Exploring the Gospel of John* (ed. R. Alan Culpepper and C. Clifton Black; Louisville, Ky.: Westminster John Knox, 1996), 317–326, here 318.

engaged in a rite of preparation for the coming one, is the first witness to Jesus' true identity (John 1:29). It is his testimony to Jesus as Lamb of God that prompts two of his own disciples to follow (ἀκολουθεῖν) Jesus; they, not he, take the first initiative. However, Jesus recognises that they are searching (τί ζητεῖτε;), and when they enquire about his dwelling he invites them to come and see, an invitation that starts a chain reaction of others, climaxing with Nathaniel's confession: "Rabbi, you are the Son of God, the King of Israel." This recognition is seen by Jesus as the beginnings of genuine belief, but "greater things" are promised in terms of a heavenly epiphany, which will manifest Jesus' true origins and identity more adequately (John 1:50–51). The "Amen, Amen" with which Jesus introduces this promise is only one of over 50 such utterances in the Gospel. Constancy with his promises is the hallmark of the Word incarnate, his sense of obligation to the truth of his word by the Word who is the truth, but also the way and the life.

When one holds this dense narrative up to the prism of Ricœur's model of identity development it is clear that the difference with Mark's account consists in their openness to a new experience because of their prior openness to the search for a new understanding, not just for themselves but for Israel. Thus Nathaniel can be designated as "an Israelite in whom there is no guile" (John 1:47). The *Idem* that created a virtually insurmountable obstacle for the Markan disciples has already been left behind by these Galileans from Bethsaida, who were in the Judean desert as members of John's retinue, a movement that already had come under the suspicion of the guardians of the status quo in Jerusalem – priests, Levites and Pharisees.

The first and only real crisis for the Johannine disciples comes at the end of the bread of life discourse in chapter 6. A division in the previously enthusiastic crowd occurs when Jesus explains what was involved in receiving the bread from heaven. Many of the disciples abandon him, which is the only indication of a larger circle of followers in the work. Only the Twelve remain and when Jesus asks if they too wish to leave, Peter as spokesperson replies: "Lord to whom shall we go? You have the words of eternal life" (John 6:60–70). They have successfully negotiated this first real test of their constancy to their word, a constancy that has developed from Jesus' repeated reassurances that their loyalty to him will be honoured by his loyalty to his word of promise to them. This relationship of trust in his word recurs in the introduction to the Lazarus story in chapter 11. Jesus' response to their hesitation with regard to the dangers that lie ahead is very different from the Markan rebuke to Peter in similar circumstances. They are challenged to continue "to work," which ironically means "to believe" (cf. John 6:23), and are reassured that their faith will be strengthened by the experience (John 11:5–16).

There was never any question of the disciples returning to the *Idem* of Galilean fishermen in the work proper, despite the evidence of the later ending in chapter 21. The remaining task is to reassure them of the promise of eternal life, despite the departure of Jesus. The note of anxiety that begins to manifest itself as Jesus seeks to console them and explain his departure, recalls again Ricœur's discussion of what often lies behind the question of identity "who am I?", namely, the more fundamental question: "what will happen to me?" The Lazarus story should have reassured them in advance with Jesus' promise of eternal life to all who believe in him "whether one lives or dies" (John 11:25–26). Yet the imminent departure of Jesus to a place where they cannot immediately follow (John 13:36), in contrast to their experience in the first encounter with him ("Rabbi where do you dwell? He said to them: come and see", John 1:38), shakes the self-confidence of their new *Ipse* as disciples of the one who promised eternal life. Queries and misunderstandings from Peter (John 13:36), Thomas (John 14:5), Philip (John 4:8) and "some of the disciples" (John 16:17–19) do not draw a rebuke from Jesus, but rather provide him with the opportunity for a further elaboration of the promise in terms of the gift of the Paraclete/Consoler, the soon return of Jesus, his going to prepare a place for them, and his indwelling in them together with the Father, as they face a hostile world. "Be of good heart, I have overcome the world" (John 16:33), is his final word before turning directly to the Father to pray for them in the trials that lie ahead.

The notion of friendship between Jesus and the disciples is particularly apt in terms of the model of keeping one's promise as this was developed by Ricœur: "[t]he perseverance of character is one thing; the constancy of friendship is quite another." The statement "you are my friends if you do what I command you" (John 15:14), is followed a little later by a second one: "you have not chosen me, but I have chosen you" (John 15:16). At first sight neither strikes the note of a friendship of equals, but seem rather to put Jesus in a position of superiority. However, these two statements enclose another assertion that links this discourse with Jesus' action of washing the feet of the disciples earlier: "I do not call you servants any longer, because the servant does not know what the master is doing, but I have called you friends because I have made known to you everything that I have heard from my Father" (John 15:15). Earlier, in the discourse after the foot washing scene, Jesus, though accepting their identification of him as Master and Teacher, performs the action of a servant in the Greco-Roman household, namely the washing of the feet of the guests at table (John 13:12–14). Jesus' friendship with the disciples is then a friendship of equals in service, not that of the typical Greco-Roman milieu of the day, namely, the friendship of unequals such as that which operated between patrons and clients or in the political arena.

The Johannine Jesus introduces the notion of friendship as descriptive of his relationship with the disciples in a context in which he wants to stress their shared experience in terms of the shared understanding of God that Jesus has imparted to them. Because of this atmosphere of trust and sharing arising from a common experience, an ethical obligation of loving one another automatically arises. The understanding of God that Jesus has imparted is that of the Father's love for the Son, and the Son's reciprocal love of the Father. This confidential understanding of the Father-Son relationship provides the pattern of love-relations that Jesus enjoins on them also, and the constancy of their friendship with him demands that they follow his example of service (ὑπόδειγμα, John 13:15). The contexts of these articulations of the love commandment are highly significant. The foot washing scene is performed as one of his intimate circle is about to betray him (ch. 13), and the discourse on friendship takes place within the setting of the world's hatred for him and them, despite the fact that his coming into the world was an act of God's love for it (John 3:16).

Thus the ethical demands of their new-found identity as friends of Jesus, that is as people whose constancy is affirmed, are both obvious and simple – to replicate the mutual love of Father and Son within their own circle. Loyalty to Jesus will mean that they must continue to resist the world and its values, while at the same time caring for the world in the light of the Father's love for it.[22] In particular the model of friendship that they are expected to replicate will challenge the dominant Greco-Roman one as this is exemplified in the trial before Pilate. The Jewish opponents of Jesus charge Pilate of not being a friend (φίλος) of Caesar, should he release Jesus (John 19:12), alluding to the distorted idea of political friendship, in which expediency rather than mutual love and trust was the controlling force. At the same time the rarefied atmosphere of their relationships based on the shared knowledge of God's love that Jesus has imparted to them, could easily distort their views of those outside their intimate circle, making it difficult for them to acknowledge God's love for the whole of creation, even the world that was hostile to his designs. Warren Carter has recently argued that it is the "imperial context of oppression" that constitutes the world as far as the Johannine Christians are concerned, but it

---

[22] I agree with Richard A. Burridge, *Imitating Jesus: An Inclusive Approach to New Testament Ethics* (Grand Rapids, Mich.: Eerdmans, 2007), 332–334, who demonstrates that in the Fourth Gospel, the term *kosmos* has both positive and negative connotation. As Burridge notes, it is interesting that the more negative usages occur towards the end of the work, whereas the positive ones are to be found in the opening chapters.

would also seem to have limited to the in-group the scope of the commandment, in sharp contradistinction to the more universal "love your enemies" of the Synoptic tradition.[23]

3. Christian Discipleship and Moral Agency

This attempt to uncover the different ways in which Christian identity is constructed around the group of permanent disciples in the two gospels, aided by the reflections of Paul Ricœur, calls for taking the further step with him to see how a narrative approach to identity formation can lead to a narrative approach to Christian ethics. When the issue of the NT and morality is discussed, too often the focus is on the content rather than the agent, with the hotly debated question of whether the New Testament moral teaching is distinctive or derivative in terms of both contemporary Jewish and Greco-Roman moral teaching. By focusing on the "who" of the moral agent rather than the "what" of the moral teaching we are inevitably drawn into the question of the ways in which a Christian self-identity is constructed and maintained. Our exploration would suggest that the *Idem/Ipse* tension is a fruitful way to explore this issue, with the interesting result that Christian moral agency is formed in different ways and with somewhat different consequences.

Mark's narrative account of discipleship-formation in terms of a shift from a stable character identity to a radically different one, illustrates the many factors that come into play. Among these were the relation of individual to group, the role of gender, the attachment to particular cultural and social forms of living, especially when these involved trans-generational loyalty and commitments, and the fear of change, but above all the existential threat to selfhood itself, once one embarks on such a journey of self-discovery. As we move through the stages of the Markan narrative all these elements emerge at various points in the story, inviting us as readers to enter into the dynamic, ponder the obstacles and consequences that emerge for different individuals and evaluate the differing points of view on what constitutes the good life in response to the reign of God, the issue that is at the heart of the story. In this respect other Markan characters provide an interesting contrast to the disciples, not least the women who had "followed him in Galilee" and who stood by the cross and

---

[23] Warren Carter, *John and Empire: Initial Explorations* (New York, N.Y.: T&T Clark, 2008), 278–281.

attended to Jesus' burial, when the male disciples had all abandoned him and fled (Mark 14:50; 15:40–41).[24]

This kind of active engagement with a story line can take place in any good narrative and lead to self-evaluation and reflection, but in the case of Christian readers the gospels are not just read for pleasure but for insight and direction in dealing with the moral dilemmas that confront us as individuals and communities on a daily basis. What Ricœur elsewhere describes as Mimesis 3, namely, the re-figuration involved in the reception of a work by actively engaging with both its pre-figuration, that is the symbolic universe to which the discourse belongs (Mimesis 1), and its configuration, namely, the textual world that is represented in the work (Mimesis 2), calls for full and active participation on our part, where our own self-identity and assumptions come under scrutiny in and through those of the characters in the story.[25] What that reading exercise will mean for different readers or groups of readers (local Christian communities e.g.) will be determined by many factors – their attachment to tradition, their openness to the search for new and more fulfilling life patterns, their sense of concern for the other, especially the least of all, their political and religious affiliations. One thing seems certain on the basis of our reading of Mark's narrative of the disciples as characters, the process of Christian self-identification is an open-ended and on-going struggle with the demons in ourselves and in our world, demons that seek to prevent us from exploring new and challenging horizons of possibility, to which the gospel summons us. It should not be forgotten however, that in seeking to enter into the self-understanding of the Markan disciples and the other characters, one is thereby also entering into the self-understanding of Jesus, whose call and life example provide the parameters and the values with which Christians are called on to engage.

Turning to John's account, the difference of perspective in comparison with Mark's realistic narrative becomes strikingly obvious when one focuses on the representation of the disciples in each work. This clearly affects the understanding of selfhood and moral agency that the work projects. The role of narrative, which Ricœur had seen as vital in maintaining the notion of permanence over time is less obvious, though not entirely absent in the Fourth Gospel, as the development of the disciples' response is charted within the plot, as outlined above. The disciples are already in

---

[24] Struthers Malbon, "Disciples/Crowds/Whoever" (n. 13).

[25] Paul Ricœur, *Time and Narrative* (vol. 1 of 3 vols.; Chicago: Chicago University Press, 1984–1985; English trans. of *Temps et Récit*; Paris: Éditions du Soleil, 1983), 52–90. Cf. Hille Haker, "Narrative and Moral Identity in Paul Ricoeur," in *Creating Identity* (*Concilium* 2002/2; ed. Hermann Haring, Maureen Junker Kenny and Dietmar Mieth; London: SCM Press, 2000), 59–67.

search of a new hero when they encounter Jesus, and that discovery provides them with both a new *Idem* and the possibility of a new *Ipse*, which,
as the narrative progresses tends to coalesce, even when anxiety and uncer-
tainty occur at various moments along the way. From the outset they believe *in* Jesus, a belief which, at the narrative level, involves not just trusting his word but being loyal to his way. Thus the word of Jesus is both
descriptive in terms of its revelatory capacity with regard to the truth, the
way, and the life, but also prescriptive in terms of the love-commandment
as the summation of the gospel's moral vision. Yet, as we have seen, in the
development of the friendship motif as a way of cementing the sense of
union between the disciples and Jesus, this can have the effect of narrow-
ing the vision to the in-group in a manner that borders on the sectarian.

From its earliest reception the re-figuration of the Fourth Gospel has
been to see it as the spiritual gospel, and this has very much influenced
what Meeks has described as a series of mis-readings which have allowed
it to have a profound influence on Western culture, including its moral
culture.[26] Meek's own reading is to show "what is wrong with John" before making any attempt to retrieve some possible meaning for contemporary Christian living. He finds its narrative world into which readers are
invited to enter, as "profoundly troubling to rational forms of moral discourse." Ironically, it is the "sectarian" dimension of John that Meeks finally identifies as being most relevant for contemporary Christian witness,
insofar as "this sharply sectarian voice is culturally and politically subversive." It is only when one stands in radical opposition to the world without
any accommodation to its values, that it is possible to challenge these with
any authenticity.[27] This view of John is not far distant from Warren
Carter's post-colonial reading of John in the context of Roman imperial
presence, without taking such a negative view of the Jesus-believing
group, as does Meeks' criticism of the almost blind obedience that is expected from the disciples. Yet the problem with Carter's fresh reading is
that now all opposition to the Jesus-group, including that coming from "the
Jews," is ultimately attributable to Roman imperial domination. The demons to be encountered may well be more diverse and more subtle.[28]

Perhaps another way to recover the narrative search for Christian self-
identity by the disciples in the Fourth Gospel is not to read the story se-

---

[26]   Meeks, 'Ethics' (n. 21), 317.

[27]   Meeks, 'Ethics' (n. 21), 319 and 324–325, citing Mennonite scholar, David Rens-
berger, *Johannine Faith and Liberating Community* (Philadelphia, Pa.: Westminster John
Knox, 1988), 27–28.

[28]   For a different, 'post-modern' approach to a post-colonial reading of John cf. Ste-
phen Moore, "'The Romans will come and destroy our holy place and our nation:'
Representing Empire in John," in *Empire and Apocalypse: Postcolonialism and the New
Testament* (ed. Stephen Moore; Sheffield: Phoenix Press, 2006), 45–76.

quentially, but diachronically in terms of the history of the community, as many recent studies of the Johannine writings suggest.[29] In this way we can begin to see how a group of Jesus-believers, with standard Jewish messianic expectations as indicated in John 1:19–51, are transmuted into Johannine Christians through force of circumstances. The high Christology to which the disciples subscribe is, then, the result of exclusion, persecution and vilification as reflected in many of the Gospel's narratives, especially in its use of the Son of man image.[30]

Once this approach is adopted many other characters enter the picture as representatives of different points of view and a more inclusive outlook. Nicodemus, the cripple at the pool of Bethesda, the Samaritan woman, the blind man whom Jesus healed and his parents, Mary, Martha and Lazarus, the Greeks who wanted to come to Jesus, all suggest a sense of cultural, social and religious and gender diversity, that a focus on the disciples alone within the narrative unity of the finished text can obscure. The "sectarianism" of the end redaction of the work, if that is how we are to describe it, is the result of external as well as internal social factors, and was to continue on within the community as we can discern from the Johannine epistles. This diachronic story of Christian self-identification becoming more and more inward looking and isolationist originated from a starting point of Jewish messianic hopes that were by no means as hostile to the world as the Johannine community was later to become. The reception of this and other works of the so-called Johannine school into the Canon of early Christian writings shows that second century Christians did not find the work as exclusive or anti-world as some moderns have done.[31] Perhaps the lesson for Christian self-understanding and notions of moral agency to be derived from that alternative story is the need to remain in touch with its larger heritage, one that is not just based on Jewish messianic hopes alone, but which also leaves room for the Greeks who sought to join the Jesus movement according to John. Faith *and* reason did have mutually supporting roles to play, even in the earliest stages of the Jesus movement,

---

[29] Cf. James L. Martyn, *History and Theology in the Fourth Gospel* (Nashville, Tenn.: Abingdon, 1968); Raymond E. Brown, *The Community of the Beloved Disciple,* (London: Chapman, 1979); Nils Dahl, "The Johannine Church and History," in *Jesus in the Memory of the Early Church* (ed. Nils Dahl; Minneapolis, Minn.: Augsburg Press, 1976), 99–120.

[30] Wayne A. Meeks, "The man from Heaven in Johannine Sectarianism," *JBL* 91 (1972): 44–72.

[31] Burridge, *Imitating Jesus* (n. 22), 339–343 also questions the use of this label for the Johannine gospel in view of the 'mixed' community of believers that he detects as represented in the variety of characters who are positively treated within the work.

and this is as true of the Fourth Gospel as it is of any other New Testament writing.[32]

---

[32] Peder Borgen, "The Gospel of John and Hellenism," in *Exploring the Gospel of John* (ed. R. Alan Culpepper and C. Clifton Black; Louisville, Ky.: Westminster John Knox, 1996), 65–97.

II. Jesus and the Gospels

Jesus' "Conception of Man" as an Expression of his "Ethics"

KARL-WILHELM NIEBUHR

With regard to an "anthropology" of Jesus that can be derived from his ministry, exegesis has been taking the route only, if at all, to reconstruct individual pieces of the pre-literary, primarily pre-synoptic Jesus tradition; it may have been taking into consideration also his ministry as a healer; and it has been attempting to historically capture and theologically interpret his road to the cross. Jesus' conception of man garners scarce attention in this process. Evidence external to the synoptic gospels is ignored in the same way as is the complete narrative picture of Jesus' ministry, as it was apparently prescribed in the Gospel narratives. The situation with regard to Jesus' "ethics" is similar. Generally, the exegesis only has been attempting to reconstruct the contours of Jesus' preaching of the Kingdom of God, to identify his relationship to ancient Jewish Torah and wisdom traditions and, from this point perhaps, to classify his ethical instructions in the context of ancient Jewish and Hellenistic-Roman paraenetic *topoi*. Again, there is seldom reflection on Jesus' ministry as an expression of his "ethics."

This paper will attempt a different approach. It will not examine the individual ethical *topoi* or paraenetic genres found in the Jesus tradition. Instead, it will be a search for Jesus' "conception of man" as an expression of his "ethics." Of course, in doing this, one cannot abandon the texts of the Jesus tradition or the ethical topics, structures and objects that appear in them. However, it will be the contours of the ministry and the person of Jesus as a whole, which can be interpreted as an expression of his ethical orientation, that are definitive for this examination. The relationship to the theme of the conference "Ethics and Language" arises from the place in which the complete narrative structure of the Jesus tradition and some of its narrative complexes are understood as an expression of an ethical intention.

Text analysis, whether it be the Gospel narratives as a whole on the literary-editorial level or individual complexes of tradition with the support of historic-traditional analysis, is not of central interest here. Instead, a search will be carried out for the narrative structures "behind" the Gospel narratives and the individual traditions incorporated in them that express

Jesus' "ethics." In this process, it will become clear that we are dealing primarily with linguistic forms that arise out of the characteristic peculiarities of Jesus' ministry and teaching, his way and his destiny. Explicitly admonitory or paraenetic linguistic forms, which of course are also found in and are important to the Jesus tradition, will be correspondingly evaluated as expressions of Jesus' "ethics" only if they can be classified into the framework of such a narratively-structured, overall ethical intention of his ministry.

The approach chosen here is based on a larger representation of the anthropology of the New Testament that proceeds from similar methodological premises.[1] With this approach, I will attempt to overcome the prevalent division in Jesus research between detailed historic-exegetic studies within the framework of the reconstruction of the "historical" Jesus and overall, theological-hermeneutic interpretations of Jesus' preaching within the context of biblical and systematic theology. In my opinion, New Testament anthropology and ethics would benefit if biblical-exegetic studies were to go beyond the level of text analysis and take a purposeful (and methodologically-reflexive) step into the realities of history that both underlie and follow these texts.

1. The Center of Jesus' Ministry

In order to capture the contours of Jesus' conception of man and the structures of his ethics, one must begin at the center of his ministry – with his preaching on and realization of the Kingdom of God.[2] In the Jesus tradition, mankind has, above all, the function of addressee and receiver of Jesus' message about the Kingdom of God. Jesus' preaching on the Kingdom of God is not only a sermon, a lesson in words, but also an event – the advent of the Kingdom of God as pronounced by Jesus and the inclusion of the addressees in this event. Thus, Jesus' message is both heard and seen (cf. Matt 12:38–42 par. Luke 11:29–32; Mark 8:11–12 parr.; Matt 13:16–

---

[1]   The present writer is working on a textbook on New Testament anthropology to be published in German in the series "Grundrisse zum Neuen Testament" with Vandenhoeck & Ruprecht in Göttingen. The paper published here gives an outline of part of the chapter on Jesus.

[2]   Cf. Martin Hengel and Anna Maria Schwemer, *Jesus und das Judentum* (Tübingen: Mohr Siebeck, 2007), 377–430; Christoph Niemand, *Jesus und sein Weg zum Kreuz: Ein historisch-rekonstruktives und theologisches Modellbild* (Stuttgart: Kohlhammer, 2007), 39–49; James D. G. Dunn, *Jesus Remembered: Christianity in the Making* (vol. 1; Grand Rapids, Mich.: Eerdmans, 2003), 383–487; Helmut Merklein, *Jesu Botschaft von der Gottesherrschaft: Eine Skizze* (SBS 111; 3rd ed.; Stuttgart: Katholisches Bibelwerk, 1989).

17 par. Luke 10:23–24). It is – like all acts of God towards mankind in the sense of the biblical and ancient Jewish tradition – the living word.

The Kingdom of God is seen not only in Jesus' message but also in his ministry as a healer of the sick. Jesus devotes himself to individuals in need. Healing occurs through encounter with Jesus and through his touch. The deliverance from personal and often bodily suffering is simultaneously the creation of a salutary relationship with God. The event of becoming healthy out of the encounter with Jesus cannot be separated from the person of Jesus as a healer. In this event, Jesus proves himself to be the representative of God who heals all illness (cf. Mark 2:1–12 parr.). Therefore, he who denies or opposes Jesus' ministry, also opposes God (cf. Matt 11:21–24 par. Luke 10:12–15).

The relationship between word and action, between the present and the future of the Kingdom of God in Jesus' ministry can be illuminated by the example of the beatitudes (cf. Matt 5:3–10 par. Luke 6:20–21).[3] Through them, listeners experience today already the transition from need and suffering to salvation and fulfillment that will be the permanent, future state in communion with Jesus. Thus, the beatitudes express the unity of Jesus' ministry and his preaching. They are, in a heightened sense, healing through the medium of the word. They are an example of that which the prayer of the Psalm confesses about God's healing acts: "he sent out his word and healed them, and delivered them from destruction" (Ps 107:20). The eschatological rootedness and direction of Jesus' preaching can also be seen clearly in the beatitudes. They are entirely defined by the notion of the fulfillment of the eschatological prophecies of Holy Scripture for Israel. Jesus devotes himself to the needy, whether it be through his words in the form of the beatitudes or through his ministry, for example in sharing the table with the needy or in his healing of the sick. Through this devotion, he communicates and he creates such a salutary communion as was expected for the eschatological communion of God with his people of Israel.

2. Contexts of Jesus' Preaching

The contours of Jesus' conception of man become sharper when they are placed in the contexts or scopes of his ministry as a whole and can be con-

---

[3]   Cf. Karl-Wilhelm Niebuhr, "Die Makarismen Jesu als Ausdruck seines Menschenbildes," in *Evangelium ecclesiasticum: Matthäus und die Gestalt der Kirche* (ed. Christfried Böttrich et al.; Festschrift Christoph Kähler; Frankfurt am Main: Hansisches Druck- und Verlagshaus, 2009), 329–352.

sidered from this position.[4] Three contexts in particular are definitive for the conception of man: the scope of creation, the scope of Israel and the scope of the eschaton.

In the scope of creation, people appear as children of God, who provides for them as their father (cf. Matt 6:25–34 par. Luke 12:22–32). Their characteristic position in relationship to God is that of asking and receiving and, not least, of praying (cf. Matt 7:7–11 par. Luke 11:9–13; Matt 6:9–13 par. Luke 11:1–4). In parables and proverbs that are close to the biblical and ancient Jewish wisdom tradition, Jesus describes important characteristics of the Kingdom of God with motifs from the creation and from the (mostly rural) daily life of his listeners. For Jesus' preaching, creation is not "untouched nature" in the modern sense but rather the habitat of mankind and the object of God's providence. The suppliant and grateful devotion towards God, the Creator and Father, does not separate Jesus and his followers from Judaism but connects them to it.

In the scope of God's promises to Israel, people find in Jesus the one who, through his ministry, brings such promises to life in the present day. The twelve disciples symbolically represent the twelve tribes of Israel, which are restored for the last days through Jesus' ministry (cf. Mark 6:7–13 parr.; Matt 10:1–16 par. Luke 9:1–6; 10:1–12; Matt 19:28 par. Luke 22:30). God's promise that, at the end of time, Israel will be purged of all sickness is fulfilled in Jesus' healing of the sick (cf. Matt 11:2–6 par. Luke 7:18–23). The challenge to cleanse the "entire person" and to fulfill the "entire Torah" applies to those who, in meeting Jesus, meet the demands and the will of the God of Israel (Mark 7:15 par. Matt 15:11).

In the scope of the eschatological Kingdom of God, which Jesus pronounces and delivers, his demand to follow the will of God also leads people to the Last Judgement (cf. Mark 9:42–50 parr.). There they must prove themselves and take responsibility as the "doers of the word." Jesus vividly expresses the connection between doing and condition, between a lifestyle that corresponds to the will of God and the promise of eschatological reward with metaphors and parables that are often defined by the tension between present and future (cf. Matt 7:16–20 par. Luke 6:43–45; Matt 12:33–35; Matt 7:24–27 par. Luke 6:47–49; Matt 25:31–46). In the future eschatological judgement, mankind will be judged by none other than Je-

---

[4] Martin Ebner, *Jesus – ein Weisheitslehrer? Synoptische Weisheitslogien im Traditionsprozeß* (HBSt 15; Freiburg: Herder, 1998); Volker Hampel, *Menschensohn und historischer Jesus: Ein Rätselwort als Schlüssel zum messianischen Selbstverständnis Jesu* (Neukirchen-Vluyn: Neukirchener Verlag, 1990); Hermann von Lips, *Weisheitliche Traditionen im Neuen Testament* (WMANT 64; Neukirchen-Vluyn: Neukirchener Verlag, 1990), 193–266; Marius Reiser, *Die Gerichtspredigt Jesu: Eine Untersuchung zur eschatologischen Verkündigung Jesu und ihrem frühjüdischen Hintergrund* (NTA 23; Münster: Aschendorff, 1990).

sus himself, the Son of Man, who, in his present day ministry, lays claim to the lives of those whom he meets and simultaneously claims for himself God's authority for the forgiveness of sins (cf. Mark 8:34–38 parr.).

One of the particular challenges and one of the most objectionable aspects of Jesus' ministry and message is that he expected, from the people he encountered, complete identification with his own claim to be acting on behalf of God. This expectation was heightened by the fact that Jesus created an interrelation between such identification and the eschatological fate of those who behaved positively or negatively towards him. This eschatological scope belongs no less to Jesus' ministry than do the contexts of creation or Israel and indeed has a direct relationship to these scopes, as the identifiable references to biblical and ancient Jewish traditions demonstrate.

Simultaneously, Jesus connected this demand for identification with himself to a challenge to do the right thing, as was prescribed by the biblical and ancient Jewish traditions for moral conduct in accordance with the will of God. In the framework of a biblical and Jewish faith, such an obligation was underpinned and paraenetically accentuated with reference to God's final judgement, which promised to reward the just with life and threatened the unjust with the loss of exactly this life. This leads more or less seamlessly into Jesus' own preaching. Jesus, however, had a specific focus in that he claimed not only the authority to enforce, with eschatological pressure, God's demands on mankind but also the power, like God, to forgive sins. Through his healing he allowed mankind to emblematically experience the deliverance of Israel from all sickness and, in the same way, through the forgiveness of sins, he exemplarily demonstrated the unlimited mercy of God in the deliverance of mankind from sin.

3. Jesus' "Ethics" as a Consequence of his Conception of Man

One cannot speak of "Jesus' ethics" in the strict sense of a systematic reflection of the requirements, guidelines and impetus of human action.[5] Nevertheless, his preaching and ministry were aimed at human actions that, for Jesus, could not be separated from the human "being" as well as was the case for the biblical and Jewish tradition. Israel's relationship with God is created and maintained by God's covenant with his people. The Torah is a definitive element of this covenant relationship – God created

---

[5] Cf. Friedrich Wilhelm Horn, "Die Nachfolgeethik Jesu und die urchristliche Gemeindeethik: Ihre Darstellung innerhalb Ferdinand Hahns Theologie des Neuen Testaments," in *Aufgabe und Durchführung einer Theologie des Neuen Testaments* (ed. Cilliers Breytenbach and Jörg Frey; WUNT 205; Tübingen: Mohr Siebeck, 2007), 287–307.

the covenant with Israel through the Torah. It is the record of the covenant and the guarantee for Israel's existence in its faith history. It is God's gift to his people and the foundation for the identity of his people in their commitment to their God. It is a guideline for faith and life in Israel for the nation as a whole as well as for every Israelite.[6] For Jesus also, the gift of the Torah is anchored, in this sense, in the relationship between God and Israel as a set of life instructions.[7] From this point of view, Jesus' "ethics" are also anchored in his ministry and preaching as a whole and substantively connected to them. The wisdom orientation of his teaching corresponds to the scope of creation in his conception of man. His handling of the Torah and its commandments signals his commitment to God's fundamental instructions to his people of Israel but can best be understood in the context of ancient Jewish wisdom tradition and its reception of the Torah and thus differs characteristically from a rabbinical-halakhic Torah interpretation. The end-time orientation of his preaching on the Kingdom of God also lends eschatological emphasis to his teaching.

Jesus' treatment of the Sabbath commandment (cf. Mark 2:23–28 parr.; 3:1–5 parr.) demonstrates, in characteristic accentuation, the emphasis of his ministry with regard to the Torah.[8] He neither invalidates the Torah as such or the institution of the Sabbath, nor does he define, in the sense of rabbinical-halakhic regulations, norms of behaviour for the Sabbath. Instead, his intentions are aimed, with radical consistency, at God's beneficial will for Israel and for mankind, which exhibits itself in the Sabbath commandment and which Jesus also brings to light there.

Jesus' teachings on interpersonal behaviour, summarized in the antitheses in the Sermon on the Mount (Matt 5:21–48 parr.), pertain to ethical areas of application that are important also in the ancient Jewish Torah reception (murder, adultery, divorce, oaths, retaliation, brotherly love).[9] Only in Matthew do these traditions take the form of antitheses.[10] There-

---

[6] For this concept of "covenantal nomism" cf. Ed P. Sanders, *Paul and Palestinian Judaism: A Comparison of Patterns of Religion* (London: SCM Press, 1977); idem, "Jesus, Paul and Judaism," *ANRW* 2.25.1 (1981): 390–450.

[7] Cf. Ingo Broer, ed., *Jesus und das jüdische Gesetz* (Stuttgart: Kohlhammer, 1992); Dunn, *Jesus Remembered* (n. 2), 563–592; Hengel and Schwemer, *Jesus und das Judentum* (n. 2), 431–451.

[8] Cf. Lutz Doering, *Schabbat: Sabbathalacha und -praxis im antiken Judentum und Urchristentum* (TSAJ 78; Tübingen: Mohr Siebeck, 1999), 398–478.

[9] Cf. Karl-Wilhelm Niebuhr, *Gesetz und Paränese: Katechismusartige Weisungsreihen in der frühjüdischen Literatur* (WUNT 2/28; Tübingen: Mohr Siebeck, 1987).

[10] Cf. for this Karl-Wilhelm Niebuhr, "Die Antithesen des Matthäus: Jesus als Toralehrer und die frühjüdische weisheitlich geprägte Torarezeption," in *Gedenkt an das Wort* (ed. Christoph Kähler et al.; Festschrift Werner Vogler; Leipzig: Evangelische Verlagsanstalt, 1999), 175–200.

fore, in view of Jesus' own understanding of the Torah and its ethical instructions, one cannot make any assumptions based on the antithetical structure nor can one in any way derive from this structure a fundamental opposition of Jesus to the Torah. Already with regard to the individual ethical domains of action, it is clear that Jesus contemporarily interpreted the corresponding demands of individual Torah commandments, which were also received in paraenetically-oriented texts in ancient Jewish literature, and changed them into fundamental teachings that describe a way of life according to God's will. The commandment of love of the enemies that finishes off the antitheses series in Matthew (Matt 5:43–48) is objectively connected to and derived from the love commandment of the Torah (Lev 19:18). This is also demonstrated by the antithetical version of the tradition in Matthew (see Matt 5:43). In the same way that the comprehensive commandment of love must be seen, in its reception by Jesus, as a part of his ethical teachings, its culmination in the commandment of loving the enemy also belongs to the specific contents of Jesus' preaching but cannot be placed in fundamental opposition to other ancient Jewish traditions of Torah reception.[11] Both in Matthew's and in Luke's versions, the fundamental attitude demanded here is derived from God's fundamental attitude towards man.[12] This, in a strict sense, theological explanation of "Jesus' ethics" closely reflects the rootedness of his teachings in God's will towards mankind.

For Jesus' position on divorce the starting point is seen in Mark's version of the argument with the Pharisees (Mark 10:4–9).[13] In this case, Jesus' teaching is indeed in opposition to the Torah option on divorce. Jesus invokes God, the Creator, in order to override the commandment of Moses. The intention of Jesus' teaching and thus his strict prohibition of divorce[14] are thus rooted in the good guideline of life that God gave to mankind by his creation. When, in his words and deeds, Jesus emphasizes God's will to create life, he places his teachings above the laws of the Torah. Jesus' authority to do this is rooted in his claim to be the eschatological messenger of God's healing grace for Israel and for his creation. In the end, neither an ethical position nor an argument is definitive to Jesus' position on divorce,

---

[11] Cf. Karl-Wilhelm Niebuhr, "Weisheit als Thema biblischer Theologie," *KuD* 44 (1998): 40–60.

[12] Matt 5:48: "Be perfect, therefore, as your heavenly Father is perfect." Luke 6:35: "Your reward will be great, and you will be children of the Most High; for he is kind to the ungrateful and the wicked."

[13] Cf. Traugott Holtz, ",Ich aber sage euch': Bemerkungen zum Verhältnis Jesu zur Tora," in Broer, *Jesus und das jüdische Gesetz* (n. 7), 135–143.

[14] See Mark's version of the Logion in vv. 11–12 in contrast to those in Matthew and Luke.

but rather the claim he places on himself to eschatologically re-validate this life-creating will for mankind.

The concentration on shaping behaviour towards the commandment to love God and one's neighbour also corresponds to a tendency of ancient Jewish Torah paraenesis, although Jesus is the first to identifiably articulate it with such conciseness, as can be seen in the double commandment according to Mark 12:28–34.[15] Surely, we see here a specification of Jesus' ethics, which, however, cannot be contrasted with an ancient Jewish understanding of the Torah. In the same way, the golden rule can be seen as a characteristic expression and part of Jesus' ethics because it cannot be placed in opposition to any fundamental ethical position well-known in Hellenistic-Roman times.

The fact that people want to fulfill God's will as it is defined in the Torah for Israel if they turn towards Jesus is demonstrated by traditions in which the actions connected to such attitude are not explicitly described in words. Tradition clearly records the fact that Jesus' relationship to his family was extraordinarily tense (cf. Mark 3:35 parr.; Luke 11:28). Jesus obviously did not reduce his exclusive claim to authority even in his relationship with his family; instead he felt justified in continuing to assume this authority as, in doing this, he fulfilled God's will. Conversely, this record demonstrates that the behaviour demanded by Jesus cannot be separated from the claim he places on himself to make the Kingdom of God accessible in his ministry. The first commandment of the Decalogue does not limit such a claim but rather emphasizes it (cf. Mark 12:28–34!) in order to point to the importance of God's will for the lives of people who follow him.

Finally, the eschatological accentuation of Jesus' ethical demands must be understood in the context of the eschatological scope of his ministry as a whole.[16] In this case, again, one must recognize the clear influence of the ancient Jewish definitions of the relationship between eschatology and ethics on Jesus' ethics without thereby forgetting the distinctiveness of his eschatological teachings. The decisive difference is found in the specific role that is assigned to Jesus himself for the eschatological events and in the eschatological judgement of human actions. An eschatological judgement based on works can be separated neither from the teaching of Jesus nor from Christian eschatology; however, the decisive factor is the identity of the judge!

---

[15] Cf. Niebuhr, "Weisheit" (n. 11), 51–59.

[16] See above, p. 93.

4. Fundamental Human Attitudes and Experiences in the Encounter with Jesus

People appear as receivers in relationship to Jesus. Among these the needy, the sick, the poor and sometimes also children stand out in particular. Jesus includes those at the edges of society ("tax collectors," "prostitutes," "sinners") in his personal community.[17] He attends directly upon individual sufferers; the poor receive his direct attention and assistance.

The multifaceted healing narratives[18] create a conception of mankind that is made up of the experience of need as well as the deliverance from need, of the suffering from reduction of the ability to live life fully as well as its restoration, of the threat to human life through death as well as newly-given life.[19] In the Jesus tradition, there is neither a term for nor a comprehensive narrative representation of "health;" however, when all of Jesus' healings are put together, there emerges a conception of man that is painted along the contours of a healthy person, created by God, in the sense of the biblical and ancient Jewish tradition. The characteristics of such a healthy human life are not only the unlimited use of one's limbs and senses and the ability to speak and listen and to move one's body, but also a community with one's fellow man that is not limited or inhibited by hygienic or religious taboos.

God is praised in the Psalms as he "who forgives all your iniquity, who heals all your diseases" (Ps 103:3–4; cf. Ps 41; 146; Isa 33:24; Isa 35:5–6), and those who have been healed by Jesus can attest to this from the experience of their encounter with Jesus (cf. Matt 11:2–6 par. Luke 7:18–23).[20]

---

[17] Cf. Martin Ebner, *Jesus von Nazaret in seiner Zeit: Sozialgeschichtliche Zugänge* (SBS 196; 2nd ed.; Stuttgart: Katholisches Bibelwerk, 2004), 153–177.

[18] Cf. John P. Meier, *Mentor, Message, and Miracles* (vol. 2 of *A Marginal Jew: Rethinking the Historical Jesus*; New York, N.Y.: Doubleday, 1994), 509–873; Hengel and Schwemer, *Jesus und das Judentum* (n. 2), 461–497; Dunn, *Jesus Remembered* (n. 2), 489–541.

[19] Cf. Reinhard von Bendemann and Josef N. Neumann, "Bedrohungen des Lebens," in *Neues Testament und Antike Kultur: Familie – Gesellschaft – Wirtschaft* (vol 2 of *Neues Testament und Antike Kultur*; ed. Klaus Scherberich; Neukirchen-Vluyn: Neukirchener Verlag, 2005), 64–74.

[20] For the biblical background of Jesus' healing ministry cf. Karl-Wilhelm Niebuhr, "Die Werke des eschatologischen Freudenboten (4Q521 und die Jesusüberlieferung)," in *The Scriptures in the Gospels* (ed. Christopher M. Tuckett; BETL 131; Leuven: Leuven University Press, 1997), 637–646. On the connection between healing and the forgiveness of sins see Mark 2:1–12 parrs., cf. for this Karl-Wilhelm Niebuhr, "Jesu Heilungen und Exorzismen: Ein Stück Theologie des Neuen Testaments," in *Frühjudentum und Neues Testament im Horizont Biblischer Theologie. Mit einem Anhang zum Corpus Judaeo-Hellenisticum Novi Testamenti* (ed. Wolfgang Kraus and Karl-Wilhelm Niebuhr; WUNT 162; Tübingen: Mohr Siebeck, 2003), 99–112.

Even the resurrection of the dead is a part of Israel's hopes for the future
(cf. Isa 26:19; Hos 6:1–2; 1 Sam 2:6; Dtn 32:39). Such hopes for the future
become, in Jesus' ministry as a healer of the sick, emblematic experiences
in the present-day. Sickness can be regarded and accepted from the perspective of deliverance and healing, even if Jesus has only eliminated it in
individual cases. From this viewpoint, sickness is a highly visible, besieg-
ing aspect of human life; however, an aspect that is exemplarily overcome
by Jesus. Jesus' overcoming of sickness demonstrates God's healing will,
even if the complete and universal implementation of this will has yet to
come to pass.

A characteristic trait of Jesus' healing is that those who are healed are
re-integrated into the social community or are accepted into this community for the first time. Within this motif, Jesus' healing is connected to his
particular devotion to the poor and those "on the edges" of the social and
religious community of his time. This is particularly clear in the examples
of healing of leprosy – an illness that, due to ritual reasons, led in Jesus'
world to religious and social ostracism. The amplitude of the evidence in
various levels and genres of the Jesus tradition (cf. Mark 1:40–44; Matt
11:4 par. Luke 7:22; Luke 17:11–19; Matt 10:8; Mark 14:3 parr.) indicates
that this is a particularly striking attribute of Jesus' ministry as healer that
has remained in memory. With regard to "leprosy," sickness appears very
clearly as a socio-religious construct that is used for orientation and classification within the community.[21] In view of Jesus' healing, this is a fundamentally important aspect of the understanding of sickness. Jesus' understanding and treatment of "leprosy" clearly demonstrates how he attacks
the use of sickness to separate and classify and thereby emblematically
creates an intact community such as God has promised for the eschatological future of Israel.

In addition to the sick, the poor play an important role as the receivers
of salvation by the encounter with Jesus.[22] The preaching of Jesus, the eschatological messenger of joy, is particularly valid for them (Matt 11:5
par. Luke 7:22, cf. Luke 4:18). They are addressed in a beatitude (Matt 5:3
par. Luke 6:20). They are to receive the gifts of the rich (cf. Matt 6:1–4;
Luke 11:41; 12:33) and are clearly much better suited than the rich to gain
entrance to the Kingdom of God (Mark 10:23–25 parr.). They are promised
places of honor at Jesus' table alongside the crippled, the lame and the
blind (cf. Luke 14:13, 21).

---

[21] For this aspect see the contemporary evidence in Josephus, *Ap.* 1.281–283.

[22] Cf. Elisabeth Herrmann-Otto, "Reiche und Arme," in *Neues Testament und Antike
Kultur 2* (n. 19), 86–90; Ekkehard W. Stegemann and Wolfgang Stegemann, *Urchristliche Sozialgeschichte: Die Anfänge im Judentum und die Christusgemeinden in der medi-
terranen Welt* (Stuttgart: Kohlhammer, 1995), 171–189.

Jesus' challenge to attend to the socially weak cannot be taken out of the context of his ministry and made an absolute; however, it does represent a characteristic attribute of his ministry. In the sense of a holistic dedication of life to the needy, it constitutes not only the foundation of his ethical preaching, but also the principle of his own ministry. In this way, similar to the case of the healing tradition, characteristics of the conception of man must emerge that demonstrate mankind's suffering, social need and need for help. Again, it can be seen that Jesus' conception of man is not one of an individual, fixated on himself, who, more or less successfully, attempts to realize his life ideals and moral concepts. Rather an image emerges here of people in relationship with one another and with Jesus. In this dual relationship – in the relationship with Jesus and one's fellow man – there comes to fruition, for Jesus, a salutary relationship between God and mankind.

It is, however, not only the poor who sit at Jesus' table. There are also other figures who are characteristically found in his society: tax collectors, prostitutes and sinners (cf. Mark 2:15–17 parr.; Matt 11:19 par. Luke 7:34; Matt 21:31–32; Luke 18:9–14; 19:1–10). Tax collectors[23] and prostitutes are relatively easily recognized as such. The sinners are more difficult to identify, although they also hold an influential position in Jesus' viewpoint (cf. Luke 7:36–50). Similarly, children in particular act as role models for mankind in this view (Cf. Mark 9:36–37 parr.; 10:13–16 parr.). According to the conventions of Jesus' social and religious environment, children were seen as the weak members of society who needed particular care and protection.[24] It is from exactly this position that they appear as role models of reception, of the fundamental position of mankind that corresponds to mankind's encounter with the Kingdom of God.

Thus, it is particularly those people who have lost their place in the established social and religious community or who never had a place in this community to whom Jesus devotes himself. It is their image that gives his conception of man its characteristic attributes. Such a conception of man is not at all idealized, but rather it is realistically exaggerated. This results in the fact that hardship, sickness, poverty, societal isolation and affliction are particularly noticeable here. The statement "Those who are well have no need of a physician, but those who are sick" (Mark 2:17 parr.) identifies Jesus' particular view of the people to whom he devotes himself and his

---

[23] Cf. Werner Rieß, "Randgruppen: Banditen, Zöllner und andere," in *Neues Testament und Antike Kultur 2* (n. 19), 100–104; Fritz Herrenbrück, *Jesus und die Zöllner* (WUNT 2/41; Tübingen: Mohr Siebeck, 1990).

[24] Peter Balla, *The Child-Parent Relationship in the New Testament and its Environment* (WUNT 155; Tübingen: Mohr Siebeck, 2003); Peter Müller, *In der Mitte der Gemeinde: Kinder im Neuen Testament* (Neukirchen-Vluyn: Neukirchener Verlag, 1992).

healing. This contains an implicit ethical accent that results from the fundamental narrative structure of the Jesus narrative.

5. Life emerging from the Encounter with Jesus

Faith is the answer when people receive the Kingdom of God through the encounter with Jesus. In the Jesus tradition, faith comprehensively denotes the belief in Jesus' claim that he is carrying out God's saving ministry for mankind when he turns towards men in personal devotion. Healing that is experienced through encounter with Jesus is communicated to people through the medium of faith and, in the faith act, it is simultaneously attributed to God as its actual originator (cf. Mark 5:25–34 parr.; 10:46–52 parr.; Matt 8:5–13 par. Luke 7:1–10). Thus, in Jesus' understanding of faith there is both an element of answering and an element of confessing. For Jesus, faith is not primarily an activity of mankind but is rather a fundamental attitude towards Jesus and the God who is encountered in him. Permanent communion with God arises out of the salvation received through the encounter with Jesus.

The life that emerges from encountering Jesus can be received and "lived out" in many different ways. To be a disciple in the sense of a personal follower of Jesus is one of the possibilities; however, according to the evidence of the Jesus tradition, not the only one. Those who were healed by Jesus continued on with their lives in their previous contexts. Women who owned houses and property allowed themselves to be attracted by Jesus, but remained owners of their houses and property and by this manner supported the Jesus movement. Most of the witnesses to Jesus' healing allowed themselves to be captivated by his acts of power and praised God for these acts without giving up immediately their previous way of life and following Jesus. Such attitudes also demonstrate that Jesus' message about the Kingdom of God was received by people and enabled new life. Personally following Jesus and assuming his way of life are thus not the only appropriate or even possible results of an encounter with him.

Jesus' attention towards his addressees thus affects their lifestyles in many different ways. The sick are healed – and go on their way, the hungry are satisfied – that is enough. Tax collectors give away the goods that they have unjustly confiscated and some of them, but certainly not all, become followers of Jesus. It is those who profit from Jesus who, in contact with him, experience long-term salutary communion. It is not that which they bring with them and submit to Jesus that relieves or saves them. Often they discover only during the encounter with Jesus what is wrong with them and what they can receive from him. The personal communion with

Jesus that expresses itself through faith in him can, according to the evidence of the Jesus tradition, not be narrowed down and limited to "a call to follow" in the sense of the adoption of Jesus' way of life. Instead it consists of many different ways of life. All of these ways of life, however, find their center in the gift of the eschatological communion with God which Jesus authenticates and imparts in his ministry.

At the same time, the traditions regarding the twelve disciples and followers of Jesus are characteristic of a comprehensive and fundamental description of that which following Jesus can mean for mankind.[25] This is the surrender of life for the Kingdom of God, which Jesus delivers and embodies. Such complete surrender of life to the Kingdom of God is carried out in the process of becoming one with Jesus in the way of life, the content of his preaching and his active ministry for the benefit of his fellow man who is suffering. In this sense, the twelve disciples have the character of role models for people who want to devote themselves completely to Jesus. This identification with Jesus thus also expressly contains a sharing of his fate, the taking up of the cross (cf. Mark 8:34–9:1 parr.; Mark 10:28–31 parr.).

6. The Surrender of Life as a Principle of Jesus' "Ethics"

In this process, we see a lifestyle that Jesus himself lived out in his ministry in Galilee and Jerusalem and out of which his entire journey, including its end in Jerusalem, becomes understandable. This principle of life has given the Christian conception of mankind and Christian ethics unmistakeable contours. The term "surrender of life" carries in it a narrative structure (in previous research, the term "pro-existence" has been used more often[26]). Surrender of life as a fundamental attitude is a principle in which Jesus' pre-Easter ministry, his death on the cross and the Easter belief, which assigns a salvific meaning to this death, have their common central point. Semantically it is indeterminate enough in order to be able to include people's individual deeds and behaviours as well as a fundamental

---

[25] Cf. Hengel and Schwemer, *Jesus und das Judentum* (n. 2), 360–376; Dunn, *Jesus Remembered* (n. 2), 539–562; John P. Meier, *Companions and Competitors* (vol. 3 of *A Marginal Jew: Rethinking the Historical Jesus*; New York, N.Y.: Doubleday, 2001), 19–285.

[26] Cf. Heinz Schürmann, ",Pro-Existenz' als christologischer Grundbegriff," in idem, *Jesus – Gestalt und Geheimnis: Gesammelte Beiträge* (ed. Klaus Scholtissek; Paderborn: Bonifatius, 1994), 286–315; Wilhelm Thüsing, *Kriterien aufgrund der Rückfrage nach Jesus und des Glaubens an seine Auferweckung* (vol. 1 of *Die neutestamentlichen Theologien und Jesus Christus: Grundlegung einer Theologie des Neuen Testaments*; 2nd ed.; Münster: Aschendorff, 1996), 93–94, 100–101, 110–112, 165, 177–180.

attitude of human life. Finally it is also suitable for understanding the deeds, behaviours and the fate of Jesus as well as the deeds, behaviour and fate of those who want to live as his followers. Therefore, it seems to be particularly suitable as a meta-linguistic term for the description of his "ethics."

The surrender of life that Jesus demands from people can consist of giving those things away to the needy that one has received as one of God's creatures and that support one's own life (cf. Mark 10:17–22 parr.; Matt 6:1–4; Luke 19:1–10). It is also demonstrated in the fact that people entrust their own worries to God rather than to their own power (see Matt 6:25–34 par. Luke 12:22–32). It is expressed particularly well through the phenomenon that, through their encounter with Jesus and in community with him, people are granted exactly that which they think they give up in the form of possessions – in other words, life (cf. Mark 8:35–38 parr.). The fact that life is a gift that emerges from encounter with Jesus gives structure to mankind's way of life. The surrender of life as a fundamental ethical structure grows out of the reversal of the experience of life given.

The surrender of life can, however, also be a comprehensive expression of Jesus' own lifestyle as it is seen through the contours of the Jesus tradition of the Gospels. His emblematic celibacy, his lack of possessions, his homelessness and his voluntary unemployment are aimed towards the needy and ostracized members of society. In his ministry as a healer of the sick, he distributes intact and healthy life from the inexhaustible stocks of the Creator of Man and Father of Israel. His preaching about the presence of the Kingdom of God and the celebratory table fellowship into which he particularly invites those who are otherwise excluded allows one to experience the fulfillment of life in the present day through the hearing of his message.

Finally, from the fundamental attitude of the surrender of life, we can understand Jesus' journey and fate in his suffering and death as a consequence of his ministry. Even in its earliest recognizable layers, the Jesus tradition allows us to see that the fate of his death was determined by thoughts of the surrender of life for others.[27] Anyone who has suitable arguments may deny that Jesus saw it this way himself.

7. Conclusion

Tying into the theme of this conference "Ethics and language," I would like to summarize my thoughts as follows:

---

[27] See particularly the tradition about the last Supper (1 Cor 11:23–26; Mark 14:22–25 parr.) as well as Mark 10:45.

The basic narrative structures of the Jesus story as they are seen in the Gospel narratives and the pre-literary traditions that underlie the Gospels make up the foundation of Jesus' "ethics." The narrated devotion of Jesus to individuals in their social need, their personal suffering and their lack of religious orientation create images of human attitudes that text-pragmatically have the function of implicit impulses for action. A "role model ethics" that obtains its contours from the fundamental narrative patterns of the Jesus story can tie in here. Particularly striking are the social aspects of Jesus' "conception of man" that are also relevant to his "ethics." Patterns of behaviour, heightened to corresponding action through Jesus' explicit teachings, are reflected in Jesus' particular attention towards the sick, the poor and towards social outcasts. Or vice versa – teachings about socially-oriented behaviour towards the needy experience theological heightening and deepening through the corresponding narrative structures of the Jesus story.

According to the evidence of the Gospels and the pre-literary traditions transmitted by them, the material ethical demands that Jesus directs towards mankind point beyond such a "role model ethics." The contexts in which such instructions of Jesus appear must be taken into consideration. From the traditional-historical viewpoint, Jesus' paraenesis is closely connected to the ancient Jewish Torah paraenesis, which can already be seen in the linguistic forms of his teaching. From the biblical-theological viewpoint, the integration of Jesus' ministry and his "ethics" in the faith history of Israel in an eschatological perspective is reflected here. From the literary viewpoint, the Gospels and the pre-literary traditions leave no doubt that the behaviour demanded by Jesus cannot be separated from the attitude towards him which the people receiving his teachings shall express. The theological idiosyncrasy of Jesus' "ethics," which cannot be separated from his ministry as a whole, is rooted here.

An "Israel structure" in Jesus' "ethics" is seen, first of all, in the relationship of Jesus' teachings to ancient Jewish Torah paraenesis but then, even more strongly, through their classification into the entire context of Jesus' ministry as the eschatological representative of God. Jesus' ministry as a healer of the sick and his preaching about the eschatological as well as actually present Kingdom of God cannot be understood without their internal relationship with the biblical prophecies for Israel. Similarly, Jesus' ethical impulses come into their own theologically only in the framework of the biblical "large narrative" about the actions of God towards his creation and his people.

Jesus' ethical teachings and Jesus' fate find their internal relationship and center in the fundamental narrative structure of the surrender of life for others. Jesus calls people into a personal connection with him and in this personal connection, he turns God's healing presence towards them. This enables these people to identify with Jesus and through this identification they can and should participate in his principle of the surrender of life for others as determined by his ministry.

"Whoever humbles himself like this child …"

The Ethical Instruction in Matthew's Community Discourse (Matt 18) and Its Narrative Setting

MATTHIAS KONRADT

To a large extent, Matthew's gospel is an ethical gospel. As is well-known, one of its characteristic features is the composition of five large discourses which include a significant range of ethical material. To this, a series of shorter pieces of instructions (like e.g. 16:24–28; 20:25–28; 23:8–12) and of ethically relevant controversy stories can be added, e.g. the Sabbath controversies (12:1–8, 9–14), the dispute on divorce (19:3–12) or on the greatest commandment in 22:34–40. However, it would be more than insufficient to try to extract Matthew's ethics just by juxtaposing the ethically relevant admonitions from these sections.[1] Matthew conveys his ethics by constructing and unfolding a narrative world, of which the discourses are an integral part. Matthew does not just offer a catechetical handbook, but he narrates a story in which he articulates the foundation of his view of the world. His ethical convictions are embedded in this world view, and they gain their plausibility within it.

I would like to illustrate this by an analysis of the ethical teaching in Matt 18 by reading it as an integral part of the communication process of the entire gospel. My thesis is that the ethical reasoning in Matt 18 cannot be sufficiently comprehended, if the discourse is read as a "closed" section by itself, but only if the embeddedness into the narrative thread of the gospel is taken into account. The narration informs the ethical admonition.

I

Together with other scholars, I define 16:21–20:34 as the narrative section of which Matt 18 is a part. The new thematic focus or Christological perspective which is introduced into the story in this section manifests itself in the triple announcement of Jesus' passion (16:21; 17:22–23; 20:17–19).

---

[1] Cf. Richard A. Burridge, *Imitating Jesus: An Inclusive Approach to New Testament Ethics* (Grand Rapids, Mich.: Eerdmans, 2007), 188, 191. – I thank Esther Schläpfer and Greta Konradt for their assistance.

In Matt 16:21 the Matthean Jesus begins "to show his disciples that he must go to Jerusalem and suffer many things ... and be killed ..." In Matthew, Jerusalem is already explicitly mentioned at this point. In 17:22, Matthew has introduced the second announcement of the passion with the words that Jesus and his disciples had *gathered* in Galilee. The signal toward the impending pilgrimage to Jerusalem, given by the explicit mention of the gathering, is underlined by the insertion of the temple tax pericope in 17:24–27, since the temple tax is collected before the feast.[2] In 19:1, the stereotypic note about the completion of the discourse is directly followed by the remark that Jesus has left Galilee and has gone into the region of Judea. Thus, Matthew presents chapter 18 as the discourse of Jesus in the face of his path to Jerusalem to suffer and die.

The designation of the composition in Matt 18 as "Gemeinderede"[3] or even "Gemeindeordnung"[4] could be misleading insofar as it might evoke

---

[2] Cf. Donald J. Verseput, "Jesus' Pilgrimage to Jerusalem and Encounter in the Temple: A Geographical Motif in Matthew's Gospel," *NovT* 36 (1994): 105–121, 111–112. For συστρεφομένων αὐτῶν ἐν τῇ Γαλιλαίᾳ in 17:22 as a signal toward the impending pilgrimage to Jerusalem see also Margaret Hannan, *The Nature and Demands of the Sovereign Rule of God in the Gospel of Matthew* (Library of New Testament Studies 308; London: Continuum, 2006), 154–155.

[3] So e.g. Alexander Sand, *Das Evangelium nach Matthäus* (RNT; Regensburg: Pustet, 1986), 363; Rudolf Schnackenburg, *Matthäusevangelium* (vol. 2; NEchtB 1.2; Würzburg: Echter, 1987), 167; Ulrich Luck, *Das Evangelium nach Matthäus* (ZBK.NT 1; Zurich: Theologischer Verlag, 1993), 199. Cf. Jacques Dupont, "La parabole de la brebis perdue (Mt 18,12–14; Lc 15,4–7)," in idem, *Études sur les Évangiles Synoptiques* (ed. Frans Neirynck; vol. 2; BETL 70.B; Leuven: University Press, 1985), 624–646, 625: "Discours communautaire."

[4] So Martin Dibelius, *Die Formgeschichte des Evangeliums* (6th ed.; Tübingen: Mohr Siebeck, 1971), 259; Rudolf Bultmann, *Die Geschichte der synoptischen Tradition* (10th ed.; FRLANT 29; Göttingen: Vandenhoeck & Ruprecht, 1995), 160–161; Eduard Schweizer, *Das Evangelium nach Matthäus* (4[16]th ed.; NTD 2; Göttingen: Vandenhoeck & Ruprecht, 1986), 233–234 (page header); Walter Grundmann, *Das Evangelium nach Matthäus* (6th ed.; THKNT 1; Berlin: Evangelische Verlagsanstalt, 1986), 411 ("Ordnung der Gemeinde"); Hans Klein, *Bewährung im Glauben: Studien zum Sondergut des Evangelisten Matthäus* (Biblisch-theologische Studien 26; Neukirchen-Vluyn: Neukirchener Verlag, 1996), 51; Wolfgang Wiefel, *Das Evangelium nach Matthäus* (THKNT 1; Berlin: Evangelische Verlagsanstalt, 1998), 318; see also J. Andrew Overman, *Church and Community in Crisis: The Gospel According to Matthew* (The New Testament in Context; Valley Forge, Pa.: Trinity Press International, 1996), 262: "Discipline and Order in the Church."
There is no lack of further designations: "Rede über brüderliches Verhalten" (Ernst Lohmeyer, *Das Evangelium des Matthäus: Nachgelassene Ausarbeitungen und Entwürfe zur Übersetzung und Erklärung* [ed. Werner Schmauch; 3rd ed.; KEK.S; Göttingen: Vandenhoeck & Ruprecht, 1962], 276); "Rede vom praktischen Verhalten der Söhne der Basileia" (Hubert Frankemölle, *Jahwe-Bund und Kirche Christi: Studien zur Form- und Traditionsgeschichte des „Evangeliums" nach Matthäus* [2nd ed.; NTAbh 10; Münster:

the expectation that, among other things, the discourse includes passages on certain functions or duties in the community. Matt 18, however, solely deals with community life among the disciples, who are addressed as a whole.[5] This occurs from a quite distinct perspective. The Matthean Jesus impresses an ethos of humility or lowliness on his disciples; and he concretizes this primarily with reference to the topic of forgiveness. As will be shown, both aspects directly relate to the Matthean understanding of Jesus'

Aschendorff, 1984], 36); "Rede von den Kleinen und den Brüdern" (Joachim Gnilka, *Das Matthäusevangelium* [vol. 2; 2nd ed.; HTKNT 1.2; Freiburg: Herder, 1992], 119); "Brotherhood in the Church" (Robert H. Gundry, *Matthew: A Commentary on His Handbook for a Mixed Church under Persecution* [2nd ed.; Grand Rapids, Mich.: Eerdmans, 1994], 358); "Rede über die Gemeinschaft" (Ulrich Luz, *Das Evangelium nach Matthäus: Mt 18–25* [EKKNT 1/3; Zurich: Benziger, 1997], 5; in the English translation of Luz' commentary, the common title "community discourse" appears, see Ulrich Luz, *Matthew 8–20: A commentary* [ed. Helmut Koester; trans. James E. Crouch; Hermeneia; Minneapolis, Minn.: Fortress Press, 2001], 423); "Life in the Community of the Kingdom" (Donald A. Hagner, *Matthew 14–28* [WBC 33B; Dallas, Tex.: Word Books, 1995], 514); "discourse on true greatness" (Daniel W. Ulrich, *True Greatness: Matthew 18 in Its Literary Context* [Ph.D. diss., Union Theological Seminary Richmond [Va.], 1996], 3); "Vom geschwisterlichen Verhalten in der Basileia" (Hubert Frankemölle, *Matthäus: Kommentar* [vol. 2; Düsseldorf: Patmos, 1997], 248); "Das Zusammenleben in der Gemeinde" (Peter Fiedler, *Das Matthäusevangelium* [Theologischer Kommentar zum Neuen Testament 1; Stuttgart: Kohlhammer, 2006], 302); "Living Together as Disciples: *The Discourse on Relationships*" (Richard T. France, *The Gospel of Matthew* [NICNT; Grand Rapids, Mich.: Eerdmans, 2007], 672 [italics in the original]). In short: In contrast to Matt 5–7, there is no fixed designation for Matt 18.

5   The discourse is not directed to the leaders of the community in particular, but to the disciples in general. See Wilhelm Pesch, *Matthäus der Seelsorger: Das neue Verständnis der Evangelien dargestellt am Beispiel von Matthäus 18* (SBS 2; Stuttgart: Katholisches Bibelwerk, 1966), 68–71; William G. Thompson, *Matthew's Advice to a Divided Community (Matthew 17:22–18:35)* (AnBib 44; Rome: Biblical Institute Press, 1970), 71–72; Ingrid Goldhahn-Müller, *Die Grenze der Gemeinde: Studien zum Problem der Zweiten Buße im Neuen Testament unter Berücksichtigung der Entwicklung im 2. Jh. bis Tertullian* (GTA 39; Göttingen: Vandenhoeck & Ruprecht, 1989), 191; Ingrid Maisch, "Christsein in der Gemeinschaft (Mt 18)," in *Salz der Erde – Licht der Welt: Exegetische Studien zum Matthäusevangelium* (Festschrift Anton Vögtle; ed. Lorenz Oberlinner and Peter Fiedler; Stuttgart: Katholisches Bibelwerk, 1991), 239–266, 251; Luz, *Matthew II* (n. 4), 423; France, *Matthew* (n. 4), 672–673 et al. Differently George D. Kilpatrick, *The Origins of the Gospel According to St. Matthew* (Oxford: Clarenden, 1946), 79; Joachim Jeremias, *Die Gleichnisse Jesu* (10th ed.; Göttingen: Vandenhoeck & Ruprecht, 1984), 36 ("Anweisung für die Führer der Gemeinden"); Jan Lambrecht, *Out of the Treasure: The Parables in the Gospel of Matthew* (Louvain theological and pastoral monographs 10; Leuven: Peeters, 1998), 37–38, 41, 51–52; Arland J. Hultgren, *The Parables of Jesus: A Commentary* (Grand Rapids, Mich.: Eerdmans, 2000), 54; Jacobus Liebenberg, *The Language of the Kingdom and Jesus: Parable, Aphorism, and Metaphor in the Sayings Material Common to the Synoptic Tradition and the Gospel of Thomas* (BZNW 102; Berlin: de Gruyter, 2001), 422–424.

death. In other words: Matt 18 is closely linked to the narrative context thematically.[6] The ethical (and ecclesiological) orientation developed in Matt 18 is, to put it succinctly, applied Christology. Or in a different manner: the Christological story, or more precisely, the thematic focus of the Christological story in the direct context of Matt 18 lays the foundation for, substantiates and informs the ethical statements in this chapter. The following passage is an attempt to outline this.

II

The discourse begins with a question put to Jesus by his disciples: "who is the greatest in the kingdom of heaven?"[7] This question not only defines the theme of 18:1–5, but it gives the whole discourse its thematic direction. In other words: the introductory pericope Matt 18:1–5, in which Matthew has significantly reworked his Markan source (Mark 9:33–37), has fundamental significance.[8]

In Matthew, Jesus' reaction begins with a symbolic act. Jesus calls a child and puts him in their midst. The child shall serve as a model for the disciples, as it is shown by the two-part explanation following in vv. 3–4 which Matthew has introduced in the Markan text and to which he has given significance by the solemn introduction "Amen, I say to you." Matthew first inserts a logion about entering the Basileia in the form of a con-

---

[6]   Differently Luz, *Matthäus III* (EKKNT; n. 4), 5, according to whom the discourse in Matt 18 is, in contrast to the other discourses, "kompositionell nicht deutlich mit der sie umgebenden Erzählung verklammert."

[7]   In Matt 18:1, ἐν τῇ βασιλείᾳ τῶν οὐρανῶν is a Matthean addition. In the immediate context, the addition of ἐν τῇ βασιλείᾳ τῶν οὐρανῶν in Matt 18:1 refers back to 17:25: Jesus and his disciples are sons of the heavenly king and as such they are free. Now, the disciples ask about the ranking in the heavenly kingdom (cf. Gundry, *Matthew* [n. 4], 359). Jesus' response in 18:3–4 suggests that despite the present tense ἐστίν, Matthew thinks – at least primarily – of the eschatological future in 18:1 (cf. 20:21) (likewise e.g. Luz, *Matthew II* [n. 4], 426 contra e.g. Wolfgang Trilling, *Das wahre Israel: Studien zur Theologie des Matthäus-Evangeliums* [3rd ed.; SANT 10; Munich: Kösel, 1964], 107). However, this does not mean that a reference to the present social structure of the community can be ruled out. Rather, with the topic of greatness in the kingdom of heaven, the earthly assignment of status positions is implied. One can easily illustrate this connection by Jesus' response to the question of the Zebedees' mother (Matt 20:20–21) in 20:25–28. Similarly, the question about the greatest in the kingdom of heaven in Matt 18:1 induces the Matthean Jesus to a discourse that deals with the behaviour within the community *hic et nunc*.

[8]   Cf. e.g. Sand, *Matthäus* (n. 3), 365 ("das Fundament der Gemeinderede"); Luz, *Matthew II* (n. 4), 429 ("basic demand").

ditional clause (cf. 5:20).[9] Instead of speaking about a certain position in the kingdom of heaven, the main concern is attaining entrance at all, which requires a fundamental change in orientation ("if you do not turn"). On the story level, the phrase "if you do not turn" seems to imply the assumption that the disciples have not asked their question solely out of intellectual curiosity, but because they themselves are striving to be great. "And become like the children" explains the intended turn, however, without defining what "to become like the children" exactly means.[10]

V. 4 elucidates that it is not naivety, innocence, obedience to parents, openness for novelties or other qualities sometimes attributed to children which constitute the point of comparison, but their generally low status in ancient societies.[11] "To humble oneself" comprises the inner attitude of humility as well as social lowliness, or the concrete renunciation of status.[12] Thus, instead of striving for greatness (v. 1, cf. 20:26–27), the disciples should "humble themselves;"[13] and instead of aiming at seats of honour and prestige (cf. negatively 23:6–7), they should orient themselves downwards. The succeeding context concretizes this general attitude. V. 4b explicitly refers to the opening question of the disciples – and results in a paradox: those who orient themselves downwards will be the greatest in the kingdom of heaven.

Thus, at the beginning of the discourse, Matthew lets Jesus propound a fundamental reorientation of values, an inversion of the accepted scale of values, as a sign of discipleship.[14] Instead of seeking greatness and prestige, Christians ought to orient themselves downwards and humble themselves. This admonition serves as a guiding principle or fundamental statement for the rest of the discourse, which exemplifies the ethos of humility with regard to the question of how the disciples should treat the little ones and the sinners in the community.

The narrative embedding of the discourse on community life in the context of the announcements of Jesus' passion indicates that for Matthew, humility and the renunciation of one's status are ethical implications of the

---

[9]   See further Matt 7:21; 19:23, 24; 23:13, cf. also 7:13; 18:8, 9; 19:17; 22:12.

[10]   Matt 18:3 provides an alternative to the logion in Mark 10:15 which Matthew omitted in Matt 19:13–15.

[11]   Cf. Luz, *Matthew II* (n. 4), 428–429; William D. Davies and Dale C. Allison, *The Gospel According to Saint Matthew* (vol. 2; ICC; Edinburgh: T&T Clark, 1991), 757; France, *Matthew* (n. 4), 676 as well as Gundry, *Matthew* (n. 4), 361.

[12]   Cf. Rudolf Schnackenburg, "Großsein im Gottesreich: Zu Mt 18,1–5," in *Studien zum Matthäusevangelium* (Festschrift Wilhelm Pesch; ed. Ludger Schenke; SBS; Stuttgart: Katholisches Bibelwerk, 1988), 269–282: 279–280; Luz, *Matthew II* (n. 4), 429.

[13]   Cf. Gnilka, *Matthäusevangelium II* (n. 4), 122: "Es ist das Gegenteil jener Haltung gemeint, die die Größe für sich in Anspruch nehmen möchte."

[14]   Cf. Hannan, *Nature* (n. 2), 157.

path which Jesus took in his passion. This becomes evident in the thematically related instruction in 20:25–28 where Jesus contrasts the ethos which
he expects from his disciples with the common demeanour of the mighty.
Among the disciples, the one who desires to be great or the first shall be
the servant and slave of the others. This instruction culminates in Jesus'
reference to his own way in v. 28. For he has come to serve and – now
Jesus' passion is mentioned – to give his live as a ransom for the many.
Moreover, Jesus' path of suffering up to his despicable death on the cross
is characterized by a deliberate renunciation of using and demonstrating
his power.[15] To illustrate this, I confine myself to only one example from
Matthew's special material in the Passion narrative. In Matthew, Jesus explicitly resists the sword stroke of a disciple in Gethsemane (26:52) and
comments on this with the words: "do you think that I cannot appeal to my
Father, and he will at once send me more than twelve legions of angels?"
(26:53). The crucified, however, will be exalted and enthroned as the lord
of the world (28:18). By analogy, Christians have the promise: "whoever
humbles himself like this child, is the greatest in the kingdom of heaven"
(18:4).

With v. 5 Matthew turns back to his Markan text. Whereas the child
served as a model for behaviour in vv. 2–4, the focus now shifts to the attitude towards a child.[16] However, vv. 3–4 and v. 5 are not thematically unrelated, but closely linked. V. 5 portrays a kind of behaviour which results
from the orientation required in vv. 3–4. In other words: in the Matthean
context, receiving a child is to be read as a first concretization of self-
humiliation. Whoever humbles himself like a child and thus encounters
him at "eye level," does not treat him contemptuously in his low social
status, but "receives him." This includes a friendly-respectful attitude, and
might also have concrete support in view. One may thereby think of (temporary) hospitality (cf. 10:40–42) and also, more comprehensively, of

---

[15] For this cf. Matthias Konradt, "Die Taufe des Gottessohnes: Erwägungen zur Taufe Jesu im Matthäusevangelium," in *Neutestamentliche Exegese im Dialog: Hermeneutik
– Wirkungsgeschichte – Matthäusevangelium* (Festschrift Ulrich Luz; ed. Peter Lampe,
Moisés Mayordomo and Migaku Sato; Neukirchen-Vluyn: Neukirchener Verlag, 2008),
257–273, 268–269.

[16] In Matt 18:5, "child" does not change its meaning to a metaphor for the disciple
who has humbled himself like a child, but Matthew continues to speak about a child in a
literal sense. A literal understanding is also suggested by Luz, *Matthew II* (n. 4), 429;
Davies/Allison, *Matthew II* (n. 11), 754 et al. Differently Thompson, *Advice* (n. 5), 105;
Göran Forkman, *The Limits of the Religious Community: Expulsion from the Religious
Community within the Qumran Sect, within Rabbinic Judaism, and within Primitive
Christianity* (ConBNT 5; Lund: Gleerup, 1972), 119; Schnackenburg, "Großsein" (n. 12),
273, 280–281; Gnilka, *Matthäusevangelium II* (n. 4), 125–126; Hagner, *Matthew II* (n.
4), 514, 520, 521.

(continued) support of children – probably orphaned[17] – who are in need of help.

V. 5 clearly implies an admonition for certain behaviour, but does not *directly* pronounce it. Rather, the Matthean Jesus explains to his disciples that receiving a child means receiving himself.[18] Thus, the leading idea is that no one less than Jesus himself is encountered in the child. Furthermore, the reception of a child is already Christological oriented in the relative clause by the expression "in my name."[19] Thus, 18:5 is a close parallel to Matt 25:40, 45, where Jesus declares his solidarity towards "the least of his brothers." The intended change in behavioural orientation in v. 3 is linked to a new interpretation of the situation or, to put it more broadly, of the order of the world, and this provides the basis of plausibility for the admonished behaviour. In addition to the eschatological motivation of behaviour by means of the motif of entering the kingdom of heaven, there is a Christological argument which makes the behaviour plausible through a Christological oriented perspective of the world, in which the small ones are ennobled by the solidarity of Jesus towards them (for Jesus' behaviour towards children cf. 19:13–15). Jesus, who – being ταπεινός himself (cf. 11:29) – trod the path to the despicable lowliness of the cross, is encountered in the lowly ones. Concerning the linguistic form, imperatives appear neither in v. 5 nor in vv. 3–4. Nevertheless, these verses also contain an implicit appeal to behave in a certain manner, namely by explaining the order of the world to the disciples, of which the entrance requirements for the kingdom of heaven are a constitutive part. In short: Matt 18:1–5 is a good example for conveying strong ethical "imperatives" by means of descriptive language.

---

[17] So e.g. Fiedler, *Matthäusevangelium* (n. 4), 303.

[18] The phrase ἐν μέσῳ αὐτῶν from 18:2 recurs in v. 20: Jesus promises his disciples to be ἐν μέσῳ αὐτῶν where two or three are gathered in his name. It is remarkable that Matthew does not use the formulation analogous to 28:20 that Jesus is "with them." One might consider that in v. 20, Matthew intentionally refers back to 18:2. If this is correct, the idea of v. 5 would be emphasized. Gundry, *Matthew* (n. 4), 370 interprets the connection between 18:2 and 18:20 differently by qualifying the statement of 18:20 by 18:2: "Matthew is making Jesus himself like a child, a model of humility in the midst of his disciples."

[19] Cf. Gundry, *Matthew* (n. 4), 361; Davies/Allison, *Matthew II* (n. 11), 760 ("'In my name' is the key to this line. To receive a child in Christ's name ... is to perceive Christ in that child and act accordingly"); John Nolland, *The Gospel of Matthew: A Commentary on the Greek Text* (NIGTC; Grand Rapids, Mich.: Eerdmans, 2005), 733 ("The challenge is to treat the lowly figure of the child with the respect that would come naturally in relating to Jesus himself").

III

The linguistic form of the instruction in v. 5 continues in v. 6.[20] Analogous to v. 5a, v. 6a formulates a certain behaviour in a relative clause which is placed at the beginning of the sentence: someone causes one of these little ones to stumble. Matthew defines the little ones as Christ-believers by the attached participle. Further matters are discussed controversially, especially whether the phrase relates – at least potentially – to *all* the disciples of Jesus in a positively qualifying sense,[21] to disciples who are in danger or not yet steadfast in their fellowship,[22] or to a group of Christians defined by their social position.[23] Furthermore, the question who causes the

---

[20] Matthew has omitted the toleration of a miracle worker exorcising in the name of Jesus who does not belong to the community, which follows in the Markan thread in 9:38–41. The Markan pericope does not fit into the Matthean concept of community and, above all, not into the thematic spectrum of the Matthean community discourse. Following the Markan text, Matthew continues in 18:6–9 with a warning against the σκάνδαλα (cf. Mark 9:42–48). In v. 7, he has inserted a logion from a thematically related passage of the sayings source (cf. Luke 17:1[–2]).

[21] So e.g. Luz, *Matthew II* (n. 4), 434 ("All Matthean Christians are little ones to the degree that they affirm this insignificance and practice it as humility and love."); Hagner, *Matthew II* (n. 4), 522; Jeongsoo Park, *Sündenvergebung: Ihre religiöse und soziale Dimension im MtEv* (Ph.D. diss., Heidelberg 2001), 184.

[22] So Georg Künzel, *Studien zum Gemeindeverständnis des Matthäus-Evangeliums* (Calwer theologische Monographien, Reihe A, 10; Stuttgart: Calwer, 1978), 159–162 ("Chiffre für den in seinem Christsein angefochtenen Jünger" [162]); Günter Bornkamm, "Die Binde- und Lösegewalt in der Kirche des Matthäus," in *Geschichte und Glaube* (ed. Günter Bornkamm; vol. 2 [vol. 4 of *Gesammelte Aufsätze*]; BEvT 53; Munich: Kaiser, 1971), 37–50, 41; Gerhard Barth, "Auseinandersetzungen um die Kirchenzucht im Umkreis des Matthäusevangeliums," *ZNW* 69 (1978): 158–177, 174–175; Simon Légasse, "μικρός," *Exegetisches Wörterbuch zum Neuen Testament* 2 (1981): 1051–1052; Sand, *Matthäus* (n. 3), 368; Lambrecht, *Treasure* (n. 5), 37–38, 52; Petri Luomanen, *Entering the Kingdom of Heaven: A Study on the Structure of Matthew's View of Salvation* (WUNT 2/101; Tübingen: Mohr Siebeck, 1998), 23 ("Matthew was not thinking just of the disciples in general but especially of those who are in danger of being incited to sin"). Nolland, *Matthew* (n. 19), 735 speaks about "a disciple whose discipleship operates at a modest level." Ambivalently Goldhahn-Müller, *Grenze* (n. 5), 187: the "little ones" are "die Jünger Jesu, denen in der Nachfolge Selbstlosigkeit, Verzicht auf menschliche Größe und Demut eignet und die im Kontext speziell in ihrer Glaubensgefährdung, Schwachheit und Hilflosigkeit und Verirrung gesehen werden."

[23] See Julius Schniewind, *Das Evangelium nach Matthäus* (10th ed.; NTD 2; Göttingen: Vandenhoeck & Ruprecht, 1962), 199 ("die Geringen im weitesten Sinn, die Armen"); Erich Klostermann, *Das Matthäusevangelium* (2nd ed.; HNT 4; Tübingen: Mohr Siebeck, 1927), 147; Grundmann, *Matthäus* (n. 4), 415–416 (die "schlichten und geringen Christen innerhalb der Gemeinden"); Gnilka, *Matthäusevangelium II* (n. 4), 131 (the "little ones" are linked with the notion "daß sie in sozialer Hinsicht verunsichert, gesellschaftlich schwach sind"). See also Trilling, *Israel* (n. 7), 113. – Some authors combine

σκάνδαλα is also a point of controversy.[24] If the "little ones" mean Christian believers in general, it suggests itself that outsiders are the subject of the σκάνδαλα; the logion would then provide consolation for the disciples. Those who endanger them will receive punishment.[25] However, if the little ones constitute a subgroup of the community, community members are also possible subjects. Taken by itself, v. 6 does not provide any criterion for a decision. This is different, however, in the editorial verse 10, in which the disciples are addressed imperatively not to disdain the little ones. Thus, we may suggest viewing them as a subgroup.[26] Furthermore, 18:10–14 helps to define them, since the search for the sheep gone astray, which is linked with the hope that this one will not get lost (18:14), appears as a positively formulated counterpart to the admonition not to disdain the little ones. The little ones thus appear as endangered Christ-believers who are (still) instable in their new life orientation. On the basis of this interpretation, a continuous thread can be detected in Matt 18:6–35: the discourse deals with the attitude towards Christ-believers who are still labile in their orientation, who sin or are in danger of going astray. In the light of 18:1–5 as the fundamental opening statement, the proper attitude towards these Christ-believers appears as a concretization of humbling oneself like a child.

One detail should be explicitly mentioned: Matthew added εἰς ἐμέ to τῶν πιστευόντων in v. 6, which takes up ἐμὲ δέχεται in v. 5. Thus, v. 6 is not only linked to v. 5 by the analogous syntax, but also by the Christological focus in both verses. According to v. 5, Jesus himself is encountered in a child; in v. 6, the reference to the relationship of the little ones to Jesus underlines the warning not to cause them to stumble. In this context, Matthew's omission not only of Mark 9:38–41,[27] but also of Mark 9:37b, has

---

the social dimension with a religious aspect. See e.g. Wilhelm Pesch, "Die sogenannte Gemeindeordnung Mt 18," *BZ NF* 7 (1963): 220–235, 226 (a "soziologisch und religiös verstandene Schicht seiner [sc. Matthew's, MK] Gemeinden"); Jürgen Roloff, "Das Kirchenverständnis des Matthäus im Spiegel seiner Gleichnisse," *NTS* 38 (1992): 337–356, 342 (the "little ones" are "die schlichten ortsansässigen Gemeindeglieder ..., die nicht den rigorosen Anforderungen radikal verstandener Nachfolge zu genügen vermögen"); Georg Scheuermann, *Gemeinde im Umbruch: Eine sozialgeschichtliche Studie zum Matthäusevangelium* (FB 77; Würzburg: Echter, 1996), 190–191 ("die religiös und sozial Bedeutungslosen in der christlichen Gemeinde" [190]).

[24] Some think (primarily) of outsiders (so e.g. Gnilka, *Matthäusevangelium II* [n. 4], 126), others explicitly include community members (so e.g. Frankemölle, *Matthäus II* [n. 4], 253).

[25] Cf. Luz, *Matthew II* (n. 4), 434.

[26] This fits well with 10:40–42, where "you" in v. 40, directed to the disciples in general, is followed by the more specific designations a "prophet," a "righteous person" and "one of these little ones" (vv. 41–42).

[27] See above note 20.

to be taken into account, since only this paves the way for the direct Christological connection in vv. 5, 6. This explicit Christological perspective of the instruction supports the proposal that the discourse is to be read in the light of Christological orientation of the story in its context, i.e., Jesus' way serves as a main element of the plausibility structure of the expected attitude towards a child or the little ones.

V. 6 does not specify any details about how the little ones are caused to stumble. The interpretation of the "little ones" presented above implies that community members are also possible subjects of σκανδαλίζειν. With regard to the analogy of the sentence structure in v. 6 with v. 5, where the disciples' behaviour is in view, it even seems to be preferable to primarily think of disciples as those who cause others to stumble. Σκανδαλίζειν does not exclusively refer to the seduction to moral wrongdoing, but might also refer to the problem that instable Christ-believers do not receive the necessary attention in the community, but are treated disrespectfully and thus driven out of it.[28] Understood in this manner, 18:6 would connect very well with the preceding verses. Additionally, 17:24–27 can be taken into account, since the verb σκανδαλίζειν already occurs here in v. 27. 17:24–27 has paradigmatic significance: a behaviour to which one does not feel obliged (as here to the payment of the temple tax) is nevertheless practised out of consideration or in order to avoid a conflict. In this light, 18:6 can be understood in the manner that conservative Christ-believing Jews who have turned away from the synagogue dominated by the Pharisees and joined the community[29] should not unnecessarily be irritated by ostentatious demonstrations of a liberal treatment of food taboos or Sabbath regulations and be brought away from their adherence to the community (cf. Rom 14:13; 1 Cor 8:13).[30] Considering the social situation of the community and its continuous effort to win other Jews over, it is obvious that conflicts could emerge here. The threat for the one who causes others to stumble is massive: in the light of the eschatological punishment which such a person has to expect, even brutal death by drowning, weighted with a millstone, would be better for him.

---

[28] Frankemölle, *Matthäus II* (n. 4), 253 suggests that community members "durch ihr Reden und Tun anderen Christen Anlaß gaben, an ihrem Glauben irre zu werden und dadurch zu Fall zu kommen." Cf. also France, *Matthew* (n. 4), 682: "To lead a person into sin is one means of causing them to 'stumble,' but their life and development as disciples may equally be damaged by discouragement or unfair criticism, by a lack of pastoral care, or by the failure to forgive."

[29] For the situational background of the gospel of Matthew cf. the considerations in Matthias Konradt, *Israel, Kirche und die Völker im Matthäusevangelium* (WUNT 215; Tübingen: Mohr Siebeck, 2007), 379–391.

[30] Cf. Eduard Schweizer, *Matthäus und seine Gemeinde* (SBS 71; Stuttgart: Katholisches Bibelwerk, 1974), 110.

With a double cry of woe, v. 7 puts the σκάνδαλα into an apocalyptic context. Thereby, it is important that those who cause σκάνδαλα are not discharged and excused by the fact that the coming of σκάνδαλα is inevitable as such.

Vv. 8–9 turn the perspective towards one's own susceptibility to stumble. The logia, which Matthew has already similarly used in 5:29–30, are adopted from Mark, whereby Mark 9:43 (hand, cf. Matt 5:30) and 9:45 (foot) are combined in one logion in Matt 18:8. As in 5:29–30, actual self-mutilation is not meant;[31] rather, hyperbolic metaphoric speech is utilized. Some exegetes relate hand, foot and eye to community members so that 18:8–9 would be about gaining distance from those or excommunication.[32] For this, one can refer to Quintilian *Inst.* 8.3.75, who attests to the comparison of the separation from corruptive people with the amputation of invalid limbs by a doctor as a common metaphor in antiquity.[33] However, the Matthean application of the metaphors in 5:29–30 stands against this interpretation. To put it positively: Matt 5:29–30 suggests that seduction to misbehaviour by one's own limbs is meant in 18:8–9.[34] The link with vv. 6–7 can be seen in the fact that one's own susceptibility to stumble could also lead others astray.[35] When one additionally takes 18:1–5 into account, another option emerges: those who are in danger of treating the little ones contemptuously (18:10) or of endangering them by their behaviour (18:6) are confronted with their own endangerment in vv. 8–9; not considering

---

[31] Likewise e.g. Davies/Allison, *Matthew II* (n. 11), 766.

[32] Pesch, *Seelsorger* (n. 5), 27–28; Forkman, *Limits* (n. 16), 122–124; Heinz Giesen, "Zum Problem der Exkommunikation nach dem Matthäus-Evangelium," in *Beiträge zur Exegese und Theologie des Matthäus- und Markus-Evangeliums* (ed. Heinz Giesen; vol. 1 of *Glaube und Handeln;* Europäische Hochschulschriften Theologie 205; Frankfurt am Main: Lang, 1983), 17–83, 61–66; Gnilka, *Matthäusevangelium II* (n. 4), 127–128; Scheuermann, *Gemeinde* (n. 23), 173, 185; Luz, *Matthew II* (n. 4), 436.

[33] Quintilian, *Inst.* 8.3.75: the following examples may seem too ordinary, and useful only for winning credibility: "... As doctors amputate limbs which disease has alienated from the body, so wicked and dangerous men, even if they are related to us by blood, must be cut off." / Illa vulgaria videri possunt et utilia tantum ad conciliandum fidem: ... ut medici abalienata morbis membra praecidant, ita turpes ac perniciosos, etiam si nobis sanguine cohaereant, amputandos. (Quintilian, *The Orator's Education*, Books 6–8 [ed. and trans. Donald A. Russell; LCL 126; Cambridge, Mass.: Harvard University Press, 2001], 382–383).

[34] In this sense also Goldhahn-Müller, *Grenze* (n. 5), 188; Davies/Allison, *Matthew II* (n. 11), 765; Ulrich, *Greatness* (n. 4), 218–219; Nolland, *Matthew* (n. 19), 738–739 and Maisch, "Christsein" (n. 5), 255: "Die leiblichen Glieder stehen stellvertretend für alles, was zum Einfallstor des Bösen werden und sich in jeder Situation neu und anders konkretisieren kann."

[35] Cf. Davies/Allison, *Matthew II* (n. 11), 765: "Perhaps the connexion with vv. 6–7 is to be found in this, that occasions of sin in oneself lead to the stumbling of others; thus in order to avoid offending one's brother, one must first take care of oneself."

oneself to be secure, however, belongs to the attitude of humility that is demanded in 18:3–4.

IV

Whereas individuals were addressed in vv. 8–9, v. 10, which changes to the second person plural, is again directed to the disciples on the whole in order to continue the teaching about the behaviour towards the little ones begun in 18:6. The addressees should pay attention not to treat one[36] of these little ones contemptuously.[37] V. 10b, therefore, provides a first argument by referring to the heavenly order, in which the personal angels of the little ones hold the privileged position of continuously seeing the face of God. Thereby, it is stated: God assigns particular value to the little ones. Accordingly, they are not to be disregarded or to be treated contemptuously in the community.

In a positive sense, this means caring for the little ones. The parable following in vv. 12–13 carries this out in a specific regard, namely with regard to the case that a little one has gone astray, and offers at the same time a further argument against the disdain of the little ones. The parable has a parallel in Luke 15:3–7. Presumably, it originates, despite the minor conformity of words between Matt 18:12–14 and Luke 15:3–7, from the sayings source since the Lukan / Matthean differences can be plausibly explained as different developments from a common basis.[38] Whereas the Lukan version focuses on the actual finding of the sheep and emphasizes

---

[36] Gnilka, *Matthäusevangelium II* (n. 4), 129 understands ἑνός in 18:10 in the light of 18:14 in a neutral sense. However, this is hardly correct since ἑνὸς τῶν μικρῶν τούτων picks up ἕνα τῶν μικρῶν τούτων from 18:6. The change to the neuter ἓν τῶν μικρῶν τούτων in 18:14 can be explained by the influence of πρόβατον in the parable in vv. 12–13.

[37] To illustrate the community problem behind 18:6, one can refer to Matt 20:1–16, since the parable of the labourers in the vineyard suggests that there were tensions between different groups in the community (cf. Luomanen, *Kingdom* [n. 22], 150–151, 256).

[38] Ascription to Q, e.g. by Bornkamm, "Binde- und Lösegewalt" (n. 22), 38; Gnilka, *Matthäusevangelium II* (n. 4), 130; Davies/Allison, *Matthew II* (n. 11), 753, 768; Hagner, *Matthew II* (n. 4), 525; Scheuermann, *Gemeinde* (n. 23), 158–159; Lambrecht, *Treasure* (n. 5), 39, 42–44; Luomanen, *Kingdom* (n. 22), 241–242. Luz, *Matthew II* (n. 4), 439, however, argues for oral tradition. – Presumably, the parable of the lost drachma, which follows after the parable of the lost sheep in Luke 15:8–10, but is missing in Matthew, was extant in the sayings source as well. The omission by Matthew can be sufficiently explained by the fact that Matthew could not revise this parable in analogy with the parable of the sheep, since one can hardly speak about a stray drachma (cf. Davies/Allison, *Matthew II* [n. 11], 769).

the joy about it, Matthew speaks about the searching, while the actual finding appears in v. 13 as only *one* possible option. V. 14 underlines that the main emphasis is not on the joy mentioned in v. 13, but on the admonition to the searching.[39] Above all, Matthew does not speak about the lost sheep, but about the one which has gone astray, which generally and correctly is considered to be secondary.[40] In Matthew, the parable of the lost sheep has thus become the parable of the stray sheep. A sheep gone astray *can* get lost – v. 14 refers to this –, but it has not yet.[41]

This new orientation is connected with the placement of the parable into the community discourse. Matthew himself speaks of *lost* sheep in the context of the mission of Jesus and his disciples to Israel (10:6; 15:24). In Matt 18, however, the situation of those is addressed, who have turned towards the congregation of the disciples, but then stray from the pursued path and are in danger of getting lost again (v. 14, cf. Matt 13:19–22) if one does not follow and "find" them, or if they do not allow themselves to be "found." In short: while the parable originally dealt with the devotion of Jesus to the lost ones, Matthew offers a paraenetically oriented adaptation related to intracongregational concerns.

Matthew does not actually *narrate* a parable, but rather, he describes a case in metaphorical language by means of a conditional clause whose apodosis is formulated as a rhetorical question which, as it is prepared by the introduction "what do you think?," intends to provoke the recipients to an affirmative reaction.[42] In v. 13, a second conditional clause follows which introduces a possible sub-case (the sheep is found) and offers a "hy-

---

[39] Cf. Trilling, *Israel* (n. 7), 112–113; David Hill, *The Gospel of Matthew* (NCB; London: Oliphants, 1972), 274; Franz Schnider, "Das Gleichnis vom verlorenen Schaf und seine Redaktoren," *Kairos* 19 (1977): 146–154, 149; Scheuermann, *Gemeinde* (n. 23), 159–160; Luz, *Matthew II* (n. 4), 440; Young S. Chae, *Jesus as the Eschatological Davidic Shepherd: Studies in the Old Testament, Second Temple Judaism, and in the Gospel of Matthew* (WUNT 2/216; Tübingen: Mohr Siebeck, 2006), 241. Luz, *Matthew II* (n. 4), 437 correctly notes that "[v]erse 14 appears to refer more to the behavior of the shepherd described in v. 12 than to his joy." Differently, Detlev Dormeyer et al., "Neunundneunzig sind nicht genug! (Vom verlorenen Schaf): Q 15,4–5a.7 (Mt 18,12–14 / Lk 15,3–7 / EvThom 107)," in *Kompendium der Gleichnisse Jesu* (ed. Ruben Zimmermann; Gütersloh: Gütersloher Verlag, 2007), 205–219, 214: "Die Freude über den Fund wird bei Matthäus als Wille des Vaters interpretiert."

[40] See e.g. Davies/Allison, *Matthew II* (n. 11), 773; Luz, *Matthew II* (n. 4), 438; Lambrecht, *Treasure* (n. 5), 43.

[41] Dupont, "Parabole" (n. 3), 634 points to the fact that "au plan de l'image, il n'y a pas de différence entre une brebis 'perdue' et une brebis 'égarée,' tandis que la différence est très importante au plan de l'application." Likewise Thompson, *Advice* (n. 5), 157.

[42] Cf. Luz, *Matthew II* (n. 4), 437: "Unlike its parallel in Luke 15:4–7, the parable is an argument in a debate rather than a narrated story."

pothesis" solemnly pronounced as an amen saying in the apodosis.[43] This linguistic style provides the parable with a strong argumentative character.[44]

The rhetorical achievement of the parable consists in the fact that the behaviour towards the little ones is made accessible in a new manner by comparing it with the care of a shepherd for a sheep gone astray. Simultaneously, the situation of the little ones is made accessible in a new manner. Their straying off is no reason for condemnation (cf. Matt 7:1), but can only be a cause to devote oneself to them graciously. This gains profile in the Matthean context if one notes the major importance of the shepherd imagery in the Matthean story: Matthew presents Jesus as the messianic shepherd of Israel (Matt 2:6) who devotes himself to the neglected and lost sheep (9:36; 15:24) and, according to the mission discourse in Matt 10, lets his disciples participate in his shepherding (9:36; 10:6).[45] Thus, for those who follow him and participate in his shepherding, who let themselves be determined by him in their life orientation, it should be self-evident that one ought not disdain community members who are instable or who have gone astray, but should meet them with the same mercy and care which is characteristic of the activity of the messianic shepherd.[46]

This can be underlined further by taking the Old Testament background of the Matthean reception of the shepherd's imagery into account, in which Ezek 34 possesses major significance, not only for the entire gospel, but especially for Matt 18:12–13 as well.[47] The admonition to devote oneself to the ones gone astray coincides with the saving action of God as shepherd of his people (Ezek 34:11–22) through the divinely appointed Davidic-messianic shepherd (Ezek 34:34; 37:24), which was promised in Scripture. Thus, the admonition is supported by the authority of Scripture. Accordingly, Matthew refers to the (saving) will of *God* in v. 14: the little ones shall not get lost (in the final judgement). In short: the evidence sug-

---

[43] Cf. Luz, *Matthew II* (n. 4), 437: "a pronouncement in the form of an authoritative amen saying."

[44] Cf. Gnilka, *Matthäusevangelium II* (n. 4), 129–130; Luz, *Matthew II* (n. 4), 437.

[45] Cf. for this Konradt, *Israel* (n. 29), 81–83.

[46] Cf. Luomanen, *Kingdom* (n. 22), 248: "The care for straying members of the congregation is seen in direct continuance with Jesus' own activity."

[47] For references to Ezek 34 in Matt 18:10–14 cf. Thompson, *Advice* (n. 5), 159–160; Davies/Allison, *Matthew II* (n. 11), 769; Hagner, *Matthew II* (n. 4), 527; Nolland, *Matthew* (n. 19), 743; Chae, *Jesus* (n. 39), 240–243. In this context, it is worth mentioning that the discourse about searching (ζητεῖν) for the sheep (Matt 18:12, cf. Ezek 34:11–12, 16) as well as the one about the πλανᾶν (Matt 18:12–13, cf. Ezek 34:4, 16, but also Isa 53:6; Jer 27:17 LXX) and the localisation of the ninety-nine sheep ἐπὶ τὰ ὄρη (Matt 18:12, cf. Ezek 34:13, [14], but also Jer 27:6 LXX) are peculiar to the Matthean version (ζητεῖν occurs, however, in Luke 15:8 in the parable about the lost drachma omitted by Matthew [cf. above, note 38]).

gested by the question in v. 12 is underlined by the intratextual references to the presentation of Jesus as messianic shepherd and its intertextual references to Scripture. The disciples who believe in God, who searches for the lost and turns the ones gone astray (Ezek 34:16 LXX), shall prove themselves as good shepherds in the succession of Jesus by seeking those gone astray.[48]

V

The regulations about the practice of admonition following in 18:15–17 continue not only the style of conditional clauses, which originated from the evangelist's hand in 18:12–13,[49] but also the theme of the parable of the sheep.[50] If the shorter reading without εἰς σέ is to be preferred in 18:15a,[51] so that 18:15 speaks about sinning in general[52] and not particu-

---

[48] With regard to the link to Ezek 34, Nolland, *Matthew* (n. 19), 743 considers the option that "the rescue effort is perhaps to be thought of as a participation in that of God himself as the good shepherd." On the theological overtones linked with the reference to Ezek 34 cf. Luz, *Matthew II* (n. 4), 443.

[49] However, with the exception of 18:15b, there are now imperatives in the apodosis in 18:15–17.

[50] To place the main break in Matt 18 between Matt 18:14 and 18:15 (so e.g. Pesch, *Seelsorger* [n. 5], 32–33; Forkman, *Limits* [n. 16], 118–119; Giesen, "Problem" [n. 32], 19–20; Gnilka, *Matthäusevangelium II* [n. 4], 119–120; Hannan, *Nature* [n. 2], 153–154) ignores this connection which is to be further developed in the following. Aptly Thompson, *Advice* (n. 5), 188: "This division cannot be reconciled with the sequence of thought."

[51] The phrase is reliably evidenced by manuscripts, but it is missing in very important manuscripts like the Vaticanus and the Sinaiticus. For the hypothesis of a secondary omission, some scholars argue that this can be explained by the influence of the parallel in Luke 17:3. However, it is at least equally plausible that εἰς σέ in Matt 18:15 is "a back-influence from v. 21" (Nolland, *Matthew* [n. 19], 744). The tradition-historical evidence does not help to come to a clear decision. As will be shown below, Matt 18:15–17 is influenced by the Early Jewish exegesis of Lev 19:17–18 which itself refers to the case that someone is personally wronged. This constellation reappears in *T. Gad* 6:3–7, a close parallel to Matt 18:15–17 (s. below). However, this does not apply to the passage in 1QS V, 24 – VI, 1 to which Matt 18:15–17 also displays some affinity, especially since both passages share the reference to the community. In the context of Matt 18, the shorter reading fits better. If εἰς σέ were original, one would have to explain the participation of the community in the vv. 16–17 by the fact that in a rather small group, a conflict between two community members affects the community as a whole as well. However, it is remarkable that the reconciliation between the sinner and the one who admonishes does not play a role in 18:15–18, not even in 18:15b, where the focus is on the salvation of the sinner (see below). While this already suggests that 18:15 does not deal with the special case of someone being *personally* wronged, the expansion of the simple personal admonition in Q 17:3–4 to a procedure, which amounts to three-steps from individual admoni-

larly about the case that someone is personally wronged, then, the protasis takes up what was metaphorically described as a sheep's straying-off in vv. 12–13. In v. 15, the sinner is explicitly designated as "your brother," bringing up the aspect of closeness and mutual responsibility within the *familia Dei* (cf. 12:46–50).

Thus, whereas ἁμαρτάνειν in v. 15a takes up the image of "a sheep's straying-off," the new aspect follows only in the apodosis. 18:12 does not mention *how* the search for the one gone astray should proceed. 18:15 discloses precisely this: if someone notices that a "brother" goes astray, he should admonish him,[53] and namely – this is important – in a conversation *in private*. The affinity of the pastoral imagery and the admonition can be well illustrated by Sir 18:13 where both issues are directly linked in the context of a statement about God's mercy (!): God "admonishes (ἐλέγχων) and disciplines and teaches and brings back, as a shepherd his flock."

---

tion to involvement of the community in the worst case of the sinner's continuous lack of insight, points into the same direction. Moreover, if 18:12–14 is taken into account, one can add that the shorter reading without εἰς σέ better fits the Matthean joining of 18:15–17 with the sheep parable, since with the shorter reading, as will be shown, a smooth connection of 18:12–14 with 18:15–17 emerges. Finally, the sequence from the absolute ἁμαρτάνειν to ἁμαρτάνειν εἰς σέ corresponds to Luke 17:3–4. If this is also to be favoured in Matt 18:15, 21, one may suppose that this sequence was already extant in Q 17:3–4. – However, there is no consensus concerning the text critical problem in 18:15a. For the shorter reading without εἰς σέ cf. Pesch, *Seelsorger* (n. 5), 37 n. 1; Barth, "Kirchenzucht" (n. 22), 168 n. 32; Thompson, *Advice* (n. 5), 176 n. 1; Goldhahn-Müller, *Grenze* (n. 5), 180 n. 253; Giesen, "Problem" (n. 32), 23; Maisch, "Christsein" (n. 5), 248–249; Alois Schenk-Ziegler, *Correctio fraterna im Neuen Testament: Die "brüderliche Zurechtweisung" in biblischen, frühjüdischen und hellenistischen Schriften* (FB 84; Würzburg: Echter, 1997), 301; Gnilka, *Matthäusevangelium II* (n. 4), 136; Nolland, *Matthew* (n. 19), 744, 745; France, *Matthew* (n. 4), 689, n. 3. For the reading with εἰς σέ cf. Gundry, *Matthew* (n. 4), 367; Davies/Allison, *Matthew II* (n. 11), 782 n. 3; Luz, *Matthew II* (n. 4), 448 n. 1; Park, *Sündenvergebung* (n. 21), 189.

[52] Contrary to Christoph Kähler, "Kirchenleitung und Kirchenzucht nach Matthäus 18," in *Christus bezeugen* (Festschrift Wolfgang Trilling; ed. Karl Kertelge, Traugott Holtz and Claus-Peter März; Freiburg: Herder, 1990), 136–145, 140, there is no indication that the meaning of ἁμαρτάνειν can be constrained to cases, "daß ein Christ dem anderen nach dem Leben trachtet oder ihn zum Abfall vom Glauben verleitet."

[53] Similarly, Armin Wouters, *"... wer den Willen meines Vaters tut": Eine Untersuchung zum Verständnis vom Handeln im Matthäusevangelium* (Biblische Untersuchungen 23; Regensburg: Pustet, 1992), 350–351, argues that the care for those gone astray is put in concrete terms in 18:15–17. See further Luomanen, *Kingdom* (n. 22), 255: "the rules concerning the reproving of one's brother are to be seen as a concrete example how one should go after his brother. The care for one's brother materializes in reproving him." Nevertheless, Luomanen inadequately designates 18:15–17 as "excommunication rules" (see below, note 86). According to Thompson, *Advice* (n. 5), 187, the regulations in 18:15–17 "apply the parable to a concrete situation in the Matthean community."

With ἔλεγξον αὐτόν the evangelist[54] refers to Lev 19:17[55] and thus to the immediate context of the love command which is part of a thematic unit in Lev 19:17–18 revolving around the problem how to deal with a sinner.[56] If this intertextual horizon is taken into account, the admonition is to be read as an expression of love.[57]

This can be substantiated by including the reception history of Lev 19:17–18[58] as it is documented by CD IX, 2–8; 1QS V, 24 – VI, 1 on the one hand,[59] and by the Testaments of the Twelve Patriarchs, especially by

---

[54] Thereby, it is not relevant whether ἔλεγξον is to be attributed to Matthean redaction (so e.g. Gundry, *Matthew* [n. 4], 367) or whether it was already found in the tradition underlying 18:15–17 (to this see below, note 89) by the evangelist, since one can assume for the latter case as well that the evangelist was conscious of the reference to Lev 19:17.

[55] Cf. Forkman, *Limits* (n. 16), 124–125; Schenk-Ziegler, *Correctio fraterna* (n. 51), 298; Gundry, *Matthew* (n. 4), 367; Gnilka, *Matthäusevangelium II* (n. 4), 137; Davies/Allison, *Matthew II* (n. 11), 782–783; Luz, *Matthew II* (n. 4), 451; Ulrich, *Greatness* (n. 4), 230–231; Dennis C. Duling, "Matthew 18:15–17: Conflict, Confrontation, and Conflict Resolution in a 'Fictive Kin' Association," *SBLSP* 37/1 (1998): 253–295, (268–) 273.

[56] Hans-Peter Mathys, *Liebe deinen Nächsten wie dich selbst: Untersuchungen zum alttestamentlichen Gebot der Nächstenliebe (Lev 19,18)* (OBO 71; Göttingen: Vandenhoeck & Ruprecht, 1986), 67.

[57] Apart from the early Jewish reception history of Lev 19:17–18 outlined in the following, cf. also Prov 27:5 where ἔλεγχοι and φιλία are connected: κρείσσους ἔλεγχοι ἀποκεκαλυμμένοι κρυπτομένης φιλίας.

[58] For the early reception history of Lev 19:17 cf. James L. Kugel, "On Hidden Hatred and Open Reproach: Early Exegesis of Leviticus 19:17," *HTR* 80 (1987): 43–61. For the love command in particular cf. Michael Ebersohn, *Das Nächstenliebegebot in der synoptischen Tradition* (Marburger theologische Studien 37; Marburg: Elwert, 1993), 56–142; Thomas Söding, *Das Liebesgebot bei Paulus: Die Mahnung zur Agape im Rahmen der paulinischen Ethik* (NTAbh NF 26; Münster: Aschendorff, 1995), 56–66.

[59] In CD IX, 2–8, passages from Lev 19:17–18 are explicitly cited. To bring a charge against one's neighbour without having previously admonished him before witnesses is regarded as an offence against the commandment in Lev 19:18 not to take vengeance and not to keep a grudge (CD IX, 2 – 4). And whoever is silent at first, but then, in "burning wrath," brings a charge against another person, violates the obligation to admonish (CD IX, 6 – 8). According to 1QS V, 24 – VI, 1, admonition (להוכיח, cf. הוכח תוכיח in Lev 19:17) of one's neighbour has to take place "in truth, humility and merciful *love*" (1QS V, 24–25: חסד אהבת, shorter version in 4Q258 1 II, 4, where only the last part of the triad חסד אהבת appears). As in Matt 18, admonition is considered as a task of everyone (רעהו את איש) (cf. CD VII, 2). The introductory admonition is then – with clear references to Lev 19:17 – further elaborated in 1QS V, 25 – VI, 1: hate is explicitly rejected, and the warning is pronounced not to incur guilt on oneself because of the sinner. Concerning the connection of admonition and love in 1QS V, 24–25, one can, furthermore, refer to the commandments for the *maskil* in 1QS IX, 12–15, since in 1QS IX, 16–19, admonition is confined to members of the community, whereas the admonition of the "men of the pit," i.e. of outsiders, is prohibited. The latter corresponds to the hate which has to be directed against the "men of the pit" (IX, 21–22, cf. I, 10), whereas, according-

T. Gad 4:2–3; 6:3–7, on the other. The Qumran texts offer an analogy to the sequence in Matt 18:16–17.[60] According to 1QS VI, 1, an issue is to be brought before the community only after an interlocution has taken place in front of witnesses[61] (cf. CD IX, 3).[62] This suggests that Matt 18:16–17 is

---

ly, admonition appears to be an expression of love towards the "sons of light" (I, 9; IX, 21). Cf. Hermann Lichtenberger, *Studien zum Menschenbild in Texten der Qumrangemeinde* (SUNT 15; Göttingen: Vandenhoeck & Ruprecht, 1980), 213–214. – For the reception of Lev 19:17–18 see further 1QS VII, 8–9; IX, 16–19; CD VII, 2–3; XIX, 18.

[60] Michael A. Knibb, *The Qumran Community* (Cambridge commentaries on writings of the Jewish and Christian world 2; Cambridge: Cambridge University Press, 1987), 115 detects three steps in 1QS V, 24 – VI, 1, in analogy to Matt 18:15–17, which implies that he understands 1QS V, 24–25 in the sense of a private admonition as a first step before the admonition in the presence of witnesses (so also James VanderKam and Peter Flint, *The Meaning of the Dead Sea Scrolls: Their Significance for Understanding the Bible, Judaism, Jesus, and Christianity* [London: T&T Clark, 2002], 339, cf. also Giesen, "Problem" [n. 32], 74 and Timothy R. Carmody, "Matt 18:15–17 in Relation to Three Texts from Qumran Literature [CD 9,2–8, 16–22; 1QS 5:25–6:1]," in *To Touch the Text* [Festschrift Joseph A. Fitzmyer; ed. Maurya P. Horgan and Paul J. Kobelski; New York, N.Y.: Crossroad, 1989], 141–158, 147–150). However, it is not clear how a possible individual admonition and the admonition in front of witnesses are related to each other, not to mention the problem that V, 24–25 does not make a precise statement about the personal constellation. Schenk-Ziegler, *Correctio fraterna* (n. 51), 133–134 argues for a two-step procedure in 1QS V, 24 – VI, 1.

[61] Cf. the rendering of 1QS VI, 1 by Geza Vermes, *The Dead Sea Scrolls in English* (3rd ed.; London: Penguin, 1987), 69: "let no man accuse his companion before the Congregation without having first admonished him in the presence of witnesses."

[62] It is not sufficiently evident from 1QS VI, 1 which function the admonition before witnesses exactly has (cf. Schenk-Ziegler, *Correctio fraterna* [n. 51], 133); and thus, whether here, as in Matt 18:15–17, different steps of a procedure, in which moving on to the next step is dependent on the sinner's reaction to the admonition, are in view or not. Neither 1QS V, 24 – VI, 1 nor CD IX, 2–8 reflect on the reaction of the sinner or deal with the question of what will happen to him (accordingly, excommunication from the community is also not mentioned here). The admonition before witnesses could also have the function to clarify whether the accusation is justified, before someone is accused of misconduct in front of the community. The texts under discussion present "halachische ... Schriftinterpretation" (Schenk-Ziegler, *Correctio fraterna* [n. 51], 144 with reference to CD IX, 2–5) which aims at precisely defining the correct observance of the commandments from Lev 19:17–18: whoever disregards the prescribed procedure violates Lev 19:17–18 and is thus guilty of an infringement of the law (cf. the reception of Lev 19:17 in 1QS V, 25 – VI, 1: "but he should not incur guilt because of him").

Furthermore, it is noteworthy that the admonition in 1QS VI, 1; CD IX, 3 appears as a part of a judicial procedure (cf. Lawrence H. Schiffman, *Sectarian Law in the Dead Sea Scrolls: Courts, Testimony and the Penal Code* [BJS 33; Chico, Calif.: Scholars Press, 1983], 94–96; Kugel, "Hatred" [n. 58], 54; Schenk-Ziegler, *Correctio fraterna* [n. 51], 143–145 [with reference to CD IX, 2b–5]). However, the formulation in 1QS VI, 1 does not exclude that there was also private admonition and that the introductory admonition in 1QS V, 24–25 includes this one as well. Perhaps, the members of the Qumran community differentiated according to the gravity of the sin. Individual admonition was suffi-

based on an early Jewish exegetical tradition of Lev 19:17–18.[63] Even more important, however, is the fact that *T. Gad* 4:2–3 exemplifies the disregard of the love command by means of the public display of someone else's sin: a hating person who does not want to listen to the words of God's commandments about neighbourly love (v. 2) strives, in the case of a brother's misconduct, to make it public to everyone immediately (v. 3). Positively, this means that whoever follows the love command does not publicly expose others.[64] Rather, he will confront the person concerned and admonish or rebuke him – as is to be added on the basis of the instructions in Lev 19:17–18 which are in the background here as well.[65] *T. Gad* 6:3–7 elaborates this. Here, the command to love one another from the heart (v. 3a) is linked with the reflection on conduct towards the sinner, which is – presumably different from Matt 18:15 – focused on the case that someone

---

cient for minor sins, whereas more severe ones had to be reported (so Hartmut Stege-mann, *Die Essener, Qumran, Johannes der Täufer und Jesus* [Freiburg: Herder, 1993], 276) and could lead to penalties such as a (temporary) exclusion from the community (cf. the penal code in 1QS VI, 24 – VII, 25). In this regard, one can further refer to CD IX, 16–23: someone who observes, without any other witness, that someone else is committing a capital offence, has to admonish the sinner and has to report him to the "examiner" who has to write it down (cf. the list of reproofs in 4Q477!). If the sinner is then reported by two other witnesses for the same sin, he is to be excluded on the basis of the triple testimony. By contrast, two witnesses are sufficient in cases concerning property according to CD IX, 22–23 (for this differentiation see Schiffman, *Law*, 73–75 and Carmody, "Matt 18:15–17" [n. 60], 144–145). The admonition is here "Teil einer juridischen Verfahrensordnung, die auf die Bestrafung dessen, der eine schwere Verfehlung begangen hat, ausgerichtet ist" (Schenk-Ziegler, *Correctio fraterna* [n. 51], 149). It is noteworthy that forgiveness is not explicitly mentioned in any of the texts above. – It has to be added that 1QS V, 24 – VI, 1 and CD IX, 2–8 do not deal with the specific case that someone has been personally wronged, but with sins of others in general.

[63] Matt 18:15–17 or the tradition adapted in Matt 18:15–17 (cf. for this below, note 89) is hardly directly influenced by the Qumran texts (likewise e.g. Trilling, *Israel* [n. 7], 120; Goldhahn-Müller, *Grenze* [n. 5], 185; Scheuermann, *Gemeinde* [n. 23], 167; Stephanie von Dobbeler, "Die Versammlung 'auf meinen Namen hin' [Mt 18:20] als Identitäts- und Differenzkriterium," *NT* 44 [2002]: 209–230, 220; differently Luomanen, *Kingdom* [n. 22], 243). The Qumran texts are important for Matt 18:15–17 as testimony of an obviously broader early Jewish adoption of Lev 19:17–18 which is also testified by the *T. 12 Patr.* (to this below) and into which one has to insert Matthew as well.

[64] In an extreme form, the *T. 12 Patr.* illustrate this by the figure of Joseph who appears as *the* model of neighbourly love (as well as generally of virtuous conduct). Joseph showed love to his brothers not only by not bearing malice against them (*T. Sim.* 4:4; *T. Zeb.* 8:4–6), but out of love for them, he also kept their misconduct secret from outsiders, in order not to shame them (*T. Jos.* 11:2; 15:3; 17:1). To love one another is linked with the mutual and patient hiding of sins (*T. Jos.* 17:2).

[65] Cf. Kugel, "Hatred" (n. 58), 50.

is personally wronged: "if a man sins against you, speak to him in peace[66] after having cast away the poison of the hate. And do not hold deceit in your soul!" (*T. Gad* 6:3b). Here, the constellation of a conversation in private is assumed (cf. *T. Gad* 6:5!). Thus, according to the *T. 12 Patr.*, love manifests itself (among other things) by not exposing the sinner in front of other people. If one reads Matt 18:15 in this light, the instruction that one should first have a conversation in private, gains contours. In the background, there is the motif that the sin of the brother is not to be made public immediately,[67] in order not to cast a poor light on him in the community.[68] "Es soll mit dem Bruder gesprochen werden und nicht über ihn."[69]

The positive case that the sinner accepts the admonition is commented on in Matt 18:15 by the words that the brother is gained. Different from *T. Gad* 6:3–7, the personal relationship between the one who admonishes and the sinner is not treated here, but rather the salvation of the sinner. "To gain people" is an uncommon phrase in non-Christian antiquity,[70] but occurs in 1 Cor 9:19–22 and 1 Pet 3:1 as a term of early Christian mission language. In the context of Matt 18, the phrase "you have gained your brother" emphasizes the connection with 18:12–14 since it resumes the soteriological dimension of 18:14.[71] The admonition or reproof serves the positive goal of winning back the brother so that he does not get lost (cf. Jas 5:19–20).[72]

Whereas *T. Gad* 6:3 mentions the alternative whether a sinner confesses or denies his deed,[73] Matthew differentiates whether the sinner listens to

---

[66] Cf. *Did*. 15:3a: Ἐλέγχετε δὲ ἀλλήλους μὴ ἐν ὀργῇ ἀλλ' ἐν εἰρήνῃ ὡς ἔχετε ἐν τῷ εὐαγγελίῳ.

[67] One might refer to Matt 1:19 to illustrate this: Joseph displays his righteousness by not exposing Mary to public disgrace.

[68] Cf. Davies/Allison, *Matthew II* (n. 11), 786 as well as Nolland, *Matthew* (n. 19), 746: "The privacy of the initial contact allows the sin to be dealt with without any need for wider awareness or of public shaming."

[69] Wouters, *Willen* (n. 53), 351–352. – Likewise Grundmann, *Matthäus* (n. 4), 419.

[70] Cf. Luz, *Matthew II* (n. 4), 451–452.

[71] Cf. Gundry, *Matthew* (n. 4), 367–368. The focus of the text is not that the initiator of the admonition has "einen Erfolg zu verbuchen" (differently Sand, *Matthäus* [n. 3], 372).

[72] Accordingly, this is not in tension with Matt 7:1–5. Matt 7:1 is directed against the unloving condemnation of the brother, but not, as 7:3–5 shows, against addressing the misconduct of the other in general (see rather 7:5b).

[73] According to *T. Gad* 6:4, one should not be contentious with the sinner, if he denies. This is motivated by the warning that one should not sin twice. Already in Lev 19:17, admonition is linked with the idea that one should not incur sin on oneself because of the other. As with the explicit mention of "hate" in 6:3, Lev 19:17 is in the background here as well (likewise e.g. Kugel, "Hatred" [n. 58], 50–52; Schenk-Ziegler, *Correctio fraterna* [n. 51], 169, 170). "To sin twice" (*T. Gad* 6:4) may refer to violating the command previously mentioned (one should speak to the other in peace) on the one hand

the person who admonishes him or not. The possibility that the sinner denies the misconduct which he is charged with, obviously does not play a role. Rather, one can consider that the reason for the disregard of the admonition is a disagreement about the norms of judgement and thus about the acceptance of Jesus' interpretation of the law which is valid in the community. In short: the controversial issue is not the conduct as such, but its assessment.

If the admonition particularly intends to explain to the sinner that his conduct is incongruent with the norms of the group and to present and impress the group norms as the will of God, the next steps of the procedure becomes plausible. If the conversation in private has no effect, then, the limited number of one to two other community members should be involved. Matthew justifies this step by a quotation of Deut 19:15 whose sense, however, appears to be significantly shifted in the Matthean context. It is, as was repeatedly noted,[74] not evident, that the persons were themselves witnesses of the deed and could, accordingly, contribute the reliable statements of the facts necessary in court.[75] That the admonition is justified (and necessary) is, as already in 18:15a, not at issue.[76] The function of the second admonition seems to be to emphasize the vote of the one who ad-

---

and on causing the other to affirm his denial of his sins by a false oath on the other. Already here, the focus is on one's own well-being, and this remains the main perspective in the following. In a *digressio* (often considered as a secondary insertion), v. 5 reflects on the possible escalation of the conflict: if one does not pay attention that the issue remains among the persons involved, so that others hear about the accusation, one is in danger of being exposed to further and heavier attacks from the conflict partner (the subject of the ἵνα-phrase in *T. Gad* 6:5 is hardly the ἀλλότριος, but rather the conflict partner, i.e. the sinner from 6:3–4). This would be, as the end of 6:5 shows, one's own fault insofar as the other has received the poison (of the hate) which one should have removed according to v. 3.

The option that the sinner denies is detailed by a sub-case in v. 6: the sinner denies because he is ashamed of being convicted or admonished – here, the verb ἐλέγχειν, which occurs also in Matt 18:15, appears. In this case, one should not pursue the issue any longer because it can be assumed that the sinner tacitly repents and will be peaceful from now on. Thus, the consequences for oneself are in view here as well: one can live in peace from then on. Finally, *T. Gad* 6:7 deals with the "worst case" that the sinner is not insightful at all and insists on his wickedness. As already in v. 3, the admonition "forgive him" follows in the apodosis, now, however, supplemented by the words: "leave vengeance to God!" (see to this also below, note 91).

[74] See e.g. Gnilka, *Matthäusevangelium II* (n. 4), 137; Gundry, *Matthew* (n. 4), 368; Luz, *Matthew II* (n. 4), 452.

[75] By contrast, CD IX, 16–23 is concerned with the reliable verification of the facts.

[76] Cf. Giesen, "Problem" (n. 32), 24: "Es steht von vornherein fest, daß derjenige, der zurechtgewiesen wird, im Unrecht ist."

monished him first[77] and, thus, to motivate him to change his conduct. This, however, conforms well with the thesis just presented that not the deed as such, but its judgement is controversial.[78]

The issue should only be brought before the community if this second attempt does not show any success as well. Now, the sinner is not only confronted with his conduct by individuals, but by the whole community which shows him that his behaviour is considered as a disregard of the will of God as it was revealed by Jesus. If the Qumran texts are taken into account again, a significant difference can be recognized. Whereas the function of the community meeting in 1QS VI, 1 and CD IX, 3 seems to be to deliver a verdict on the basis of the reliably ascertained facts, the first obligation of the congregation in Matt 18:17 is to undertake another attempt to admonish and regain the sinner.[79]

If this attempt remains unfruitful as well, one has to state the failure of the admonition. To the initiator of the admonition – and accordingly also to the other members of the community – he shall be "as the Gentile and the tax-collector" from now on, that means, he shall not be considered as a "brother" (18:15) any longer, but as an outsider.[80] The sinner has shown that he does not share the community's understanding of the will of God based on the teaching of Jesus and, thereby, he has expressed his extraneousness. The exclusion from the community[81] implied in 18:17 draws the formal consequence of it.[82]

---

[77] Cf. Joachim Gnilka, "Die Kirche des Matthäus und die Gemeinde von Qumrân," *BZ* 7 (1963): 43–63, 54; Thompson, *Advice* (n. 5), 183 ("They witness to the truth of his fraternal correction and encourage their brother to accept the fact that his conduct has been sinful."); Gundry, *Matthew* (n. 4), 368; Schenk-Ziegler, *Correctio fraterna* (n. 51), 306.

[78] Deut 19:15 is interpreted by Matthew in the way that two or three testify that a certain behaviour is not in accordance with the will of God.

[79] Cf. Carmody, "Matt 18:15–17" (n. 60), 155–156.

[80] This can be compared with the refusal of the disciples' message in Matt 10:14 (καὶ ὃς ἂν μὴ δέξηται ὑμᾶς μηδὲ ἀκούσῃ τοὺς λόγους ὑμῶν). Here as well, the result is that those who do not want to listen to the words of the disciples exclude themselves from salvation (cf. 10:15!).

[81] One cannot evade the insight that exclusion from the community is implied in Matt 18:17 by referring to the fact that, according to Matt 9:9–13, Jesus, the "friend of tax-collectors and sinners" (11:19), particularly turned to the tax-collectors (differently Jean Galot, "Qu'il soit pour toi comme le païen et le publicain," *NRTh* 106 [1974]: 1009–1030, 1023–1024). The two other occurrences of ἐθνικός in the gospel of Matthew (5:47; 6:7) point to a clearly negative connotation in Matthew's use of the word, and in 5:46–47, as in 18:17, τελώνης and ἐθνικός constitute a pair. However, Matt 18:17b does not imply an irrevocable condemnation. Cf. further note 94.

[82] Cf. Sand, *Matthäus* (n. 3), 372: "Durch seine Verweigerung, Einsicht zu üben und zu bereuen, steht der Sünder bereits außerhalb der Gemeinde und wird nun von dieser ausdrücklich als ‚Draußenstehender' angesehen." Cf. further Goldhahn-Müller, *Grenze*

With the logion about binding and loosing in v. 18, which here refers to the forgiveness or the keeping of sins,[83] the decisions of the community receive the promise of validity in heaven and thus are credited with an unsurpassable authority.[84] For the sinner, Matt 18:18 means that his lack of insight not only has social consequences, such as the exclusion from the community, but also soteriological ones. Inversely, this is also valid for forgiveness which is not only an interpersonal act renewing social cooperation, but implies that God has forgiven the sinner as well.

For the general understanding it is fundamentally important that the exclusion from the community is by no means the aim of the admonition, but only the worst-case-scenario. One misses the Matthean intention in 18:15–17 if one places the weight one-sidedly on 18:17b[85] and only looks at the first half of v. 18 mentioning the *binding* of sins. Accordingly, it is mis-

---

(n. 5), 180; Giesen, "Problem" (n. 32), 23; Maisch, "Christsein" (n. 5), 258–259; Schenk-Ziegler, *Correctio fraterna* (n. 51), 307.

[83] "Binding and loosing" was already mentioned in 16:19, there in the sense of the authorisation of Peter for halakhic decisions, which, in the general context of the gospel, is linked to Jesus' interpretation of the Torah (see for this Matthias Konradt, "Die vollkommene Erfüllung der Tora und der Konflikt mit den Pharisäern im Matthäusevangelium," in *Das Gesetz im frühen Judentum und im Neuen Testament* [Festschrift Christoph Burchard; ed. Matthias Konradt and Dieter Sänger; NTOA/SUNT 57; Göttingen: Vandenhoeck & Ruprecht, 2006], 129–152). Thus, Peter is presented as the guarantor for the correct interpretation of the Torah which goes back to Jesus as the one and true teacher (cf. 23:8). In 18:18, however, the context suggests that "binding and loosing" refers to forgiveness and keeping of sins (likewise e.g. Luz, *Matthew II* [n. 4], 454, but differently Davies/Allison, *Matthew II* [n. 11], 787, who interpret 18:18 in line with 16:19: "the halakhic decisions of the community have the authority of heaven itself"). The latter presupposes, however, a communal consensus about the ethical guidelines. Independent of the controversial question about the traditio-historical priority of Matt 16:19 or 18:18, it should be noted that the sequence of the logia in the Matthean composition makes sense, since the halakhic authority of 16:19 is the presupposition for 18:18 (cf. Bornkamm, "Binde- und Lösegewalt" [n. 22], 49). The connection of both verses is further underlined by the fact that in the verses directly preceding (16:18; 18:17) the only evidences of ἐκκλησία in the gospel of Matthew appear.

The authority of the community to forgive sins was already implied in 9:8. By mentioning the "binding" of sins, 18:18 adds the negative counterpart to forgiveness.

[84] It is noteworthy that the motif implied in Matt 18:17, that the sinner should *listen* to the community, already pointed to the authority of the community (cf. von Dobbeler, "Versammlung" [n. 63], 216–217).

[85] Goldhahn-Müller, *Grenze* (n. 5), 181 postulates for the pre-Matthean tradition that the emphasis of the text is on 18:17b: "Bei der Bestimmung einer festgezogenen Grenze der Gemeindezugehörigkeit liegt der Schwerpunkt der halachischen Regel" (cf. to this below, note 89). See further Bornkamm, "Binde- und Lösegewalt" (n. 22), 41–42; Barth, "Kirchenzucht" (n. 22), 175.

leading to speak of "excommunication rules"[86] in Matt 18:15–17. The goal
of the admonition is, as was mentioned before, to gain the sinner back.[87]
And it is exactly this focus which Matthew has emphasized throughout his
composition. He related 18:15–17 to the admonition to "search for those
astray" as concretizing guidelines. And, vice versa, he placed the poimenic
care for the sinner as a guiding principle in front of 18:15–17:[88] the admonition and the search for those gone astray belong to the pastoral duties of
the disciples who are in the fellowship of the messianic shepherd.[89]

---

[86] Luomanen, *Kingdom* (n. 22), 232, 233, 253, 258. Elsewhere, Luomanen speaks
about "excommunication procedure" (242, 248) and about a "process of expulsion"
(251). Cf. further Luz, *Matthew* (n. 4), 451, 461 ("rule of excommunication"); von Dobbeler, "Versammlung" (n. 63), 216, 220 ("Ausschlussverfahren"). To speak of a "Diszi-
plinarverfahren" (Gnilka, "Kirche" [n. 77], 54), also sets an inadequate emphasis.

[87] Cf. e.g. Wouters, *Willen* (n. 53), 354; Overman, *Church* (n. 4), 268.

[88] Cf. Goldhahn-Müller, *Grenze* (n. 5), 190, according to whom the focus is on the
"intensive ... Bemühung um Wiedergewinnung des einzelnen sündigen Bruders" in the
Matthean composition. In a contrasting manner, Goldhahn-Müller sets the Matthean emphasis apart from the – postulated – rigorism of the underlying community tradition (see
to this below, note 89). Barth, "Kirchenzucht" (n. 22), 176 sees the "Kirchenzuchtsregel
18 15–17 gewissermaßen gegen den Strich gebürstet" by embedding it into Matt 18. According to Gnilka, *Matthäusevangelium II* (n. 4), 139 Matthew has shifted the emphasis
by means of the composition "vom Rechtsdenken auf ein pastoral-ekklesiologisches
Anliegen."

[89] Since Matt 18:15–17 is based on community tradition (cf. for many Jean Zumstein, *La condition du croyant dans l'Évangile selon Matthieu* [OBO 16; Fribourg: Vandenhoeck & Ruprecht, 1977], 387–388; Goldhahn-Müller, *Grenze* [n. 5], 170–172;
Gnilka, *Matthäusevangelium II* [n. 4], 135; Scheuermann, *Gemeinde* [n. 23], 167;
Schenk-Ziegler, *Correctio fraterna* [n. 51], 297; Luomanen, *Kingdom* [n. 22], 242–243,
differently, however, Stephenson H. Brooks, *Matthew's Community: The Evidence of His
Special Sayings Material* [JSNTSup 16; Sheffield: JSOT Press, 1987], 103), one may
consider that Matthew opposes a group in the community which gave priority to the
community's holiness instead to their mercy to sinners, through the placement of the
tradition in the context of Matt 18 (cf. Schenk-Ziegler, *Correctio fraterna* [n. 51], 298 as
well as Gnilka, *Matthäusevangelium II* [n. 4], 140: Matthew has "das den VV 15–17
zugrunde liegende Bild einer heilig und rein zu erhaltenden Kirche dahingehend korri-
giert, daß das Bemühen um den irrenden oder sich verfehlenden Bruder im Vordergrund
zu stehen hat"; cf. also Scheuermann, *Gemeinde* [n. 23], 193–194). But this can be no
more than speculation. In any case, it is not at all compelling that the tradition underlying
18:15–17, taken by itself, mirrors "eine in der Gemeinde geübte, relativ rigorose Praxis"
(Gnilka, *Matthäusevangelium II* [n. 4], 141). Likewise, we cannot categorically claim for
the pre-Matthean text that "Umkehr und Wiederaufnahme nach der disziplinarischen
Maßnahme der ‚Exkommunikation' nicht mehr vorgesehen sind" (Schenk-Ziegler,
Correctio fraterna [n. 51], 298; cf. Forkman, *Limits* [n. 16], 129; Goldhahn-Müller,
Grenze [n. 5], 181–182, 194). The text, taken by itself, does not say anything about how
one ought to proceed in the case of a late insight of the sinner. Above all, it is, to say the
least, not at all impossible that the evangelist takes up the context, in which the admonition typically occurs in the community, and "only" emphasizes it by means of his compo-

With regard to the ethical message of this section, one central aspect is that the sinner is protected by the rule that the admonition has to take place first of all apart from the public; he is not exposed before the forum of the community. This is an expression of love (cf. *T. Gad* 4:2–3).[90] Second, the obligation to a multistage procedure[91] makes evident that the "search for those gone astray" is not already to be terminated after a first failure; it

---

sition, trying to substantiate it. Schweizer, *Matthäus und seine Gemeinde* (n. 30), 112–113 considers that 18:15–17 was already linked with the parable of the sheep in the pre-Matthean text.

[90] It is noteworthy that in the epistle of James, which stands close to the gospel of Matthew, the same aspect occurs as an application of the love command (Jas 4:11–12, cf. also Jas 5:19–20). Cf. for this Matthias Konradt, *Christliche Existenz nach dem Jakobusbrief: Eine Studie zu seiner soteriologischen und ethischen Konzeption* (SUNT 22; Göttingen: Vandenhoeck & Ruprecht, 1998), 187–193.

[91] Different from Matt 18:15–17, *T. Gad* 6:3–7 does not develop a sequence of steps or the aspect of multiple attempts of admonition at all; it only deals with different options of possible reactions of the sinner. This difference documents the diverging social contexts. In contrast to *T. Gad* 6, Matthew not only treats the admonition on the private level of the relationship between two persons (for *T. Gad* 6:3–7 in this respect cf. Jürgen Becker, *Untersuchungen zur Entstehungsgeschichte der Testamente der Zwölf Patriarchen* [AGJU 8; Leiden: Brill, 1970], 360–361), but rather in the ecclesial horizon, whereby he comes closer to 1QS V, 24 – VI, 1. It is noteworthy that 1QS and Matt 18 offer regulations for special communities in Israel. Differently, the Testaments of the Twelve Patriarchs reflect the synagogal practice of Torah paraenesis, which is influenced by sapiental motifs, with regard to everyday life. Accordingly, the instructions in *T. Gad* 6:3–7 and Matt 18:15–17 are led by different aims of action: *T. Gad* 6:3–7 deals with the problem of a disturbance of the social relationship between two persons under the perspective that afterwards, a peaceful coexistence in everyday life becomes possible again. The soteriological prospects of the sinner are not in focus: it is not the central purpose to lead the sinner (back) to salvation. Rather, the text ends with the outlook that revenge is to be left to God, i.e. the sinner will receive his punishment. This perspective of the judgement of God should motivate not to pursue the issue any longer (cf. Prov 20:22; 1QS X, 17–18; *2 En.* 50:4; Ps.-Phoc. 77; *Jos. Asen.* 28:14; Rom 12:19). In other words, the focus in *T. Gad* 6 is one's own situation – with the purpose to live in peace from now on. By contrast, Matt 18:15–17 asks, in an ecclesial horizon, how one should treat members of the community who stray from the way which is considered as right on the basis of Jesus' interpretation of the Torah. Thereby, the view is particularly focused on the "winning back" of the sinner, and thus, on his salvation (cf. 18:12–14). Furthermore, the difference between *T. Gad* 6:3–7 and Matt 18:15–17 manifests itself in different understandings of forgiveness. When *T. Gad* 6:7 commands to forgive the sinner even in the case that he persists in his wrongdoing, only the interpersonal relationship is in perspective, as the final sentence, that the revenge is to be left to God, makes evident. Thus, the interpersonal forgiveness does not effect that the sins are also cancelled before God. By contrast, Matt 18:18 explains that forgiveness pronounced by the community (or its members) is valid also in heaven. Therefore, it is understandable that Matthew does not know the option of silent repentance without a confession of sins, which is mentioned in *T. Gad* 6:6.

requires more patience. At the same time, a limit is set to it.[92] If the sinner also disregards the admonition of the community, one can only document the existent difference by the exclusion from the community.[93]

This does not necessarily mean that all communication with him in everyday life is strictly prohibited from now on.[94] It "only" means that he cur-

---

[92] Wouters, *Willen* (n. 53), 353–354 understands the statement in 18:17–18 as follows: 18:17b says "im vorliegenden Kontext ..., daß eine den mahnenden Bruder verpflichtende Gemeinschaft mit dem Sünder nicht mehr besteht. Das bedeutet, der Bruder ist aus der Verantwortung für den Sünder entlassen, als Initiator des Verfahrens trägt er keine individuelle Verantwortung mehr für das weitere Geschehen."

[93] In contrast to the previous interpretation of 18:10–18 as a coherent, consistent line of thought, in which the textual parts interpret or complete each other, some exegetes postulate an irresolvable tension between the admonition to search for the lost in 18:10–14 and the unlimited forgiveness in 18:21–22 on the one hand, and the exclusion from the community in 18:15–18 on the other (see e.g. Bornkamm, "Binde- und Lösegewalt" [n. 22], 41–42; C. J. A. Hickling, *Conflicting Motives in the Redaction of Matthew: Some Considerations on the Sermon on the Mount and Matthew 18:15–20* [SE 7; ed. Elizabeth A. Livingstone; TU 126; Berlin: Akademie, 1982], 247–260, 259; Schenk-Ziegler, *Correctio fraterna* [n. 51], 297, 307; Luz, *Matthew II* [n. 4], 450, 466–467). Luz, *Matthew II* (n. 4), 462 explains the tension by means of the material's origins: "The rule of vv. 15–17 that originated in the early church and its supporting saying about binding and loosing in v. 18 reflect the situation of the beginning institutionalization of the Jesus community which had to distinguish itself from the majority society which did not believe in Jesus. Verses 21–22 and also 12–14, on the other hand, go back to Jesus himself and are not originally concerned with the problem of institutionalization." The evangelist would then not have balanced the tension between the different passages in the compilation of the material. However, this ignores that already in 18:12–14 the possibility is present that the "sheep gone astray" gets lost; this negative case appears to be more deeply reflected in 18:16–17. Moreover, 18:21 undoubtedly presupposes the repentance of the sinner. Inversely, 18:15–18 cannot be reduced to the aspect of the exclusion from the community. The case mentioned in v. 13a, that the sheep is found, finds a counterpart in v. 15b. With regard to 18:21–22 it is furthermore noteworthy that 18:17b limits the attempts of the admonition, but not of the willingness to forgive. If the sinner returns later on his own, a new situation emerges. Moreover, this means that 18:18 does not imply an anticipation of the judgement (differently e.g. Goldhahn-Müller, *Grenze* [n. 5], 190–191; Luz, *Matthew II* [n. 4], 454) because late repentance is not principally excluded. At least in the light of 18:21–35 there is no doubt that the community would then have to receive the sinner again.

[94] Similarly Nolland, *Matthew* (n. 19), 748. By contrast, Schenk-Ziegler, *Correctio fraterna* (n. 51), 307 argues for an interpretation of 18:17b in the sense of a cessation of communication (cf. *Did.* 15:3b as well as 1 Cor 5:11, for early Judaism cf. 1QS VII, 24–25). But from Matt 18:17, it can only be inferred that the *admonition* does not have a continuation. It is not automatically stated therewith that from now on one has to change the side of the street if one meets the "sinner." To talk of the cessation of communication in general, is thus undifferentiated. John P. Heil reads 18:17 in the light of Matthew's overall picture of Jesus' attitude: "the community is still to extend to the sinner the same mercy, fellowship, and love Jesus demonstrated to pagans and tax collectors" ([Warren

rently does not belong to the group anymore, and that there is no admonition anymore for him in the sense of caring for a "stray sheep," because this is an intracommunal task. However, it is already implied in 18:19–20 and is underlined in 18:21–22 that he needs not be a *persona non grata* for the community forever; a return is not principally ruled out.

In v. 19, Matthew has inserted a logion about praying which, when taken by itself, deals with the answering of prayers in general. Its insertion into the context of the community discourse after 18:15–18, however, poses the question about a specific point of reference for the prayers of the disciples, especially since a thematic connection with the preceding verses is supposed by various linguistic points of contact.[95] The context suggests that the members of the community should include the sinner in their prayers to effect his repentance.[96] This may refer to the admonition, or, to pick up vv. 10–14, to the search for the one gone astray, but also to intercession after the failure of the procedure. If the admonition was unsuccessful, prayers for the sinner still remain for the disciples.[97] The promise that their plea will be answered is grounded by the Matthean Jesus in v. 20 by the fact that he himself is present (cf. 28:20) where two or three are gathered in his name. In other words: the presence of Jesus among his disciples guarantees the answering of prayers by the heavenly father of Jesus (see παρὰ τοῦ πατρός μου τοῦ ἐν οὐρανοῖς in Matt 18:19!).[98]

Carter/]John P. Heil, *Matthew's Parables: Audience-Oriented Perspectives* [CBQMS 30; Washington, D.C.: Catholic Biblical Association, 1998], 123).

[95] The juxtaposition ἐπὶ τῆς γῆς – ἐν οὐρανοῖς links 18:19 with 18:18. Δύο refers back to v. 16. – Cf. Luz, *Matthew II* (n. 4), 458.

[96] Gnilka, *Matthäusevangelium II* (n. 4), 140. Petr Pokorný, "'Wo zwei oder drei versammelt sind in meinem Namen ...' (Mt 18,20)," in *Gemeinde ohne Tempel: Zur Substituierung und Transformation des Jerusalemer Tempels und seines Kultes im Alten Testament, antiken Judentum und frühen Christentum* (ed. Beate Ego, Armin Lange and Peter Pilhofer; WUNT 118; Tübingen: Mohr Siebeck, 1999), 477–488, 480 refers to the plea "für die Verlorenen" and the possibility of solving "Konflikte im Lichte der Vergebung Gottes." In contrast, Bornkamm, "Binde- und Lösegewalt" (n. 22), 43 assigns the function to Matt 18:19–20 "die unmittelbar zuvor der Gemeinde zugesprochene Binde- und Lösevollmacht zu begründen." Cf. also David D. Kupp, *Matthew's Emmanuel: Divine Presence and God's People in the First Gospel* (SNTSMS 90; Cambridge: Cambridge University Press, 1996), 181–182: "The 'agreement' of v. 19 corresponds to and reinforces the decision 'to bind' or 'to loose' in v. 18 – and provides the corporate application for the binding and loosing authority promised initially to Peter alone in 16.19."

[97] Luz, *Matthew II* (n. 4), 458 correctly refers to the fact that „the church naturally will pray not for the destruction but for the salvation and the return of erring brothers or sisters." In my opinion, one must emphasize more clearly than Luz, that the purpose that no "brother" gets lost is the leading principle of 18:15–20 on the whole.

[98] Cf. Gundry, *Matthew* (n. 4), 370: "His dynamic presence provides the reason for the heavenly Father's answering their prayers."

Furthermore, one can consider that the reference to Jesus' presence shall evoke the Christological foundation on which the entire discourse is based.[99] According to 18:14, the saving will of God intends that no one should be lost. In 1:21, Matthew has programmatically centred the task of Jesus in salvation from the sins by means of an interpretation of Jesus' *name*. This is realized in Matthew by the concrete encounter with Jesus during his earthly mission (9:2–8) on the one hand, and on the other hand, and primarily, by the death of Jesus, as 26:28[100] makes clear, and as is also indicated by the insertion of Jesus' name in the *titulus crucis* (27:37). The impending passion of Jesus is, as we have seen, the Christological thematic focus in the narrative context of the community discourse. Interpreted within this frame of reference, gathering in the *name* of Jesus (18:20) means that the one is present whose blood has been shed for the many for the forgiveness of sins (26:28) and whose effort for the sinners obliges those who are gathered in his name to care for the sinners.

VI

In v. 21, Matthew further develops the topic of forgiveness which was implied in the positive case of regaining the brother in 18:15b[101] and to which he also related in 18:18b. Thereby, a new aspect comes to the fore. Matthew takes up the Q-thread from 18:15, but rearranges the teaching of Jesus from Q 17:4 to a dialogue. Whereas the disciples have come to Jesus in 18:1 to confront him with a question, now, Peter comes forward with a question. He has understood that he has to forgive the brother who has taken the admonition to heart,[102] but now, he raises the still open question

---

[99] Luz, *Matthew II* (n. 4), 458 sees in v. 20 "the christological center of the entire chapter."

[100] Matthew has inserted εἰς ἄφεσιν ἁμαρτιῶν in 26:28, and at the same time he has not adopted the Markan designation of John's baptism as βάπτισμα μετανοίας εἰς ἄφεσιν ἁμαρτιῶν (Mark 1:4). In Matthew those who want to be baptized confess their sins as well (Matt 3:6), but actual forgiveness of sins is not mentioned here (cf. e.g. Joachim Gnilka, *Das Matthäusevangelium* [vol. 1; 2nd ed.; HTKNT 1.1; Freiburg: Herder, 1988], 68).

[101] In the parallel text in Luke 17:3, which may come very close to the Q-version (cf. James M. Robinson et al., eds., *The Critical Edition of Q* [Leuven: Peeters, 2000], 488–489), forgiveness of sins is explicitly mentioned.

[102] The repentance which is explicitly mentioned in Luke 17:3–4 (*The Critical Edition of Q* [see n. 101] presupposes this motif also for Q 17:3) is implied in Matt 18:21 (likewise e.g. Hagner, *Matthew II* [n. 4], 537, 541; Ulrich, *Greatness* [n. 4], 251; Elaine L. Ramshaw, "Power and Forgiveness in Matthew 18," *WW* 18 [1998]: 397–404, 400). Ποσάκις ἁμαρτήσει εἰς ἐμὲ ὁ ἀδελφός μου picks up ἐὰν δὲ ἁμαρτήσῃ ὁ ἀδελφός σου from v. 15. In 18:15, ἐὰν σου ἀκούσῃ implies repentance. Now, the case is treated that

about the limits of forgiveness, and thereby shifts the focus to the case that someone is personally wronged. Both aspects are connected with each other insofar as the question of the limit of forgiveness becomes even more pressing when one is affected by the sin of the other. Peter's subsequent question "as many as seven times?," following "Lord, how often shall my brother sin against me, and I forgive him?," may be meant as a generous offer.[103] Yet this is even surpassed by Jesus with seventy-seven times,[104] which actually means that forgiveness does not know any limits.[105] The possibility of receiving forgiveness is never lost, and this undoubtedly applies also for the one who has ignored the threefold admonition in 18:15–17, but then sees reason. For the one who ought to forgive, Jesus' answer in 18:22 means a radical challenge, especially since now, as we have seen, the focus is on the case that someone is personally wronged.

In his answer, however, Jesus does not confine himself to this radical demand, but adds a parable whose main features are quickly summarized. A servant owes his lord a huge amount of 10.000 talents.[106] On the day of payment he supplicates his lord for extension of payment, but then, he gets much more than that by his merciful lord who cancels his entire debt. Along the way, he meets a fellow servant, who owes him a comparatively small amount,[107] and claims the money back from him. Now, the fellow

---

one and the same brother is repeatedly guilty, but accepts the admonition (or comes to the conclusion by himself that he committed a sin).

[103] Cf. Nolland, *Matthew* (n. 19), 754. Luz, *Matthew II* (n. 4), 465 points out that "[s]even is the traditional number of perfection." Thus, "the sense of Peter's question is: 'Is perfect forgiveness expected of me?'"

[104] The meaning of ἑβδομηκοντάκις ἑπτά is – just as in the reference text in Gen 4:24 (see below, note 105) – not evident. As an alternative to the reading presented above, one can also read 7 x 70. Arguing for the above interpretation, Luz, *Matthew II* (n. 4), 465 refers to the Hebrew source of the LXX in Gen 4:24.

[105] Matt 18:22 alludes to the Lamech-song in Gen 4:24 ("If Cain is avenged sevenfold, truly Lamech seventy-sevenfold;" cf. for many Davies/Allison, *Matthew II* [n. 11], 793). The reader or the hearer of the gospel may hardly not have heard this. Unlimited forgiveness substitutes revenge.

[106] With the selling advised in 18:25, only a fraction of this sum could be covered (cf. Nolland, *Matthew* [n. 19], 757). With regard to the narrative logic, one can assume that originally, the amount was smaller, although still high (so e.g. Davies/Allison, *Matthew II* [n. 11], 795–796; Nolland, *Matthew* [n. 19], 756–757), so that it could realistically have been raised by the selling of the slave, the wife, the children and the possession (Martinus C. de Boer, "Ten Thousand Talents? Matthew's Interpretation and Redaction of the Parable of the Unforgiving Servant [Matt 18:23–35]," *CBQ* 50 [1988]: 214–232, 228 supposes 10.000 denarii). Matthew would then drastically have augmented the sum in order to emphasize God's mercy towards the sinners.

[107] Here, "it is about one six hundred thousandth of the figure that has just been forgiven him [sc. the servant]" (Luz, *Matthew II* [n. 4], 473).

slave falls to the ground before him[108] and begs with the words which he himself used before in addressing his lord: "have patience with me, and I will pay you." But the slave does not show compassion and casts the fellow slave into prison until he could pay the debt. When the lord hears about this, he immediately summons the slave and rebukes him: "you wicked slave! I forgave you that entire debt because you pleaded with me; should you not have had mercy on your fellow slave even as I had on you?" (18:32–33). With this pitilessness, the slave has forfeited the mercy which has been shown to him. He is now judged according to the measure with which he himself had measured (Matt 7:2b),[109] and is delivered to the torturers (v. 34).

The function of the parable could be seen in the fact that Jesus substantiates his radical demand with a massive threat. Stating this is not wrong, but it is nevertheless insufficient. In the context of Matt 18, the central function of the parable is that it subtly involves Peter in a change of roles with its metaphorical language. The form of the parable allows Peter to view his question in the mirror of a story without being coerced to directly identify himself with one of the *personae dramatis*. In the parable, the question of Peter corresponds to the relationship between the slave and the fellow slave. Taken by itself, it appears to be an everyday and absolutely legitimate issue to claim the payment of the debt from the fellow slave, that is, to insist on one's rights. But in the parable, this aspect is preceded by another scene. Thereby, the slave is presented as someone whose immense debt has been cancelled. His conduct thus appears in an absolutely different light.[110] It appears grotesque, absurd and in fact highly unmerciful.[111] If one relates this to Peter's question, how often one has to forgive the sinner after having been personally wronged, it becomes evident that the question cannot be adequately answered in the context of an isolated consideration of the relationship between the sinner and the one who

---

[108] Πεσὼν οὖν ὁ σύνδουλος αὐτοῦ (v. 29) takes up πεσὼν οὖν ὁ δοῦλος in v. 26, but προσεκύνει is missing now, of course.

[109] Cf. Luz, *Matthew II* (n. 4), 474.

[110] Cf. Gnilka, *Matthäusevangelium II* (n. 4), 146; Luz, *Matthew II* (n. 4), 473 ("Because of what happened earlier, the normal brutality of life is seen as something that is truly shocking"); Johanna Hess, "Zwischenmenschliche Vergebung und Versöhnung im Neuen Testament," in *Gewalt und Gewaltüberwindung in der Bibel* (ed. Walter Dietrich and Moisés Mayordomo; Zurich: Theologischer Verlag, 2005), 243–250, 248; Hanna Roose, "Das Aufheben der Schuld und das Aufheben des Schuldenerlasses (Vom unbarmherzigen Knecht): Mt 18,23–35," in *Kompendium der Gleichnisse Jesu* (ed. Ruben Zimmermann; Gütersloh: Gütersloher Verlag, 2007), 445–460, 447.

[111] Further, the servant breaks the Golden Rule (cf. Davies/Allison, *Matthew II* [n. 11], 801; Nolland, *Matthew* [n. 19], 758): he withholds from his fellow slave what he himself has asked for.

should forgive. The central function of the parable is to define the role of the one who ought to forgive anew.[112] He is not only the one who should forgive, but he is at the same time someone who himself lives by virtue of the forgiveness of God.[113] Because of this, it would be absurd to withhold forgiveness from one's neighbour. At the same time, the motif of the *imitatio Dei* (cf. 5:48) comes to the fore.[114] Whereas in 18:12–14, the motif of orienting oneself in accordance with God's action was suggested by the intertextual references, this motif becomes explicit in 18:23–35: "Gottes Handeln ... wirkt normbildend für das Miteinander in der Gemeinde."[115]

As has been mentioned already, Matthew has reshaped the Q-text into a dialogue in 18:21–22 and introduced Peter. Of course, one can simply point to the fact that Peter functions as the spokesman of the disciples elsewhere in the gospel of Matthew.[116] Quite often, however, all the disciples are involved in the dialogue with Jesus.[117] In particular, it should be mentioned that Peter does not appear as speaker in any of the other four discourses. In the parable discourse, elements of dialogue appear, but here, the disciples in general are the interlocutors (13:10, 36). The introduction of Peter in Matt 18:21 gains profile when one considers this in the context of the rest of the story. For here, it is Peter who has indeed incurred a great debt upon himself.[118] He is the one who has denied Jesus, but nevertheless belongs to the disciples again after Jesus' resurrection, and, even more, he is ennobled as the rock on which Jesus builds his church (16:18). Peter thus can serve excellently as a symbol for forgiveness as a basic principle of the church, as a *nota ecclesiae*.[119] In this context, one can furthermore

---

[112] It has often been postulated that the parable does not fit exactly into the present context, since it does not deal with the aspect of *repeated* forgiveness (see, e.g., William R. Herzog II, "What If the Messiah Came and Nothing Changed? The Parable of the Unmerciful Servant [Matt. 18:23–35]," in *Parables as Subversive Speech: Jesus as Pedagogue of the Oppressed* [Louisville, Ky.: Westminster John Knox, 1994], 131–149, 132). While this difference is obvious, the parable nonetheless fits into the context quite well, since it takes up the question posed in v. 21 in a more fundamental way by reflecting on the person who shall forgive.

[113] This holds, even if it has to be conceded that the concrete debt sum cannot be generalized, particularly as the 10.000 talents are to be read as intentionally exaggerated information.

[114] Cf. Davies/Allison, *Matthew II* (n. 11), 802, 804; Luz, *Matthew II* (n. 4), 474.

[115] Roloff, "Kirchenverständnis" (n. 23), 343.

[116] See Matt 15:15; 16:16; 17:4; 19:27, cf. further 17:24–27. – Cf. e.g. Scheuermann, *Gemeinde* (n. 23), 187–188.

[117] See Matt 13:10, 36; 14:15; 15:12, 23, 33; 17:(10), 19; 19:10, 25; 21:20; 24:3.

[118] Cf. Ulrich, *Greatness* (n. 4), 249–250, 254–255.

[119] It is noteworthy that the prediction of the denial of Peter in Matt 26:34–35 directly follows on the announcement of Jesus, quoting Zech 13:7, that the *shepherd* will be beaten and the *sheep* be scattered (26:31). Therefore, the pastoral imagery, which is also

point to a sideline of the parable. In v. 31, fellow slaves appear complaining about the mercilessness of the slave. In this context, one can surmise that the group of slaves is transparent for the community.[120] V. 31 would then emphasize that the refusal to forgive constitutes a violation of the group ethos. The ending of the parable in v. 34 and the application of the parable in v. 35 show that community members who behave unmercifully in this manner exclude themselves from salvation (cf. Jas 2:13).[121]

In short: the role of the slave in the parable fits brilliantly in illuminating the situation of Peter for whom a big debt has been cancelled as well, but who should behave differently towards others than the figure in the parable. Conversely, Peter was outstandingly qualified to pose the question in 18:21, in order to make the radical demand for unlimited forgiveness plausible by means of the parable. Interpersonal forgiveness is nothing else than a consequence of the forgiveness that one has received oneself.[122] The question raised by Peter in v. 21 is to be viewed in the light of the forgiveness granted by God. The person, who has been wronged and is asked for forgiveness by the sinner, ought not meet the sinner in arrogant self-righteousness. Rather, he should bear in mind that he himself lives from God's mercy and is dependent upon it. In other words: he does not have a reason to meet the other by looking down on him (cf. 7:1–5). If 18:1–5 is included, the ethos of humility presented there is concretized here.[123] In view of the acquittance which one has received, it is absurd to disdain the little ones.

---

used in the community discourse in 18:12–13, appears in direct connection with the prediction of the denial of Peter.

[120] Cf. Martin Leutzsch, "Verschuldung und Überschuldung, Schuldenerlaß und Sündenvergebung. Zum Verständnis des Gleichnisses Mt 18,23–35," in Schuld und Schulden: Biblische Traditionen in gegenwärtigen Konflikten (ed. Marlene Crüsemann and Willy Schottroff; Munich: Kaiser, 1992), 104–131, 107; Luz, Matthew II (n. 4), 470.

[121] It would be hardly according to Matthew's intention to draw the conclusion from the judgment scene in v. 34(–35) that withholding forgiveness once is a trespass that cannot be forgiven and thus excludes form salvation in an unrevisable manner (for this problem cf. Bernard B. Scott, "The King's Accounting: Matthew 18:23–34," JBL 104 [1985]: 429–442, 430–431). Matthew uses the judgment scene to impress the importance and necessity (cf. οὐκ ἔδει in v. 33) of granting forgiveness on his readers/hearers.

[122] Cf. Nolland, Matthew (n. 19), 753.

[123] Cf. Ulrich, Greatness (n. 4), 203: "the people whom God considers great are humble to the point that they are like slaves before the divine Master, completely dependent on God's mercy and grace."

VII

I would like to summarize the findings in three points:

1. In the course of the preceding analysis, Matt 18 presented itself as thematically coherent discourse. At its beginning, Jesus establishes an ethos of humility and lowliness as the ethical guideline (18:1–5). The rest of the discourse exemplifies this fundamental orientation.[124] Humility and lowliness manifest themselves in receiving children at "eye level," in caring for the "little ones," as a shepherd takes care of a sheep gone astray, instead of despising them (18:10–20), in an unlimited willingness to forgive, even if one was personally wronged (18:21–22), bearing in mind that everyone lives by virtue of the forgiveness of God (18:23–35) and is himself in danger of stumbling (18:8–9) so that there is no reason for any pride or arrogance.

2. Matthew's Gospel is well-known for its radical ethical demands. The disciples shall love their enemies (5:44). If anyone strikes them on the right cheek, they shall turn to him the other as well (5:39). Someone who calls his brother "fool" is liable to the hell of fire (5:22); and someone who looks at another's wife lustfully, has already committed adultery with her (5:28), and so on. In short: the disciples shall be perfect (5:48, cf. 19:21). Furthermore, there is also a radical demand to forgive the sinner. This, however, also means that the radical demands are counterbalanced by the realistic assessment that sins and failures are a matter of fact also among the followers of Jesus and by an exceedingly merciful attitude towards sinners. Matthew does not conceive of the congregation as an unblemished holy community in which the strife to reach the summit of highest virtuousness does not leave any space for the ethically weak, for the little ones. Matthew calls for a perfect fulfillment of the will of God, but he also knows that Christ-believers are sinners who may trust in God's mercy which at the same time obligates them to show mercy towards others as well. In modern terms, one could say that Matthew's approach is oscillating between a sect-like rigorism and the openness of a "Volkskirche," a people's church.

3. Matthew's ethics cannot be sufficiently understood without considering the relation between ethical admonitions and the story. His ethical convictions form an integral part of his view of the world which he unfolds by narrating a story. In Matt 18, this can be illustrated by several intra- (and also inter-)textual links.

– The discourse is part of the narrative section of the Gospel in which Jesus' passion emerges as the dominant Christological perspective. If this

---

[124] Cf. Luz, *Matthew II* (n. 4), 429.

context is taken into account, the ethos of humility and lowliness, which is unfolded in the discourse, appears as applied Christology. Jesus, the humble king (21:5, cf. 11:29), takes the cross upon himself and takes the path of lowliness to save the "many" (26:28) from their sins. Matt 18 draws the ethical consequences from believing that this Jesus is the Messiah.

– Moreover, the demand to search for the "stray sheep" is linked to Matthew's presentation of Jesus as the merciful messianic shepherd and, to include the intertextual dimension, to the presentation of God as the shepherd of his people and the promise of the Davidic messianic shepherd in Scripture (Ezek 34:23; 37:24).

– Finally, the anthropological presupposition of the discourse that human beings are not immune against weakness and sin and are dependent on God's mercy, gains contours in the context of the story by introducing the figure of Peter, since Peter symbolizes that it would be absurd and presumptuous to withhold forgiveness from one's neighbor.

Ethics through the Power of Language:

Some Explorations in the Gospel according to John

JAN G. VAN DER WATT

1. Introduction

Ethics is normally not regarded as a major or even a prominent theme in John's[1] Gospel.[2] Theobald, for instance, is of the opinion that „Ein *ethi-*

---

[1] From now the Gospel of John will simply be referred to as "John" for the sake of convenience.

[2] Frank Matera, *New Testament Ethics: The legacies of Jesus and Paul* (Louisville, Ky.: Westminster John Knox, 1996), 92; Heinz-Dietrich Wendland, *Ethik des Neuen Testaments: Eine Einführung* (Göttingen: Vandenhoeck & Ruprecht, 1975), 109; Wolfgang Schrage, *The Ethics of the New Testament* (Edinburgh: T&T Clark, 1996), 297 remarks, "we may ask whether a chapter on the Johannine writings even belongs in a book on the ethics of the New Testament". Birger Gerhardsson, *The ethos of the Bible* (Philadelphia, Pa.: Fortress Press, 1981), 98 regards love as the only ethical theme of significance in John; Klaus Berger, *Im Anfang war Johannes: Datierung und Theologie des vierten Evangeliums* (Stuttgart: Quell, 1997) does not give attention to the ethics in John in his "theology" of this Gospel; James L. Houlden, *Ethics and the New Testament* (London: Mowbrays, 1973), 35–36; R. Alan Culpepper, "Anti-Judaism in the Fourth Gospel as a theological problem for Christian interpreters," in *Anti-Judaism and the Fourth Gospel* (ed. Reimund Bieringer, Didier Pollefeyt and Frederique Vandecasteele-Vanneuville; Louisville, Ky.: Westminster John Knox, 2001), 61–82, 79; Richard A. Burridge, *Imitating Jesus: An inclusive approach to New Testament ethics* (Grand Rapids, Mich.: Eerdmans, 2007); Gerald L. Borchert, *The American Commentary: John 12–21* (Nashville, Tenn.: Broadman & Holman, 2002), 355 remarks that "[a]lthough the Johannine Gospel does not spend much time outlining the characteristics of the Christian life and ethical behavior, it epitomizes the transformed life in the commandment 'to love.'" See also Jan G. van der Watt, "'Julle moet mekaar liefhê.' Etiek in die Johannesevangelie," *Scriptura Suppl.* 9a (1992): 74–96 for a discussion of this issue; Siegfried Schulz, *Neutestamentliche Ethik* (Zurich: Theologischer Verlag, 1987), 486–488; Leon Morris, "Love in the Fourth Gospel," in *Saved by hope* (Festschrift Richard C. Oudersluys; ed. James I. Cook; Grand Rapids, Mich.: Eerdmans, 1978), 27–43; Ian H. Marshall, *New Testament Theology* (Downers Grove, Ill.: Intervarsity, 2004), 522–523; János Bolyki, "Ethics in the Gospel of John," *Communio Viatorum* 45 (2003): 198–208, 198; for the law in John see Jörg Augenstein, "Jesus und das Gesetz im Johannesevangelium," *KuI* 14 (1999): 161–179; William R. G. Loader, *Jesus' attitude towards the Law* (Grand Rapids, Mich.: Eerdmans,

sches Interesse an der Gestaltung der Lebensbereiche der Gemeinde wird im Buch nirgends greifbar."[3] Scholars like Meeks contend that one should not, and could not, speak of ethics in John's Gospel. Rather, he chooses to approach the Gospel simply as an "instrument for moral formation."[4]

The question that will be addressed here in part is whether there are possibilities of broadening the analytical framework for unlocking ethical material in John's Gospel.[5] To answer this question the influence of language on the dynamics of ethics and the way the author of this Gospel uses language to attain his ethical goals will come into focus.

2. Ethics in John?

Analyzing "ethics" requires a clear definition or description of ethics, especially as it presents itself in John. A major clue as to the essence of all ethical actions in John is given when the crowd approached Jesus as Rabbi (6:25) with an *ethical* question about the required behaviour to please God and receive eternal life (6:28). Jesus' answer shifts the focus from the specific requirements of the law to the person of Jesus (6:29): "this is the works of God: that *you believe in the One He has sent.*" The basic ethical requirement is clearly stated: it is not the law but faith in Jesus that forms the central thrust of all ethical action.[6] This is what it means to do τὸ ἔργον τοῦ θεου. The essential and most basic ethical *deed* that is required is *faith in Jesus*.

The implication of this on the ethical thinking of John is profound indeed. The following should be noted:

When faith is regarded as the central ethical action in this Gospel, it elevates ethics to a *relational* phenomenon, i.e. relationships/identity de-

---

2002); for the concept of sin see Rainer Metzner, *Das Verständnis der Sünde im Johannesevangelium* (WUNT 122; Tübingen: Mohr Siebeck, 2000).

[3] Michael Theobald, *Herrenworte im Johannesevangelium* (HBS 34; Freiburg: Herder, 2002), 565.

[4] Wayne A. Meeks, "The ethics of the Fourth Evangelist," in *Exploring the Gospel of John: In honor of D. Moody Smith* (ed. R. Alan Culpepper and C. Clifton Black; Louisville, Ky.: Westminster John Knox, 1996), 317–326, 317; idem, "Understanding early Christian ethics," *JBL* 105 (1986): 3–11.

[5] See Jan G. van der Watt, "Ethics and ethos in the gospel according to John," *ZNW* 97 (2006): 147–176.

[6] See D. Rudolf Liechtenhan, *Gottes Gebot im Neuen Testament: Sein ursprünglicher Sinn und seine bleibende Bedeutung* (Basel: Helbling & Lichtenhahn, 1942), 122–123.

termine one's actions. Salvific faith[7] points to the establishment of a relationship between Jesus and a particular person based on a self-sacrificing, intellectual, and existential, acceptance of the message and person of Jesus by that particular person to the extent that it completely transforms the person's thoughts and deeds in accordance with this message. This in turn leads to an obedient life of doing what a child of God should do.

The relational dimension (based on faith) is expressed through the central concept of eternal life which invokes family imagery as a result.[8] From the identity of a believer as member of God's family flow his or her behavioural patterns (8:38–41; 13:15; 14:10–11).

The ethical system of John proved to be primarily relational, grounded in Christology. Actions cannot be separated from identity and the one flows naturally into the other, so much so that accepting Jesus in faith becomes the primary ethical action in John. This has the following implication for our analysis: material relevant for ethical analysis can be found wherever there is reference to an acceptance of Jesus, or where the language touches on this issue in some way. Our attention will now shift to the way in which the language is used in John's Gospel to attain this goal.

3. Performative Texts? John 20:28–31 in the Light of some Theoretical Considerations

3.1 John 20:28–31 as a Performative Text

In John 20:30–31 John formulates a central purpose of this Gospel in performative terms, namely, to bring the readers to faith or to strengthen their faith through the words written in his Gospel. John 20:30–31 should be

---

[7] In this Gospel the word πιστεύω is used in different ways – its meaning is contextually determined. The 'full story' of what faith involves is not told in each case, but is gradually developed through this Gospel, with the full description in the narrative of the blind man in chapter 9 with confirmation in chapter 11 (see Ruben Zimmermann, "The Narrative Hermeneutics of John 11. Learning with Lazarus How to Understand Death, Life, and Resurrection, in: *The Resurrection of Jesus in the Gospel of John* (ed. Craig R. Koester and Reimund Bieringer; WUNT 222; Tübingen: Mohr Siebeck, 2008), 75–101. The different contexts provide different aspects or building blocks of the total picture of what salvific faith implies.

[8] For a detailed argument linking these two concepts, see Jan G. van der Watt, *Family of the King: Dynamics of metaphor in the Gospel according to John* (Biblical Interpretation Series 47; Leiden: Brill, 2000).

read in context with the preceding verses.[9] The presence of the divine and resurrected Jesus led to Thomas' climactic[10] confession (20:28): "my Lord and my God,"[11] changing his status from that of an unbeliever to that of a believer (καὶ μὴ γίνου ἄπιστος ἀλλὰ πιστός – 20:27; see also 20:25).[12] Henceforth people will not be in the privileged position of Thomas[13] to see the risen Jesus *physically*; they will come to faith without the "assistance" of the physical presence of the resurrected Jesus (20:29).[14] How will this happen? Through the *written Gospel* people will "meet" Jesus and come to faith (v. 29). Faith stands central, not only structurally, but also in the argument itself. In 20:30–31, it is stated that the signs[15] were narrated with

---

[9] See Jan G. van der Watt, "The cross/resurrection-events in the Gospel of John with special emphasis on the confession of Thomas (20:28)," *Neot* 37 (2003): 127–145 for similar argumentation.

[10] Frederik W. Grosheide, *Het Heilig Evangelie volgens Johannes* (Amsterdam: H. A. van Bottenburg, 1950), 546; Charles K. Barrett, *The Gospel according to St John* (2nd ed.; London: SPCK, 1978), 573; Frederick F. Bruce, *The Gospel of John* (Grand Rapids, Mich.: Eerdmans, 1983), 394; Robert Kysar, *John* (Augsburg Commentary on the New Testament; Minneapolis, Minn.: Fortress Press, 1986), 307; Donald A. Carson, *The Gospel according to John* (Grand Rapids, Mich.: Eerdmans, 1992), 659; Ludger Schenke, *Johannes: Kommentar* (Düsseldorf: Patmos, 1998), 380. Rodney A. Whitacre, *John* (Leicester: Intervarsity, 1999), 485–486 points out that this confession is indeed climactic, not only because it forms the apex of the development of the narrative, but also because it expresses the heart of the confession about Jesus.

[11] Johannes Riedl, *Das Heilswerk Jesu nach Johannes* (Freiburg: Herder, 1973), 200; D. Bruce Woll, *Johannine Christianity in conflict: authority, rank, and succession in the first farewell discourse* (Chico, Calif.: Scholars Press, 1981), 51; Raymond E. Brown, *The Gospel according to John* (vol. 1; London: Chapman, 1971), 218; Hermann Strathmann and Gustav Stählin, *Das Evangelium nach Johannes. Die Apostelgeschichte* (NTD 2; Göttingen: Vandenhoeck & Ruprecht, 1962), 104. See Carson, *Gospel* (n. 10), 658 on the content of the confession.

[12] In 20:25 the unbelief of Thomas is formulated – he sets conditions on which he will start to believe. Carson, *Gospel* (n. 10), 659 correctly remarked: "The most unyielding skeptic has bequeathed to us the most profound confession."

[13] Barclay M. Newman and Eugene A. Nida, *A translator's handbook on the Gospel of John* (New York: United Bible Society, 1980), *ad loc.* points out that the aorist participium (πιστεύσαντες) may point to an "action that is past from the viewpoint of Jesus or the author of the Gospel" (which implies that the verse refers to people who have already believed before Thomas), or "as representing timeless action." The latter is preferable.

[14] See Jürgen Becker, *Das Evangelium nach Johannes Kapitel 11–21* (ÖTK 4/2; Würzburg: GVH Wissenschaft & Gemeindepraxis, 1981), 631.

[15] Some are of the opinion that the signs only refer to the first section of the Gospel, up to chapter 12. Raymond E. Brown, *The Gospel according to John* (vol. 2; London: Chapman, 1972), 1059, for instance, maintains that the resurrection should not be seen as a sign. However, the death and resurrection of Jesus should be seen as the biggest sign in the Gospel. In 2:18–22, it is implied that the death and resurrection of Jesus is indeed a sign. See also George H. C. Macgregor, *The Gospel of John* (London: Hodder & Stoughton, 1933), 366–367; Rudolf Bultmann, *Das Evangelium des Johannes* (Göttingen: Van-

the purpose of (ἵνα) leading people to faith and assisting them to remain faithful in Jesus as the Christ, the Son of God. Thus they would get eternal life as a consequence of their belief.[16] People who are no longer in the position of Thomas to "see" Jesus physically, have the Gospel narrative through which they can discover the identity of this Jesus and get to know him as the Christ. This should result in faith, in the same manner that the physical appearance of Jesus to Thomas resulted in faith. In this sense the Gospel functions as a means by which the physically absent Jesus now becomes present among people.[17] The rhetorical power[18] of the Gospel lies in the fact that the author of the text cannot take a person to the physical Jesus, but he can invite that person to accompany him through the narrative of the Gospel, listening to the words of Jesus, "seeing" his signs through "the eyes of literature," and by doing this persons can come to faith, or have their existing faith strengthened. This truth is rehearsed over and again in the narrative for every reader to "see." By understanding John 20:28–31 in the above manner, one can maintain that the author of the text was fully aware of the performative power of the text. Naturally this implies a radical involvement by the reader (interpreted within an ethical framework by John) as well as a radical challenge by the text.[19]

---

denhoeck & Ruprecht, 1978), 541 also points out that in John the signs and words should be seen as a unity.

[16] See Andrew Steward, "The supreme claim," *EvQ* 8 (1936): 423–433, 432 and Leon Morris, *The Gospel according to John* (Grand Rapids, Mich.: Eerdmans, 1974), 231.

[17] Ulrich Wilckens, *Das Evangelium nach Johannes* (Göttingen: Vandenhoeck & Ruprecht, 1998), 318–319; Ulrich Schnelle, *Das Evangelium nach Johannes* (Leipzig: Evangelische Verlagsanstalt, 1998), 312; See also Carson, *Gospel* (n. 10), 660.

[18] The way in which the Gospel itself invites the reader to partake in the narrative by choosing sides (see Jan G. van der Watt and Lizel Voges, "Metaforiese elemente in die forensiese taalgebruik van die Johannesevangelie," *Skrif en Kerk* 21 (2000): 387–405 as illustration of how the forensic imagery in the Gospel is used to involve the reader), the use of irony or misunderstanding, the effective portrayal of the opposition of Jesus and what happens to them, etc. are all rhetorical mechanisms to "move," influence and convince the readers in a dynamic and participatory way. See also Anthony E. Harvey, *Jesus on trail: A study in the fourth gospel* (London: SCM Press, 1976).

[19] Wilckens, *Evangelium* (n. 17), 318; Schnelle, *Evangelium* (n. 17), 307; Barnabas Lindars, *The Gospel of John* (Grand Rapids, Mich.: Eerdmans, 1987), 616; John N. Suggit, *The Sign of Life: Studies in the Fourth Gospel and the Liturgy of the Church* (Pietermaritzburg: Cluster Publications, 1993), 167.

3.2 Is the Concept of 'Performative Text' a Modern Construct or an Ancient Practice?

Before exploring the performative nature of John further, the following theoretical point should first be made: ancient authors were aware or conscious of the performative nature of texts.

Olbricht[20] has aptly illustrated this.[21] For our purposes it is Olbricht's[22] conclusion that should be taken seriously: "[t]he rhetoricians [of ancient discourse – added JvdW] conceived analogical features of discourse as essentially stylistic devices. In the communication that took place in the church and synagogue, however, analogical approaches reflected a fundamental vision of reality. It is for this reason that increased attention needs to be given to how these features of religious discourses work as well as the manner in which they possess rhetorical power." This remark is important for two reasons: a) ancient authors were intensely aware of the performative nature of a text and used language to reach their communicative intentions. John seemingly fits into this pattern. b) The evidence Olbricht offers, shows that the performative nature of the text should not be restricted, rather he demonstrates its varied nature. This implies that as readers (and re-readers) of an ancient text like the Gospel of John we should be sensitive to possible rhetorical features that could function performatively.

Within this light we are ready to further explore the performative nature of John's language *inter alia*. A few remarks about the theory of language followed in this discourse would be helpful at this stage.

---

[20] Thomas H. Olbricht, "Analogy and allegory in classical rhetoric in Early Christianity and classical culture" in *Early Christianity and Classical Culture: Comparative studies in honor of Abraham J. Malherbe* (ed. John T. Fitzgerald, Thomas H. Olbricht and L. Michael White; Leiden: Brill, 2003), 371–389.

[21] [ps-]Demetrius *On Style* mentions four "levels of style: the grand, the elegant, the plain and the forceful" (Olbricht, "Analogy and allegory" [n. 20], 375). "Clearly [ps-] Demetrius believed that analogical devices make discourse arresting and provide force, but they have more to do with attractiveness and understanding than with substance." (Olbricht, "Analogy and allegory" [n. 20], 376). According to the *ad Herennium*, "the contributions of similes to style are to embellish, clarify and make vivid, much as declared by Aristotle." (Olbricht, "Analogy and allegory" [n. 20], 376). Similar examples from Cicero (*De Oratore*), Longinus *On the Sublime*, Quintilian, etc. illustrate the point more than aptly that ancient rhetoricians were more than aware of the performative nature of texts. Olbricht, "Analogy and allegory" [n. 20], 379 concludes "From this perusal of the rhetoricians, the power of analogical material first of all lies in clarity, especially in regard to literal or historical comparison. Fictional or allegorical analogies supply vivacity, liveliness and emotion. They function both to enhance style, and to contribute toward proof by way of πάθος ('affect')."

[22] Olbricht, "Analogy and allegory" [n. 20], 388–389.

4. John, Language and Ethics

The narrative structure of John is complicated by the literary features of the text, i.e. it contains long discussions and monologues, makes use of multiple imageries, comparisons, metaphors, etc. This asks for a multidi-mensional literary approach[23] based on a complex theory of language, which will be briefly outlined here.[24] A diagram of the elements of a text may look as follows:

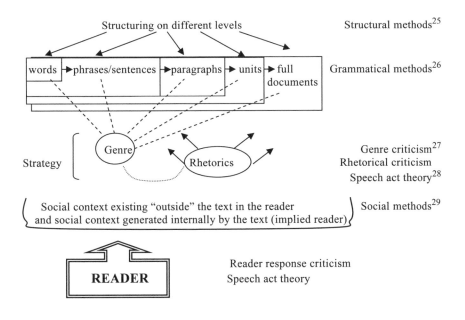

---

[23] No theory can cover all the language features in this Gospel, neither can one theory of reception or understanding of the text explain the reading process in full.

[24] Obviously, matters are more complex than could be discussed here, but the aim is simply to provide a working perspective.

[25] Examples of methods used: discourse analysis, structural analysis, narrative analysis.

[26] Examples of methods used: word grammar, TGG, syntactical grammar, linguistic criticism, stylistic analysis.

[27] Examples of methods used: genres, form criticism.

[28] Speech act theory tries to address multiple features in the text.

[29] Examples of methods used: sociology, socio-scientific, socio-historic, social methods, background studies, archaeology, etc.

Texts consist of progressively growing language units starting with words, and ending in a full document. This "interrelated grouping together" of language units (structuring) is based on the language conventions of that particular language. Inherently part of the communication process is the chosen genre, which serves as the overall discourse compositional template. Some theorists even argue that *genre* is the most determinative aspect in the process of communication,[30] since genre sets the stage for interpreting words, phrases, etc. and influences decisions on all levels of the creation of the text. *Rhetoric*[31] is also a communication strategy that influences the text from the very moment of its formation. The way in which words and phrases are formed, choices as to which stylistic features should be included, etc. all relate to rhetoric.[32] Genre and rhetoric are also interrelated, since the genre will depend on the rhetorical strategy and *vice versa*.

The total textual process is *socially* determined, from the meaning of words, the way syntax and structures work, the function and characteristics of language as well as rhetoric. Language is a social phenomenon and social knowledge plays a determinative role in constituting communication.

The communication process discussed above does not unfold in a linear manner, rather it is circular in nature, implying that the reader constantly "returns" to what he has already read and re-interprets that in the light of newly acquired information. For instance, one might not realize at first that somebody is telling a joke, but as the person continues to talk you soon realize and understand the content and means of the communication more clearly. This will lead to a reinterpretation and re-evaluation of information that has already been acquired. Rhetoric or genre does not exist apart from the surface level of the text. Conclusions about the rhetorical strategy and the genre are based on the way in which the text itself is structurally presented. This questions methods that pretend to be "full interpretations" of a text but only focus on one or two of these aspects.

Then there is the *reader*. He or she is confronted through the text with all the features in their interrelatedness as they are described above. The measure to which the readers allows themselves to be drawn into this integrated process, and equip themselves to do so, will result in the effectiveness of the communication that takes place. The reader is basically con-

---

[30] For instance, if you tell a joke (genre = joke) and somebody thinks your statement is factual, or to be taken seriously, it might have dire consequences. Conversely if you warn somebody that a car is coming and he thinks it is a joke the consequences might be just as bad.

[31] Stephen Motyer, *Your father the devil? A new approach to John and 'the Jews'* (Carlisle: Paternoster Press, 1997), 116 describes rhetoric as "techniques employed in order to exercise persuasive power." In this way the discourse is infused with persuasive force and even feeling.

[32] See Lucian's *Nigrinus* 35–36 for the powerful effect of rhetoric.

fronted with "codes" presented by the text that contain information that is socially determined. On the one hand there are the conventions of the original language on the basis of which the communication process takes place. As current day readers we are expected to interpret those conventions, yet we must concede that we are at a disadvantage: we do not belong to the original interpretative framework of the text. Readers should be aware of the possibility of loss of the possibly intended meaning (by not recognizing or only partly recognizing the rhetorical signals in the text) or on the other hand, the possibility of over-interpreting the text (by applying current day conventions to such an ancient text). The measure to which the reader can responsibly interpret these codes (ranging from words or stylistic features to genre and rhetorical strategies) will directly contribute towards his or her understanding of the text. The more codes there are, or the more complicated the social setting becomes, the better are the chances for multiple readings/understandings or even misunderstanding.[33]

Although there are theories that claim that the reader determines meaning *in toto* in the reading process and degrades the influence of the text to virtually zero, reading a text is quite an interactive process between the text and the reader (or between the written text and the text represented by the reader, in inter-textual terms) where the origin of communication starts with the text, but it is unfolded in an interaction with the reader. The text presents signals to the reader that are interpreted by the reader, who in this sense is in charge of the interpretative process.[34] The interpretation of the reader can (and should) then be checked against the signals of the text for validity.[35] There will be a specific range of possible and valid interpretations. The moment the interpreter moves outside of this range that interpretation will (and should) be falsified by other (especially academic) readers.[36]

---

[33] I regard misunderstanding as interpreting the text against its own grain or apparent meaning.

[34] Terms like "text-pragmatism" or "reader response" are often used to indicate the interaction between the text (acknowledging its contribution to the communication process) but also not denying the contribution the reader makes in the interpretation of the text. Motyer, *Your father* (n. 31), 107, quoting Rebell, points out that the principal idea of text-pragmatism is to investigate the effect of the text on its recipients, in other words, how is what done to the reader? He continues (108) by mentioning that text-pragmatism not only focuses on the original recipients but also on recipients in general.

[35] Texts communicate on multiple levels and can consequently carry multiple meanings. One can therefore not speak of the meaning, but of plausible meanings. The challenge is to determine when and where a meaning becomes implausible and why.

[36] Alexander S. Jensen, *John's Gospel as Witness: The development of the Early Christian language of faith* (Ashgate: Hampshire, 2004), 42.

Emotive meaning[37] and perlocution is difficult to determine and not much attention will be given to this aspect in this article. It is usually studied through methods like speech act theory.

In the light of the above, the Johannine text will be approached with the following assumptions: a) that the author(s) of the Gospel indeed intended the text to be performative and that such signals are to be found in the text. b) In order to recognize these performative features a close reading of the text is the starting point. Close attention should be paid to the expectations and reactions within the flow of the text itself, i.e. if misunderstanding occurs, what is the immediate reaction (or expectation) that is apparent in the text itself. Cues must be taken from the text itself. It is obviously not possible to predict how a reader will respond to any specific text. By reading the text closely it becomes possible to give clear indications of the direction the text encourages the reader to take. The broad ideological thrust as well as the smaller linguistic features of the text will work together in determining this "encouragement" of the text. The functionality of the text with its features will form the main focus. c) We will focus on the relation between text (language) and the ethical dynamics of the text.

5. The Role of Language in John with Special Emphasis on John 8

Chapter 8 will serve as our basic text for analysis because it is one of the primary texts in this Gospel that deals with ethics.

It was already established that the *first and major ethical act* in John is to bring people to faith in Jesus (20:30–31). We will focus on the numerous linguistic techniques on different levels that are employed to attain this goal.

5.1 Words (Word Grammar) and Ethics

5.1.1 The Use of Particular Words in Ethical Meanings

Ethically related words and concepts confirm the ethical dynamics of this narrative. Although a variety of ethical words used belongs to the broad

---

[37] Quintilian (*Inst.* 6.2.2,5–6; 5.8.3; 4.1.14; 3.5.2) calls the emotive approach the most effective way of conquering an audience: "There is some advantage to be gained by pleasing our audience and a great deal by stirring their emotions" (*Inst.* 5.8.3). "As soon as they begin to be angry, to feel favorably disposed, to hate or to pity, they begin to take a personal interest in the case ...; the judge, when overcome by his emotions, abandons all attempt to enquire into the truth of the arguments, is swept along by the tide of passion and yields himself unquestioning to the torrent" (6.2.6; cf. 6.2.3; 12.10.62) "Pity alone may move even a strict judge" (4.1.14).

semantic field of ethics, there is a focus on the following; a) The sin of the opponents (ἁμαρτία – vv. 21, 24, 34; see also v. 46) is concretely expressed in their unbelief in Jesus (vv. 24, 45) and consequently in their lying about him (vv. 48, 52, 55 – see especially ψεύστης) and even wanting to kill him (vv. 37, 40 – ἀποκτείνω; see also vv. 20, 59). These are all things that the devil does (8:44). b) The programmatic phrase in 8:12 with ethically related words like ἀκολουθέω[38] and περιπατέω[39] sets an ethical tone for what is to follow. There are several positive ethical references, like doing (ποιέω – vv. 28, 29) what the Father requires. In a similar vein there is a positive reference to the works or behaviour of Abraham (v. 39 – τὰ ἔργα ... ἐποιεῖτε). The proposition that a child does what his father does (vv. 38, 41) is basic to the ethical training of a child. Keeping/holding to the word of Jesus (μείνητε ἐν τῷ λόγῳ τῷ ἐμῷ – v. 31, see also 5:38; τὸν ἐμὸν λόγον τηρήσῃ – vv. 51, 52) implies behaving in accordance with what Jesus taught and determines the actions of those who hold to the word. Love (ἀγαπάω – v. 42), giving honor (τιμάω – vv. 49, 50)/ glorifying (δοξάζω – v. 54) or dishonoring (ἀτιμάζω – v. 49) somebody, were all ethically loaded actions in ancient times. Active knowledge about the "law" (νόμος – v. 17) is shown. The frequent references to ἀληθής / ἀλήθεια (as contrast to ψεύστης, see also v. 44) in chapter 8 (vv. 14, 26, 32, 40, 45, 46; see also vv. 13 and 17 where it is used in a direct forensic context) give the witness and words of Jesus a positive ethical quality. God is true (v. 26) and since Jesus' witness is also true, it is aligned with God.

Because of the use of these words this text acquires an ethical nature. The conceptual issues are ethical. In the sense of introducing ethical topics, words and combinations of words (phrases and propositions) play a crucial role.

5.1.2 The Use of Literary Features related to Word Grammar

5.1.2.1 Irony

Irony is a literary device that is widely used,[40] but ironically difficult to define.[41] Duke,[42] following Muecke, points out that there is no watertight,

---

[38] Ἀκολουθέω is predominantly used to indicate disciples following Jesus with commitment, obviously with strong ethical implications for their lives.

[39] Περιπατέω is predominantly used in the Gospel to indicate people going around without any ethical undertones, especially Jesus (1:36; 6:19; 7:1; 10:23; 11:54) and in some cases other people like the healed man who must take his bed and go (5:8, 9, 11, 12) or Peter (21:18). In 6:66 the term is used with ethical undertones, where some of his followers decide not to "walk with him" any more, based on what Jesus asked from them.

[40] Paul D. Duke, *Irony in the Fourth Gospel* (Atlanta, Ga.: Westminster John Knox, 1985), 2–3 warns against undisciplined discoveries of "irony" in a text revealing "more

comprehensive definition of irony, but nevertheless suggests the following definition of irony: "irony as a literary device is a double-leveled literary phenomenon in which two tiers of meaning stand in some opposition to each other and in which some degree of unawareness is expressed or implied."[43]

Basic to this description is the fact that the reader (implicit or real) shares some knowledge with the implicit author. The character who utters these particular words, however, is not aware of this additional knowledge that will shed a different light on what is said. In a certain sense, what is said is true, but not in the sense that it is meant or intended by the speaker. This results in the speaker speaking and acting in an inappropriate, erroneous and often humorous way. An important point to note is that "virtually all irony is indirect communication, inviting the observer into some initiative of perception."[44] Irony expects the reader to participate in and indeed draws him into this two level communication, based on his superior knowledge of what is being said.[45] This influences readers cognitively and emotionally in their relationship to what is being said.

This brings us to irony and its relationship to ethics in John 8. It becomes clear in 8:19 that there is a serious problem in the opponents' understanding of who Jesus is. This is exactly the knowledge the implicit (and real) reader shares with the implicit author and which makes irony possible. The opponents talk without understanding what they are *truly* saying. This becomes apparent when Jesus tells them that he is going away

---

creativity from the critic than from the author." He remarks, "Irony, it should be remembered, laughs at all pretensions, especially the pretension of claiming to have grasped irony" (4).

[41] The appearance of Duke's study on irony in John's Gospel gave the debate a new impetus, although this is by no way the first work on this topic. He was stimulated by R. Alan Culpepper, *Anatomy of the Fourth Gospel* (Philadelphia, Pa.: Fortress Press, 1983). It is called different things like a "form of misunderstanding" (Raymond E. Brown, *An introduction to the Gospel of John* [ed. Frances J. Moloney; New York, N.Y.: Doubleday, 2003], 290) or "a mode of revelatory language" (Gail R. O'Day, *Revelation in the Fourth Gospel: Narrative mode and theological claim* [Philadelphia, Pa.: Fortress Press, 1986], 31). Duke, *Irony* (n. 40), 8–10. shows that irony was known and effectively used in ancient times, both among the Greeks and Jews.

[42] Duke, *Irony* (n. 40), 13–17.

[43] Duke, *Irony* (n. 40), 18–21. distinguishes between many different types of irony, like stable and unstable, verbal or dramatic; it is not necessary to discuss this issue in full here.

[44] Duke, *Irony* (n. 40), 17.

[45] Andrew T. Lincoln, *Truth on trial: The lawsuit motif in the Fourth Gospel* (Peabody, Mass.: Hendrickson, 2000), 19 also locates irony in the frequent misunderstanding. He continues: "This way of structuring the narrative coaxes its readers into sharing the implied author's point of view about Jesus ..."

and that they cannot follow him. In 8:22 the opponents wonder whether Jesus is going to kill himself. This remark is usually seen as ironic.[46] What the opponents say (that Jesus is going to "kill himself") is true, but not in the sense they thought. He is going away and this is best interpreted in the light of 10:17–18 where Jesus lays down his own life. The opponents are not only unaware of their role in Jesus' death (see also 8:20, 59) but also that he would indeed lay down his life voluntarily (10:17–18). Seen in this light the statement of the opponents is ironic indeed (see also 8:27). This lack of understanding of Jesus' death will cause the opponents to die in their sin (8:21, 24) – indeed a strong ethical remark.

Ironically Jesus is also accused of being possessed by a demon (8:48).[47] The irony is that people who are accusing Jesus of being possesed by a demon are themselves without God (8:47) and are indeed children of the devil (8:44) blaming Jesus, who is from God (8:47). The irony lies in their lack of knowledge of their own status. The ethical implications are clear. In seeing Jesus as demon possessed disqualifies them from recognizing who Jesus is and they will therefore never come to the light (8:12). Accordingly, they will miss their chance of becoming children of God.

Irony is a mechanism that rhetorically invites choice and performance. By using irony here the reader is challenged to get involved in the narrative by siding with Jesus against his opponents who are characterized by their lack of knowledge. Recognizing Jesus for who he really is, is of course a basic ethical action, a prerequisite for becoming part of the family of God with all its consequences.

5.1.2.2 Contextual-semantic Influence and the Ethical Meaning of a Word: Murder or Execution? – The Use of ἀποκτείνω

The interpretative context has a very determinative influence on the meaning of a word's semantic (and therefore also its ethical) significance. The meaning of a word is (at least) determined by its potential (lexicographical meaning) and its meaning when used in a specific context (associative meaning determined largely from the co-text). Take the sentence: "They *killed* him." If this action was the result of a valid legal process, the action will be good, i.e. a valid execution. However, if there is no justifiable rea-

---

[46] Brown, *Introduction* (n. 41), 290; Duke, *Irony* (n. 40), 85–86.

[47] Jesus does not defend himself against the accusation that he is a Samaritan (8:48). This also seems to have an ironic tone, since he associated himself with Samaritans (chapter 4). Jesus' message is not only for the Jews (chapter 3) but also for the Samaritans (chapter 4) and therefore such slander does not affect Jesus – to the contrary he is a "Samaritan" in the sense that God loved the world and the Samaritans too. Everybody is welcome with him (see Duke, *Irony* [n. 40], 75).

son for the particular action and it was not done lawfully, it will be murder and therefore ethically extremely negative.

This happens in 8:37, 40. There it is remarked that the opponents want to kill (ἀποκτείνω) Jesus. When it is used by Jesus to refer to his opponents, this word is indeed negative – it amounts to *murder*, since that is the characteristic of the devil, their father whose will they seek (v. 44). However, there are indications in this text (v. 20, where there is reference to an arrest[48] – see also 7:30; 10:39; 11:57) and even more in the rest of the Gospel (11:53 – a decision of the council; 18:31) that the opponents see it as an execution.[49] The question is: is this an execution or a murder? In the end the reader is confronted with this very same question: murder or execution?

5.2 Breaks in the Structural Flow of the Argument
and their Ethical Implications: Openness/Open Spaces,
Discontinuous and Conflicting Dialogue

"*Openness*" in a text serves as provocation and invites participation from the implied reader.[50] Obviously the (correct and false) answer is implied but not given – the *implicature* (also a term borrowed from reception theorists) is there, but the realization of the meaning is "open." These are gaps in the narrative that provoke or tempt the reader into getting involved in the narrative world by filling those gaps. An example is found in the question whether Jesus' witness is true (8:18, 19, 21) while the Pharisees declare it as invalid (8:13); or Jesus being called a Samaritan, and again when he calls himself older than Abraham (8:48). *Discontinuous dialogue*[51] is related to this openness and is a helpful tool in identifying surprises in the dialogue, since it often functions in an incongruent manner.

---

[48] Οὐδεὶς ἐπίασεν αὐτόν – this phrase creates the idea of a lawful action by the opponents. In 11:57 the authorities give the green light for the arrest.

[49] Both 12:10 and 16:2 refer to decisions to kill people by the socially dominating group, which implies that the consequences for them are not juridical, therefore amounting to executions.

[50] See Motyer, *Your father* (n. 31), 118.

[51] Motyer, *Your father* (n. 31), 117 refers to the stylistic feature of "discontinuous dialogue," something that was identified by people like Stibbe, Warner, Jasper and Nuttall. Mark W. G. Stibbe, "The elusive Christ: A new reading of the Fourth Gospel," *JSNT* 44 (1991): 19–37, 28 mentions "the systematic absence of logical fit" within a particular discussion. This technique can be used in different ways, but Stibbe, "The elusive Christ" (see above), 28 refers to Nuttall who interprets it as a means of communicating mystery and deliberate transcendence. This lies more in the interpretation than in the technique itself, as Stibbe, "The elusive Christ" (see above), 117 also points out.

Motyer[52] mentions that the *unexpectedness* of Jesus' responses, the *sideways* logic creates breaks in the flow of the argument. This has the effect of throwing "the reader off balance" makes him look for the logic in the narrative, and thus compels him to become "involved in the text, adjusting the focus and pitch, negotiating the implications of discussions carried out under such odd conditions." [53]

This literary technique is, for instance, used with positive ethical impact in 8:30, 31. Many believed in Jesus (8:30) and then Jesus spoke to them (8:31). The following discussion with these "believing Jews" holds one surprise after another. The discussion gets more and more aggressive up to the point where Jesus calls these "believers" children of the devil (8:44) and they call him a Samaritan who is demon possessed (8:48). They even want to kill him in the end (8:59). However, if we accept the unity of the text, which I do, this tension in the text between believers who are eventually called children of the devil becomes functional. The reader is surprised and forced to rethink what is being said – this process is intensified with the increasing level of conflict in the narrative. But what should the reader rethink? – Obviously the answer would seem to be that the reader should consider why "believers" are not really children of God, but could be called children of the devil.

Conflicting dialogue, again, refers to statements within the same context that deal with the same issue yet communicate seemingly opposite things. This is, of course, a very effective rhetorical technique of drawing the reader's attention to a particular matter. The conflict in the text must be solved and the reader then considers possibilities for solving the tension created by the conflict. Let's look at the following example:

In 8:37 Jesus acknowledges that the opponents are children of Abraham, yet in 8:39–41 Jesus seems to deny that they are children of Abraham. They have another father. So, are they children of Abraham or not? Obviously, the two levels of reality hold the key to the solution of this tension. They are physically the children of Abraham, but through their behaviour they illustrated that on a spiritual level they actually have the devil as their father (41, 44). The spiritual level is of course the more important level. What therefore happened and should be accepted is that the opponents denied their physical ancestry. Their ethical behaviour serves as proof. Through conflicting dialogue the reader is not only challenged on a cognitive level to clearly understand the essence of the conflict but is also

---

[52] Motyer, *Your father* (n. 31), 117.

[53] See Stibbe, "The elusive Christ" (n. 51), 117; Walter Rebell, *Gemeinde als Gegenwelt: zur soziologischen und didaktischen Funktion des Johannesevangeliums* (Frankfurt am Main: Lang, 1987), 200–201.

drawn into becoming part of the conflict through a decision for or against Jesus. This again underlines the performative nature of the text.

The implications for the ethical dynamics are evident. Choosing Jesus' side is per implication an ethical act, since it is a choice for truth and life and not for death and lies. The choice itself *is* an action and *is* living in truth and walking in the light. "Openness" or discontinuity constantly creates opportunities for the reader to make these choices.

5.3 Discourse Grammar with Ethical Implications

5.3.1 Propositions and Proverbial Statements

The influence of the associative context/co-text on the meaning of words or phrases can barely be overestimated. But how does such a context/co-text come about in the construction of a text? One of the important rhetorical mechanisms used in chapter 8 is the use of propositions or proverbial statements. This chapter is packed with revelatory material that takes the form of propositions by Jesus. Obviously all these statements are functional and important. I want to point out that certain of these propositions form corner stones in the development of the argument. If you do not accept that proposition, the argument falls flat and becomes unconvincing. This means that through these propositions the framework is created for sustainable argumentation. Let us briefly look at *some* of these statements and their contribution to the ethical argument in this section.[54]

Proposition/and or proverbial expression	Contribution to context
v. 12: ἐγώ εἰμι τὸ φῶς τοῦ κόσμου· ὁ ἀκολουθῶν ἐμοὶ οὐ μὴ περιπατήσῃ ἐν τῇ σκοτίᾳ, ἀλλ' ἕξει τὸ φῶς τῆς ζωῆς.	a) Establishes the identity of Jesus in terms of the world and life – he is the source of light b) His ethical superiority is established c) Eternal life comes from him *Established fact: The ethical superiority of Jesus is established and authentic behaviour (walk in light) should be defined in terms of him.*
v. 14: ἀληθής ἐστιν ἡ μαρτυρία μου, ὅτι οἶδα πόθεν ἦλθον καὶ ποῦ ὑπάγω· ὑμεῖς δὲ οὐκ οἴδατε πόθεν ἔρχομαι ἢ ποῦ ὑπάγω.	Believers are ignorant of Jesus' origin and destination and can therefore not appreciate his judgment. *Dualism* is established – this forms the framework for understanding the ignorance of the opponents but also for Jesus' right to reveal and judge (see also vv. 16, 18, 21, etc.).

---

[54] Not all the statements Jesus makes will be considered, especially not all the statements he makes about himself. I will only select some of those that form a foundation of the argument.

v.23 ὑμεῖς ἐκ τῶν κάτω ἐστέ, ἐγὼ ἐκ τῶν ἄνω εἰμί· ὑμεῖς ἐκ τούτου τοῦ κόσμου ἐστέ, ἐγὼ οὐκ εἰμὶ ἐκ τοῦ κόσμου τούτου.

v. 28: καὶ ἀπ' ἐμαυτοῦ ποιῶ οὐδέν, ἀλλὰ καθὼς ἐδίδαξέν με ὁ πατὴρ ταῦτα λαλῶ.
v. 29: καὶ ὁ πέμψας με μετ' ἐμοῦ ἐστιν· οὐκ ἀφῆκέν με μόνον, ὅτι ἐγὼ τὰ ἀρεστὰ αὐτῷ ποιῶ πάντοτε.

The intense *relationship* between Jesus and the Father is established, pointing to the importance of Jesus' mission (see, for instance, also 42, 54, 55). -The obedience of Jesus, doing his Father's will is established and will serve as example for his disciples (see v. 38).

v. 38: ἃ ἐγὼ ἑώρακα παρὰ τῷ πατρὶ λαλῶ· καὶ ὑμεῖς οὖν ἃ ἠκούσατε παρὰ τοῦ πατρὸς ποιεῖτε.
v. 41: ὑμεῖς ποιεῖτε τὰ ἔργα τοῦ πατρὸς ὑμῶν.

The proverbial-like remark that a *child does what his father does* forms the basis for the rest of the argumentation that takes behaviour as indication of identity.

v. 44: ἐκεῖνος ἀνθρωποκτόνος ἦν ἀπ' ἀρχῆς καὶ ἐν τῇ ἀληθείᾳ οὐκ ἔστηκεν, ὅτι οὐκ ἔστιν ἀλήθεια ἐν αὐτῷ. ὅταν λαλῇ τὸ ψεῦδος, ἐκ τῶν ἰδίων λαλεῖ, ὅτι ψεύστης ἐστὶν καὶ ὁ πατὴρ αὐτοῦ.

The *devil* is defined according to his basic characteristics. These characteristics are used to evaluate the behaviour of the opponents and identify them as being of the devil and not of God.

The following should be noted:

a) Without the proverbial-like statement about a child that should act like his father (8:38, 41), the argumentation that a person's identity can be established through his behaviour would not make sense. This is the major proposition on which the ethical argument in this section is built.

b) Without defining the characteristics of the devil by way of proposition (8:44), it would have been difficult to identify the behaviour of the opponents as devilish.

c) The "ethical atmosphere" of who is right is established by the proverbial-like expression in 8:12. Jesus is the light and what he says, is thus the truth. This immediately elevates Jesus to a higher moral level. In light of this remark his further remarks about himself become plausible and carry authority.

The rationale of these basic ethical propositions is not argued in this section, but assumed. They can be proposed because Jesus the "light of this world" proposes them or because they are commonly accepted knowledge (like the son copying his father). The ethical tone within the context of the section is therefore established through basic statements presented as propositions or proverbial statements. If one agrees with these notions one cannot deny the logic of the argument.

5.3.2 Characterization

5.3.2.1 Functionality of Characterization

Culpepper[55] did some groundbreaking work in the Johannine field of characterization by emphasizing the importance of characters and their symbolic value in a narrative. Culpepper[56] remarks: "The characters, who illustrate a variety of responses, allow the reader to examine the alternatives. The shape of the narrative and the voice of the narrator lead the reader to identify or interact variously with each character ... readers may place themselves in the role of each character successively while searching for the response they will choose." This results in drawing the reader by default into the narrative by positioning himself. The author can thus manipulate (or at least try to manipulate) the reader through his positive or negative representation of characters.[57]

The presentation of characters in chapter 8 is varied and vivid. This is done in several ways, for instance, semantic dissonance, dualistic descriptions or contrasts, as well as examples. The people Jesus engages in dialogue are the Pharisees in the first section (8:12–30) and "believers" in the second section (8:31–59). The dialogue with the believers deals directly with their ethical behavior and how it is to be identified, while the dialogue with the Pharisees deals with witness and understanding (or not understanding) the witness.

The characterization is stylistically and semantically done in strong *dualistic fashion*. For instance, Jesus is presented as a divine (pre-existent) character who stands in a solid relationship with God, the Father, while the Pharisees are dynamically pictured as people from below who do not know God at all and therefore do not recognize Jesus because of misguided judgments (i.e., according to the flesh). The reader is not left with any doubt about what an association with any of the characters would entail. Dualism plays an important role in the sense that grey areas are completely excluded. This is part of the rhetorical strategy of the plot based on the ideology of the author. This brings us to the other dialogue partner, those who believed (8:30–31).[58]

---

[55] Culpepper, *Anatomy* (n. 41), *ad loc.*

[56] Culpepper, *Anatomy* (n. 41), 148.

[57] See Culpepper's study, *Anatomy* (n. 41, though not the first, but to my mind the most influential) that opened a floodgate of studies on characters and their influence on readers.

[58] There are other characters that function in a less prominent position in the dialogue, like God, Abraham, the disciples, and the devil. Each makes his own contribution to the narrative, but time does not allow further investigation.

In short, characterization is functional, not only in bringing out the nature of ethical behavior as a relational process, but also as motivating the reader to come to an ethical choice in favor of Jesus.

5.3.2.2 Vilification of Characters

Vilification[59] plays an important role in this section, supporting the thrust in the narrative to convince the (implicit) reader to accept Jesus and reject the alternative. Rhetorically this technique was aimed at discrediting people by dishonoring them.[60] In this way it encourages disassociation by the reader with particular people.[61]

The vilification against the opponents[62] is aimed at pointing to their real identity as sinners who are from below and are children of the devil; they are estranged from God and unwilling to believe Jesus. On the other hand the opponents also discredit Jesus because they are not really from God.[63] The implication for the reader is: With whom do you want to associate yourself and with whom do you want to dissociate yourself? Vilification encourages positive choice by showing the negative aspects of what should not be chosen.

---

[59] Vilification is not a stylistic technique but a rhetorical one. Different stylistic techniques (can) work together in order to discredit characters in a text.

[60] Andrie B. du Toit, "Vilification as pragmatic device in Early Christian epistolography," *Biblica* 75 (1994): 403–412; Heinrich Lausberg, *Handbuch der literarischen Rhetorik* (vol. 1; Munich: Max Hueber Verlag, 1960) 55, 61; 131–138; 205–206; 542; Bruce J. Malina and Jerome H. Neyrey, "Conflict in Luke-Acts: Labeling and Deviance Theory," in *The Social World of Luke-Acts: Models for Interpretation* (ed. Jerome H. Neyrey; Peabody, Mass.: Hendrickson, 1991), 100 remark: "Negative labels, in fact, are accusations of *deviance.* Behavior is deviant when it violates the sense of order or the set of classification which people perceive to structure their world." See also Bruce J. Malina and Richard L. Rohrbauch, *Social-science commentary on the Gospel of John* (Minneapolis, Minn.: Fortress Press, 1998), 33.

[61] Du Toit, "Vilification" (n. 60), 404; Luke T. Johnson, "The New Testament's anti-Jewish slander and the conventions of ancient polemic," *JBL* 108 (1989): 419–441.

[62] See: Opponents judge according to flesh (15); ... will die in their sin (21, 24); ... are from below/of this world (23); ... are not Abraham's children (39); ... have the devil as their father (44); ... are not of God (47); ... do not know God (54–55); ... are liars (55); ... do not want to believe Jesus (46).

[63] Jesus is a Samaritan (48); ... has a demon (48, 52); ... presumes he is greater than Abraham (53).

5.4 Imagery in Service of Ethics

5.4.1 The Imagery of Light[64] in Chapter 8

The ἐγώ εἰμι proclamation by Jesus in 8:12 is programmatic for what follows (even up to chapter 12). What concerns us here is the relationship between ethics and the metaphors of light/darkness and life.

5.4.1.1 The Use of the Metaphor of Light in 8:12

In 8:12 Jesus reveals himself as the light of/for the world,[65] and the "location" where the light is present in this world.[66] Those who stay close to him will have light and will walk in light and not in darkness.

But it is also stated in verse 12 that those who are close to him will have the light of life (ἕξει τὸ φῶς τῆς ζωῆς). Carson assumes that the phrase should be interpreted as "the light that produces life."[67] Jesus, as personified light, will also give life to people. Another possibility is to see the light as belonging to the life, that is, it shines where life is. To have the "light of life" implies that those who live/have life, will also have light to walk in,[68] and will therefore know how to live (act and relate) as children of God since those persons have eternal life. The context supports both interpretations,[69] although the evidence for the latter receives more support from the immediate context of chapter 8.

In the presence of Jesus, as light, one can see where to walk, yes, how to live.[70] Light represents the revelation to people concerning how to be-

---

[64] The imagery of light also occurs throughout the first part of the Gospel (1: 4, 5, 7, 8, 9; 3:19, 20, 21; 5:35; 8:12; 9:5; 11:9, 10; 12:35, 36, 46. See also Riedl, *Heilswerk* (n. 11), 298–299). Craig R. Koester, *Symbolism in the Fourth Gospel: Meaning, Mystery, Community* (Minneapolis, Minn.: Fortress Press, 1995), 123 calls it probably the most striking motif in the Gospel, but this is debatable. See also Alan F. Segal, *Two powers in heaven: early Rabbinic reports about Christianity and Gnosticism* (Leiden: Brill, 1977), 214; Brown, *Gospel* 1 (n. 11), 343 and Rudolf Schnackenburg, *Das Johannesevangelium, III. Teil, Kommentar zu Kap. 13–21* (Freiburg: Herder, 1977), *ad loc.*

[65] Both Bultmann, *Evangelium* (n. 15), 260 and Schnackenburg, *Johannesevangelium* (n. 64), 240 see τοῦ κόσμου as an objective genitive, or light for the world. See also Josef Blank, *Krisis: Untersuchungen zur johanneischen Christologie und Eschatologie* (Freiburg: Herder, 1964), 186–188.

[66] See Barrett, *Gospel* (n. 10), 337; Riedl, *Heilswerk* (n. 11), 299. This is also the implication of the saying in 9:5, where Jesus says that while he is in the world, he is the light of the world (ὅταν ἐν τῷ κόσμῳ ὦ).

[67] Carson, *Gospel* (n. 10), 338.

[68] See 10:27; 12:26 and read 1:37–43 with 21:19–22.

[69] In 10:10 and 11:25–26 Jesus is indeed described as the giver of life.

[70] Lindars, *Gospel* (n. 19), 86 gives a broad description of light as total enlightenment, both intellectually and religiously. Joseph N. Sanders and Brian A. Mastin, *A commentary on the Gospel according to St John* (London: Black, 1968), 72 sees light in

have (live) as a member of those who have life, in other words, who belong to God's family.

5.4.1.2 The Imagery of Light and Life in Service of Communicating Ethical Material in Chapter 8

As was already mentioned, 8:12 is programmatic for what is to follow. Interestingly, none of the key words (life[71], light[72] or darkness[73]) are used again in chapter 8, although they are all used in subsequent chapters. This does not mean that 8:12 is not thematically linked to the rest of chapter 8. The contrast between the two ways of living (light and darkness) is programmatic in the rest of chapter 8, since there is a contrast between those who have life (will never see death) and those who will die in their sin. The metaphorical language, expressing the same message, changes from light to familial language, heralded by the use of the familial metaphor of life in 8:12.

It was substantially argued elsewhere that ζωή is a key term representing familial language in this Gospel.[74] To have life implies being part of the family of God or being a child of God, since one is born into this family (1:13; 3:3, 5). Jesus is the light of life, in other words, light makes it possible for people to see and act correctly. This basic argument in 8:13–15. dealing with the relationship between identity and ethics is based on familial imagery. A son obeys his father, seeks to fulfil the desires of the father (vv. 29, 44) and acts as his father does (vv. 38, 41). This is typical of ideal sonship in ancient times. Jesus is of course the prime and ideal example of such sonship (8:19, 26, 28, 29, 38, 40, 49, 55). The example Jesus sets is that of an obedient son that "copies" his father in order to honor and please him. His words and deeds are completely in line with what his Father does and says. He confirms the basic proposition that a child does what his father does (38). He reveals the words and deeds of God that are true (vv. 14, 16, 26, 40, 45, 46). Moreover, the person who keeps Jesus' words (vv. 31, 51 – in other words, staying close to the light) shows that he is Jesus' disciple (v. 31). Such a person will never see death (v. 51). If a person associates with the Son, the Son will make him free of sin or dark-

---

terms of revelation, while Alfred Plummer, *The Gospel according to S. John* (Cambridge: Cambridge University Press, 1929), 66 describes it as "intellectual and moral." Archibald M. Hunter, *The Gospel according to John* (The Cambridge Commentary on the New English Bible; Cambridge: Cambridge University Press, 1975), 17 again refers to "moral and spiritual illumination."

[71]   Life is used in chapters 10:10, 28; 11:25; 12:25, 50, following chapter 8.

[72]   This word is picked up in chapters 9:5; 11:9, 10; 12:35, 36, 46.

[73]   This term is again used in 12:35, 46.

[74]   Van der Watt, *Family* (n. 8), 201–245.

ness.[75] The message is thoroughly ethical. A child follows his father – as an example Jesus follows his Father and those who have life (are children of God) should follow the example of Jesus. Those who do not belong to Jesus walk in darkness and will die in their sin. Jesus is the ultimate ethical example for believers to follow – a child does what his father does. Jesus sets the example which should be followed by his disciples. The ethical implications are clear: in this framework the major task of the child of God is obedience to the will and desires of God as they are revealed through Jesus. The imageries of light and family serve as the interpretative framework for communicating the above-mentioned ethical material.

5.4.2 Forensic Imagery with a Performative Function

One of the major literary features in the Gospel is the use of forensic[76] language.[77] This is an effective way of convincing people, since the forensic process involves people and their views and eventually judgment on a particular issue. What is of interest is of course the performative nature of these forensic passages.

The author uses a forensic[78]-like narrative[79] which, with the exception of four asides (vv. 20, 27, 30, 59), is constructed in the form of a dialogue

---

[75] There are also other remarks expressed in filial language: as the Father taught Jesus (v. 28 – a familial expression of moral education) Jesus also teaches (v. 20). Jesus identifies himself as the one who came from the Father, witnessing about the truth, which the Father substantiates (vv. 13–19). He is the one who reveals the Father's will to them, although some do not want to accept it (for instance, 8:23–28, 34–38, 45–47, 55). The revelation of Jesus' self-identity is emphasized, to indicate that he really is the light.

[76] The *term "forensic"* should be qualified. Technically, it covers all matters pertaining to the law court (Mairi Robinson [ed.], *Chambers 21st Century Dictionary* [Edinburgh: Chambers Harrap, 1996], 518; Philip B. Gove, *Webster's Third New International Dictionary of the English Language* [Springfield: Merriam-Webster, 1981], 889). John uses those matters selectively. In the sections in John where forensic material is found the emphasis falls more on the arguments about the actions and person of Jesus. In the end, he appears before the High Priest and Pilate and thus the focus shifts to penal law.

[77] Jerome H. Neyrey, "The trials (forensic) and tribulations (honor challenges) of Jesus: John 7 in Social Science Perspective," *BTB* 26 (1996): 107–124, 107; Lincoln, *Truth* (n. 45), 22 even go so far as to maintain that the way the motif is used in the Gospel, encourages the reader to "view the narrative, as a whole, from the perspective of a trial." He identifies explicit occurances of the trial motif in 5:19–47 (vv. 22, 24, 27, 29–39, 45), 8:12–59 (vv. 13–18, 26, 50), also 2:25; 3:11, 17–19, 26–28, 32, 33; 4:39, 44; 7:7, 14–52; 9:39. See also the Advocate (14:16, 26; 15:26, 27; 16:7–11; 21:24, and obviously, 18:1–19:42. Lincoln, *Truth* (n. 45), 170) even wants to describe the genre of the Gospel as "a testimony or defense speech in a trial." Though he acknowledges that the genre of the narrative is indeed an ancient biography, he argues that it is a biography dominated by the motif of a trial.

[78] An important question is which legal system underlies the Johannine narrative? In Van der Watt and Voges, "Metaforiese elemente" (n. 18) it is argued that in many cases

with questions and counter questions (8:19, 22, 25, 33, 43, 46, 48, 53, 57). This dialogical pattern with all the repetitions "forces itself upon the reader, reinforces the sense of a cut-and-thrust debate, and makes it impossible to avoid taking sides."[80] The performative nature[81] of the text is one of the most evident rhetorical characteristics of the dialogue in chapter 8.

It will be illustrated that it is up to the reader to weigh, deliberate and decide certain issues, based on the available information, but also to do so based on what is left unsaid ("open spaces"). The reason why it is argued that the reader is drawn into the text is because forensic procedures create certain expectations, namely, that there would be an accused, witnesses, an accuser, a judge, a charge, judgment, etc. Judgment is, for instance, not given explicitly in the text and is left open for the reader to say, "yes, I concur" or not. Such words are performative in the sense that it would place the reader in the judge's seat. Jesus does not pronounce direct explicit judgment, though he interprets the position of his opponents as being without God (8:47). The assumption is that the implied reader should take sides.

There seem to be multiple juridical procedures taking place simultaneously in chapter 8, depending on the perspective taken.

---

the Jewish legal system seems to be basic to the argument, although the Roman system is also present, especially in the Pilate narrative (chapters 18–20). It may be assumed that where Roman influence was strong for military and administrative reasons (see Thomas W. Mason, *Ethics and the Gospel* [London: SCM, 1974], 27) the same applied to the Roman legal system. The Gospel was indeed addressed to a diverse group of people that most probably included Greeks, Jews, Romans and even Samaritans (see Marian Maye Thompson, "John, the Gospel of," in *Dictionary of Jesus and the Gospels* (ed. Joel B. Green and Scott McKnight [Downers Grove, Ill.: Intervarsity, 1992], 368–383, 371). It would therefore be fair to assume that the readers were acquainted with Jewish as well as Roman law (Frances Lyall, *Slaves, Citizens, Sons: Legal Metaphors in the Epistles* [Grand Rapids, Mich.: Zondervan, 1984], 24–25, 225–226), even if most of them most probably belonged to the lower classes (see Otto Eger, *Rechtsgeschichtliches zum Neuen Testament* [Basel: Friedrich Reinhardt, 1919], 29–31; Raphael Taubenschlag, *The Law of Greco-Roman Egypt in the Light of the Papyry: 332 B C – 640 A D* [Milan: Cisalpino-Goliardica, 1972], 1–55; William E. Ball, *Saint Paul and the Roman Law* [Edinburgh: T&T Clark, 1901], 2 – what they say of Paul equally applies to the Johannine situation). This means that one should not think of a single judicial system, but these systems overlapped.

[79] Μαρτυρέω (vv. 13, 14, 18); μαρτυρία (vv. 13, 14, 17); κρίνω (vv. 15, 16, 26, 50); κρίσις (v. 16); πιάζω (v. 20); νόμος (v. 17); perhaps ἐλέγχω as accusation (v. 46) and ὑψόω as execution (v. 28). The effort to throw stones at him (v. 59) might also imply execution that usually followed a verdict.

[80] Motyer, *Your father* (n. 31), 144.

[81] Obviously the reaction of readers cannot be predicted, but the communicative signs in the text which help constituting the implied reader provide some indication of the direction in which the implied author intends the communication to develop.

Juridical procedure 1: the Jewish opponents reject the witness of Jesus (8:12) and pass a verdict that Jesus' witness cannot be accepted on the basis of an assumed proposition that self-witness is not acceptable according to law (8:13). Jesus indeed calls them judges in 8:15 but questions the criteria used in their judgment. The judgment of the Pharisees is impaired, since they use fleshly, earthly criteria (8:15). Jesus uses different criteria, based on his origin and mission (8:16).

Juridical procedure 2: in defense Jesus confirms himself as the eschatological judge because of his relationship with the Father (5:16, 30). As judge he can also evaluate the value of his own witness (8:14). In the same context where he is the accused (8:13) he also refers to himself as judge. This clearly indicates the presence of a second forensic process where roles are reversed. Jesus has two strong witnesses; himself and another witness, namely, his Father, and that makes two trustworthy witnesses (8:18).[82] The Pharisees, however, do not accept his witness and do not know or recognize the second witness, because they do not know God. They do not recognize the second juridical procedure in which they are the accused and Jesus and his Father are the judges (8:16, 24).[83]The accusers of the first process become the accused in the second and vice versa.

It must be noted that this section does not portray judgment in a neutral way as if any verdict is morally the correct verdict. The moral high ground of Jesus' judgment is established in 8:16, and reconfirmed in 8:50: God, the Father, is also named as judge, with Jesus. In a Jewish context God is regarded as the supreme eschatological judge, and in 5:22 he shares this judgment with Jesus. By accepting the judgment of Jesus, the eschatological judge, God, is also accepted. This places the forensic nature of this section as well as the outcome on a completely different level.

Juridical procedure 3: there is a third juridical procedure, involving the reader. The judgment for or against Jesus is not explicitly given at the end, although the implicit (and real) reader realizes what the judgment would be. If you are not on the side of God, you will be judged. If you are on his side, you will not see death, but live, or in terms of 8:12: "they will not walk in darkness, but will have the light of life," a direct and clear ethical statement. Neutrality does not exist.

The implied reader is thus maneuvered into the position of a judge, especially through the intense dialogue offering arguments from and in fa-

---

[82] Trustworthy witnesses were crucial in both Jewish and Roman juridical procedures.

[83] Lincoln, *Truth* (n. 45), 25 also emphasizes that "the Jews" and Pilate in the end turn out to be the people on trial.

vour of both sides.[84] This implies and indeed constitutes a third juridical procedure in which the reader becomes the judge. The "accused" are Jesus and his opponents and the issue is the true identity of these two groups in light of their relationship with the true God. The reader is provided with the necessary information to make a judgment. Paradoxically, the reader also comes under judgment through his or her own judgment (this can indeed be seen as a fourth juridical procedure). The reader is simultaneously the judge and the judged. By making the verdict he positions himself and actually pronounces a verdict over himself. What the reader decides as a judge, will determine the reader's own fate – either he will not see death but will have eternal life (vv. 12, 51–52) or he will die in his sins (vv. 21, 24). In the end the decision of the reader can also be seen as a witness – for or against Jesus. This means that the role of the reader alternates from judge, to accused, to witness, the outcome depending on the decision of the reader.

6. Some Concluding Remarks

The investigation into the relationship and interaction between ethics and language in John's Gospel, focusing on chapter 8, resulted in a rich and varied picture.[85] What became clear is that John integrates a wide variety of language features and techniques in a symbiotic way in order to attain his communicative goal(s).

The following remarks are aimed at pointing out the most important conclusions that could be made regarding ethics and its relation with language in John:

---

[84] By choosing a forensic setting, certain expectations are created: there must be an accused and accusations, there must be witnesses, there must be deliberation (reasons) and there must be an outcome (judgment). Especially the latter is important for our purposes. A judgment must be made. If the judgment is not given in the text itself, the reader (both implicit and presumably the real reader) becomes the judge. This is simply the performative nature of forensic language. Reception theorists refer to *implicature*, which means that there is an "open space" in the information flow of the text which must be filled by the reader.

[85] Although chapter 8 is a central text in John's ethical argumentation and most of the language features John uses are found in this dense text, there are features used by John that do not occur in chapter 8.

a) Two central ethical truths are formative to the argumentative structure of the Gospel:

The structure of the argument is based on the assumption of the *interrelatedness of identity and behavior.* This is stated in 8:12 already where following Jesus (an expression of relationship) will result in not walking in darkness but rather walking in light (an expression of behavior). There is a strong focus on Jesus' identity based on his relationship with the Father (8:14, 18, 19, 21, 23, 26–29). The argument consequently shifts focus to deeds and the origin of deeds – people do as their fathers do (8:38, 41). This is exactly what Jesus was arguing about himself up to this point (8:28–29). The forensic arguments in this section are based on exactly this assumption – identity determines deeds and deeds show identity. Deeds are determined by identity (8:39, 42). That is why Jesus could identify the identity of the opponents (8:47) based on their deeds.

Jesus is presented in a refined way in this argument as the *example* to follow to his followers. He knows his identity (8:14) and that the Father is acting with him (8:16, 18). Through his behavior people can "see the Father" (8:19 per implication in the light of 14:6–8). Jesus always does what is pleasing to the Father (8:28–29) and declares what he has heard from the Father (8:26). The transition is in 8:38 where Jesus compares his own behavior to that of the opponents. Both follow their respective fathers. A follower of Jesus will act like Abraham and Jesus, following the truth that set them free (8:32, 39–40) and listening to the words of God (8:47, 52). They will act according to the words of God, like Jesus does (8:28–29, 43, 47).

b) Language and ethical expression:

A clear and founded definition of ethics in a particular document as well as proper analytical categories are necessary prerequisites for even starting the analysis of the ethical nature of texts and the language used. We have seen that the ethical system of John proved to be primarily relational, grounded in Christology, which implies that material relevant for analysis can be found wherever there is reference to an acceptance of Jesus, or where the language touches on this issue in any way. Distortions would result from any attempt at forcing other definitions of ethics onto the text of John.

Literary features abound in this dense text (John 8) with ethics as a main theme. Different language features on all levels were used in this informative and performative communicative process.

Most literary features were not ethical in themselves, but simply a means of attaining a specific communicative goal in order to facilitate communication. As such they are not ethical, but neutral and would function in the same way, whether it is communication about ethical matters or something else. Features like irony, the use of propositions or asides, discontinuous of conflicting dialogue, "open spaces," etc. all have functional value in the process of communication, but are not ethical as such.

Some literary features are also not specifically ethical, but are specifically suited for ethical argumentation. For instance, forensic language, of which dialogue is a part, can easily be aligned to deal with two contrasting positions, like what is right or wrong. It is evident that certain genres are more suitable for presenting ethical material than others. John has chosen to use forensic and argumentative dialogical genres that suited his aim of convincing people to believe in Jesus. Obviously, if he had a different view of ethics and a decision for Jesus was not so important, he could have used a different type of genre. Again, this underlines the importance of the relationship between form and content/message.

c) It seems that most of the literary features are functional without being specifically ethical. They are not necessarily dependent on the content but represent a strategy for presenting the material, for instance, discontinuous dialogue or "open spaces" want to draw attention, propositions want to inform, vilification wants to influence, examples want to educate, etc. They each contribute in different ways to the communication process:

Informative nature (presenting information): there are features that want to draw the attention of (and, of course, influence) the reader, like some uses of proverbial-like expressions, imagery, vilification.

Performative nature: there are features that actively invite participation and give the text its performative nature, for instance, forensic and dialogical language presented in an inconclusive way, so that the reader is expected to make a decision. Features like discontinuous or conflicting dialogues, "open spaces," chiasm or repetition usually also fall under this category. It became clear that many of the literary features used in this section contribute to the performative nature of the text and therefore functionally assist in actively promoting an ethical decision in favour of Jesus.

Functionally the literary features do not operate on the same level and with the same intention. For this reason they could be used in symbiosis, cumulatively adding to the total communicative effect of the text. One can speak of a *total communication strategy* and interpreters should approach the text as such. This is because a text like this one has different requirements, namely, to inform, convince, motivate, change opinion, etc. Different literary features are therefore employed to facilitate the different requirements.

d) The next step is to ask what exactly in the language process makes this text an ethical text? Is "ethics" inherent to the language, or is the ethical nature derived from somewhere else? Up to now it was argued that most language features are functionally "neutral" and not inherently ethical.

Informing

Through the surface level of the text: it seems to me that the building blocks in making the context ethical is the most basic element of language, namely, the words or phrases used. Words, phrases (also in the form of propositions or proverbs) like, *doing* what the father desires or requires, to *follow* Jesus, to *walk* in darkness, to *keep* words, to *kill*, to *lie*, to *believe*, to *love*, etc. are semantically related to the idea of behaviour that is defined as an ethical category. The basic subject matter relates to ethical issues. Using these words in association with other words also belonging to the semantic field of behaviour strengthens the ethical nature of the passage. The way in which the material is presented, namely, by way of irony, or forensic or dialogical structure, etc. implies molding the basic ethical material to communicate as effectively as possible. Content and strategy should be distinguished. The content, determined by words and phrases, is determinably ethical, while the strategy is not ethical as such.

Through reader recognition (outside the text): a second aspect that should be considered when one is asked what makes a text ethical, is the social context, or the social expectations of the readers. Words are social phenomena and work on the basis of social conventions. Words or phrases will be identified as ethical if they fit into what is socially perceived as ethical. Being able to identify the "language codes" adequately is crucial. If a person is not able to identify the social value of a language code like irony, or of the meaning of light or life in John, loss of understanding will be considerable. In this case figurative language originates from familial contexts, the contexts of light and darkness, slavery, juridical procedures and if the reader is not able to interpret them within their intended social framework, the reader's understanding will suffer. For instance, the proposition that a child will do what his father does is a socially determined statement. It only serves as an effective ethical expression because it is a socially accepted practice. Here "external social knowledge" is needed for correct interpretation. The text as narrative also generates its own shared (internal) social knowledge that determines interpretative perspectives within the text. For instance, the question whether killing Jesus amounts to murder or execution depends on the internal perspective of the text itself. The information given in the text determines the ethical quality of the expression. This takes us back to the discussion about the assumption of what ethics in this particular Gospel is, or how it is conceptualized. Words, fitting into that conceptual framework of what is ethical and what is not will add ethical value to the discussion.

Performative nature

In our definition of ethics in John it was pointed out that the decision for Christ is the basic ethical action according to the Gospel. Performative language aimed at bringing about such a decision therefore stands directly in service of ethics. In this context it contributes to ethical actions, but is not ethical language as such. A distinction between the literary technique and the effect of the technique should be made.

e) Form and content/message are closely connected. However, by observing the use of language in John 8 it becomes clear that the message enjoys precedence over the form, meaning that the form can be changed to serve a better communication of the message, but the message is not adapted in order to facilitate a better, or aesthetically more acceptable, image or expression. For instance, 8:12 starts with the light/darkness imagery, but through the connection with the concept of life ("light of life") it moves to the familiar imagery in the rest of chapter 8. The slavery imagery is also introduced to move to the child imagery (children of Abraham). Forensic imagery is used performatively and together these imageries all contribute towards motivating readers in line with the ideology of the author. Form has functional use aimed at conveying the message more effectively.

As the Father has sent me, I send you:

Towards a missional-incarnational Ethos in John 4

Kobus Kok[1]

1. Introduction

A few remarks with regard to the method and presuppositions of this paper seem in order. First, it will be explained how the terms ethics and ethos are to be understood, what serves as the basis or motivation thereof and how it functions in the macro-narrative of the Gospel of John. Thereafter it will be illustrated how the narrative of the Samaritan woman in the Gospel of John could be understood as a narrative of moral language with specific reference to what I would like to call a *missional-incarnational ethos*. Here the term incarnational is metaphorically used to refer to the concrete crossing of boundaries in cultural perspective and the concrete embodiment of 'n lived Christ-like ethos that flows from an understanding of God's mission in the world (*Missio Dei*).[2] It will also be argued how this particular micro-narrative is integrated with the ethical dimension of the macro-narrative of the Gospel as a whole and in which way it motivates behaviour and creates a particular symbolic universe which revolves around the continuing missional motive that started with the mission of Jesus.

By way of introduction it could be agreed with Pierre Lévy[3] that the language of ritual, religion, morality, law, economic regulations etc., are all social mechanisms for virtualizing violence, and dealing with relations of force, impulse, instinct and desires. Therefore, it could thus be argued that moral language could be seen as a virtualization of social relations in that language in itself is symbolic, virtually referring to particular realities,

[1] Kobus (Jacobus) Kok (Ph.D.) is a senior lecturer in the department of New Testament Studies at the University of Pretoria, South Africa. Some parts of the present chapter were published as an article by Jacobus Kok and Cornelius J.P. Niemandt, "(Re)discovering a missional incarnational ethos," *HvTSt* 65/1 (2009): 502-507 (see also http://www.hts.org.za/index.php/HTS/article/viewFile/274/705).
[2] Cf. David Jacobus Bosch, *Believing in the Future: Toward a Missiology of Western Culture* (Valley Forge, Pa.: Trinity Press, 1995).
[3] See Pierre Lévy, *Collective Intelligence: Mankind's Emerging World in Cyberspace* (trans. Robert Bononno; New York: Plenum Press, 1997).

but removed from the material reality thereof. Take for instance the reality of legal contracts. A particular desired or preferred reality is constructed through language and terms which are embedded within a particular juridical language and meaning system. A virtual, desired reality is constructed and behaviour is directed towards the actualization of the desired state by the use of inherent value systems, limitational structures, borders, contractional expectations, penalties of misconduct etc. – in other words a particular virtual reality is constructed with its own norms, expected behaviours, limitations, borders, etc.

In the same way, moral language entails a particular ordering of beliefs, norms and behaviour in terms of a particular constructed reality which is related to but in reality removed from actual reality. In the same instance we find moral or ethical ideas which are expressed through the use of narratives in John's Gospel. In the telling of the story, the ethical basis and motivation of particular behaviour (ethos) becomes clear, against the background of the macro-narrative of the Gospel. By using language to construct a story, the evangelist moved into the realm of virtuality in the sense that a particular narrative world is created that might or might not correspond with actual reality. In constructing such a narrative world, the writer is creating a fictive or virtual world which has the experiential power to transform the actual world in any given time in the future, by changing perceptions, challenge norms (ethics) and direct behaviour (ethos) by firstly establishing a new basis of motivation. In order for the basis of motivation to change norms and behaviour, a particular world-view should to a certain extent be deconstructed and a new world-view constructed, which inherently entails a new view of God, self and others which will be actualized by creating a new symbolic universe. In John's Gospel for instance, Jesus' message is set against a particular narrative background which is *inter alia* created by using the metaphor and story of a King (cf. 1:49; 12:13, 15; 19:14, 19, 21), his Son the Agent (17:21, 23, 25; 20:21) and a new family which came to be (cf. 1:12; 8:44),[4] which will be the main approach taken in this article.

---

[4] Cf. Jan G. van der Watt, *Family of the King: Dynamics of Metaphor in the Gospel according to John* (Biblical Interpretation Series 47; Leiden: Brill, 2000). The metaphor of the King and his family is not the only way of understanding the plot of the Gospel of John within the framework of a narrative reading thereof. In this regard there are also other scholars who contributed much to the narrative understanding of John's Gospel and take somewhat different approaches to the understanding of the plot of the gospel. Some of the most prominent scholars will be mentioned: cf. Alan Culpepper, *Anatomy of the Fourth Gospel: A study in literary designs* (Philadelphia, Pa.: Fortress Press, 1983); Mark W. G. Stibbe, *John as storyteller: Narrative criticism and the Fourth Gospel* (New York: Cambridge University Press, 1992), who gives a good history of development with regards to the narrative reading of John in his first chapter. In his book Stibbe rightly

In the Gospels, the virtual world the writer created in a micro-narrative for instance has an intra-textual relational correspondence to the macro-narrative of the Gospel. Closer investigation reveals that this relational correspondence exists on the intra and inter-textual levels with regards to ethics, (which could be understood as particular norms built on a particular basis which constitutes the motivation for the norm) and on the level of ethos (which could be understood as the consequent appeal to a lived or particularized ethics).

2. Basis, Ethics, Ethos, and Context

A distinction could be made between ethos and ethics.[5] The term ethics is to be understood as the values we live by, on the basis (motivation) of how we understand ourselves, our relationship to God and the world and the values, rules and principles we defer from that. Ethos is to be understood as the practical way we live out our ethics (*Lebensstil*[6] – practical life style) in a given socio-historical and cultural context.[7] As Christians, the

---

argues that John's Gospel is a multi-story phenomenon that calls for a multi-disciplinary narrative methodology. Consequently he constructed a method which looks at John's narrative at the level of text, context and pre-text – in other words, the surface level of the narrative, the social context and lastly the historical reference, sources and tradition of the narrative. Stibbe illustrated that narrative criticism which is only concerned with the "technical" literary issues of characterization, plot and structure restricts the functions of the narrative, especially when one takes the possibility of the narrative for the social reconstruction of history. To this I would like to add the fact that it also has the potential to influence the identity, ethics, and ethos of the church in the twenty first century by reshaping or realigning the church to the "way of Jesus and his earliest followers." See also Andries G. van Aarde, "Narrative criticism applied to John 4:43–54," in *Text and Interpretation: New approaches in the criticism of the New Testament* (ed. Patrick J. Hartin and Jacobus H. Petzer; Leiden: Brill, 1991), 101–128; cf. also Sjef van Tilborg, *Imaginative love in John* (Leiden: Brill, 1993), who notes that there are different exegetical possibilities to the reading of John and that narrative reading is but one possible choice. In his reading Van Tilborg investigated that way in which the important Johannine concept of love is given form in a narrative manner and in which way the characters in the story realized this pivotal element in John (see Van Tilborg, *Imaginative love in John*, 241–247).

[5]   Cf. Jan G. van der Watt, ed., *Identity, Ethics and Ethos in the New Testament* (BZNW 141; Berlin: de Gruyter, 2006), v–ix.

[6]   Leander E. Keck, "Das Ethos der Frühen Christen," in *Zur Soziologie des Urchristentums* (ed. Wayne A. Meeks; TB 62; Munich: Kaiser, 1979), 13–36, 13–26 understands ethos as: "Lebensstil einer Gruppe oder Gesellschaft."

[7]   Jan G. van der Watt, "Directives for the Ethics and Ethos Research Project" (Unpublished paper delivered at the Identity, Ethics and Ethos project meeting in Pretoria; University of Pretoria, South Africa, 2004), 2–3.

basis or motivation of our being is built on the basis of a particular understanding of God, the world and God's story for the world.

In John God loved the world (3:16), which is caught up in darkness, sin
and blindness (5:24; 9:41; 12:40), who in essence became evil children of
the devil (8:44). For this reason God sent his only Son so that those who
believe in him could have eternal life (3:16; 20:30–31) and become part of
a new family, the children of God (1:12). In John, soteriology also implies
re-socialization and entrance into a new social reality, which also serves as
the basis for the formulation of the believers' ethics. Therefore, a fundamental dialectic relationship exists between ethics and ethos. Conduct is a
result of identity and therefore ethos is always a result of ethics, rooted in a
particular understanding of the Universal Godly Narrative. Ethos is in other words the *Lebensstil* or conduct of those who share a common identity.
The understanding of ethics and ethos is a dynamic social process due to
its realization within a specific socio-historical context.[8] Van Rensburg explains it as follows: "[t]he basis motivates the ethics, which in turn is practiced as ethos, which receives approval and/or disapproval from society.
This may result in the ethos being reconsidered in the light of the basis,
and this either reinforces or reconstitutes specific behavior (ethos), etc."
The ethos also has a heuristic function in the sense that it refers to the ethics. In other words, to develop a missional-incarnational ethos, we have to
have a particular view of ethics, which is based on a particular understanding of God and his story with the world.

3. The Basis of Ethics and Ethos

Something of the reality of our world resonates with John's world-view in
the sense that he recognizes the reality of brokenness, destruction and dis-
connection in this world.[9] In John's theology the world is ruled by the

---

[8]   Fika J. van Rensburg, "Ethics in 1 Peter" (Unpublished paper delivered at the
Identity, Ethics and Ethos project meeting in Pretoria; University of Pretoria, South Africa, 2005), 3.

[9]   Rob Bell, *Velvet Elvis: Repainting the Christian Faith* (Grand Rapids, Mich.:
Zondervan, 2005). Rob Bell is of the opinion that much has changed over the centuries,
but that some things are quite *recognizable human* experiences that do not change over
time. If one looks at the normal cycles of life and death and phenomena like sorrow,
pain, brokenness, sin, destruction, love, hope, joy, peace, etc. – one finds a striking resemblance to the reality of life and certain similarities of experience across the spectrum
of cultures, religions and time. Of course one will find different meanings attached to
these typical life experiences, due to the diverse symbolic universes in particular cultures
and in different times (cf. the difference of the pre-modern period, the "*Aufklärung*" and

ἄρχων τοῦ κόσμου, the prince of this world (cf. 12:31). This prince is the father of all evil, a murderer from the beginning, one who steals and destroys and takes away life in abundance – he is the father of destruction, lies and murder since the dawn of time (cf. 8:44). In this he is not alone, for he has many children, who embody the lifestyle of their father (8:44), they are agents of the same destruction and in them there is no true love for God or the children of God to be found (5:42). Most people on earth are fundamentally caught up in a life situation of crisis and disorientation for they are spiritually dead (5:24), fundamentally lost (3:16), in desperate need for the life they lost or that they never really had. They are not only spiritually dead but also spiritually sick – for they are blind (9:41; 12:40), in desperate need of healing and restoration. The incarnation and mission of the Son is thus seen against the narrative background of this broken reality.

John's view of reality corresponds in some ways with our view of reality – it seems to be an accurate description of the way life is. We do not have to look far to see the destruction when we look in the eyes of women and children who have been abused by men, the victims of genocide, of war, of poverty, of indescribable acts of violence against humanity, even in the destruction of mother earth, global warming, etc. It seems that we still live in a reality filled with brokenness, desperately in need of healing and restoration.

John's Jesus incarnated into this world as God's Agent,[10] to restore life, to bring light, truth, faith, hope, restoration and reconciliation, to heal those who are spiritually blind (cf. 9:41; 12:40), to restore life in abundance (10:10) and reveal truth (1:18). After his death and his resurrection – the culminating restorative act[11] – he breathed over the disciples and they received the Spirit (20:22), became a new creation – equipped to become empowered agents, called to embody the same mission as the Son (20:21 – καθὼς ἀπέσταλκέν με ὁ πατήρ, κἀγὼ πέμπω ὑμᾶς). We are fundamentally

---

the scientific post modern period we currently live in). Still, one recognizes something similar in many instances, at least then on a purely hermeneutical level.

[10] Cf. Peder Borgen, "God's Agent in the Fourth Gospel," in *The Interpretation of John* (ed. John Ashton; London: SPCK, 1986), 67–78. Cf. 5:24, 37–38; 8:18, 42; 12:49; 14:24. Cf. also Van der Watt, *Family* (n. 4). See also Ruben Zimmermann, "Metaphoric Networks as Hermeneutic Keys in the Gospel of John: Using the example of the Mission imagery" in *Repetitions and Variations in the Gospel of John: Style, Text, Interpretation* (ed. Gilbert van Belle, Michael Labahn and Petrus Maritz; BETL 223; Leuven: Peeters, 2009), for a very good article on the missionary imagery in John, and in which way the mission imagery serves as an example of a coherence network.

[11] Cf. Jacobus Kok, *Siekte en Gebrokenheid teenoor Genesing en Restourasie in Johannes* (Ph.D. diss.; University of Pretoria: ETDs, 2008) for a thorough discussion of the resurrection as the culminating healing act in John.

called to become agents of healing and restoration in the world (*Weltoffen-heit*), to live the way of Jesus (*Gottoffenheit*).[12] In today's day and age we need to regain a missional-incarnational ethos with a heart for healing and restoration of a world caught up in brokenness and loss of true life. Maybe we might come to see something of this in the way Jesus restored the Samaritan woman who according to John's Gospel became the first missionary to the Samaritans, by looking through a new lens at an old story we have heard so many times before.

4. The Samaritans: a Story of Crisis, Disorientation, and Socio-religious Brokenness[13]

According to John the Pharisees have heard that Jesus was making and baptizing more followers than John (4:1–2). Jesus knew that the Pharisees had heard about him, and therefore left the unsafe Judea and went back to Galilee (4:3). On his way there he had[14] to go through Samaria and entered the town called Sychar, which is near the field Jacob gave to his son Joseph (4:5), and Jacob's well (4:6). Being tired and thirsty from the long exhausted trip, Jesus went and sat down beside Jacob's well, round about twelve o'clock noon (4:6). Jesus' disciples were not with him for they had gone to buy some food (4:8). At that very moment a Samaritan woman came to the well to gather some water and Jesus asked her to give him a drink (4:7). Surprised the Samaritan woman said to Jesus: πῶς σὺ Ἰουδαῖος

---

[12] For a discussion on the terms *Weltoffenheit* and *Gottoffenheit,* see Wolfhart Pannenberg, *Was ist der Mensch? Die Anthropologie der Gegenwart im Lichte der Theologie* (Göttingen: Vandenhoeck & Ruprecht, 1976), 5–13.

[13] Cf. Jonathan Campbell, *The way of Jesus: A journey of freedom for pilgrims and wanderers* (San Francisco, Calif.: Jossey Bass, 2005), 199: Campbell also uses the narrative of Jesus and the Samaritan woman as illustration of how Jesus broke through the major religious and cultural mores of his day. Ingrid Hjelm, "What do Samaritans and Jews have in common? Recent trends in Samaritan studies," in *Currents in Biblical Research* 3/1 (2004): 9–59, notes that "Apart from the later period of the Hasmonaean kingdom, Samaritans and Jews were always separate peoples who had either Gerizim or Jerusalem as their main cult place. While Jewish perspectives on Samaritan origin and history still prevail in recent research, future research will have to broaden the perspective and take into consideration Samaritan claims for authenticity in respect to origin, belief and traditions. These claims have recently been substantiated by excavations on Mount Gerizim, which have unearthed structures of a major Persian Period cult place that may date as early as the sixth century BCE. These finds, as well as finds of about 400 inscriptions and 13,000 coins, have just begun to be published." In her article Hjelm presents the most recent development in research on Samaritan history and literature, in order to offer a base for the necessary rewriting of both Samaritan and Jewish history.

[14] Cf. ἔδει in 4:4.

ὧν παρ' ἐμοῦ πεῖν αἰτεῖς γυναικὸς Σαμαρίτιδος οὔσης; οὐ γὰρ συγχρῶνται Ἰουδαῖοι Σαμαρίταις.

In Jesus' time Jews never spoke to Samaritans, for in the eyes of the Jews they were unclean, a people judged and rejected by God, a damned nation.[15] The deeply rooted antipathy and aversion between Jews and Samaritans goes back to the origins of the Samaritans as a mixed race, settled in the northern kingdom by the king of Assyria (see the account in 2 Kgs 17:24–41).[16] The crisis appeared round about 720 B.C.E. and intensified over the centuries.[17]

The fact that the Samaritans once were located at an ideal position of life possibilities within the Jewish symbolic universe, does not guarantee their current positioning[18] because in the time of Jesus they were seen as ritually impure.[19] Barrett rightly points to the fact that from the point of view of the purity laws of the Jews, "the daughters of the Samaritans are menstruants from their cradle (*Niddah* 4.1)."[20] Therefore all Samaritan women were viewed as unclean, and therefore also the utensils and vessels such a woman would hold. If Jesus would have drunk from such a vessel,

---

[15] The Samaritans nevertheless viewed themselves as true Israel, and heirs of the promises of God to Israel, and their version of the Pentateuch as the original one, direct from Moses.

[16] Cf. George R. Beasley-Murray, *John* (WBC 36; Waco, Tex.: Word Books, 2002), 60 (Electronic edition).

[17] Cf. Beasley-Murray, *John* (n. 16), 60; and especially Ferdinand Dexinger, "Limits of Tolerance in Judaism: The Samaritan Example," in *Jewish and Christian self-Definition* (vol. 2; ed. Ed P. Sanders et al.; London: SCM Press, 1981), 89–96, for a good discussion of the survey on this matter. For a recent updated bibliography of the Samaritans see e.g. Alan D. Crown and Reinhard Pummer, *A Bibliography of the Samaritans: Revised, Expanded and Annotated* (Atla Bibliography Series; 3rd ed.; Lanham, Md.: Scarecrow Press, 2005). John 4 and the story of Jesus and the Samaritan woman always played an important role in discussions of the relationship between Jesus (Christianity) and the Samaritans and much has been published on the matter: cf. Reinhard Pummer, "Einführung in den Stand der Samaritanerforschung," in *Die Samaritaner* (ed. Ferdinand Dexinger and Reinhard Pummer; Wege der Forschung 604; Darmstadt: Wissenschaftliche Buchgesellschaft, 1992) and more recently the more sympathetic work of Jürgen Zangenberg, *SAMAREIA: Antike Quellen zur Geschichte und Kultur der Samaritaner in deutscher Übersetzung* (Tübingen: Francke, 1994), 54 (cf. also a summary in: „Die Samaritaner," in *Neues Testament und Antike Kultur: Weltauffassung – Kult – Ethos* [vol. 3 of *Neues Testament und Antike Kultur*; ed. Jürgen Zangenberg; Neukirchen-Vluyn: Neukirchener Verlag, 2005], 47–50); cf. also Robert T. Anderson and Terry Giles, *The Keepers: An Introduction to the History and Culture of the Samaritans* (Peabody, Mass.: Hendrickson, 2002).

[18] Cf. Charles K. Barrett, *The Gospel According to St. John* (2nd ed.; Philadelphia, Pa.: Westminster Press, 1955), 194.

[19] Raymond E. Brown, *The Gospel according to John I–XII* (AB 29; New York: Doubleday, 1966), 170.

[20] Barrett, *St. John* (n. 18), 194.

he would become unclean (*Kelim passim*). According to the concentric Jewish maps of persons and places,[21] the Samaritans were seen as fundamentally out of place, and cut off from God's chosen people – on the symbolic maps they were positioned on the periphery, marginalized to the fullest sense of the word.[22]

It would be interesting to look at this narrative through the eye of an ancient temple oriented Jew: here, Jesus, who in John is presented as the holy son of God sent by God the father (John 3:16) is found *talking to an unclean Samaritan* and *drinking* something that was given by a Samaritan[23] (cf. *m. Aboth* 1:5).[24] This was something a true Rabbi would never do. Barclay notes the following interesting facts:

> There was still another way in which Jesus was taking down the barriers: "[t]he Samaritan was a woman. The strict Rabbis forbade a Rabbi to greet a woman in public. A Rabbi might not even speak to his own wife or daughter or sister in public. There were even Pharisees who were called "the bruised and bleeding Pharisees" because they shut their eyes when they saw a woman on the street and so walked into walls and houses! For a Rabbi to be seen speaking to a woman in public was the end of his reputation – and yet

---

[21] Cf. Jerome H. Neyrey, *The Social World of Luke-Acts: Models for Interpretation* (Peabody, Mass.: Hendrickson, 1991).

[22] Neyrey, *Social World* (n. 21), 279 says: "There are ten progressive degrees of 'holiness:' one moves upward and inward to the centre, from non-temple to temple, from outer courts to the Holy of Holies where God is enthroned on the cherubim. The principle of classification (and hence, of 'holiness') is proximity to the heart of the temple." Interesting enough, some are of the opinion that this is still the way some traditional Jews feel about the Samaritans: See Lawrence H. Schiffman, *Text and Traditions: A Source Reader for the Study of Second Temple and Rabbinic Judaism* (Hoboken, N.J.: KTAV, 1998), 96–98. See also in this regard Pieter W. van der Horst, "Anti-Samaritan propaganda in early Judaism," in *Persuasion and Dissuasion in early Christianity, ancient Judaism, and Hellenism* (ed. Pieter W. van der Horst et al.; Leuven: Peeters, 2003), 25–44.

[23] Cf. Barrett, *St. John* (n. 18), 194; Brown, *John* (n. 19), 170 remarks: "[S]amaritans were ritually impure. A Jewish regulation of A. D. 65–66 warned that one could never count on the ritual purity of Samaritan woman since they were menstruants from their cradle – seen Lev xv 19."

[24] According to Bruce J. Malina and Richard L. Rohrbaugh, *Social-Science Commentary on the Gospel of John* (Minneapolis, Minn.: Fortress Press, 1998), 100 the woman's reputation and honor status was far beyond retrieval. It might be suggested that we have here a situation with strong sexual connotations (see συγχράομαι in 4:9). See in this regard Ruben Zimmermann, *Christologie der Bilder im Johannesevangelium* (WUNT 171; Tübingen: Mohr Siebeck, 2004), 142–149, who *inter alia* thoroughly explains the "*Symboltraditionen*" in John 4 with specific reference to the Symbol of water and the connection to the "*Wasser als Liebessymbol*" against the background of the "*Brautmotivik*" in John (chs. 2–4 especially). Zimmermann, *Christologie der Bilder*, 144 correctly draws attention to Prov 5:15–19 where "die Wassermetaphorik [steht] zugleich in der Funktion der Warnung vor der 'fremden Frau' und vor Ehebruch." When these elements are taken in consideration, Jesus is even more so crossing the boundaries and the writer of John intends the reader to understand it in just such a way.

Jesus spoke to this woman. Not only was she a woman; she was also a woman of notorious character. No decent man, let alone a Rabbi, would have been seen in her company, or even exchanging a word with her – and yet Jesus spoke to her.[25]

According to Keener even the Samaritans would have judged the woman "which would have resulted in ostracism from the Samaritan religious community – which would have been nearly coextensive with the whole Samaritan community."[26] The crisis and disorientation of the life situation in this narrative lies therefore on two levels. In a sense the a) personal crisis and disorientation of the Samaritan woman creates the opportunity of addressing the b) larger societal crisis of marginalization, loss of life possibilities etc. of the Samaritans as a socio-religious group. It also creates an opportunity for this narrative to be a sign or a vehicle to illustrate greater truths in John's typical way of using the everyday situations to illustrate divine truths. Using this narrative, John could not have chosen a worse case scenario to illustrate the way Jesus gives life! It seems that John always takes such worse case scenarios in illustrating the way Jesus gives life: in John 4:43–54 the boy is close to death, in John 5:1–9 the man had been sick for 38 years, in John 9 the blind man has been born blind, in John 11 Lazarus loses his life completely.[27] John's healing acts as signs of his ability to give life, are thus set against a *hyperbolic background* in order to accentuate and intensify Jesus' ability to give qualitative life, and restore a life situation of brokenness to a life situation of life in abundance (cf. 10:10).

5. Jesus as Transformation Agent offers the Gift of Life (4:7–18)

Above we argued that through the eyes of the Jews, the Samaritans were in a marginalized socio-religious position, disconnected from the heart of the temple, and therefore the heart and presence of God. According to the Jews the Samaritans have no part in God's chosen people and his saving light and life (Eccl 50:25, 26 depicts God as saying: "[w]ith two nations is my soul vexed, and the third is no nation; they that sit upon the mountain of Samaria, and the Philistines, and that foolish people that dwell in Sichem."). They have lost life and are therefore a damned nation. This means that we have here a socio-religious crisis, which resulted in a disorientated life situation relative to the purity maps of the Jews. In this situation of

---

[25] William Barclay, *The Gospel of John: The new Daily Study bible* (vol. 1; revised ed.; Philadelphia, Pa.: Westminster Press, 2000), *ad loc.*

[26] Cf. Craig S. Keener, *The Gospel of John* (2 vols.; Peabody, Mass.: Hendrickson, 1993), *ad loc.*

[27] Cf. Brown, *John* (n. 19), 175–176.

crisis and disorientation, Jesus as transformation agent, again appears right in the middle between the Jews and the marginalized Samaritans, *breaking down the barriers* that separated them for many centuries,[28] which reminds the reader of the incarnational reality in which Jesus became a man and narrowed the gap between God and man, creating a symbolic bridge (1:10–11; 1:14, 18; 3:16) in which people will hear the voice of God in a new way (cf. John 1:18; 10:1–18).

It is clear that a certain dynamic interaction took place: Jesus initiated the interaction with the unclean Samaritan woman (4:7) at the well,[29] asking her for something to drink.[30] As we have already said, in asking the Samaritan woman for something to drink, Jesus is socio-religiously speaking, moving beyond the *status quo* of the day.[31] The specific character of the social interaction Jesus initiates, has the aim/effect of creating a symbolic bridge in order to meaningfully relate to the Samaritan woman on a social level. Jesus thus creates the possibility of open communication between himself and the woman – the possibility of exchanging or sharing ideas.[32] *The Jews built and maintained the symbolic socio-religious walls of separation and exclusivity, whereas Jesus became a bridge builder, breaking down the barriers and particularised an incarnational way of relating to those who were marginalized and seen as outcasts, all because of his mission, his calling (cf. John 3:16) (which is ultimately also our mission [John 20:21 – καθὼς ἀπέσταλκέν με ὁ πατήρ, κἀγὼ πέμπω ὑμᾶς]).*

Jesus shares the true spiritual reality with the Samaritan woman and offers her the gift (τὴν δωρεὰν) of redeeming life (4:10 – ὕδωρ ζῶν; cf. also 6:35 ἄρτος τῆς ζωῆς) and living[33] water that will quench all spiritual thirst

---

[28] According to Barclay, *Gospel of John* (n. 25), *ad loc.*

[29] The theme of men and women meeting at wells has also some deep roots in Scripture (cf. Gen 24; 1 Sam 9:11; 1 Kgs 17:10).

[30] Cf. Barrett, *St. John* (n. 18), 195. See also the article by Ruben Zimmermann and Mirjam Zimmermann, "Brautwerbung in Samarien. Von der moralischen zur metaphorischen Interpretation von Joh 4," *ZNT* 1 (1998/2): 40–51.

[31] Cf. Malina and Rohrbaugh, *Gospel of John* (n. 24), 98–99.

[32] Malina and Rohrbaugh, *Gospel of John* (n. 24), 99 go so far as to say that interpersonally the woman becomes part of Jesus' in-group due to the fact that the "public space" is transformed to "private space" because of the sharing of utensils. This of course is a serious polluting act by Pharisees standards.

[33] The term "living water" is a metaphor that is not commonly used in rabbinic literature (Barrett, *St. John* [n. 18], 195) although the metaphor water is often used (cf. Strack-Billerbeck II, 433–436). The metaphor "water" in John is pre-eminently the Holy Spirit, which gives life (cf. 6:63). This of course, is something only God can do (4:10, 14). The living water Jesus offers will create and maintain life in God's new family (Barrett, *St. John* [n. 18], 195; Dwight M. Smith, *John* [Abingdon New Testament Commentaries; Nashville, Tenn.: Abingdon, 1999], 113; cf. Jer 2:13; Zech 14:8; Ezek 47:9).

(metaphor for the spirit, cf. John 7:37–39), something that only God can do.[34]

6. Revelation and Transformational Ethos

Still the woman shows a complete lack of understanding[35] – she interprets the words of Jesus in a non-spiritual way,[36] hears his words through spiritual ears of unbelief.[37] In John 3:6 Jesus says: τὸ γεγεννημένον ἐκ τῆς σαρκὸς σάρξ ἐστιν, καὶ τὸ γεγεννημένον ἐκ τοῦ πνεύματος πνεῦμά ἐστιν. In other words, until one has not been born by the spirit, one will see and hear Jesus' words through spiritual eyes and ears of unbelief, and not be able to see the kingdom of God (3:3 – ἐὰν μή τις γεννηθῇ ἄνωθεν, οὐ δύναται ἰδεῖν τὴν βασι-λείαν τοῦ θεοῦ). Ironically enough, the woman asks the most fundamental important questions,[38] without even realizing it:[39]

1) πόθεν[40] οὖν ἔχεις τὸ ὕδωρ τὸ ζῶν; (4:11), – where is the source (1:46; 7:4–42, 52) of living water to be found?
2) and in what way is Jesus greater than the tradition (4:12).[41]

---

[34] Brown, *John* (n. 19), 178 narrows the term "living waters" down to two possibilities within the scope of Johannine theology: a) it refers to Jesus' revelation to mankind b) or the Spirit Jesus gives to men. According to Beasley-Murray, *John* (n. 16), *ad loc*: "The 'gift of God' denotes the salvation of God in an inclusive sense. The 'living water' from Jesus is here virtually equated with it. It is evident that 'living water' has a variety of nuances that must be taken into account; chiefly it appears to denote *the life mediated by the Spirit sent from the (crucified and exalted) Revealer-Redeemer.*"

[35] Cf. Barrett, *St. John* (n. 18), 196.

[36] Cf. Smith, *John* (n. 33), 114.

[37] In John's Gospel *salvific faith* (πιστεύω and its 98 occurrences) does not only entail acceptance of Jesus as the Son of God, but also existentially influences and determines one's deeds (Jan G. van der Watt, *Salvation in the New Testament: perspectives on soteriology* [NovTSup 121; Leiden: Brill, 2005], 121). In this sense it clearly is linked to ethics.

[38] Cf. Smith, *John* (n. 33), 114.

[39] Cf. Gerald L. Borchert, *John 1–11* (The New American Commentary 25A; Nashville, Tenn.: Broadman & Holman, 2001), 204; cf. John Macdonald, *The Theology of the Samaritans* (London: SCM Press, 1964).

[40] The word πόθεν (whence?) is one of the key words in John, used 13 times in this gospel. According to John most people do not know from whence Jesus came (e.g., 7:27 and 8:14; also see 6:41–42). Similarly the woman did not know or understand from whence Jesus received this living water (4:11). It seems that at the heart of human misunderstanding about Jesus is the question of recognizing his origin (See Borchert, *John* [n. 38], 204).

Excursion: Representation and Reorientation – where and with whom is God? (4:19–26)

In order for Jesus to be able to give life, God has to be actively involved and present with Jesus. According to Van der Watt the major question in John's Gospel (and the resulting conflict) revolves around the question of the centre: "where and with whom is God?"[42] This question was answered differently by the disciples of Jesus and the disciples of Moses, although both groups claimed the same God.[43] In Jesus' interaction with the Samaritan woman he remarks: "ὑμεῖς προσκυνεῖτε ὃ οὐκ οἴδατε· ἡμεῖς προσκυνοῦμεν ὃ οἴδαμεν, ὅτι ἡ σωτηρία ἐκ τῶν Ἰουδαίων ἐστίν). Above we argued that the Samaritans viewed themselves as true Israel, and heirs of the promises of God to Israel, and their version of the Pentateuch as the original one, direct from Moses.[44] Jesus' discussion with the Samaritan woman thus has to do with the whole problematic issue regarding worship of the true God (cf. 4:19–24). At least in this particular narrative, we have three distinctive groups, each claiming true worship of the real God and the fact that God was to be found exclusively with them. This of course resulted in the socio-religious exclusion of one another (cf. 10:33; 19:7 and 8:19, 24, 54–55).

Was it Jesus' intension to bring a new god or a new religion, or to continue the true religion of the God of Abraham and Moses? Jesus did not try to establish a new religion but to integrate the Jews and the Samaritans (the world – 3:16) into the new centre. If it was not Jesus' intension to bring a new god or a new religion,[45] the implication would be that those who reject Jesus are cut off from the true God, and expelled from the centre. They become spiritually blind and dead (cf. 5:24; 9:39–40). On the other side of the coin, it would mean that those who were previously opposed to one another would be reconciled with each other in and through Jesus, as the new centre. Being the new centre, Jesus does not only reconcile people with himself and God (3:16), he also reconciles people with one another (4:21–24). In Jesus as the new centre, believing Jews and Samaritans become part of the same family of the Father and the Son. Jesus thus not only presents a new centre, but also represents reality. Suddenly God's true reality, his plan and God's family on earth become visible. In the process it also happens that the previous polarization and mutual exclusion, the broken relationship that existed between Jew and Samaritan and Gentile (cf. John 4:43–54) is being restored. In becoming the centre, and drawing the whole world to himself, Jesus not only "heals" but also restores and reconciles on multi-dimensional levels.

---

[41] In John Jesus becomes the new centre. He replaces or is superior to most of the cultic or historic symbols in Israel's faith. See John 6 where Jesus is said to be the bread from heaven, parallel and even greater to that which was once given by Moses. To eat the bread which is Jesus is to believe in him and have communion with him. In the same way to drink the water is to believe. It is thus clear that John uses the well known traditions from Holy Scripture in arguing that Jesus is the true fulfilment of all expectations. Lightfoot (Robert H. Lightfoot, *St. John's Gospel* [Oxford: Oxford University Press, 1956], 134) is thus correct when he remarks: "St. John's purpose in each case is no doubt to emphasize the measureless superiority of the new order to anyone or anything representative of the old order."

[42] Cf. Van der Watt, *Salvation* (n. 37), 102.

[43] Cf. Van der Watt, *Salvation* (n. 37), 103.

[44] Cf. Beasley-Murray, *John* (n. 16), 60.

[45] Cf. Van der Watt, *Salvation* (n. 37), 104.

This is also illustrated in Jesus' priestly prayer in John 17. There Jesus prays to the Father regarding the unity of the new family he created (17:22) as well as the unity with the future believers (17:20) by saying: ²²κἀγὼ τὴν δόξαν ἣν δέδωκάς μοι δέδωκα αὐτοῖς, ἵνα ὦσιν ἓν καθὼς ἡμεῖς ἕν·²³ἐγὼ ἐν αὐτοῖς καὶ σὺ ἐν ἐμοί, ἵνα ὦσιν τετελειωμένοι εἰς ἕν, ἵνα γινώσκῃ ὁ κόσμος ὅτι σύ με ἀπέστειλας καὶ ἠγάπησας αὐτοὺς καθὼς ἐμὲ ἠγάπησας (cf. also 15:9). Here Jesus presents the new symbolic universe of the new family of God over against the Jewish symbolic universe by using a concentric argument. God is in the centre, as with the Jewish symbolic universe, but then followed by Jesus and the believers. The new concentric symbolic universe differs from the Jewish symbolic universe in the sense that Jesus is closely linked with the centre (God) and that the progressive degrees of holiness are represented in a three dimensional paradigm of unity. This unity is fundamentally established within the context of love (20:26), closely linked with revelation (2:25). It could also be argued that the unity will be revealed in the context of the love that exists in the family of God (15:9; contra 5:42). Elsewhere (cf. 13:1–17) Jesus uses the same argument with the disciples: ³⁴Ἐντολὴν καινὴν δίδωμι ὑμῖν, ἵνα ἀγαπᾶτε ἀλλήλους, καθὼς ἠγάπησα ὑμᾶς ἵνα καὶ ὑμεῖς ἀγαπᾶτε ἀλλήλους (13:34). In John, the symbolic universe of the Jews is being represented and set against the background of the creation of a new community. Jesus is the new centre where God is present. Wherever Jesus is, there is God, and there love will be found within the new family matrix that Jesus created. It is this same love that was the original motivation for the sending of the son (3:16). It was this love that sought to restore the multidimensional brokenness that existed before the incarnation of the Son.

Jesus responded to this question by saying πᾶς ὁ πίνων ἐκ τοῦ ὕδατος τούτου διψήσει πάλιν· ¹⁴ὃς δ' ἂν πίῃ ἐκ τοῦ ὕδατος οὗ ἐγὼ δώσω αὐτῷ, οὐ μὴ διψήσει εἰς τὸν αἰῶνα, ἀλλὰ τὸ ὕδωρ ὃ δώσω αὐτῷ γενήσεται ἐν αὐτῷ πηγὴ ὕδατος ἁλλομένου εἰς ζωὴν αἰώνιον (4:13–14). What Jesus is saying is that he is the new source of true life, of living water.[46] For a second time the woman interprets Jesus' words in a non-spiritual way, showing her lack of understanding. At this point of the social dynamics of this conversation the question would be if Jesus is going to stand up and leave the woman at this point of unbelief, or if he is going to "heal" her spiritual blindness (cf. John 9:40–41; 12:41) by illustrating his divine origin by per-

---

[46] In Isa 55:1–5 it is promised that the thirsty and hungry would receive the gift of water and bread, and that outsiders will become part of the fold. Later in the wisdom writings this theme was taken up as a symbol for the desire of God's way of wisdom (Sir 24:21; *1 En.* 48:1). In John's narrative however, we see how Jesus offers life to the thirsty, rejected half-breeds of Jewish society. This eventually results in one of the earliest confessions in John's Gospel (cf. 4:42).

forming a "sign" in a transformation interaction? The implicit reader is left in narratological tension.

Suddenly the level of the current social interaction is transposed to a next level of abstraction – the level of *revelation*.[47] Jesus speaks a soul penetrating, revelatory word in 4:16 – ὕπαγε φώνησον τὸν ἄνδρα σου καὶ ἐλθὲ ἐνθάδε.[48] Jesus *reveals* to the Samaritan woman that he has supernatural knowledge of her most intimate personal life, knowing of her unusual many husbands[49] (4:17–18 – καλῶς εἶπας ὅτι ἄνδρα οὐκ ἔχω· [18] πέντε γὰρ ἄνδρας ἔσχες καὶ νῦν ὃν ἔχεις οὐκ ἔστιν σου ἀνήρ· τοῦτο ἀληθὲς εἴρηκας), which essentially paints a picture of brokenness and shame. This makes the interaction between Jesus and the woman even more profound – he engaged meaningfully with her, knowing of her brokenness and shame, her unclean state of being. It is clear that the Samaritan woman experienced these revelatory words as a sign (cf. 4:29, 39) – a sign that Jesus is not just a mere man, but that he is the awaited prophet (*Taheb* – cf. Deut 18:15–18), a man sent from God (cf. 4:19 – θεωρῶ ὅτι προφήτης εἶ σύ; cf. 4:39). According to Beasley-Murray this is indeed a "faithful reflection of the Samaritans' messianic expectation,[50] which was defined not by the

---

[47] According to Barrett, *St. John* (n. 18), 196 the woman continues to misunderstand, but then Jesus initiates the process and takes a fresh approach.

[48] Cf. Leon Morris, *The Gospel according to John* (NICNT; Grand Rapids, Mich.: Eerdmans, 1975), 283.

[49] The question of the many husbands could be a question to the notorious character of the woman, or to the fact that no man wanted to marry her, making her a victim of men. In ancient times men decided whether they wanted to marry a certain woman. In my opinion the life situation of this woman was possibly one of brokenness and rejection (cf. Stanley E. Porter and Craig A. Evans, eds., *Dictionary of New Testament background: A compendium of contemporary biblical scholarship* [electronic ed.; Downers Grove, Ill.: Intervarsity Press, 2000], *ad loc* on the article regarding divorce in the New Testament world).

[50] Wengst (Klaus Wengst, *Das Johannesevangelium: 1. Teilband Kapitel 1–10* [Theologischer Kommentar zum Neuen Testament 4,1; Stuttgart: Kohlhammer, 2000], 162) argues: "Mit dieser Erkenntnis weiß sie schon viel mehr über Jesus als am Anfang der Begegnung. Aber sie weiß noch nicht genug." Thyen (Hartwig Thyen, *Das Johannesevangelium* [HNT 6; Tübingen: Mohr Siebeck, 2005], 268) argues: "Auch wenn Wilckens den ‚Propheten wie Mose‘ von Deut 18:15–18 wohl zu Unrecht mit dem Taheb identifiziert und dieses als ‚die Zentralgestalt der samaritanischen Messiaserwartung‘ bestimmt, macht er doch zu Recht darauf aufmerksam, dass Jesus sich mit seinem ἐγώ εἰμι nicht direkt mit dem von der Frau erwarteten Messias identifiziert." Barrett, *St. John* (n. 18), 197 on the other hand, argues that the Samaritan woman here merely believes that Jesus is a prophet like in 1:21, thus incorrectly understanding who Jesus is, and therefore not truly believing for the Samaritans did not accept the authority of the prophets. Elsewhere, in his commentary on 4:39, Barrett, *St. John* (n. 18), 204 states that: "To bear witness (seen on 1.7) is the task of a disciple. The woman joins with John the Baptist as witness, and in fact precedes the apostles." It is in other words clear that the

prophetic books but by the Pentateuch,[51] notably Deut 18:15–18."[52] They believed that the *Taheb*, as another Moses, will restore true belief in God, he will reveal the truth and he will also restore true worship of God,[53] elements which are explicitly referred to in this particular text.[54] Morris agrees and remarks: "[f]or her to speak of Jesus as a prophet was thus to move into the area of messianic speculation."[55]

What Jesus has just done was to open the woman's spiritual eyes. Suddenly she could see something new, something unexpected, to such a degree that she later relates the coming of the Messiah with what she has experienced in her interaction with Jesus (4:25 – οἶδα ὅτι Μεσσίας ἔρχεται ὁ λεγόμενος χρι- στός· ὅταν ἔλθῃ ἐκεῖνος, ἀναγγελεῖ ἡμῖν ἅπαντα). Το

Samaritan woman's testimony eventually lead others to faith. Her words and her testimony pointed towards positive belief in Jesus and in eventually recognizing his true identity (4:42). According to Hindson and Kroll (Edward E. Hindson and Woodrow Michael Kroll, eds., *KJV Bible commentary* [Nashville, Tenn.: Thomas Nelson, 1997], *ad loc*) the Samaritan woman first saw a Jew, then a prophet, and finally the Messiah (cf. Wengst, *Johannesevangelium* [see above], 162). Her faith thus represents progressive degrees of development.

[51] Cf. Beasley-Murray, *John* (n. 16), *ad loc*. Cf. Donald A. Carson, *New Bible commentary: 21st century edition* (4th ed.; Leicester: Intervarsity Press, 1994; rev. ed. of Donald Guthrie and John A. Motyer, eds., *The new Bible commentary* [3rd ed.; Downers Grove, Ill.: InterVarsity Press, 1970], *ad loc*): According to Carson Jesus was prepared to let himself be described as a prophet by the Samaritan woman on account of their unique Messianic expectations, but not to the Jews whose Messianic hopes did not fit in with Jesus' mission.

[52] Cf. also Brown, *John* (n. 19), 171.

[53] Cf. Keener, *The Gospel of John* (n. 26), *ad loc* argues that the frequent designation "Prophet" for Jesus in John illustrates inadequate faith (cf. 4:44; 6:14; 7:40; 9:17). He also notes that the Samaritans awaited not just any prophet, but indeed the greatest prophet of all time, one like Moses (Deut 18:15–18); see also John 4:25. But still, this seems to be inadequate faith in John.

[54] Cf. Macdonald, *Theology* (n. 39), 362–365. See Thyen, *Johannesevangelium* (n. 50), 256 who argues: "Denn mit der Qualifikation Jesus als ‚Prophet' zeigt die Samaritanerin, dass sie auf dem Wege ist zu begreifen ..., und mit der prophetischen *Sendung* Jesu erkennt sie, wie ihre folgende Frage zeigt, zugleich seine religiöse Kompetenz und Gottesnähe an ..." Thyen then goes on to argue that the Samaritans rejected the prophetic books. The only prophet they recognized was the one who was to return (Deut 18:15–18). According to Thyen, in the woman's mind Jesus was simply a Jewish prophet (Thyen, *Johannesevangelium* [n. 50], 256). Thyen's interpretation cannot be agreed with for the following reasons. By saying that "we know that *when* the Messiah comes he will reveal to us everything" (cf. 4:25), the woman's words are embedded within the Samaritan expectation of the Messiah. In 4:16 Jesus gives a self-revelation by saying to her that he is indeed the awaited Messiah. In the following scene the woman leaves everything there, and runs to the Samaritans to share her message.

[55] Morris, *John* (n. 48), 266.

this Jesus could then immediately reply:[56] ἐγώ εἰμι, ὁ λαλῶν σοι (4:26), and reveal his true identity to her.[57]

7. Missional Ethos and Ethics

In the following scene the narrator introduces the disciples (4:27), almost interrupting the conversation,[58] and the woman *energetically* left the scene and went her way into the city (4:28) *where she gave testimony* (cf. 4:29 – μήτι οὗτός ἐστιν ὁ χριστός;, 4:39 – μαρτυρούσης) of the transformational interaction she experienced (4:28, 39), in a world where women never did such things, especially women with a notorious character. The result of this testimony was that it was not only a sign to the Samaritan woman, but also became a personal testimony that would eventually convince others of Jesus' true identity[59] (cf. 4:39):[60] The Samaritan woman first saw a Jew, then a prophet, and finally the Messiah.[61] In this narrative there are in other

---

[56] Here we find the first ἐγώ εἰμι self-revelatory in the Gospel of John spoken through the lips of Jesus himself (cf. Smith, *John* [n. 33], 118).

[57] According to Van der Watt (Jan G. van der Watt, *Die Teologie van die Johannes-evangelie en Briewe* [Unpublished lecture material; Department of New Testament, University of Pretoria, 1999], *ad loc*) it is ironic that the woman says that when the Messiah comes, he will reveal all. If Jesus is indeed the Messiah, she just got the answer and revelation of the truth. And then Jesus himself says that he is the Messiah (4:26), the gift of God (4:10). Here Jesus brings her to the point of no return – she has to make a life changing choice, or not. In the following verses it becomes clear that the woman indeed made the right choice, to such an extent that she became one of the first witnesses to the Samaritans. In this narrative it seems that the Samaritans were not moved by visible miracles or signs (cf. 2:23; 7:31; 10:42; 11:45; 12:42), but by the life changing testimony of the Samaritan woman on the basis of what Jesus has told her.

[58] Cf. Smith, *John* [n. 33], 118.

[59] Campbell, *The way of Jesus* (n. 13), 200 rightly remarks: "The woman was transfixed by her encounter with Jesus, and she ran to tell anyone who'd listen. So much was she a dramatically changed woman that the people of Sychar were drawn into the message of Jesus."

[60] Cf. R. Alan Culpepper, *Anatomy of the Fourth Gospel: A study in literary design* (Philadelphia, Pa.: Fortress, 1983), 91; Mark Edwards, *John* (Blackwell Bible Commentaries; Oxford: Blackwell, 2004), 60; Morris, *John* (n. 48), 283; Keener, *The Gospel of John* (n. 26), *ad loc* is correct in saying that the woman's witness indeed reminds us of the way Philip had witnessed (1:46). Culpepper, *Anatomy* (see above), 91 agrees that the woman came to faith: "The Samaritan woman hails him as the Christ, and many in her village say he is the 'saviour of the world' (4:29, 39–42)."

[61] Cf. Hindson and Kroll, *KJV Bible commentary* (n. 50), *ad loc*; Wengst, Johannes-evangelium (n. 50), 162. According to Hindson and Kroll, *KJV Bible commentary* (n. 50), it seems that there were definite developments in her faith to such an extent that she eventually becomes a true believer in the Johannine sense of the word. Mostly, in instances where it is connected to the Christology, it revolves around recognizing Jesus as

words progressive degrees of development, to such an extent that it culminates in true Johannine confession, becoming a witness to Jesus' true identity – the first *missionary* to the Samaritans, spreading the good news of the Christ's coming to the world almost like a rock that is thrown into the water and creates the ring-like effect. Wengst is thus correct in postulating: "[d]as Zeugnis der Frau weckt also Glauben, und es entsteht Gemeinde als neue Sozialität."[62] This becomes especially clear when one investigates John 4:39:

Ἐκ δὲ τῆς πόλεως ἐκείνης πολλοὶ
ἐπίστευσαν εἰς αὐτὸν τῶν Σαμαριτῶν
διὰ τὸν λόγον τῆς γυναικὸς *μαρτυρούσης*
ὅτι εἶπέν μοι πάντα ἃ ἐποίησα.

It is clear that the Samaritans came to faith in Jesus (πολλοὶ ἐπίστευσαν εἰς αὐτόν),[63] on account of (διά) the woman's testimony (τὸν λόγον τῆς γυναικὸς μαρτυρούσης),[64] qualified as the transformational interaction she experienced with Jesus who revealed truth in her life,[65] something that the *Taheb* will do.[66] The faith of this woman reminds the reader of salvific

---

the redeemer of the world. The particular images are also employed to develop this recognition. See in this regard Ruben Zimmermann, *Christologie der Bilder* (n. 24), 142–149.

[62] Wengst, *Johannesevangelium* (n. 50), 184.

[63] John H. Bernard, *A Critical and Exegetical Commentary on the Gospel according to St. John* (ICC 1; Edinburgh: T&T Clark, 1928; repr. 1953), 160 argues that πολλοὶ ἐπίστευσαν εἰς αὐτὸν is a favourite with John, occurring no less than six times in this gospel (cf. 7:31; 8:30; 10:42; 11:45; 12:42). He postulates that "The aorist seems to indicate a definite, but not necessarily lasting, movement of faith evoked by special words or deeds of Jesus."

[64] According to Archibald T. Robertson, *Word Pictures in the New Testament* (Oak Harbor: Logos Research Systems, 1997), *ad loc*, the Samaritan woman is already convinced herself (vv. 26–27), but she puts the question in a hesitant form in order to avoid arousing opposition. Therefore she avoided the use of οὐκ and instead used μητι. By doing this she piques the Samaritans' curiosity, according to Robertson. See also Brown, *John* (n. 19), 174–175 who argues that the λόγον of the woman should be contrasted with the λόγον of Jesus in that there is a qualitative difference between the faith on account of Jesus' λόγον (cf. 4:41) and faith on account of the woman's λόγον. Brown is indeed correct that there exists a qualitative difference, but the question is on what level the qualitative difference rests. Certainly it does not mean that a person who receives "second hand" λόγον by means of the testimony of a believer has wrong or qualitatively less valued faith than those who came to believe in Jesus on account of direct interaction with him. In John 17 Jesus prays for those who will believe on account of the second hand witness of Him in the future.

[65] Cf. Culpepper, *Anatomy* (n. 60), 91; Wengst, *Johannesevangelium* (n. 50), 184.

[66] Cf. Macdonald, *Theology* (n. 39). According to Thyen, *Johannesevangelium* (n. 50), 282 the faith of the Samaritans is only provisional ("vorläufig") in nature. Smith,

faith.[67] In John's Gospel *salvific faith* (πιστεύω and its 98 occurrences) does not only entail acceptance of Jesus as the Son of God, but also existentially influences and determines one's deeds.[68] It seems that the woman and the Samaritans (cf. 4:42) eventually came to true faith in the source of living water. In John, those who believe become reborn children of God, and receive the right (ἐξουσίαν in 1:12) to be called God's children (1:12).

Later, in their interaction with Jesus, even more of the Samaritan people experienced Jesus' words and could confess that they also believe in him (4:41 – καὶ πολλῷ πλείους ἐπίστευσαν διὰ τὸν λόγον αὐτοῦ). The only difference is that they now do not believe in him because of the woman's testimony alone, but due to their own personal experience with Jesus (4:42 – ὅτι οὐκέτι διὰ τὴν σὴν λαλιὰν πιστεύομεν).[69] Jesus has touched their personal lives to such an extent that their spiritual eyes and ears were opened[70], and they could see and know the true reality[71] (αὐτοὶ γὰρ ἀκηκόαμεν καὶ οἴδαμεν), namely that Jesus is indeed ἀληθῶς ὁ σωτὴρ τοῦ κόσμου[72] (4:42).[73]

John (n. 33), 121 argues that the Samaritan woman's testimony (cf. 4:17–18, 29) leads many Samaritans to faith, but only to sign faith at second hand.

[67] According to Barclay, *Gospel of John* (n. 25), 172 the Samaritan woman is a great example of his saving power. He argues that the town where she stayed would no doubt have labelled her a character beyond reformation; but here Jesus saved and restored her; he enabled her to break away from the past and he opened a new future to her. Naturally then, there is no title adequate to describe Jesus except Saviour of the World.

[68] Cf. Van der Watt, *Salvation* (n. 37), 121.

[69] Cf. also Campbell, *The way of Jesus* (n. 13), 200. In his discussion of the dynamics of movements, Alan Hirsch, *The Forgotten Ways: Reactivating the Missional Church* (Grand Rapids, Mich.: Brazos, 2006), 194 remarks that "[N]ew missional movements almost always begin on the edges of society/culture and among the common people. They are nonlitist. And they have the ability to excite and enlist others as leaders and participants." This is in sync with others like Harvey Cox who argued that the main stimulus for the renewal of Christianity more than often comes from the bottom and from the edge, from exactly those sectors of the Christian world that are on the margins of society (cf. also quoted by Hirsch, *Forgotten Ways* [see above], 194). In the narrative of Jesus and the Samaritan woman, it became clear that the unclean, marginalized Samaritan woman became the first missionary to the unclean, common Samaritans and that the stimulus for this renewal came from the bottom and from the edge, from the margins of society.

[70] Cf. Bernard, *St. John* (n. 63), 160. In the Johannine community people come to believe on account of the words of those who testify.

[71] Bernard, *St. John* (n. 63), 161 argues that the initial stages of belief may be brought about by the testimony of others, but the belief in Jesus that is complete and assured is realized in the context of personal contact and association with the living Christ. This passage is rightly referred to as the mission to the Samaritans.

[72] Brown, *John* (n. 19), 185 rightly points to the fact that "Nicodemus, the rabbi of Jerusalem, could not understand Jesus' message that God had sent the Son into the world so that the world might be saved though him (iii 17); yet the peasants of Samaria readily come to know that Jesus is really the Saviour of the world." This whole narrative also

8. As the Father has sent me I also send you

The question now logically follows whether this has got anything to do with Christian ethics or moral language and whether or not John 4 and the sending motive (John 20:21, etc.) of the disciples can be linked to each other on a textual level. Although there is no evidence of sending seman-temes in the chapter itself, apart from the stereotypical use of πέμπω, it is certainly implied, and also a consequence of a life that imitates Christ. The fact that John does not explicitly link the sending motive of John 20:21, for instance with that of John 4:1–42 does not mean that he does not wish to do so by implication. In John, the disciples are often presented as not un-

---

revolves around the important truth that Jesus is the source of living water and that the hour is coming (cf. 4:21; 5:25, 28; 16:2, 32) that the true worshippers shall worship the Father in Spirit and in truth, and that the Father seeks such people to be his worshippers (4:23). The result of this truth will then be that the Father will not be worshipped on this mountain (Gerizim), nor in Jerusalem. The reason is clear: there will be a new source of life – God has moved to a new address. Beasley-Murray, *John* (n. 16), 58 is thus correct in arguing that just as the cleansing of the temple entails a contrast between the old tem-ple and the new temple of Christ's body, so the worship of Jerusalem and Gerizim is declared to be superseded by the worship of the new age introduced by Christ and the Spirit he sends. The pivotal question in John thus revolves around the question of the true centre: where, and with whom is God to be found?

[73] Jesus' interaction with the Samaritan woman could be interpreted within the framework of a restorative hermeneutic of representation. In John, God has moved from the localized materialistic to the "glocal" (global and local) spiritualistic. With "glocal" it is meant that God will be localized wherever Jesus is, but "globalistic" in the sense that Jesus is to be found not only with the Jews but also with the Samaritans (4:1–42) and even the gentiles (4:43–54). Wherever Jesus is, the Father is, and the life the Father of-fers, becomes apparent (cf. the healing narratives). In this narrative it is clear that it was not only the broken relationship between the Samaritan woman and God that had been restored, but also the *potential restoration* of the broken relationship between the Samari-tans and the Jews. This narrative *represents reality* to such an extent that *reconciliation* between Jew and Samaritan becomes possible. It becomes possible the moment Jesus becomes the new (glocal) centre through faith and love (17:23). Through faith people are born into the new family of the King (Van der Watt, *Family* [n. 4]). Soteriology in John leads to resocialization and reconciliation (Van der Watt, *Salvation* [n. 37], 123). In this way a new restored and reconciled existential reality is (re)presented: reconciliation and restoration on horizontal (people/nations) and vertical (people and God) levels. Jesus' interaction with the Samaritan woman is thus much more than just mere communication interaction – it could indeed be seen as a transformational interaction, a proto-type of *a restorative hermeneutic of representation*, or a healing act in John's symbolic universe. This healing act in John's understanding not only serves as a vehicle (sign) to illustrate that Jesus is the Messiah, but also that he is the true centre, the source of living water, of life itself. In this way the narrative serves the core purpose of the Gospel (20:30–31), namely to serve as a sign that Jesus is indeed the Son of God and the source of life, the new temple (cf. 2:17–22).

derstanding the complete picture during the time they lived with Christ. Only after his death and resurrection they came to a fuller understanding of the implications (cf. 2:22). In other words, the disciples are in many instances not the ideal understanding followers of Jesus and in John 4 we almost do not expect them to understand the full picture. However, in my opinion the implicit reader of John is guided throughout the gospel of John to understand the implications thereof. John presents the life of Jesus as the prototype to be followed, and implicitly guides the reader to eventually live the way Jesus lived, embody the ethics and ethos of Jesus. This is *inter alia* clearly seen in John 13:15 where Jesus gives the inner circle a ὑπόδειγμα (an example) and tells them to follow his example and serve one another. The motive of the ὑπόδειγμα of Jesus, or a life that imitates Jesus, is certainly not exclusively limited to the warm inner circle of the disciples. Within the framework of the ancient family, as Van der Watt argued convincingly, the Father sends and educates his Son who does the will of the Father in an intimate way (cf. 5:19).[74] When Jesus teaches his followers (children cf. 1:12), he guides them to unfold the story of the mission further, for they are also taken up in the mission of the family of God and should carry on with the mission for which they as children of the King were called. If there should be any doubt whether John explicitly links the missional ethos of Jesus to the life of the faith community as a whole, John 17:18 will certainly prove the fact:

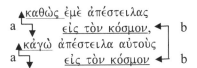

Clearly, here we have evidence (cf. the a-b a-b structure) that John leads the implicit reader to understand that Jesus' mission (3:16 – cf. ἀπέστειλεν ὁ θεὸς τὸν υἱὸν εἰς τὸν κόσμον) to the unloving (cf. 1:11) *world* (εἰς τὸν κόσμον) will by implication also be the mission of the followers of Jesus. The nature of those in the world are portrayed by John as those who not only hated Jesus and God (1:11) but will also hate the followers of Jesus (17:14). This is not a picture of a mission to the inner circle, but a mission away from safe spaces to hostile territory where the followers of Jesus will have to embody the missional ethos of love as Jesus states in John 17:26: καὶ ἐγνώρισα αὐτοῖς τὸ ὄνομά σου καὶ γνωρίσω, ἵνα ἡ ἀγάπη ἣν ἠγάπησάς με ἐν αὐτοῖς ᾖ κἀγὼ ἐν αὐτοῖς. Again, when one investigates the priestly prayer of Jesus in John 17 carefully one will see that the universal mission of love is not only meant for the inner circle, but also for those who will become part of the family of God in the future, presuppos-

---

[74] Cf. Van der Watt, *Family* (n. 4), 277.

ing an inherent inclusive missional-incarnational ethos (cf. John 17:20–21:
[20] Οὐ περὶ τούτων δὲ ἐρωτῶ μόνον, ἀλλὰ καὶ περὶ τῶν πιστευόντων διὰ
τοῦ λόγου αὐτῶν εἰς ἐμέ, [21] ἵνα πάντες ἓν ὦσιν, καθὼς σύ, πάτερ, ἐν
ἐμοὶ κἀγὼ ἐν σοί, ἵνα καὶ αὐτοὶ ἐν ἡμῖν ὦσιν, ἵνα ὁ κόσμος πιστεύῃ
ὅτι σύ με ἀπέστειλας). From the above investigation, it could thus be argued that although it is not explicitly mentioned in John 4:1–42, the sending motive is certainly implied in John, as I will further argue below.

According to John, Jesus came to this world because he was sent (ἀποστέλλω) by God (3:16–17), thereby becoming incarnated as a man and
lived among us (1:12, 14). It is a well-known fact in Johannine literature
that the ἀποστέλλω motive forms one of the most important elements in the
understanding of the mission of Jesus and therefore it will not be discussed
in detail here due to the fact that literature on the subject is extensive (cf.
4:34).[75] The important thing is that Jesus' mission originated from God
(3:16) and the primary motive for the sending of the Son was God's love
(ἠγάπησεν in 3:16) for the world which is caught up in sin and darkness
(8:34) and the ultimate outcome of this mission culminates in the gift of
life (cf. ζωὴν in 3:16 and 20:30–31) for those who believe (cf. πιστεύων).
In John, Jesus as the ideal sent agent of the King, resembles the one who
has sent him (5:19). Therefore John argues that those who see and hear
Jesus, see and hear the Father (cf. 5:19; 14:9). In John 5:16 Jesus clearly
states that what he teaches comes not from himself, but comes from the
one that sent him (ἡ ἐμὴ διδαχὴ οὐκ ἔστιν ἐμὴ ἀλλὰ τοῦ πέμψαντος με).
God educates Jesus like a Father educated his son in the context of antiqui-

---

[75] Cf. Kok, *Gebrokenheid* (n. 11); Van der Watt, *Family* (n. 4), 296–302 and idem,
Identity, Ethics and Ethos (n. 5), 434. See Teresa Okure, *The Johannine Approach to
Mission: A Contextual Study of John 4:1–42* (WUNT 2/31; Tübingen: Mohr Siebeck,
1988), 285; Anthony E. Harvey, *Christ as Agent* in *The Glory of Christ in the New Testament* (ed. Lincoln D. Hurst and Nicholas T. Wright; Oxford: Clarendon, 1987), 239–
242; Michael Waldstein, "Die Sendung Jesu und der Jünger im Johannesevangelium," in
Internationale katholische Zeitschrift 19 (1990): 203–221 (= "The Mission of Jesus and
the Disciples in John, Communio," in *International Catholic Review* 17 [1990]: 311–
333). See also Klaus Haaker, "Sendung/Mission" in *Theologisches Begriffslexikon zum
Neuen Testament* 2 (2000): 1654–1667. See Zimmermann, *Christologie der Bilder* (n.
24), 183–192 as well as idem, "Metaphoric Networks" (n. 10), 395, where he discusses
the narrative plot of the sending motive in John and postulates that all the mission declarations in John are written in the past tense: "Narratives are constituted in a space-time
framework and both basic parts of the narrative are also found within the mission declarations. First, the aspect of time. Up to now I have not alluded to the fact that in all mission declarations a form of time, namely the Greek past tense aorist is used. Only twice is
a perfect form used (Jn 5,36; 20,21); all instances of future are related to the Advocates
(Jn 14,26; 15,26; 16,7); the present tense is used only once and, not by chance, in the
sending out of the disciples (Jn 20,21). The mission of Jesus expressed with the aorist
thus refers to an event that happened in the past. The evangelist continues to consistently
implement his retrospective."

ty (8:28). For this reason, Zimmermann is correct in arguing that John's metaphor of mission is always simultaneously a metaphor of relationship.[76] Jesus' mission was thus not only *incarnational* in nature but also strongly *relational*. Sweet is correct in speaking of the mission of the church that should be essentially characterized by a MRI-ethos – *missional*, *relational* and *incarnational*.[77]

Jesus' mission *inter alia* resulted in people being healed from spiritual blindness (cf. the implication of 12:40–41 and 9:4) and freed from slavery to sin (8:34) with the implication that they became part of and re-socialized into the new family of God (cf. 1:12). This is exactly what happened to the Samaritan woman. Jesus offered her living water and life, she believed and became part of God's family. If Jesus did not cross the socio-cultural boundaries, the Samaritan woman would not have experienced what she did. The initiative and action of Jesus, motivated by love, thus resulted in her conversion and her spiritual restoration.

Jesus argues that those who love him and the Father will also do and live the way Jesus lived (cf. 13:15) and do even more than he did (14:12). In John 15 Jesus uses the imagery or metaphor of a vine to illustrate the fact that those who follow him are and should be in a close relationship with him (cf. 15:7) with the implication that the fruit (deeds) they produce not only originates from but is also determined by the vine as the source. Jesus then argues that his example is that of love, and therefore the follow-ers of Jesus as the branches should exemplify the life of Jesus.[78] It is thus clear that we have in this metaphor of the vine an example of moral lan-guage or an ethical dimension because it appeals to a moral life, a lived ethos.

At this point of the argument it is in others words clear that there exists an important link between the motive of the sending of the Son and the moral reality of love (cf. 3:16; 5:19, and especially 17:26). The main mo-tive for the sending of the Son as was already stated, is God's love for the world (3:16), which Jesus also inherently embodied and demanded from his followers (15:9–17; 17:26) as it is explicitly mentioned in 15:8–10: [8]ἐν τούτῳ ἐδοξάσθη ὁ πατήρ μου, ἵνα καρπὸν πολὺν φέρητε καὶ γένησθε ἐμοὶ μαθηταί.[9]Καθὼς ἠγάπησέν με ὁ πατήρ, κἀγὼ ὑμᾶς ἠγάπησα· μείνατε ἐν τῇ ἀγάπῃ τῇ ἐμῇ.[10]ἐὰν τὰς ἐντολάς μου τηρήσητε, μενεῖτε ἐν τῇ ἀγάπῃ μου, καθὼς ἐγὼ τὰς ἐντολὰς τοῦ πατρός μου τετήρηκα καὶ μένω αὐτοῦ ἐν τῇ ἀγάπῃ. It could be argued that the love spoken about here is only meant for those inside the church or those who believe in Jesus, in other words an

---

[76] Cf. Zimmermann, "Metaphoric Networks" (n. 10), 395.

[77] Cf. Leonard Sweet, *So Beautiful: Divine Design for Life and the Church* (Colora-do Springs, Colo.: David C. Cook, 2009).

[78] Cf. also Van der Watt, *Identity, Ethics and Ethos* (n. 5), 446.

exclusive inward-directed love towards insiders. In my opinion this could
be no further from the truth, especially when the inherent dynamics and
scope of the ἀποστέλλω (mission) motive of Jesus on the one hand, and the
explicit moral appeal towards the followers of Jesus on the other hand is
taken into serious consideration (cf. 17:26 discussed above). Furthermore
it is to be remembered that Jesus' interaction with the Samaritan woman
was also not an exclusive in-group directed action, in fact! Jesus, as God's
Son who was sent to give life, crossed socio-cultural and religious boundaries in a missional-incarnational way to offer living water to the Samaritan
woman and it indeed transformed her life. In John 20:21 Jesus explicitly
says καθὼς ἀπέσταλκέν με ὁ πατήρ, κἀγὼ πέμπω ὑμᾶς. Just as the Father
has sent Jesus, so Jesus sends his followers. *This expression inherently
implies action, reaction or movement, and therefore it has a moral, ethical
or imperative dimension.*[79] In other words, within the dynamics of the linguistic statement of John 20:21 lies the inherent dynamics of a movement
ethos. In my opinion Jesus is in no way referring to an exclusive inward
directed love towards insiders, but to a missional-incarnational way of life
which follows his way. In using the words καθὼς ἀπέσταλκέν the associative elements of Jesus' mission are drawn into the frame of reference (cf.
love, faith, life), which surely include and recall the story of Jesus' interaction with the Samaritan woman and the way he crossed the socio-cultural
and religious boundaries of the day. In the narrative of Jesus and the Samaritan woman we see a well constructed narrative that inherently embodies a
missional-incarnational ethos which was of course written in a time when
such mission most probably on a historical level already had taken place
for several decades (John was probably written after 90 C.E.). Even if this
narrative represented a primitive oral tradition, it might in the early stages
have served as a catalyst for a missional-incarnational ethos, motivating
followers of Jesus to spread the gospel to those outside the socio-cultural
boundaries of the time, especially those who were viewed as being out of
place – the untouchables, the poor, the Samaritans, the heathens as we indeed see in the later developments in Acts (cf. Acts 10–15).[80] The missional-incarnational ethos motivated by an understanding of the continual mis-

---

[79] See Ruben Zimmermann, "Ethics in the New Testament and Language," in this
volume), 28–45 for an important discussion on the different forms of ethical language in
the New Testament where he discusses the ethical quality of linguistic statements or
requests on an intra-textual level. He argues that grammatical imperatives might sometimes express a request and not a real imperative (cf. Matt 6:11b – Lord's Prayer) and in
other instances we have simple requests or statements that actually function like an imperative (cf. the future indicative in Matt 5:43 – love your neighbor). In my opinion John
20:21 is such an example where we do not find a grammatical imperative, but it nevertheless has the dynamics and effect of an imperative.

[80] Cf. Kok, *Gebrokenheid* (n. 11).

sional ethics of Jesus' sending in my opinion serves as an imperative for the church's self-understanding. The implication of a missional-incarnational ethos is that those who are motivated by love (17:26), will *inter alia* cross socio-cultural boundaries and go to those who are regarded as out of place, as outcasts, the poor – those in need of restoration, those who are on the periphery of the socio-cultural boundaries of our day.[81]

9. Conclusion

When the mission-motive of Jesus and the narrative of the Samaritan woman are integrated a particular virtual reality is constructed with its own norms, expected behaviours, limitations, borders, etc. Furthermore, a particular moral dimension was discovered in the narrative as a virtualization of social relations and a new symbolic universe was not only created but also illustrated by particularizing the macro world-view of John's universal godly narrative creating an example not only of how Jesus lived but also how his followers are to live. As was mentioned above, the Jews maintained the symbolic socio-religious walls of separation and exclusivity, whereas Jesus became a bridge builder, breaking down the barriers and particularised an incarnational way of relating to those who were marginalized and seen as outcasts, all because of his mission, his calling (cf. John 3:16) – which is ultimately and essentially also our mission (John 20:21).

By accepting Jesus as the Son of God, and as a result thereof, the Samaritan woman experienced a conversion which in its essence implies a destruction of her old world-view and the reconstruction of a new world-view which entails her becoming part of a new symbolic universe (cf. 1:12). This new world-view leads not only to a new way of life (ethos) but also to a new understanding of God, self and others which could be seen as the motivation or basis from which the new lived identity is realized. Those who read the narrative are also challenged with regards to their own world-view, their ethical basis and their ethos and thus it functions as a self-reflecting narrative that motivates people to continue the missional-incarnational ethos of Jesus. Jesus' interaction with the Samaritan woman eventually developed into a magnificent transformational interaction leading to a spiritual *reorientation* and *representation of reality* and the dynamic energy associated with a missionary impulse.[82] Suddenly everything changed for the Samaritan woman, she was transformed from an unclean, marginalized, stigmatized Samaritan woman to a faithful witness, someone whose brokenness has been radically restored. Even her eschatological life

---

[81] Cf. Kok, *Gebrokenheid* (n. 11).

[82] Cf. Hirsch, *Forgotten Ways* (n. 69), 193–194.

possibilities changed.[83] According to John 5:24 those who hear His word, and believe Him who sent Jesus, already have eternal life, and do not come into judgment, but have already passed from death to life. In this way the dynamics in this micro-narrative is taken up within the dynamics of the macro-narrative of the Gospel.

From the investigation above it becomes clear that it was Jesus' missional-incarnational ethos that culminated not only in the reality of transformation and restoration, but also in the activation of the dynamics of a movement. In other words, Jesus' presence gives birth to spiritual movement and lives that are transformed – leading to transformed and restored people who move and invite others. A missional-incarnational spirituality and ethos results in the bringing of the presence of Christ in marginalized places/spaces where such presence is not recognized, which leads to revelation (when people's spiritual eyes are opened) and restoration –, which then leads to a dynamic missional movement when they share the transformational wonder they have experienced and invite others to participate. Plainly said: Jesus' presence reaches out, builds bridges, invites, restores, heals, transforms and moves people to missional action. That, in my opinion, is as close to the dynamics of a movement ethos one might get!

Jesus' missional activity originated in God's mission (John 3:16), but the dynamics of that movement should continue (imperative dimension of John 20:21) in the missional-incarnational ethos of the church, the organic, vibrant, living body of Christ as Alan Hirsch[84] correctly postulates:

> At its very heart, Christianity is therefore a messianic movement, one that seeks to consistently embody the life, spirituality, and mission of its Founder. We have made it so many other things, but this is its utter simplicity. Discipleship, becoming like Jesus our Lord and Founder, lies at the epicentre of the church's task. It means that Christology must define all that we do and say. It also means that in order to recover the ethos of authentic Christianity, we need to refocus our attention back to the Root of it all, to recalibrate ourselves and our organizations around the person and work of Jesus the Lord. It will mean taking the Gospels seriously as the primary texts that define us. It will mean acting like Jesus in relation to people outside of the faith.

Jesus' mission is fundamentally also our mission, as Jesus himself sent his disciples forth in John 20:21 before he was to depart back to the Father. Therefore the church is called to live a missional-incarnational ethos that is built on a particular ethical basis which is the result of a particular understanding of God's story and view of the world and our understanding of our own place and role in this story. According to John 17:17–19 believers

---

[83] Wengst, *Johannesevangelium* (n. 50), 180–181 remarks: "In der Gemeinde fanden Menschen neue Lebensmöglichkeiten, deren bedrücktes Leben perspektivlos erschien, die durch Lebensbrüche hindurchgegangen waren. Sie fanden in geteilten Leben in der Gemeinde erfülltes Leben."

[84] Hirsch, *Forgotten Ways* (n. 69), 94.

are also sent like Jesus was sent, and the aim of that sending revolves around the ἁγίασον of those that were sent, in other words, the sanctification of all who will come to faith. Therefore Bosch was right when he said that in the first place the church should understand and become part of the *Missio Dei*.[85] Practically this virtual narrative and the dynamics of the moral language thereof will challenge the church's ethical perspective and missional ethos with reference to the reality of *inter alia* HIV and Aids for instance in the South African context. Like the story of the Samaritan woman, this phenomenon has to do with stigmatization, symbolic bridges that marginalize and exclude, and call for a missional-incarnational ethos of healing, restoration and reconciliation. In the end, Jesus' mission has become our mission and therefore it has to become part of our ethical conduct, derived and motivated from the basis of our understanding of God, ourselves and others and our calling with regards to the *Missio Dei* (cf. John 17:18; 20:21).

In conclusion it could thus be argued that those who seek to speak of moral language in John (at least on a textual level) should probably also include the reality of a missional-incarnational ethos that will transcend all boundaries (cultural, social, economical, racial, etc.) to show love and be accepting of everyone.[86] From the investigation above, it becomes clear that the narrative of Jesus and the Samaritan woman should be integrated not only with the sending motive and ethos of the Son, but also with the imperative of the missional ethos of the followers of Jesus (cf. John 20:21). Together these elements form a(n inclusive) moral language or ethical paradigm of mission and give the reader a full and integrated picture of the essence of behavior in following the way of Jesus, or in the words of Burridge *a life that imitates Jesus* – the loving friend of sinners and outcasts – those who are often on the periphery of this life.[87] The community of Christ is thus called to incarnationally embody the implicit "love-ethics" of Jesus that missionally transcends and breaks through socio-religious, cultural and other man-made boundaries. Let us therefore remind ourselves once again of the words of Jesus in John 20:21:

καθὼς ἀπέσταλκέν με ὁ πατήρ, κἀγὼ πέμπω ὑμᾶς –
Just as the Father has sent me,
I send you …

---

[85] Bosch, *Believing in the Future* (n. 2), 32.

[86] Cf. Richard A. Burridge, *Imitating Jesus: An Inclusive Approach to New Testament Ethics* (Grand Rapids, Mich.: Eerdmans, 2007).

[87] Cf. Burridge, *Imitating Jesus* (n. 86), 335.

III. Pauline Literature

The Exposition of Moral Rules and Principles in Pauline Letters

Preliminary Observations on Moral Language in Earliest Christianity

HERMUT LÖHR[*]

1. Introduction

There is no consensus in present scholarship whether or not one can properly speak – or if it is even justifiable to speak – of New Testament ethics. Obviously the answer given depends on how one defines "ethics" – and its textual representation – in the context of antiquity. While this might appear as a quandary, I am, nevertheless, not convinced that searching for the "ethos" of the early Christians *instead of* their "ethics" would solve the problem: to describe the "ethos," aptly defined e.g. by Clifford Geertz as "the tone, character, and quality of their life, its moral and aesthetic style and mood; it is the underlying attitude toward themselves and their world that life reflects,"[1] seems to be even a greater challenge to historians of earliest Christianity than to sketch the ethics of the respective New Testament author or of the canon as a whole. Indeed to me it seems quite possible to describe some characteristics, presuppositions and assumptions of *implicit* New Testament ethics.[2]

But this is not necessarily the first step in investigating the question at hand. Without a doubt moral instruction is present in most of the New Testament writings, and one wonders, for example, what the Pauline letters

---

[*]   I wish to thank Dr. Martin Dorn, Lübeck (Germany), for a revision of the English text. All extant mistakes are mine.

[1]   Clifford Geertz, "Ethos, World View, and the Analysis of Sacred Symbols," in *The Interpretation of Cultures: Selected Essays* (ed. Clifford Geertz; New York, N.Y.: Basic Books, 1973), 126–141, 127. New Testament scholars who have tried to advance definitions include Michael Wolter, "Die ethische Identität christlicher Gemeinden in neutestamentlicher Zeit," in *Woran orientiert sich Ethik?* (ed. Wilfried Härle and Reiner Preul; Marburg: Elwert, 2001), 61; Jan G. van der Watt, "Ethics and Ethos in the Gospel according to John," *ZNW* 97 (2006): 147–176, 150–151.

[2]   Instead of "ethics" we could also speak of "moral thought," an expression which lacks, however, an exact German equivalent.

would be like *without* this moral instruction. Even though the word "moral" in combinations such as "moral instruction," "moral language," "moral thought" or "moral philosophy" is quite common and used neutrally in philosophical discourse, theologians, especially Protestants, might hesitate to use it: the idea of morals or morality may spontaneously evoke negative connotations such as unreflected or bourgeois rules of behaviour. While such connotations do exist in everyday language, I think we should not allow that to influence our work in the academic context. For this reason I do not hesitate to refer to "moral instruction," understood as instruction with the goal of influencing the human mindset, intentions, and actions, or to refer to "moral language" in New Testament writings.

Furthermore, a study of implicit New Testament ethics has to begin with a description of the moral language, the terms and categories used, the exposition of the argument, and the rhetorical techniques applied. The importance of a linguistic and rhetorical analysis of the moral statements and arguments in New Testament literature can be illustrated as follows.

We cannot be sure of the (still widely accepted) description of the relationship between soteriology and ethics in Pauline thought as within the categories of "indicative" and "imperative" as long as we cannot demonstrate this connection from the textual construction of the argument, and its inherent logic. And demonstrating this connection is no easy task – a problem acknowledged by an increasing number of scholars.[3]

Nor can we be sure of the importance of the love commandment or the idea of the community as *corpus Christi* for Pauline ethics, as long as we are not able to describe the linguistic means by which this importance is signalled in the text.

More generally speaking – and this does not only refer to New Testament ethics, but also to New Testament theology in general – our analysis should not only isolate the propositions implied in the argumentations presented, but also pay attention to the manner of presentation itself. In addition, we need to pay attention to the forms of rhetorical technique in a very general sense.

This task could be considered easy,[4] and therefore superfluous. Nevertheless it has to be done. And if we take a look into current reference

---

[3] Cf. Ruben Zimmermann, "Jenseits von Indikativ und Imperativ: Entwurf einer 'impliziten Ethik' des Paulus am Beispiel des 1. Korintherbriefes," *ThLZ* 132 (2007): 259–284, 260–265. No small part of the investigation of moral language by Richard Marvin Hare shows that, in the terms of a logical analysis of everyday language, a moral imperative *never* follows from a factual (indicative) statement; cf. Richard M. Hare, *The Language of Morals* (Oxford: Clarendon, 1952; repr. Oxford: Clarendon, 1972).

[4] Or as Johannes Weiß put it succinctly: „Ich beschränke mich auf Mitteilung einiger Einzelbeobachtungen, die weiter kein Verdienst für sich beanspruchen, da jeder sie machen kann;" cf. Johannes Weiß, "Beiträge zur Paulinischen Rhetorik," in *Theologische*

books on New Testament ethics, one might get the impression that there is still much left to be done (or at least brought back into discussion) in the analysis of moral language in the Pauline letters.[5]

I will not dwell here on questions of methodology and categories of analysis. Suffice it to say that the open approach of the "nouvelle rhétorique," as developed prominently in the "Traité de l'argumentation" of Chaim Perelman and Lucie Olbrechts-Tyteca, seems to be especially helpful for our purposes.[6] Additionally, it might be useful to learn from the methods used by philosophers such as Bernard Williams to analyse the ethical impact of non-philosophical texts from antiquity.[7]

Let us return to the question of New Testament ethics, or of ethics implied in New Testament writings, and to Paul in particular. It seems important to me to raise the question as to whether the moral instructions in Paul's diverse letters are limited to scattered pieces of advice for this or

---

Studien: Herrn Wirkl. Oberkonsistorialrath Professor D. Bernhard Weiss zu seinem 70. Geburtstage dargebracht (ed. Caspar R. Gregory et al.; Göttingen: Vandenhoeck & Ruprecht, 1897), 165–247, 166.

[5] To illustrate this point, in the following publications no section is devoted to moral language in the NT: Wolfgang Schrage, *Ethik des Neuen Testaments* (GNT 4; 4th ed.; Göttingen: Vandenhoeck & Ruprecht, 1982); Rudolf Schnackenburg, *Die sittliche Botschaft des Neuen Testaments* (HTKNT Supplement I/II; 2 vols.; Freiburg: Herder, 1986/1988); Eduard Lohse, *Theologische Ethik des Neuen Testaments* (Theologische Wissenschaft 5/2; Stuttgart: Kohlhammer, 1988); Frank J. Matera, *New Testament Ethics: The Legacies of Jesus and Paul* (Louisville, Ky.: Westminster John Knox, 1996); Richard B. Hays, *The Moral Vision of the New Testament: A Contemporary Introduction to New Testament Ethics* (San Francisco, Calif.: Harper, 1996; repr. Edinburgh: T&T Clark, 1998); Matthias Pfeiffer, *Einweisung in das neue Sein: Neutestamentliche Erwägungen zur Grundlegung der Ethik* (BEvT 119; Gütersloh: Gütersloher Verlag, 2001). In my own overview (cf. Hermut Löhr, "Ethik und Tugendlehre," in *Neues Testament und Antike Kultur: Weltauffassung – Kult – Ethos* [vol. 3 of *Neues Testament und Antike Kultur*; ed. Jürgen Zangenberg; Neukirchen-Vluyn: Neukirchener Verlag, 2005], 151–180), a section devoted to "Stile und Gattungen" had to be left out for the publication, cf. 178 n. 218.

[6] Cf. Chaim Perelman and Lucie Olbrechts-Tyteca, *Traité de l'argumentation: La nouvelle rhétorique* (5th ed.; Brussels: Édition de l'Université de Bruxelles, 1992). This approach, though drawing heavily from reference books on antiquity, attempts to establish its own system and categories of description. It stresses the assumption that rhetorical technique and semantics are interconnected. To my knowledge the categories of the "nouvelle rhétorique" have unfortunately not been developed into a generally accepted and common tool of investigation in New Testament scholarship. But cf. Folker Siegert, *Argumentation bei Paulus: Gezeigt an Römer 9–11* (WUNT 34; Tübingen: Mohr Siebeck, 1985). Cf. also the discussion in: Roger D. Anderson Jr., *Glossary of Greek Rhetorical Terms connected to Methods of Argumentation, Figures and Tropes from Anaximenes to Quintilian* (CBET 24; Leuven: Peeters, 2000).

[7] Cf. e.g. Bernard A. O. Williams, *Shame and Necessity* (Sather Classical Lectures 57; 2nd ed.; Berkeley, Calif.: University of California Press, 2008).

that urgent problem concerning the individuals addressed (or the congregation as a whole), or if they instead indicate casuistic rules of an if-then-logic. Or do we come across some basic principles, some central moral rules or instructions, which could provide orientation in completely different situations, and which could have been transferred by the addressees to new situations and dilemmas? Do the instructions and their rationale open areas of creative adaptation and application? Or are they casuistic and situation-bound? The fact that we have no ἐπιτομή to Paul's moral instruction, no testament, "famous last words" or κύριαι δόξαι is certainly no mere accident, but instead tells us something about Paul's aims and intentions in moral instruction. However, we cannot exclude the possibility that the ephemeral Pauline writings intentionally include basic, perhaps even universal, moral rules and principles. The only way to surmise what really mattered to Paul is to look for the signals provided in the texts themselves. Certainly Paul was no theoretician of ethics, and I am quite sure that he did not want to construct a consistent system of morality, but he may have been moving in the direction of formulating coherent moral thought. By searching Paul's writings for fundamental moral rules and principles, and their linguistic representation in the texts, we also raise the questions of the freedom of choice Paul poses for his addressees with his instructions, of the assumed rationality of the addressees, and we also raise the question of the possibility and justification of transferring these principles to our own time.

2. The Exposition of Fundamental Moral Rules and Principles in Pauline Letters

Beginning with the result, we can state that the Pauline letters contain phrases which can be understood as basic moral rules and principles, and which can be applied to varying cases and situations. These passages demonstrate that, in the majority of cases, Pauline moral thought goes beyond *ad hoc*-advice free of governing principles, and they may even help us to find the focal point of Pauline ethics, both in the individual letters and in the *Corpus Paulinum* as a whole.

In what follows I will name some of the linguistic and rhetorical means by which Paul seems to present fundamental moral rules or principles.[8] Although an exhaustive study is not possible at this point, it is my aim to

---

[8] Speaking of "rules" and "principles" leaves the possibility open for a variety of syntactical representations.

show at least some of the more important features present in Paul, and to illustrate them by examples from different letters.

2.1 Repetition and Extension

One of the simplest rhetorical means for emphasizing a statement is to repeat it. This becomes even more effective when the repetition does not occur only once and in the immediate context, but repeatedly and at different points in the argumentation.

Indeed Paul uses this common rhetorical device in his moral instruction. One of the most prominent examples can be found in Phil, a text that uses the concept of "joy" (χαίρειν is the verb used) to admonish the readers and thus, while aiming primarily at the mental attitude of the addressees rather than concrete action, it nevertheless becomes part of the Apostle's ethical language.

While the motif of joy is already introduced in Phil 2:17–18 and serves as a link between the author and his addressees (made explicit by the use of the composite verb συγχαίρειν), in 3:1 and 4:4 we find direct exhortations to rejoice. These are emphasized not only through their double occurrence, but also by making the repetition explicit through reference to written or oral communication: "Rejoice in the Lord. To *write* the same things to you is not troublesome to me, and for you it is a safeguard"[9] (3:1), "Rejoice in the Lord always; again I will *say*: Rejoice" (4:4).

Other examples of repetition in moral instruction as an indication of basic principles include the double reference to ἀγάπη in Rom 12:9–10 and 13:8–10 (ἀγάπη is already mentioned before in Rom 5:5, 8; 8:35, 39, but only with recourse to God's or Christ's love) and the exhortation to freedom in Gal 5:1, 13 (ἐλευθερία occurred already in 2:4), followed by more detailed advice to the readers. Perhaps one could also adduce the repeated rhetorical question οὐκ οἴδατε in 1 Cor 6:2, 3, 9, 15, 16, 19, followed by different, but partly convergent, moral statements, or the formula πάντα (μοι) ἔξεστιν in 1 Cor 6:12; 10:23. The validity of this last example, however, is relativized by the additions and explanations resulting from the given specific cases.

The praise of ἀγάπη in 1 Cor 13, though it is marked by seven occurrences of the noun (and by repeated parallelism), is nevertheless more properly described as an extension: the argumentation dwells exhaustively on a single concept, the length of which alone signals its outstanding importance in its literary context. The same could be said of 1 Cor 12:12–27, a passage in which the imagery of the ἐκκλησία as a body is developed at

---

[9] If not noted otherwise, all English translations of biblical texts are from the NRSV.

length for the purpose of exhortation. Passages such as Gal 5:16–25 and
Rom 8:1–17, which are discussed below, could also be cited as extensions
of moral instruction.

2.2 Generalizations

One of the most striking characteristics of Pauline moral language is its
tendency towards generalization. Our overall impression that Paul's moral
instruction is not limited to actual problems and questions can be explained
to a great extent by this rhetorical device.

2.2.1 Agents

Different types of generalization can be observed. While Paul addresses,
for the most part, specific Christian communities and, less frequently, individual persons,[10] he nevertheless also formulates moral rules in the third
person singular, and thus rhetorically goes beyond the context of direct
dialogue, see e.g. Gal 6:5, 7–8 and Rom 12:8. Other phrases using the pronoun πᾶς can be found in Rom 13:1–2 and 1 Cor 9:25a, while 1 Cor 7:7
contrasts a hypothetical universal moral concept with the differentiating
power of the πνεῦμα. In this context one should also refer to the statement
on justification by faith, which has moral implications, to say the least, and
which has πᾶσα σάρξ or ἄνθρωπος as subject (Gal 2:16; Rom 3:28). Correspondingly, there are negative rules constructed with μηδείς (1 Cor 10:24;
2 Cor 6:3).

In 1 Cor 11:4–5 Paul speaks of πᾶς ἀνὴρ προσευχόμενος ἢ προφητεύων
and πᾶσα γυνὴ προσευχομένη ἢ προφητεύουσα, thus formulating general
rules for men and women separately. Here Paul addresses a specific situation, which also shows that the emphatic negation of gender difference in
Gal 3:28 is not to be understood in terms of moral instruction. Other examples for this *non sequitur* include the different cases discussed in 1 Cor
7 or the (Pauline?) passage 14:33b–36.

In some important passages moral instruction (not only description!) is
based on dichotomic anthropology. This is the case in Gal 5:16–25, where
a catalogue of vices and virtues is framed by the distinction of (divine)
πνεῦμα and σάρξ, the vices being the "works of the flesh," the virtues labelled as fruit of the spirit. The use of ἔργα and καρπός implies a difference between specific types of action and the anthropological capacities
upon which they are based. This distinction is taken up again in Gal 6:8,
this time combined with the imagery of seed and harvest. "Flesh" and
"spirit" are placed in analogy to the field that is sown. The use of "flesh"
and "spirit" in Rom 8:1–17 is slightly different: instead of ἔργον or

---

[10] Not only in Phlm, but also in Phil 4:2–3.

καρπός, Paul uses a variety of phrases, mostly κατὰ σάρκα – κατὰ πνεῦμα, but also ἐν σαρκί – ἐν πνεύματι and τῇ σαρκί – πνεύματι. Once, in v. 13, the text speaks of πράξεις τοῦ σώματος, while σῶμα is used positively in Rom 12:1. In some other passages the anthropological notion of νοῦς is introduced into the moral argumentation, both negatively and positively (cf. Rom 1:28; 7:23; 12:2).

To illustrate by comparison Paul's use of terms: the imagery of darkness and light, traditionally a part of both Jewish and pagan language of conversion, is extended to the realm of ethics. While 1 Thess 5:5 addresses the readers as "children of light and day" and contrasts them to those belonging to night and darkness, Rom 13:12 combines the same categories of darkness and light with the terms "works" and "weapons."

In other instances general moral regulations are expressed by the use of present participles with or without an object. By using this form of speech Pauline moral language tends to create types of agents – stereotypes of moral practice. Here the Pauline rhetoric turns the discussion of even specific questions of everyday congregational life into more general moral statements. In Rom 14, for example, Paul generalizes forms of behaviour into stereotypes including ὁ ἀσθενῶν (Rom 14:1–2), ὁ ἐσθίων (Rom 14:3, 6) and ὁ μὴ ἐσθίων (Rom 14:6), ὁ κρίνων (Rom 14:4) and ὁ μὴ κρίνων (Rom 14:22), ὁ φρονῶν (Rom 14:6), ὁ δουλεύων (Rom 14:18). We could add ὁ ἀγαπῶν (Rom 13:8), or ὁ σπείρων in 2 Cor 9:6 and Gal 6:8.[11] Apart from these participial expressions, there are also cases in which Paul names various forms of negative behaviour and presents them stereotypified in noun form (instead of naming the vices themselves, 1 Cor 5:11; 6:9–10).

Paul not only uses the first person singular to express his personal view, but also to affirm general moral standards. See, for example, 1 Cor 4:4 and, above all, Rom 7:7–25 – a text which makes extensive use of this rhetorical method to express the moral dilemma of humanity.

More limited to the communities addressed, but nevertheless open to transfer, are general rules of reciprocal behaviour in Gal 6:2; Rom 12:10, 16; 13:8; 14:13 and 15:7.

2.2.2 Objects and Actions

The same tendency can be observed in statements generalizing the possible *object* or *result* of an action.

So the praise of love in 1 Cor 13, after an enumeration of what love does and does not (vv. 4–6), concludes most effectively with short repeti-

---

[11]   Cf. also 1 Cor 9:13 οἱ τὰ ἱερὰ ἐργαζόμενοι, but, as emphasized in v. 15, Paul does *not* bow to the general rule.

tive phrases which have πάντα as their object (v. 7): "(Love) bears all things, believes all things, hopes all things, endures all things."

Here love is indeed introduced as a virtue to be practiced regardless of any possible benefits. Similar phrases can be found in 1 Cor 16:14 (πάντα ὑμῶν ἐν ἀγάπῃ γινέσθω), Phil 2:14 or Rom 14:23 (πίστις). Correspondingly, there are also admonitions using the pronoun μηδέν (1 Thess 4:12; Phil 4:6; Rom 13:8); see also Rom 14:23.

That the realm and the effect of action is not limited to the Christian community, but concerns all human beings, is expressed by explicitly mentioning them as the objects of Christian behaviour (1 Thess 3:12; 5:15; Phil 4:5; Gal 6:10, πρός πάντας).

2.2.3 Norms and Virtues

Throughout his letters, Paul's moral instruction is characterized, above all, by the introduction of nouns or phrases which do not represent specific virtues or vices, but which are used as general moral norms and categories. Such moral terminology includes words such as "love," "freedom," "belief," "joy," "the good" (the adjective form of this term is also used repeatedly), "sanctification" and others. Behavioural categories to be avoided include "sin," "evil," "fornication," "lust," "uncleanness" etc., adjectives such as αἰσχρός and φαῦλος, but also more formal notions such as τὰ ἑτέρων (as opposed to τὰ ἑαυτῶν) in Phil 2:4, τὰ ἴδια in 1 Thess 4:11 or τὰ ὑψηλά in Rom 12:16.

However, we find no exact definitions of the terms, and no effort is made to describe or to delineate these concepts more precisely. It appears that the author builds his argument on common knowledge, an elementary and conventional (mostly Jewish) encyclopaedia of moral notions, and he may also assume the evocative and emotional force of the words he chooses.

An even greater number of theological concepts ("the Gospel," "the vocation," "the Lord," "the Spirit," "the reign of God") is used in various contexts of ethical argumentation throughout the letters. The relationship between those concepts and the agents addressed is established with the aid of imagery such as, e.g. body, participation, clothing, entering or indwelling. The moral impact of those categories is less evident, but sometimes it is explained in the context (cf. 1 Thess 4:3–8 for sanctification; 1 Cor 6:12–20 and Rom 12:4–8 for the imagery of the body).

The exposition of one of the most prominent examples of general moral understanding in Paul, ἀγάπη, will be discussed in more detail below. Suffice it here to note that ἀγάπη was always part of Paul's moral language beginning with his first extant letter. While he equates mutual ἀγάπη and φιλαδελφία in 1 Thess 4:9, the formula εἰς ἀλλήλους καὶ εἰς πάντας, already mentioned above, shows that even in the early period of his ministry, Paul does not restrict ἀγάπη to the community.

Less noticeable than ἀγάπη, but equally striking to me, is the presence of the abstract τὸ ἀγαθόν in Pauline letters, especially in Rom, where it occurs no less than 15 times. Its moral impact can be shown by the fact that τὸ ἀγαθόν appears recurrently in connection with *verba agendi* (cf. Rom 2:10; 3:8; 7:19; 9:11; 13:3).[12] The text does not provide an extensive reflection on the nature of the good – ἀγαθόν is used as a predicative (or an attribute), not as an object of analysis or critique. This fact leaves it up to the addressees to judge what is good and evil in every new situation. The prominent presence of the concept in Paul's moral language shows its close connection to general or universal everyday standards of morality.[13]

The use of πορνεία as a negative moral norm in 1 Cor 5 is an interesting case. As we have already seen, the use of general moral terminology, both positive and negative, always implies the task to relate it to facts, to interpret data from everyday life in terms of the categories of moral language: good and bad, preferable and harmful, but also vice and virtue are not self-evident, they are interpretative concepts, not objects. Though the meaning of πορνεία is more specific than just an indication of immorality, it is not specific enough to mean a fixed set of behavioural patterns. In 1 Cor 5 Paul evidently takes a short-cut in juxtaposing the general concept and the specific case (1b), "that someone has the wife of his father" (my translation), adding a remark which rhetorically underlines the judgement on the specific case at hand and which is indicative of the implicit world view of the Apostle (1a): "fornication of a kind which is not found even among the gentiles!" (my translation).

This is moral rhetoric. A more thorough argumentation would certainly have to show *why exactly* having "the wife of his father" is πορνεία. At least the norm would have to be made explicit.[14] Whether the first addressees of the letter did in fact agree with Paul's equation, or whether they were astonished to hear about his categorizing, we cannot know. After exposing in some detail how to deal with the fornicator, and after illustrating this by *mazzot* imagery, Paul comes back to the concept of πορνεία (this time using πόρνος) in v. 9 by referring to an earlier letter. It is not clear whether Paul in this earlier letter dwelt on πορνεία in general, or whether another specific case of πορνεία was mentioned. It seems quite probable to me, however, that the earlier letter did not discuss the case which is under scrutiny in 1 Cor – the man living with the wife of his father. Thus from the presentation in 1 Cor 5 itself it becomes clear that within the ongoing

---

[12] Also in Gal 6:10.

[13] A more detailed analysis has to be reserved for a subsequent publication.

[14] Paul probably has Lev 18:8 in mind, but makes no direct reference to it.

dialogue between the apostle and the Corinthians, πορνεία has the status of a general ethical principle which allows for interpretation and for judgement of varying situations in community life.[15]

While a series of norms is mentioned in Phil 4:8, followed by a very general reference to the apostolic moral teaching, in Rom 12:2 such a set of general norms is identified as the will of God. In these cases the effect of generalization is reached by accumulation: the individual statements as well as their combination give the impression of a general rule of behaviour.

To conclude our search for techniques of generalization, there is no better passage than 2 Cor 9:8, a text in which various modes of these techniques appear in combination: δυνατεῖ δὲ ὁ θεὸς πᾶσαν χάριν περισσεῦσαι εἰς ὑμᾶς, ἵνα ἐν παντὶ πάντοτε πᾶσαν αὐτάρκειαν ἔχοντες περισσεύητε εἰς πᾶν ἔργον ἀγαθόν ("And God is able to provide you with every blessing in abundance, so that by always having enough of everything, you may share abundantly in every good work").

2.3 Personification

The use of general and abstract terminology in Paul's moral language has its counterweight in personification.

The most prominent example for this can be found once again in 1 Cor 13. In this chapter ἀγάπη is never made into an object of a direct admonition, but it is introduced in a chain of short phrases as the subject of action (cf. vv. 4–7). It is interesting to notice, however, that in the first three verses, Paul uses the phrase "to have love" (ἀγάπην ἔχειν), thus possibly exposing "love" as a virtue or a good both behind, and extending beyond, visible deeds (v. 3).[16]

In the first line personification is a stylistic device that adds to the liveliness of the argumentation (the underlying principle obviously being that a person is best characterized by his behaviour – which reveals a lot about anthropological notions in early Christianity) and stresses the importance of the concept of love. But at the same time a virtue is more tangible when presented as a(n attractive) person, the subject of the action. The personification, whether attractive and convincing or not, leaves open the possibility of choice. For the reader it creates more the impression of recommendation, guideline and illustration than that of advice and authoritative in-

---

[15] It goes beyond the scope of the present article to describe the context of the argument more precisely. Let it suffice to say that 1 Cor 6 (cf. esp. 6:18–19) provides further reasons for avoiding fornication without explicit reference to Torah interdictions.

[16] The phrase seems to have been used for the first time in early Christianity, cf. 1 Cor 13:1–3; Phil 2:2; John 13:35; 15:13; 1 Pet 4:8; 1 John 4:16. I thank my assistant David C. Bienert for drawing my attention to this fact.

struction: the ethical discourse changes from commandment and obedience to example and imitation, hence making its addressee the subject of moral decision.

While that could be part of the author's way of entering into dialogue with the specific community in Corinth (other texts testifying quite to the contrary), it is certainly also an expression of the underlying notion of ἀγάπη, which in itself seems to require openness, self-responsibility and personal commitment resulting from personal choice.

Let us consider the presentation of ἀγάπη in Rom 13:8–10, a passage which begins with imperatives, not with personifications. In the text love is related to a second and more precise moral norm, the law. However, it would miss the thrust of the argument to interpret the verses only with regard to the problem of the law, its validity and its different *usus*. The context in the chapter is not about the concept of the law, but about the question of how to act. So reference to the law or, to be more exact, to some (but not all) precepts of the Decalogue, seems to serve as a common ground for the argument on which it is built, i.e. the commendation of love. It adds to the rhetorical effect that the *positive* love commandment is placed side by side with *interdictions* taken from the Decalogue, while it is made clear already in v. 8, but also in the negation of v. 10, that the love commandment itself goes beyond the respective precept or prohibition.

Finally, in v. 10 the same stylistic device is used as in 1 Cor 13: personification. Love becomes the subject of the phrase, the agent. While v. 10a formulates what love does with regard to other human beings, v. 10b takes up the concept of the law again and speaks of fulfilment, thus connecting two distinct approaches for describing the moral impact of love. It is not far-fetched, I think, to see this argument in a well-constructed contradistinction to the personifications used in chapter 6 and 7: while sin, in misusing the ἐντολή of the law, deceives and kills me (7:11–12), love – as the summation and fulfilment of the Law's different ἐντολαί – does no harm to one's (Christian?) neighbour. For Paul this would not be enough in terms of soteriology; with regard to ethics, it is.

It should be added that in Rom 6:15–23 personification is used not only with regard to "sin," but also "justice," "uncleanness," and "iniquity;" see also Rom 8:3–4 for positive personifications. It would be misleading to see in this rhetorical device the expression of some underlying notion of suprahuman, cosmic powers or entities, an understanding that would not fully take account of the construction of the argument. This is also why I am increasingly hesitant to speak of a so-called "transmoral" understanding of sin in Paul, a category which seems to be alien to the Jewish-Christian tradition in antiquity.

2.4 Authority and Example

The reference to personal authority and example is an important part of the strategy of persuasion in Pauline argumentation. While apostolic authority is the basis of most of the interaction with the communities addressed, and while it is made explicit in moral advice or admonition, e.g. in 1 Thess 1:6; 1 Cor 5:3; 7:12, the apostle himself and Christ also serve as ethical examples (cf. 1 Cor 4:6–16; 7:7–8; 8:13; 11:1[17]; 2 Cor 10:1; Rom 15).[18]

While the passages from 1 Thess, or 1 Cor 7 and 8, mention or discuss a number of specific cases, in texts such as 1 Cor 4:6; 11:1 (cf. the generalizing statement in 10:31!) and 2 Cor 10:1 personal example and general rules of behaviour are linked together.

The somewhat enigmatic introductory phrase ὃ καὶ ἐν Χριστῷ Ἰησοῦ in Phil 2:5 *might* be understood without alluding to Christ's example,[19] but from the context of the christological hymn in Phil 2:6–11 it becomes quite clear that the way described, including the active humbling of the self, serves as a general moral example for the community addressed (cf. esp. vv. 2–4 and the introduction in v. 12: ὥστε). This is also why Paul can admonish his readers in 3:17 to become his συμμιμηταί, thus linking the examples of the apostle and of Christ.

The overall impression made by these and other texts, though, is that the reference to personal example is not the most prominent or efficient rhetorical method for the exposition of moral rules or principles in the Pauline writings.

2.5 Climax and Progress

One of the biggest challenges for any serious ethical reflection or responsible moral advice is to argue convincingly for a hierarchy of values or practical options that enables the addressee to decide on preferences or priorities of action and to avoid moral dilemmas – while at the same time avoiding any oversimplification. The field of ethics is not only about good

---

[17]   The threefold structure: the Christ as the example for Paul, Paul in turn as the example for the community, has its parallels in Seneca's letters (cf. *Ep.* 70.9, 71.1, 7) where Socrates is the paragon.

[18]   The notion of ethical *imitatio* in the Pauline writings is described by Anselm Schulz, *Nachfolgen und Nachahmen: Studien über das Verhältnis der neutestamentlichen Jüngerschaft zur urchristlichen Vorbildethik* (StANT 6; Munich: Kösel, 1962), 201–331. I thank Prof. Dr. Sean Freyne, Dublin, for drawing my attention to this useful monograph. Cf. also Hans Dieter Betz, *Nachfolge und Nachahmung Jesu Christi im Neuen Testament* (BHT 37; Tübingen: Mohr Siebeck, 1967), 137–189.

[19]   Cf. Gerald F. Hawthorne, *Philippians* (WBC 43; Waco, Tex.: Word Books, 1983), 79–81; Nikolaus Walter, Eckart Reinmuth and Peter Lampe, *Die Briefe an die Philipper, Thessalonicher und an Philemon* (NTD 8/2; Göttingen: Vandenhoeck & Ruprecht, 1998), 55.

and bad or "do's" and "don'ts," but also about better and (a little bit) worse, both with regard to acts, aims and benefits, but also to agents of behaviour and their mindsets.

This is also reflected in Pauline moral language, which thus expresses not only better options in specific cases (as in 1 Cor 7:21), but every now and then also establishes gradations to illuminate the general rules of behaviour to be adopted.

So the praise of ἀγάπη as a virtue in 1 Cor 13 (the verses 1–3 and 13 once being labelled as "Wertepriambel" by Klaus Berger[20]) is introduced in 12:31 by a two-step climax: to conclude the argument on different χαρίσματα in the community Paul admonishes his readers to strive for the better (μείζονα) ones. But instead of introducing ἀγάπη as one of these better gifts of the spirit, the author adds the remark (v. 31b) "And I will show you a still more excellent way."

The expression "way" (ὁδός) signals the practical concern of what follows and, by indicating a difference between the better χαρίσματα and the way καθ' ὑπερβολήν, thus expresses that ἀγάπη is definitely more than one of the capacities discussed in the preceding chapter. This construction not only emphasizes ἀγάπη as a basic moral principle, but at the same time expresses that for Paul, the χαρίσματα mentioned in chapter 12 (cf. esp. vv. 4–11) belong to a different category than love (together with hope and faith). The same differentiation is also mirrored in 14:1, which concludes the praise of love: "Pursue love and strive for the spiritual gifts."

The fundamental difference evidently is that while love (singular!) is possible for everyone to enact, not every single χάρισμα (in this verse Paul uses the plural noun πνευματικά) is available for every member of the community. In other words: love, together with faith and hope, is a general moral rule to be followed, while prophecy or healing are not and cannot be.

As a corollary to these remarks on climax one may ask whether the use of the phrase (τὸ) λοιπόν in moral instruction (1 Thess 4:1; 2 Cor 13:11; Phil 4:8) could be understood as an anti-climax, introducing what should be said even though it is of minor importance. But Phil 4:8, to name at least one textual reference, speaks against this assumption. Here the phrase marks a swing back from exhortation of individuals to that of the entire community. We may note in this context that, in some instances, general rules originating in basic moral categories serve to conclude discussions of

---

[20]   Cf. Klaus Berger, "Hellenistische Gattungen im Neuen Testament," *ANRW* 2.25.2 (1984): 1031–1432 and 1831–1885, cf. esp. 1204–1208. The category was not retained in: Klaus Berger, *Formen und Gattungen im Neuen Testament* (Tübingen: Francke, 2005).

more specific character, see for example 1 Thess 5:15, 22; 1 Cor 5:13; 16:13–14, Gal 6:10 or Rom 12:21; 14:23.

In other passages the concepts of "growing" or "perfection" can be used to affirm fundamental moral values such as love (1 Thess 4:10), justice (1 Cor 3:6–7; 2 Cor 9:10) or faith (2 Cor 10:15). These texts clearly imply a concept of moral progress, which otherwise plays an important role especially in Phil (cf. 1:6, 9–11, 25; 3:16).

3. Conclusion

Our investigation into Paul's moral language can be summarized as follows:

1.   The letters of Paul do not provide systematic ethical reflection or general theory. Nevertheless they are clearly shaped by moral instructions. An analysis of the moral language used, including its rhetoric and logic, can help us to identify basic moral rules and develop an understanding of their implicit ethics.

2.   Our selective overview showed Paul as a vivid and versatile counsellor of his congregations. The author's argument is not restricted to detailed advice in specific situations, but it makes partial use of general or universal rules or principles, which are sometimes even the subject of more intensive reflection in longer passages.

3.   Those rules and principles, however, are never developed into a fixed set of benefits, values or virtues. The tendency toward basic statements is more rhetorical than systematic, but it is not *only* rhetorical.

4.   This being the case, the prominent position of ἀγάπη in Pauline moral instruction can be shown by analyzing passages in 1 Cor and Rom. In these passages, but also in 1 Thess, ἀγάπη is not limited to a "brotherly love" exclusively within the community.

5.   The fact that we do find moral rules and principles in the Pauline letters, and are able to single out some (but not all) of the means by which they are presented in the texts, might tell us something about the kind of ethics involved. The type of ethics implied in the Pauline text is apparently halfway between authoritative ethics based on a notion of specific or general commandments and their subsequent obedience and fulfilment, and an ethics relying on rationality, persuasion, reflection and choice. Linguistic and rhetorical analysis thus corroborate that Paul's ethics seems to be on

the border between "Gebotsethik" (ethics based on commandments) and "Einsichtsethik" (ethics based on insight or understanding).[21]

---

[21] The differentiation between "Gebotsethik" and "Einsichtsethik" should not be understood as equivalent to the difference between Jewish and Hellenistic ethics in New Testament times, *pace* Gerd Theißen, *Das Neue Testament* (Munich: Beck, 2002), 10.

"Unethical" Language in the Pauline Letters?

Stereotyping, Vilification and Identity Matters[1]

JEREMY PUNT

1. Introduction

The innovative and interesting ways in which language was used in various New Testament documents in their consistent and ongoing processes of identity negotiation has received more attention since the "linguistic turn" in biblical hermeneutics. For example, a widespread mechanism that was often employed in issues concerning identity in New Testament times, namely stereotyping or labelling people, and its close ally, vilification or rhetorical and often groundless derision, is now acknowledged as important means towards negotiating identity.[2] First-century stereotyping was in the first instance generally not about the language of simple description and certainly not the accurate portrayal of people, of *other* people, but rather about identity politics: marking out identity of self and others, reinforcing the self through denigrating the other. Thus, accusations levelled by some Roman authors against the early Christians, such as ritualistic infanticide and cannibalism (e.g. Fronto), "may be understood as entirely believable to his audience – not because the accusation was thought to be 'true' but because it efficiently expressed a collective distaste for the characteristic Christian refusal to participate in the common culture of city and empire."[3] In the end stereotyping was often not so much about the na-

---

[1] Paper read at a Humboldt *Kolleg*, "Moral Language in the New Testament," Pretoria, 8–10 September 2008.

[2] Cf. Andrie du Toit, "Vilification as a Pragmatic Device in Early Christian Epistolography," *Biblica* 75 (1994): 403–412; Sean Freyne, "Vilifying the Other and Defining the Self: Matthew's and John's Anti-Jewish Polemic in Focus," in *"To See Ourselves As Others See Us:" Christians, Jews, "Others" in Late Antiquity* (ed. Jacob Neusner and Ernest S. Frerichs; Scholars Press Studies in the Humanities; Chico, Calif.: Scholars Press, 1985), 117–143; Luke T. Johnson, "The New Testament's Anti-Jewish Slander and the Conventions of Ancient Polemic," *Journal of Biblical Literature* 108 (1989): 419–441.

[3] Jennifer W. Knust, *Abandoned to Lust: Sexual Slander and Ancient Christianity* (Gender, Theory, and Religion; New York, N.Y.: Columbia University Press, 2006), 7. "It is the prior understanding of the other as a dangerous threat to society that leads

ture of the stereotyped objects as about the identity of the ones making use of stereotyping, defining the self through others.[4]

The use of stereotype and vilifying language is evident throughout the New Testament, and is perhaps most easily discernible in the later traditions. Amidst increased levels of acrimony and heightened intensity of differences between insiders and outsiders, a letter such as Jude levelled serious accusations against the "ungodly" (ἀσεβεῖς) ones (Jude 4, 15, 18). As probably one of the most aggressive documents in the New Testament, the letter of Jude[5] unreservedly attacked the opponents identified in the letter, not allowing for any compromise.[6] Although the letter is concerned with more than the issue of opponents and difference, the dominant concern of Jude's letter[7] was apparently the issue of how to deal with the opponents, who were identified in vague and ambiguous ways only.[8]

---

ancient authors, whether in history or fiction, to draw on a common stockpile of typical anti-societal actions," Philip A. Harland, "'These People Are … Men Eaters:' Banquets of the Anti-Associations and Perceptions of Minority Cultural Groups," in *Identity and Interaction in the Ancient Mediterranean: Jews, Christians and Others* (Essays in Honour of Stephen G. Wilson; ed. Zeba A. Crook and Philip A. Harland; New Testament Monographs 18; Sheffield: Sheffield Phoenix, 2007), 56–75, 74.

[4] Notwithstanding modern claims to unprejudiced and truthful description and reporting, and if the axioms that all perception is theory-laden, and all theory is value-laden are to be trusted, it also does not augur well for the modernist project of "truth" in a positivistic sense, especially not when it comes to the description of other people.

[5] The letter of Jude is generally dated around the turn of the first century CE. Some disagree, and so after evaluating Jude according to the categories of the imminent expectation of the parousia; the evidence of an institutionalised church with an elaborate set of officials; and, indications of a fixed set of doctrine of belief; Bauckham (Richard J. Bauckham, *Jude, 2 Peter* [WBC 50; Waco, Tex.: Word Books, 1983], 9) for example challenged the consensus in scholarship regarding the letter of Jude representing early Catholicism, concluding: "[s]o there is not just a lack of evidence for Jude's 'early Catholicism,' there is compelling evidence against it."

[6] An equally irredeemable position is constructed for the Pharisaic group in the Fourth Gospel, when the charge of blindness is given an ironic twist in John 9: although they can see (sc. Jesus, the saviour of the world), they are blind because they persist in their sin of not acknowledging Jesus, and will therefore die in their sin (John 8:23) (Freyne, "Vilifying" [n. 2], 135–136).

[7] And also of 2 Peter, which often forms part of any discussion on the letter of Jude, because of the large degree of correspondence of Jude with 2 Pet; however, although 2 Pet was in the past often seen to be primary, the current consensus is that, whatever the nature of the relationship, 2 Pet probably to a large extent depended upon Jude's letter on which 2 Pet then expanded (cf. e.g. Bauckham, *Jude* [n. 5], xii; Donald A. Carson, "Jude," in *Commentary on the New Testament Use of the Old Testament* (ed. Gregory K. Beale and Donald A. Carson; Grand Rapids, Mich.: Baker Academic, 2007), 1069–1079, 1069.

[8] Jeremy Punt, "Jude and the Others: Hermeneutics, Identity, Conflict," *South African Baptist Journal of Theology* 17 (2008): 149–162.

However, problems with opposing or disagreeing groups of different types and appearances were fairly common in New Testament letters generally, although understanding the trouble they were portrayed to have caused *and* the way that they were represented has historically, to say the least, not been *un*problematic. In fact, in the Pauline documents with their strong moral tenor, the use of stereotype language was not limited to the opponents only but used against some members of the Pauline communities, too. In this brief investigation of one aspect of his use of language, Paul's use of stereotype and to some extent vilifying language, its purpose and some consequences will be discussed, focusing mainly on the letter to the Galatians.[9]

2. First-century Language and Discourse

Investigations on the use of language within the wider ambit of the New Testament's moral discourse have to proceed beyond the distinction between orality and literacy, no matter how helpful this distinction is at a certain level.[10] It is for example increasingly recognised that – in a more modern idiom – the followers of Jesus were less a people of the (canonical) book and more a group translating and passing around paperbacks among themselves. The first-century world's oral character extended to religious communication and propaganda, shared also by the early followers of Jesus but they engaged in a revolutionary kind of "oral literacy," showing independence and originality in their use of culture and tradition. Their focus was on *imitatio Jesu* rather than submission to the Torah or another canon, and when by the second century the use of codices became characteristic in Christianity, the focus of this practice was on their practical rather than cultic use.[11] And while the early followers of Jesus inha-

---

[9]   While focusing on Paul's letter to the Galatians to situate the argument – no exhaustive discussion is provided of Galatians, not even regarding the topic under discussion – this paper assumes a distinction between this letter together with the other authentic Pauline letters, and the deutero-Pauline letters (2 Thess, Eph, Col and the Pastoral Epistles). To frame the argument, it is from time to time set against the broader scope of other New Testament documents as well.

[10] Cf. e.g. Pieter J. J. Botha, "Mute Manuscripts: Analysing a Neglected Aspect of Ancient Communication," *Theologica Evangelica* 23 (1990): 35–47; Joanna Dewey, "Textuality in an Oral Culture: A Survey of the Pauline Traditions," *Semeia* 65 (1994): 37–65; J. Keith Elliot, "Manuscripts, the Codex and the Canon," *JSNT* 63 (1996): 105–123; Johannes A. Loubser, "Orality and Literacy in the Pauline Epistles: Some New Hermeneutical Implications," *Neotestamentica* 29 (1995): 61–74.

[11] Guy G. Stroumsa, "Early Christianity – a Religion of the Book?," in *Homer, the Bible, and Beyond: Literary and Religious Canons in the Ancient World* (ed. Margalit

bited a world which was oral in nature and populated by a variety of oral traditions and cultures including those from the Jewish context, they increasingly carved out a language and an ethos which incorporated beliefs about Jesus Christ, formatting a social world where they could construct a new identity and celebrate it. "[T]he early Christian talk about a newly created ego does not *describe*, mirror or represent an already *existing* reality. No, it *creates* this reality of a new ego ... The entire realm of social relationships is based on words and information that *create* reality."[12]

This concern for a new identity in Christ, or at least for negotiating such an identity, is prominent in the Pauline letters[13] – without arguing for either the similarity of different Pauline letters or for a generalised version of "the" Pauline letter. Paul's concern about identity[14] is, partly, borne out by the presence and indeed pervasiveness of his moral discourse, as both a framework for and set of specific themes and issues in his letters. In other words, the identity that Paul was constantly negotiating constituted the

---

Finkelberg and Guy G. Stroumsa; Jerusalem Studies in Religion and Culture 2; Leiden: Brill, 2003), 153–173. Stroumsa is at great pains to point out various misunderstandings related to the characterisation of early Christianity as a "religion of the book" in a way similar as was found in Jewish and Muslim circles, showing upon the early Christians' differences in attitude towards written texts.

[12] Peter Lampe, "Identification with Christ: A Psychological View of Pauline Theology," in *Texts and Contexts: Biblical Texts in their Textual and Situational Contexts* (Essays in Honor of Lars Hartman; ed. Tord Fornberg and David Hellholm; Oslo: Scandinavian University Press, 1995), 930–943, 940, emphasis in the original. Psychoanalytically, the difference between one who imitates and one who identifies with the model person is that the latter not only displays similar behaviour but adopts the model person's motivations, goals and emotions, as well. This requires a "libido impulse" or affection between Christ and believers, and eventually leads to "a radical restructuring of the Ego by identification with Christ," initiated by the ritual identification process of baptism (Lampe, "Identification" [see above], 940). Given the imperial setting of the first century CE, a postcolonial perspective and especially the notion of mimicry may describe this relationship between model and follower better: *viz* mimicry as the ambivalent mixture of deference and disobedience, which often amounts to a counter-strategy brought into play by the colonised or the subalterns.

[13] Jeremy Punt, "A politics of difference in the New Testament: Identity and the Others in Paul," in *The New Testament interpreted* (Essays in honour of Bernard C. Lategan; ed. Cilliers Breytenbach, Johan C. Thom and Jeremy Punt; NovTSup 124; Leiden: Brill, 2006), 199–225.

[14] As has been argued in a different context, identity concerns were and are not peripheral to people's social and personal lives, and should not in the New Testament documents be portrayed as being in contrast to theological concerns such as the love command. "The search for and the preoccupation with defining the self are symptoms of our condition, both Jewish and Christian – especially, it would seem, when we are confronted with the experience of a God who seeks to destroy such deep-seated longings within us" (Freyne, "Vilifying" [n. 2], 141).

new ethos[15] he envisioned for the communities he worked with. Dealing with Pauline ethos would include both his ethical considerations and exhortation, but also his use of the language of stereotyping.

The letter to the Galatians is sometimes viewed with some suspicion when it comes to a discussion of moral discourse in the Pauline corpus. However, it has been shown quite convincingly that, rather than containing an ethical deficit in the midst of a controversy about the law, Paul's emphasis on ethics in the last two chapters of Galatians in particular, which revolved around two central exhortations, to stand in the freedom that Christ made possible (5:1) and to walk in the Spirit (5:25), was characterised by his appeal for the specific nature and style of ethics. Avoiding the substitution of the law with another legal system, Paul opted to stress responsibility for independent and founded decision making, informed by a multiplicity of "sources," and in the process redefined the nature of early Christian ethics. This shift in the basis of ethical decision-making was accompanied by a new style of ethical discernment, since Galatians also reflected Paul's ideal of participating and creative ethics, a new understanding of what ethical responsibility entails.[16] Galatians stands within the broader context of Paul's new moral and ethical discernment,[17] and is indicative of another lifestyle or ethos.[18]

---

[15] The apostle's letters sit more comfortably with the notion of ethos as identity incorporating moral discourse, than ethics as (reflected upon) moral discourse.

[16] Bernard C. Lategan, "Is Paul Developing a Specifically Christian Ethics in Galatia?," in *Greeks, Romans and Christians* (Essays in Honor of Abraham J. Malherbe; ed. David L. Balch, Everett Ferguson and Wayne A. Meeks; Minneapolis, Minn.: Fortress Press, 1990), 318–328.

[17] Allen Verhey, *The Great Reversal: Ethics and the New Testament* (Grand Rapids, Mich.: Eerdmans, 1994), 103–113.

[18] At this stage a few caveats are required, which at the same time indicate where further investigation is needed. Firstly, Paul's stereotyping requires attention also for other elements of Paul's language, including his use of the Scriptures of Israel, a language of embodiment (his "body theology"), etc. Secondly, stereotype language intersects with other discourses such as an ontological gender discourse (Caroline Vander Stichele and Todd Penner, "Paul and the Rhetoric of Gender," in *Her Master's Tools? Feminist and Postcolonial Engagements of Historical-Critical Discourse* [ed. Caroline Vander Stichele and Todd Penner; Global perspectives on biblical scholarship 9; Atlanta, Ga.: SBL, 2005], 287–310) which was present within the broader framework of an ontological philosophical discourse about the "chain of being" (Elisabeth Schüssler Fiorenza, *The Power of the Word: Scripture and the Rhetoric of Empire* [Minneapolis, Minn.: Fortress Press, 2007], 99) in the first century CE. E.g. stereotypical slander operated within "an early Christian 'gendered disciplinary apparatus' designed to control insiders [and] shame outsiders" (Knust, *Abandoned* [n. 3], 13; Elizabeth A. Clark, "Sex, Shame, and Rhetoric: Engendering Early Christian Ethics," *Journal of the American Academy of Religion* 59 [1991]: 221–245, 221) – cf. further below. This meant that the ideological frameworks which defined people and their place in society were largely

At the same time, however, Paul's advocacy of a new identity and ethos in Galatians was accompanied by the language of stereotype typical of his contemporary context – and other letters. Stereotype language which often led to the vilification of outsiders as well as those insiders opposing him played an important role in Paul's rhetoric, of which the following would have been some of his strategies and its consequences.

3. Pauline Language, and Stereotyping and Vilification

The earliest New Testament documents such as the letters directed to the Galatians and the Philippians provide evidence of insider-outsider conflicts, and how boundaries are tightened when initial gestures of inclusivity were reversed. In these and other letters, the fibre of the community or the veracity of Paul's expressed convictions and commitments are protected from those considered to threaten them, and those posing the threat are in the process marginalised, vilified and even excluded.[19] Those who rejected the Pauline understanding of the Christian message were referred to with sarcasm, dealt with rather harshly in terms of social categories, and were even accused of vile acts. The rhetorical situation of a letter such as Galatians might be taken to suggest that exclusion was the result of invoking essentialist-sounding categories such as ethnic identity;[20] the problem, it seems, was rather whether the position people assumed was in line with Paul's understanding of God and life.[21]

---

fixed, but at the same time also overwhelmingly forceful and determinative for the lives of people. Thirdly, further work is needed on the complex relationship between stereotyping and vilification, where on the one hand the former can be ground for vilification, while on the other hand vilification can at times also simply become stereotyped.

[19] Cf. Punt, "A politics" (n. 8), 199–225.

[20] The claim that Paul eschewed any particular ethnic identity in favour of an all-inclusive community of the Lord fails to deal with the broader array of evidence. "[S]ometimes Paul's opponents must be Christians as well as, presumably, Jews. I would include in that category gentile Christians who had already been circumcised, making them Jews for all intents and purposes," Alan F. Segal, "Response: Some aspects of conversion and identity formation in the Christian community of Paul's time," in *Paul and politics: Ekklesia, Israel, Imperium, Interpretation* (Essays in honour of Krister Stendahl; ed. Richard A. Horsley; Harrisburg, Pa.: Trinity Press International, 2000), 184–190, 186. Cf. below on stereotyping and racial and ethnic identity.

[21] Claims such as "Paul's mission implies an alternative vision of the path toward global reconciliation," and "[s]ince God's grace is equally available to all, no claim of superiority remains valid and therewith the basis for every kind of imperialism has been removed" (Robert Jewett, "Response: Exegetical support from Romans and other letters," in *Paul and politics* [n. 20], 58–71, 71) can be sustained to some degree, but ultimately

Many questions and the complexity of interpretation are even more pronounced in a contribution which is written from the perspective that language is an important component in our construction of reality, and more particularly – and building on insights gained from social identity theory – that language is vital in identity formation. Since it is used between and about people, language is inevitably social: "[o]ur social reality is largely constructed and renewed in conversations."[22] Amidst the volatile and fragile nature of identity processes in the changing first-century environment, stereotyping and vilification proved to be valuable linguistic tools in the precarious undertaking of formulating (communal) identity.

3.1 First-century Stereotyping and Vilification

Stereotype language was present in different formats in the first century CE, with character, ethnic and social role stereotypes probably being most pervasive.[23] In Aristotle's *Politics* 7.6.1–2 people from Europe (spirited but not so intelligent) are contrasted with those from Asia (intelligent but not so spirited), before the philosopher concluded that "the Greek race" occupied the middle position (intelligent and spirited) in character, as much as in geography. Ethnocentrism and accompanying stereotyping abounded: Josephus (*Vita* 352) described Scythians as wild beasts taking pleasure in murdering people; Strabo (*Geogr.* 16.2.23) thought Phoenicians were superior to all other people; and Vergil (*Aen.* 2.65) was convinced that Greeks as a whole could be known by any one of them. Ethnic stereotyping was expanded to include the evaluation of others based on geography, trade and social groupings or factions. Social roles which were related to recurrent social expectations formed the basis of yet another set of stereotypes, functioning in the household or family (father, mother, etc.) as much as in the political structures (king, governor, etc.) or in village and city life (scribes, fishermen, etc.).

Stereotyping has never been restricted to collectivist societies only, but it typically plays a more important role where the group is prioritised.[24]

---

breaks down within (or, at least becomes relegated to) the broader picture where the Pauline notion of identity ruled the day.

[22] Sik Hung Ng, "Power: An Essay in Honour of Henri Tajfel," in *Social Groups and Identities: Developing the Legacy of Henri Tajfel* (ed. William Peter Robinson; International Series in Social Psychology; Oxford: Butterworth-Heinemann, 1996), 191–214, 194.

[23] Bruce J. Malina and Jerome H. Neyrey, *Portraits of Paul: An Archeology of Ancient Personality* (Louisville, Ky.: Westminster John Knox, 1996), 169–174.

[24] Along with embeddedness; socialisation through appeal to tradition and loyalty; and, the use of sanctions and rewards with regard to what was considered appropriate duties, piety and virtues, thinking in stereotypes can be listed as the primary indications of first-century group-oriented people. "Persons socialized into group-oriented societies

Coupled with the socially harsh environment of the first century CE with its strong agonistic tendencies, great emphasis was put on social values in New Testament times as was evident in constant attempts of people and groups to increase honour and elude shame. The honour-and-shame society of the time period was not only informed by and structured according to various hierarchies, but it was patriarchy in particular that defined and inscribed male power and dominance. With the focus primarily on the group, people dealt with each other and with outsiders in particular in terms of stereotype and slander,[25] often amounting to vilification. In fact, stereotyping was often accompanied by vilification,[26] which was also a well-established pragmatic device in ancient epistolography,[27] functioning as the opposite side of praise speech. Used as a tool of persuasion in ancient letters, explicit and implicit vilification is often found in New Testament letters where authors wanted to persuade their audiences to accept and affirm their views against those of their opponents.[28]

Language of stereotype in collectivist societies served the all important purpose of maintaining and negotiating the identity of the own social group, through ascribing identity to those outside the own group. Stereotyping was at one level about simplification: "[e]xperiencing life in terms of stereotypes means to approach everyday reality with its persons and things by using general conceptions rather than taking time to construct customized designs."[29] But stereotyping was even more important for identity negotiation since stereotypes "had social as well as individual functions; in particular they provided group members with positively valued intergroup differences which enhanced their social identity, and explained and justified intergroup relations. They served collective aspects of psy-

---

invariably make sense of other people by assessing them 'sociologically' rather than 'psychologically.' In other words, people in collectivist cultures appraise others in terms of the stereotypes they share with their in-group" (Malina and Neyrey, *Portraits* [n. 23], 169). Other scholars connect stereotyping and the accompanying polemic also to the Hellenistic tradition of philosophical schools where disputes often relied on conventional expressions (cf. Johnson, "Anti-Jewish Slander" [n. 2], 429–430).

[25] Malina and Neyrey, *Portraits* (n. 23), 169–174.

[26] Here one should not merely focus on crude stereotypes only, since "even the most trivial of category distinctions can be the cue for the most extreme forms of discrimination," J. Richard Eiser, "Accentuation Revisited," in *Social Groups* (n. 22), 121–142, 139.

[27] *Vituperatio* or vituperative rhetoric was learned in rhetorical schools, "aimed at destroying the social and political *persona* of one's adversary" (Freyne, "Vilification" [n. 2], 118).

[28] Du Toit, "Vilification" (n. 2), 403–404.

[29] Malina and Neyrey, *Portraits* (n. 23), 170.

chology, ideologizing and giving social meaning and value to action."[30]
Taking stereotype language as vital for identity negotiation as point of departure, at least four important aspects, namely racial and ethnic identification, constructing opponents and othering, curse rhetoric, and sexual
slander can be identified in Paul's stereotyping strategy in Galatians.

3.1.1 Racial and Ethnic Identification as Stereotyping

Racial and ethnic categorisation was basic to ancient stereotyping but is
unfortunately today often denied in the interest of contemporary concerns
and interests. In contrast to early Christian texts' invocation of racial and
ethnic categories, but also in light of the ascendency of scientific racism in
the late nineteenth century, historical constructions of early Christianity
widely assumed that the notion of Christian identity excluded any racial
connotations.[31] Both those mainline scholars who insist on the perceived

---

[30] John C. Turner, "Henri Tajfel: An Introduction," in *Social Groups* (n. 22), 1–23,
14. A helpful theoretical framework for establishing the link between processes of
identity formation and negotiation, and stereotyping is social identity theory. This theory
was developed to address issues of group prejudice, where groups' reasoning and
behaviour were influenced and distorted at a larger scale and through complex
mechanisms by social values. Dealing with the intricate relationship between human
psychological functioning and large-scale social processes and events which affect and
are affected by such functioning, social identity theory want to understand the conditions
within which individuals choose a certain (group) identity and act accordingly as
members of a group. Such group identity is not dependent upon group cohesion or
physical and direct interaction with other people, and not even those associating with the
same group (Henri Tajfel, "Introduction," in *Social Identity and Intergroup Relations*
[ed. Henri Tajfel; European Studies in Social Psychology; Cambridge: Cambridge
University Press, 1982], 2–11, 4; John C. Turner, "Towards a Cognitive Redefinition of
the Social Group," in *Social Identity* [see above], 15–40). Stereotyping is inevitably
involved in social identity, and linked to social categorisation which is an inevitable if
regrettable part of human society which has generally been explained in two ways:
categorisation as simplification of perception, or categorisation as enhancing group and
individual self-definition. Cf. Penelope Oakes, "The Categorization Process: Cognition
and the Group in the Social Psychology of Stereotyping," in *Social Groups* (n. 22), 95–
119, 105–115 on the tension between these two views, which she resolves in favour of
categorisation as identity.

[31] Denise K. Buell, "Rethinking the Relevance of Race for Early Christian Self-
Definition," *Harvard Theological Review* 94 (2001): 449–476. Buell focused her
attention on authors around the time of early Christianity, including Christian authors
such as Diogenes, Clement of Alexandria, Athenagoras, Justin Martyr, and Origin, but
also a wider array of ancient authors of a wider temporal spectrum such as Philo of
Alexandria, Isocrates, Dionysius of Halicarnassus, and so on. Biblical references to race
and ethnicity include e.g. Matt 21:43 (*genos*); John 1:46 (Nazareth), 7:52 (Galileans);
1 Pet 2:9–10 (*genos, ethnos, laos*) etc.

universality of early Christian thought as authoritative ideology,[32] and scholarly voices from the margin that emphasise the apparent inclusive nature of early Christianity as embracing the vulnerable,[33] share the modern opinion of race as biological, natural identity *and* the conviction that early Christian thought detaches itself from racial or ethnic categories.

However, an understanding of race and ethnicity which is more appropriately aligned with the first-century CE context, allows for the recognition of the ability and even propensity of the early followers of Jesus to stereotype others: to "use ethnoracial language to denounce Christian rivals as barbarians and Jews."[34] In the first-century Greco-Roman world kinship and ethnicity were expressed with a variety of different terms.[35] Such terms were, regardless of their link to birth and descent, used interchangeably, signifying a different understanding of race and ethnicity than what has pertained in history since then. Race or ethnicity were closely associated with religious practice, and were mutable terms that did not presuppose "essences" and "givens"[36] – they could therefore accommodate

---

[32] Together with erasure, silencing and marginalisation, universality can be an ideological strategy in racialised thinking, intend on reinforcing the Euro-American perspective, cf. Shawn Kelley, "Race," in *Handbook of Postmodern Biblical Interpretation* (ed. Andrew K. M. Adam; St Louis, Mo.: Chalice Press, 2000), 213–219, 214.

[33] A number of texts in the New Testament are often invoked in the debate about whether the Bible promoted universalism or particularism. One of these, the Pauline text of Gal 3:28, has over many decades evoked much discussion with some scholars seeing the text and Paul in general as model for harmonious, multicultural communities, e.g. John M. G. Barclay, "'Neither Jew nor Greek:' Multiculturalism and the New Perspective on Paul," in *Ethnicity and the Bible* (ed. Mark G. Brett; Biblical Interpretation Series 19; Leiden: Brill, 1996), 197–214. More recently others have argued that Paul's rhetoric relied on ethnicity rather than trying to obliterate it, and that his concept of ethnicity was not static and monolithic but flexible and complex as he differentiated between gentiles and Jews in Christ, and those who were not in Christ. Paul has been connected to universalism even from a decidedly non-confessional point of view, stressing a philosophical concern to identify the subject and the universal through singularity, Alain Badiou, *Saint Paul: The Foundation of Universalism* (Cultural Memory in the Present; trans. Ray Brassier; Stanford, Calif.: Stanford University Press, 2003).

[34] Buell, "Rethinking" (n. 31), 473.

[35] *Genos, ethnos, laos,* and *phylos* can all four be translated interchangeably with terms such as "people," "race," and "ethnicity," although some other uses can also be identified. When early Christian literature referred to the "Christian race," *laos* or *phylos* were mostly used; in the Roman imperial period the terms *genos* and *ethnos* were preferred for referring to ethnoracial groupings, amidst great variance on how such groups were defined; *ethnos* as reference to the inhabitants of a *polis* or *poleis* were used interchangeably with *genos* with the same reference in mind, while *genos* was also used to refer to family group (Buell, "Rethinking" [n. 31], 456–457 n. 20).

[36] "Early Christians inhabited a world in which many facets of one's self, including race or ethnicity, were perceived as mutable – sex, status, citizenship, even humanness" so that "boundaries between animals, humans, and gods, those between slave and free,

both changes between and ranking of ethnicities, tolerate both an insistence on ethnic particularity and a universal ideal,[37] and allowed Christian
conversion to be expressed in ethnic terms.[38] "Race" and "ethnicity" were
terms that were therefore inevitably involved in identity negotiation in
communities of Jesus followers.[39]

In the "idiot *Galatians*"-remark ('Ω ἀνόητοι Γαλάται, Gal 3:1) more
than just an emotional outburst of anger may be present. If this phrase was
supposed to pick up on ethnic identity, there would have been more behind
it. Especially if as some scholars reckon, the letter was directed to a community located in the Roman province of Galatia, in the south of Asia Minor rather than in the northern territory on the subcontinent,[40] this may
have served as an ethnic slur. For the citizens of the Roman province to be
addressed as "Galatians" and "foolish" on top of that would be a grave
insult, an ethnic insult invoking connotations of being equated with the
descendants of the rather infamous Celtic people of the North. The accusation of foolishness (Gal 3:1, 3) also could have been in the hierarchical
first-century a gendered insult incurring downward slippage[41] for the men
of the Galatian community, being aligned with one of the stock traits ascribed to women.

Although Paul operated with a fluid ethnicity in relating both Jewish
and gentile identity to Christ (Gal 3:28), he had a rather fixed notion in the
sense of ideologies of kinship (Gal 4:21–5:1) and understandings of the
Spirit in baptism (Gal 3:1–2). An interesting if convoluted logic is at work
regarding claims of Jewish identity and heritage. Starting out with his insistence upon a biologically-defined Jewish identity in Gal 2:15, and ar-

---

and those between male and female were all seen to be breachable." Rather than understanding race or ethnicity as givens, early Christians used these concepts when speaking
of conversion (Buell, "Rethinking" [n. 31], 466–467; 467 n. 50).

[37] Christian universalism was at times expressed in ethnic terms (cf. 1 Pet 2:9–10),
demonstrating that it was less about the incorporation of other ethnicities into an agglom-
eration where such distinctions were unimportant, than about other ethnicities co-con-
stituting a new race or ethnicity: it was more about enlisting for a new identity than being
included in non-ethnic or race-less obliqueness. Cf. Buell, "Rethinking" (n. 31), 473.

[38] Buell, "Rethinking" (n. 31), 469, 473.

[39] Early Christians found race and ethnicity useful for self-definition against
outsiders, as "central organizing concept for Christianness" as well as for authorising
specific forms of Christian conviction and practice as universal norm, and also against
other insiders, in competition with rival groups and in asserting a particular form of
Christian identity (Buell, "Rethinking" [n. 31], 451).

[40] Cf. David A. Fiensy, "The Roman Empire and Asia Minor," in *The Face of New
Testament Studies: A Survey of Recent Research* (ed. Scot McKnight and Grant R.
Osborne; Grand Rapids, Mich.: Baker Academic, 2004), 36–56, 48–50.

[41] Jouette M. Bassler, *Navigating Paul: An Introduction to Key Theological
Concepts* (Louisville, Ky.: Westminster John Knox, 2007), 45.

guing along the line of the promise taking precedence over the law in the next chapter, Paul argued for a new understanding of the "real" Jewish people towards the end of chapter 4. In the end, Paul forged a notion of identity that did not erase ethnic and cultural differences,[42] but combined them in a hybrid existence,[43] which still posed Israel as the umbrella concept (cf. Gal 4:28), and which therefore retained a complex and asymmetrical relationship between Jews in Christ and Gentiles in Christ.[44] This negotiation of identity relied upon stereotyping, embedded in the social fibre of the time.

3.1.2 Stereotyped Othering in the New Testament: the Identification of Opponents and Beyond

New Testament letters often described the opponents by means of stereotyping slander. In various contexts in the New Testament and in all its major corpora strong binaries from the outset distinguish between in-group and out-group, leading to an us-them perspective. The strong anti-Judaic tone which dominates the gospels surfaces repeatedly,[45] and while the gospels generally reveal two strata of the Jesus story, both are infused with insider-outsider rhetoric. In the Fourth Gospel, the Jews are portrayed as people who deserve aggression, and become the symbol for all who rejected God (John 5:16; 8:57–59; 18:12; 19:10). This could be understood against the background of the early Jesus followers' fear of exclusion from the side of the Jewish authorities, while at the same time dreading the might of the Roman Empire to obliterate whole communities presumed guilty of discord.[46]

---

[42] Although universalising tendencies can be identified in Paul, his use of ethnicity can neither be essentialised nor can his sense of universalism be seen as opposed to ethnicity, Denise K. Buell and Caroline J. Hodge, "The Politics of Interpretation: The Rhetoric of Race and Ethnicity in Paul," *Journal of Biblical Literature* 123 (2004): 235–251, 250.

[43] Sze-kar Wan, "Does Diaspora Identity Imply Some Sort of Universality? An Asian-American Reading of Galatians," in *Interpreting Beyond Borders* (ed. Fernando F. Segovia; Bible and Postcolonialism 3; Sheffield: Sheffield Academic Press, 2000), 107–131, 126.

[44] Buell and Hodge, "Politics" (n. 42), 249. Paul used totalising categories when he took over the often used contrast between those descendants from a chosen lineage of Abraham, and other peoples, applying this well-known ethnic reasoning in what amounted to oppositional ethnic self-definition (Buell and Hodge, "Politics" [n. 42], 244).

[45] Cf. Freyne, "Vilifying" (n. 2), 117–143; Johnson, "Anti-Jewish Slander" (n. 2), 419–441.

[46] In the Fourth Gospel, it is the insiders who are early on already identified as the real outsiders (John 1:11), setting the tone for what follows. Echoes of the concern with the insiders and outsiders can be heard throughout the Johannine writings and in the Jo-

Identifying the others of Paul's letters is a complex task and often unattainable goal;[47] a discussion for which space allows only a few brief remarks. The epistolary accounts simply presupposed and rather briefly referenced aspects related to their identity, a problem which is further complicated by the rather sparse information on the applicable socio-historical context, providing little if any corroborating evidence. The difference between encoded and real-life opponents, along with further qualifications,[48] should therefore be maintained.[49] Moreover, the likelihood of constructing one-sided accounts together with the danger of mirror-reading[50] becomes a real threat for ethical biblical interpretation. This is not to mention the difficulty of determining whether the opponents were deemed such by the authors or also by the communities towards which the authors' letters were directed, or the extent to which the contemporary reader's theological, political, ideological and other commitments would predispose him or her towards alignment with Paul, his opponents, or the community.

---

hannine letters the categories are starkly divided between the saved and the damned, the insiders and the outsiders, Judith M. Lieu, *The Second and Third Epistles of John: History and background* (Studies of the New Testament and its world; Edinburgh: T&T Clark, 1986), 145–148. The boundaries of the new covenant group in Rev 21 and 22 are clearly drawn: "[t]he boundary of the redeemed sets up a system of opposites expressed as insider and outsider, Christian and non-Christian, and fornicators and virgins. There is no room for dissent and no place for women's power and women's voices," Tina Pippin, *Death and desire: The rhetoric of gender in the Apocalypse of John* (Literary Currents in Biblical Interpretation; Louisville, Ky.: Westminster John Knox, 1992), 55–56.

[47] Cf. recently Stanley E. Porter, "Introduction to the Study of Paul's Opponents," in *Paul and His Opponents* (ed. Stanley E. Porter; Pauline Studies 2; Leiden: Brill, 2005), 1–5; Jerry L. Sumney, "Studying Paul's Opponents: Advances and Challenges," in *Paul and His Opponents* (see above), 7–58.

[48] E.g. sometimes the relation between encoded and real-life opponents is vastly different, so that in some cases encoded opponents may have no real-life equivalents, as in the case of paradigmatic or even simply hypothetical opponents, Du Toit, "Vilification" (n. 2), 404.

[49] E.g. Du Toit, "Vilification" (n. 2), 411–412.

[50] While mirror-reading often forms part of the interpretation of the New Testament, in the case of mirror-reading polemical texts an even greater amount of caution is required. As much as legends of violence were used to provide a hegemonic group or culture the pretence of persecution or suffering, and the concomitant identity of being a victim, with the purpose of mobilising and legitimising violence against the other who often were minority groups (David Frankfurter, "Violence and Religious Formation: An Afterword," in *Violence in the New Testament* [ed. Shelly Matthews and E. Leigh Gibson; New York, N.Y.: T&T Clark International, 2005], 140–152, 144–150), stereotyping often served in an analogical way the purpose of defining the self or in-group through others or the outside-group. For mirror-reading, cf. e.g. John M. G. Barclay, "Mirror-Reading a Polemical Letter: Galatians as a Test Case," *JSNT* 31 (1987): 73–93; Du Toit, "Vilification" (n. 2), 403–412.

In Galatians, the opponents that have become known as the Judaisers, an epithet flowing from Paul's disgust at Gentiles "living like Jews" (ἰου-δαΐζειν, Gal 2:14), are portrayed as people who questioned both his apostolic credentials and the adequacy of his message. While accuracy or vitality of the threat perceived by Paul is difficult to determine, his response is emphatic.

The baptismal reference (Gal 3:27–28) underscores the notion that a community of people with the same focus is established through their commitment to Christ. However, Paul argued, in contrast to the faithful, the Others are guilty of proclaiming an *other* (ἕτερον) gospel (1:6) and following an *other* (of the) apostle(s) (1:19); their identity is rather that of being "false brothers" (2:4) with the accompanying danger that a fellow member of the community (6:4) may also become one of the Others. Using harsh language (e.g. 3:3), emotionally-laden rhetoric (e.g. 1:6) and sarcasm (e.g. 5:12) towards his opponents as well as the wavering within the Galatian community, they are vilified in stereotypical manner as unfaithful (1:6), obscure (2:4), hypocritical (2:13), sorcerers and foolish (3:1), unreliable (5:7), seditious (5:12), braggarts (6:13), and selfish (6:12–13).

3.1.3 Curse Rhetoric

A curse functioned as rhetorical violence, but with serving the further purpose of self-understanding it also extended towards mapping a pattern for understanding the Other. In this way boundaries are established for the community between the insiders and outsiders, and thus the "righteous" and the "wicked" – while again effectively creating rather than identifying the very nature of these groups. In the end a great deal of social power is exercised in this way, by appealing to and hoping to generate obedience to community expectations.[51]

The invocation of curses is at an early stage already part of Galatians, when the traditional thanksgiving of Greco-Roman letters is changed by Paul into an exclamation of astonishment (Θαυμάζω, Gal 1:6). In keeping with the emotional and polemical nature of the letter, he pronounced a curse (ἀνάθεμα,[52] Gal 1:8) and in fact stressed that he already, previously announced the curse (Gal 1:9) on anyone – including an angel from heaven or even himself! – who dared to oppose his earlier preaching to the Galatians. In Gal 3:10–14 the rhetoric of curse returns, where curse (κατάρα) was contrasted with blessing (εὐλογία) and directed at "those who rely on

---

[51] Cf. Kimberly B. Stratton, "Curse Rhetoric and the Violence of Identity in Early Judaism and Christianity," in *Identity and Interaction* (n. 3), 18–30 on the use of curse rhetoric to establish identity in Revelation.

[52] Used also in 1 Cor 12:3; 16:22; cf. Rom 9:3; elsewhere only in Acts 23:14 and Acts 23:12, 14, 24 as verb; and Mark 14:71 as verb.

works of the law" ("Ὅσοι γὰρ ἔργων νόμου εἰσίν, 3:10), namely Paul's opponents who castigated him for not insisting upon the law as requirement for Gentile believers.

The expression of curses was established as the dividing line between the in-group and the Others, between the Pauline faithful and Paul's opponents, and so drawing out the boundaries of the community. In Galatians with its typical appeal to the "brothers,"[53] the curses served a further purpose, namely protecting the identity and integrity of the community by threatening[54] that even the insiders may find themselves on the wrong side of the community's boundaries, if they failed to give heed.

3.1.4 Stereotyped Sexual Slander

A particularly pervasive form of stereotyping in the first-century CE and beyond was sexual slander, which also amounted to invented categories of social identity and which was often invoked in the New Testament[55] for purposes of exercising social control.[56] Openly hostile toward troublemakers, Paul invoked a sexual slur, expressing the wish that "those who upset you would castrate themselves" (5:12), an exhortation and its implied consequences pregnant with religious and socio-cultural implications. The exhortation to the community to practice self-mastery (ἐγκράτεια, Gal 5:23) because Christ has crucified "the flesh with its passions and desires" (τὴν σάρκα ... σὺν τοῖς παθήμασιν καὶ ταῖς ἐπιθυμίαις, Gal 5:24; cf. Gal 5:16–26), plays on the sexual stereotype of Gentile sexual perversion and deviance. By appealing to the community to control their desires, Paul aligned himself with the stereotype that Gentiles are enslaved to their de-

---

[53] Though with a heightened sense, in defining the brothers in Gal 1:2 as "all the brothers who are with me" (οἱ σὺν ἐμοὶ πάντες ἀδελφοὶ); cf. also the stark contrast with the ψευδαδέλφους ("false brothers," 2:4).

[54] Du Toit sees the curse rhetoric as "nothing but an invoking of God's eschatological wrath on the false teachers of Galatia (Du Toit, "Vilification" [n. 2], 410).

[55] The accusation that the opponents in the letter of Jude "perverted the grace of God into licentiousness" (Jude 4), correlates with the typical first-century CE claim or accusation that one's opponents lacked sexual self-control (Du Toit, "Vilification" [n. 2], 408; Knust, *Abandoned* [n. 3], 1–13; Jerome H. Neyrey, "Clean/Unclean, Pure/Polluted, and Holy/Profane: The Idea and System of Purity," in *The Social Sciences and New Testament Interpretation* [ed. Richard L. Rohrbaugh; Peabody, Mass.: Hendrickson, 1996], 80–104 [99–100], and were therefore sexually debauched, depraved or perverse (cf. Jude 6–7). Such stereotyping and vilification played an important role in exercising control in society. Cf. also Jennifer W. Knust, "Paul and the Politics of Virtue and Vice," in *Paul and the Roman Imperial Order* (ed. Richard A. Horsley; Harrisburg, Pa.: Trinity Press International, 2004), 155–173; Punt, "Jude and the Others" (n. 8).

[56] Cf. Knust, *Abandoned* (n. 3), 51–87.

sires.[57] But using this stereotype, Paul also insisted that in construing their identity according to Christ, they can exhibit exceptional virtue in contrast to others' vice.[58]

In his letter to the Galatians, Paul was hard at work to persuade the recipients of the letter to reconfirm their new identity, and moving from the believers' new identity in Christ to focus on the implications of their new identity for their lives.[59] In order to persuade the Galatians about the legitimacy of his claims, Paul at times resorted to stereotyping and vilification. In addition to (or maybe as sub-category of) identity negotiation, the letter is also evidence of his attempts to take up and (re)assert his social control over the Galatian community. The pragmatic purpose of Paul's and other New Testament authors' use of stereotype, slander, and vilification, was twofold: large scale negotiation (invention and maintenance) of categories of social identity, accompanied by attempts at exercising control.[60]

3.2 The Power of Stereotyping and Vilification: Identity and (Social) Control

In a context where the divisions between the followers of Jesus and other Jewish groups kept on growing, the emerging "Christianity" had to find other ways to present itself as a legal and respectable religion,[61] inevitably resulting in tensions and conflict with (amongst others) what would later become known as "Judaism" – the greatest danger to any community or organisation has always been the one from within.[62] Despite the difficulties involved, the identification of self and others was part of being a faith community built around core beliefs, regardless of the community's ability

---

[57] Space prevents a discussion of the ambiguity in Paul's use of the slavery stereotype, in a context where slavery was linked to desire and slaves were associated with moral suspicion, and its possible implications for Gal 3–4, cf. Knust, *Abandoned* (n. 3), 67–70.

[58] "Sexual slander ... cuts both ways. It can never be wholly insider or outsider directed. It is always both," Knust, *Abandoned* (n. 3), 174 n. 74.

[59] Especially if the notion of Joop F. Smit, "The Letter of Paul to the Galatians: A Deliberative Speech," *NTS* 35 (1989): 1–26 and others is accepted that the letter is deliberative rather than juridical rhetoric, as Hans Dieter Betz, *Galatians: A Commentary on Paul's Letter to the Churches of Galatia* (Hermeneia; Philadelphia, Pa.: Fortress Press, 1979) suggested.

[60] Cf. Frankfurter, "Violence" (n. 50), 143.

[61] As the Acts of the Apostles and later also e.g. Diognetus (1–3) and Origen (*Cels.* 2.1; 2.4) showed, Christianity had to defend itself against accusations of being little more than a novel superstition, unwilling to participate in other religious activities of the day.

[62] William S. Green, "Otherness within: Towards a Theory of Difference in Rabbinic Judaism," in *"To See Ourselves"* (n. 2), 49–69; Simmel, in Shelly Matthews and E. Leigh Gibson, "Introduction," in *Violence in the New Testament* (n. 50), 1–12, 4; Frankfurter, "Violence" (n. 50), 142; Punt, "Jude and the others" (n. 8).

to maintain such beliefs or the level at which these were posed as normative. Such beliefs generally exuded and even encouraged a certain ethical
practice.[63] This was the case with early Christianity too, with often divergent beliefs centering on Jesus Christ, accompanied by the promotion of a
strong ethos in the nascent Christian communities.[64] Early Christian communities, at times, evidently advanced the notion of inclusivity and
claimed the universal impact of Jesus Christ, trimming down on religious
ritual and entrance requirements which could have posed barriers for new
recruits. At the same time, from an early stage the New Testament documents also attest to identifying and allocating people into groups, under-
writing such practices and their accompanying claims with both religious
fervour and argument.

Paul's consistent referrals to his past interaction with the Galatians and
especially his claim that they then acceded to his position (e.g. Gal 1:6;
5:7), as well as his ongoing direct appeals to the community, both to get
rid of the opponents (Gal 4:30; strengthened further by using the words
from Gen 21:10) and to take up their new identity in Christ (Gal 5:1), that
is, to take up and stand firm in the freedom of Christ, underlines Paul's
attempts to regain control over the community. Using stereotyping and
vilification assisted Paul in his efforts, accusing the community of stupidity (3:1), expressing his anguish over what he portrays as their fickleness
("I am afraid I have labored over you in vain," 4:11); "You were running
so well, who has hindered you from obeying the truth?" (5:7). But also the
equally sharp oppositions Paul established in the letter between slavery
and freedom, between flesh and spirit, between law and faith, and between
death and life, as seen at its best probably in his use of the Scriptures of
Israel (esp. Gal 4:21–5:1) were directed in re-establishing Paul's position
in and his control over the community.

Using stereotypes to align the Judaising opponents and their sympathis-
ers with the first elements of such binaries, and conversely himself and
those in agreement with his position with the second elements, Paul sought
to re-establish and enforce his control among the Galatians. But it should
not be forgotten that such control has to be plotted on the broader canvas

---

[63] In the Old Testament, with its strong monotheistic stance and theocratic setting,
the people of Israel not only identified themselves accordingly, but also other people in
contrast to such claims and ideals. The accuracy and legitimacy of such claims regarding
self as well as regarding the Others is a discussion reserved for another time.

[64] The argument that Jude urged "control of the body as an indication of orthodox
theology" (Neyrey, "Clean/Unclean" [n. 55], 100), although implying a linear relationship between the two and not admitting adequately to the reciprocal relationship between
moral injunctions and faith, is helpful to underline that first-century belief in Christ was
more than a singularly cognitive position.

of imperial ideology and hegemony, and the latter's influence on early Christian discourse.

3.3 Resisting or Confirming Imperial Rhetoric?

Stereotyping as a generally important identity negotiation-mechanism in the first-century CE, was prevalent in Roman imperial rhetoric, as seen in for example Horace's and Juvenal's depiction of the Jewish people, and generally had the aim of establishing *omonoia* in the colonies. In the first-century's imperialist context stereotyping could function as strategic subversion of empire, and thus in another way serve the purpose of both identity negotiation as well as exercising power and (social) control.[65] But in taking up the moral discourse of those by whose power relations they felt themselves marginalised, and while aiming to reverse it, early Jesus-followers confirmed and at times augmented the social and moral status quo.[66] One element in Paul's identity negotiation in the Jesus follower-communities was his challenge, often rather ambivalent, to the Roman Empire and its accompanying ideology. "His [Paul's] critique of Roman imperial pretensions, framed, in part, in terms of sexual virtue and vice, depended upon and reinscribed hierarchical theories of sex and gender that, historically, has been used by Romans and Greeks to claim their own privileged status while undermining the claims of their rivals."[67] However, Paul's use of the same conventional rhetorical strategies of stereotyping and vilification meant that his invective towards the imperial order implicitly had an uneasy relationship with imperial standards and ideology.

The broader first-century CE context was partly defined by the interests and mechanisms of the Roman Empire and its reach into most communities, bringing a further element of harshness and stronger need for group identity. This was especially true in the case of the followers of Jesus, who as a new community and marginalised group, with internal group-

---

[65] Winter's theory is that the Galatian community's concern for longing for Jewish identity markers was not related to religious or soteriological concerns (earning salvation through good works) but that it was rather about the ability to claim a Jewish identity. Such identity would have given them religious legitimacy in the eyes of the Roman authorities, complete with certain social privileges, Bruce W. Winter, *Seek the Welfare of the City: Christians As Benefactors and Citizens* (Grand Rapids, Mich.: Eerdmans, 1994), 134–142; cf. earlier work by Lütgert and guarded support for this hypothesis in Winter, *Welfare* (see above), 75–76.

[66] Knust, *Abandoned* (n. 3), 12.

[67] Knust, "Politics" (n. 55), 173. For the imperial cult as Paul's primary opponent in the Corinthian correspondence, cf. Ross Saunders, "Paul and the Imperial Cult," in *Paul and His Opponents* (n. 47), 227–238.

differences,[68] resembled a situation where subordinates or subalterns engaged in conflict with each other within an authoritarian and hegemonic imperial society. People had vested interests in their groups who in their quests for self-definition were constantly constructing, disputing, and negotiating identity (both their own and their perception of the identity of others) and were therefore also involved in group-formation.[69] With intra-communal conflict such as probably also expressed in the letter to the Galatians[70] – notwithstanding Gal 6:10 – the definition of the community is sometimes more specific than in other instances, where even friends or neighbours are included[71] – on which a text such as Gal 6:10 may be an exception.

The ambivalence of using stereotype as anti-imperial mechanism is situated in the notion that "resistance occurs in power," in the sense that the dominated need to use the language of the dominators, with the danger of implicating themselves. It is in the very nature of language that the contravention of discursive, linguistic norms through a phenomenon such as "slang," is based on the very existence of norms. Similarly, resistance occurs within language and imagery that has already defined what direction the contravention will take. The contravention of the conventional, the status quo, in the name of resistance would not of necessity challenge the conventional. Ironically, the status quo predetermines the format of the resistance and, regardless of its intention, the resistance becomes complicit

---

[68] As different "Jewish-like" groupings; with varying interpretations of Jesus and events surrounding him, and their implications; and so on; cf. Johnson, "Anti-Jewish Slander" (n. 2), 425.

[69] Cf. Frankfurter, "Violence" (n. 50), 140–144.

[70] Cf. Nanos' proposal that the opponents in Galatia should not be understood according to an intra- (i.e. other Jewish) but rather an intergroup conflict, with the opponents from outside the community of Jesus followers, Mark Nanos, "Intruding 'Spies' and 'Pseudo-Brethren:' The Jewish Intra-Group Politics of Paul's Jerusalem Meeting (Gal 2:1–10)," in *Paul and His Opponents* (ed. Stanley E. Porter; Pauline Studies 2; Leiden: Brill, 2005), 59–97. For similar intra-Jesus follower conflicts about contending identities and constructions of the Other, cf. e.g. David Frankfurter, "Jews or Not? Reconstructing the 'Other' in Rev 2:9 and 3:9," *HTR* 94 (2001): 403–425.

[71] The difficulties are evident from a related 1st century CE issue, non-retaliation, which often appeared in Jewish and Christian writings. Non-retaliation in distinguished in intra-communal conflict and persecution, and external oppression of the community related to the concern with reconciliation and harmony, and the hope for God's vengeance respectively. Inter-personal conflict posited non-retaliation as forgiveness, love and good deeds aimed at reconciliation, but in some texts, reconciliation is restricted by "sharp socio-economic divisions, moral elitism or personal enmities" and in yet other documents, non-retaliation applies regardless, even including Gentiles "in the horizon of application", Gordon M. Zerbe, *Non-Retaliation in Early Jewish and New Testament Texts. Ethical Themes in Social Contexts* (JSPSS 13; Sheffield: JSOT, 1993), 219–294.

in (at least) partially confirming and re-inscribing the status quo.[72] While appropriating the vituperative rhetoric of their contemporaries, the followers of Jesus rearticulated the moral categories of their neighbours and adversaries, but for their own persuasive purposes.

4. Conclusion

Paul's constant efforts to negotiate the substance and boundaries of identity in Christ, was closely connected to his vision of a new community and their practices. It was in this vision that notions of identity, a new community and ethos or moral life were connected, and together constituted the new identity within Pauline communities. Stereotyping, far from standing in opposition to the triad of identity, community and morality, informed and directed the construction and negotiation of all three. And central to the triad was, of course, language, as can be seen in stereotyping and vilifying language as well![73]

Paul's use of stereotyping language is not restricted to letters where his anger was palpable or even manifestly present (Galatians and 2 Cor 10–14) but is also found in friendship and "personal" letters (Philippians and Philemon).[74] Was such stereotyping language unethical? Maybe the question should rather be about its purposes and consequences. On the one hand, it served a very important purpose from Paul's point of view in that it was a constituent element in maintaining and negotiating the identity of the communities he was involved with. On the other hand, Paul's stereotyping underwrote the ideological purposes to which language can be put, and played into the hands of imperial logic if not ideology – a trend which may have become clearer only in subsequent Christian generations. First century stereotyping and vilifying language (and its successors) serves to remind about the complex and ambiguous place of language, also in moral discourse.

---

[72] Knust, *Abandoned* (n. 3), 173 n. 71, referring to Bourdieu.

[73] The meta-text here is of course the increased focus on the performative aspect of language, which has often been neglected in biblical studies in favour of focusing on its propositional dimension and use (cf. e.g. Du Toit, "Vilification" [n. 2], 403–404).

[74] Since the ancient stereotype held that the inherent character of the slave was at best faithful, most often childlike and incompetent, and at worst dangerously hostile (Jennifer A. Glancy, *Slavery in Early Christianity* [Minneapolis, Minn.: Fortress Press, 2006], 137), and slaveholder mentality in the first century therefore viewed slaves as lazy, untrustworthy, dishonest, deceitful and especially prone to steal, the remark that Onesimus may possibly have wronged Philemon or be indebted to him (Phlm 18), may be ascribed to embellishment through stereotyping, cf. Jeremy Punt, *Paul, power and Philemon: A postcolonial reading (forthcoming)*.

Putting on Christ

On the Relation of Sacramental and Ethical Language in the Pauline Epistles

FRIEDRICH WILHELM HORN

I would like to begin by discussing an often mentioned and well-known problem in Pauline studies, where contradictory or possibly also just see-mingly contradictory statements stand side by side. Rudolf Bultmann clearly addressed the issue at the beginning of a significant essay in the year 1924: "[n]eben Aussagen, nach denen der Gerechtfertigte von der Sünde frei, der Sünde gestorben ist, nicht mehr im Fleisch, sondern im Geiste lebt, finden sich solche, in denen zum Kampf gegen die Sünde ge-mahnt wird, der auch für den Gerechtfertigten gilt ... Die Eigenart des Problems wird dadurch deutlich, dass sich die verschiedenen Aussagen – die Indikative und die Imperative – nicht nur an auseinander liegenden Stellen der Briefe finden, sondern aufs engste miteinander verbunden sind und eine Antinomie bilden."[1] This is by no means a marginal problem in the Pauline exegesis, in fact the text passage must be viewed as a central theological issue which is open to interpretation. It may have been rated as a side aspect, when all questions of ethics within Pauline exegesis were relatively insignificant.[2] This, however, has fundamentally changed in the

---

[1] Rudolf Bultmann, "Das Problem der Ethik bei Paulus," in *Exegetica: Aufsätze zur Erforschung des Neuen Testaments* (selected, introduced and ed. Erich Dinkler; Tübin-gen: Mohr Siebeck, 1967), 36–54, 36. Bultmann reverts in this matter to the older publication of Paul Wernle, *Der Christ und die Sünde bei Paulus* (Freiburg: Mohr Sie-beck, 1897). Here on p. 89 a conception of indicative and imperative can be found, in fact rather in the sence of a grammatical statement. Furtheron Bultmann refers to Hans Windisch, *Taufe und Sünde im ältesten Christentum bis auf Origenes: Ein Beitrag zur altkirchlichen Dogmengeschichte* (Tübingen: Mohr Siebeck, 1908): see Bultmann, "Prob-lem," 36 (see above). This latter book originally owned by Rudolf Bultmann passed into the ownership of the library of the Faculty of Protestant Theology of the Johannes Gutenberg-Universität Mainz on the occasion of a purchase of his estate. I was able to look at underlined text passages and notes made by Bultmann throughout this special volume. Bultmann's essay was published simultaneously with Hans Windisch's essay, "Das Problem des paulinischen Indikativs" in the same volume of *ZNW* 23 (1924): 265–281.
[2] Cf. the brief report on related research: Friedrich Wilhelm Horn, "Die Nachfolge-ethik Jesu und die urchristliche Gemeindeethik," in *Aufgabe und Durchführung einer*

past decades. The so called imperative, which illustrates the ethical statements in the Pauline epistles in multifaceted ways, has been subject to an
entirely new and thoughtful interpretation, examining the ethical content of
the statements and establishing religio-historical links to Jewish and pagan
ethics or general anthropological considerations. Today, the task of assign-
ing indicative and imperative is different from what it was in Rudolf Bultmann's time. Essentially, he based his research on the theological question
if statements of salvation and imperatives could coexist. For Rudolf Bultmann and his contemporaries the problem of this point of view lay in the
imperative and not in the indicative mood. From the very beginning in this
theological approach imperatives were viewed as subordinate and secondary, their ethical and linguistic content having been of little interest. Today, many scholars understandably criticize the attempt to categorize all
these statements in the Pauline epistles into either indicative or imperative
as counterproductive and they take into consideration that the research
should distance itself from the indicative-imperative model as a leading
explanation pattern of Pauline ethics.[3] The criticism of this paradigm relates to different aspects, among them also linguistic-philosophical considerations, which are the focus of this Humboldt Kolleg that explores "language and ethics in the New Testament." My task here is to focus on the
linguistic form and content of ethical statements rather than intentionally
searching for an approach of comprehensive concepts such as indicative
and imperative.

In my article I would like to elaborate on an imagery encountered twice
in the Pauline epistles that speaks of "putting on the Lord Jesus Christ" in
Rom 13:14 and "putting on Christ" in Gal 3:27. In Rom 13:14 this statement is unambiguously anchored in an ethical, in Gal 3:27, however, in a
sacramental context.[4] In the literature, both statements are readily assigned
to the imperative and indicative mood respectively, and occasionally it has
been problematized in what way an ontological or ontic metaphor can be

---

Theologie des Neuen Testaments (ed. Cilliers Breytenbach and Jörg Frey; WUNT 205;
Tübingen: Mohr Siebeck, 2007), 287–307, esp. 287–292; idem, "Ethik des Neuen Testaments 1982–1992," *ThR* 60 (1995): 32–86.

[3]   Knut Backhaus, "Evangelium als Lebensraum: Christologie und Ethik bei Paulus,"
in *Paulinische Christologie: Exegetische Beiträge* (Festschrift Hans Hübner; ed. Udo
Schnelle and Thomas Söding; Göttingen: Vandenhoeck & Ruprecht, 2000), 9–31. Backhaus, "Evangelium," (see above), 10, has collected fundamental literature as well as research surveys referring to the indicative-imperative-model. Furthermore Udo Schnelle,
Paulus: Leben und Denken (Berlin: de Gruyter, 2003), 629–631. Recently Ruben Zimmermann, "Jenseits von Indikativ und Imperativ: Entwurf einer 'impliziten Ethik' des
Paulus am Beispiel des 1. Korintherbriefes," *ThLZ* 132 (2007): 259–284, esp. 265.

[4]   I would like to remind, that Augustine, *Conf.* 8.12.28–29 associated Rom 13:13–
14 with his 'conversion experience.'

related to an ethical metaphor.[5] The ethical argumentation uses a metaphor in a nearly identical linguistic form as employed elsewhere in a purely sacramental context. The early church interpretation of both statements is almost exclusively dominated by the ethical perspective that links "putting on Christ" with Christian virtues or characteristics. According to a fundamental article by Alois Kehl, however, a distinct explanation containing the ontic understanding is difficult to find in the early church interpretation.[6] Returning to Paul, what does this finding imply for the linguistic form of the ethical argumentation and what theological conclusions can be drawn?

1. Linguistic Conditions

In the following the focus is on relatively few statements in the Pauline epistles that use the verbs ἐνδύομαι τι (all statements in the medium, to put on something: Rom 13:12, 14; 1 Cor 15:53–54; 2 Cor 5:3; Gal 3:27; 1 Thess 5:8; but also cf. Col 3:10, 12; Eph 4:24; 6:11, 14), ἐπενδύομαι (medium, to be clothed upon; 2 Cor 5:2, 4), ἐκδύομαι (medium, to be unclothed: 2 Cor 5:4), ἀπεκδύομαι (Col 2:15: to disarm; 3:9: to put off) and the noun ἀπέκδυσις (putting off the body of the sins of the flesh: Col 2:11) to express a clothing imagery.[7] Outside the Pauline epistles the clothing

---

[5] Martin Hengel and Anna Maria Schwemer, *Paulus zwischen Damaskus und Antiochien: Die unbekannten Jahre des Apostels* (with a contribution by Ernst A. Knauf; WUNT 108; Tübingen: Mohr Siebeck, 1998), 443 (see also excursus VII: Zur Gewand-Metaphorik, 443–446). For Hengel and Schwemer the opposition of ontic and ethic describes an "irreführende Alternative" (443), which has its origin in our modern categories. The adopted division into ontic and ethical metaphors at this point in fact seems to be a problem since the metaphor is not defined on any domain.

[6] Alois Kehl, "Gewand (der Seele)," *RAC* 10 (1978): 1014.

[7] Jung H. Kim, *The Significance of Clothing Imagery in the Pauline Corpus* (JSNTSup 268; London: T&T Clark, 2004), informs quite extensively about the clothing imagery in the Pauline letters and in the history of religion. In this monograph he also discusses Gal 3:28 und Rom 13:14 in detail (108–151). Part I of the study analyses 'Clothing Imagery in its History-of-Religions Background,' Part II 'The Clothing Imagery in the Pauline Corpus.' From Kim's survey on the related research history a reference has to be made esp. to Michael B. Thompson, *Clothed with Christ: The Example and Teaching of Jesus in Romans 12.1–15.13* (JSNTSup 59; Sheffield: Sheffield University Press, 1991). However, Kim seems to be right in complaining that "we do not find a sufficient treatment of the significance of the Pauline clothing imagery from these writings, though they do contain highly valuable insights" (4).

imagery using this word stem in the NT is only resumed in Rev 1:13; 15:6 and 19:14. The Apostolic Fathers often use ἐνδύω in metaphorical speech.[8]

2. The Usage of the Evidence in the Pauline Corpus

The earliest evidence in the Pauline corpus in 1 Thess 5:8 assigns a clear-cut and traditional metaphorical pair to its two elements. On the one hand there are light, day, to watch and to be sober, standing as attributes, here for the Christian community. On the other hand there are night, darkness, to sleep, and to be drunk, standing for the opposite pagan world. God's wrath comes down on the last mentioned lifestyle, but through their connection with Jesus Christ, the Christian community is salvaged from its effects. Up to this moment the community puts on (ἐνδύω τι) a spiritual armour, the breastplate (θώραξ) of faith and love and the helmet of hope (περικεφαλαία), thereby virtually concealing the future salvation. Paul hereby draws upon the description of the armour and clothing imagery of LXX, primarily upon Isa 59:17 and Wis 5:18.[9] This imagery is reactivated in Rom 13:11–13 (day, night, light, darkness, to put on the armour, to sleep, salvation), but also the outlook onto the coming judgment day. We can view these statements as a virtually classic example of traditional Jewish, often also eschatologically oriented clothing imagery, insofar virtues or characteristics allegorise a new garment. This garment is simultaneously the changed, the new identity of a person, and this garment assists in prevailing over the forces of evil in an apocalyptic battle.

1 Cor 15:53–54 and 2 Cor 5:3–4 use the clothing imagery to describe the transition of the mortal body into the immortal body (1 Cor 15:53–54:

---

[8]   Within the linguistic requirements it is necessary to allude to metaphor as a text phenomenon. I would like to point to Ruben Zimmermann, *Geschlechtermetaphorik und Gottesverhältnis: Traditionsgeschichte und Theologie eines Bildfelds in Urchristentum und antiker Umwelt* (WUNT 2/122; Tübingen: Mohr Siebeck, 2001), 40: "Die Metapher bezeichnet in diesem Sinn ein Textphänomen, bei dem zwei üblicherweise nicht aufeinander bezogene Sinneinheiten prädikativ in Beziehung gesetzt werden, so dass eine neue semantische Kohärenz entsteht, die konventionellen Bedeutungsinhalte innerhalb dieses Sinngeschehens aber transparent bleiben." In fact with regard to the imagination of "putting on Jesus" it is necessary to name it a "necessary metaphor." These necessary metaphors replace blanks in the semantic catalogue if a denomination for a certain thing is not available within the language; cf. Oda Wischmeyer, *Hermeneutik des Neuen Testaments: Ein Lehrbuch* (NET 8; Tübingen: Francke, 2004), 145–146, rather adopting a definition from *Metzler Lexikon Literatur- und Kulturtheorie* (²2001): 301.

[9]   Thomas Söding, *Die Trias Glaube, Hoffnung, Liebe bei Paulus: Eine exegetische Studie* (SBS 150; Stuttgart: Katholisches Bibelwerk, 1992), 77–78; Abraham J. Malherbe, *The Letters to the Thessalonians* (AncB 32B; New York, N.Y.: Doubleday, 2000), 297–298.

φθαρτὸν τοῦτο ἐνδύσασθαι ἀφθαρσίαν καὶ τὸ θνητὸν τοῦτο ἐνδύσασθαι ἀθανασίαν).[10] Here, too, it is about the question of a new identity after the individual death, which is mentioned in 2 Cor 5:3–4 ἐκδύειν.

In the Pauline epistles, the figurative use of the clothing imagery in Rom 13:14 and Gal 3:27, now speaking of putting on a person, namely the Lord Jesus Christ, and not just putting on certain characteristics or virtues (faith, hope, love) or also an entity (immortality), illustrates a conspicuous, even audacious picture.[11] In Gal 3:27 Paul uses the aorist indicative medium: Χριστὸν ἐνεδύσασθε, in Rom 13:14 the imperative: ἀλλὰ ἐνδύσασθε τὸν κύριον Ἰησοῦν Χριστόν. At first, I will present these two evidences within their context. Finally Col 3:10–11 (as well as Eph 4:24) also have to be considered, since the baptism tradition in this deuteropauline epistle has the same background as Gal 3:26–28 (and 1 Cor 12:13), likewise displaying the clothing imagery.

3. Gal 3:27

The connection with baptism is ensured by the anterior sentence: ὅσοι γὰρ εἰς Χριστὸν ἐβαπτίσθητε, Χριστὸν ἐνεδύσασθε. But also the direct context Gal 3:26, 28 ensures the sacramental background. Probably Paul is reporting a baptism tradition, as the parallels in 1 Cor 12:13 and Col 3:11, but also the stringent composition suggests, which reminds of a relatively fixed formula. Alone the formula διὰ τῆς πίστεως (ἐν Χριστῷ Ἰησοῦ)[12] (Gal 3:26) and the entire verse Gal 3:27 may be a Pauline extension of the formula, resulting from the conflicts among Paul, the Galatian communities, and the adversaries who appeared in the meantime.[13] However, it is

---

[10] With regard to the usage of clothing imagery in these texts cf. Manuel Vogel, *Commentatio mortis: 2 Kor 5,1–10 auf dem Hintergrund antiker ars moriendi* (FRLANT 214; Göttingen: Vandenhoeck & Ruprecht, 2006), 223–378; preliminarily Egon Brandenburger, *Fleisch und Geist: Paulus und die dualistische Weisheit* (WMANT 29; Neukirchen-Vluyn: Neukirchener Verlag, 1968), 175–177.

[11] Bauer-Aland, 533: "Kühn ist d. Bild τὸν κύριον Ἰησοῦν Χριστὸν ἐ. d. *Herrn Jesus Chr. anziehen.*" Cf. also for both text passages: Jost Eckert, "Zieht den Herrn Jesus Christus an…! (Röm 13,14): Zu einer enthusiastischen Metapher der neutestamentlichen Verkündigung," *TThZ* 105 (1996): 39–60.

[12] The prepositional determination ἐν Χριστῷ Ἰησοῦ does probably not relate to διὰ τῆς πίστεως but to πάντες γὰρ υἱοὶ θεοῦ ἐστε. The prepositional connection of διὰ τῆς πίστεως and ἐν would be unusual; cf. in detail Franz Mußner, *Der Galaterbrief* (4th ed.; HThK 9; Freiburg: Herder, 1981), 261.

[13] I would like to point to the evidence in Hans Dieter Betz, *Galatians: A Commentary on Paul's letter to the Churches in Galatia* (Hermeneia; Philadelphia, Pa.: Fortress Press, 1979), 181–185.

also assumed that Gal 3:27 is part of this baptism tradition.[14] The two sentences beginning with πάντες γὰρ form a frame: for in Christ Jesus you are all children of God through faith (Gal 3:26a) – for all of you are one in Jesus Christ (Gal 3:28b). The separate groups are abolished and united in Christ: of Jews and gentiles, slaves and free, man and woman (Gal 3:28a). This unity exists among those who are baptized (Gal 3:27a). However, now Gal 3:27b continues this line of thought with an additional and new argument. For as many of you as have been baptized into Christ have put on Christ.[15] The aorist ἐνεδύσασθε looks back at the previous unique event of baptism, when the new garment was put on. The abolition of the separate groups, therefore, is effected by the new garment (= Christ), which connects everything and, in Gal 3:28b, results in the unity of those baptized in Christ.

The religio-historical question, which Paul based the concept of "putting on Christ" on, will not be dealt with yet or even answered. It must be established, though, that the metaphor "putting on Christ," first found in the Pauline corpus in Gal 3:27b, is not a foreign body in the argumentation of Gal 3:26–28. Whereas Gal 3:26 (πάντες υἱοὶ θεοῦ ἐν Χριστῷ Ἰησοῦ) and 3:28a (πάντες ... εἷς ἐστε ἐν Χριστῷ Ἰησοῦ) are concerned with addressing the baptized as a unity, regardless of their religious, social, and gender difference, Gal 3:27 denotes baptism as that place where unity is realized in such a way that Christ, like a garment, encompasses the numerous baptized.

4. Rom 13:14

In the sequence covered in Rom 13:11–14 Paul thematises the attitude of Roman Christians towards the καιρός, the time or eschaton by means of the metaphorical pairs night and day, light and darkness.[16] The clothing im-

---

[14] Udo Schnelle, *Gerechtigkeit und Christusgegenwart. Vorpaulinische und paulinische Tauftheologie* (GTA 24; Göttingen: Vandenhoeck & Ruprecht, 1983), 58–59. The Letter to the Colossians that very well may be a deuteropauline one also contains the clothing imagery, even in relation to the new man. This may surely be a secondary modification. Nevertheless, the occurrence of the clothing imagery in Col 3:10–11 may attest the affiliation to tradition.

[15] The medium ἐνεδύσασθε is mostly translated actively: you have put on. However, some exegetes proclaim a passive translation: you have let you put on (Ulrich Mell, *Neue Schöpfung: Eine traditionsgeschichtliche und exegetische Studie zu einem soteriologischen Grundsatz paulinischer Theologie* [BZNW 56; Berlin: de Gruyter, 1989], 308).

[16] For the interpretation of Rom 13:14 in a direct context cf. also Michael Theobald, "*Concupiscentia* im Römerbrief: Exegetische Beobachtungen anlässlich der lutherischen Formel 'simul iustus et peccator,'" in *Studien zum Römerbrief* (ed. Michael Theobald;

agery is then utilized in Rom 13:12 in both directions, as casting off the works of darkness and as putting on the armour of light (cf. also Eph 6:10–17). Rom 13:13 illustrates to both sides, but mentions only one single virtue and altogether six vices the Roman community should renounce. Concluding with ἀλλά in Rom 13:14 and resuming the verb ἐνδύω from Rom 13:12, this negative behaviour, three times introduced by μή, is contrastingly juxtaposed with the putting on of the Lord Jesus Christ. The context is ethical-eschatological throughout. Especially the conclusion, saying that who puts on the Lord Jesus Christ makes no provision for the flesh to fulfil the lusts thereof, is in this respect unambiguous. In Rom 13:14 the clothing imagery of putting on the Lord Jesus Christ stands quite isolated in the context. It appears appended by reinserting the verb ἐνδύω but now as in Gal 3:27 relating to a person. This person, of course, is not the worldly Jesus, whose behaviour could serve as an orientation for the community.[17] Since κύριος Ἰησοῦς Χριστός is mentioned beyond Gal 3:27b, Paul is thinking of the elevated Lord. Different from Gal 3:27, putting on Christ is not performed once, but should rather be performed consistently, especially also in renouncing the mentioned vices.

5. Col 3:10–11

The possibly deuteropauline Epistle to the Colossians reverts to the pre-Pauline baptism tradition, conveyed in Gal 3:27–28; 6:5; 1 Cor 12:13; 7:19–21 by addressing the pairs pagan–Jew, circumcised–uncircumcised, slave–free. But simultaneously the presumed wording and most notably the context of this tradition are changed.[18] Col 3:9–10 speaks of putting off the old man with his deeds and of putting on the new man. According to Col 2:12, this new man died in baptism, but was raised from the dead through faith by the working of God. Col 3:11 recalls this baptism reality. Putting off the old or putting on the new man, here expressed as an aorist parti-

---

WUNT 136; Tübingen: Mohr Siebeck, 2001), 250–276, here 267–269 and 273–274; Klaus Haacker, *Der Brief des Paulus an die Römer* (3rd ed.; ThHK 6; Leipzig: Evangelische Verlagsanstalt, 2006), 293–295, provides a broad collection of the latest literature concerning this text.

[17] Charles E. B. Cranfield, *The Epistle to the Romans* (vol. 2; ICC; Edinburgh: T&T Clark, 1998), 688–689: "It means to follow Him in the way of discipleship and to strive to let our lives be moulded according to the pattern of the humanity of His earthly life."

[18] Detailed proof in Michael Wolter, *Der Brief an die Kolosser. Der Brief an Philemon* (ÖTK 12; Gütersloh: Gütersloher Verlag, 1993), 181. Jürgen Becker, *Paulus: Der Apostel der Völker* (Tübingen: Mohr Siebeck, 1989), 110–113, introduced these and further texts as compounds of pre-Pauline Antiochian theology and stressed their baptismal orientated context.

ciple, is therefore a memory of the past baptism and not an imperative.[19] The Epistle to the Colossians assumes that Christians had resurrected in the presence with Christ and that their identity is already, even though still in a concealed manner, tied to Christ (Col 3:1–4). While Gal 3:27 speaks in the baptismal context about putting on Christ without linking it to the resurrection reality, Col 3:11 interprets this picture further: putting on the new man is putting on the resurrected man, who has been linked to Christ since baptism. In Col 3:10–11 the clothing imagery looks at a past event, at the baptism, and the author links it with a creational-theological interpretation, almost overloading the text: in Christ, the image of God (Col 1:15), the εἰκὼν θεοῦ, man regains in this recreation his actual destination. Col 3:10–12 appears to be the first interpretation of the older metaphor of putting on Christ. In Col 3:12, however, the letter, reinstating the verb ἐν-δύω, introduces a short catalogue of virtues, and here ἐνδύω is clearly an imperative.

6. The religio-historical context of the imagery

The clothing imagery, especially expressed by the verb ἐνδύω κτλ, is frequently found in the ancient literature.[20] Martin Hengel recognized in this context "... eine gemeinantike religiöse Koine und Vorstellungswelt, an der alle antiken Religionen und Kulte, einschließlich des Alten Testaments und Judentums, partizipieren und die die religiöse Verkündigung und Propaganda überhaupt erst möglich macht."[21] This mindscape is not only accessible in literature by correlating certain characteristics or virtues with clothes or even weapons, thereby illustrating a clothing imagery. Many examples of the Jewish sphere are found in LXX, Philo, and Josephus, which can be easily complemented by parallels from the Graeco-Hellenistic and Latin literature. At the same time, this mindscape had an

---

[19] Detailed in this respect Joachim Gnilka, *Der Kolosserbrief* (HThK 10/1; Freiburg: Herder, 1980), 185–186.

[20] Cf. the surveys by Albrecht Oepke, "δύω κτλ.," *TWNT* 2 (1935): 318–321; Pieter W. van der Horst, "Observations on a Pauline Expression," *NTS* 19 (1972/73): 181–187; Kehl, "Gewand" (n. 6), 945–1025; Hengel and Schwemer, *Paulus* (n. 5), 443–446; Kim, *Significance* (n. 7), 8–103, investigates the clothing imagery in selected Jewish, Christian und pagan writings or in religious contexts of antiquity.

[21] Hengel and Schwemer, *Paulus* (n. 5), 445. Astrid Böhme-Schönberger, "Kleidung und Schmuck," in *Neues Testament und Antike Kultur: Familie, Gesellschaft, Wirtschaft* (vol. 2 of *Neues Testament und Antike Kultur*; ed. Klaus Scherberich; Neukirchen-Vluyn: Neukirchener Verlag, 2005), 42–47, deals with the clothing imagery but not sufficiently and much too brief in the chapter in question. The article "Kleidung" in *DNP* 6 (1999): 505–513, only remains on the level of real clothing and disregards the clothing imagery.

obvious reference to the public and religious daily life, where priests publicly wore the clothing of the deities in cults. In the exegetic literature the clothing imagery as used by Paul is often directly related to initiation rites in mystery religions. In connection with this interpretation of Col 3:9 Eduard Lohse recalled, "dass der Myste in der Weihehandlung zwölfmal bekleidet wird und ein Gewand empfängt, das mit Tierbildern geschmückt ist. Durch das Anlegen der Kleider wird er geheiligt, das bedeutet: Er wird mit den Kräften des Kosmos erfüllt und erfährt eine physisch-substantielle Veränderung an sich, durch die er göttlicher Lebenskraft teilhaftig wird. In gnostischen Texten wird das Bild vom Anlegen bzw. Empfangen des Gewandes als Ausdruck für die Verwirklichung der Erlösung verstanden, die sich vollzieht, indem der Mensch in die göttliche Welt aufgehoben und mit deren Licht und Kraft durchströmt wird."[22]

But is a rather general reference to the appearance of the clothing imagery in the ancient world helpful? Henning Paulsen considered, "ob nicht die religionsgeschichtliche Erklärung stärker die differenzierte Verwendung von ε. innerhalb des NT zum Ausgangspunkt ihrer Überlegungen machen sollte."[23]

Now the usage of the clothing imagery in Gal 3:27 and Rom 13:14 differs fundamentally from the general usage as they talk about putting on a person and not characteristics or virtues. After reviewing the parallels in the ancient literature, Pieter W. van der Horst concludes: "[t]he verbs 'putting off' and 'putting on' appear nowhere with *man* as their object, except in Paul's letters."[24] He assumed that Paul, inspired by general statements of the clothing imagery, had arrived at his two statements in Gal 3:27 and Rom 13:14, at best having experienced additional stimulation in the theatrical events (see below). Günter Wagner also asked, "ob die alttestamentlichen Parallelen und die sinnfällige, nicht unbekannte Metapher nicht doch genügen, um den Ausdruck dem Apostel als selbständige Formulierung belassen zu können."[25] Wagner also did not want to categorically exclude the influence of mystery religions, especially of Gnosticism. On the contrary, Hans Dieter Betz assumes: "... but the 'putting on' of a redeemer figure has parallels only in the mystery religions and in Gnosticism."[26] Together with the predominantly older religio-historical studies Hans Dieter Betz objects to the attempt of tracing this metaphor to

---

[22] Eduard Lohse, *Die Briefe an die Kolosser und an Philemon* (KEK 9; Göttingen: Vandenhoeck & Ruprecht, 1968), 204.

[23] Henning Paulsen, "ἐνδύω (ἐνδύνω), ἐπενδύομαι," *Exegetisches Wörterbuch zum Neuen Testament* 1 (²1980): 1103–1105, 1104.

[24] Van der Horst, "Observations" (n. 20), 182.

[25] Günter Wagner, *Das religionsgeschichtliche Problem von Römer 6,1–11* (AThANT 39; Zurich: Zwingli-Verlag, 1962), 286.

[26] Betz, *Galatians* (n. 13), 188.

the context of an either Gnostic[27] or mystery religious[28] idea of a redeemer figure.[29] The criticism of this derivation is manifold and indicates among others that the listed evidence is usually without any exception post Christian emanating from totally different contexts.[30]

Oepke referred to the theatre for the next and probably only parallel use of ἐνδύω with a personal object, and Van der Horst supported him in this thesis (Dionysios of Halikarnassos, *Ant. rom.* 11,5: τὸν Ταρκύνιον ἐκεῖνον ἐνδυόμενοι/acting the part of Tarquin[31]; furthermore Libanus, *epist.* 1048.2: ῥίψας στρατιώτην ἐνέδυ τὸν σοφιστήν).[32] Martin Hengel has partially agreed to this thesis, too. He reminds us that the clothing of deities was publicly worn especially in processions and draws an indirect relation to the Pauline language use: "[w]eil diese Gewänder von Menschen im Kult (aber auch im Triumphzug, im Theater oder von den Kaisern) verwendet wurden, konnte die Metapher 'mit Christus bekleidet werden' von ehemaligen Heiden analog verstanden werden."[33] Thus, with the metaphor 'putting on Christ' Paul must have considered the reception horizon of his community.

However, initially one should restrictively view the first use of this metaphor 'putting on Christ' in Gal 3:27b as occurring in a context that supports it with parallel metaphors. On the one hand εἰς Χριστὸν ἐβαπτίσθητε

---

[27] Betz points to the Hymn of the Pearl in the *Acts Thom.* 108–113; *Gos. Thom.* 36–37 (NHC 2.2); *Gos. Phil.* 24 (NHC 2.57.19–24); *Gos. Truth* 20.30–43 (NHC 1.3/12.2); Thom. *Cont.* P 143.37 (NHC 2.7). Although these texts deal with the clothing imagery, they do not understand it as an act like Gal 3:27; Rom 13:14, in which the redeemer is clothed.

[28] Betz quotes inter alia Ephippus in *Athen.* 12.53, p. 537 E (here from the edition used by Bauer-Aland, 533: "Alex. d. Gr. legte gern die ἱερὰς ἐσθητὰς der Götter an und wurde so Ammon, Artemis, Hermes, Herakles" (see also Hengel and Schwemer, *Paulus* [n. 5], 445 n. 1828); besides that Betz points to Plutarch, *Is. Os.* 352B (critical comment in this respect by Alexander J. M. Wedderburn, *Baptism and Resurrection: Studies in Pauline Theology against Its Graeco-Roman Background* [WUNT 44; Tübingen: Mohr Siebeck, 1987], 338–339); Apuleius, *Metam.* 11.24 (critical comment by Wedderburn, *Baptism*, 333–335); Philo, *Fug.* 110.

[29] Also Robert Jewett, *Romans: A Commentary* (Hermeneia; Minneapolis, Minn.: Fortress Press, 2007), 827.

[30] Cf. Van der Horst, "Observations" (n. 20), 181–182; Wagner, *Problem* (n. 25), 286; Hengel and Schwemer, *Paulus* (n. 5), 444.

[31] See *Neuer Wettstein: Texte zum Neuen Testament aus Griechentum und Hellenismus* (ed. Georg Strecker and Udo Schnelle; vol. 2/1; Berlin: de Gruyter, 1996), 210, where an additional reference to Lucianus, *Gall.* 16–17.19 can be found. A cock reports about the sequence of several resurrections. The vocabulary ἐνδύω and ἀποδύω is used.

[32] Oepke, *TWNT* 2 (n. 20): 319–320; referred to by Van der Horst, "Observation" (n. 20), 182–183; critical comment by Schneider, *Galaterbrief* (n. 12), 263 n. 89.

[33] Hengel and Schwemer, *Paulus* (n. 5), 445; similar before: Wedderburn, *Baptism* (n. 28), 338–339.

(Gal 3:27a) is to be recalled. A spatial understanding of this baptism formula is apparent, the person to be baptized is baptized into Christ. On the other hand, as a consequence of baptism, the baptized persons are promised: εἷς ἐστε ἐν Χριστῷ Ἰησοῦ (Gal 3:28c). This, however, means that Paul mentions the metaphor 'putting on Christ' in connection with baptism for the first time and that this is the base where it may not have its linguistic form but rather its interpretational horizon.[34] Col 3:9–10 clearly postulates this connection to baptism, too. Opposed to Robert Jewett, I am of the opinion that it is just a postulate, a mystical use in early Christianity, chronologically postulated even before being applied to baptism, a problematic postulate, since it is based on religio-historical Gnostic evidences, which, admittedly, are all clearly post Christian.[35] In my opinion, Udo Schnelle described the intention of these baptismal formulas and also additional Pauline texts appropriately as "participatory Christology." Since their baptism, the believers participate in the elevated Christ and in the power of his resurrection.[36]

7. The Ethical Use of the Metaphor

The ethical use of the metaphor "to put on the Lord Jesus Christ" cannot be explained by the indicative-imperative-model, although the secondary lite-

---

[34] Again Paulsen, "ἐνδύω (ἐνδύνω), ἐπενδύομαι" (n. 23), here 1104. Hermann-Josef Venetz, "'Christus anziehen:' Eine Exegese zu Gal 3,26–27 als Beitrag zum paulinischen Taufverständnis," *FZPhTh* 20 (1973): 3–36, rightly emphasizes, that putting on Christ coincides with being baptised. Also Hans Dieter Betz, "Geist, Freiheit und Gesetz: Die Botschaft des Paulus an die Gemeinden in Galatien," in *Paulinische Studien: Gesammelte Aufsätze III* (ed. Hans Dieter Betz; Tübingen: Mohr Siebeck, 1994), 46–62: "Diejenigen, die zum Glauben an Christus kamen und getauft wurden, wurden Teilhaber am gegenwärtigen Christus selbst: sie 'zogen Christus an' (3,27), Christus 'nahm unter ihnen Gestalt an' (4,19), sie waren nun 'in Jesus Christus' (ἐν Χριστῷ Ἰησοῦ)." Some more parallel metaphors, which occur in the context of baptism as well and show a clear relation to the community of Christ by using the preposition σύν, are contained in Rom 6:4–6: to be buried with him (συνετάφημεν), to be united with him (σύμφυτοι), to be crucified with him (συνεσταυρώθη); cf. again Hans Dieter Betz, "Transferring a Ritual: Paul's Interpretation of Baptism in Romans," in *Paulinische Studien: Gesammelte Aufsätze III* (ed. Hans Dieter Betz; Tübingen: Mohr Siebeck, 1994), 240–271, esp. 267–270.

[35] Contrary to Jewett, *Romans* (n. 29), 827.

[36] Udo Schnelle, "Transformation und Partizipation als Grundgedanken paulinischer Theologie," *NTS* 47 (2001): 58–75; idem, *Paulus: Leben und Denken* (Berlin: de Gruyter, 2003), 463–465; idem, *Theologie des Neuen Testaments* (Göttingen: Vandenhoeck & Ruprecht, 2007), 200–221. Schnelle connects the transformation of Jesus Christ, e.g. his change in status from the crucified to a godlike, with the believers' participation in this process insofar as he describes the aim of Christ's transformation to be the believers' participation in this process.

rature consistently uses this interpretation.[37] In the argumentation of Rom 13:11–14 a reference to an indicative is missing, comparable to Gal 3:27. It is in fact significant that Paul uses the metaphor "to put on the Lord Jesus Christ" without supporting it by a preceding indicative. One also cannot assume that the Roman community, different from the reader today, was immediately able to relate to the Epistle to the Galatians and also to the use of the metaphor in Gal 3:27.[38] But what does the claim in Rom 13:14 imply? First we need to consider the closer context. The metaphor of putting on the armour of light (Rom 13:12b) is reintroduced by ἐνδύω so that both metaphors support each other. Similarly, the request ἐν ἡμέρα εὐσχημόνως περιπατεῖν (Rom 13:13a) relates to this statement, as light and day are positively assigned to one another. In the narrower context the altogether six vices, three times introduced by μή are antithetically juxtaposed with the subsequent ἀλλά-sentence. Therefore, resulting from the narrower context, "putting on the Lord Jesus Christ" is a life in light and day and a renunciation of the vices: μὴ κώμοις καὶ μέθαις, μὴ κοίταις καὶ ἀσελγείαις, μὴ ἔριδι καὶ ζήλῳ. In addition, it is a renunciation of a lifestyle that is oriented at ἐπιθυμίαι (Rom 13:14b).

If the usage of the metaphor "putting on the Lord Jesus Christ" in Gal 3:27 was explained in a participatory Christology, hence Christ accommodating the believers like a room and ordaining them, then this explanation is also applicable to Rom 13:14. Thus, Paul has in mind not only the admission to the reality of Christ and putting on the Kyrios, but also a life in the presence of the elevated Christ, where salvation is conveyed. This concept serves at the same time as a fundamental basis of ethics.[39] Tearing apart indicative and imperative would be totally inadequate here, since the Christian life consists of the unity of "putting on Christ." The ethical content of this "putting on Christ" does not fundamentally differ from what

---

[37] Haacker, *Römer* (n. 16), 308: "Der Ruf zum 'Anziehen' des Herrn Jesus Christus verwandelt den Indikativ von Gal 3,27 in einen Imperativ;" also James D. G. Dunn, *Romans 9–16* (WBC 38B; Dallas, Tex.: Word Books, 1988), 791; also with emphasis Cranfield, *Romans* (n. 17), 688–689. Folker Blischke, *Die Begründung und die Durchsetzung der Ethik bei Paulus* (ABG 25; Leipzig: Evangelische Verlagsanstalt, 2007), 361, intends to overcome an orientation at the indicative-imperative-model and he recognizes in Rom 13:11–14 a "Vergegenwärtigung der Taufentscheidung."

[38] Ulrich Wilckens, *Der Brief an die Römer* (EKK 6/3; Neukirchen-Vluyn: Neukirchener Verlag, 1982), 75, identifies the antithetic parenesis in Rom 13:13–14 as a topos of baptismal catechesis.

[39] Backhaus, "Evangelium" (n. 3), 22: "Ursprungsort dieser Lebens- und Handlungseinheit ist die Taufe, in der sich der Glaubende mit Christus bekleidet (ἐνδύω), um so zu seiner neuen, Christus-konformen Existenzgestalt zu finden (Gal 3,27; vgl. 1 Thess 5,8–10; Röm 13,14)." Simon Légasse, *L'épître de Paul aux Romains* (LeDiv. Comm. 10; Paris: Cerf, 2002), 847–848, additionally points to the Holy Spirit through whose action the connection with Christ takes place.

Paul can say in view of the vices: μὴ κώμοις καὶ μέθαις, μὴ κοίταις καὶ ἀσελγείαις, μὴ ἔριδι καὶ ζήλῳ in a different passage. And yet there is a difference between knowing not to yield to the "works of the flesh" (Gal 5:19) by renouncing the vices or living under the awareness of putting on Christ in this way. That is why Klaus Haacker, subsequent to Rom 13:14a, spoke of a Christian ethic as Christ aesthetics, with the aim to portray the Lord Jesus Christ.[40]

With the question of ethics and language in mind, it seems important to me to recognize the diversity of ethical argumentation in the New Testament and not forcing it into a superior pattern. The metaphor of putting on the Lord Jesus Christ is met just once within an ethical context in the Pauline epistles. It is a building block within the ethical argumentation of the Epistle to the Romans, which is substantially determined by other text passages, such as Rom 6:1–23 or 12:1–2. The distinctiveness of this metaphor and its use by Paul lies in the fact that here the clothing imagery is postulated but relating to a person and utilized in the sense of a participatory Christology encompassing the complete Christian life.

---

[40] Haacker, *Römer* (n. 16), 308. I would rather agree with Jewett, *Romans* (n. 29), 827, in this respect, who recognizes a form of early Christian mysticism which aims at a life within the community with Christ, although he puts emphasis on slightly different details.

Moral Language in the New Testament:

Language and Ethics in 2 Corinthians 3

FRANÇOIS S. MALAN

1. The implied moral impact of 2 Corinthians 3

2 Corinthians 3 is not a typical ethical text with imperatives, prescriptions and prohibitions. At first glance Paul is defending his ministry against an unfavourable comparison with Moses, as being weak and without glory. He describes his weak position in 4:7–15 and 6:4–10, but sees it as strength in weakness (12:9, 10). The glory and power of his message comes from God who works through the weakness of the cross of Christ (4:7; 5:15; 13:4). But he *involves* his readers in such a way in his defence that they should rethink their way of life. For example, throughout chapter 3 Paul refers to himself in the plural, as "we," not with verbs in the first person singular ("I"). With the *pluralis sociativus* Paul involves his readers in his own actions.[1] It especially bears on the *motivation* and direction of their beliefs and behaviour.

The congregation is a letter of Christ (v. 3). At the same time they themselves are Paul's credential (v. 2). Their faith in Christ and their way of life as a congregation, inscribed in their hearts and minds through the service of Paul, is universally known and read as being Christ's witness, as well as Paul's credential, which he carries in his heart.[2] By labelling them as Christ's letter, read by all people, Paul *sensitizes* them to their responsibility to live up to it.

Although vv. 4–6 deal with Paul's adequacy as a servant of the new covenant, the Corinthians are God's partners in this new covenant. Their responsibility to live as God's partners is *implied*. Their empowerment is

---

[1] Friedrich Blass, Albert Debrunner, and Friedrich Rehkopf, *Grammatik des neutestamentlichen Griechisch* (Göttingen: Vandenhoek & Ruprecht, 1976) (= BDR), § 280.

[2] See Ben Witherington III, *Conflict and community in Corinth: A socio-rhetorical commentary on 1 and 2 Corinthians* (Grand Rapids, Mich.: Eerdmans, 1995), 378. Carol K. Stockhausen, *Moses' veil and the glory of the new covenant* (Rome: Pontificio, 1989), 80–81 compares 'written in Paul's heart' with Aaron's breastplate on his heart, containing the names of the tribes of Israel engraved on stones, when he enters the presence of God, Exod 36:21 (LXX).

also from God, and it is to them that the Spirit gives life, the kind of life expected from God's covenant partners.

Vv. 7–11 state the glory of the ministry of the Spirit that puts the congregation in the right relationship with God, and to do what God requires, to do what is right.[3] V. 18 states clearly that the plural "we" embraces all who are being transformed by the Spirit into the likeness of Christ. The statement that the goal of the Spirit is to transform the believers into the likeness of Christ *challenges* every Christian to adapt his or her way of life to Christ's example.

While the text in its context is an apologia of Paul's ministry, the sub-text is an *appeal* to the Corinthians to be what they are, to live as a letter of Christ. From v. 3b through v. 18 Paul *entices* them to a new way of life by comparing the glory of being Christ's message to the world, with the glory attached to the old covenant with its ethical instruction on tablets of stone. And it explains the way in which God is busy transforming them to be a letter of Christ.

2. The context and course of 2 Corinthians 3

Paul wrote 2 Corinthians after he experienced the rejection of his authority in the Corinthian congregation, as well as their renewed acceptance following his "Painful Letter"[4] and Titus' visit to the congregation.[5]

Chapter 3 is part of a major argumentative section, 2 Cor 2:14–7:4, which is situated between the autobiographical narratives 1:8–2:13 and 7:5–16.[6] Its sub-section 2:14–4:6 describes the ministry of the new covenant and its glory, 4:7–5:10 our present distress and future glory, and 5:11–7:4 the new life of reconciliation and commitment to God. Chapter 3 is encased between an introduction 2:14–17 and a conclusion 4:1–6. The preface uses the image of vital fragrance that brings life, versus deadly fume that kills (2:14–17), chapter 3 employs the *metaphors* of letters, tablets, and a veil, and its conclusion the similes of darkness and light (4:1–6).

---

[3] See Johannes P. Louw and Eugene A. Nida, *Greek-English lexicon of the New Testament based on semantic domains* (New York, N.Y.: United Bible Societies, 1988) on δικαιοσύνη § 34.46 – to cause someone to be in a proper or right relation with someone else, probably in the context of the covenant relationship; § 88.13 the act of doing what God requires.

[4] See 2:4, 9; 7:8, 12.

[5] See 2:13; 7:6, 13; 12:18(?).

[6] See Jan Lambrecht, *Second Corinthians* (Sacra Pagina 8; Collegeville, Pa.: Liturgical Press, 1999), 43; Craig S. Keener, *1–2 Corinthians* (New Cambridge Bible Commentary; Cambridge: Cambridge University Press, 2005), 163.

In chapter 3 he refers to the renewed acceptance of Moses' authority by Israel, after his dismissal by them on account of his lengthy absence on Mount Sinai, as recorded in Exodus 32–34.[7] Paul expands on the second set of stone tablets as basis of God's renewed covenant after Moses' intervention for Israel. He reminds the Corinthians of the sign with which God ratified Moses' authority as his intermediary by the supernatural light that glowed on Moses' face when he descended from Mount Sinai, and which was seen by the Israelites whenever he came from the presence of God. Paul employed elements from this history as *metaphors* to re-establish his own adequacy (ἱκανότης, 3:5; see 2:16) as intermediary of God's new covenant. He applied the unveiling of Moses' face as recorded in Exodus 34 to the Christians' privilege of communication with God through the incarnated and risen Christ. With this *metaphor* he calls on believers to a way of life that is daily being conformed to, or transformed into the image of the humble triumphant Christ (v. 18), to be letters that are read by everyone (v. 2).

3. Consider the kind of attestation needed – 3:1–3a

Chapter 3 starts off with two balanced rhetorical questions opposing "ourselves" with the derogatory "some people," with words corresponding in sound (assonance, παρήχησις).

> Ἀρχόμεθα πάλιν ἑαυτοὺς συνιστάνειν;
> ἢ μὴ χρήζομεν ὥς τινες συστατικῶν ἐπιστολῶν
> πρὸς ὑμᾶς ἢ ἐξ ὑμῶν;

The first question whether "we are starting (Ἀρχόμεθα with rho, chi and *ometha*) again to recommend (συνιστάνειν with sigma, upsilon/ jota, sigma, tau/ ending with nun) ourselves," suggests a negative answer in comparison ("or") with the second question where μή indicates a negative answer "whether we are in need of (χρήζομεν with chi, rho and *omen*) recommendation (συστατικῶν with sigma, upsilon, ending with nun) letters (ἐπιστολῶν with jota, sigma, tau/ ending with nun) like some people." The second question ends with the contrast "to you" or "from you" directing both questions to the readers to reconsider their opinion of Paul, and to think again about some people's need of attestation. "Some people" could refer to "the many who adulterate the word of God for profit" (2:17). These two questions are an euphonious invitation to choose between two ways of life. It also introduces a list of opposing propositions that grow in intensity throughout chapter 3, and climax in v. 18.

---

[7]   John I. Durham, *Exodus* (WBC 3; Waco, Tex.: Word Books, 1987), 469.

Paul's answer (v. 2) to the two questions contains five gammas and three participles ending in *mene* following the feminine word *epistole*. Note the paronomasia of the two passive participles γινωσκομένη καὶ ἀναγινωσκομένη and the placing first of "knowledge" that logically follows from "reading."

ἡ ἐπιστολὴ ἡμῶν ὑμεῖς ἐστε,
    ἐγγεγραμμένη ἐν ταῖς καρδίαις ἡμῶν,
    γινωσκομένη καὶ ἀναγινωσκομένη ὑπὸ
πάντων ἀνθρώπων

Why and how it happened will be discussed in the following verse, but the irrefutable fact is that they are themselves Paul's letter of commendation through their way of life. The perfect tense of the first participle indicates that it is indelibly written in Paul's and their hearts. The present tense of the following two participles describes the ongoing testimony of their way of life. It is known by all their acquaintances and read by all. These statements of fact also appeal to the responsibility of the Corinthian congregation.

The why and the how are explained by the next statement (v. 3a). It opens with the emphasized present participle φανερούμενοι to indicate the reason why it is clear to all. Their way of life is a witness to Christ. He is the real author. The aorist participle διακονηθεῖσα refers to the foundational service rendered by "us," Paul as amanuensis of Christ, with the co-operation of the believers. How it happened is explained in contrast to the credentials of "some people" that is written (perfect participle) with ink. The founding and life of the congregation is the work of the living God by means of his Spirit. This statement calls on the Corinthians to consider their position before God to be a visible letter of Christ guided by the Spirit of God through the words of Paul and their response to it.

4. Life under the law vs. life through the Spirit – 3:3b–6

In v. 3b there is a shift of imagery, from a letter of recommendation, to a comparison with the Ten Commandments written on stone tablets by Moses.[8] The Spirit of the living God wrote on the tablets of their hearts.[9] The perfect participle ἐγγεγραμμένη in vv. 2 and 3 refers to the continuance of their completed conversion in the past.[10] The comparison calls attention to the superiority of life through the Spirit over life under the law.

---

[8] See Exod 31:18; 34:1.
[9] See Jer 38:33 (LXX) ἐπὶ καρδίας αὐτῶν γράψω αὐτούς referring to νόμους.
[10] See BDR (n. 1), § 340.

The comparison of stone tablets with fleshy[11] heart tablets implies a *warning* against hardness of heart, or impenitence, and it *advises* a sensitive feeling heart, or willing obedience.[12] In the light of the word for conversion (ἐπιστρέφω) in v. 16, σαρκίνος hints at a heart that can change. The allusions to the promises of God through Ezekiel and Jeremiah[13] verify Paul's claim for his gospel as coming from God (2:17), and confirm that the church in Corinth is the fulfilment of God's promises.

Paul emphasizes that it is through Christ's active presence that "we" have this confidence that they are Christ's letter and his credential (v. 4). While it speaks of Paul's position before God (πρὸς τὸν θεόν), in the sight and judgment of God (see κατέναντι θεοῦ in 2:17), it implies that, through the grace of Christ, they are also living before God, *coram Deo*, and must be worthy of it.

Paul speaks of his and the congregation's adequacy (ἱκανότης) for their service before God (vv. 5, 6a; see 2:17). With two *parallelesmi membrorum*[14] Paul emphasizes that, of ourselves, we are not adequate to consider anything as deriving from ourselves, but that our adequacy is from God,[15] who made us adequate to be servants of his new treaty (when Moses complained that he was not adequate, οὐχ ἱκανός, for his calling, God said "I will be with you;" LXX, Exod 3:11, 12; see 4:10, 11). These two double assurances refer to Paul's apostleship in the first place, but it is also true of the congregation, calling them very seriously not to trust their own ability, but to rely wholly upon God to make "us" his adequate servants.

Next Paul introduces the new motif of the covenant (v. 6). God enables us to be servants of a new covenant.[16] The nature of this new covenant is juxtaposed with the old covenant of Sinai, with "of the Spirit" (πνεύματος) against "of the letter" (γράμματος). The law written on stone tablets kills (see 2:15, 16 "to those on the way to destruction ... a fume from death to death"), but the law written in human hearts, by the Spirit of the living God, imparts life, life from God as the creator of the new covenant with its new way of life (see 2:16 "we are ... a fragrance from life to life" (ἐκ ζωῆς εἰς ζωήν). This comes as an *indirect warning* to the readers not to rely on an externally written, not executed, hence powerless law,[17] which leads to

---

[11] "Σαρκινός has an unusual meaning for Paul," Ralph P. Martin, *2 Corinthians* (WBC 40; Waco, Tex.: Word Books, 1986), 45; not typical human or worldly. It follows the prophecy of Ezekiel.

[12] See Ezek 11:19; 36:26–27 τὴν καρδίαν τὴν λιθίνην ... σαρκίνην. καὶ πνεῦμα καινὸν δώσω ἐν ὑμῖν.

[13] Jer 31:33.

[14] See BDR (n. 1), § 490.

[15] See ἀλλ᾿ ὡς ἐκ θεοῦ in 2:17.

[16] Διακόνους καινῆς διαθήκης, see Jer 38:31 (LXX); 1 Cor 11:25.

[17] See Lambrecht, *Second Corinthians* (n. 6), 43.

transgression of the law and eternal death. It also *exalts* the new covenant that leads to final salvation to *persuade* the Corinthians to allow the Spirit to change their way of life from within.[18] *This represents the major change of motivation for ethical living from an external law, enforced with threats, to an inward drive from conviction.*

5. The glory of the old vs. the glory of the new – 3:7–11

The next sub-paragraph starts and ends with the passing or fading glory (καταργουμένην, vv. 7, 11, also in vv. 11, 13), and puts forward three comparisons about the glory of the ministries of: death vs. Spirit, condemnation vs. justification, and transience vs. permanence. The method of arguing is the conventional logical argument "from the lesser to the greater" (μᾶλλον),[19] as well as the rhetorical devices of antithesis and repetition.[20] Although there is not one personal verb in the sub-section, the comparisons are placed before the readers to persuade them to follow the new covenant, which refers to the new arrangement by Christ's death (1 Cor 11:25).

In the first comparison (vv. 7–8) the ministry of the old covenant with its law inscribed on stone tablets is negatively described as *a ministry that leads to death.* Its ministry is paradoxically described as coming into existence with such a glory that the Israelites could not keep their eyes fixed on Moses' face. Its glory came from the glorious presence of God, and was reflected on the face of its intermediary (Exod 34:29). But the radiance on the face of Moses was dying away (καταργουμένην) every time Moses departed from God's presence. With the certainty expressed with a rhetorical question (v. 8), *the agency of the Spirit will be characterized by glory,* more so than the agency of Moses. Against the ministry that leads to death, with its externally inscribed law and its fading glory, is placed the glory of the life-giving Spirit, engraved in hearts and minds (see vv. 3, 6). This should already *convince* the readers, but the second comparison increases the difference between the two ways to serve God.

The second comparison (vv. 9–10) focuses on *God's reaction to the two ministries,* and leads to the climax of the three comparisons. The ministry of the old covenant is called the ministry of *condemnation* (κατάκρισις). Its end result is divine judgement. The ministry of the new covenant is called

---

[18] In Ezek 11:20 the Lord promises that with the new spirit in a heart of flesh they will walk in my commandments, and keep my ordinances, and do them; see 36:27.

[19] *A minore ad maius,* like the rabbinical method of "light and heavy," קל וחומר, cf. *Kommentar zum Neuen Testament aus Talmud und Midrasch* (ed. Hermann L. Strack und Paul Billerbeck; vol. 3; 4th ed.; Munich: Beck, 1965), 233–236.

[20] See Keener, *1–2 Corinthians* (n. 6), 168.

the ministry of *righteousness* (τῆς δικαιοσύνης). It restores the relationship with God. If glory is attached to the ministry of condemnation (τῇ διακο-νίᾳ ... δόξα, dative ... nominative) the ministry of righteousness is attached to glory (ἡ διακονία ... δόξῃ, nominative ... dative). This chiasm of cases suggests that the glory attached to the old ministry only lasted while Moses was in the presence of God, while the ministry of the Spirit attaches us to the glory of God. Therefore Paul is jubilant. With three words (πολλῷ μᾶλλον περισσεύει) he expresses the overabundance and flourishing in glory of the ministry that dispenses righteousness. To the readers it is a *joyful invitation* to leave the old, and wholeheartedly to dedicate them to the new.

The comparisons reach their climax in the description of v. 10. The reason for the excellence of the ministry of the Spirit is that its astounding glory *totally eclipses* the fading glory of Moses and of the old covenant. It is described with a paradoxical statement: "what has been glorified has not been glorified" (οὐ δεδόξασται τὸ δεδοξασμένον) in this case (ἐν τούτῳ τῷ μέρει),[21] because of the extraordinary glory of the ministry of righteousness. The absoluteness of the statement is an *appeal* to the readers to leave the old and to embrace the new completely.

The concluding reason without a verb (v. 11) compares the *durability* of the two ministries, which implies the lifetime of the two covenants. The old ministry and covenant is in the process of abolition (τὸ καταργούμενον, present participle) ever since the inauguration of the new covenant. The *transience* of the old covenant was symbolized by the fading (v. 7, τὴν καταργουμένην) glory on Moses' face. On the contrary the ministry of the Spirit and the new covenant is *permanent*. The old covenant is described as διὰ δόξης, and the new as ἐν δόξῃ. In the light of the chiasm in v. 9 the old can be seen as accomplished through the glorious presence of God *attached to* it,[22] and the new as *consisting of* the glorious presence of God[23] as the Spirit, in the hearts of the believers.[24] The same *a fortiori* reasoning as in vv. 8 and 9 is used: "[f]or if the vanishing (is) accomplished through glory, *much more* the abiding (is) consisting of glory." The endurance of the new covenant invites the readers to their lifelong participation in its glory, which is comprised of the right relationship with God. While the glory of the old covenant consisted of visible brilliance that led to death, the glory of the new covenant that gives life paradoxically consists of the

---

[21] See Lambrecht, *Second Corinthians* (n. 6), 51.

[22] Διὰ as marker of the instrument by which something is accomplished; see Louw and Nida, *Greek-English lexicon* (n. 3), § 90.8.

[23] Ἐν as marker of that of which something consists; see Louw and Nida, *Greek-English lexicon* (n. 3), § 89.141.

[24] Most commentators see no difference intended by the different prepositional phrases, and refer to ἐν δόξῃ for both in v. 7.

visible indignity of a crucified Christ (1 Cor 2:2; 2 Cor 13:4), of his hu-
miliated apostle (2 Cor 4:7–15; 6:4–10), and his self-sacrificing "dying"
followers (2 Cor 5:15).

6. Veiled vs. unveiled – 3:12–18

Moses had to veil his face in order to hide from his people the *fading away*
of the radiance on his face (see Exod 34:33–35; the reason given in Exod
34:30 is that they were afraid to approach him). Paul, on the other hand,
relies on the *permanence* of the new covenant as the basis of his hope.[25]
Therefore he has nothing to hide from his readers, and can speak openly
(3:12). They can trust his ministry and his message to be transparent. But
the verb χρώμεθα is first person plural, "we behave," to *involve* his readers.
They should cherish the same hope, and act with the same freeness (πολλῇ
παρρησίᾳ, *Freimütigkeit*) as Paul.

Paul sees Moses' veiling of himself, whenever he left the presence of
God,[26] as indication of his lack of openness, which he blames on Israel's
unbelief in v. 14. According to Paul's version, Moses veiled himself to
keep the Israelites from fixing their eyes on the end of what was fading
away, namely the radiance of his face, which Paul sees as the symbol of
the passing away of the old covenant (v. 13).

Israel's minds were closed, hardened, made insensitive (v. 14), which is
symbolized by the law written on stone (v. 7). According to the conclusion
of the pericope the unbelieving minds were blinded by the god of this passing age (4:4). Their resistance to the truth in the days of Moses persisted
even in the time of Paul. He sees that the same veil or barrier to grasp the
real purpose of the Mosaic law remains (μὴ ἀνακαλυπτόμενον, is not removed) up to the present, whenever the Scriptures of the Old Covenant are
read in the synagogue. He pictures their insensitiveness as an inward veil
that covers their minds, which is only abolished by Christ. With the last
remark he directs the readers to Christ to open their minds for the abundant
glory of the new covenant, and to act with the same freeness that Paul has
(see v. 12). V. 15 repeats v. 14 in abbreviated form to emphasize that even
at present "whenever Moses is read a veil lies on their heart." It refers to
an internal obstruction in the seat of their feelings and thoughts whenever
the Scriptures of Moses are read. The conclusion warns the readers that

---

[25] See Louw and Nida, *Greek-English lexicon* (n. 3), § 25.61 on ἐλπίς for the basis
for hope.

[26] The imperfect ἐτίθει indicates the frequency of Moses' covering of his face. Exod
34:35 says "and Moses put the veil over his face till ever (ἄν) he went in to speak with
him."

this stoppage blinds the unbelievers even to the light from the glorious gospel about Christ, who is the image of God (4:4).

V. 16 is ambiguous. It alludes to the removal of the veil whenever Moses returned (ἐπιστρέφω) to the Lord. The Septuagint's rendering of Exodus 34:34, 35 uses the words "go in to" (ἐισπορεύομαι and ἐισέρχομαι). But following on vv. 14–15, which speak of the Jews of his day, Paul's change of the verb from "enter" to "turn" suggests that the veil will be removed by Christ (see v. 14) for every person who turns to Him. The word ἐπιστρέφω *suggests* a turn-about of opinion and behaviour, a conversion.

V. 17 connects the Lord, mentioned in v. 16, with the Spirit of the living God, who writes on the hearts of people of the new covenant to cause them to live (see vv. 3 and 6).[27] Although the Lord of v. 16 alludes to Moses' communication with God in Exod 34, Paul calls Christ Jesus our Lord or Lord, and in 2 Corinthians he calls God our Father or Father.[28] It is Christ who abolishes the veil that bars understanding (3:14). To Paul, Christ is the image of God (4:4), and it is Christ Jesus whom "we" proclaim as Lord (4:5).

Paul uses Moses' turning to God as the paradigm for conversion to Christ as Lord, which is effected by the working of the Spirit in the hearts and minds of people (in 6:6 he calls him the Holy Spirit). These workings of the Spirit, to accept Christ as Lord, are the *deepest motivation* to live according to the will of God that is engraved in one's heart and mind. Therefore Paul says "where the Spirit of the Lord (is, there is) freedom." Freedom *from* death (vv. 6, 7), transience (vv. 7, 11), condemnation (v. 9), incomprehension (vv. 14, 15); freedom *for* witness (v. 3), adequate service (v. 6), righteousness, doing what God requires (v. 9), sharing in God's glory (v. 9), permanence (v. 11), freeness, *Freimütigkeit* (v. 12), comprehension (vv. 14, 16).

The emphasis on the transforming power of the message of life reaches its climax in v. 18. In the old covenant with its outward law, engraved on stone tablets, only Moses went into the presence of God to speak to Him, and only Moses' face shone with glory after such a meeting. In the new covenant every believer (v. 18; "all of us") is a reflector of Christ's glory. The Greek word κατοπτρίζομαι has two meanings: "to reflect"[29] and "to

---

[27] On the different identifications of "the Lord" see Margaret E. Thrall, *A critical and exegetical commentary on the second epistle to the Corinthians* (ICC; 2 vols.; Edinburgh: T&T Clark, 1994), 274–282; Lambrecht, *Second Corinthians* (n. 6), 54–55.

[28] See 1:1, 2, 3, 14; 2:12; 4:5 etc.

[29] To reflect light or visual patterns coming from some source; see Louw and Nida, *Greek-English lexicon* (n. 3), § 14.52.

behold as in a mirror" or "to behold by reflection."[30] Probably Paul had both in mind, thinking of Moses, who beheld God's reflecting glory,[31] and who thereafter reflected God's glory on his face. With a face uncovered by Christ (see v. 14) every Christian reflects the glory of the Lord.[32] The perfect ἀνακεκαλυμμένῳ refers to the "unveiling" of the believers' minds and hearts as something that happened in the past with lasting results. By beholding the glory of Christ, we are in the process of transformation or change[33] into the same image.[34] The passive voice of the verb implies that the transformation is the work of the Holy Spirit (see vv. 6, 17, 18b). The "mirror" or indirect way in which we see Christ can refer the work of the Spirit through the witness about Christ and the Christ-event.[35] The way in which the glory of the Lord becomes visible would be through the believer's *Christ-like behaviour.*

The transformation is described as a progression from one state of glory to a further state of glory, which suggests that the believer becomes more and more like the self-sacrificing Christ (see 8:9), "precisely as[36] from the Spirit of the Lord."[37] Through the service that proclaims the undistorted word of God (2:17; 4:2) that describes the glory of Christ as our Lord (4:4–5), the Spirit changes our hearts and minds, so that we will *change* our way of life, to become living letters of Christ, known and read by all people (vv. 2, 3, 6).

---

[30] To see indirectly or by reflection in a mirror; see Louw and Nida, *Greek-English lexicon* (n. 3), § 24.44.

[31] See Exod 33:23 "My face will not be seen by you;" Num 12:8 "... he saw the glory of the Lord."

[32] 3:18a: ἡμεῖς δὲ πάντες ἀνακεκαλυμμένῳ προσώπῳ τὴν δόξαν κυρίου κατοπτριζόμενοι.

[33] Μεταμορφούμεθα present tense indicating duration.

[34] 3:18b: κατοπτριζόμενοι τὴν αὐτὴν εἰκόνα μεταμορφούμεθα, reading κατοπτριζόμενοι in its second meaning.

[35] By equating δόξα and εἰκών Thrall (*Corinthians* [n. 27], 283) sees κύριος in vv. 17, 18 as referring to God, whose image is seen reflected in Christ.

[36] Καθάπερ as an emphatic marker of comparison, see Louw and Nida, *Greek-English lexicon* (n. 3), § 64.15.

[37] For the different ways to explain this clause, see Thrall, *Corinthians* (n. 27), 286–287.

Moral Language in Philemon

PIETER G. R. DE VILLIERS

1. Introduction

Philemon and the two letters to Timothy are often described as personal letters which form a different category of letters next to those who were written to churches.[1] In the case of Paul's letter to Philemon it is traditionally seen as having been written to Philemon, a close associate of Paul, about a specific problem which Paul hoped to solve by reconciling Philemon with his slave, Onesimus.

The devastating *Wirkungsgeschichte* of the letter[2] and especially its role in the support of slavery nevertheless show how it impacted morally much wider than on an individual level.[3] But it was not only the reception history of Philemon which showed the comprehensive nature of its ethos. Paul himself already understood that this issue about Philemon's slave had implications beyond the mere personal. This is clear from the formal presen-

---

[1]   For major introductory issues, cf. e.g. Joachim Gnilka, *Der Philemonbrief* (HTKNT 10/4; Freiburg: Herder, 1982); Michael Wolter, *Der Brief an die Kolosser. Der Brief an Philemon* (ÖTK 12; Gütersloh: Gütersloher Verlag, 1993); James D. G. Dunn, *The Epistles to the Colossians and to Philemon* (NIGTC; Grand Rapids, Mich.: Eerdmans, 1996); John M. G. Barclay, *Colossians and Philemon* (New Testament Guides 12; Sheffield: Sheffield Academic Press, 1997); Markus Barth, *The Letter to Philemon* (Eerdmans Critical Commentary; Grand Rapids, Mich.: Eerdmans, 2000); Joseph A. Fitzmyer, *The Letter to Philemon* (Anchor Bible 34C; New York, N.Y.: Doubleday, 2000); Eckart Reinmuth, *Der Brief des Paulus an Philemon* (THKNT 11/2; Leipzig: Evangelische Verlagsanstalt, 2006). Most of these commentaries reflect how scholarship focussed on the issue of slavery as major topic of research, with less attention to its theological and moral pronouncements.

[2]   For discussion of slavery, cf. S. Scott Bartchy, "Slavery," *ABD* (1992): 58–74; Peter Lampe, "Keine 'Sklavenflucht' des Onesimus," *ZNW* 76 (1985): 135–137. Cf. also Isak J. du Plessis, "How Christians can survive in a hostile social-economic environment: Paul's mind concerning difficult social conditions in the letter to Philemon" in *Identity, Ethics, and Ethos in the New Testament* (ed. Jan G. van der Watt; BZNW 141; Berlin: de Gruyter, 2006), who provides an informative discussion of slavery as context within which to understand Philemon. He indicates how some slaves enjoyed great privileges and a good lifestyle, though he also points out the negative, exploitative face of slavery.

[3]   Du Plessis, "Christians" (n. 2), 387–390 correctly points out how this letter has gender and labour implications.

tation of the letter. He embeds the conflict between Philemon and Onesimus within a wider readership through his introduction and conclusion with which he frames this letter. In them he mentions several people (Timothy, Apphia, Archippus, Epaphras, Mark, Aristarchus, Demas and Luke and the church; Phlm 1, 23–24).[4] He also concludes the letter with the plural ὑμῶν through which he refers to his addressees (Phlm 25). Paul thus integrates an individual issue within a corporate, collective setting. The way in which Philemon traditionally has been read as a "personal" letter, therefore should not obscure its nature as a letter written to a house church.[5]

It is important for a proper understanding of the moral impact of this letter to keep this collective perspective in mind. The letter to Philemon reflects, as will become clear below, a situation with moral implications for a number of people within the Pauline missionary team and house churches. It furthermore provides insights in the identity and ethos of early Christianity, particularly within the Pauline tradition or within groups who responded to the Pauline proclamation of the gospel. In this sense it confronts the interpreter of the letter with the question of Ruben Zimmermann: "in welcher Beziehung steht der ethische Entscheidungsträger zu anderen Personen oder übergeordneten Instanzen, Kräften oder Mächten ... Wie verhalten sich Individualethik und Sozialethik zueinander, kann das Subjekt etwa auch eine kollektive Größe sein?"[6]

In a nutshell, then, Paul writes his text to end Philemon's conflict with his slave, Onesimus. Philemon's behavior created a crisis which required ethical reflection. Both Onesimus and Paul thought that the situation needed to change. But, even more so, the letter suggests that Philemon's behavior affected the ethos of the community of believers. It challenged established relationships between members who shared a social system.[7] Paul's letter is, therefore, a direct result of this conflict – something which

---

[4]   Cf. the close reading of the text in section 4.1 below.

[5]   Du Plessis, "Christians" (n. 2), 411 also stresses this corporate insight. For another interesting perspective on the corporate structures that are implied in this letter, cf. e.g. Chris Frilingos, "'For my Child, Onesimus:' Paul and Domestic Power in Philemon," *JBL* 119 (2000): 91–104.

[6]   Cf. Ruben Zimmermann, "Jenseits von Indikativ und Imperativ: Entwurf einer impliziten Ethik des Paulus am Beispiel des 1. Korintherbriefes," *TLZ* 132 (2007): 259–284, 276. As will become clear below, the motif of κοινωνία τῆς πίστεώς in Phlm 6 will be an important indication of the corporate nature of the letter. Cf. also Dunn, *Philemon* (n. 1), 319.

[7]   Cf. Michael Wolter, "Ethos und Identität in paulinischen Gemeinden," *NTS* 43 (1997): 430–444 for a further discussion of the meaning of the term ethos and its relationship with identity.

often motivated moral reflection.[8] By noting Paul's response to this conflict one can therefore gain insight in his moral views and ethos.

2. Philemon and Ethics

In a few cases Paul reflected in an explicit manner on ethics. Paul mentions in Phlm 9 that he is appealing to Philemon on behalf of Onesimus "out of love" (διὰ τὴν ἀγάπην μᾶλλον παρακαλῶ). His intervention is, therefore, in accordance with the normative function of love. Related to this, is his appeal in Phlm 14 that Philemon must do good willingly, "out of benevolence," not because he is forced to do so. There is another interesting example in Phlm 8 where Paul remarks that he could be bold and order Philemon to do what he "ought" to do or what his "duty" is (ἐπιτάσσειν σοι τὸ ἀνῆκον).[9] Paul here indicates in a direct manner that the Christian community lives according to binding norms and values which can be enforced on its members.[10]

Yet Paul did not design an ethics in the sense of Aristotle's ἠθικὴ θεωρία. His letters, including Philemon, cannot be read in terms of a systematic-theoretical reflection on the ethos of his community. They are mostly practical, expressed in moral language which is metaphorical and implicit in nature rather than philosophical and technical.[11] The challenge is to extrapolate Paul's moral convictions and arguments from these indirect, practical pronouncements, as will be done now.

3. Fellowship as Norm

Paul's moral language in Philemon is grounded in a faith context. He writes about the required behavior for the conflicting parties in terms of

---

[8] This point is well made by Zimmermann, "Indikativ und Imperativ" (n. 6), 273. He observes, "Gerade und besonders in Konfliktsituationen, dann, wenn die Beurteilung einer Handlung strittig ist, ist 'Ethik' erforderlich."

[9] Morton S. Enslin, *The Ethics of Paul* (New York, N.Y.: Abingdon Press, 1957), 215 compares Paul's claim to demand obedience with Pythagorean and Orphic groups among whom the word of the master was final.

[10] Cf. also Zimmermann, "Indikativ und Imperativ" (n. 6), 272–273.

[11] Cf. Zimmermann, "Indikativ und Imperativ" (n. 6), 272 for a discussion of terms like ethos, moral, ethics. Enslin, *Ethics* (n. 9), 77–78 commented on the prominent "ethical note" throughout Paul's letters but added that his ethical exhortations, "for the most part were called forth to meet the specific needs of the Christians to whom he ministered, and thus were intensely practical and timely in their nature and a far step from the ordered sequence of a Greek moralist like Aristotle."

the new reality in Christ in which they participated since their conversion. Paul argues deontologically[12] from this context to address the conflict in Philemon's house church, as will be argued now.

The language in Philemon is traditional in nature.[13] Paul speaks of well-known motifs like grace and peace (Phlm 3, 25), refers to the divine with such established descriptions like God as Father (Phlm 3) and Jesus as Christ and Lord (Phlm 3, 9, 25). His language reflects the decisive role of the salvific events of God in Christ with several references to Christ (cf. e.g. Phlm 1, 3, 5, 6, 8, 9, 16, 20, 23, 25). The salvific nature of these events comes to the fore in Paul's typical corporate language. He repeatedly uses the phrases "in" Christ / the Lord (Phlm 8, 16, 20) or "of" Christ Jesus (Phlm 9).[14]

This language refers to a transformative, loving relationship of the divine with humanity. This language also contains terms like faith, love, joy, fellowship and prayer to describe the human response to God's salvific offer (e.g. Phlm 4–7). As such they also have moral meaning. These are qualities that he values highly, as is clear when he commends them in believers in Thessalonica (1 Thess 1:3; 2 Thess 1:3). For Paul believers have a new identity in Christ because of their faith, but to be in Christ implies a particular lifestyle.[15] Faith and morality are so intertwined that they can hardly be distinguished in terms of the indicative and imperative, as happened so often in New Testament scholarship.[16]

This statement can be motivated by a passage at the beginning of the letter to Philemon (Phlm 4–7). In it Paul commends Philemon for his love

---

[12] For the term, cf. Dirk J. Smit, "Oor 'n Nuwe-Testamentiese Etiek," in *Geloof en Opdrag: Perspektiewe op die Etiek van die Nuwe Testament* (ed. Cilliers Breytenbach and Bernard C. Lategan; Scriptura S9a; Pretoria: Unisa, 1992), 303–325 and Zimmermann, "Indikativ und Imperativ" (n. 6), 275, who traces it to Broad's well-known work, published in 1935, on the five types of ethical theory.

[13] Cf. Richard B. Hays, *The Moral Vision of the New Testament: Community, Cross, New Creation. A Contemporary Introduction to New Testament Ethics* (New York, N.Y.: Harper Collins, 1996), 39 who remarks that for Paul, God's transforming act in Christ conditions all of reality. "Insofar as we perceive the truth about God's redemptive work in the world, we will participate gladly in the outworking of God's purpose."

[14] Cf. James D. G. Dunn, *The Theology of Paul the Apostle* (Grand Rapids, Mich.: Eerdmans, 1998), 388–404 for a discussion of the various uses of the "in"- and "with"-formulae in Paul's theology. Also still relevant are the observations of Herman Ridderbos, *Paulus: Ontwerp van zijn Theologie* (Kampen: Kok, 1966), 56–62.

[15] Hays, *Moral Vision* (n. 13), 36–41 discusses Paul's moral logic in terms of warrants, norms and power for moral life and observes (*Moral Vision* [n. 13], 39) that one warrant is that "through union with Christ, we undergo transformation that should cause us to 'walk in newness of life.'"

[16] Cf. the discussion in Wolfgang Schrage, *The Ethics of the New Testament* (Edinburgh: T&T Clark, 1988), 167–186.

and faith – both well-known theological motifs which he often uses in his letters (cf. e.g. 1 Thess 1:4; Eph 1:15; Col 1:4, 8 and further below). When Paul uses these motifs in Philemon to argue a course of moral action, they attain a unique meaning. The two motifs in Philemon therefore differ from their use in other Pauline texts.

Before this can be discussed, some linguistic observations must be made. It is, first of all, vital for the understanding of this passage to recognize that Paul presents the material in vv. 4–7 as a ring composition.[17] The motifs of faith and love are decisively determined by it. Where scholars fail to detect the ring composition, the interpretation of these motifs is rather confusing. Literally the Greek text reads, "I always thank God ... hearing of your love and faith which you have for the Lord Jesus and for all the saints." One of the problems is that faith is linked to both Jesus and believers. Scholars who regard this as impossible, bring some order by interpreting faith vertically in terms of the divine and love horizontally in terms of the holy ones. They argue that Paul commends Philemon for his faith in the Lord, whilst his praise for his love had to do with his behavior towards other believers.[18] Wolter also distinguishes faith and love in this way, "Glaube und Liebe bilden ein Begriffspaar, das die fundamentalen Dimensionen der christlichen Identität benennt. Der Glaube beschreibt die

---

[17] The letter as a whole is also a ring composition, confirming the author's inclination towards this structuring device. An author, who composes his material in terms of a ring composition, will do so not only on macro-level but such literary techniques will also most likely be found on micro-level as well. Several authors have written about Philemon as a ring composition. One of the first was Nils W. Lund, *Chiasmus in the New Testament: A Study in Formgeschichte* (Chapel Hill, N.C.: University of North Carolina Press, 1942), 219, followed later by John W. Welch, *Chiasmus in Antiquity: Structures, Analyses, Exegesis* (Hildesheim: Gerstenberg, 1981), 225 and John P. Heil, "The Chiastic Stucture and Meaning of Paul's Letter to Philemon," *Biblica* 82 (2001): 178–206; Recently the results of these attempts were evaluated positively by David E. Aune, *The Westminster Dictionary of New Testament and Early Christian Literature and Rhetorics* (Louisville, Ky.: Westminster John Knox, 2003), 355. The notion of chiasm is mostly understood as referring to a stylistic device with a specific structure (A, B, B', A'). A and B are repeated in an inverse order: B is immediately discussed by B' whereafter A' follows as repetition of the first element. In the case of a larger text, it is better to use the term ring composition which also expresses this logic of repetition. There can be little doubt that the letter contains distinct units, each with its own conceptual motifs and coherence, whilst these units are mutually and hierarchically related in reverse order on syntactical and semantical levels.

[18] Nicholas T. Wright, *The Epistles of Paul to the Colossians and Philemon* (TNTC 12; Grand Rapids, Mich.: Eerdmans, 1988), 175 argues that it is possible that love and faith could be directed towards Jesus and other Christians. Cf. also Dunn, *Philemon* (n. 1), 317 who observes that there is no reason why Paul could not have thought of love and faith as the sum of the Christian lifestyle and "therefore of both as related to both 'the Lord Jesus' and 'all the saints.'"

'vertikale,' soteriologische (das Verhältnis zum erhöhten Herrn) und die Liebe die ihn realisierende 'horizontale,' ethische (das Verhältnis zum Mitchristen) Dimension."[19] The influence of this reading is visible in translations like the NIV which contains the version, "because I hear about your faith in the Lord Jesus and your love for all the saints."

The ring composition, however, questions this reading, as will become clear from the following close reading of the passage:

A Ε̲ὐ̲χ̲α̲ρ̲ι̲σ̲τ̲ῶ̲ τῷ θεῷ μου πάντοτε μνείαν σου ποιούμενος ἐπὶ τῶν προσευχῶν μου,[20] ἀκούων σου τ̲ὴ̲ν̲ ἀ̲γ̲ά̲π̲η̲ν̲

    B καὶ τ̲ὴ̲ν̲ π̲ί̲σ̲τ̲ι̲ν̲, ἣν ἔχεις πρὸς τὸν κύριον Ἰησοῦν καὶ ε̲ἰ̲ς̲ π̲ά̲ν̲τ̲α̲ς̲ τ̲ο̲ὺ̲ς̲ ἁ̲γ̲ί̲ο̲υ̲ς̲,

    B' ὅπως ἡ κοινωνία τ̲ῆ̲ς̲ π̲ί̲σ̲τ̲ε̲ώ̲ς̲ σου ἐνεργὴς γένηται ἐν ἐπιγνώσει παντὸς ἀγαθοῦ τοῦ ἐν ἡμῖν ε̲ἰ̲ς̲ Χ̲ρ̲ι̲σ̲τ̲ό̲ν̲.[21]

A' χ̲α̲ρ̲ὰ̲ν̲ γ̲ὰ̲ρ̲ π̲ο̲λ̲λ̲ὴ̲ν̲ ἔ̲σ̲χ̲ο̲ν̲ κ̲α̲ὶ̲ π̲α̲ρ̲ά̲κ̲λ̲η̲σ̲ι̲ν̲ ἐπὶ τ̲ῇ̲ ἀ̲γ̲ά̲π̲ῃ̲ σου, ὅτι τὰ σπλάγχνα τῶν ἁγίων ἀναπέπαυται διὰ σοῦ, ἀδελφέ.[22]

This close reading reveals the careful use and repetition of the motifs of love and faith. They play a seminal role in the ring composition, being the key motifs in it. Paul first expresses his thanks and joy in the outside frame (A / A') and then announces love and faith as two of Philemon's exceptional qualities which he is celebrating. In the first element of its inner core he then develops the motif of faith first in B and then in even more depth in B'. In a subtle move in B' he, however, speaks of *"the koinonia"* (ἡ κοινωνία; fellowship/sharing) of faith that he finds so commendable in Philemon's case. This intensifies the notion of faith by qualifying it with the notion of fellowship. Paul gives this seminal concept, traditionally interpreted in terms of a vertical relationship as faith in the Lord, a *horizontal* slant as faith that reaches out in fellowship. He accentuates fellowship and sharing as a key quality of faith, thereby mooting faith's moral implications and thus its horizontal effects (v. 6).[23]

---

    [19] Wolter, *Philemon* (n. 1), 253.

    [20] Note how the alliteration functions as a marker here. For the style of Philemon, cf. Gert J. Steyn, "Some Figures of Style in the Epistle to Philemon: Their Contribution towards the Persuasive Nature of the Epistle," *Ekklesiastikos Pharos* 77 (1995): 64–80. He refers to such figures of style like assonance, polysyndeton, inclusion, ellipse, chiasmus, repetition of propositions, antithesis, isocolons, paranomasia, and anacoluthon.

    [21] B and B' are both separate units, as is spelled out by their similar endings, beginning with an εἰς-phrase.

    [22] A' is a unit, indicated formally by the insertion of γάρ in v. 7.

    [23] For the role of *koinonia* in Philemon, cf. Johnny H. Roberts, "Vryheid, Gelykheid en Broederskap in die Brief aan Filemon: Die Evangelie as Maatskappy-Omvormende Krag" in *Geloof en Opdrag* (n. 12), 259–274. Recently Christian Strecker, *Die liminale*

This emphasis is further confirmed by the combination of love and faith, with love framing faith in the ring composition. This horizontal slant is, furthermore, *formally* underlined by the fact that, uncharacteristically for Paul, he mentions love first, thereby emphasizing it.[24] This contrasts with the order of faith and love in instances like Ephesians 1:15; Colossians 1:4, 8; 1 Thessalonians 1:4. At the same time he adds references to the Lord Jesus and all the saints in both cases, which prevents any of these terms to be read only in a vertical sense.

This introductory passage sets the tone for the rest of the letter. Paul's arguments about the conflict later in the letter when he suggests that Philemon should extend his love to Onesimus (Phlm 16) develop these initial remarks. Philemon should uphold his reputation of a loving relationship with the saints (Phlm 5). In this way, the horizontal nature of love is further stressed. Paul's reading of faith *as fellowship* (Phlm 6) is also confirmed later through Paul's repetition of the koinonia-motif. This motif is taken up again when Paul refers to its cognate (κοινωνόν) in v. 17 to indicate his own intimate relationship with Philemon. He reminds Philemon in that verse of the special fellowship between them, "So if you consider me a partner,[25] welcome him (Onesimus) as you would welcome me." Even more striking is that this is one of the few prescriptive remarks in this letter: Philemon is explicitly asked by Paul to share his fellowship with Onesimus in the same way that he shares his faith in fellowship with the apostle himself. Though faith in its vertical sense is adumbrated in v. 7, Paul focuses on faith as fellowship.

This descriptive language sets the boundaries and the example for the actions required from Philemon. Paul offers this presentation of faith as fellowship to promote his argument in the letter: since Onesimus is now a believer, having converted under Paul's guidance (Phlm 10), Philemon's *koinonia* should extend to him as well. In doing so, Philemon will live up

---

Theologie des Paulus: Zugänge zur paulinischen Theologie aus kulturanthropologischer Perspektive (FRLANT 185; Göttingen: Vandenhoeck & Ruprecht, 1999), 376 also investigated the motif and referred to the "hohe Relevanz sozialer Communitas für das Gemeindeverständnis des Apostels."

[24] Cf. the discussion in Barth, *Philemon* (n. 1), 272; Peter T. O'Brien, *Colossians, Philemon* (WBC 44; Waco, Tex.: Word Books, 1982), 53. Robert W. Wall, *Colossians and Philemon* (IVP New Testament Commentary Series 12; Downers Grove, Il.: Intervarsity, 1993), 20.

[25] This term has financial overtones. Cf. on the financial nature of Paul's language, Ernst Lohmeyer, *Die Briefe an die Philipper, an die Kolosser und an Philemon* (KEK 9; Göttingen: Vandenhoeck & Ruprecht, 1956), 189; Eduard Lohse, *Die Briefe an die Philipper, an die Kolosser und an Philemon* (KEK 9; 14th ed.; Göttingen: Vandenhoeck & Ruprecht, 1968), 284. Peter Stuhlmacher, *Der Brief an Philemon* (EKKNT 18; Zurich: Benziger, 1975), 49–50. Though Paul uses commercial language here, he integrates it in a religious context. As a result the religious meaning dominates.

to the reputation which he has built up among other believers who experienced his love and fellowship. Through these formal pronouncements, Paul thus prepares the way for the extra-textual impact of this passage. His language wishes to stabilize the ethos of the churches by underlining the significance of love and fellowship among believers. Their ethos has love and faith as key motifs, but then in this particular case it is made significant in so far as it promotes *koinonia*. Believers like Philemon are required to heed the full consequences of faith. In this way, Paul's ethics is deontologically grounded in faith as fellowship.

At the beginning of this letter, Paul's language about Philemon's faith therefore already in itself has an ethical character with appellative force.[26] Believers are confronted with the challenge inherent in their faith to live in an intimate, warm mutual relationship. Paul portrays the life in faith as a life in community, encompassing the other – even and especially those who are normally not part of one's inner circle. One has here an illustration of Engberg-Pedersen's remark: "[t]hen a person has Christ faith, (a) not only will he do everything that he *should* do … (b) he will also do it freely and as a direct consequence of his new self-understanding. He will do it because he *wants* to, not merely because he must or because it is a means to something else that he wishes to obtain."[27]

Faith is used here in Philemon in a different way than, for example, in a polemical situation regarding the Jewish traditions of early Christianity. It does not function in tension with the law (as in Galatians), but questions separation, alienation and broken relationships between people. The appellative force is intensified by the fact that this language is placed at the beginning of the letter where Paul sets the tone and announces the themes that he will be mooting in the rest of his text. Not only the nature of the language, but also the way in which it is emphasized formally through location, implicitly provides moral guidance. From the very beginning the way in which Paul speaks of Philemon prepares the ground for his later requests to him.

Finally, one further dimension must be mooted here in order to underline the specific nature of Paul's emphasis on fellowship and his indirect request to Philemon to share it with his slave. One could understand the special nature of Paul's call also in the light of the ethos of his Graeco-Roman context in which fellowship is extended only to equals.[28] Paul's

---

26 Zimmermann, "Indikativ und Imperativ" (n. 6), 269.

27 Troels Engberg-Pedersen, *Paul and the Stoics* (Edinburgh: T&T Clark, 2000), 234.

28 Cf. Wolter, *Philemon* (n. 1), 274. Strecker, *Theologie* (n. 23), 376. The intertextual relationship of Philemon with the surrounding ethos cannot be pursued in detail in this essay because of restricted space. For theoretical observations about the sociological approach to ethics and ethos, cf. Zimmermann, "Indikativ und Imperativ" (n. 6), 270–

argument for sharing fellowship with Onesimus according to the early Christian norm of equality implicitly questions this ethos of the wider community. The theological and Christological language in which he expresses his remarks about fellowship with all its major consequences for human relationships within the believing community, implicitly functions to outline that the own identity of believers is shared by all who believe, despite social status. Their identity which is grounded in God's salvific actions and which contributed to their particular Christian ethos, thus determined the potentially radical modification of their surrounding ethos.

4. Love as Norm

Although love[29] has been mentioned briefly in the previous section, it deserves further attention in terms of its place in the letter to Philemon as a whole.

4.1 Love in Philemon

Love is crucial for an understanding of the letter to Philemon. A close reading of the text shows how it is a recurring motif that gives coherence to the letter as a whole. Before this is explained in more detail, a short note is necessary to point out that even though the word love is not specifically used in the various parts of the letter, other terms of intimacy and endearment that presuppose and reflect love are used. These include such sibling terms like child, brother,[30] sister, father and emotional terms like "my heart" and "refreshing." What counts, therefore, is not the actual words for love in the letter, but the semantic field which represents love. If the se-

---

272. The relationship is mentioned here in order to illustrate the implications of Paul's emphasis on faith as fellowship.

[29] Cf. Schrage, *Ethics* (n. 16), 211–217 for an extensive discussion of love as a motif in Pauline texts.

[30] Ethelbert Stauffer, "ἀγαπάω κτλ," *TWNT* 1 (1933): 20–55, 51 thus correctly observes, "Das organische Prinzip, das ein für allemal mit der Richtung der Liebe auf den Nächsten gegeben ist, wirkt sich hier organisierend aus: Nächstenliebe, einst die Hilfsbereitschaft gegen den Genossen des israelitischen Bundesvolks, heißt jetzt Dienst am Genossen des neuen Gottesvolkes, heißt das Heil der Bruderschaft zum Leitgesichtspunkt der Lebensführung machen.'Αγαπητός und ἀδελφός werden *Wechselbegriffe* (1 Th. 2,8; Phlm 16)" (secondary italics). In the footnote to this passage, he also refers to Phlm 5 to point out that love of the other as brother is implied through this word.

mantic field of love, affection and compassion is taken as guideline,[31] the following outline reveals the central[32] place of love in this letter:

A. Paul writes to Philemon as a "*beloved*" brother (1–3) about
>   B his fellowship in faith and for his <u>refreshing</u> *love* for the Lord and for others (4–6).
>>   C. Paul then appeals on the basis of *love* to Philemon to do "what is fitting" towards Onesimus (7–11).
>>>   D. Paul is reluctantly *sending back* Onesimus who is Paul's "*heart*," though he would like to keep him (12–13).
>>>>   E. Paul embeds an explanation that he wanted to do nothing without Philemon's knowledge. Philemon should *do good* voluntarily – out of choice, rather than being forced (14).
>>>   D'. Paul then returns to the sending back. Onesimus is *sent back* to Philemon to be welcomed as a "*beloved brother*" (15–17).
>>   C'. Paul will stand in for anything that stands in the way of Philemon's reconciliation with Onesimus and prevents them from living as (beloved) brethren (18–19).
>   B'. Philemon's benevolent love towards Onesimus will <u>refresh</u>[33] Paul (20–22).
A'. Philemon is remembered by the community of believers (23–35).

Paul's language in this letter is, therefore, deeply permeated by the love motif. Love is for him an essential characteristic of a believers' lifestyle. It is love that will solve the conflict between Philemon and Onesimus. Love is ultimately the foundation of Paul's desire that the relationship between them should be deepened and further transformed beyond that of master and slave.

4.2 Characterization in Philemon: Believers, Brothers and Beloved

Love does not only run as a golden thread through this letter, but is also used as central motif in the characterization of Philemon and Onesimus.

Paul occasionally uses general terms to describe Christians like, for example, the "holy ones" (Phlm 4, 7), "partner" (κοινωνόν, v. 17) or "coworkers" (Philemon, Mark, Aristarchus, Demas and Luke in Phlm 1 and 23). The latter creates a special bond between him and his addressees, since it reveals their fellowship in their missionary work. By referring to their missionary struggle with terms like prisoner of Jesus Christ (for himself; Phlm 1, 9), Epaphras as fellow captive (Phlm 23) and Archippus as fellow soldier (Phlm 1) he creates an even stronger bond between his cha-

---

[31] Johannes P. Louw and Eugene A. Nida, *Greek-English lexicon of the New Testament based on semantic domains* (New York, N.Y.: United Bible Societies, 1988), 288–296.

[32] Cf. Schrage, *Ethics* (n. 16), 213 for other examples of the central position of love in Pauline texts.

[33] The motif of ἀναπέπαυται / ἀνάπαυσον appears in both B and B'.

racters. They are not only sharing his ministry, but also its negative consequences.

Paul mostly describes his characters with sibling terminology (Timothy, Apphia in v. 1 as brother and sister) and Onesimus as Paul's "child" whom he has "begotten" (ἐγέννησα) in prison (v. 10).[34] Through this emphatic use of intimate, sibling language Paul projects a picture of a close group of believers who through their shared faith and mission is as close to one another as was the case in families of his time. Even more important, such language suggested concrete moral behavior. Aasgaard aptly observed in his study on siblingship in Paul, "[a]bove all ... the sibling relationship was associated with love: siblings were expected to display love towards one another (ἀγάπη; ἀγαπᾶν) ... Thus, more than other family relationships, the sibling relation was thought to be distinguished by mutual love." He adds that Paul, in agreement with his social context, "alludes again and again to ideas of love, and exhorts his co-Christians to attitudes and actions of love towards one another, which, as noted involved both emotions and practical obligations."[35]

The letter reserves even more intimate terms for Onesimus and Philemon. Of all the names mentioned in this letter (Timothy, Apphia, Archippus, Epaphras, Mark, Aristarchus, Demas and Luke), only Philemon is described as "beloved" (Phlm 1). This caught the attention of early readers of the text, as is evident from the fact that some manuscripts used the same word for Apphia so that she is also the "beloved" (D², Ψ, M, sy^p, sa^mss). But this is an inferior reading. Paul singled out Philemon by characterizing only him as beloved.

Paul develops this intimacy also in Phlm 16 where he wants Philemon to receive Onesimus back, not as a slave, but as "more than a slave." He then adds "as a beloved brother." This is the only time in the letter that these two terms (beloved/brother) are linked. It happens, strikingly, in the middle section of the letter (D–D') where Paul focuses on the healing of the relationship between Philemon and Onesimus (Phlm 18). In this section Paul also speaks emotionally and affectively of Onesimus as Paul's "heart"

---

[34]   Beloved or beloved brothers as designations for co-believers are well-known in the Pauline tradition. Cf. e.g. 1 Cor 10:14 (beloved), 15:58 (beloved brothers), Phil 4:1 (ἀδελφοί μου ἀγαπητοὶ καὶ ἐπιπόθητοι); 2 Cor 7:1; 12:19 (beloved); Phil 2:12 (beloved); 1 Thess 1:4 (brothers, loved by God); Rom 1:7 (beloved of – or loved by God); cf. also 1 Tim 6:2. A most helpful instance is to be found in 1 Thess 1:4: ἀδελφοὶ ἠγαπημένοι ὑπὸ θεοῦ. Here the origin of the love is traced to God. A similar usage is found in Romans 1:7 (ἀγαπητοῖς θεοῦ).

[35]   Cf. e.g. Reidar Aasgard, *'My Beloved Brothers and Sisters!' Christian Siblingship in Paul* (JSNTSup 265; London: T&T Clark, 2004), 309 and 311.

(τὰ ἐμὰ σπλάγχνα;[36] Phlm 12). It is this affective relationship that he wants Philemon to extend to Onesimus.

Paul's moral language in this letter is given a further intensity if it is read in terms of contemporary Graeco-Roman texts about brotherly love. Such an intertextual reading illuminates a vital dimension of the early Christian ethos as reflected in such Pauline letters like Philemon. Brotherly love was an important ideal in antiquity. Already Aristotle reflected on the nature of the relationship between brothers which he described as a loving relationship, based on brothers being born of the same parents. Their identity and biological link with their parents makes them identical with each other (Nichomachean Ethics 1160b 29). Much later Plutarch also wrote a treatise which quite tellingly had as title "Fraternal Affection" (cf. *Mor.* 488A). In it he criticized any conflict or jealousy in a family. Brothers should rather make mutual concessions and live in peace. In these cases the mutual bond between people is determined by birth from the same parents. Paul's religious portrait of brotherhood is, in contrast, not based on biological links, but on believers' relationship with God.[37] Intimacy is extended beyond the family because of this religious relationship. In contrast to their surrounding social system, believers relate to the socially lowly as one relates to the closest of friends, even to one's own natural family. Paul's affectionate language for Philemon and Onesimus reflects the caring, affectionate and intimate relationship for those who are part of the believing community and Paul's general concern that Christians should "treat one another honorably internally," should "harbour positive and strong emotions toward one another" and should "further unity among diversity."[38]

Paul's language in Philemon modifies this insight. Philemon has become part of the new family of God when he joined the Pauline mission. But he needed to grow into a deeper understanding of its religious ethos which he inherited as believer.[39] He has to reconsider his relationship with his slave and to understand how his faith in Christ modifies or even questions the social conventions of his time. The reconsideration of human relations is spelled out in personal and concrete terms. It affects not only religious, but also everyday life. There is little room for misunderstanding.

---

[36] Louw and Nida, *Lexicon* (n. 31), 295 discuss this expression as part of the semantic domain of love, affection, compassion and interpret the phrase in Phlm 12 as an indication of "one for whom one had deep affection or compassion – 'object of affection.'"

[37] Cf. the full and useful discussion in Aasgaard, *Brothers and Sisters* (n. 35), 513–530.

[38] Aasgaard, *Brothers and Sisters* (n. 35), 307.

[39] In this regard, the discussion between Bornkamm and Bultmann on eschatological dialectics is important. Cf. Schrage, *Ethics* (n. 16), 170 who refers to Paul's paraenesis which is addressed to the saints as those who "are pilgrims in the new life that is theirs."

Paul writes to Philemon: "so, if you consider me as a partner, welcome him as you would welcome *me*." Philemon will have Onesimus back "both *in the flesh* and in the Lord" (Phlm 17).

All this shows how early Christian language with such motifs like faith and love steered moral behavior. The early Christian vocabulary empowered Paul to manage this conflict, even if he did modify it to fit his particular setting and time. Language creates worlds that determine lives and lifestyles, as is well illustrated by the destructive nature of racist, sexist and ageist language. In the case of Philemon, the Christian "text" with its language of unconditional, intimate fellowship indicated the lifestyle which Philemon and the Pauline church needed. Paul is not requiring something new from Philemon, he is spelling out the implications of the new dispensation of Christ which he proclaimed in his gospel.

5. The Aim of Love

There is another dimension of language in this letter which deserves more attention, because it spells out the consequences of the implicit ethics in the Letter to Philemon. It will illustrate that Paul's ethical arguments are not only deontological in nature, as indicated in the previous sections, but also teleological.

It has already been noted above that Paul often refers to the close relationship between God and believers when he uses the phrases "in" and "through" Christ / the Lord (e.g. Phlm 5, 8, 16, 20, 23). In Phlm 6 Paul speaks of the fellowship that needs to become powerful in the recognition of all the good that is among believers *for* Christ (ἡμῖν εἰς Χριστόν). The expression "εἰς Χριστόν" suggests that fellowship promotes a deeper, mystical unity with Christ. When Philemon seeks the deeper fellowship with Onesimus like he had already been doing with other saints, it will by implication bring both of them into a closer relationship with Christ. Wright remarked about this phrase, "Being already 'in Christ,' the church is to grow more fully 'into him,' that is, to explore and realize more completely what true corporate Christian maturity means in practice."[40] Dunn referred to the "mystical overtones" of this phrase which speaks of "bringing us into (closer) relationship to Christ."[41] There is therefore a special bond between believers and Christ which is strengthened and intensified by their mutual harmony. This insight by implication represents a powerful

---

[40] Cf. Nicholas T. Wright, *The Climax of the Covenant: Christ and Law in Pauline Theology* (London: T&T Clark, 1991), 54 who provides a thorough discussion of this verse.

[41] Dunn, *Theology of Paul* (n. 14), 405.

incentive for Philemon: his moral response to Onesimus will have major spiritual consequences.[42]

This picture of the intimate relationship with the Lord is to be compared with Phlm 15b which explains that the separation of Philemon from Onesimus happened so that Paul may have him back forever (αἰώνιον). This does not indicate, as Strecker correctly stated, that Philemon receives Onesimus back as a possession for good, but that they will be mutually joined forever, "d.h. als christusgläubigen Initiierten und damit als Gefährten, mit dem er in die Ewigkeit Gottes verbunden ist."[43] It is an intensification of *koinonia* which, because of its eternal character, reminds one of the eternal link between Christ and believers as portrayed elsewhere in Pauline letters (cf. also 1 Thess 4:17).

The remark therefore "envisions the Christological aim or direction of spiritual formation," as Wall remarked.[44] Moral action thus deepens the spiritual unity with Christ. The unity with Christ does not merely precede or elicit moral behavior, but, it also accompanies it and, especially follows on it.[45] In this sense Paul integrates both a deontological and teleological approach in his moral argumentation. His moral language is not only linked with God's past redemptive work in Christ, but also with the future union with Christ. Ethics thus is steered by the relationship with Christ in faith which extends towards the future. This is vitally important, since ethics has to do with the ongoing spiritual journey of believers in the present. Faith is about ethics, but ethics also deepens faith – one can almost speak of the soteriological nature of ethics and ethos in this letter. At stake for Paul in this letter is therefore a deeper unity with Christ. This reflects to some extent the remark of Backhaus: "Christus prädisponiert in umfassender Weise den *Lebensgrund,* insofern der Glaubende in und aus der Gemeinschaft mit Christus lebt (I), das *Lebensziel,* insofern Christus den Bewegungsfeldern sittlichen Handelns die Finalität einstiftet (II), den *Le-*

---

[42] Note the remarks by Enslin, *Ethics* (n. 9), 78: Paul's ethics expressed "the deep-seated principles governing his life – of the facts and implicates of union with Christ and their corollary, the union of fellow believers in Christ. We might almost say this sense of *koinonia* produced his ethics, or at least gave to it its distinctive form." Cf. also his remarks on 127.

[43] Strecker, *Theologie* (n. 23), 371.

[44] Cf. Wall, *Colossians* (n. 24), 20.

[45] This remark needs to be considered in the light of the questions of Zimmermann, "Indikativ und Imperativ" (n. 6), 260, "Wurden die Glaubenden nur auf Bewährung in die Freiheit entlassen und müssen sie die Neuheit des neuen Seins erst noch durch ein entsprechendes Handeln verwirklichen oder gar 'vollenden' (2 Kor 7,1)? Wenn der Mensch synergistisch dem Heilshandeln Gottes nachhelfen muss, wie ist es dann um den Wert und die Wirklichkeit des göttlichen Heils bestellt?"

bensmaßstab, insofern sittliche Existenz unter den Bedingungen des alten Aion dauerhaft auf den Rückbezug auf Christus verwiesen ist (III)."[46]

6. The Role of Mission in Philemon's Moral Language

There are other motifs in Philemon which function in a normative way just like love and faith. In fact, there are deeper dynamics at work behind these two norms that require further attention in order to understand the moral language of Philemon.

Recently Heil concluded his close reading of the letter as a ring composition as follows:

"[m]any surmise that what Paul wants of Philemon is unclear. The chiastic structure of the letter, however, indicates not only what Paul wants from Philemon, namely, Onesimus to serve on his behalf in the work of the gospel (v. 13), but also why he wants it, namely, as a further good that Philemon can do under benevolence (v. 14) for Paul and the holy ones based on love and in response to grace."[47]

Heil's remarks reflect Paul's wish for Philemon to act ethically in such a way as to promote his mission.[48] There is good reason why Paul would have regarded such a request as important. He had an eschatological perspective on his ministry as a key instrument in God's hands in the end times.[49] Through his ministry the offer of salvation went out to the gen-

---

[46] Knut Backhaus, "Evangelium als Lebensraum: Christologie und Ethik bei Paulus," in *Paulinische Christologie: Exegetische Beiträge* (Festschrift Hans Hübner; ed. Udo Schnelle and Thomas Söding; Göttingen: Vandenhoeck & Ruprecht, 1998), 9–31, 21.

[47] Heil, "Chiastic Structure" (n. 17), 201.

[48] Cf. also the illuminating discussion about Paul's exact request in this letter by Du Plessis, "Christians" (n. 2), 401–408. It should be noted here that Paul's request for Onesimus to join him could contribute to the impression that this implied his manumission. Paul, however, does not explicitly request it. Peter Arzt-Grabner, *Philemon* (PKNT 1; Göttingen: Vandenhoeck & Ruprecht, 2003) interprets Paul's request to Philemon to receive Onesimus back as meaning that *Philemon* should entrust his slave with a responsible task, make him a business partner or entrust him with a leading role in the Christian community. Whilst this and other proposals regarding the request of Paul, show the open-ended nature of Paul's remarks, they also reveal the surplus of meaning in the letter. Whatever the precise request, it clearly impacts on the wider ecclesiological and missiological setting of Pauline communities. Scholars mostly suggest two options: that Paul wanted Onesimus back as a missionary co-worker or that Paul wanted Philemon to accept Onesimus as a brother. For a discussion of German literature on these theories, cf. Strecker, *Theologie* (n. 23), 370 n. 70.

[49] Cf. James D. G. Dunn, *Jesus and the Spirit: a study of the religious and charismatic experience of Jesus and the first Christians as reflected in the New Testament* (Grand Rapids, Mich.: Eerdmans, 1997), 308 who writes that Paul had a sense of eschatological apostleship and thought he had a decisive role to play in "bringing about the

tiles, bringing them to turn away from their idols to worship the living God (1 Thess 1:9–10).

Paul's awareness of the significance of his mission is reflected not only in his request for Onesimus to share in his mission. It is also to be seen in his language elsewhere in Philemon when, for example, he describes his addressees in terms of his eschatological ministry. Paul, as has been pointed out above, writes this letter with Timothy to Philemon as "co-worker" in the Pauline mission (Phlm 1) and as part of a group and church who are fellow soldiers (Phlm 1, 23) and co-workers (Phlm 24). With this, Paul refers to their corporate involvement in mission as a key element of their identity. They are not only converts, but also proclaimers of the gospel.

This participation in mission would have had certain consequences. The participants in the Pauline mission who are mentioned in the letter would all have been affected by the tension between Philemon and Onesimus. Potentially several aspects of this situation could have been harmful and detrimental to their missionary work. Personal discord between Philemon and Onesimus would have intensified the difficult situation in the Pauline mission for which Paul was already suffering imprisonment (Phlm 10). As Du Plessis observed, Philemon "will also be judged by the members of his church in how he responds to Paul's request."[50]

Onesimus' presence with Paul (Phlm 11, 13), furthermore, would also have affected Philemon's involvement in the Pauline mission. In addition, the mere harboring of an absconding slave could have caused a serious problem for the Pauline mission. Outsiders could have reacted negatively or even reported the matter. The reputation of Philemon, of Paul, of the Christian community and the Pauline mission was under threat and their well-being at stake.

At the same time, the handling of this conflict could have been an example of the reconciling power of the gospel. The suggestion of Du Plessis that "the correct treatment of his (Paul's) request regarding Onesimus would be seen by unbelievers and might lead them to accept Christianity" makes sense.[51] Or, as Wall observed more specifically in terms of the communal values expressed in the letter itself,

"[m]ore important, Paul's prayer (4–7) introduces in a positive way what the main body of his letter develops: that the compassion and so *koinonia* of the congregation are now

---

climax and conclusion of God's purposes in this age." Cf. also L. Jan Lietaert Peerbolte, *Paul the Missionary* (Contributions to biblical exegesis and theology 34; Leuven: Peeters, 2003), 255 who notes that Paul viewed his new communities as "the new creation" that God was about to establish.

[50] Cf. Du Plessis, "Christians" (n. 2), 399.

[51] Cf. Du Plessis, "Christians" (n. 2), 400.

threatened by the problem between Onesimus and Philemon. Given Paul's twofold peti-
tion, then, the reader realizes that Philemon's response to Paul's appeal will largely determine whether the congregation's witness to the gospel in Colosse will survive."[52]

One should, however, look a bit deeper than all this in order to explain
adequately the passion with which Paul writes this letter and to understand
the moral language fully. The Pauline mission was threatened in a more
fundamental manner than merely by tension between Philemon and Onesimus. At stake was its often repeated proclamation of the inclusive nature
of the gospel of Christ. Paul's proclamation consistently rejected any attempts to exclude people because of some inherent, natural qualities. The
outreach to the gentile nations and the openness towards women are normally regarded as examples of Paul's inclusive ministry. But Paul also
placed a high premium on the fact that the gospel specifically rejected the
exclusion of someone on the grounds of their social location, specifically
on the grounds of their status as slaves (esp. Gal 3:28 and Col 3:11, but
also 1 Cor 7:21–24). This meant that full fellowship should be accorded to
all who are family in Christ. In the case of Philemon, this implied that Philemon should nurture a relationship with the slave Onesimus that tran-
scended societal norms and conventions, that promoted the well-being of
the gospel and of Onesimus as person.[53] Paul's message of reconciliation
and salvation formed the heart of his missionary work and preaching. This
guaranteed the integrity of his mission. In this sense the inclusive nature of
his missionary work practically functioned as an ethical norm.

One should therefore view Paul's communication with Philemon
beyond situational ethics. It is a letter that reflects supra-situational and
universally valid motifs that had to do with the nature of the gospel itself
and with the heart of his ministry to the gentiles.[54] When Paul writes to
Philemon, he does not only address a particular conflict, but in fact de-
fends the integrity of his gospel. He wants everyone in his mission to understand the full implications of the gospel for interpersonal relationships.
Whilst he developed the consequences of his inclusive gospel by rejecting
a salvific function of the law, as in Galatians, he focuses on another implication in his letter to Philemon. Here the issue is not that of faith against
the law, but of faith against human prejudices. Paul insists that the gospel

---

[52] Wall, *Colossians* (n. 24), *ad loc.*

[53] Strecker, *Theologie* (n. 23), 371 also points out the transformative impact of
Paul's remarks. Especially in Phlm 15b Paul depicts Philemon's separation from
Onesimus as directed towards "eine Statustransformation ... die eine Transformation der
Beziehung zwischen Sklave und Herrn zwangsläufig einschließt." It is important to note
that the often recorded pronouncements on the humane treatment of slaves did not transform the system of slavery itself. On this cf. also Strecker, *Theologie* (n. 23), 373. Cf. for
a sober discussion of Philemon, Ridderbos, *Paulus* (n. 14), 353–354.

[54] Cf. Zimmermann, "Indikativ und Imperativ" (n. 6), 283.

message creates a faith community across human boundaries and prejudices. Faith in this letter is about *koinonia* and intimate love which transcends social prejudices, restrictions and conventions. Where this is not understood, Paul's ministry and the gospel itself are under threat.

7. Conclusion

Philemon is not a polemical letter. In the conflict situation, Paul uses highly affective, motivating language, refraining from "tough" love talk or from heavy handed demands (e.g. requesting Onesimus' manumission[55] or for Onesimus to remain with him as leader of the mission). In addition Paul does not reject the ethos of Roman society outright, though he strikes a blow at its very roots. And, finally, though Paul brings Philemon to a deeper understanding of his faith and love, he himself does not fathom their full implications: a slave must be returned to the master and possible damage repaid as is required in his society (Phlm 18–19). He nowhere shows any sign of reflecting on the demand in Hebrew Scriptures that slaves were to be released every six years. Paul's mind is not occupied with the problem of slavery as a social institution and he (sadly) fails to move on to the important issue of addressing structural injustice and systemic oppression.

Paul's mind is preoccupied with matters of more concern to him. He is concerned about the conflict between Philemon and Onesimus and desires that they live in a loving fellowship.[56] Paul does not see this loving relationship as only a personal matter between the two. Love and fellowship find concrete application within the social context of his mission and community.[57] Paul wants the community to understand the need to retain close, intimate relations that reflect their common faith, bring about greater unity with Christ and respect the integrity of his mission. This unity should not be qualified in any way by social, familial or biological status.

---

[55] So, correctly, Ridderbos, *Paulus* (n. 14), who notes that there is no indication that Paul requested the intricate judicial process for manumission to begin.

[56] Roberts, "Vryheid" (n. 23), 245–246 argues that in its request to Philemon to receive Onesimus back, Paul redefines the relationship between Philemon and Onesimus.

[57] Cf. Schrage, *Ethics* (n. 16), 212 and also 215–216 with specific reference to Philemon.

IV. Later New Testament
and Early Christian Writings

Disparagement as Argument:

The Polemical Use of Moral Language in Second Peter[*]

JÖRG FREY

The predominant issues between the author of Second Peter and his opponents are the question of the eschatological expectation, the hope for the parousia (2 Pet 3:3–4) and, as an implication, the reliability of the prophetic word (2 Pet 1:19). But in the whole of 2 Peter 2, the so-called "false teachers" are only accused of immoral behavior and described as people of not only dangerous and erroneous teaching but also morally corrupt conduct and an animal-like nature. In the climax of this massive polemic, the author adopts two drastic proverbs otherwise unparalleled within the New Testament: "a dog returns to his own vomit," and "a sow, having washed, [returns] to her wallowing in the mire" (2 Pet 2:22).

Does the author compare his opponents with unclean animals, instead of taking their arguments seriously? In any case, the argument is discredited before being introduced by the rhetorical device of the moral disparagement of the opponents' conduct and character. It is not particularly astonishing that such a fierce mode of polemics has raised the question to what extent the author himself still acts according to the ethical standards of the gospel, or fails to meet them by his own way of writing.[1] It is not my pri-

---

[*] Revised and expanded version of the paper presented to the symposium on Moral Language in the New Testament at the University of Pretoria, South Africa, on September 10, 2008. The author is a Research Associate of the Department of New Testament of the Theological Faculty of the University of Pretoria and in the academic year 2008/09 senior fellow of the Alfried-Krupp-Wissenschaftskolleg (Institute for Advanced Studies) in Greifswald. The present article was completed in that period, and I am grateful to the Krupp foundation for granting me this prestigious scholarship. – Thanks are due to the organizers of the symposium, my colleagues and friends Prof. Dr. Jan van der Watt and Prof. Dr. Ruben Zimmermann, for the invitation and the preparation of the Kolleg, to the Alexander-von-Humboldt-Stiftung for funding it, to the participants of the conference for the vivid discussion, to my friend and colleague James A. Kelhoffer (St. Louis) for reading my English draft and to Dr. Anni Hentschel (Würzburg) and Nadine Kessler (Munich/Zurich) for invaluable help with the corrections.

[1] Cf. e.g., the massive criticism by Edwin A. Abbott, "The Second Epistle of St. Peter contrasted with The Gospel of John," in *From Letter to Spirit* (ed. Edwin A. Abbott; Diatessarica 3; London 1903), 443–460, 447: "This Epistle is not Christian in spirit,

mary aim to address the issue as a moral one. In view of much premature criticism[2] I am convinced that the author of this letter should not be condemned too rapidly. A balanced judgment, however, can only be made on the basis of an analysis of the form and function of the moral language in Second Peter and, especially, of the polemics in chapter 2.

1. Preliminaries

For the present purpose, there is no need to discuss the introductory matters.[3] With the majority of critical scholarship, I presuppose that Second Peter is not written by the apostle Peter himself, but composed much later, roughly in the second quarter of the second century, as a pseudonymous "testament of Peter." There is also a very strong case for the assumption that the author of 2 Peter utilized the epistle of Jude, not only but predominantly in his polemical section in 2 Pet 2:1–3:3.[4] We can, therefore, analyze how the author adopted Jude's polemics, omitting certain phrases, while inserting others, and adjusting his "Vorlage" to his own polemical purposes. Such a comparison can also help to see to what extent the author utilizes polemical patterns in order to disparage his opponents and how he

---

much less apostolically Christian." See also Günter Klein, "Der zweite Petrusbrief und der neutestamentliche Kanon," in *Ärgernisse: Konfrontationen mit dem Neuen Testament* (ed. Günter Klein; Munich: Kaiser, 1970), 109–114, 113, according to whom the author's polemics sounds "wie ein grausiges Vorzeichen künftiger Scheiterhaufen."

[2]   Cf., e.g., the harsh criticism of the author's eschatology by Ernst Käsemann, "An Apologia for Primitive Christian Eschatology," in *Essays on New Testament Themes* (ed. Ernst Käsemann; London: SCM Press, 1964); German original: "Eine Apologie der urchristlichen Eschatologie," in *Exegetische Versuche und Besinnungen* (ed. Ernst Käsemann; vol. 1; Göttingen: Vandenhoeck & Ruprecht, 1964), 135–157.

[3]   For details, I would like to point to my commentary *Der Judasbrief und der zweite Petrusbrief* (THKNT 15,2; Leipzig: Evangelische Verlagsanstalt, *forthcoming*).

[4]   In this passage the parallels occur with only one exception (the Balaam example in 2:15–16) according to the sequence of Jude's text. In other parts of 2 Peter, there are some more allusions to Jude (cf. 2 Pet 1:5 // Jude 3; 2 Pet 1:12 // Jude 5a; 2 Pet 1:10 // Jud 24; 2 Pet 3:14 // Jud 24; 2 Pet 3:18 // Jud 25), but they do not follow the textual order of Jude. Cf. recently Thomas J. Kraus, *Sprache, Stil und historischer Ort des Zweiten Petrusbriefes* (WUNT 2/136; Tübingen: Mohr Siebeck, 2001), 368–376; Terrance Callan, "Use of the Letter of Jude by the Second Letter of Peter," *Bib* 85 (2004): 42–64; Lauri Thurén, "The Relationship between 2 Peter and Jude: A classical problem resolved?," in *The Catholic Epistles and Tradition* (ed. Jacques Schlosser; BETL 176; Leuven: Peeters, 2004), 451–460, and with refined criteria Tommy Wasserman, *The Epistle of Jude: Its Text and Transmission* (CB.NT 43; Stockholm: Almqvist & Wiksell International, 2006), 73–98.

uses the rhetorical technique of vilifying his opponents.[5] In any case we have to keep in mind that "the depiction of opponents ... is a construct of the author. We should therefore differentiate between the 'encoded opponents' and their real-life counterparts."[6] Especially with regard to the blame of immoral conduct, there is reason to infer that the author does not actually describe the opponents as they were but rather fabricates a polemical image of the immorality of "heretics" in order to distance his audience from his opponents and to throw further suspicion on their "dogmatic" views. [7]

The literary structure of the epistle can best be determined from the epistolary framework: it is clear that there is a prescript (1:1–2) and an extensive prooemium (1:3–11) and also an epistolary closing with a final exhortation and a doxology but without a concluding formula of salutations or blessings (3:17–18).[8]

Structuring the central section is more difficult. In my view, the body of the letter is opened by a particular "testament of the apostle" (1:12–15), followed by a reference to the transfiguration (1:16–18) by which the author wants to appear as an eyewitness of Jesus, "in order to underscore his authority to confirm the prophetic word of Scripture and to tell his readers how to interpret it" (1:19–21).[9] The body is closed by a paraenesis moti-

---

[5] On the rhetorical techniques of vilification in early Christian literature see the lucid article by Andrie du Toit, "Vilification in Early Christian Epistolography," *Bib* 75 (1994): 403–412; see also Sean Freyne, "Vilifying the Other and Defining the Self: Matthew's and John's Anti-Jewish Polemic in Focus," in *"To See Ourselves as Others See Us": Christians, Jews, 'Others' in Late Antiquity* (ed. Jacob Neusner and Ernest S. Frerichs; Chico, Calif.: Scholars Press, 1985), 117–143, and Adela Yarbro Collins, "Vilification and Self-Definition in the Book of Revelation," *HTR* 79 (1986): 308–320; on the comparison with the convention of ancient polemics see Luke T. Johnson, "The New Testament's Anti-Jewish Slander and the Conventions of Ancient Polemic," *JBL* 103 (1989): 419–441. On the polemics of the Church Fathers see Carsten Colpe, "Formen der Intoleranz: Altkirchliche Autoren und ihre antipagane Polemik," in *Wahrnehmung des Fremden: Christentum und andere Religionen* (ed. Rainer Kampling and Bruno Schlegelberger; Schriften der Diözesanakademie Berlin 12; Berlin: Morus, 1996), 87–123. On Second Peter in particular see Troy A. Miller, "Dogs, adulterers, and the way of Balaam: The forms and socio-rhetorical function of the polemical rhetoric in 2 Peter," *Irish Biblical Studies* 22 (2000): 123–144 and 189–191.

[6] Du Toit, "Vilification" (n. 5), 404.

[7] Although the differences between the polemics in chapter 2 and the theological argument in chapter 3 caused some scholars to postulate two different groups of opponents (or to question the unity of the epistle), I presuppose with the vast majority of recent scholarship that the whole epistle is about one group of opponents.

[8] Cf. Hans-Josef Klauck, *Ancient Letters and the New Testament: A Guide to Context and Exegesis* (Waco, Tex.: Baylor University Press, 2006), 408–413. Cf. also the syntactical structure given in Kraus, *Sprache, Stil und historischer Ort* (n. 4), 401–404.

[9] Klauck, *Ancient Letters* (n. 8), 410.

vated by the legacy of Paul (3:14–16).[10] Most important is the composition of the two-part body middle: whereas the first part (2:1–22) predicts the appearance of false teachers and the judgment against them (2:1–10a) and then enters a lengthy disparagement of the opponents (2:10b–22), an idea of their teachings and views is only given in the second part (3:1–13), where the opponents are presented as the scoffers of the last days (3:3–4). Their teaching is verbally quoted or summarized here, and their views are refuted by the author's own eschatological and cosmological teaching.

Thus, the primary issue between the author and his opponents is only exposed in the second half of the body middle (in 3:3–13), whereas an extensive earlier part merely polemicizes against them without revealing any clear idea of their actual teaching. Polemical invective precedes the argument, with the effect that the views of the opponents are already discredited long before they are mentioned and finally refuted.

2. Polemical Rhetoric and the Use of Moral Accusations in 2 Peter 2

The present paper will focus on the first part of the body middle, the introduction and disparagement of the so-called "false teachers" (2:1–22). In this section, the author largely draws on Jude, which is a similarly polemic letter, but written by a different author in a different situation and, most probably, in view of quite different opponents. These differences should not be ignored, if we want to reconstruct precisely the situation and the profile of the opponents of each letter.[11]

Without going into detail, we can say that the opponents of Jude are primarily accused of "slandering" or disregard of angels, whereas the author himself seems to be strongly impressed by Enochic traditions in which

---

[10] Klauck, *Ancient Letters* (n. 8), 412. Other authors think that the paraeneses are already part of the epistolary closing, thus, e.g. Marlis Gielen, "Der zweite Petrusbrief," in *Einleitung in das Neue Testament* (ed. Martin Ebner and Stefan Schreiber; Kohlhammer Studienbücher Theologie 6; Stuttgart: Kohlhammer, 2008), 522–529, 523.

[11] Quite frequently, scholars lack precision here. Thus, e.g. Anton Vögtle, *Der Judasbrief: Der Zweite Petrusbrief* (EKK 22; Neukirchen-Vluyn: Neukirchener Verlag, 1994), 95–98, who claims that already the opponents of Jude questioned the parousia, or also Gielen, "Petrusbrief" (n. 10), 527, when she assumes that not only the opponents of Jude but also those of Second Peter rejected the veneration of angels. Especially the moral charges of libertinism or sexual misconduct are often seen as a characteristic of the opponents in both letters – thus also Gielen, "Petrusbrief" (n. 10), 527. It must be considered, however, that Second Peter adopts some of the accusations from Jude, and that charges of immorality are quite often used as standard charges against heretics.

angels have a predominant position.[12] By contrast, the opponents of Second Peter explicitly deny the expectation of Christ's parousia (including a last judgment). In view of his situation, the author of Second Peter alters Jude's polemic in various aspects. He omits the quotation from *1 Enoch* 1:9 in Jude 14 and smoothens down the references to particular angelic traditions (Jude 6, 7, 9), as well as the more precise hints to the profile of the opponents and to the charge against them (Jude 8–9, 12). On the other hand, the author of Second Peter retains the elements of a general polemic against heretics and adds even more accusations, mostly focused on moral matters. Apparently, he found the polemic pattern from Jude useful for his own purposes. Most probably he also agreed with Jude on some important points, e.g. that the judgment of the ungodly is determined by the Scriptures, and that the appearance of the ungodly is a confirmation that the end of times is at hand. But when he adopts the accusations from Jude or even inserts additional standard charges, especially of immoral conduct and selfish behavior, these charges primarily serve the purpose of denouncing the opponents. The question is thus unavoidable, whether the opponents actually were as immoral, as the author depicts them, or whether the use of moral charges is simply a rhetorical device in preparation for the theological argument in 2 Pet 3:1–13.

Of course, the question raised is hard to answer, since our only source for the opponents is the polemical letter of our author. It thus is hardly possible to reconstruct the precise profile of the opponents accurately. Most of the suggestions in scholarship – Gnostics of various schools,[13] radical Paulinists,[14] anti-Roman revolutionists,[15] Essenizing Christians,[16]

---

[12] For further argument cf. Jörg Frey, "Judgment on the Ungodly and the Parousia of Christ: Eschatology in Jude and 2 Peter," in *Eschatology in the New Testament* (ed. Jan van der Watt; WUNT II; Tübingen: Mohr Siebeck, *forthcoming*); idem, *Der Judasbrief und der Zweite Petrusbrief* (n. 3). Cf. also the precise argument in Henning Paulsen, *Der Zweite Petrusbrief und der Judasbrief* (KEK 12,2; Göttingen: Vandenhoeck & Ruprecht, 1992), 48–49 and 95–97.

[13] Thus already Hugo Grotius, who wanted to identify the opponents of Jude and Second Peter with the Carpocratians. For the Gnostic view, cf. especially, the monograph by Hermann Werdermann, *Die Irrlehrer des Judas- und 2. Petrusbriefes* (Beiträge zur Förderung christlicher Theologie 17,6; Gütersloh: Bertelsmann, 1913). Cf. still Thomas S. Caulley, "The False Teachers in 2 Peter," *SBTh* 12 (1982): 27–42.

[14] Thus Friedrich Spitta, *Der zweite Brief des Petrus und der Brief des Judas* (Halle: Waisenhaus, 1885), 503–515.

[15] So Bo Reicke, *The Epistles of James, Peter and Jude* (AncB 37; Garden City, N.Y.: Doubleday, 1964), 171.

[16] Thus the view of Rainer Riesner, "Der zweite Petrusbrief und die Eschatologie," in *Zukunftserwartung in biblischer Sicht* (ed. Gerhard Maier; Wuppertal: Brockhaus, 1984), 124–143.

Christians compromizing with Paganism[17] or others – are based on conjectures from other texts, or on an uncritical type of mirror reading from the polemical accusations of the epistle.[18] Especially the question of the opponents' "positive religious teaching" can hardly be answered.[19]

Any reconstruction has to start from the only thing we can know with some degree of certainty, namely that the opponents questioned the expectation of Christ's parousia and, most probably together with that, a general expectation of salvation and judgment connected with the hope for the parousia.[20] This kind of scepticism is quoted or at least summarized in 2 Pet 3:3–4, and in 2 Pet 3:5–13 the author enters a detailed argument on the expectation of the end of the present world and the hope for a new heaven and earth where justice dwells (2 Pet 3:13). Probably the remarks on the prophetic word in 2 Pet 1:19–21 are also connected with the debate on eschatology, and possibly also the note on the misinterpretation of Paul's letters in 2 Pet 3:15–16. Instead, most of the polemical charges in 2 Peter 2 appear unrelated to the "dogmatic" issue of eschatology. This nourishes the suspicion that they are rather used for disparaging the opponents. Thus the traditional harmonistic view that the opponents "combined scepticism with the parousia with moral libertinism"[21] is unpersuasive.

In the following passages, I shall analyze the means and elements of the polemical disparagement in the opening of the letter and primarily in chapter 2, i.e. before the author enters the debate on the subject matter of eschatology.

2.1 Implicit References to the Opponents before Their Explicit Introduction

Presupposing the epistles of James, Jude and First Peter (cf. 2 Pet 3:1), a collection of Pauline epistles and numerous elements of the Synoptic tradition (perhaps Matthew), the author of Second Peter chooses and constructs a pseudonymous authorization of his message, using the figure of Peter

---

[17] Thus Tord Fornberg, *An Early Church in a Pluralistic Society: A Study of 2 Peter* (CB.NT 9; Lund: Gleerup, 1977), 31–32.

[18] On the methodological problem of mirror reading cf. John M. G. Barclay, "Mirror-Reading a Polemical Letter: Galatians as a Test Case," *JSNT* 31 (1987): 73–93, and Klaus Berger, "Die impliziten Gegner: Zur Methodik des Erschließens von Gegnern in neutestamentlichen Texten," in *Kirche* (Festschrift Günther Bornkamm; ed. Dieter Lührmann and Georg Strecker; Tübingen: Mohr Siebeck, 1980), 373–400.

[19] Thus Richard J. Bauckham, "2 Peter: An Account of Research," *ANRW* 2.25.5 (1988): 3713–3752, 3728 in his conclusion of the discussion.

[20] It is a question, therefore, whether the scepticism against the idea of a judgment connected with the parousia leads to an immoral conduct, or whether the author just conjectures this or views it as a necessary consequence.

[21] Thus the assumption of Bauckham, "2 Peter" (n. 19), 3724.

who was a recognized authority in the church.[22] Compared with other pseudonymous epistles such as First Peter, James or Jude, the mode of pseudonymous legitimation in Second Peter is quite daring,[23] starting from the solemn introduction of the author as *Symeon Petros* (2 Pet 1:1), down to the claim to be the eye witness of Jesus' transfiguration and eschatological glory (2 Pet 1:16–18) and to the final "reconciliation" with the "dear brother Paul" (2 Pet 3:15–16). All these elements of legitimization should be understood as an effort to successfully convey his message and to convince his audience, not to follow the opponents' views.

From the very beginning, the author ties the alliance with his readers and thereby enables them to achieve some distance from the opponents: thus in the prescript "Peter" addresses "those who have received a faith which … is of equal value with ours" (2 Pet 1:1). That is, he confirms that his readers, if they follow the author's ideas, are in the true, "apostolic" line of faith, sharing with "Peter" and the genuine apostles the same kind of salvific faith, and also its ultimate benefit, namely eternal salvation. And in the solemn proemium "Peter" confirms that the divine power "has bestowed on us," i.e. Peter *and* the readers, "everything which is necessary for life and godliness" (2 Pet 1:3). So the fictive person of the apostolic author Peter (and of course, the real author as well) is united with his readers – or at least with those who faithfully follow his argument.

At the beginning of the proemium, the author also shows his ethical interests: the aspects of a "godly" conduct are exposed by a catalogue of virtues (2 Pet 1:5–7).[24] The author's aim of introducing them is obviously paraenetic but implicitly polemic as well. "Peter" encourages the addressees to take effort to produce these virtues, in order not to be "idle or fruitless" (οὐκ ἀργοὺς οὐδὲ ἀκάρπους) in the knowledge of Christ (2 Pet 1:8). For our purpose it is interesting that the author makes up a first distinction on the basis of the virtues mentioned: those who have *not* produced those

---

[22] It is most significant that especially within the second century a large number of pseudonymous Petrine writings were composed, such as the *Apocalypse of Peter*, the *Gospel of Peter*, the *Kerygma Petrou* (as part of the Pseudo-Clementines).

[23] On the mode of pseudonymous legitimation in Second Peter, see Jörg Frey, "Autorfiktion und Gegnerbild im Judasbrief und im Zweiten Petrusbrief," in *Pseudepigraphie und Verfasserfiktion in frühchristlichen Briefen* (ed. Jörg Frey et al.; WUNT 246; Tübingen: Mohr Siebeck, 2009), 683–732.

[24] The list is formed by eight terms (ἄπιστις, ἀρετή, γνῶσις, ἐγκράτεια, ὑπομονή, εὐσέβεια, φιλαδελφία, ἀγάπη). For comparison, see Richard J. Bauckham, *Jude. 2 Peter* (WBC 50; Waco, Tex.: Word Books, 1984), 174–176. Πίστις at the beginning and ἀγάπη at the end may be characteristic for a Christian catalogue of virtues (cf. 2 Cor 8:7 and *Herm. Vis.* 3.8.7; but the other terms (ἀρετή, γνῶσις, ἐγκράτεια, ὑπομονή, εὐσέβεια, φιλαδελφία) are more common in Hellenistic moral philosophy and show the strong Hellenistic influence on the author.

virtues and do *not* possess them, are said to be short-sighted, or even blind, having forgotten that they once had been cleansed from their former sins (2 Pet 1:9). But now they have dropped back into the unclean state of sinners, i.e. into the situation they were before they came to belief – or even worse (cf. 2 Pet 2:20). Although not mentioned explicitly, we can assume that the author has in mind already his opponents:[25] they are described as former Christians, as people who had once been cleansed from their sins by baptism,[26] but have now forgotten and lost out of sight their saving knowledge (2 Pet 1:9), being blind and ignorant, yet also unclean, sinful and subject to eternal judgment. Since they do not live according to the virtues mentioned, they will not enter the eternal kingdom of Christ (1:11).

At the end of Peter's "eye-witness"-testimony, there is another implicit charge, which may refer more directly to the theological issues at stake. When the author states that "no prophecy of Scripture is a matter of one's own interpretation" (1:20), this may be hint that – in the view of the author – the opponents actually interpreted scriptural prophecies according to their own fashion, not according to the Spirit, when refusing to accept the common belief in the parousia.[27]

However, apart from those implicit references to the theological issues, there is no mention of the opponents in the first chapter. They are only introduced at the beginning of the middle part of the epistolary body. From this point on, the author closely follows the polemical text of Jude which is rephrased, shortened or expanded but always taken as the red thread of the author's own polemics.

---

[25] Vögtle, *Der Judasbrief. Der Zweite Petrusbrief* (n. 11), 152–153, explains the strange combination of "short-sighted" and "blind" from the consideration of the opponents who were once able to see (cf. 2 Pet 2:20a) but now deny their master, forget their former state and become short-sighted. Contra Paulsen, *Der Zweite Petrusbrief und der Judasbrief* (n. 12), 111, who thinks that this is only a "topische Antithese."

[26] The metaphor of purification refers to baptism, cf. Acts 22:16; 1 Cor 6:11; Eph 5:26; Tit 3:5; *Barn.* 11:11.

[27] This view is shared by most of the commentaries. Bauckham, *Jude. 2 Peter* (n. 24), 229–230, however, points to the fact that ἴδιος in 1:20 seems to address the question of the prophecies' origin and nature, which is not human but from the divine spirit. But this observation does not exclude that the author refers to the differences in the interpretation of the prophetic writings (as he also acknowledges the differences in the interpretation of Paul's letters in 3:16). While the opponents might have considered the biblical prophecies as mere human guesswork or human interpretation of the prophets' visions, the author rejects such a sceptical view as inadequate and contradictory to the insight and truth of the apostolic faith and claims that the prophetic word – including the promise of the parousia – are reliable and will come to fulfillment.

2.2 The Introduction and First Characterization of the Opponents in 2:1–3a

2 Pet 2:1 mentions the presence of false prophets (ψευδοπροφῆται) in Biblical times, as opposed to the truly divine and inspired prophets (1:21), then he turns to the present, or – within the fictive perspective of the pseudonymous author – to the future, for which "Peter" predicts "that (likewise) there will be false teachers among you" (καὶ ἐν ὑμῖν ἔσονται ψευδοδιδάσκαλοι[28]). Now the interests of the real author are openly addressed: he is concerned about his and his readers' present, which is addressed in the predictive mode of Peter's "testament," seeking "to label his opponents as the false teachers whom the apostles predicted."[29]

For the sake of this fiction, Jude's text is changed significantly: whereas Jude addresses his audience as contemporaries and introduces his opponents also as a group of "certain persons" (τίνες ἄνθρωποι) who have already crept into the community (Jude 4), the author of Second Peter must use the mode of prediction: Peter, who is already dead (cf. 2 Pet 1:13–14) but knew about the impending tribulations (2 Pet 3:3, 17) and foretold the coming of false teachers, who are now present.[30]

Although the author rephrases most of this opening, the utilization of Jude is clear:[31] interestingly 2 Pet 2:1 utilizes Jude's idea that the opponents

---

[28] Cf. ψευδοδιδασκαλία *Polycarp Phil.* 7:2. Ψευδοδιδάσκαλοι does not occur before Justin, *Dial.* 82.1. Probably the author avoids to talk of prophets for his own time; for him, prophecy is a phenomenon of the past, cf. Paulsen, *Der Zweite Petrusbrief und der Judasbrief* (n. 12), 127.

[29] Thus David Horrell, *The Epistles of Peter and Jude* (London: Epworth, 1998), 161.

[30] One reason might be that Peter's death in the 60s is quite well-known whereas Jude, the brother of the Lord, is a more marginal figure in early Christianity, who was possibly alive until the late first century. But Jude is also a pseudonymous letter, ascribed to Jude, the brother of James and thus also the brother of the Lord (Jude 1). It is, however, quite uncertain whether the addressees of Jude had closer relations to that figure or whether the fictive author is only chosen in relation to his more prominent brother and to the epistle of James which is alluded to in Jude. See further Jörg Frey, "Der Judasbrief zwischen Judentum und Hellenismus," in *Frühjudentum und Neues Testament* (ed. Wolfgang Kraus and Karl-Wilhelm Niebuhr; WUNT 162; Tübingen: Mohr Siebeck, 2003), 180–210, English translation: "The Epistle of Jude between Judaism and Hellenism," in *The Catholic Epistles and the Apostolic Tradition* (ed. Karl-Wilhelm Niebuhr and Robert W. Wall; Waco, Tex.: Baylor University Press, 2009), 309-330, 463-475. In any case, the authorial fiction of Second Peter is worked out more consequently than that in Jude, where the author unwillingly shows his post-apostolic point of view when he calls his readers to „remember the predictions of the apostles of our Lord Jesus Christ how they said ..." (Jude 17–18). According to the parallel in 2 Pet 3:2, the addressees are called to remember the commandments, not a prophecy of the apostles of Christ. Such a phrasing better fits Peter's place in history.

[31] There is a verbal accordance in δεσπότην ἀρνούμενοι and τὸ κρίμα, the ἀσέλγεια is adopted in the plural, and there is a close correspondence in the use of two verbs with

used the side door, acting not openly but in a hidden and dishonest manner. But whereas Jude says that they "crept in" from outside (παρεισέδυσαν),[32] the author of Second Peter adopts a different verb with the same double prefix παρεισ- stating that they "will introduce" or rather "will insinuate"[33] (παρεισάξουσιν) heretical teachings that lead to destruction. Thus, the teaching of the opponents is characterized as an alien one, which comes from outside and is not in accordance with the true, apostolic tradition. In contrast with Jude, there is no idea that the teachers themselves entered the community from outside. More important is that this characterization serves to distance the addressees from the opponents' teaching and, implicitly, from the "false" teachers themselves who are characterized by a notion of *dishonesty*.[34] Such a characterization is more often used for heretics in later times.[35]

Other aspects of the characterization in Second Peter are more explicit: probably being Christian teachers, they are characterized as "false" teachers and put in one line with the false prophets from biblical times. Moreover their teachings are characterized as destructive or leading to destruction (αἱρέσεις ἀπωλείας), i.e. to the eschatological judgment. Thus the "apostolic" author and his faithful addressees are linked with the inspired prophets and brought into a "dualistic" contrast with the unfaithful group of the false prophets and the "heretical" false teachers. Both groups share an opposite eschatological fate, and when the heretics are said to face judgment (2 Pet 2:1, 3b), as the biblical examples taken from Jude demonstrate (2 Pet 2:4–6; cf. Jude 5–7), the readers striving for salvation are effectively drawn to the lips of the author.[36]

Even more alarmingly, the opponents are said to "deny their master (δεσπότης) who has bought them, thus bringing on themselves quick destruction" (2 Pet 2:1). So they are characterized not only as erroneous and seductive teachers but even more strongly as apostates (cf. 2 Pet 2:20) –

---

the prefix παρεισ-, finally the verb βλασφημεῖν is so frequent in Jude that its use in 2 Pet 2:1 might be influenced from there.

[32] This was sometimes interpreted as referring to wandering prophets who did not belong to the community of addressees. But the term may simply serve to mark a distance between the addressees and the τίνες ἄνθρωποι in Jude 4.

[33] Thus Bauckham, *Jude. 2 Peter* (n. 24), 239.

[34] Cf. already Gal 2:4 παρεισάκτοι ψευδαδελφοί. Cf. Kraus, *Sprache, Stil und historischer Ort* (n. 4), 297–298; also Bauckham, *Jude. 2 Peter* (n. 24), 239: "connotation of something underhanded or surreptitious."

[35] Cf. Hegesippus in Eusebius, *Hist. eccl.* 4.22.5; Hippolytus, *Haer.* 5.17.10; 7.29.8.

[36] Possibly even the term αἵρεσις has already lost its neutral meaning, towards the sense of "heretical teaching" (as used in Ignatius, *Eph.* 6:2 and *Trall.* 6:1), at least by the addition of ἀπωλείας (thus Paulsen, *Der Zweite Petrusbrief und der Judasbrief* [n. 12], 128).

who have deliberately abandoned their former state of salvation. It remains unclear how we should imagine their denial of Christ. Certainly the denial of the parousia or the reliability of the prophetic word could be interpreted as such, and Peter's claim to have seen his majesty and heard his glory proclaimed (2 Pet 1:16–17) might be an argument in this direction. But the use of the term δεσπότης ("master;" cf. Jude 4) and the image of the transferral of slaves to new ownership implied in the use of the verb ἀγοράζειν[37] suggest that in the view of the author there is also a lack of obedience in practical life.[38] Thus the further accusation of immorality is well prepared. By renouncing their master who lawfully owns them, the opponents actually disown Jesus. Thus they are liable to judgment facing eschatological condemnation. If this inference is accepted, it is quite clear that the faithful readers cannot follow their teaching any more. The disparagement of the opponents is effective from the beginning.

But now "doctrinal" arguments are supplemented by other, chiefly moral aspects. The false teachers are explicitly said to lead an immoral, licentious life (ἀσελγείαι)[39] by which the way of the truth will be maligned. The indictment of ἀσέλγεια, however, is not original in 2 Peter but probably adopted from Jude, where it is said that the ungodly people who crept in "turn the grace of God into licentiousness (ἀσέλγεια)" (Jude 4). The term "is sexually toned,"[40] and of course, "it is possible that the false teachers promoted a libertine lifestyle in the name of Christian freedom. But it is also possible that the charge of sexual misconduct is being used here without much thought or evidence, simply to vilify the opponents and their teachings,"[41] and the fact that the word is just taken from Jude makes this suggestion plausible.

The accusation is further strengthened by the note that the false teachers will have many followers (πολλοὶ ἐξακολουθήσουσιν αὐτῶν) in their lifestyle which is thereby said to appear attractive and seductive, so that the opponents must appear even more dangerous. The idea that their immoral and licentious life is attractive (perhaps even more than the strict ethics of

---

[37] Cf. the term in 1 Cor 6:20; 7:23; Rev 5:9; 14:3–4.

[38] Cf. Bauckham, *Jude. 2 Peter* (n. 24), 240–241.

[39] W. Bauer, *A Greek-Englisch Lexicon of the New Testament and Other Christian Literature* (3rd ed., rev. and ed. F. W. Danker; Chicago: University of Chicago Press, 2000), 141: „lack of self-constraint which involves one in conduct that violates all bounds of what is socially acceptable."

[40] Thus Peter H. Davids, *The Letters of 2 Peter and Jude* (Grand Rapids, Minn.: Eerdmans, 2006), 222 who refers to the terms that appear along with ἀσέλγεια in other vice lists.

[41] Thus Daniel J. Harrington, "Jude and 2 Peter," in *1 Peter, Jude and 2 Peter* (ed. Donald P. Senior and Daniel J. Harrington; Sacra Pagina 15; Collegeville, Minn.: Liturgical Press, 2003), 161–299, 262.

the author's teaching) and the additional idea that its attractivity for others might defame the "true" Christian lifestyle – called "way of the truth" – in the eyes of outsiders and corrupt it for insiders,[42] is a very effective argument to discredit the false teachers.

This is complemented by use of the charge of greed (πλεονεξία), which is repeated in 2 Pet 2:14. The opponents are said to be greedy and to "buy" (ἐμπορεύσονται) the addressees, i.e. to attract them with the promise of some benefit, but ultimately for their own selfish interests. But the notion of selfishness and cupidity – which was also conveyed in the image of the opponents in Jude[43] – is likewise a stereotyped charge against religious or philosophical rivals.[44] Regardless whether such a charge had a reason in the behavior of the opponents, it could be used to darken their character and to efficiently disparage them.

A further charge linked with the accusation of cupidity turns back to theological questions. The opponents operate with "self-fabricated" words (πλαστοῖς λόγοις),[45] i.e. they strive for their own benefit even by use of stories they have made up by themselves, or even stronger, by pretension and forgery. If it is true that the opponents charged the author to follow "cleverly invented myths" (2 Pet 1:16), the author just turns the argument against them claiming that they use stories they have made up deceitfully.[46] In any case, their words are not only opposed to the true and inspired word of the prophets (1:19–21), but are also weak and invalid, so that they cannot lead to salvation but only to destruction.

Accordingly, it follows that already the introduction of the opponents is designed in order to discredit them thoroughly. They are introduced as "false teachers," with self-fabricated, false and divisive teachings that lead to destruction, yet they themselves are apostates, denying Christ and their former salvation and defaming Christian doctrine and conduct. Yet, even more significant seems the use of standard charges for the moral disparagement of the opponents. They are not only said to live a licentious and immoral lifestyle, but also to be guided by greed and avarice, i.e. by dishonest motives. Both charges are standard motives of polemic against reli-

---

[42] Cf. Harrington, "Jude and 2 Peter" (n. 41), 262. The phenomenon that the teaching was brought into a bad light by adherents who lived in a way otherwise considered as immoral, is also confirmed by Rom 2:24.

[43] Jude 12: ἑαυτοὺς ποιμαίνοντες ("shepherding themselves"); Jude 16: "they flatter others for the sake of gain."

[44] Cf. Harrington, "Jude and 2 Peter" (n. 41), 262. See already 1 Thess 2:5. From pagan polemics, cf. the examples from Dio of Prusa or Aelius Aristides mentioned by Johnson, "Anti-Jewish Slander" (n. 5), 430.

[45] As Bauckham, *Jude. 2 Peter* (n. 24), 243, observes, the term is "a classical expression ... for deceitful speech" and especially for myths.

[46] Cf. Davids, *The Letters of 2 Peter and Jude* (n. 40), 223–224.

gious rivals and heretics, which could be used for vilifying opponents, regardless of their actual behavior. Whether some of the charges were justified or not, is hard to decide from our only source, but we must distinguish "between the 'encoded opponents' and their real-life counterparts,"[47] and there is a strong possibility that these charges are "less actual statements of what the author's opponents did or said than projections of what their errors lead to."[48] But before we can decide on these issues, we must first consider the remaining portions of the text.

2.3 The Utilization of the Biblical Examples from Jude (2:4–10a)

In the following passage, the author draws extensively, but as always very freely, on the the text of Jude and the biblical examples mentioned there. In Jude 5–7, three examples – the wilderness generation, the Watchers and the Sodomites (Jude 5–7) – prove that the condemnation of the ungodly is written down long ago, i.e. in Scripture (including the prophecy of Enoch in Jude 14). In his adoption of Jude's examples, Second Peter not only rearranges their sequence in accordance with the Biblical narrative, but also changes their number and intention: he only adopts two of Jude's examples of judgment, the Watchers and Sodom and Gomorrah, but inserts two positive examples of salvation from the destruction, namely Noah and Lot (2 Pet 2:5, 7). This demonstrates that the author's aims are not simply to demonstrate the necessity of the ungodly's future judgment but more comprehensively to confirm the truth of the eschatological expectation as summarized in 2 Pet 2:9: „the Lord knows to rescue the pious from trial and to hold the unrighteous for the day of judgment."

Even more significant is that from the text of Jude all the elements which point to the precise profile of Jude's opponents, are either omitted or at least reduced. 2 Pet 2:4 simply mentions the "sin" (ἁμαρτάνειν) of the angels, not the detail that they had left their realm or transgressed the border between heavenly and human creatures (Jude 5), and 2 Pet 2:6 similarly omits the notion that the Sodomites went after "foreign flesh" (Jude 7), which was also a hint to the transgression of the border between angels and humans.

The idea of such a transgression which is implied in Jude's accusation of slandering the angels (cf. Jude 8–9) is not shared by the author of Second Peter. In adapting the phrase from Jude 7, he just stresses that judgment will meet at most (μάλιστα) those "who go after the flesh in the

---

[47] Du Toit, "Vilification" (n. 5), 404.

[48] Jerome H. Neyrey, *2 Peter, Jude* (AB 37C; New York, N.Y.: Doubleday, 1993), 192. This conclusion is rejected by Davids, *The Letters of 2 Peter and Jude* (n. 40), 223, by the argument that in Second Peter "the main charges against the false teachers are ethical." But Davids seems to underestimate the eschatological argument in 2 Peter 3.

desire of pollution and despise the Lordship" (2:10). The phrase "going after (the) flesh" is certainly taken from Jude 7, but now transferred from the example to the polemical application at the end of the passage. Thus, the author addresses a disobedient, lust-oriented and even "dirty" lifestyle but not the particular idea of a violation of the majesty of the angels. The extensive period (that runs from vv. 4–10b) ends in the same polemical tone which was already established in the introduction of the "false teachers" (vv. 1–3). Echoing the charges already made in Jude 8 but adapting them to his own aims, the author accuses his opponents of living according to the flesh in an unclean desire and neglecting the authority of God or Christ.

Thus the utilization of the biblical examples is again focused on the opponents, although their doctrinal views are not mentioned. Possibly they uttered scepticism against the teaching that "the Lord is capable to save and to keep for judgment," i.e. against the expectation of a final judgment or also against God's and Christ's activity within history. But it is not that scepticism which is accused here, but very generally an immoral, "fleshly" conduct which is additionally "darkened" by the use of metaphors of pollution. Thus, the opponents are actually put in line with the sinful angels and the immoral Sodomites, so that the idea that people with such conduct[49] will face eternal condemnation is expressed as strongly as in Jude.

2.4 The Ultimate Vilification of the Opponents (2:10b–22)

Having returned to the theme of the opponents, the author now continues with an otherwise unparalleled polemics[50] against his opponents, whose immoral conduct and nature are described in yet another series of accusations, which reach a climax in the two proverbs in 2 Pet 2:22. Still utilizing the polemical patterns from Jude, the author rephrases large parts of the argument and removes the references to the particular situation addressed in Jude.[51] He changes the sequence of the motifs in one passage[52] and in-

---

[49] The teaching of the opponents is totally ignored here.

[50] John N. D. Kelly, *The Epistles of Peter and of Jude* (BNTC; London: Black, 1969), 337, characterizes it as "the most violent and colourfully expressed tirade in the NT." Rhetorically, the passage is sometimes seen as a "digressio" – thus Duane F. Watson, *Invention, Arrangement and Style: Rhetorical Criticism of Jude and 2 Peter* (SBLDS 104; Atlanta, Ga.: Scholars Press, 1988), 124–126, and also Paulsen (*Der Zweite Petrusbrief und der Judasbrief* [n. 12], 137), but the function of vilifying the opponents seems to be well calculated and fits into the whole of chapter 2.

[51] Thus especially the mention of the community meals in Jude 12 is not adopted in 2 Pet 2:13, so that the feasts now no longer appear in a community context, but rather in a private one.

[52] The Balaam example of 2 Pet 2:15–16 (cf. Jude 11) is transferred after the charges 2 Pet 2:13–14 (cf. Jude 12a).

serts a new passage (2 Pet 2:18–22) phrased independently with new and specific charges and with the proverbs mentioned as the polemical climax of the whole section.

The passage opens with an outraged exclamation, which is inserted into the text adopted from Jude and breaks the syntactical structure:[53] "Bold and arrogant ones!" This offence resumes the previous charges that the opponents deny their Master (2 Pet 2:1) and despise the Lordship (2 Pet 2:10a), but it is now turned into a polemical verdict on their character: they *are* bold and arrogant, i.e. habitually disrespectful and without any fear – not even in face of δόξαι.[54]

In the use of the term δόξαι and the phrase δόξας οὐ τρέμουσιν βλασφημοῦντες which is adopted from Jude 8 with only minor alterations we can see a remnant of Jude's main charge against his opponents who were accused of "slandering the angels" (δόξας δὲ βλασφημοῦσιν), i.e. pronouncing pejorative words against them. It is unclear whether the charge could apply also to the opponents of Second Peter, but considering that the main point of dispute was eschatology, the differences between Jude's text and its reception in 2 Pet 2:10b–11 are significant. In Jude, the charge of slandering the angels is illustrated by the contrasting example of the contest between Michael and the Satan on the corpse of Moses (Jude 9) taken from the Jewish apocryphal tradition of the *Assumption of Moses*.[55] Even the archangel did not dare what the opponents of Jude apparently did: pronouncing a slanderous verdict against an(other) angel, namely Satan. The use of this example in Jude suggests that the addressees knew the apocryphal tradition and could take Michael as a positive example over against the disrespectful opponents. In Second Peter the charge from Jude 8 is adopted, but the illustrating example from Jude is considerably shortened. Michael and the Satan are not mentioned any more, the quotation of Michael's words is omitted, and the shortening even causes some lack of syntactic clarity,[56] so that the whole matter remains somewhat foggy. If

---

[53] The last part of Jude 8 (κυριότητα δὲ ἀθετοῦσιν δόξας δὲ βλασφημοῦσιν) is split, so that the exclamation Τολμηταὶ αὐθάδεις inserted by the author of Second Peter now divides κυριότητος καταφρονοῦντας (which is now the end of the preceding passage) and δόξας οὐ τρέμουσιν βλασφημοῦντες (which now belongs to a new passage, beginning with the exclamation Τολμηταὶ αὐθάδεις).

[54] For αὐθάδεις cf. Tit 1:7. Τολμηταί is a New Testament *hapax legomenon*. The verb, however, is used in Jude 9, so that the author might be inspired from there. The two terms occur together in *1 Clem.* 30:8.

[55] Cf. most extensively Bauckham, *Jude. 2 Peter* (n. 24), 65–76.

[56] The reference of the κατ' αὐτῶν in 2 Pet 2:11 is uncertain, so it remains unclear in 2 Peter against whom the angels should pronounce a slanderous word or judgment. The numerous suggestions to understand the text cannot be discussed here; cf. recently, Davids, *The Letters of 2 Peter and Jude* (n. 40), 234–236.

Second Peter's readers lacked a detailed knowledge of the apocryphal tradition utilized in Jude, they were certainly unable to conjecture the scene
which was originally alluded to in Jude.[57] We should thus suppose that the
whole charge of slandering angels did not really apply to the opponents of
Second Peter, although the author adopts the charge from Jude 8. What is
left (and could be adopted from Jude) is just the idea that even the powerful angels humbly avoid what the opponents do in their undue disrespect.
Thus the accusation δόξας οὐ τρέμουσιν βλασφημοῦντες functions as an
illustration of the arrogance and lack of respect the author very generally
ascribes to his opponents.

The following vv. 12–14 likewise focus on vilifying the opponents.
"These men" (οὗτοι)[58] are now the subject of a sequence of insults most of
which the author adopts from Jude, but intensifies their rhetorical power.
Most significant is that the author now turns to a description of the opponent's nature which is characterized as non-human, animal-like. The opponents are "like irrational animals" (ὡς ἄλογα ζῷα) simply "born with a
body" (γεγεννημένα φυσικά), i.e. without reason or spirit, and with the
sheer destiny of being caught and destroyed (εἰς ἅλωσιν καὶ φθοράν).[59]
The comparison with Jude is again significant: there it is only said that the
opponents "understand things by nature like the irrational animals,"[60] so
the phrase remains a mere comparison regarding the opponents' way of
understanding. The author of Second Peter changes the syntax and the
word position so that the phrase ὡς ἄλογα ζῷα appears more strongly
linked with the opening οὗτοι and thus more independent from the main
verb, so that there is a stronger articulation of the opponents' nature.[61]

---

[57] Therefore, interpreters should not conjecture the context of the charge from Jude
in Second Peter.

[58] The οὗτοι is the typical and recurring reference to the opponents in Jude where it
has a structuring function, introducing the application of the biblical examples to the
opponents (Jude 8, 10, 12, 16, 19). 2 Pet 2:12 takes the οὗτοι literally from Jude 10, although it does not shape the structure of the argument in Second Peter. The deictic reference to the opponents helps to avoid mentioning them by name. This is also a very common element of (not only) ancient polemics. Cf. also Paul's use of τινες (Rom 3:8; 1 Cor
4:18; 1 Cor 15:12; 2 Cor 3:1; Gal 1:7; further 1 Tim 1:6; 6:21; Jud 4).

[59] Bauckham, *Jude. 2 Peter* (n. 24), 263, mentions ancient passages showing that
"the idea that certain animals were born to be slaughtered and eaten was common in the
ancient world."

[60] Syntactically, this is an adverbial construction embedded into a relative clause:
ὅσα δὲ φυσικῶς ὡς τὰ ἄλογα ζῷα ἐπίστανται (Jude 10).

[61] Of course, the expression ὡς ἄλογα ζῷα γεγεννημένα φυσικὰ εἰς ἅλωσιν καὶ
φθοράν can still be read as a complement to the following relative structure ἐν οἷς ἀγ-
νοοῦσιν βλασφημοῦντες, ἐν τῇ φθορᾷ αὐτῶν καὶ φθαρήσονται. But its position before
the relative pronoun suggests a reading as an almost independent insult. Especially in the
end of v. 12 the construction lacks syntactical clarity. In the phrase ἐν τῇ φθορᾷ αὐτῶν

They not only act or understand like irrational animals, but are really comparable to them: like them, the false teachers are just created for destruction, without having any enduring value or destiny.

The second part of v. 12 adopts and intensifies the charge from Jude 10: the opponents slander what they do not understand – or conversely, they are purely ignorant of what they slander. They are ignorant not simply of the angels or the heavenly creatures but of possibly everything they claim to know. They are irrational beings, although they may utter rational scepticism against the Christian hope, and their alleged ignorance is in strong contrast with the true knowledge claimed by the author (2 Pet 1:2, 3, 8, 12, 16).[62]

The following staccato of charges[63] and insults can hardly be conveyed adequately by any translation: the charges, however, appear unrelated to the charge of ignorance expressed before. Without further specification, the "false teachers" are generally said to be evildoers who will "suffer the reward of unrighteousness" (in a fine word-play: ἀδικούμενοι μισθὸν ἀδικίας). Afterward, the licentious lifestyle of the opponents is addressed, when they are said to "consider as pleasure (ἡδονή) reveling in the daytime" (instead of in the evening),[64] which points to their dissolute and shameless behavior. With metaphors of uncleanness, they are called "blots and blemishes" (σπίλοι καὶ μῶμοι), and another metaphoric expression combines the aspects of feasting and inhonesty: they "revel in their deceits when feasting with you" (ἐντρυφῶντες ἐν ταῖς ἀπάταις αὐτῶν συνευωχούμενοι ὑμῖν). Interestingly, the author has changed the text of Jude in two significant ways by just altering a few letters: from the metaphor of "cliffs" (σπιλάδες), dangerous for a ship, he gets "blots" (σπίλοι), and from the ἀγάπαι (the communal meals) mentioned in Jude 12 he switches to

---

καὶ φθαρήσονται "and in their destruction they too will be destroyed" it remains unclear whose destruction is meant. Does αὐτῶν refer to evil angels which according to some interpreters' view were slandered by the opponents (cf. Horrell, *Epistles of Peter and Jude* [n. 29], 168, following Bauckham, *Jude. 2 Peter* [n. 24], 264), or does it simply refer to the slaughtering of the animals (thus, e.g., Kelly, *Epistles of Peter and of Jude* [n. 50], 339: "a destruction similar in its finality to that which befalls wild beasts;" Davids, *Letters of 2 Peter and Jude* [n. 40], 237–238; Paulsen, *Der zweite Petrusbrief und der Judasbrief* [n. 12], 140)? The decisive point is, however, the destruction that the opponents will face.

[62] Harrington, "Jude and 2 Peter" (n. 41), 272.

[63] The staccato is syntactically shaped by a sequence of only nominal expressions and participles.

[64] Τρυφή has a broad range of meaning: It denotes not necessarily feasting but luxury and indulgence (which could be linked with meals). But especially meals were commonly held only at night whereas feasting in the day was viewed negatively both in Jewish and Greco-Roman eyes (cf. Eccl 10:16; Isa 5:11; *T. Mos.* 7:4; Juvenal 1.103); cf. Davids, *The Letters of 2 Peter and Jude* (n. 40), 239.

ἀπάται to express the deceitful nature of the opponents or, possibly, the danger of being caught during common meals or feasts considered as events of shamelessness.

Three supplementary insults in v. 14 express the habituality of the opponents' sins: they have "eyes full of adultery," "never stop sinning;" and "have a heart trained in greed." All these reproaches intensify the previous ones by adding an aspect of continuity and habituality. One additional charge, however, may point to a particular danger sensed by the author: the opponents "seduce the unstable." This is the accusation which will be adopted again in the final verses of the passage (vv. 18–20).

A concluding insult corresponds to the opening τολμηταὶ αὐθάδεις and marks the climax of the series of reproaches: formally in a curse, the opponents are called κατάρας τέκνα, "children of the curse," or "accursed brood!"

Such a series of insults is definitely not a description of the opponents' actual conduct but rather a mere disparagement and vilification. The opponents are accused of a luxurious, desire-oriented or even animal-like lifestyle governed by greed, food, drinks and sex. Feasting not only in the evening but already in the daylight, the continuous desire for sexual intercourse or, as it is said, adultery, the training in greed – all these expressions are simply general denunciations of the opponents' sinful nature, which not only illustrate the general charge of injustice but also make the opponents appear like beasts and dangerously seductive evildoers.

We can briefly pass over vv. 15–16 where the author adopts only one of the three short biblical examples from Jude 11, the paradigm of Balaam which is slightly expanded. The description of this figure who was considered a false prophet in Jewish exegesis was particularly appropriate to be applied to the false teachers. When following the way of Balaam they have left the "right way" (εὐθεῖαν ὁδόν) and gone astray (ἐπλανήθησαν), as it is said. As in Jude 11, the example of Balaam is used to express the charges of injustice and greed and the comparison with animals, when it is said that he loved the gain from injustice and was rebuked even by a donkey.

After the brief biblical comparison, the author turns again to a series of denunciations and charges which lead to the proverbial climax in v. 22. The first two expressions adopt two of the metaphors of nature from Jude 12, but simplify them for the sake of rhetorical efficiency: the opponents[65] are said to be "waterless springs," i.e. fruitless, and "mists driven by a storm," i.e. empty, without substance and transitory. The shortened adoption of the four metaphors from Jude 12b–13 and especially the omission

---

[65] As already v. 12, v. 17 is opened by the οὗτοι which points to the opponents. It is adopted here from Jude 12a and functions as a paragraph marker, although Second Peter does not use the οὗτοι as consistently as does Jude.

of the image of the "wandering stars" (Jude 13) again result in a lack of clarity. The phrase οἷς ὁ ζόφος τοῦ σκότους τετήρηται „for which the black darkness is reserved" which is exactly borrowed from Jude, has now lost its original connection to the planets (and the fallen angels),[66] but it is still effective and useful as an expression of the impending judgment the opponents have to face.

The next charges are phrased without any reference to Jude, but they repeat the accusations made before: the opponents are again charged of uttering boastful and empty words (cf. vv. 3, 10b.) and of enticing others in the lustful desires of the flesh (cf. v. 2). But the accusation is intensified by mentioning that they entice especially those who had just come to faith in Christ and are escaping from error, i.e. they "entice the unstables" (v. 14). Here the author apparently touches a point which is really significant for the situation he addresses. This theme is expanded in vv. 18–21. This the most extensive treatment of a single charge in the whole of the chapter. We may, therefore, conclude that this touches upon a very concrete aspect of the opponents' agitation. They were quite possibly successful in winning converts for their views and – in the author's view – caused them to return to paganism.

The author further alleges that the opponents are charged to promise freedom (2:19) while being themselves slaves of depravity. It is a matter of discussion what kind of freedom they promised. This might be a clue for reconstructing their identity or their views more precisely. But within the polemics of our author, the contradiction is stressed: while promising freedom, they are themselves slaves of corruption. Thus their promise consists of "empty" (cf. v. 18) or "self-fabricated" (cf. v. 3) words and is, therefore, invalid. Whereas escaping from the corruption of the world is an important expression of the author's view of salvation (cf. 2 Pet 1:4), the opponents as apostates do not share that fate, but rather face judgment and destruction instead.

But according to a widespread conviction[67] our author states that the situation of those who have turned from their saving knowledge of Christ is even worse than before (2 Pet 2:20–21). This conviction is brought to a climax by the two proverbs which serve to decisively vilify the opponents: "[o]f them the proverbs are true: 'a dog returns to his own vomit,' and, 'a

---

[66] Probably the author did not want to evoke the cosmological and angelological implications of Jude 13 and its Enochic background. This is again a confirmation that the author is not interested in the matter of angels.

[67] Cf. already the logion Matt 12:45 // Luke 11:26 which is closely parallel with 2 Pet 2:20, or the stance of the author of Hebrews on the impossibility of a second conversion.

sow, having washed, (returns) to her wallowing in the mire'" (2 Pet 2:22).[68]

Using proverbs[69] for argument or proof or as a brief summary was a customary rhetorical device. But the two proverbs bring the harsh polemics to an ultimate climax. Serving "as commentaries on the spiritual condition of the false teachers"[70] and of all others following them, they particularly stress the aspect of uncleanness and pollution and, again, the earlier comparison with animals. Both are about unclean animals, and, while probably taken from different sources, both make the same point: in contrast with modern views, dogs were normally despised in ancient cultures.[71] The proverb expresses "an often observed behavior of dogs, that is, their returning to, sniffing, and sometimes eating what they have vomited."[72] In a very similar manner, the image of the dog returning to its vomit is used for a fool in Prov 26:11. But the mention of vomit also strengthens the aspect of uncleanness, which is likewise expressed by the second proverb of the pig that, after having washed, returns to the mud.[73] Both proverbs are used to polemically characterize the conduct and nature of the opponents. What they have done and cause others to do is returning to uncleanness and pollution, thus they merely demonstrate that they are like unclean and despised animals.

3. The Image of the Opponents in 2 Peter 2: the Accusations Systematized

The present section will summarize systematically the charges directed against the opponents in 2 Peter 2. Few of the charges refer to the teaching of the opponents and its effects. Much more accusations refer to the moral conduct of the opponents, and some even to their "nature."

---

[68] On the surface, these phrases are related not to the opponents but to the people they caused to turn away from faith. But of course the opponents are also viewed to be apostates (cf. 2 Pet 2:1 and already 1:9), and the rhetorical strength of these last phrases of the chapter is only conceivable if the author has the opponents in view.

[69] Different from other NT usage (cf. John 10:16; 16:25, 29), παροιμία is used here for a proverb.

[70] Thus Harrington, "Jude and 2 Peter" (n. 41), 278.

[71] According to Harrington, "Jude and 2 Peter" (n. 41), 278, the image of the "dog" was used to describe enemies (Ps 22:16; Isa 56:10–11), the unclean (Matt 15:26–27; Rev 22:15) or male prostitutes (Deut 23:18).

[72] Davids, *Letters of 2 Peter and Jude* (n. 40), 252.

[73] This saying probably comes from pagan sources, and its closest parallel appears in a version of the *Story of Ahikar* 8:18. Cf. Bauckham, *Jude. 2 Peter* (n. 24), 279.

3.1 The Opponents' Teaching and its Effect

Some of the charges imply a doctrinal aspect of their teaching and its effect. Most of these charges occur in the introduction of the opponents (2 Pet 2:1–3), although in this passage we do not get any precise idea of their teachings or views which are not explained before the beginning of 2 Peter 3.

- The opponents are called "false teachers" (ψευδοδιδάσκαλοι) and paralleled with the biblical "false prophets" (ψευδοπροφῆται). Later they will be called "scoffers" (2 Pet 3:3) with their teachings (αἱρέσεις)[74] being mentioned. As the "false prophets" from biblical times they cannot be trusted.
- Their words are said to be self-fabricated (2 Pet 2:3), i.e. empty and worthless (2 Pet 2:18), and thus opposed to the inspired words of prophecy (2 Pet 1:21).
- The opponents are accused to deny the master who has bought them, i.e. to disown Christ (2 Pet 2:1). Being apostate, they are in a situation which is even worse than it was before they came to belief (2 Pet 2:20–21).
- Their teachings are said to be destructive or bring destruction (αἱρέσεις ἀπωλείας, 2 Pet 2:1) to their followers, as they will also face destruction themselves (ἐπάγοντες ἑαυτοῖς ταχινὴν ἀπώλειαν, 2 Pet 2:1; cf. 2:19).

3.2 The Mode of the Opponents' Agitation

A number of charges do not refer to their doctrines but to the mode of their agitation. Instead, we already find moral categories, especially the charge of inhonesty.

- The "false teachers" are said to introduce their teachings secretly, through the side door (παρεισάξουσιν 2 Pet 2:1).
- They are accused to utter empty and boastful words (2 Pet 2:17), yet to get followers through self-fabricated words (2 Pet 2:3), i.e. deceive their followers (2 Pet 2:13).
- Furthermore, the opponents are charged with being greedy (πλεονεξία, 2 Pet 2:3; cf. 2:15), and their relationship with the addressees is described in economic terms: they try to exploit them for their own benefit.
- The opponents are said to promise freedom and to attract followers by such a false promise (2 Pet 2:19) and by their own licentious lifestyle (2 Pet 2:2; cf. 2:18).

---

[74] The meaning of αἵρησις is not easy to determine here. It is not simply "heresy," but the use of the term implies the notion of a deviant teaching, cf. 1 Cor 11:19; Gal 5:20.

- A particular effect is that the opponents successfully entice the unstable and especially fresh converts (2 Pet 2:14, 18).

3.3 The Opponents' Immoral Lifestyle

The majority of charges refers to immoral conduct and behavior. Such accusations are already expressed when the opponents are introduced in 2:1–3. They are prepared even earlier, in the context of the catalogue of virtues in chapter 1. However, in the course of chapter 2 "moral" charges become dominant. This is striking since they are apparently unrelated with the opponents' teaching and with the eschatological subject matter discussed in chapter 3.

- The opponents' conduct is generally characterized by licentiousness (ἀσέλγεια; cf. 2 Pet 2:2, 7, 18).
- The licentiousness and lust-orientation is effectively illustrated by the notion of feasting (i.e. eating and also drinking!) at daylight (2 Pet 2:13), which may imply a neglect of one's regular duties of daily work.
- In that context we also find the term "pleasure" (ἡδονή) with a negative connotation (2 Pet 2:13). When regarding feasting at daylight as a pleasure, the opponents obviously like and enjoy what is shameful in the author's eyes.
- Their conduct is further characterized by the term "desire" (ἐπιθυμία), which is a technical term for sin (as used in the Decalogue) (2:10) and is further specified to pertain to the fleshly human nature (2:18).
- Such desire is sexually specified by mention of adultery (2:14). The "false teachers" always look for an adulterous woman (μοιχαλίς).
- Such desire is further characterized metaphorically by the notion of pollution (μιασμάς, 2 Pet 2:10, cf. 2:20) or uncleanness (cf. 2 Pet 2:13 "blots and blemishes" and also the proverbs in 2 Pet 2:22).
- In this context the author also uses the term "flesh" (σάρξ). The opponents go after the flesh, instead of following the Lord (2 Pet 2:10). Here, "flesh" seems to imply the sinful desire for goods and also sexual desire.
- The opponents are also said to entice others in the desires of the flesh (2:18), i.e. to seduce them to a similar conduct, or try to "buy" them by promising the liberty for such a lifestyle. Here, the charge of immoral agitation and the charge of immoral conduct are connected.
- Furthermore, they are generally charged to "despise authority," or more clearly, the Lordship (of Christ) which is meant by the term κυριότης (2 Pet 2:10).
- This leads to the general accusations of arrogance and lack of respect (2 Pet 2:10). The opponents do not even respect heavenly beings or things.

- In close connection with these charges, the opponents are said to be totally ignorant. They do not understand what they despise (2 Pet 2:12).
- Without further specification, their deeds are characterized as unjust (ἀδικεῖν) (2 Pet 2:13). Even stronger, it is said that they continuously sin (2 Pet 2:14).

3.4 The Opponents' Sinful and Animal-like "Nature"

Here we can see that some of the charges mentioned are phrased in a manner so that the immorality appears to be the "nature" of the opponents:

- They sin without end (2 Pet 2:14).
- They are trained in greed (2 Pet 2:14).
- Their eyes are full of adultery (2 Pet 2:14).

In some metaphors – partly taken from Jude – the nature of the opponents is illustrated. And, much beyond the phrasing in Jude, the form of the expressions is not only a comparison, but of a metaphoric characterization:

- The opponents are waterless springs (2 Pet 2:17).
- They are mists driven by a storm (2 Pet 2:17).

The idea that they do not understand the matters they slander leads to a further step of mere disparagement of their nature:

- They are like irrational animals, not like human beings (2 Pet 2:12), born just in a physical nature, i.e. devoid of any spiritual insight.
- They are just born "to be caught and destroyed" (2 Pet 2:12). Their ultimate destiny is not life, but perishing and corruption.
- In the climax of the passage, the opponents are again polemically compared with unclean and despised animals, characterized by images of dirt and pollution: vomit and mud (2 Pet 2:22).
- At the end of one series of accusations, the opponents are even cursed and addressed as "children of curse" (2 Pet 2:14).

3.5 The Eschatological Condemnation

We must also add the expressions of eschatological condemnation because the opponents are strongly viewed within that context.

- Generally, the last judgment is thought to be the reward for the evil deeds, so that the ungodly receive the reward for their wickedness (2 Pet 2:13; cf. 2:3, 5, 6, 9, 15).

– In agreement with Jude, the author states that the judgment on such people like the "false teachers" was determined long ago (ἔκπαλαι).[75] The reality of the eschatological judgment is confirmed at least by one of the biblical examples from Jude, the angels who had sinned and who were not spared. They are rather kept in darkness for the impending judgment (2 Pet 2:4; cf. Jude 5).[76] Here, the author of Second Peter alludes to the Greek notion of the netherworld, the "Tartarus" when using the *hapax legomenon* ταρταρόω.[77]
– The exclamation of the curse in 2 Pet 2:14 pronounces the eschatological condemnation on the opponents.

4. Reality or Fiction?
The Polemical Image of the Opponents and the Question of their Actual Profile

I have already addressed the question to what extent the charges against the opponents are mere vilification and disparagement and how far we can see them as offering an adequate description of their conduct. Of course, we must be aware that the image of the "false teachers" in 2 Peter 2 is primarily a literary construct, so the real-life opponents must be distinguished from the "encoded" opponents.[78] Conversely, the literary image of the opponents might possibly tell us more about the author's own views and interests than about the actual conduct and nature of the opponents.[79] It is hard to find criteria to decide the question. The following three points may offer a way forward.

a) First, we can ask about the charges simply adopted from Jude. Of course, even a charge adopted from a source may actually fit the opponents in view, at least in the imagination of the author. But the question is, then, how the different points fit into an overall image of the opponents. And if

---

[75] However, in contrast to Jude 4, the author Peter does not say that the judgment is written down in advance or that the ungodly are predetermined. Instead, he states that "their condemnation is not idle and that their destruction is not asleep." This might be in contrast to some claims of the opponents that the expected judgment will not come. Or should they think that God himself is idle or even asleep?

[76] The other examples – the judgment on the flood generation and on the people of Sodom and Gomorrah – are, strictly speaking, not examples for the last judgment, but for a judgment within history. They only serve as hint to a future judgment by analogy.

[77] Cf. Kraus, *Sprache, Stil und historischer Ort* (n. 4), 337. Cf. also Birger A. Pearson, "A Reminiscence of Classical Myth at II Peter 2.4," *GRBS* 10 (1969): 71–80.

[78] Cf. Du Toit, "Vilification" (n. 5), 404.

[79] Cf. Michel R. Desjardins, "The Portrayal of the Dissidents in 2 Peter and Jude: Does It Tell Us More about the 'Godly' and the 'Ungodly?,'" *JSNT* 30 (1987): 89–102.

the charges adopted from Jude seem unrelated to the main concerns of Second Peter, there is reason to be sceptical.[80]

b) Second, from the parallels in other polemic texts in the New Testament, the Apostolic Fathers and later Church Fathers, or also in Greco-Roman and Early Jewish polemics, we can identify a number of accusations which were often used as standard charges against religious or philosophical rivals, regardless whether the charges were actually "justified" or not.[81]

c) Third, we can look for charges in Second Peter which appear not to be standard charges but sound rather particular and may give a clue for reconstructing the situation or the profile of the opponents.[82]

4.1 Charges Adopted from Jude

Browsing through the list of accusations, we can observe that a very large number of them were already used by the author of Jude against his opponents. Some of them, however, are significantly changed in Second Peter.

– In Jude, there is already notion of *false teachers* (without using that term) who crept in and allegedly change the teaching (Jude 3–4). Their activity (and especially the judgment prescribed for them) is explained by biblical examples, among which those in Jude 11 (Cain, Balaam, and Korah) are particularly significant.
– Already in Jude, the opponents – who are not addressed, nor mentioned by name, but only addressed by the repeated pronoun οὗτοι – are charged to be disrespectful, to *reject authority* (Jude 8) and even to deny their Master and Lord (Jude 4). The charge of disrespect might be a common accusation against rivaling teachers or people questioning traditional values. In Jude, however, the charge is focused on the particular accusation of slandering the angels (Jude 8–10) and transgressing the border set between humans and angels (cf. Jude 6–7), whereas the charge of disrespect in Second Peter appears to be less specific and

---

[80] Needless to say, some Jude's accusations against his opponents may be also standard charges or mere diffamations. But this is not our topic here.

[81] Cf. e.g., Du Toit, "Vilification" (n. 5), 405–410, who mentions from the New Testament and the Apostolic Fathers nine prominent vilifying trends: "1. Hypocrisy and falseness ... 2. Obscure, shadowy characters ... 3. Sorcery ... 4. Inflated self-esteem ... 5. Moral depravity ... 6. A perversive influence ... 7. Associated with dubious historical characters ... 8. Prone to judgment ... 9. Ludicrous characters." For elements from the broader ancient polemic, see also Johnson, "New Testament Anti-Jewish Slander" (n. 5) and Arnd Rehn, "Vomunt ut edant, edunt ut vomant: Beobachtungen zur Epikurpolemik in der römischen Literatur," in *Die Heiden* (ed. Reinhard Feldmeier and Ulrich Heckel; WUNT 70; Tübingen: Mohr Siebeck, 1994), 381–399.

[82] Cf. especially Jerome Neyrey, "The Form and Background of the Polemic in 2 Peter," *JBL* 99 (1980): 407–431.

more general, since the mention of the angels and the accusation of slandering angels is considerably reduced.

– Consequently, the opponents of Jude are also viewed to be *apostates*. But of course, such an accusation does not reveal anything about the way the opponents viewed themselves. Possibly they regarded themselves as true members of the community when participating in the community meals (Jude 12). The author of Jude, however, considers this inappropriate and an act of shamelessness. In Second Peter, the opponents are also considered to be apostates, although they probably considered themselves as true members of the community. A remarkable difference, however, is that the community aspect is less prominent in Second Peter than in Jude.

– In Jude, the opponents are charged with a *lack of understanding* of spiritual things, in particular regarding the angels they slander (Jude 10). The former verdict is adopted and even radicalized in Second Peter, but the link with the angels is weakened (2 Pet 2:12), so that the charge is a more general lack of understanding of spiritual things.

– Already in Jude, this leads to a *comparison with irrational animals* and to the idea that the opponents are in some respect people of nature and instinct (φυσικῶς in Jude 10; ψυχικοί, πνεῦμα μὴ ἔχοντες in Jude 19). In Second Peter, the motif is adopted, because it appeared particularly useful for the polemical disparagement of the opponents. Thus, the degree of diffamation is strengthened, especially regarding the "animal-like" nature of the opponents.

– In Jude, the opponents are described as *shameless*, doing what is inappropriate for them (Jude 12). The charge is adopted in Second Peter and linked with other accusations.

– In Jude, the opponents are charged with being *selfish*, caring only for themselves (ἑαυτοὺς ποιμαίνοντες) and for their own gain (Jude 16). Second Peter even intensifies the notion of greed and economic interests.

– Already in Jude, the opponents are described as a *stumbling stone*, or – in a fine metaphorical expression – as a cliff (Jude 12) which endangers others of losing their way (cf. Jude 21). Second Peter changes this into an accusation of being "blots and blemishes" (by a slight change of the word), but keeps the idea that the opponents mislead others, especially new converts, to lose the way of righteousness.

– In Jude, the opponents are viewed as *deceitful* (metaphorically: waterless clouds) and fruitless (v. 12: autumn trees without fruit). Second Peter changes and shortens the metaphors (2 Pet 2:17), but also characterizes his opponents as "false" and deceitful (2 Pet 2:1, 3, 19).

- Metaphorically, Jude's opponents are characterized as *transitory* (v. 12: clouds, carried along by the winds); 2 Pet 2:17 adopts the metaphor and also the notion that the opponents will definitely perish (2 Pet 2:12 etc.).
- The conduct of Jude's opponents is characterized by the term ἐπιθυμία: they are walking according to their own ungodly *desires* (Jude 16). The same is said about the Second Peter's opponents (2 Pet 2:10, 18).
- Already in Jude, this is linked with metaphors of uncleanness: the opponents are viewed as *unclean* and shameful (v. 13: spewing out the foam of their shame; cf. also V. 8: defile the flesh). This is strongly adopted in 2 Peter, with the climax in the two proverbs in 2 Pet 2:22.
- In Jude, the opponents are described as *scoffers* (ἐμπαῖκται) but without any reference to the hope for the parousia (Jude 18; cf. 2 Pet 3:3). This is then adopted in 2 Pet 3:3 when the scoffing of the opponents is more precisely introduced.
- Already in Jude, the opponents are charged of *undue and bombastic speeches* (Jude 16).
- Jude's opponents are regarded as *dead* (v. 12: twice dead, uprooted), and, of course, liable to the judgment, as the wandering stars „for whom the utter depths of eternal darkness have been reserved" (v. 13).
- In Jude, there is no direct curse on the opponents, but a woe-exclamation related to the notion of the prescribed judgment (v. 11). The author of Second Peter even accurses his opponents (2 Pet 2:14).

4.2 Standard Charges and Polemical Stereotypes

Many of the accusations phrased in Second Peter (and also several of those phrased in Jude) can be regarded as standard charges in early Christian polemic against rivals or heretics or in the wider horizon of ancient polemics. From the list of vilifying trends given by Du Toit,[83] we can take a number of points:

- The characterization of the opponents by attributes of *"falseness,"*[84] as "false" teachers (including the notion of "liars"), is, of course a stereotype which is used by those considering themselves to be right, honest, or orthodox. In Second Peter there is the direct charge of *dishonesty*, of fraud (2 Pet 2:13: ἀπάτη), and the idea that the opponents try to "buy" their followers by false and invalid promises (2 Pet 2:18–19). In the same context we should note the idea that the opponents (who belonged to the Christian community) "smuggled" their teaching through the side door (2 Pet 2:1). This is a rhetorical device intended to alienate their

---

[83] Du Toit, "Vilification" (n. 5), 405–410. See above, n. 81.
[84] Cf. the examples collected by Du Toit, "Vilification" (n. 5), 405 who points to the ψευδ-prefix in general.

teaching from the addressees, but it does not tell anything about the actual origin or content of the teaching.

- A clear polemical stereotype is also the charge of inflated self-esteem,[85] disrespect or *arrogance* (2 Pet 2:10). Such a charge could easily be linked with the notion of blasphemy or violation of the majesty of God, disrespect against the "Lordship" (Jude 8; 2 Pet 2:10), God's servants (e.g. the angels or the apostles) or the Divine commandments and words. As Du Toit notes, this assertion "surely was one of the gravest labels which could be attached to anyone."[86] As in Jude the opponents' lack of respect for the angelic powers (cf. Jude 8).[87] In Second Peter the opponents' scepticism against the expectation of the parousia (2 Pet 3:3–4) could easily be interpreted to be such an unduly arrogant attitude towards the prophetic word (cf. 2 Pet 1:20–21) or even the majesty of the Lord himself (cf. 2 Pet 1:16–17) for which Peter is introduced as an eyewitness.

- Another very common charge is that the opponents' moral integrity is questioned by the accusation of greed, avarice and a "*profiteering intention*" (2 Pet 2:3, 14).[88] As Du Toit states: "[t]he connection between religion and money-making does not only have a long history," e.g., in the polemics against all types of "sophists,"[89] "it constitutes also a stereotyped technique of vilification."[90] Such a charge was effective to denigrate the opponent's credibility and also to evoke suspicion against their teaching among the addressees.

- Quite prominent among the standard charges against opponents and "heretics" was also the accusation of moral licentiousness (ἀσέλγεια, 2 Pet 2:2, 7, 18; cf. Jud 1:4), especially *sexual misconduct*, fleshly lust (2 Pet 2:18) or *adultery* (2 Pet 2:10, 14). There are numerous parallels in early

---

[85] Du Toit, "Vilification" (n. 5), 407–408, points to the use of ἀλαζονεία (Jas 4:16; 2 Tim 3:2; *1 Clem.* 14:1; 16:2; 21:5; 35:5), αὐδάδεια (*1 Clem.* 1:1; 30:8; *Barn.* 20:1) and ὑπερηφανία (2 Tim 3:2; *1 Clem.* 16:2; 30:1–2; Ign. *Eph.* 5:3; *Barn.* 20:1), to the label of καύχησις (Rom 2:17, 23; 2 Cor 10:12–18; 11:12, 18; Gal 6:13; Jas 4:16; *1 Clem.* 21:5; Ign. *Eph.* 18:1) and the charge of self-exaltation (2 Cor 11:20; *1 Clem.* 14:1; 16:1; 21:5; 39:1).

[86] Du Toit, "Vilification" (n. 5), 408.

[87] On the background of this charge and its links with the (Deutero-)Pauline tradition, see Frey, "Der Judasbrief zwischen Judentum und Hellenismus" (n. 30) and – extensively, Roman Heiligenthal, *Zwischen Henoch und Paulus: Studien zum theologiegeschichtlichen Ort des Judasbriefes* (TANZ 6; Tübingen: Francke, 1992), 157.

[88] Du Toit, "Vilification" (n. 5), 408 mentions also 1 Tim 6:5; Tit 1:11; *Barn.* 20:2 and *Did* 5:2.

[89] Cf. examples from Dio Chrysostom (*Or.* 13) in Johnson, "Anti-Jewish Slander" (n. 5), 430.

[90] Du Toit, "Vilification" (n. 5), 408.

Christian polemics against heretics,[91] especially against later Gnostics, but also in ancient anti-Epicurean polemics.[92] In Second Peter, the charge is partly adopted from Jude, where the opponents are also charged of licentiousness (Jude 4), and the biblical examples include the notion of πορνεύειν and intercourse with "foreign flesh" (Jude 7). The author of Second Peter removes such a specification and accuses his opponents of simply going after the flesh (2 Pet 2:10) which is connected with other terms of sin, such as ἐπιθυμία (2 Pet 2:10, 18; cf. Jude 16, 18) and metaphors such as pollution (μιασμός 2 Pet 2:10) and uncleanness (2 Pet 2:22). Such an accusation, especially when it is intensified towards a habitual element of the opponents' nature, functions as a potent element of vilification. It is even likely to be merely a form of vilification, although it is conceivable that in the imagination of our author people who deny the parousia and the final judgment of God and Christ might feel licenced to sin in every respect, and especially in the field of sexual relations.

- Another common aspect of denunciation which also pertains the field of moral depravity and licentiousness is the charge of *gluttony* (2 Pet 2:13).[93] Adopted from Jude (Jude 12), the author intensifies the accusation by use of two motifs, the notion of reveling at daytime and the aspect of "pleasure."

- It is also a very customary charge against heretics that they seduce others and have a potential *perversive influence* on the addressees.[94] This is also part of the polemics in Second Peter (cf. 2 Pet 2:2, 18–22), where it is stated that the "way of truth" is blasphemed due to the conduct of the opponents and their lifestyle (2 Pet 2:2). However, the length of the passage and the particularity of the charge seem in this instance to indicate that the problem was a very urgent one and that we might have a hint about the situation of the addressees or at least the problem, as the author defines it.

- Another vilifying trend mentioned by Du Toit is the association with dubious historical characters.[95] Here, the example of Balaam must be mentioned who is used as a negative tag for oppositional groups in Jude 11, 2 Pet 2:15 and in Rev 2:14. It is improbable to construct a historical

---

91 Cf. also Jude 4:16, 18, 23; Rev 2:14, 20–22; *Barn.* 20:1.

92 On this, see generally Rehn, "Vomunt ut edant" (n. 81).

93 Du Toit, "Vilification" (n. 5), 408, who refers to Rom 16:18; Phil 3:19 and Jude 12.

94 Cf. Du Toit, "Vilification" (n. 5), 409.

95 Du Toit, "Vilification" (n. 5), 410.

link between Revelation and Jude / 2 Peter on this basis;[96] the author of
Second Peter adopts this biblical example from Jude but develops it because the figure of Balaam could appear especially appropriate to be
linked with "false teachers," since the figure was denigrated in post-
biblical Judaism and viewed especially as a false prophet who seduced
the Israelites to idolatry.

– One final forceful vilifying technique merits attention: the threat of
judgment pronounced upon the opponents (and, of course, those who
might follow them). In 2 Peter, the threat is pronounced strongly and
repeatedly. In contrast with Jude (Jude 4–7, 14–15) it is not primarily
taken from biblical or written prophecy, although the examples (2 Pet
2:4, 6) are forcefully introduced. The conviction that the judgment on
the ungodly "is not idle" (2 Pet 2:3) or that God "is able to keep the unrighteous for the day of judgment" (2 Pet 2:9), that there is a reward of
unrighteousness (2 Pet 2:13, 15–16), is just stated as a common belief
(as opposed to the scepticism of the opponents). Climactically, the
judgment is pronounced in the curse on the false teachers in 2 Pet 2:14.
But we should note that these threats aim primarily at shocking the audience thus discouraging them from following the heretics.[97]

4.3 Particular Charges and Hints about the Actual Situation

Let us now look at some of the differences between Jude and Second Peter
and their significance for reconstructing the situation and the profile of the
opponents in Second Peter. We can in silence pass over the changes due to
the authorial fiction (cf. 2 Pet 2:1–2; 3:1–3) and also the omission of the
references to the situation and the profile of Jude's opponents. These
changes only demonstrate that Second Peter was written in a different situation and had different opponents in view. Any assumption of a common
milieu for both letters[98] or of similar challenges is questionable in view of
these observations.

Some of the particular elements in Second Peter might be important for
reconstructing the situation of the addressees. An interesting expansion of
Jude's "Vorlage" is, in this respect, the prediction that the false teachers
will have many followers (2 Pet 2:2). Together with the note on the seduction of the unstable (2 Pet 2:14) and the relatively long passage on the

---

[96] Such an attempt was made by Anders Gerdmar, *Rethinking the Judaism-Hellenism
Dichotomy: A Historiographical Case Study of Second Peter and Jude* (CB.NT 36;
Stockholm: Almqvist & Wiksell International, 2001), 324–342.

[97] Thus Du Toit, "Vilification" (n. 5), 410; Freyne, "Vilifying" (n. 5), 137–138.

[98] Thus, on an unclear reconstruction of the literary relationship between Second Peter and Jude, the study by Gerdmar, *Rethinking* (n. 96); cf. my review in *TLZ* 128 (2003):
393–395.

backdrop of recent converts (2 Pet 2:19–22), we can conclude that the rivaling teachers had some success. They could appear as a danger to the
churches because they had won many new believers.

We can also mention the particular stress on the fact that the Lord can
also save the pious from trial (2 Pet 2:9). Should this indicate that the addressees were themselves in danger of following the teaching of the opponents, or that the author foresaw such a danger, which he calls a "trial"
from which he hopes to be saved, together with his faithful addressees? Or
did the author and his followers just suffer from the situation, when they
had to realize the attractiveness of a rival teaching they considered to be
dangerously misleading? This might at least partly explain the fierce mode
of the author's polemic.

A significant feature is also the mention of meals. Interestingly, the
readers are directly addressed when the author phrases that "they feast together with you" (συνευωχούμενοι ὑμῖν) in 2 Pet 2:13. Does this mean that
the addressees had good contacts with the opposed teachers who had some
influence on the members of the communities, at the occasion of meals?
The absence of any hint to communal meals (in marked contrast with Jude
12, where the ἀγάπαι are mentioned) might point to the importance of private invitations. Such invitations could be considered as pleasure (ἡδονή, 2
Pet 2:14). In the view of the author of Second Peter, however, they are
viewed quite negatively, and linked with the suspicion of any kind of inappropriate luxury and immorality. This might also shed some light on the
attitude of the author himself. For him, those meals are a source of licentiousness, and the opponents act as „blots and blemishes,"[99] that is, they
cause pollution and dishonor for those with whom they feast, so that the
addressees can only keep in distance from them.

One of the most important keywords is ἐλευθερία in 2 Pet 2:19.[100] The
opponents "promise 'freedom'" to those who follow them, although they
themselves are – in the view of the author – "slaves of corruption." Probably the opponents used this word themselves, so this could be a hint to
their actual teaching before the introduction of their eschatological views
in 2 Pet 3:3–4. The question is, however, what kind of liberty is meant, and
which context can be assumed for the message of ἐλευθερία. If the opponents are not Gnostics, the suggestion that they propagate freedom from
the "world" or from its demiurge, can be dismissed.[101] The suggestion that

---

[99] Cf. the changing of the text of Jude 12 in 2 Pet 2:13.

[100] Cf. basically Neyrey, "The Form and Background" (n. 82), 419–420, most recently, Thomas Scott Caulley, "They Promise Them Freedom: Once again, the ψευδοδιδάσκαλοι in 2 Peter," *ZNW* 99 (2008): 129–138.

[101] Cf. Bauckham, *Jude. 2 Peter* (n. 24), 275.

freedom from φθορά ("perishability")[102] is meant due to a "realized eschatology" (cf. 2 Tim 2:18) is also implausible in view of the eschatological argument in chapter 3.[103] It was often suggested that the opponents preached freedom from moral law[104] which could be understood as a license for sin. But the idea of "freedom" should be viewed in connection with the issue of eschatology, and it should be considered that freedom was a central theme of the Pauline tradition (including some of Paul's opponents), so that the question arises whether the opponents adopted some aspects of the Pauline tradition and used them in their own terms (cf. 2 Pet 3:15–16).[105] But we should consider that the opponents are particularly said to seduce new converts (2 Pet 2:18), for whom the issue of freedom from the Jewish law or even the issue of a wider form of moral law was probably not the most distinctive issue. The most plausible view that combines the aspect of eschatology, Hellenistic scepticism, and Pauline catchwords, was suggested by Jerome Neyrey, who thinks that the opponents promised freedom from concern over future judgment or, in a broader Epicurean context, from Divine retribution or freedom from "trouble."[106] In any case, the issue is primarily theological, not ethical,[107] although it might have had implications on ethical issues, and the author of Second Peter focuses on the (presumed) ethical consequences before he starts discussing and refuting the theological and eschatological issue.

Thus, the aspect of "freedom" might be seen as one aspect of the real profile of the opponents, but the mention of the "promise of freedom" is certainly not sufficient to view all the moral charges of licentiousness, adultery, greed etc. as describing the real conduct of the opponents.

---

[102] Cf. Käsemann, "Apologia" (n. 2), 171.

[103] Cf. Bauckham, *Jude. 2 Peter* (n. 24), 275.

[104] Thus, e.g., Fornberg, *Early Church* (n. 17), 106–107. With a different argument also Caulley, "They Promise Them Freedom" (n. 100), 138: "freedom from doctrinal 'tyranny' and accompanying moral constraints." See also Bauckham, *Jude. 2 Peter* (n. 24), 280.

[105] Bauckham, *Jude. 2 Peter* (n. 24), 275, points to Rom 3:8, Gal 5:13 and 1 Pet 2:16 for the fact that Paul's teaching of freedom was open to antinomian abuse. But the opponents of Second Peter are not simply a prolongation of the Corinthian libertines (cf. 1 Cor 8:9; 10:23). Already in Jude 4, the charge of "turning the grace of our God into licentiousness" is not simply an antinomian position but embedded into a distinctive view of the possession of the pneuma (Jude 19) and on the relevance or non-relevance of cosmic powers (i.e. the angels).

[106] Cf. Neyrey, "The Form and Background" (n. 82); idem, "The Apologetic Use of the Transfiguration in II Peter 1.16–21," *CBQ* 42 (1980): 504–519; idem, *2 Peter. Jude* (n. 48).

[107] Cf. Neyrey, "The Form and Background" (n. 82), 430.

4.4 Tentative Historical Conclusions

A more precise description of the "true" profile of the opponents is almost impossible. Moreover, the question whether they were as immoral as the author depicts them, or whether the use of moral accusations is just a rhetorical device in preparation of the theological argument put forward in 2 Pet 3:3–13 can only be answered tentatively.

But I have demonstrated that numerous elements of the opponents' image are primarily if not solely intended to vilify and to disparage them without being based in the actual conduct of those people.

- This is, first, the *diffamation of their nature* as animal-like and purely somatic, which deliberately ignores the humanity of the fellow-teachers.
- One could add the *expansion of moral charges towards a habituality* of continuous sinning.
- Mention should also be made of the *metaphorical expansion of charges* by the motif of uncleanness, which is a consequence of the author's views of communal "purity."
- Furthermore, it is plausible that many of the *accusations adopted from Jude*, especially the charges of moral depravity (avarice, licentiousness, adultery), are largely part of the author's construct and a product of the author's conjecturing or suspicion.

If the author thought (as numerous interpreters still do) that denying a last judgment should necessarily lead to unlimited immorality, he could use such a suspicion as a rhetorical device to disparage the opponents, whose views appeared so dangerously seductive to believers he wished to protect.

Of course, we cannot exclude the possibility that the opponents, in their proclamation of freedom, held a more liberal or even libertinistic view than the author could accept. But very often the charge of libertinism or immorality is used as a standard charge against religious or philosophical rivals or heretics.[108] And in view of the author's vilificatory rhetoric this seems much more probable than simply to assume that the opponents "combined scepticism with the parousia with moral libertinism."[109]

---

[108] As noted above, this was particularly common in the ancient polemics against Epicureans.

[109] Thus Bauckham, "2 Peter: An Account of Research" (n. 19), 3724, and similarly numerous interpreters.

5. Afterthoughts: Immoral Usage of Moral Language?

Theologically our author is convinced (from Jude and other writings) that the judgment on the ungodly is predetermined. Teachers who nourish scepticism against the validity of biblical prophecy and against the early Christian tradition, denying the hope for the parousia and questioning the salvific power and activity of God, cannot share the divine nature and escape the corruptible world but will face a severe judgment. He is also convinced that apostasy of people once converted makes their situation even worse than it was before. Thus, the opponents are, in his view, a dangerous challenge that requires all possible efforts to be refuted – predominantly by theological and moral argument.

For the sake of protecting his audience against the intellectual fascination of their views, our author is able to take up their argument and counter it in a creative manner. No other New Testament writer develops such a detailed cosmological view as the author of Second Peter does. He counters the scepticism of the opponents with a combination of the Stoic idea of a final destruction of the world by fire (ἐκπύρωσις) with the biblical tradition of the antidiluvian, the present, and a future "heaven and earth" (2 Pet 3:3–13). His eschatological argument is an interesting example of inculturation of the early Christian hope into a thoroughly Hellenistic world of ideas. In these respects, the theological qualities of our author should not be underestimated.[110]

We do not know whether the author's refutation might have convinced the sceptics, or even those of his addressees who were inclined to follow them. Presumably being aware of these difficulties, he chose his rhetorical devices: not only a very daring pseudonymous legitimation, the fiction of the apostle Peter writing his testament, but also a thorough disparagement of his opponents before entering the argument with them or even mentioning their views. Thus, the disparagement of the opponents in 2 Peter 2 serves as an additional "argument" in the theological struggle for the eschatological expectation and the "true" apostolic teaching.

Such an "argument" is, of course, very questionable, historically, theologically and also morally. It is a historical fabrication of the author's persona and the opponents' character. Theologically, it does not really contribute to the task of refuting the opponents' views. But the moral questions are most urgent: the idea cannot be easily dismissed that such a polemical

---

[110] Therefore, some of the criticism of Second Peter in New Testament scholarship as expressed, e.g., by Ernst Käsemann, seems to be quite inappropriate. Cf. Käsemann, "Apologia" (n. 2), 169–195. On the eschatology of Second Peter see also Frey, "Judgment on the Ungodly and the Parousia of Christ" (n. 12).

rhetoric is far away from the Gospel's call for love for one's neighbours or even enemies.

Some interpreters might feel the apologetical duty to protect our author (and other biblical authors) against undue and anachronistic moral charges.[111] Often the case is smoothened down by historical and rhetorical arguments: polemic vilification of opponents was a customary rhetorical device in antiquity (as it is still in many modern contexts), among Jews and Gentiles,[112] so why should it be different among rivaling Christian groups? But is the vilification of the opponents just "mere" rhetoric in the sense that nobody who was familiar with the communicative "code" really took seriously what was actually said? Should we just explain the texts as examples of an ancient polemical convention? Of course, the addressees did not consider the opponents to be animals, but the comparison with unclean animals had its vilificatory force, and the series of abuses of the opponents and the curse on them should not be belittled too early. In 2 Peter 2, "moral language" and high moral claims are used for rather immoral purposes.

The contextualization of such texts within the polemical rhetoric of antiquity is certainly helpful and necessary for a better understanding of the forms and functions of these texts.[113] It excludes an anachronistic reading from modern ethical viewpoints shaped by humanism, pluralism and postmodernism, and it can also prevent the abuse of these "dangerous" texts for polemical purposes in current theological and ethical debates. This is quite important for any use of the Bible that tries to meet ethical standards.

However, a theologically responsible and ethically sensitive interpretation cannot stop here. We must at least allow for the insight that within Christian theology, and even within the biblical canon, there are texts with an inhuman and destructive force which call for a critical interpretation instead of emulation. This is often admitted in view of the anti-Jewish polemics in 1 Thess 2:14–16, in John 8, or in Revelation, or for some of the antifeminist texts such as 1 Cor 14:34 or 1 Tim 2:12–15, but is definitively needed for the fierce disparagement of the opponents in 2 Peter 2 and other

---

[111] I am especially grateful to Jan van der Watt and Friedrich Wilhelm Horn for the challenge to reformulate and even sharpen this paragraph.

[112] Such a kind of apologetics is quite often used in view of the problematic passages of biblical texts, e.g. the Anti-Jewish polemics in the Gospel of John and elsewhere; cf. Johnson, "Anti-Jewish Slander" (n. 5), 441.

[113] A comprehensive history of early Christian polemics within the context of ancient polemics is still to be written. Cf., most recently, the interesting work by Jeremy F. Hultin, *The Ethics of Obscene Speech in Early Christianity and Its Environment* (NovTSup 128; Leiden: Brill, 2008).

polemical texts as well. In this, Ernst Käsemann was right:[114] there is theological reason for canonical criticism and for the distinction between right and wrong within the biblical canon. 2 Peter 2 with its extreme mode of dehumanizing polemics offers a striking example of Scripture that we must learn not to imitate.

---

[114] Cf. his collection *Das Neue Testament als Kanon* (ed. Ernst Käsemann, Göttingen: Vandenhoeck & Ruprecht, 1970) and numerous of his articles in idem, *Exegetische Versuche und Besinnungen* (2 vols.; Göttingen: Vandenhoeck & Ruprecht, 1960/1964); partly translated into English in idem, *Essays on New Testament Themes* (London: SCM, 1964).

Some Possible Intertextual Influences from the Jewish Scriptures on the (Moral) Language of Hebrews

GERT J. STEYN

"By three things the world is sustained: by the [study of] law, by worship,
and by deeds of charity"
(Simon the Just; *Aboth* 1.2)

"For whatever was written in former days was written for our instruction, so that by
steadfastness and by the encouragement of the scriptures we might have hope" (Paul;
Rom 15:4)

1. Introduction

Religion and morality were in general not closely associated with each other in the Greek world.[1] Judaism and Christianity, however, connected ethics and religion based on divine revelation.[2] Early Judaism and early Christianity stood in a tradition of divine revelation which was transmitted via the oral and written traditions of those religions. It can thus be assumed that the Jewish Scriptures and their interpretation would play an important role on an intertextual level during the writing of (moral) texts. The book of Hebrews is a good example in this regard. It is an early Christian document that interacts with the tradition of divine revelation in the light of the Christ-event (cf. Heb 1:1–4), as well as making an appeal on the behaviour of its readers in the light of that Christ-event as divine revelation. It connects ethics and religion. Similar to some of the other epistolary[3] literature in the NT, one might identify doctrinal ("indicative") and ethical ("imperative") sections in Hebrews. It presents a perspective on the theoretical-confessional basis of the early Christian religion on the one hand (Heb 1:1–10:31), followed by a practical-instructional part which presents the expectation of a lifestyle that is in accordance with the religious beliefs on

---

[1] "Consciousness of sin was not so acute nor was there a desire for a new ethical life" (Everett Ferguson, *Backgrounds of Early Christianity* [2nd ed.; Grand Rapids: Eerdmans, 1993], 281).

[2] Cf. Ferguson, *Backgrounds* (n. 1), 165.

[3] With this statement it is definitely *not* implied that *Ad Hebraeos* should be typified as "a letter" or "an epistle." It should rather be taken as a sermon.

the other hand (Heb 10:32–13:22). The role of the Scriptures as *divine revelation* in both these parts is undeniably prominent. Almost all the explicit quotations, for instance, are introduced with a verb of *saying* and are connected to a *"promise"* (ἐπαγγελία) of God. It is thus God who "speaks" through Scripture.

However, apart from the written tradition of the divine revelation, also the oral tradition of that revelation played an important role. The retelling of the stories of religious heroes from the past from one generation to the next, as well as the collective memory of the Jewish people as celebrated during the Jewish festivals (where Scripture also featured prominently), provided examples for the religio-ethical lifestyle of the current generation. One of the best examples in this regard is Heb 11 – not only in Hebrews, but also in the whole of the NT.

The intention of this study is then to investigate the role of three areas of possible intertextual influences on the moral language of Hebrews pertaining to the Jewish Scriptures. "Moral language" is taken here in its widest sense, namely in the sense of the expected virtuous or pious behaviour of its readers and not in the narrow sense of morality (chastity) only. Attention will firstly be paid to the possible intertextual influences from the *moral language of the Decalogue* and other laws on the language and theology of Hebrews. Secondly, the list of narrative intertexts of the *commemoratio* of Heb 10–12 will be investigated. Thirdly, two of the maxim-like ethical formulas of Heb 13 will be studied against the backdrop of the Jewish festival traditions with its intertextual Scriptural connections.

2. Possible Intertextual Influences from the Moral Language of the Decalogue and other Laws on the Language and Theology of Hebrews

It seems likely that the author of Hebrews might have included different elements from Deut 4 and Deut 9 (including the quotation from Deut 9:19) into the broader context of his argument. "Both experiences happen at Mount Sinai (4:11; 9:8), and both focus on the Ten Commandments (4:13; 9:9–11). In both passages the mountain burns with fire (4:11; 9:15), and Moses speaks with the Lord (4:14; 9:19)."[4] The author of Hebrews composes the narrative about the events at Sinai in Heb 12:18–25 from his own perspective by selecting different elements from different episodes and

---

[4] George H. Guthrie, "Hebrews in Its First-Century Contexts," in *The Face of New Testament Studies: A Survey of Recent Research* (ed. Scot McKnight and Grant R. Osborne; Grand Rapids, Mich.: Baker Academic, 2004), 988.

conflating phrases from different narratives. The event of receiving the law on Sinai during the old compensation through the mediation of Moses, is now contrasted by the author of Hebrews with the event of those who gathered on Mount Zion, who arrived at the "congregation of the firstborn" (ἐκκλησία πρωτοτόκων, 12:23), and who came to Jesus the mediator of a new covenant (διαθήκης νέας μεσίτῃ Ἰησοῦ, 12:24). It is to be expected then, against the backdrop of this contrast between the old covenant and the new covenant, that a different interpretation of the Mosaic Law would feature in the light of the Jesus-event. The divine revelation within the Jewish history is now being re-interpreted by early Christianity in terms of Christ.

2.1 Possible Intertextual Connections with the Decalogue

One should thus be able to detect the contrast between the old dispensation and the new in the manner in which the Decalogue surfaces in the language and theology of Hebrews. It would, therefore, be appropriate to compare – as a test case – each of the Ten Commandments (the Deuteronomy 5 version is chosen here) with Hebrews.

1st Commandment: No other God
(οὐκ ἔσονταί σοι θεοὶ ἕτεροι πρὸ προσώπου μου, Deut 5:7)

The first commandment expected Jews not to worship any other God. The God of Israel holds the ultimate position for them as Eternal Being, Creator, Ruler, King and Judge. There is no other God like him and he alone should be worshiped as the sole divine entity of this people. Early Christianity understood the status of Jesus as post-Easter, resurrected and exalted Christ to be equal to the God of Israel. In Hebrews the author acknowledges the Son on the same level as King, Ruler, Judge, Creator, Eternal Being, who takes the position at the right hand of God's throne (Heb 1:8–13). Some of the explicit quotations listed here underline the exalted status of the Son (e.g. Ps 45:7–8; Ps 102:26–28; Ps 110:1). The very nature of God is described in Deut 4:24 as being like a consuming fire – a quotation being referred to by the author of Hebrews in Heb 12:29. Already in the beginning of his document, the author of Hebrews stated: "The Son radiates the glory of God and that he is the exact representation of the being of God" (Heb 1:3). When Moses blesses the Israelites before his death in Deut 33, he describes how the Lord comes down from Sinai, from the place where tens of thousands of angels live, where they have a place at his right hand (Deut 33:2). Moses says to Jeshurun that there is no one like God. He rides through the heavens in order to help Jeshurun. He rides on the clouds in his majesty (Deut 33:26). The author of Hebrews, in turn, describes how Christ went into heaven itself in order to appear before

God (Heb 9:24) and how his readers were coming to mount Zion and the city of the living God, the heavenly Jerusalem with its millions of angels (Heb 12:22). They came to God who is the Judge of all (Heb 12:23) because all are accountable to him (4:13), his is an eternal judgment (6:2) and it is his right to punish and to judge. The royal and judicial roles ascribed to Christ in Hebrews should be understood within the broader context of the book and its expectation of moral behaviour that displays perseverance in suffering, which ultimately leads to reward or rejection by God (cf. Heb 10:26–31, 38–39; 11:6, 16; 12:22–29).

2nd Commandment: Idolatry
(οὐ ποιήσεις σεαυτῷ εἴδωλον, Deut 5:8)

The second commandment expected Jews not to worship any idols. In Heb 12:15 a lengthy allusion (not a quotation) is found to the phrase "root of bitterness," which occurs also in Deut 29:(17)18. The phrase "root of bitterness" there in Deut 29:(17)18 refers to the Israelites who had become involved in idolatry. "The 'root of bitterness' parallels the developing of a hardened, unbelieving heart in Hebrews 3:12 and includes leading others to withdraw from the community into apostasy."[5] If this is true, then part of this apostasy might have been a skewed Christology in which the Son was seen merely as an angel, i.e. as just another "son of God."[6] This apostasy might even imply, although yet unproven, the possibility of angel worship by the readers of Hebrews. The allusion to angels as the heavenly mediators of the old revelation (Heb 2:2) is hinted at in Deut 33:2.[7] However, for the author of Hebrews the Son is the image of God (1:3), he is different than the angels (1:4) and the future world is submitted to him (2:5–9). The angels should in fact worship him (1:6).

3rd Commandment: The Name of God
(οὐ λήμψῃ τὸ ὄνομα κυρίου τοῦ θεοῦ σου, Deut 5:11)

The third commandment expected Jews to revere the Name of God. The author of Hebrews holds the "Name" in reverence on two levels. On the one level the *Name of God* is honoured. Jesus declares those who are holy

---

[5]   Thomas K. Oberholtzer, "The Failure to Heed His Speaking in Hebrews 12:25–29. Part 5 of The Warning Passages in Hebrews," *Bib Sac* 146/581 (1989): 67–75, 68.

[6]   Cf. Gert J. Steyn, "Addressing an angelomorphic christological myth in Hebrews?," *HTS* 59/4 (2003): 1107–1128.

[7]   According to Martin and Davids, it gained acceptance sometime prior to the first century and spread among the Hellenistic Jews with traces to be seen in Acts 7:38, 53; Gal 3:19; Josephus *Ant.* 15.5.3 §136. Ralph P. Martin and Peter H. Davids, *Dictionary of the Later New Testament and Its Developments* (Leicester: InterVarsity Press, 1997) electronic edition.

to be his brothers (2:11). By using Ps 22:23 he indicates that he will make the Name of God known amongst his brothers (2:12). The connection between the readers' moral behaviour and the Name of God is stated later when the author mentions that the believers have shown their love for God's Name by serving each other (6:10) and they are encouraged to continue bringing a sacrifice of praise to God by glorifying God with lips that confess his Name (13:15).

On another level, the *Name of the Son* is linked to his exalted status as described particularly in Hebrews 1. The fact that the author of Hebrews states that the name of the Son (given to him by God) is different than the name of the angels (1:4), might be another indication of the possible confusion by the readers with Jesus as the Son of God and the angels who were also called "sons of God."

4th Commandment: The Sabbath
(φύλαξαι τὴν ἡμέραν τῶν σαββάτων, Deut 5:12)

The fourth commandment expected Jews to honour the Sabbath as a day of "rest." When looking at Heb 3:7–4:11 and the prominence of the motif of "rest" (τὴν κατάπαυσιν, Heb 3:18; σαββατισμός, Heb 4:9), which is mainly based on the long quotation from Ps 95:7–11 and its interpretation by the author, one becomes aware of the possibility that either the author, or his readers (or both), were converts from a group that held the Sabbath in high regard. Two keywords used by the author of Hebrews within this motif are κατάπαυσιν and σήμερον. Both these are playing also a prominent role in Deuteronomy. For σήμερον compare, for instance, Deut 11:2, 8; 29:9, 14 and for κατάπαυσιν compare Deut 12:8–9. One cannot argue in favour of the author's reliance on Deuteronomy for these motifs, as they are clearly based on the author's use and application of Ps 95. However, implied familiarity with these from his Jewish background cannot be ruled out.

The motif itself is firmly rooted in the importance of the Sabbath as such and substantiated on the basis of God who rested on the seventh day after he created everything. This same motivation – that God rested on the seventh day – is to be found in the quotation from Gen 2:2.[8] In Hebrews the "rest" becomes an ultimate goal for the believers who are journeying towards it. It is meant to be a place, a period, or both, and it is the reward only of those who are obedient (Heb 4:6, 11) and who persevere to the end (Heb 4:3).[9]

---

[8] Cf. Gert J. Steyn, "A Note on the *Vorlage* of the Citation from Gen 2, 2 in Heb 4, 4," *Ekklesiastikos Pharos* (2002): 43–50.

[9] See also Heb 3:12, 14; 4:1.

5th Commandment: Honour your father and mother
(τίμα τὸν πατέρα σου καὶ τὴν μητέρα σου, Deut 5:16)

The fifth commandment expected Jews to honour their parents. The "parental" relationship between God and his Son represents a relationship of mutual respect in Hebrews. God acknowledged the Son as *his* Son and himself as the Son's *Father* (1:5). Christ as Son, in turn, is faithful to the house of God (3:6). God gave Jesus the *Sonship* (as high priest) and Jesus honoured God as *Father* (5:5–10). On another level, Jesus stated his position regarding the *children* granted to him (2:13–14). In Heb 12:4–12 the author deals with the relationship between God and the believers whom he adopted as his *children*. Those adopted by God as his *children*, he also tests (12:6 – quoted from Prov 3:11–12). The metaphorical connection between a father disciplining his children and the experience of trying times by believers as God's instruction of his children was already well established in the tradition by the time that Hebrews was written. Although the author is clearly dealing with the theodicy problem,[10] he utilises this known notion from the Jewish sapiential literature to interpret the difficult times of his recipients in the light of Scripture.[11] It is presented as if these are the direct words of God to them, hence encouraging them that what they experience is not a sign of God's rejection, but of his love and involvement.[12] They are personally addressed as "son(s)" (similar to Heb 2:10), putting their relationship with God in the same perspective as that between Christ (Son) and God (Father) as became clear from Heb 1–2. Trying times, difficulties or suffering, are thus perceived to be normal within the parent-child relationship where instruction, guidance and discipline takes place.[13] To be tested as God's children presupposes moral be-

---

[10] Erich Gräßer, *An die Hebräer: 3. Teilband: Hebr 10,19–13,25* (EKKNT 17/3; Neukirchen: Neukirchener Verlag, 1997), 257. Cf. also Hendrik van Oyen, who has an interesting perspective on this matter: "Het is niet waarschijnlijk (tegen vele patristische en ook nieuwere exegeten) bij de woorden 'niet ten bloede' te denken aan de mogelijkheid, dat de gemeente nog geen bloedige vervolgingen te verduren heeft gehad; de bedoeling moet wel zijn, dat zij zelf nog niet als de worstelaar in het stadion tot op het bloed de kamp heeft doorstaan ..." (*De bief aan de Hebreeën* [Nijkerk: Callenbach, 1962], 220, 221)

[11] Gerd Schunack, *Hebräerbrief* (ZBKNT 14; Zurich: Theologischer Verlag, 2002), 197.

[12] Cf. Schunack, *Hebräerbrief* (n. 11), 197: "Das als Züchtigung Gottes verstandene Leiden ist nicht Erfahrung heilloser Ferne von Gott, sondern Erfahrung der Nähe und liebenden Zuwendung Gottes zu Söhnen, die als Brüder des Sohns zum Heil bestimmt wird." Similar August Strobel, *Der Brief an die Hebräer* (NTD 9,2; 13th ed.; Göttingen: Vandenhoeck and Ruprecht, 1991), 232, 233.

[13] Robert M. Wilson, *Hebrews* (NCB; Grand Rapids, Mich.: Eerdmans, 1987), 22: "we must remember that in the ancient world a father's word was law within the family, his authority absolute."

haviour of honour and obedience within the context of the fifth commandment.

6th Commandment: Commit no adultery
(οὐ μοιχεύσεις, Deut 5:17)

The sixth commandment expected Jews to honour marriage. First century Jews, such as Josephus (on discussing the Jewish precepts), included sanctity of marriage.[14] Heb 13:4 picks up the same motif. It briefly refers to the state of marriage and that it ought to be honoured by all. Faithfulness to each other is emphasised because those who are unfaithful, "the adulterer and all those who are sexually immoral," will be judged by God. The maxim, or principle, is presented to the new covenant community. It should be one of their identity markers.

7th Commandment: Commit no murder
(οὐ φονεύσεις, Deut 5:18)

The seventh commandment expected Jews not to commit murder. This is clearly not an aspect that the author of Hebrews touches upon with regard to the behaviour of its readers. Nonetheless, the book makes it clear that through the death of Jesus, the one who has the power of death (i.e. the devil) is conquered, so that those in slavery of the fear of death are being set free (Heb 2:14–15). If people persist in their old lifestyle after having being converted, they crucify Christ again (Heb 6:4–6) – which actually makes them murderers in the most serious degree.

8th Commandment: Do not steal
(οὐ κλέψεις, Deut 5:19)

The eighth commandment expected Jews not to steal. Although the issue of theft as such does not receive attention from the author of Hebrews, the related aspect of greed and mutual sharing amongst each other is referred to in Heb 13:16. This is the same motif as that of Deut 15:7–8, 10–11 where an attitude of sharing amongst each other is expected as an identity marker of this new covenant community.

9th Commandment: No false oath
(οὐ ψευδομαρτυρήσεις, Deut 5:20)

The ninth commandment expected Jews not to engage in the swearing of false oaths. In Heb 6:16 the author makes reference to human oaths. Within the author's typical style of contrasts, the ultimate oath – that of God

---

[14] Cf. Josephus *C. Ap.*; cf. Ferguson, *Backgrounds* (n. 1), 457.

made by Himself – is now contrasted with these human oaths (Heb 6:17–18).

10th Commandment: Do not envy
(οὐκ ἐπιθυμήσεις, Deut 5:21)

The tenth commandment expected from believers not to envy the possessions of others. Hebrews, again, picks up on this motif: "Keep your lives free from the love of money and be content with what you have"[15] is what the author urges his readers to do (Heb 13:5–6). This directive is explicitly linked with a quotation from Deut 31:6 or Jos 1:5. The quotation already appeared by Philo of Alexandria in his *De confusione linguarum* 166. The intertextual connections of this principle might actually go back to the Jewish festival tradition – a matter that we will return to at the end of this paper.

2.2 Examples of Intertextual Connections with some other Laws and Instructions

(a) *The position of strangers:* Deuteronomy honours and protects the position of strangers or aliens (10:18–19; 24:17; 25:5; 27:19). Josephus takes a similar position on hospitality[16] – and so does the author of Hebrews (Heb 13:1–2: τῆς φιλοξενίας μὴ ἐπιλανθάνεσθε). This attitude of hospitality towards others was also a well-established expectation within the early Christian tradition.[17] Apart from Heb 13:2, it is also used in Rom 12:13 and again within a paraenetic context.[18] The same moral expectation is noticeable in other early Christian intertexts, such as in Rom 16:33; 1 Tim 3:2; Tit 1:8; 1 Pet 4:9; 2 John 10; 3 John 5–8; 1 Clem 10–12; Didache 11–13.

(b) *The number of witnesses:* According to references such as Deut 17:6[19] (with similar intertexts Deut 19:15 and Num 35:30)[20] execution can

---

[15]   Cf. also Matt 6:24 (Luke 16:13) and Matt 6:31–34 (Luke 12:29–32).

[16]   Cf. Josephus *C. Ap.* 1.2–3 on hospitality; cf. Ferguson, *Backgrounds* (n. 1), 457.

[17]   Ferguson summarises the important place that hospitality occupied in early Christianity, as "the needs of missionaries and messengers of the churches provided an extended family, giving lodging and assistance for the journey. Christians here followed and expanded a Jewish practice of caring for their own way from home (cf. Mark 6:10). Many synagogues had guest rooms attached for the use of Jews on a journey" (Ferguson, *Backgrounds* [n. 1], 82).

[18]   Horst Balz and Gerhard Schneider (eds.), *Exegetical Dictionary of the New Testament* (vol. 3; Grand Rapids: Eerdmans, 1993), 427.

[19]   Paul Ellingworth, *The Epistle to the Hebrews* (NIGTC; Grand Rapids, Mich.: Eerdmans, 2000), 537.

[20]   Gräßer refers to these three localities for the law about two or more witnesses, but states: "Hebr zieht aber ausdrücklich Dtn 17,6 in Verbindung mit Num 15,30 heran: Auf

take place on the testimony of two or three witnesses, an issue alluded to by the author of Hebrews in 10:28 with regard to the "law of Moses" (νόμον Μωϋσέως).[21]

3. Narrative Intertexts from the *Commemoratios* of Heb 10:32–12:24 and a Lifestyle of Perseverance

Heb 10:32–39 presents a general summary, or overall conclusion, to the third part of the book, namely Heb 5:11–10:39.[22] The author first lets his readers look back into the *past* by taking them on a commemorative tour of their own history. He refers to their own past and how they remained strong in difficult times. This *commemoratio* is based on narrative intertexts from early Christianity and contained mainly in the oral tradition. Then the author moves to the *present* and reminds them about the two aspects that they need to embrace: faith and perseverance. Hereafter the author reminds them about the *future* reward which is to follow on a lifestyle of faith and perseverance.[23]

This cycle of past, present and future is repeated for a second time in Heb 11–12. This time the commemorative tour of the *past* goes far beyond their own history to that of their ancestors (Heb 11). This *commemoratio* is exclusively based on narrative intertexts from Jewish history (probably including that of Maccabean times) and contained in the Jewish Scriptures. Against that historical-theological perspective, the author encourages his readers in their *present* situation. Although they have to suffer, they should see this as education by God which takes place through discipline (Heb 12:7) and they fix their eyes on Jesus "the Author and Perfecter of their faith," who himself is now sitting on the right hand of God's throne (12:2). The author then lets them peer into the future by providing them with an eschatological-apocalyptic view of where their destination is – with the Living God Himself (12:22–24).

Todesstrafe darf nur erkannt werden, wenn die Tat durch zwei oder drei Zeugen erwiesen ist" (Gräßer, *Hebräer III* [n. 10], 43).

[21] Ellingworth, *Hebrews* (n. 19), 537.

[22] Albert Vanhoye, *Situation du Christ: épître aux Hébreux 1–2* (Lectio Divina 58; Paris: Cerf, 1969), 115–182; Ellingworth, *Hebrews* (n. 19), 552.

[23] Cf. the beatitudes in Matt 5 where the same phenomenon occurs.

3.1 The First Cycle

3.1.1 The Past (Commemoratio: Heb 10:32–34)

Heb 10:32 begins thus with an appeal to its readers to recall the past days in remembrance: "remember those earlier days ..." The *commemoratio* recalls the past behaviour of early Christianity and serves to encourage them to persevere with this attitude in their present circumstances. The author reminds them about a number of past events:

–   *"They stood their ground in a great contest in the face of suffering"* (10:32). It is clear that the believers found themselves in a time of suffering. What is unclear is which period this might have been. If it is assumed that the readers found themselves in Rome and that the book could be dated in the late 80s or beginning of the 90s. If so, then Hebrews could possibly refer to the time of persecution under the rule of Domitian (81–96 A.D.). However, already since the decree of Claudius was issued in 49 A.D., instructing that all Jews should leave Rome (when also Aquila and Priscilla left), Christians experienced difficult times – as they were seen as being just another Jewish sect.

–   *Publicly exposed to insult and persecution* (10:33). The Roman writer, Tacitus, reported how Christians "were clad in the hides of beasts and torn to death by dogs; others were crucified, others set on fire to serve to illuminate the night when daylight failed" (*Ann.* 15.44) during the Neronian persecution.

–   *Siding with those who were persecuted* (10:33). This aspect is mentioned in a positive manner as part of the believers' Christian lifestyle of the *past*. The author will return to this behaviour, which is expected from them in 13:3 when they are called in the *present* to "remember those in prison as if you were their fellow prisoners."

–   *Sympathysing with those in prison* (10:34). Yet again another positive remark is made regarding the behaviour of the believers in the *past* – which would have resounded in their ears when he later calls on them to remember those in prison (13:3) – which probably refers here to Christian believers who were in prison because of their faith. These prisoners were dependent on family and friends for their emotional and material needs.

–   *Joyfully accepting the confiscation of their property because they knew they had better and lasting possessions* (10:34). The confiscation of property was a well-known Roman punishment in more serious cases of resistance. Important to notice here is the connection between perseverance in present suffering in the light of a future reward and permanence.

3.1.2 The Present (Heb 10:35–39): Continue with the Good Behaviour of the Past

Three aspects are highlighted in the following section (10:35–39) which appeals now to their present behaviour in the light of their past: confidence (παρρησία), perseverance (ὑπομονή) and faith (πίστις). This encapsulates the general attitude, or behaviour, that the author wants to convey to his readers.[24] Both confidence and perseverance ultimately lead to reward: "so do not throw away your confidence; it will be richly awarded. You need to persevere so that when you have done the will of God, you will receive what he has promised" (vv. 35–36). The reward is the salvivic gift of life.[25] It is not of the *earth* or of a material nature, but of *heaven* and of an eternal nature (10:34), it is a promise (10:36), is given by God (11:6) and consists of life with God.[26] Furthermore, the first of these parallel statements is rhetorically presented in a negative format and the second in the positive.

(a) Do not throw away our confidence (negative) (10:35)
The word for confidence (παρρησία) already surfaced in Heb 3:6; 4:16; and 10:19. It was used in the first instance in the general sense of "holding on to their courage," whereas in the latter two instances they are encouraged to "approach the throne with confidence." It is used here in 10:35 (the negative: "do not throw away") in a similar manner as in 3:6 (the positive: "hold on to"). The "possession" (their promise) should thus be treasured and not be "thrown away" like something that is worthless.[27] It carries a futuristic eschatological accent, being the gift of salvation and the eternal reward (cf. 9:15),[28] but also a present realised dimension, being a free gift that Christians already received.[29] Thus, what is at stake here is the attitude, or behaviour, of Christians in this world, the security of God's salvation and the public confession in the midst of suffering.[30]

---

[24] Harold W. Attridge, *The Epistle to the Hebrews: A commentary on the Epistle to the Hebrews* (Hermeneia; Philadelphia, Pa.: Fortress Press, 1989), 300. Gräßer reckons that perseverance (*upomone*) is the gesture of confidence (*parresia*) in times of suffering (*Hebräer III* [n. 10], 73).

[25] Schunack, *Hebräerbrief* (n. 11), 157.

[26] Ellingworth, *Hebrews* (n. 19), 551.

[27] Hans-Friedrich Weiß, *Der Brief an die Hebräer* (KEK 13; Göttingen: Vandenhoeck & Ruprecht, 1991), 546.

[28] See also Gräßer, *Hebräer III* (n. 10), 71.

[29] Weiß, *Hebräer* (n. 27), 547.

[30] Frederick F. Bruce, *The Epistle to the Hebrews* (NICNT; Grand Rapids, Mich.: Eerdmans, 2007), 270; Attridge, *Hebrews* (n. 24), 300.

(b) You need to persevere (positive) (10:36)

The virtue of perseverance (ὑπομονή) was also praised in non-Christian literature.[31] The connection with perseverance in suffering, however, was typical of Christian literature and recalled the suffering and death of Christ.[32] The implied intention of this statement is that God's promises are made to all, but that it is only realised in those who persevere to the end.[33] Thus, it is salvation through *perseverance* in faith. In retrospection the believers did show an attitude of perseverance in the past (cf. Heb 10:32). Now, however, the perspective is towards their present and future behaviour.[34] They are encouraged, on the one hand, by looking back at their own history, but also by the example of Jesus himself who endured his suffering and was rewarded.[35] Perseverance means here to continue to be obedient,[36] faithful and dedicated until the end in the actions of Christian discipleship.[37]

The readers need to be patient, loyal and not give up. They should not stop *doing* God's will,[38] as God will fulfil his promise and they will share in extreme joy. "Patience" should be understood in the light of the classical Greek literature where characters such as Heracles and Odysseus displayed *active* perseverance in the midst of the actions of their gods.[39] The focal point is an *ethically* directed and brave steadfastness in the midst of opposition and threats. This patience is not without purpose.[40] It is closely connected with actively doing the will of God[41] as an expression of patiently waiting[42] for the eschatological fulfilment of God's promises. It deals with faithfulness that is rewarded and with hope that is fulfilled.[43]

There is thus ultimately a close connection between "perseverance" and "faith,"[44] between behaviour and belief, ethics and doctrine in Hebrews. This is an important difference with regard to Paul where those who merely *believe* are saved (Rom 1:17; Gal 3:11). In Hebrews only those who actively *persevere* in their faith are saved. It is interesting that also Mark and

---

[31] Cf. Seneca, *Lucil.* 5.67.10.

[32] Ellingworth, *Hebrews* (n. 19), 552.

[33] Ellingworth, *Hebrews* (n. 19), 551.

[34] Attridge, *Hebrews* (n. 24), 301; Ellingworth, *Hebrews* (n. 19), 552.

[35] Attridge, *Hebrews* (n. 24), 301.

[36] Andrie B. Du Toit, *Hebreërs vir vandag. 'n Bybelstudie vir dieper delwers* (Vereeniging: CUM, 2002), 182.

[37] Ellingworth, *Hebrews* (n. 19), 553.

[38] Bruce, *Hebrews* (n. 30), 271.

[39] Gräßer, *Hebräer III* (n. 10), 73.

[40] Gräßer *Hebräer III* (n. 10), 71.

[41] Schunack, *Hebräerbrief* (n. 11), 157.

[42] Weiß, *Hebräer* (n. 27), 548.

[43] Gräßer, *Hebräer III* (n. 10), 71.

[44] Attridge, *Hebrews* (n. 24), 301

Matthew (60s–70s A.D.) emphasised salvation rather on the basis of *perseverance* in faith until the end (cf. Mk 13:13; Mt 24:13), than salvation based on faith only. It is then especially on these aspects that the author of Hebrews expands upon in chapter 11.

3.2 The Second Cycle

3.2.1 The Past (Commemoratio: Heb 11)

The second cycle starts with a long list of examples from history of how perseverance in faith often resulted in behaviour that exceeds what is comprehensible. The list is a presentation of narrative intertexts from Jewish history and a commemoration of the exemplary behaviour of each of the characters.[45] Each of these exemplary faith characters is introduced with πίστει. Their behaviour – what they have *done* or achieved – is the direct result of their faith according to Hebrews. Thus, the list is proof that true faith leads to obedient behaviour despite the fact that its results often cannot be seen immediately. The author describes the persevering qualities and continuing actions of this faith without perceiving immediate results. The actions for which these characters are remembered are thus directly connected with the fact that they believed.

Heb 11:4–7: in three great leaps the author deals with the periods of *Abel, Enoch and Noah*. The tenor of the three examples is a dedicated life to God. The sincerity (δίκαιος) of Abel, pleasingness (εὐάρεστος) of Enoch, and the devoutness (εὐλαβής) of Noah – as desired by God – distinguished these persons from their contemporaries. The author includes his own theological commentary between the references to Enoch and Noah: "and without faith, it is impossible to please God" (11:6).

Heb 11:8–16: in Heb 11:8–12 the story of the patriarch *Abraham* and his wife Sarah is presented. The author gives his own theological commentary on this in 11:13–16. These examples present blind faith, because Abraham "obeyed (ὑπήκουσεν) without knowing where he was going" (11:8) and they died "without receiving the things promised" (11:13).

Heb 11:17–22: the *patriarchs* (Abraham, Isaac and Jacob) are listed together with Joseph. The tenor here is that God's promises for the future have to be trusted. All these cases deal with an act of faith in the shadow of death. Abraham was prepared to offer Isaac as a sacrifice when he was tested by God (11:17). Isaac blessed his sons on his deathbed (11:20), and so did Jacob with the sons of Joseph as he was praying to God (11:21). Joseph, in turn, gave instructions about his bones.

---

[45] "The customs of the ancestors (*mos maiorum*) were even more binding in Rome than in Greece" (Ferguson, *Backgrounds* [n. 1], 160).

Heb 11:23–31: in this section follows the *period of Moses'* parents, himself, the Israelites and their Exodus from Egypt up to their investigation of the Promised Land. Very interesting is the inclusion here of the name Rahab, the prostitute, who helped the spies and whose life is finally saved during the entry of the Israelites. The tenor of this phase in the history of Israel is that the faith heroes had another view on life. Moses' parents "were not afraid" (οὐκ ἐφοβήθησαν, 11:23). Moses "chose to be ill-treated along with the people of God rather than to enjoy the pleasures of sin for a short time" (συγκακουχεῖσθαι τῷ λαῷ τοῦ θεοῦ ἢ πρόσκαιρον ἔχειν ἁμαρτίας ἀπόλαυσιν, 11:25). He "regarded disgrace," left Egypt not fearing (μὴ φοβηθείς) the Pharaoh's anger, "perservered (ἐκαρτέρησεν) because he saw him who is invisible" (11:26–27), and "kept the Passover" (πεποίηκεν τὸ πάσχα, 11:28). The Israelites moved through the Red Sea as if over dry land (11:28) and the prostitute Rahab welcomed the spies (11:31).

Heb 11:32–38: the author now refers in broad lines to the periods of the *Judges* (Gideon, Barak, Samson and Jephtah), the *kings* (David and Samuel/Solomon) and the *prophets* (without anyone here being singled out by name). In even broader lines he now moves on in history without listing any names, but only events. If the readers knew the history of the Jewish people, then they would have had a good idea what he is referring to. The scene moves almost unnotably further to the recent history when he refers to "others" (ἕτεροι δέ) and their martyrdom, jeers, flogging and imprisonment (11:35–38). The golden thread of believers who persevered in their faith thus runs through history. They are commended for their faith and presented by the author as examples who continued to trust God's promises, despite the fact that they had not received what was promised to them during their lifetimes.

3.2.2 The Present

After the commemoration of the ancestors, the author now appeals to his readers to stay focused in the present in their current circumstances. After their insight into the past through those retrospective lenses are they now practically advised for the present in which they find themselves. Modelled on the metaphor of an athlete running a race, they are encouraged to throw off everything (including sin) that hinders them, to run the race with perseverance, and to keep the eyes fixed on Jesus as the ultimate role model (12:1–3). In doing so they will not grow weary and lose heart (12:3).

The readers find themselves actually in position of struggling against sin (12:4). This hardship should be endured as discipline (12:7). It is proof of God treating them as his children, because he "disciplines those whom he loves" (12:6 as part of the quotation from Prov 3:11–12). Once again, as with a number of quotations in Hebrews, one also finds here a midrash on

Prov 3:11–12 in Heb 12:7–11. He uses two key concepts from his quotation on which he now elaborates: παιδείαν/παιδεύει[46] and υἱός. The latter occurs three times in this brief commentary (vv. 7, 8), the former (either the noun or the verb) five times (vv. 7, 8, 10, 11), plus the noun παιδευτής (v. 9). The meaning is probably closer along Jewish wisdom lines, than along the classic Greek training lines.[47] The author summons the readers against this background to let go of their sluggish behaviour: "strengthen your feeble arms and weak knees! Make level paths for your feet, so that the lame may not be disabled, but rather healed" (12:12–13).

The recipients were already reminded in Heb 2:1 to "pay greater attention to what we have heard, so that we do not drift away (παραρυῶμεν) from it." In Heb 6:18 the recipients are encouraged, using the phrase παράκλησιν ἔχωμεν. The same undertone of encouragement surfaces also here in the quotation from Prov 3:21: "my child, do not let these escape from your sight ..." (υἱέ, μὴ παραρρυῆς).[48] The author of Hebrews, furthermore, refers to his own work at the end as an exhortation (παράκλησις, 13:22). This purpose can be detected at a number of places throughout the book. Here, though, he links directly an explicit quotation with the term παράκλησις.

4. Scripture and Festivals as Intertexts for Some of the Maxim-like Formulas?

In this section we will only concentrate on two of the maxim-like formulas in Heb 13 and their possible intertextual connections with the Jewish feasts and their own Scriptural intertexts, namely Heb 13:2 and Heb 13:5 – the latter being connected with a quotation from Ps 118(117) as part of the great Hallel.

Ps 118(117):6 is the very last explicit quotation in *Ad Hebraeos*. The *finale* of this sermon ends in a quotation from a Psalm that was well known and widely used during the Jewish feasts, namely from the Hallel. It is closely linked with the Exodus tradition and with the new covenant motif.

---

[46] Probably with the intention of "Discipline in the form of punishment from God"? Cf. Gerhard Schneider, "παιδεύω," *EDNT III* (1993): 4; cf. also "παιδεύω," *A Greek-English Lexicon of the New Testament and other early Christian literature* (ed. William F. Arndt and Felix W. Gingrich; Chicago, Ill.: University of Chicago Press, 1957), 604. According to Paul Ellingworth, "(b)roadly speaking, the Greek tradition emphasised παιδεία as education, whereas the Hebrew tradition stressed the positive value of (especially God's) discipline of his people by punishment" (*Hebrews*, [n. 19], 649).

[47] Weiß, *Hebräer* (n. 27), 648.

[48] "Die παράκλησις, das ist hier konkret der tröstliche und zugleich ermahnende Zuspruch der Schrift" (Weiß, *Hebräer* [n. 27], 647).

Its pilgrimage character and cultic setting might provide information regarding its hermeneutical application within the context of the maxim-like ethical formulas.

Heb 13:6, however, cannot be detached from Heb 13:5. It is part of the same sentence that refers to Deut 31:6. Whereas Heb 13:5 (Deut 31:6, 8) was most probably the *pars dei*, which is God's promise, Heb 13:6 (Ps 118[117]:6) was probably the *pars populi*, the response of the people.[49] This second quotation might thus have been introduced as a response that the early Christian receivers of Hebrews, thus "we" (ἡμᾶς), made as a result of God's promise in the Torah.[50] "The use of ἐγκαταλείπω in Ps 118(LXX 117):8 may have suggested to the author the link between his two quotations in 13:5f,"[51] or merely the fact that both Deut 31 as well as Ps 118(117) were connected with the Feast of Tents.

Some Old Testament scholars understood Deut 31:9–13 to connect the reading of the Law primarily with the Sabbatical year and secondarily with the Feast of Tents (*Sukkoth*) in that year.[52] According to Lev 23:34–36, 39 the Feast of Tents was held on the 15th day of the seventh month, Tishri. It was preceded by a feast on the first day of the seventh month (Num 29:1–6) and the Day of the Atonement (*Yom Kippur*) on the tenth day of the seventh month (Lev 23:26). The Day of the Atonement is referred to in Heb 5:5, 10:4, etc. The Feast of Tents lasted for seven days (15–21 Tishri). On the last day the priests walked seven times around the altar and the singers of the temple sung Ps 118(117). The people only joined at v. 25 after which the High Priest blessed them (v. 26).[53] Verse 25 was apparently used as a supplication for rain at the Feast of Booths procession during which the procession approached the altar with branches.[54] After the Feast followed a solemn day of rest (22 Tishri).[55]

Is it co-incidental that Heb 13:5 quotes from the immediate preceding section of Deut 31:9–13 which refers to the Sabbatical year and to the Feast of Tents? "It was the most important and the most crowded of the three annual pilgrimages to the sanctuary,"[56] and referred to by Josephus to

[49] Simon J. Kistemaker, *The Psalm Citations in the Epistle to the Hebrews* (Amsterdam: van Soest: 1961), 56.

[50] Attridge, *Hebrews* (n. 24), 389 – and similarly Weiß, *Hebräer* (n. 27), 706.

[51] Ellingworth, *Hebrews* (n. 19), 701.

[52] Roland de Vaux, *Ancient Israel. Its Life and Institutions* (Grand Rapids, Mich.: Eerdmans, 1997), 502.

[53] Frank C. Fensham and Johannes P. Oberholzer, *Bybelse Aardrykskunde, Oudheidkunde en Opgrawings* (Pretoria: Interkerklike Uitgewerstrust, 1976), 305.

[54] Cf. Jakob J. Petuchowski, "'Hoshi'ah na' in Psalm CXVIII 25, – a Prayer for Rain," *VT* 5 (1955): 266–271.

[55] De Vaux, *Ancient Israel* (n. 52), 472–473.

[56] De Vaux, *Ancient Israel* (n. 52), 495. Also Ferguson, *Backgrounds* (n. 1), 525.

be the "holiest and the greatest of Hebrew feasts" (*Ant.* 8.4.1). Therefore, although it is possible that this was co-incidental, it is highly unlikely when the motifs of the new covenant, the Sabbath and the day of rest are all playing key roles in the argumentation of the unknown author of Hebrews.[57]

Deut 31:1–6 reports how Moses told the people of Israel that he came to the end of his journey and that Joshua will lead them further. They are reminded about the promises of God and that they should be strong and courageous, that they should not be afraid or terrified because the Lord their God goes with them and will never leave or forsake them (v. 6). In the following section (Deut 31:7–8), Moses calls Joshua and inspires him with the words that he should be strong and courageous and that he will enter the land promised with an oath to the ancestors of the Israelite people. "He will never leave you, nor forsake you" (v. 8). Hereafter follows Deut 31:9–13 which reports how Moses gave this Law to the Levite priests with the instruction that it should be at the end of every seventh year, "in the year for cancelling debts, during the Feast of the Tabernacles ... you shall read this law before them in their hearing. Assemble the people – men, women and children, and the aliens living in your towns ..." (Deut 31:10–12). The two maxims under discussion in Heb 13 became clearer against the backdrop of Deut 31: "do not forget to entertain strangers" (13:2) and especially that they "should keep their lives free from the love of money and be content with what they have" (13:5) – following the quotation from Deut 31:6. The context of the Sabbatical year during which the "cancelling of debt" takes place, referred to in Deut 31, contrasts the reference to the "love of money" referred to in Heb 13:5.

The author of Hebrews presents now the quotation from Ps 118(117):6 as a conclusion to the aforegoing discussion on the love of money with its reference to Deut 31:6.[58] The focus of the argument shifts to contentment. This is being done by the connecting phrase ὥστε θαρροῦντας ἡμᾶς λέγειν which combines the two quotations as part of the same argument and as part of the same sentence.

---

[57] A comparative study between Hebrews and the Therapeutae (who were very similar to the Qumran community) of whom Philo of Alexandria wrote in his *De Contemplativa*, makes it clear that the same motifs were also strongly present in the Therapeutae communities. Even the simplistic housing of these communities calls to mind the "huts" (*sukkôth*) during the Feast of Tents. These connections might point partially to Christian converts from the Therapeutae or similar groups in the desert outside Alexandria. But this is an investigation for another time.

58 William L. Lane is of the opinion that "the quotation has the sobering effect of establishing a social context for the instruction in v 5*a*" (William L. Lane, *Hebrews 9–13* [WBC 47B; Dallas, Tex.: Word Books, 1991], 520).

There is sufficient evidence from early Judaism and early Christianity that Ps 118(117) played a key role in the liturgies of the Jewish festivals as a Hallel Psalm. Particularly its links with the Jewish Sabbatical Year, the Passover and the Feast of Tents are well-known. The prominence given to Ps 118(117) by the writers of early Christianity, as well as the presence and the liturgical rootedness of βοηθός in the early Church, are clear indications that this Psalm also played a key role in early Christianity. The author of Hebrews builds on this tradition. He creates a close link between the quotations from Deut 31:6 and Ps 118(117):6 in Heb 13:5–6. Structurally both quotations are being presented by means of a single sentence and with a single introductory formula. The occurrence of ἐγκαταλείπω strengthens this link.

Behind this structural connection lies, however, a deeply rooted Jewish festival tradition that combined the two quotations. The Sabbatical Year and Feast of Tents, which were testified about in Deut 31, provides a liturgical link for the author with Ps 118(117), which was sung at these occasions as well as during the Passover. The dialogical nature of the two quotations, "*God said*" (through the words of Deut 31:6 in Heb 13:5), and "*we say*" (through the words of Ps 118(117):6 in Heb 13:6) has a liturgical tone. It thus makes sense in assuming a possible *pars dei* (Deut 31:6 in Heb 13:5) and a *pars populi* (Ps 118(117):6 in Heb 13:6). When adding to this the preceding context of the love for money (Heb 13:5) in the light of a Sabbatical Year motif in Deut 31, on the one hand, as well as the possible motif of the Eucharist (especially Heb 13:10–12) in the light of the Passover festival, on the other hand, the author and his readers' familiarity with these intertexts from a liturgical tradition, becomes clear.

5. Conclusion

This brief study intended to investigate the role of three areas of possible intertextual influence from the Jewish Scriptures on the moral language of Hebrews. Attention was firstly paid to the possible intertextual influences from the moral language of the Decalogue and other laws on the language and theology of Hebrews. It was concluded that traces of the moral language of the Decalogue and other Jewish laws from the Pentateuch might indeed be identified in Hebrews – but reinterpreted in light of the Christ-event.

Secondly, attention was paid to the list of narrative intertexts of the *commemoratios* of Heb 10–12. The second list is a presentation of narrative intertexts from Jewish history and a commemoration of the exemplary behaviour of each of the characters listed. This past exemplary behaviour serves as a general model for the current readers to persevere despite the trying circumstances in which they find themselves.

Thirdly, two of the maxim-like ethical formulas in Heb 13 (vv. 2, 5) were briefly referred to against the backdrop of the Jewish festival traditions with its intertextual Scriptural connections. The Jewish festival traditions connected passages such as Ps 118(117) with the Passover, and Deut 31 with the Sabbatical Year and with the Feast of Tents. The maxim-like formulas regarding the entertainment of strangers (Heb 13:2) as well as lives that ought to be kept free from the love of money and to be content with what they have (13:5), might have been influenced, amongst others, by these Scriptural intertexts in connection with the Jewish festival traditions – initial traces that already were observed in Philo.

The observation of this study confirms the suspicion that the Jewish Scriptures played an important role on different levels during the compilation of early Christian documents such as *Ad Hebraeos* – as can be observed in the (moral) language of this book. *Implicit influence*, being that subconsciously or unintentionally, from these Scriptures as intertexts – e.g. the Decalogue and other Pentateuchal Laws – became clear. *Explicit influence*, consciously and intentionally, from these Scriptures as intertexts – e.g. a list of narrative intertexts presented as exemplary behaviour for early Christians (and combined with the ultimate example of Christ) – could also be noted. Liturgical traditions, however, such as those from the Jewish festival traditions, played its own role during the compilation of the grid of intertextual connections between Hebrews and the Jewish Scriptures.

Protreptic Ethics in the Letter of James:

The Potential of Figurative Language in Character Formation

Susanne Luther

1. Introduction

In his daring and controversial project, A. J. Jacobs, the agnostic author of the fiction bestseller *The Year of Living Biblically*, tries to follow "every rule, every guideline, every suggestion, every nugget of advice I find in the Bible" as literally as possible for the sake of "exploring religion." Besides criticizing the notion of Biblical literalism, the novel describes the endeavour to change a person's character and convictions through adherence to Biblical instructions concerning concrete actions. The choice of the Bible as basis for this undertaking reflects the significance which is still credited to Biblical ethical advice today. More precisely, the book depicts an attempt at character formation via a cognitive psychological approach: "[M]any of the rules ... will, I hope, make me a better person by the end of the year. I'm thinking of: No lying. No coveting. No stealing. Love your neighbour. Honor your parents. Dozens of them."[1] However, the author's immense sense of freedom when finally discarding the religious rules he had authoritatively imposed upon himself discloses the difficulty of adopting specific precepts and prohibitions of conduct without a preceding basic transformation of character due to conviction, insight or faith.

This problematic phenomenon is already reflected in New Testament epistolary literature. Despite the premise of the addressees' conversion

---

[1] Cf. Arnold J. Jacobs, *The Year of Living Biblically: One Man's Humble Quest to Follow the Bible as Literally as Possible* (New York, N.Y.: Simon & Schuster, 2007), quotes from p. 8. For justified criticism concerning the detachment of Biblical rules from their context and theological intent as well as the trivialization of theological constructs cf. e.g. the New York Times review by Janet Maslin on October 18, 2007 (http://www.nytimes.com/2007/10/18/books/18masl.html?_r=1, 3.7.2009). Cf. Petra von Gemünden, "Affekte und Affektkontrolle im antiken Judentum und Urchristentum," in *Erkennen und Erleben: Beiträge zur psychologischen Erforschung des frühen Christentums* (ed. Petra von Gemünden and Gerd Theißen; Gütersloh: Gütersloher Verlag, 2007), 249–269 for the application of psychological paradigms in New Testament exegesis. The Letter of James would probably come closest to "autodynamische Affektkontrolle" in that insight ("Erkenntnis") is the key to influencing one's affects and actions.

(ἔμφυτος λόγος, 1:21) and their status as firstborn of the new creation (ἀπαρχή τῶν αὐτοῦ κτισμάτων, 1:18), empirical observations – as echoed e.g. in Jas 3:2 or 4:1–4 – do not admit the notion that Christians are able to live up to the required moral standards of their own accord, e.g. by virtue of their conversion, for conversion does not directly influence moral conduct. Ethical instruction[2] is necessary in order to collate the individual's moral judgement with Christian standards.[3] The normative imperatival instruction abounding in New Testament literature seems to imply that iterative exhortation is regarded as compulsory for a successful Christian existence, for "moral instructions aid these converts in the process of conforming their lives to their convictions. ... [M]oral instructions serve not only to define ethical norms but also to aid growth in character and discernment, both in terms of intellectual development and affective reorientation," for "reforming one's character does not happen in an instant."[4]

This is manifest in the gospels' mode of communicating ethics: R. Zimmermann emphasizes that Jesus was regarded and remembered as a parable teller[5] whose way of teaching was characterised by his use of dilemma stories that aim at moral-cognitive development and the forming of a moral judgement in the addressees instead of mediating normative ethics[6], for "[d]er Deutungsoffenheit und Polyvalenz der Parabeln korreliert gerade auch eine offene, polyvalente Ethik. Die Ethik der Parabeln ist nicht eingleisig, statisch, sondern bleibt mehrdimensional und dynamisch. Statt zwingender Imperative wird ein Handlungsspielraum eröffnet, der aus

---

[2]   Ruben Zimmermann, "Ethics in the New Testament and Language. Basic Explorations and Eph 5:21–33 as Test Case," in *Moral Language in the New Testament. Contexts and Norms of New Testament Ethics* (ed. Jan G. van der Watt and Ruben Zimmermann; Tübingen: Mohr Siebeck, 2010), 19–50; cf. also Jan van der Watt, "Preface," in *Identity, Ethics and Ethos in the New Testament* (ed. Jan van der Watt; BZNW 141; Berlin: de Gruyter, 2006), iv–ix, vii.

[3]   Cf. Michael Wolter, "Die ethische Identität christlicher Gemeinden in neutestamentlicher Zeit," in *Woran orientiert sich Ethik?* (ed. Wilfried Härle and Reiner Preul; Marburger Jahrbuch Theologie 13; Marburg: Elwert, 2001), 61–90, esp. 67–69.

[4]   J. de Waal Dryden, *Theology and Ethics in 1 Peter* (WUNT 2/209, Tübingen: Mohr Siebeck, 2006), 196–197.

[5]   Cf. Ruben Zimmermann, "Gleichnisse als Medien der Jesuserinnerung: Die Historizität der Jesusparabeln im Horizont der Gedächtnisforschung," in *Hermeneutik der Gleichnisse Jesu: Methodische Neuansätze zum Verstehen urchristlicher Parabeltexte* (ed. Ruben Zimmermann; WUNT 231; Tübingen: Mohr Siebeck, 2008), 87–121. Cf. on this Howard Kamler, "Self-Identity and Moral Maturity," in *Personal and Moral Identity* (ed. Albert W. Musschenga; Library of Ethics and Applied Philosophy 11; Dordrecht: Kluwer Academic Publishers, 2002), 123–146.

[6]   Cf. also for criticism Anton A. Bucher, *Gleichnisse verstehen lernen: Strukturgenetische Untersuchungen zur Rezeption synoptischer Parabeln* (PTD 5; Fribourg: Universitätsverlag, 1990) and Charles W. Hedrick, "Survivors of the Crucifixion: Searching for Profiles in the Parables," in Zimmermann, *Hermeneutik* (n. 5), 165–180, esp. 175.

dem Verstehensspielraum erwächst."[7] This teaching is not based on logic, it is not rational but based on affects, it is first of all narrative and only implicitly directive.[8] In that the parable stories appeal to the hearers and invite them to adopt the position of the parable teller they implicitly carry the potential for moral development and character formation. This way of teaching is not intent on conveying ethical standards by imposing prescriptive instruction via cognitive discernment but aims at a radical and lasting amelioration of character.[9]

The Letter of James attempts to tackle the problem in a distinctive way: firstly the ethical instruction conveyed is not paraenetic but protreptic, i.e. the letter does not primarily communicate specific explicit rules for concrete actions but rather advice on character formation.[10] Secondly ethics is formally conveyed through figurative language, which is able to illustrate abstract subject matters and serves well in explicating the core of Jacobean ethical instruction: protreptic ethics.[11] It is precisely a figurative rendering of instruction which promises the potential for a profound impact in ethical instruction.

The following case study in the Letter of James intends to reveal, to what *extent* and in which *forms* the linguistic and psychological potential of metaphoric and generally figurative language was used in early Christianity and which *function* and *significance* are assigned to figurative language within the argumentative context of the "post-conversional dis-

---

[7] Ruben Zimmermann, "Die Ethico-Ästhetik der Gleichnisse Jesu: Ethik durch literarische Ästhetik am Beispiel der Parabeln im Matthäus-Evangelium," in *Jenseits von Indikativ und Imperativ: Begründungszusammenhänge neutestamentlicher Ethik* (ed. Friedrich Wilhelm Horn and Ruben Zimmermann; vol. 1; WUNT 238; Tübingen: Mohr Siebeck, 2009), 235–265, 251.

[8] Zimmermann, "Ethico-Ästhetik" (n. 7), 239: "Dargestellte Erzählungen ('enacted narratives') werden dann auch zu einem Leitbegriff, oder sagen wir eher zur Leitform, in der sich Ethik manifestiert. ... Die Form der Erzählung wird somit zum bevorzugten Darstellungs- und Mitteilungsmedium der Ethik," einer Ethik der Ästhetik, der Wahrnehmung und Empfindung.

[9] Cf. *Eth. nic.* 1179b 15–30, where Aristotle states that the character of a person must be changed, before he can think and act correctly, i.e. like the land must be prepared to nurture the seed. However, by contrast to the Letter of James, Aristotle assumes that preparing the character for right conduct comes via the practice of right conduct (*Eth. nic.* 1103a 30–1103b 25).

[10] Concerning the distinction between protreptic and paraenetic ethical admonitions cf. Wolter, "Ethische Identität" (n. 3), 63–64.

[11] Cf. Gottfried Boehm, *Wie Bilder Sinn erzeugen: Die Macht des Zeigens* (2nd ed.; Berlin: Berlin University Press, 2008), 13. Rüdiger Campe, "Aktualität des Bildes: Die Zeit rhetorischer Figuration," in *Figur und Figuration: Studien zu Wahrnehmung und Wissen* (ed. Gottfried Boehm, Gabriele Brandstetter and Achatz von Müller; Text und Bild; Munich: Fink, 2007), 163–182.

course" in enhancing ethical admonition and teaching.[12] I would like to consider this issue through a close analysis of a representative variety of specific exemplary Jacobean passages in order to provide an overview of the form and function of figurative devices in the Letter of James and to demonstrate the congruence of form, content and pragmatic purport that is characteristic of the author's ethical teaching.

2. Examples of Figurative Forms of the Communication of Ethics

Within the basic argumentative framework the author employs a rather systematic conception of Christian ethics. Although this is not elaborated on systematically in the modern sense of the word, an "ethical superstructure" can be derived from the overall argumentation of the text.[13] With reference to James, it is therefore appropriate to talk of ethics[14] with regard to the extended reflection on the ethico-theological understanding of Christian existence which constitutes the *premise* for right conduct and maps out the anthropological preconditions of any adherence to concrete ethical admonitions.[15] The ethics conveyed here in the form of figurative language

---

[12] Cf. Klaus Berger, *Formen und Gattungen im Neuen Testament* (UTB 2532; Tübingen: Francke, 2005), § 50: Postkonversionale Mahnrede.

[13] Ruben Zimmermann, "The 'Implicit Ethics' of New Testament Writings: a Draft on a New Methodology for Analysing New Testament Ethics," *Neot* 43/2 (2009): 398–422, 402: "This 'ethics' should be called 'implicit' because the New Testament authors themselves render no systematic account for norms of action and contexts of reason that would be similar perhaps to the ethics of Aristotle. In spite of a lack of systematization, they still have an order of values and ethical argumentation. We, however, can retrospectively derive, from individual elements of the text, an 'ethical superstructure' underlying the specific communication of a certain writing and at the same time assemble the mosaic stones into a more systematic awareness of ethical argumentation. This underlying ethics is still strictly bound to the text itself, and cannot be misunderstood as something which is imposed upon the text from outside". Cf. Karl-Wilhelm Niebuhr, "Ethik und Anthropologie nach dem Jakobusbrief: Eine Skizze," in Horn/Zimmermann, *Indikativ und Imperativ* (n. 9), 329–246, 331–332, who speaks of 1:12–25 as the theological centre and "theologische Grundlegung" of Jacobean ethics.

[14] According to the definitional distinction between "ethos/morals" and "ethics" as proposed in this volume, ethical admonitions are concrete instructions that lead to ethical conduct and reflect the motives and norms behind the instructional directives; cf. Zimmermann, "Ethics and Language" (n. 2), 19–23; cf. also Van der Watt, "Preface" (n. 2), vii.

[15] For the concept cf. Matthias Konradt, *Christliche Existenz nach dem Jakobusbrief: Eine Studie zu seiner soteriologischen und ethischen Konzeption* (StUNT 22; Göttingen: Vandenhoeck & Ruprecht, 1998). Cf. also idem, "'Geboren durch das Wort der Wahrheit' – 'gerichtet durch das Gesetz der Freiheit:' Das Wort als Zentrum der theologischen

centre on dispositional or protreptic ethics, i.e. ethics that generally form human character. Although James contains formal-ethical principles as well as individual material-ethical maxims (e.g. Jas 4:11; 5:12 etc.), the focus of the letter is *not* primarily directed towards ethics as meta-reflection on concrete norms for concrete actions.[16] The ethics conveyed are not predominantly focussed on normative instruction for specific moral action nor are they merely the basis for moral instruction. As will become evident from the following analysis, Jacobean ethics are concerned with reflection on human theological-ethical disposition, with the ethical mind-set or the disposition of character of the addressees,[17] and hence with re-flection on the premises of all further meta-reflection of norms for actions: with *protreptic ethics*.[18]

The basic framework for conveying ethics in the epistle is an argumen-tative setting, which is repeatedly implemented by means of descriptive or figurative language: the author employs a significant amount of metaphors, miniature parables, example stories and Old Testament role models, which render the instruction inductive and invite affective involvement.

Konzeption des Jakobusbriefes," in *Der Jakobusbrief: Beiträge zur Rehabilitierung einer "strohernen Epistel"* (ed. Petra von Gemünden, Matthias Konradt and Gerd Theißen; BVB 3; Münster: LIT, 2003), 1–15 and most recently idem, "Werke als Handlungsdi-mension des Glaubens: Erwägungen zum Verhältnis von Theologie und Ethik im Jako-busbrief," in Horn/Zimmermann, *Indikativ und Imperativ* (n. 9), 309–327. Cf. also Pat-rick J. Hartin, "The Letter of James: Its vision, ethics, and ethos," in Van der Watt, *Iden-tity* (n. 14), 445–471, 445.

[16] Cf. Niebuhr, "Ethik und Anthropologie" (n. 13), 340–341: "Die konkreten ethi-schen Handlungen werden im Jakobusbrief somit nicht in Form von Handlungsanweisun-gen im Einzelnen vorgeschrieben, sondern müssen von dem, der sich dem Willen Gottes unterwerfen will, selbst aufgefunden werden. Dazu kann er Gebote der Tora als Richtli-nien, als Grenzmarkierungen oder als Wurzelboden für seine Lebensentscheidungen im Alltag heranziehen."

[17] Cf. for a content-related connection between James and Jesus concerning anthro-pology and ethics and the importance of "Ganzheitlichkeit" and perfection: Niebuhr, "Ethik und Anthropologie" (n. 13), 332–336.

[18] Cf. n. 10. M. Wolter points out that the Pauline letters detach ethos from the level of concrete actions and focus on πιστεύειν: from propositions like Rom 6:19b, Gal 5:16 or 1 Thess 2:12 and their parallel intention to Old Testament texts like Lev 19:2 he con-cludes: "Allen diesen Aufforderungen fehlt die materiale Konkretion. Die Ebene des Verhaltens bleibt von ihnen unerreicht, und aus diesem Grunde können sie als solche auch noch nicht als ethosfähige Weisungen fungieren. Paulus formuliert hier vielmehr lediglich das … Prinzip der Korrelation von Ethos und Identität." In the Letter of James a similar phenomenon can be stated concerning the conveyance of "ethics" – however in my opinion it is justifiable to propose, that the intention of James is to promote disposi-tional ethics; cf. Michael Wolter, "Ethos und Identität in paulinischen Gemeinden," *NTS* 43 (1997): 430–444.

2.1 Metaphoric Examples

The Letter of James employs genitive metaphors[19], which either depict aspects of the gospel (λόγος ἀληθείας, 1:18; νόμος τέλειος ... τῆς ἐλευθε-ρίας, 1:25; 2:12)[20] or describe abstract theological parameters like στέφανος τῆς ζωῆς (1:12)[21], πατρὸς τῶν φώτων (1:17)[22], κυρίος ... τῆς δόξης (cf. 2:1)[23] or κληρονόμοι τῆς βασιλείας (2:5)[24] with terminology bor-rowed from tradition and everyday speech. In the context of this letter it is evident, that these metaphors serve to explain abstract or complex theo-

---

[19] For the definition of "metaphor" cf. e.g. Ruben Zimmermann, "Metapher, neutes-tamentlich," *Lexikon der Bibelhermeneutik* (ed. Oda Wischmeyer et al.; Berlin: de Gruy-ter, 2009): 377–378. The metaphor ἀδελφός will not be analysed in this context, for al-though it bears a rhetorical significance it is not directly to be subsumed under figurative speech but rather has the function of a community-building metaphor. However, cf. Hu-bert Frankemölle, *Der Brief des Jakobus* (2 vols.; ÖTK.NT 17/1, 2; Gütersloh: Gütersloh-her Verlag, 1994), I 245.

[20] Concerning νόμος and λόγος in James cf. e.g. Martin Klein, *"Ein vollkommenes Werk:" Vollkommenheit, Gesetz und Gericht als theologische Themen des Jakobusbriefes* (BWANT 139; Stuttgart: Kohlhammer, 1995), 145–148; Konradt, *Christliche Existenz* (n. 15), 184–185; Karl-Wilhelm Niebuhr, "Tora ohne Tempel: Paulus und der Jakobus-brief im Zusammenhang frühjüdischer Torarezeption für die Diaspora," in *Gemeinde ohne Tempel. Community without Temple: Zur Substituierung und Transformation des Jerusalemer Tempels und seines Kults im Alten Testament, antiken Judentum und frühen Christentum* (ed. Beate Ego, Armin Lange and Peter Pilhofer; WUNT 118; Tübingen: Mohr Siebeck, 1999), 427–460; idem, *Gesetz und Paränese: Katechismusartige Wei-sungsreihen in der frühjüdischen Literatur* (WUNT 2/28; Tübingen: Mohr Siebeck, 1987); Hubert Frankemölle, "Gesetz im Jakobusbrief: Zur Tradition, kontextuellen Ver-wendung und Rezeption eines belasteten Begriffes," in *Das Gesetz im Neuen Testament* (ed. Karl Kertelge; Freiburg: Herder, 1986), 175–221; Manabu Tsuji, *Glaube zwischen Vollkommenheit und Verweltlichung: Eine Untersuchung zur literarischen Gestalt und zur inhaltlichen Kohärenz des Jakobusbriefes* (WUNT 2/93; Tübingen: Mohr Siebeck, 1997), 109–115.

[21] Cf. Wiard Popkes, *Der Brief des Jakobus* (ThHK.NT 14; Leipzig: Evangelische Verlagsanstalt, 2001), 101 with reference to Rev 2:10 and other traditional eschatological promises in the context of "Überwindersprüchen." The motif is derived from the context of sports competition, in a figurative sense it is to be found especially in wisdom litera-ture. The context of the ἀγών is also hinted at in Phil 1:30; 1 Cor 9:24–27.

[22] Cf. Popkes, *Jakobus* (n. 21), 114 with reference to *T. Ab.* 7:6; *Apoc. Mos.* 36; Philo, *Deus* 20–32; *Leg.* 2:33, 72 etc.: The term is taken from the context of creation terminology (cf. also loc. cit., 122: Gen 1:14–18 etc.).

[23] Cf. Popkes, *Jakobus* (n. 21), 156, 158 with reference to *1 En.* 22:14; 63:2–3; 1 Cor 2:8 probably taken from tradition.

[24] Cf. Popkes, *Jakobus* (n. 21), 156 the metaphor was known in early Christian cate-chetical tradition, with reference to Matt 25:34; 1 Cor 6:9–10; 15:20; Gal 5:21.

logical concepts through their correlation with specific and uncomplicated concepts.[25]

Attributive metaphors are found e.g. with the instruction to follow the νόμος ... βασιλικός (2:8) or in connection with the imperative δέξασθε τὸν ἔμφυτον λόγον τὸν δυνάμενον σῶσαι τὰς ψυχὰς ὑμῶν (1:21). It might be suggested, that the latter passage may have generated associations with the tradition of Matt 11:29 in the readers' minds[26]: the appeal ἄρατε τὸν ζυγόν μου ἐφ' ὑμᾶς parallels Jas 1:21 in semantic variation while a lexical cohesion is to be detected in the lexems πραΰς and ψυχή. In replacing the Biblical and Jewish metaphor of the ζυγός[27] with the metaphor ἔμφυτος λόγος – possibly derived from the context of Hellenistic philosophy[28] – the perception of the "law" is transformed from bearing the connotation of being a "burden" to the notion of the νόμος τέλειος ... τῆς ἐλευθερίας, i.e. the language of obligation is replaced by that of promise.[29] The intertextual reference to the Gospel of Matthew in this implicit reception of the *"Heilands-ruf"* and the use of diction derived from missionary contexts[30] generate an epistolary reminder of the recipients' baptism or conversion.[31] According to the theory of interaction, "creative metaphors" like ἔμφυτος λόγος[32] or the depictions of the νόμος/λόγος in innovative composite terms are defined by their context and in this manner have the potential to convey familiar content matter in an innovative-heuristic way.[33] Thus the addressees

---

[25] Cf. George Lakoff and Mark Johnson, *Metaphors we live by* (Chicago, Ill.: Chicago University Press, 1980; German trans.: 5th ed.; Heidelberg: Carl-Auer-Verlag, 2007); cf. also Gerhard Kurz, "Metapher, literaturwissenschaftlich" and Helge Skirl, "Metapher, textlinguistisch," *Lexikon der Bibelhermeneutik* (n. 19): 379–380, 380–381.

[26] Cf. also the association of Deut 30:1 (εἰς τὴν καρδίαν σου): Martin Dibelius, *Der Brief des Jakobus* (KEK 15; 12th ed.; Göttingen: Vandenhoeck & Ruprecht, 1984), 108.

[27] Cf. Ulrich Luz, Das Evangelium nach Matthäus (EKK I/2; Zurich: Benziger, 1990), 217 with reference to close parallels in wisdom literature, e.g. in Sir 51:23–30.

[28] Cf. Matt A. Jackson-McCabe, *Logos and Law in the Letter of James: The Law of Nature, the Law of Moses, and the Law of Freedom* (NT.S 100; Leiden: Brill, 2001): From Stoic tradition; cf. also Dibelius, *Jakobus* (n. 26), 145.

[29] Cf. also the depiction of the internalized law in Rom 7:5, 23; cf. also Jas 4:1.

[30] Cf. Walter Grundmann, "δέχομαι κτλ," *TWNT* 2 (1935): 49–59, 52–53 and Gerhard Schneider, "ἀποτίθεμαι," *EWNT* 1 (1980): 352–353.

[31] An interpretation of Jas 1:19–26 within baptismal paraenesis (cf. e.g. Franz Mußner, Der Jakobusbrief [HThK 13; 4th ed.; Freiburg: Herder, 1981], 101–102) seems not appropriate with reference to Jas 1:2–18 and the genre of the letter, cf. Popkes, *Jakobus* (n. 21), 16–26, 44–58.

[32] Hapaxlegomenon in the New Testament; cf. also Petra von Gemünden, *Vegetationsmetaphorik im Neuen Testament und seiner Umwelt: Eine Bildfelduntersuchung* (NTOA 18; Göttingen: Vandenhoeck & Ruprecht, 1993), 270–271.

[33] Cf. for an overview of the approach Von Gemünden, *Vegetationsmetaphorik* (n. 32), 6–18.

may repeatedly receive the same stimulus, which intensifies its motivating force through the startling lexical variation.

Sentence metaphors in the letter of James are e.g. καὶ ἡ γλῶσσα πῦρ (3:6) and ἀτμὶς γάρ ἐστε ἡ πρὸς ὀλίγον φαινομένη, ἔπειτα καὶ ἀφανιζομένη (4:14). Both images are traditional[34] and both recur to the characteristics of the metaphoric expressions in order to illustrate their argument: the premise for the understanding of the metaphors is the knowledge of the ephemeral nature of "smoke," which inevitably vanishes, as well as of the devastating and uncontrollable impact of "fire." Ὁ κόσμος τῆς ἀδικίας is found regularly as a Jewish creation metaphor, the comparison with fire may be derived from Sir 28:13–26.[35] By likening humanity to smoke and aspects of human effectiveness to fire the author achieves a vivid and powerful illustration, intelligible and catching for recipients from all educational levels by being taken from everyday situations.[36] The context of these metaphors implies that their ethical impetus is confined to the illustrative depiction of characteristics: those among the addressees to whom the admonition may refer – the unwise in chapter 3, the rich in chapter 4 – are paralleled with phenomena of nature, of fallen creation. Only to them is the vigorous implicit admonition addressed: to recognize the fact that they have reverted to their pre-conversion status (3:9–10; 4:16), to yield to the appeal in Jas 1:21 and to revert to conduct worthy of the new creation (3:10b; 4:13, 15; cf. 1:18). With regard to those not directly addressed, the metaphors may be intended as warnings to watch their ways.

In Jas 5:9 contextual metaphorization is employed, when picturing the judge standing πρὸ τῶν θυρῶν. In the context of a passage of instructions concerning eschatological patience (vv. 7–8) and the mention of the motif of judgement (v. 9), this image is to be understood as an illustrative metaphorical rendering of the imminent expectation of the final judgement. As parallels in Mk 13:29 and Rev 3:20 disclose, this motif is common in traditional material: it serves as an expression of the Christian expectation of

---

[34] Cf. Frankemölle, *Jakobus* (n. 19), II 500–510 (with reference to parallels in wisdom literature, e.g. Sir 28; *Pss. Sol.* 12:2–3); 635–644 (with reference to parallels in wisdom literature as well as in Graeco-Roman philosophical texts and to the distinctive feature that the use of the lexem ἀτμίς in James constitutes a hapaxlegomenon within traditional material).

[35] Cf. Frankemölle, *Jakobus* (n. 19), II 500–501; the ancient parallelization of tongue and affects is not evoked in the Jacobean context.

[36] Cf. Ruben Zimmermann, "Metapherntheorie und biblische Bildersprache: Ein methodologischer Versuch," *TZ* 56 (2000): 108–133, 124; cf. also 108: "[Sprachbilder] aktivieren die Imaginationskraft des Rezipienten, sie sprechen an, ziehen den Leser bzw. Betrachter unmittelbar in den Verstehensprozess hinein, der die ganze Person umfasst."

the παρουσία[37] and supports ethical instruction with pressing motivation arising from the eschatological perspective (cf. e.g. Rom 13:11–14; 1 Cor 7:29–31).[38] The metaphor in Jas 5:9 is employed in order to visualize drastically the impending threat of the (final) judgement that is close at hand thus motivating the addressees to adhere to the instruction provided by way of a combination of the cognitive and the affective dimension in teaching.[39]

The surplus value of metaphors supporting ethical argumentation lies in their potential to achieve a stronger impact on the recipient than mere cognitive reasoning: in their argumentative-descriptive function metaphors generate a semantic tension between the metaphorical expression and the context, create an interplay between literal and figurative meaning and most notably convey cognition and knowledge through an absurd or innovative parallelization of two fields of meaning. In their argumentative-appellative function metaphors aim at an intensification of the argumentation through vivid images which evoke the recipients' particular attention, irritation, reflexion or even fear.[40]

2.2 Typological Examples

The Letter of James employs figurative language in the form of short references to moral agents[41] from the Old Testament, such as Abraham, Ra-

---

[37] Cf. e.g. 1 Cor 15:23; 1 Thess 2:19; 3:13; 4:15; 5:23; 2 Thess 2:1, 8–9; Matt 24:3, 27, 37, 39; 2 Pet 1:16; 3:4; 1 John 2:28; Heb 6:11–12. However, W. Popkes points out, that the explicit reference to the παρουσία is singular in the New Testament (317) and that James is not intent on identifying the judge with either Christ or God (*Jakobus* [n. 21], 326).

[38] Cf. Berger, *Formen und Gattungen* (n. 12), 161, 217, 224. Concerning this perspective on the future, not the future, but the perfect formulation seems of importance with reference to the judge: "ist vor die Tür getreten."

[39] Contextual metaphorization may also be attested in 5:6, as τὸ δίκαιον in the proposition κατεδικάσατε, ἐφονεύσατε τὸν δίκαιον, οὐκ ἀντιτάσσεται ὑμῖν meaning the suffering Son of Man is only comprehensible in the context of a prophetic judgement speech evoking associations to possibly Matt 20:1–16 or Matt 21:33–46. As, however, the interpretation of τὸ δίκαιον is debated controversially, this verse will be excluded from closer examination in the context of this paper.

[40] Cf. the analysis by Petra G. Kos-Schaap, "'Metaphors we live by' im Lukasevangelium 10–20," in *Erinnern um Neues zu sagen: Die Bedeutung der Metapher für die religiöse Sprache* (ed. Jean-Pierre van Noppen; Frankfurt am Main: Athenäum, 1988), 258–274 concerning the directive function of metaphors.

[41] Moral agents are included in this treatise of figurative language, because the Old Testament *personae* mentioned are not referred to as historic figures, but as symbols for a distinctive behaviour.

hab, Elijah or Job, to back up admonitions.[42] Concerning Abraham the author comments in Jas 2:21: Ἀβραὰμ ὁ πατὴρ ἡμῶν οὐκ ἐξ ἔργων ἐδικαιώθη ἀνενέγκας Ἰσαὰκ τὸν υἱὸν αὐτοῦ ἐπὶ τὸ θυσιαστήριον; There is no further elaboration on the story of the sacrifice; the bare and abrupt reference to Abraham seems to suffice in order to render him a prime example of the argumentation.

With a view to the analysis of figurative language in James, especially in the context of an argument on the importance of ἔργα, the *semantische Leerstelle* constituted by the absence of the narrative context and thus of any directive concerning the interpretation of the verb ἀναφέρω seems problematic, if the addressees were not familiar with the Genesis story.[43] However, several aspects of the formal rendering of the passage suggest that Abraham's story and the interpretational subject matters belonged to the established tradition of the recipients' community: Abraham is brought in as a familiar figure, adorned with the attribute ὁ πατὴρ ἡμῶν, but without any elaboration of his story and background. Only two aspects of his story – his justification and the sacrifice of Isaac – are referred to in the context of a crucial argument which was possibly even directed against (presumed) false teaching.[44]

A similar (ὁμοίως) case can be stated concerning Rahab, where οἱ ἄγγελοι are mentioned (Jas 2:25) without any direct contextual exposition of the original narrative. Rahab is introduced as Ῥαὰβ ἡ πόρνη and the recipients must have been familiar with her story also in order to be able to assess and appreciate the value of referring to her example in the context of the argument. There is no moral implementation in connection with her mentioning and of the two aspects cited concerning her story the second, the ἑτέρᾳ ὁδῷ ἐκβαλοῦσα, is formulated indistinctly with a view to the meaning of ἕτερος.[45] Yet – as in the reference to Abraham's story – exact references or a re-telling of the Old Testament story do not constitute the

---

[42] Cf. Peter H. Davids, "Tradition and Citation in the Epistle of James," in *Scripture, Tradition and Interpretation* (Festschrift Everett Falconer Harrison; ed. W. Ward Gasque and S. William LaSor; Grand Rapids, Mich.: Eerdmans, 1978), 113–126; concerning tradition history cf. Gunnar Garleff, *Urchristliche Identität in Matthäusevangelium, Didache und Jakobusbrief* (BVB 9; Münster: LIT, 2004), 299–303, 307–310.

[43] Concerning further theological and exegetical problems of the passage cf. Popkes, *Jakobus* (n. 21), 186–190, 201–211. Cf. loc. cit., 203 for the proposal that ἀναφέρειν in the sense of offering is regarded as the direct presupposition for justification and for the problematization of the foreknowledge of the addressees of Jewish or Christian terminology and concepts or even more specifically of familiar Pauline theologumena.

[44] Concerning the interpretation of 2:14–26 cf. Konradt, "Werke als Handlungsdimension" (n. 15), 320–321.

[45] Cf. Popkes, *Jakobus* (n. 21), 210: "anders, als sie gekommen waren, oder: anders, als Rahab den Häschern sagte?."

main focus here. To a much greater degree the thematic stress is on the persons themselves.

Another figure of the Old Testament tradition occurs in Jas 5:17–18 as corroboration of the statement that πολὺ ἰσχύει δέησις δικαίου ἐνερ-γουμένη (v. 16b). Except for a short final clause in v. 17b, vv. 17–18 are characterized by simple narrative style consisting of a chain of paratactic sentences with finite verbs and linked with καί.[46] Elijah is introduced without any further explication as a familiar personage; his life and pro-phetic deeds are irrelevant in this context. In accordance with the stress on vegetation metaphor and creation terminology, the author associates the prophet's prayer for rain, the precondition for the fruits of the earth (Jas 5:18). Following up on Jas 5:13–16, this association may be contrary to the recipients' anticipations – an association with Elijah's raising of the dead son of the widow of Zarephath through prayer (1 Kgs 17:22) would be more pertinent in this context. The unexpected argumentation with 1 Kgs 18:42–45 pursues the chain of creation images emphasized in the Letter of James.[47] Yet despite the polyvalent possibilities of connotation in the fig-ure of Elijah in the light of Old Testament tradition as well as Christian eschatological expectations, solely his righteousness is emphasized.[48] The apparently illogical compilation of material contrary to what might be ex-pected attracts the recipients' attention and opens a space for associations – e.g. with 1 Kgs 17 – which are not explicitly mentioned in the Jacobean text but resonate implicitly in the contextual allusions.

The passage at hand has far-reaching implications: the argumentation in vv. 16–18 defines the righteous as a person who has confessed his sins and has been forgiven. Through the line of thought leading from ὁ δίκαιος (v. 16b) to Elijah (v. 17) and ending in the depiction of Elijah as ἄνθρωπος ἦν ὁμοιοπαθὴς ἡμῖν (v. 17), the recipients are paralleled with Elijah, the role model for the righteous whose prayer is fulfilled. This analogy has two pragmatic implications: in relativising the status of the prophet, the recipi-ents are invited to identify with Elijah and motivated to confident prayer. Moreover the analogy explicitly indicates a connection between Elijah, an eschatological symbolic figure (cf. e.g. Matt 11:13–15; 17:11–13), and the ecclesiological field where the eschaton has dawned and the addressees are

---

[46] Cf. Popkes, *Jakobus* (n. 21), 351.

[47] It is not to be decided whether intertextual references are intended by the author. However, the impact of his writing in the sense of perlocutionary forces can be de-scribed. For examples of interpretations, which are in danger of over-interpreting the text by drawing references between different allusions throughout the text cf. Frankemölle, *Jakobus* (n. 19), II 720–729 and Popkes, *Jakobus* (n. 21), 352–353.

[48] Cf. Christine E. Joynes, *The Return of Elijah: An Exploration of the Character and Context of the Relationship between Elijah, John the Baptist and Jesus in the Gos-pels* (electronic resource; Oxford 1998).

likewise enabled to offer righteous prayer – as well as to heal or even raise the dead. This conclusion is not explicitly mentioned, but finds corroboration in the argumentative context. The association with 1 Kgs 17 is obviously intended, as without its bridging function the argument is not logically comprehensible. The fact that the author reverts to creation metaphor instead of mentioning this traditional passage must be understood as a formal mode of drawing attention to the overall argumentation of the letter: the recipients' prayer effects the growth of the new creation and its bringing forth fruit.

The author of James seems intent on mentioning only the most distinctive features of his agents' stories for the present context in order to set a frame for associations in the minds of the addressees. In analogy to pictorial representations of the scene, the picture "painted" in the recipients' minds by the author's words resembles a scene "frozen in action."[49] Its purpose seems to be to provide the recipients with the freedom to associate other aspects of the narrative figures' lives and to prompt them with the help of sparse scattered hints referring to their individual pre-knowledge.[50] This allows the personages mentioned to develop into ideal narrative and fictive stereotypes, which are in turn associated with theological concepts, ethical admonition and advice. The succinct and hence polyvalent argumentation opens up for associations that are definitely implied by the text; through their individual associations the recipients are reminded of possibly analogous personal and affective experiences, which induce forces that exert more intense ethical stimulation than a verbose normative and structured argumentation. Hence the pragmatic function of referring to Abraham, Rahab and Elijah in this context is the reinforcement of the argument with material from the fount of common tradition that bore no necessity of discussion within the interpretative community for which the author of James is writing. In this respect an identity-building function is inherent to

---

[49] For the ethical impact of "images" cf. Otto Langer, "Bildverstehen," in *Ethik des Verstehens: Beiträge zu einer philosophischen und literarischen Hermeneutik* (ed. Susanne Kaul and Lothar van Laak; Munich: Fink, 2007), 63–81.

[50] For considerations of reader-response criticism in respect to the impact of literary images see Jörg Frey, "Das Bild als Wirkungspotenzial: Ein rezeptionsästhetischer Versuch zur Funktion der Brot-Metapher in Johannes 6," in *Bildersprache verstehen: Zur Hermeneutik der Metapher und anderer biblischer Sprachformen* (ed. Ruben Zimmermann; Übergänge 38; Munich: Fink, 2000), 321–361, 340–343: "Sind die erzählten Bilder ... elementarer und in ihren Einzelheiten und ihrer gegenseitigen Zuordnung weniger stark determiniert, dann bleibt für die Aktivität der Leser mehr Raum. Diese müssen dann selbst die Lücken füllen, die offen gelassenen Details in ihrer eigenen Vorstellung präzisieren. Das geschieht in der Regel durch die Eintragung von Elementen aus der Welt der Leser, aus dem Schatz an Bildern, den sie – aus ihrer eigenen Welt- und Lebenserfahrung, aus ihrem kulturellen Wissen oder aus der bisherigen Lektüre des Textes – in sich tragen" (341).

their stories.[51] It is the recurrence to material of the collective as well as individual memory that provides common ground for the corroboration of the author's endeavour of argumentative persuasion. Moreover, the purpose of the use of specific personages is the addressees' identification with these Old Testament role models, whose (ethical) conduct is presented as exemplary.[52]

2.3 Macaristic Examples

A similar use of moral agency can be found in Jas 5:11, where Job is mentioned as a role model for patient endurance.[53] In line with οἱ προφῆται the reward of his exemplary conduct is taken up as an admonition and promise for the recipients. Formally this is rendered as a macarism analogous to Jas 1:12, which presents the perfect state of man as enduring in πειρασμοί. The two macarisms centre on the same subject and intend to convey ethics in a non-imperative, descriptive way. In identifying desirable and required conduct and holding out the prospect of eternal reward (τὸν στέφανον τῆς ζωῆς in 1:12, πολύσπλαγχνος and οἰκτίρμων as characteristics of the κύριος' judgement in 5:11), macarisms formulate their claims in a positive way: the macarism (μακάριος) in Jas 1:12a addresses the individual[54] and is followed by a substantiating ὅτι-sentence in v. 12b indicating not an eschatological threat but the promised reward. In 5:11 the phrasing varies slightly from conventional macarisms in that the verb is inflected (μακαρίζομεν); moreover between the statement and its positive corroboration (ὅτι) and motivation, v. 11 positions the example of Job. In some ways this Old Testament role model is inserted using similar formal criteria to those discussed above: again the story is presumed to be familiar to the recipients, as only two aspects of Job's life are mentioned – his patience and his final reward. In explicitly displaying aspects of Job's character as exemplary, the recipients are prompted to consider him a positive role model. Moreover they are enabled to associate freely those facets of Job's story which are appropriate in order to render the overall statement appealing and relevant for their personal situation – these associations are

---

[51] Cf. Garleff, *Urchristliche Identität* (n. 42), 37–40, esp. 38 concerning the function of "story" in forming identity.

[52] The figure of James (Jas 1:1) will not be considered in this context, as the naming of the (fictive) author does not function as a figurative example within the ethical argumentation, but cf. Garleff, *Urchristliche Identität* (n. 42), 241–247.

[53] As the Old Testament does not portray Job as a model of endurance, it has been proposed that the author of James either refers to the *T. Job* (where endurance is a central motif) or to a contemporary figure familiar to the addressees (which in my opinion cannot be presumed with regard to the address in Jas 1:1). Cf. Popkes, *Jakobus* (n. 21), 327–331.

[54] Cf. the macarisms in Matt 5 (μακάριοι).

not defined by the author and not necessary for the progress of the argumentation.

Both macarisms display an eschatological-apocalyptic perspective[55] and revert to the *Tun-Ergehens*-correlation characteristic of traditional wisdom macarisms. However, while the latter express concern for a fulfilled temporal existence based on traditional value hierarchies, the Jacobean macarisms combine this traditional form with eschatological predications while promoting the virtues of steadfastness and perseverance in the face of temptations and suffering. In analogy to macarisms of the Gospel tradition (cf. e.g. Matt 5:3–11) they convey paradoxical propositions, which attract attention and require further argumentative reasoning. While 1:12 employs metaphors from the field of (this-worldly) competitive sports (στέφανος)[56] rendered into eschatological ethical motivation (στέφανος τῆς ζωῆς), 5:11 depicts the prophets as models of faith and endurance, who have already pursued and won the victor's promised laurels. Thus the figurative account in 5:11 promotes the prophets' example and confirms as well as corroborates the motivation of 1:12. Both the eschatological perspective and the positive verbalization aim at the recipients' disposition to comply with the proposed ideals, to adopt the aspired objectives as their own and act accordingly motivated by the positive reinforcement. The macarisms function as positive guidelines for the recipients, who are expected to act according to 1:12 as the prophets have already successfully done (5:11).

2.4 Parabolic Examples

In Jas 1:6b the author substantiates his argumentation by likening the doubter (διακρινόμενος) to a wave of the sea. This short parable[57] is introduced by ἔοικεν and operates as a pictorial corroboration of the imperative instruction in v. 6a: αἰτείτω δὲ ἐν πίστει μηδὲν διακρινόμενος. The following v. 7 pursues the argument further in hinting at the *Tun-Ergehens*-correlation, while v. 8 takes recourse to v. 6b in reviving the parable in a concrete application for the addressees: in explication of the figurative example, it describes the doubter (ἀνὴρ δίψυχος) as ἀκατάστατος ἐν πάσαις

---

[55] Cf. Popkes, *Jakobus* (n. 21), 100.

[56] For the interpretation of the laurels cf. also Ruben Zimmermann, *Geschlechtermetaphorik und Gottesverhältnis: Traditionsgeschichte und Theologie eines Bildfelds in Urchristentum und antiker Umwelt* (WUNT 2/122; Tübingen: Mohr Siebeck, 2001), 448–449.

[57] For the definition of parable as used in this essay cf. Ruben Zimmermann, "Die Gleichnisse Jesu: Eine Leseanleitung zum Kompendium," in *Kompendium der Gleichnisse Jesu* (ed. Ruben Zimmermann et al.; Gütersloh: Gütersloher Verlag, 2007), 3–46, 25–28.

ταῖς ὁδοῖς αὐτοῦ, specifying instability or double-mindedness as the central vice presented. Through the explicit interpretation of v. 6b in v. 8, the argument takes on a directive and normative aspect. However, in presenting the depiction ahead of its exegetical explication, the hearer is given some moments to find the meaning for himself and thus to learn inductively, although the exegesis is predefined in every detail. This dual way of instruction in form of persuasive description as well as explicative argumentation, covers a range of instructional possibilities and at the same time ensures the correct comprehension of the text in the absence of the author.

In Jas 1:23–25 a miniature parable finds integration in the argumentation: v. 22 introduces a general imperatival instruction (γίνεσθε δὲ ποιηταὶ λόγου καὶ μὴ μόνον ἀκροαταί), which is taken up in v. 23 in the conditional reverse (εἴ τις ἀκροατὴς λόγου ἐστὶν καὶ οὐ ποιητής ...) and illustrated by the first half of a parable story (vv. 23b–24): he who does listen but does not act is likened (ἔοικεν) to "a man," who looks in the mirror and then immediately forgets again what he looked like. V. 25 takes up the instruction from v. 22 in the indicative (ὁ δέ + aorist participle) and contrasts the forgetful hearer in vv. 23b–24 with him, ὁ παρακύψας εἰς νόμον τέλειον τὸν τῆς ἐλευθερίας καὶ παραμείνας.

The metaphor of the mirror is a well-known motif in the ancient world in literature and visual arts, and is usually associated with the semantic fields of death, memory/oblivion and transformation (instead of the modern notion of representation). Moreover mediation between the divine and the human world was achieved through mirrors.[58] For the exegesis of Jas 1:23–25 it can be stated that the addressees of the Letter of James could have been familiar with all these aspects which are present in pagan as well as Jewish tradition. However, although the Greek *termini* κατόπτρον or ἔσοπτρον or the verb κατοπτρίζεσθαι occur in the New Testament in 1 Cor 3:12, Jas 1:23 and 2 Cor 3:18, James adds a different focus by introducing the verb παρακύπτειν (Jas 1:25). This lexem occurs in the New Testament exclusively in the context of revelations: in Luke 24:12 and John 20:5, 11 it describes the disciples' stooping and looking into the empty tomb, in 1 Petr 1:12 it refers to the proclamation of the gospel.[59] Hence the parabolic image of looking into the mirror in v. 25 is not only a positive resumption of the negative part of the parable story (vv. 23–24) and an

---

[58] For attested evidence and an analysis of ancient theories of the perception through the mirror cf. Annette Weissenrieder, "Der Blick in den Spiegel: II Kor 3,18 vor dem Hintergrund antiker Spiegeltheorien und ikonographischer Abbildungen," in *Picturing the New Testament: Studies in ancient visual images* (ed. Annette Weissenrieder, Friederike Wendt and Petra von Gemünden; WUNT 2/193; Tübingen: Mohr Siebeck, 2005), 312–343.

[59] Cf. Wilhelm Michaelis, "παρακύπτω," *TWNT* 5 (1954): 812–814; cf. also Bauer-Aland, 1251.

application of the parable to the argument. It rather carries the parabolic image on by means of association: the hearer is reminded of and participates again in the life-transforming epiphany of the resurrection and equates the plerophoric expression νόμος τέλειος τῆς ἐλευθερίας with the gospel. While the volatile character perceives his πρόσωπον τῆς γενέσεως in the mirror, he who looks deeply will find the law, which must be read as a lexical variation of the "implanted word" (1:21). At this point the ancient mirror theories become significant in their core statement of the power of transformation attributed to the mirror image: the transformation referred to here is life according to the status of the new creation (1:18) through the acceptance (... καὶ παραμείνας, οὐκ ἀκροατὴς ἐπιλησμονῆς γενόμενος, v. 25) of the λόγος (1:21).

This second half of the parable constructs a direct relation between the image and the moral subject of the recipient. The passage is a pivotal point in that it explicates the type of ethics conveyed in the Letter of James: παρακύπτειν is directly identified with being ποιητὴς ἔργου, i.e. there is no distinction between cognition and action, between acceptance of the "word" and ethical conduct.[60] The argumentation at hand in James is a protreptic discourse, which purposefully and deliberately establishes and grounds theological-ethical *precepts* for ethical reflection and conduct – in other words: the focus is on the moral ethical *disposition*, concrete actions will follow from the correct, well-modelled person. Therefore in Jas 1:23–25 cognition plays an important role: the recipients are asked to look into the law as in a mirror in order to recognise their features and are motivated to remain looking and accept the transformation the λόγος works in them in order to change their character. Within the framework of the sustained argumentation the aim is to instruct the addressees in correct moral disposition through a text that constitutes a "call to remain in the covenant relationship as the constituted people of God," not a call to become members of the covenant community through proper conduct.[61] Hence from a prag-

---

[60] This finds corroboration in the passage on faith and works, Jas 2:14–26, where morally good action is linked to faith – i.e. a transformed character through faith should show a transformation with regard to actions, cf. Konradt, "Werke als Handlungsdimension" (n. 15), 320–321.

[61] John G. Gammie, "Paraenetic Literature: Toward the Morphology of a Secondary Genre," in *Paraenesis: Act and Form* (ed. John G. Gammie and Leo G. Perdue; Semeia 50; Atlanta, Ga.: Scholars Press, 1990), 41–77, 51, against Hartin, "Letter of James" (n. 15), 449, for it remains to be stressed that the addressees are Christians (1:18) and – although faith and correct moral conduct are closely correlated (2:14–26) – conversion through the "word of truth" is credited primacy (1:22) in relation to conduct (1:23–25); cf. also Stanley M. Hauerwas, *A Community of Character: Towards a constructive Christian social ethic* (Notre Dame, Ind.: University of Notre Dame Press, 1981), 131: "... because of the nature of the reality to which they have been converted, conversion is

matic perspective, the lively and memorable image in Jas 1:23–25 can play an important role in the formation of the moral character in a way similar to Jesus' parables: in antiquity the mirror is an image of self-awareness. Hence the hearer also has to identify with one of the two positions offered and account for his inner disposition. In the following the author provides an exact interpretation and evaluation of both ways of conduct in order to supply definitive instruction: the first character is said to deceive himself, the second character is promised οὗτος μακάριος ἐν τῇ ποιήσει αὐτοῦ ἔσται.

In Jas 5:7 a narrative miniature illustrates the virtue of patience: v. 7a conveys an imperative instruction to wait patiently for the παρουσία τοῦ κυρίου. With ἰδού v. 7b introduces a parable, which formally constitutes an example within the argumentative context.[62] The peasant who waits for the fruit of the earth is set before the eyes of the hearers as a model of perfect patience.[63] Although the correlation between v. 7a and the agricultural image is patently obvious, in v. 8a the author reinforces an interpretation of the parable as corroboration of v. 7a through the explicit repetition of the imperative μακροθυμήσατε καὶ ὑμεῖς ...

The image of the peasant in metaphorical correlation with the notion of hope is traditional: in Christian tradition the peasant is either portrayed as working towards the harvest (2 Tim 2:6) or the aspect is emphasized that man is not able to influence the ripening of the harvest (as e.g. in Mark 4:26–29).[64] Jas 5:7 does not follow in these lines: from the *ductus* of the argumentation and the lexical context (μακροθυμέω, ἐκδέχομαι, μακρο-θυμέω ἕως) the intended interpretation of the miniature parable as an illustration of the virtue of patience becomes evident.[65] The narrative is intended to motivate the recipients in the face of the delay of the parousia (vv. 7a, 8b, 9b) and at the same time emphasizes the prominence of vegetation metaphor in the context of Jacobean ethical argumentation as well as

---

something never merely accomplished but remains also always in front of them ... Therefore conversion denotes the necessity of a turning of the self that is so fundamental that the self is placed on a path of growth for which there is no end."

[62] Cf. Popkes, *Jakobus* (n. 21), 322: "lehrhafter Vergleich."

[63] It is neither intended nor possible within the scope of this paper to elaborate on the textcritical problem concerning the addendum of "rain" or "fruit." Cf. here Popkes, *Jakobus* (n. 21), 322–324 for a detailed presentation of the syntactic and hence exegetic problematics of this parable.

[64] Cf. Popkes, *Jakobus* (n. 21), 317–318, 320–321 – for the combination with hope cf. e.g. 1 Cor 9:7–10; Sir 6:19–20; Horace, *Ep.* II.1.139–143.

[65] Cf. Von Gemünden, *Vegetationsmetaphorik* (n. 23), 296–299. "Das [Bild des Bauern, S.L.] spiegelt kleinbäuerliche Verhältnisse, wo der Bauer und seine Familie von der Frucht der Erde leben müssen. Die Bildwahl könnte aber auch auf metaphorische Tradition zurückzuführen sein (cf. Ps 126,5. 6; Sir 6,19; Mk 4,26–29 par.)" (299).

the purport of creation theology within the letter's ethico-theological conception of Christian existence (cf. Jas 1:21).[66]

The use of parables in the Letter of James reflects a distinctive approach to the context of ethical teaching and admonition. Although the parables' purpose of adding an affective component to the cognitive argumentation is perpetuated, the basic characteristics inherent in parabolic narratives – their openness for interpretation and their ambiguity – are negated in that the syntactic or semantic context specifies the intended interpretation and classification in a rather normative way. The use of parabolic examples prevents an active participation of the recipient in the process of constructing meaning.[67] The use of figurative language within the argumentation hence shows close parallels to the application of examples in classical rhetoric.[68] This phenomenon may be due to the epistolary genre, as the communication situation presupposes the constellation of an absent speaker, who is forced to ensure the intention and pragmatics of his figurative, polyvalent examples are clear and unambiguous.

2.5 Parabolic Examples in Situational Adaptation

This paragraph focuses on parables used in a specific way: in two instances the argumentation of the Letter of James receives corroboration through example stories, i.e. short narratives introduced by ἐάν which depict a hypothetical setting or action and diatribic discourse within the recipients' community (εἰς συναγωγὴν ὑμῶν, 2:2); the recipients are part of the narrative and are imagined as interacting in an exemplary or non-exemplary manner. The example concludes with a rhetorical question through which the recipients are asked to judge their own conduct in the story. On the one hand, the examples picked are meant to illustrate a certain abstract (theological) point, not to recount actual occurrences, on the other hand the description is often exaggerated in a way that renders it implausible and carries the potential to induce the desired reaction in the recipients. These example stories are not to be counted among genuine parables as they do not narrate a parabolic story which the recipients have to transfer to their situation: the transfer is already accomplished in the narrative itself; the parable is personalized with respect to the recipients.

---

[66] Cf. Konradt, *Christliche Existenz* (n. 15) and the literature referred to in n. 15.

[67] Cf. Dieter Massa, "Verstehensbedingungen von narrativen Bildern," in Zimmermann, *Bildersprache verstehen* (n. 50), 313–330, 314.

[68] For further elaboration on parable theory in ancient rhetoric cf. Ruben Zimmermann, "Jesus' Parables and Ancient Rhetoric: The Contribution of Aristotle and Quintilian to the Form Criticism of the Parables," in Zimmermann, *Hermeneutik* (n. 5), 238–258.

In 2:2–3 the author reports the case of a wealthy man and a pauper join-ing the συναγωγή and develops fictionally the possible reactions of the members of the congregation towards the respective guest. In order to con-struct illustrative reference points between the story and the preceding in-struction (μὴ ἐν προσωπολημψίαις ἔχετε τὴν πίστιν τοῦ κυρίου ἡμῶν Ἰησοῦ Χριστοῦ τῆς δόξης, v. 1), the outward appearances of both *personae* are saliently opposed and elaborately visualized: the rich is described as χρυσοδακτύλιος ἐν ἐσθῆτι λαμπρᾷ, the poor as ἐν ῥυπαρᾷ ἐσθῆτι (v. 2). According to their appearance the guests are allocated a place of honour or a lowly footstool or no place at all (v. 3). The schematic depiction conveys the hypothetical and exemplary character of the scene; however, the por-trayal remains close enough to reality to be conceived of as relevant. In the light of the syntactic structure of the passage Jas 2:1–4, the introduction of the figurative story in v. 2 by ἐὰν γάρ and the deductive rhetorical ques-tion in v. 4, which is phrased in forensic terminology and requires a posi-tive, self-critical response, confirm the story's deployment as an example. Its purpose is to concretize what προσωπολημψία entails within the con-gregational situation and it concludes with an appeal to the recipients' power of discernment.[69]

The ethics conveyed here do not focus on the Jewish commandment for almsgiving but seem to be indicative of influences from Lev 19:15, defer-ring to judgement of the other as opposed to the love command, which is quoted in the context (Jas 2:8; cf. Lev 19:18; cf. also Jas 4:12).[70] Although James does not object to adopting imperative formulations from Old Tes-tament commandments (e.g. Jas 2:8[71], in 2:2–3 he prefers a "personal-ized" figurative rendering of his instruction, which offers exemplary fic-tional possibilities of conduct which explicitly involve the recipients. The rhetorical question aims at adequate conduct rooted in personal insight and discernment effected by way of the inductive teaching situation.

Another similar story substantiates the diatribic argumentation concern-ing the importance of the necessary interaction of πίστις and ἔργα in Jas 2:15–16, 18–19.[72] The example pictures a brother or sister in need of cloth-

---

[69] Cf. Popkes, *Jakobus* (n. 21), 160.

[70] For various suggestions for the interpretation of διακρίνεσθαι cf. Christoph Bur-chard, *Der Jakobusbrief* (HNT 15/1; Tübingen: Mohr Siebeck, 2000), 100; Popkes, *Ja-kobus* (n. 21), 164.

[71] Cf. Wiard Popkes, "James and Scripture: An Exercise in Intertextuality," *NTS* 45 (1999): 213–229.

[72] For a workable definition of diatribe cf. Stanley K. Stowers, *The Diatribe and Paul's Letter to the Romans* (SBL Dissertation Series 57; Ann Arbor, Mich.: Scholars Press, 1981); cf. also Heinrich Lausberg, *Elemente der literarischen Rhetorik: Eine Ein-führung für Studierende der klassischen, romanischen, englischen und deutschen Philo-*

ing and food and presents the fictitious reaction of τις ... ἐξ ὑμῶν (v. 16): the mere offering of a pious reply, which resumes an Old Testament as well as Christian traditional formula (ὑπάγετε ἐν εἰρήνῃ). This expression connotes the confirmation of saving faith[73] but also alludes to a denial of assistance as required by the Jewish obligation of social charity.[74] Both strands of tradition are intended to be associated by the recipients. This preposterous and farcical rendering intends drastically to illustrate the misconduct involved in neglecting the needs of the other by setting the value of words of faith above actual deeds. By selecting this incredible, hyperbolic example as a case study for his argument[75] and at the same time explicitly involving the recipients, the author can count on their indignation, possibly even their desire to defend or demarcate themselves against that sort of assumption, and may rely on their approbation of his following argument.[76]

Parables in situational adaptation or "personalized parables" constitute a device of addressing the recipients more explicitly than via the regular form of parables by personally involving them in the action as narrative personages as well as appealing to their moral judgement in the final rhetorical question. Both strategies enhance the impact of figurative teaching. In analogy to the use of absolute parables in the Letter of James, personalized parables are followed by an interpretation of the narrative miniature: a diatribic passage provides an answer in response to the rhetorical question at the end of the narrative. In this way the author predefines the intention and pragmatics and renders moral impulses and ethical instruction through the intuitive force of the images that appeal to the recipients and aim at forming their moral judgement and character. The stratagem of employing a diatribic passage makes it possible for the author not to judge the por-

---

logie (10th ed.; Ismaning: Hueber, 1990), 34 and Berger, *Formen und Gattungen* (n. 12), § 43.

[73] Ralph P. Martin, *James* (WBC 48; Waco, Tex.: Word Books, 1988), 84. Cf. e.g. Mark 5:34; Luke 7:50; 8:48.

[74] Cf. e.g. Exod 18:20; Mic 6:8; in 1:27; 2:12, 15–16; 5:1–6 the Letter of James refers to social welfare, especially concerning orphans and widows; for the tradition of these motifs cf. Gustav Stählin, "χήρα," *TWNT* 9 (1973): 428–454, esp. 436–448 and Heinrich Seesemann, "ὀρφανός," *TWNT* 5 (1954): 486–488; Mußner, *Jakobusbrief* (n. 31), 76–84; with reference to this verse cf. Burchard, *Jakobusbrief* (n. 70), 115–116; the verbs θερμαίνομαι and χορτάζω would – interpreted as passive imperatives – leave the fulfilment to the (logical) subject of the sentence, to God. Cf. Popkes, *Jakobus* (n. 21), 194.

[75] Cf. Popkes, *Jakobus* (n. 21), 192: "Fallbeispiel."

[76] Jas 2:18–19 will not be analysed within the context of this paper, as it does not involve figurative language, but rather the argumentative involvement of a fictive interlocutor, a rhetorical device which can be subsumed under the characteristics of the diatribe, cf. Frankemölle, *Jakobus* (n. 19), II 429–437 esp. concerning Jas 2:16.

trayed conduct himself but rather to have the recipients judge with the help of his guidance and then conceive of and change their conduct. Cognition plays an important role in this respect. It might be suggested that within the context of a diatribal discourse the author prefers to personalize his parabolic examples in order to incorporate the figurative illustration formally into the dialogue between the fictive speaker and his audience.

2.6 Parabolic Example based on Traditional Material

Jas 1:9–11 can operate as a generic example for the corroboration of the argumentation by way of compilations of different fragments of tradition:

9   Καυχάσθω δὲ ὁ ἀδελφὸς ὁ ταπεινὸς ἐν τῷ ὕψει αὐτοῦ,
10   ὁ δὲ πλούσιος ἐν τῇ ταπεινώσει αὐτοῦ, ὅτι ὡς ἄνθος χόρτου παρελεύσεται.
11   ἀνέτειλεν γὰρ ὁ ἥλιος σὺν τῷ καύσωνι καὶ ἐξήρανεν τὸν χόρτον καὶ τὸ ἄνθος
     αὐτοῦ ἐξέπεσεν καὶ ἡ εὐπρέπεια τοῦ προσώπου αὐτοῦ ἀπώλετο· οὕτως καὶ ὁ
     πλούσιος ἐν ταῖς πορείαις αὐτοῦ μαρανθήσεται.

The initial imperative (καυχάσθω) in v. 9 deploys a twofold link to ὁ ἀδελφὸς ὁ ταπεινὸς in v. 9 as well as to ὁ πλούσιος in v. 10 – the latter constituting a semantic incongruence but correlating with ὕψος in v. 9. Thus high and humble Christians[77] are set in opposition, offering an allusion to the tradition of Matt 23:12 (ὅστις δὲ ὑψώσει ἑαυτὸν ταπεινωθήσεται καὶ ὅστις ταπεινώσει ἑαυτὸν ὑψωθήσεται). However, only v. 9 shows lexical parallels to Matt 23:12, which is set in the context of the discussion of a person's status within the community, while 1:10a introduces the concrete parabolic example of a rich man (cf. also Jas 4:10).[78] This rich man's journey through life is described in v. 10b with images derived from the context of Isa 40[79]: Isa 40:4 speaks of vales that will be raised up and hills that shall be lowered – a metaphorical reference to what James has already said in vv. 9–10 in the words of Christian tradition.[80]

---

[77] Concerning the exegetical positions whether both rich and poor are brothers or whether the rich are *per definitionem* not part of the Christian community cf. Popkes, *Jakobus* (n. 21), 93–94.

[78] Cf. Burchard, *Jakobusbrief* (n. 70), 64; Frankemölle, *Jakobus* (n. 19), I 241 concludes from the allocation of references to the poor and the rich that the author of James intends to address problems that lie with the rich; Popkes, *Jakobus* (n. 21), 94 emphasizes the parallels concerning paradoxical boasting in traditional Christian material. This is relevant for the present study as it reveals a reversal of values. Jas 4:16 condemns the conventional form of boasting.

[79] Cf. Von Gemünden, *Vegetationsmetaphorik* (n. 32), 305–306 for further Old Testament parallels; based on a comparison with 1 Pet 1:23–24 Von Gemünden points out that James does not quote Isaiah, but shows relative latitude concerning his use of traditional material and its combination with different motifs.

[80] Cf. Burchard, *Jakobusbrief* (n. 70), 65: "Jak 1,10b–11 sind weder Zitat noch freie Anwendung von Jes 40, sondern ein neuer Text aus atl. Spolien (cf. 5,4f.)."

Vv. 6–8 compare the people of Israel with the grass and the flower of the field (simile), which perish at the breath of God. The aspect of beauty (εὐπρέπεια, *hapaxlegomenon* in the NT) does not occur in Isaiah but may refer to the tradition found in Matt 6:29.[81] It may be presupposed that the recipients were familiar with the motif of transience, which had become conventional in wisdom literature. With reference to Jas 5:2–3 it is remarkable that not prosperity is described as subject to transience, but the rich person.[82] In using the personalized form in the context of a corroborating, descriptive passage with the pragmatic intention of warning the addressees, the author achieves forceful and pointed criticism and admonition and thus aims to enhance the recipients' motivation.[83]

There is no mention of the sun in this context, but in contrast to the withering plants the word of God is said to be everlasting. As Isa 40:7–8 show a parallel structure, it may be possible to equate the breath of God with his everlasting Word, whereby the implicit context of this quotation in Jas 1:9 operates as a precursory reference to Jas 1:21, where the implanted word of God promises life. The aspect of the heat of the sun in Jas 1:11 links the passage in James to the tradition found in Matt 13:6, the parable of the sower and the seed, but shows some elaboration of the concise wording of the Matthean *dictum*, which merely says that with the rising of the sun the grass withered and dried up as it did not have roots. The problem lies with the interpretation of the parable in Matt 13:18–23, where this passage in the parable is said to refer to inconstant persons – actually the issue James discussed in vv. 5–8. Yet in the interpretation of the seed that fell among the thorns there is a reference to ἡ μέριμνα τοῦ αἰῶνος καὶ ἡ ἀπάτη τοῦ πλούτου, which keep the rich from accepting the word (Matt 13:22).

Even if these references are not straightforward, it can be stated that James deliberately chose to insert several points of reference to various Gospel traditions in order to enforce his argument with authoritative intertextual reference: he addresses the rich as well as the poor, the high in standing as well as the low, he refers to Gospel tradition and links it with Old Testament prophecy, he embeds vv. 9–11 within the context by indi-

---

[81] Οὐδὲ Σολομὼν ἐν πάσῃ τῇ δόξῃ αὐτοῦ περιεβάλετο ὡς ἓν τούτων.

[82] Cf. Frankemölle, *Jakobus* (n. 19), I 246–247; Frankemölle points out that in line with wisdom traditions James does in this passage not criticize wealth in itself, but the unsolidary attitude of the rich in social-ethical aspects and their delusive security concerning anthropological aspects (249–250).

[83] Cf. Frankemölle, *Jakobus* (n. 19), I 248: "Jeder Leser des Jak, ob niedriggestellt/arm oder reich ..., wird im Prolog [1:2–18, S.L.] angesprochen und direkt und unverhofft (nach Art einer Schocktherapie) mit seiner Vergänglichkeit konfrontiert." Concerning the device of personalization cf. Jas 1:14–15, where sin and lust are displayed as personalized powers.

rectly linking the passage with Jas 1:5–8 by way of the crosswise uptake of the parable story and the effected reference to the inconsistent believer. And most important: through the implied reference to the story of the sowing of the word – which might cause the addressees, who will have been familiar with this parable or otherwise would have had trouble understanding the authors' argumentation, to identify with one of the four parable positions – he places a link to the following instruction to accept the implanted word in Jas 1:21. Thus the author illustrates in creation terminology the opposition between the withering, destructive experience of a life lived apart from the word (Jas 1:9) and the flourishing life in the Christian existence (Jas 1:21).

Concerning the use of the parabolic potential of language in this passage it can be said that James applies traditional contents as well as traditional forms within the context of his argumentation, with which the addressees presumably were familiar.[84] Yet he does not tell the whole parable story (e.g. of the sower and the seed), but only hints at certain aspects of traditional material and uses the metaphorical content as a figurative example to strengthen his argument, thus prompting the recipients to associate the missing sections in their minds. By merely dropping hints to various strands of tradition the author provides for a certain latitude concerning which associations the individual recipient is likely to follow – possibly those which he remembers best or those which apply to his current situation;[85] however, in order to control the interpretation and pragmatic impact of his propositions, the author never fails to give his explicit interpretation of the images involved (cf. the summarizing note in v. 11b), even when he only inserts fragments or allusions to parables in his argumentation.

---

[84] See Hartin, "Letter of James" (n. 15), 450: "Social scientific interpreters would refer to this as 'high-context communication' – there is no need for James to spell out his meaning because he presumes his hearers/readers already know what he is talking about." – I would like to apply this to the passage discussed here.

[85] Cf. Hauerwas, *Community of Character* (n. 61), 66 concerning scripture as an authority: "The moral use of scripture, therefore, lies precisely in its power to help us remember the stories of God for the continual guidance of our community and individual lives." The Letter of James intends to be an aid for remembering these stories of the gospel tradition, which his recipients know already but need to remember in order to continue living according to "the word" (Jas 1:21).

2.7 Comparative Examples[86] in the Context of an Ekphrasis

The anthropological-ethical description of the character of the tongue in Jas 3:1–12, which culminates in the programmatic diagnosis of the unnatural duality of speech, is illustrated by examples from everyday life and characterized by strong metaphorical language. Parallels to the discourse can be found in Jewish wisdom literature, where two categories of the genre are especially distinguished: *ekphraseis* on vices and on virtues,[87] which treat ethical or moral topics, are characterized by a persuasive, non-argumentative *ductus* and based on empirical observations and the subsequent explicative application for the persuasive drive of the discourse. In order to demonstrate the contextual coherence and cohesion of the similes in Jas 3:1–12 it is indispensable to analyze the entire passage.

Using the directive genre of wisdom speech[88] the author presents an initial programmatic imperative admonition (v. 1a), which extends into an explicit eschatological warning according to the *Tun-Ergehens*-correlation (v. 1b). The admonition μὴ πολλοὶ διδάσκαλοι γίνεσθε is usually regarded as having been taken from topical traditional material.[89] V. 2a corroborates v. 1a by pointing out an anthropological insight quite generally and adhortatively: πολλὰ γὰρ πταίομεν ἅπαντες. The τέλειος ἀνήρ – who is able to speak and act in the right way – is set in opposition in the context of a general *sententia*, which seems to promote this Hellenistic ideal and is substantiated and elaborated on in the following descriptive passage.[90]

The main clause of v. 2b introduces the rheme χαλιναγωγεῖν, which is taken up again as theme in v. 3 and constitutes the main aspect of compari-

---

[86] Or παραβολή according to Aristotle's definition, cf. Aristotle *Rhet.* 1393 b 4–8; cf. Zimmermann, "Jesus' Parables and Ancient Rhetoric" (n. 68), 246: "the rhetorical function of examples, as in metaphors, is derived from a relation of similarity." However, as the Letter of James does not reveal a formal-logical argumentation, Aristotle's categories have to be applied to the text, especially in the case of the *ekphrasis* in 3:1–12, with great caution.

[87] Cf. e.g. *T. Benj.* 3:1; 4:1–5:3; 6:1–6; 8:2–3; cf. Max Küchler, *Frühjüdische Weisheitstraditionen: Zum Fortgang weisheitlichen Denkens im Bereich des frühjüdischen Jahweglaubens* (OBO 26; Fribourg: Universitätsverlag, 1979), 478–486 (cf. also Prov 1–9; Ps 37; 49; 73; Eccl 3:1–8).

[88] Cf. Berger, *Formen und Gattungen* (n. 12), 207, 211: Ekphrasis, cf. e.g. Wis 7:22–8:1 and 1 Cor 13:4–7, 8–10, 13 for a more abstract description and comparison of the motifs.

[89] Cf. William R. Baker, *Personal Speech-Ethics in the Epistle of James* (WUNT 2/68; Tübingen: Mohr Siebeck, 1995), 105–122; Burchard, *Jakobusbrief* (n. 70), 135–137; Sophocles *Ant.* 1023–1024; Aristotle [*Rhet. Alex.*] 37; Seneca *Clem.* I.6.3; Epictetus *Diatr.* 1.11.7; Philo *Deus* 75. However, it also alludes to ὑμεῖς δὲ μὴ κληθῆτε ῥαββί εἷς γάρ ἐστιν ὑμῶν ὁ διδάσκαλος, πάντες δὲ ὑμεῖς ἀδελφοί ἐστε in Matt 23:8.

[90] Cf. Berger, *Formen und Gattungen* (n. 12), 245: Jas 3:2b is grouped under the category of "Kennzeichensatz" which indicates when somebody commits sin.

son in vv. 2b–3, because the lexicographic resumption of σῶμα parallelizes man and animal and the formulation εἴ τις ἐν λόγῳ οὐ πταίει describes the state of the bridled tongue in analogy to the bridled horse. It marks the possibility of bridling and holds out the prospect of the subsequent ability to control the whole body.[91] The grammatical-structural connection with the copulative-coordinating construction ἰδοὺ καί (v. 4) seems to line up another example for bridling; yet the explicit lexical recourse to μετάγειν and the implicit reference to the body in the figurative depiction of the ship are overruled by a new contrastive aspect, the opposition μικρός – μεγάλη. Hence the topic shifts from the possibility of the bridling of the tongue (vv. 2–3) to a miniature parable concerned with the problem of the tongue's power (v. 4).[92] In v. 5a μικρός is applied in a comparison of the human tongue (μικρὸν μέλος) with the rudder of a ship and acquires a new aspect of meaning: while the illustration of the ship in v. 4 exemplifies an empirical fact in neutral terms, v. 5a evaluates the power of the tongue by means of the verb αὐχέω. In v. 5b ἰδού introduces a further example which varies the correspondence ἡλίκος – ἡλίκος from vv. 4–5a in the picture of the fire. The metaphor of the tongue as πῦρ in v. 6 finally presents a direct parallelization of the two powers, which is carried on in a metaphorical depiction of the tongue as fire and a series of traditional metaphorical attributes.[93] Within the context of the development of the argumentation vv. 3–4 and v. 5b constitute similes[94], *exempla*, which corroborate the persuasive aspect of the argument through vivid illustrations.

The figurative language of v. 7 alludes to the Old Testament: the polysyndetic phrase πᾶσα γὰρ φύσις θηρίων τε καὶ πετεινῶν, ἑρπετῶν τε καὶ ἐναλίων refers back to the horse in v. 3 as well as it takes up the subject of control in the verb δαμάζειν. This *exemplum* is followed by an anthropo-

---

[91] Differently Dibelius, *Jakobus* (n. 26), 227, who interprets the opposition between "great" and "small" as the comparative aspect of both examples; in my view the first example is based on the reference to "bridle/bridling" in v. 2b, the second recurs to "directing" in v. 3, but focuses on the power of direction, cf. Popkes, *Jakobus* (n. 21), 216.

[92] With Peter H. Davids, *The Epistle of James: A Commentary on the Greek Text* (NIGTC; Exeter: Paternoster Press, 1982), 135–149 against e.g. Popkes, *Jakobus* (n. 21), 218–219, 550, who proposes an ecclesiological interpretation, interpreting the body/ship as the church, the tongue/helmsman as the teacher, the winds as the "Irrungen des Lebens." Similar: Frankemölle, *Jakobus* (n. 19), II 480–513.

[93] Cf. above 2.1. In 3:6 τρόχος τῆς γενέσεως is a Hellenistic-Jewish creation metaphor; 3:7 has a lexical parallel in Gen 1:26 (LXX), which is open the association with creation terminology.

[94] *Similitudo*: both are examples of the *quaestio infinita*, which was used in classical rhetoric as adornment – or as in this case as corroboration of an argument – in connection with a *quaestio finita*; cf. Lausberg, *Elemente* (n. 72), § 82.2–3, § 83. Cf. also Von Gemünden, *Vegetationsmetaphorik* (n. 32), who lables e.g. the similes of the well and of the trees-and-fruits "Bildworte."

logical aphorism in v. 8, which explicitly opposes the tamed creation and the untameable human tongue: τὴν δὲ γλῶσσαν οὐδεὶς δαμάσαι δύναται ἀνθρώπων. This is not a contradiction to the use of χαλιναγωγεῖν in Jas 1:26 and 3:2, which describes a bridling or conscious refraining.[95] In the Letter of James the τέλειος ἀνήρ (3:2) and the wise man (3:13–18) are able *to bridle* the tongue[96], but no human creature is able *to tame* the tongue.[97] This first part of the passage, the *ekphrasis* in vv. 1–8, is structured to develop the thesis in v. 2a under four aspects: the first illustration focuses on the failure of the tongue (*exemplum*: horse), the second on the power of the tongue (*exemplum*: ship), the third illustration on the evil of the tongue (*exemplum*: fire) and the fourth on the taming of the tongue (*exemplum*: taming of animals). While the first illustration is argued inductively, the other three are developed deductively, thus increasing the high pedagogic value of the parabolic discourse.

The evil of the tongue is a *topos* frequently used in Greco-Roman literature.[98] E.g. Plutarch[99], Seneca[100] and Epictetus[101] are concerned with the destructive powers of the tongue and the difficulty of controlling it. A person's character is judged by his speech[102]: "a person who does or says harmful things [is labelled] ignorant rather than sinful."[103] This reveals the notion that it was regarded as possible to influence speech through education.[104] Hence the author seems to have been able to draw on a great variety of traditional material: the imagery employed in Jas 3:1–6 derives from Greco-Roman as well as Hellenistic Jewish literature, from Wisdom tradition, mystery religions and Stoic philosophy.[105] In the Letter of James

---

[95] Cf. Gerhard Schneider, "δαμάζω," *EWNT* I (1980): 660 and Klaus Berger, "χαλιναγωγέω," EWNT III (1983): 1084; auch Bauer-Aland, 340, 1745.

[96] This topos is derived from Jewish tradition and refers to the law-abiding person (cf. e.g. Eccl 3:7; 6:11); according to Prov 17:27 it characterizes the wise man, who is able to control the tongue; cf. also Frankemölle, *Jakobus* (n. 19), II 495–499.

[97] Cf. e.g. Mark 5:4; Dan 2:40 (LXX).

[98] Concerning the use in general Greek literature cf. Johannes Behm, "γλῶσσα κτλ," *TWNT* I (1933): 719–726.

[99] Cf. *Mor.* 1.10f–11c; 6.452e–464d, 506c, 507b.

[100] Cf. *Ira* 1.2.2.

[101] Cf. *Diatr.* 2.26.1–7; 3.2.14–15; 3.20.15–16; *Ench.* 2.48.

[102] Cf. Hesiod *Theog.* 611–614; Seneca *Vit. beat.* 20.6; Plutarch *Mor.* 1.10a.33–34; 6,464; Isokrates *Nic.* 8.

[103] Cf. Baker, *Speech-Ethics* (n. 89), 118.

[104] Cf. Baker, *Speech-Ethics* (n. 89), 117–120.

[105] For parallels in classical literature, Philo and concerning the motif of the horse, the charioteer, the ship, the helmsman, of the dominion over animals, the classification of animals, the untameable tongue, the well with sweet and salty water, the correlation of tree and fruit cf. the references to the respective verses in the commentaries of Dibelius,

these traditions are taken up, reinterpreted and strategically employed to corroborate the *ekphrasis*, thus opening its teaching to a wide range of recipients by structural and thematic affiliation to and derivation from a wide spectrum of cultural, religious, ethical and literary sources.[106] On the other hand, this new compilation of traditions asserts a claim to universal validity. From a pragmatic view, the author uses images from fields the addressees are familiar with in their everyday life, from nautics, agriculture and nature in general.[107] The human dimension is always opposed to the non-human dimension, often with reference to creation. The argumentation of this passage is characterized by an extensive use of comparisons.

Vv. 9–12 transfer the abstract and general teaching to the actual situation of the addressees by mentioning their habit of praising God the Father, the *Creator*, and swearing at man, God's *creation*. The εὐλογία καὶ κατάρα, which come ἐκ τοῦ αὐτοῦ στόματος, are taken up in v. 11 in the description of the well: ἐκ τῆς αὐτῆς ὀπῆς it cannot pour forth sweet *and* salty water.[108] This is followed by another interrogatively formulated example in v. 12a, which may be taken from the synoptic tradition (cf. Matt 7:16–20; Lk 6:43–44): the example of the fig tree, which bear olives as the vine cannot bear figs. Just as the synoptic tradition focuses on the impossibility of thorns (ἄκανθα, τρίφολος, βάτος) bearing fruit (σταφυλή, σῦκον), the author of James focuses on the identity of tree and fruit (μὴ δύναται, ἀδελφοί μου, συκῆ ἐλαίας ποιῆσαι ἢ ἄμπελος σῦκα;), but reshapes the semantic material from the combination of fruit–thorns to fruit–trees.[109] Just like Matt 12:33–37 James employs the image in the context of ethics concerning speech. Even if v. 12a is not a direct quotation, it constitutes an explicit allusion to Gospel tradition. It can be assumed that it therefore draws on its authority with the recipients in order to operate as corroborat-

---

Jakobus (n. 26), Popkes, *Jakobus* (n. 21) and Mußner, *Jakobusbrief* (n. 31); cf. esp. Ps 62:5 and Lam 3:38 for the unnatural state of good and bad coming from one mouth.

[106] Cf. *Dibelius*, Jakobus (n. 26), 232–233.

[107] Possibly the "Bildspender" fire, water, air and earth have to be considered in the context of creation metaphor, cf. Philo *Deo* 107–149; Wis 19:18–22; Sir 13:2.

[108] Cf. Von Gemünden, *Vegetationsmetaphorik* (n. 32), 268; for parallels in traditional material cf. Popkes, *Jakobus* (n. 21), 235.

[109] Cf. Popkes, *Jakobus* (n. 21), 236; cf. also Von Gemünden, *Vegetationsmetaphorik* (n. 32), 268–269, who detects a difference between the gospel ("Unvereinbarkeit von Gutem und Schlechtem") and the Jacobean ("Unvereinbarkeit von Gattungsunspezifischem") propositions derived from the respective context and gives Plutarch *Mor.* 6.472, Epictetus *Diatr.* 2.20.18–19 as parallels for Jas 3. In my opinion, however, thorns are not to be paralleled with rotten trees and therefore the connotation of good and bad of the Gospel tradition is not inherent to the example, but indicated by the Gospel context; as James employs the tradition apart from this context and situates it within the new context of the unnaturalness of the sweet and salty well, this interpretation may be associated by the recipients, but is not necessarily intended by the author.

ing example for the preceding rhetorical question in v. 11, which is answered in the very brief metaphorical conclusion of the whole paragraph in v. 12b: οὔτε ἁλυκὸν γλυκὺ ποιῆσαι ὕδωρ. For the sake of the parallelization of στόμα and πηγή in v. 11 no further parallelization is necessary in order for the mention of the well to awake a chain of connotations in the recipients (πηγή = στόμα = εὐλογία καὶ κατάρα), which leads to the conclusion that as the salty well cannot give sweet water, corrupted creation cannot speak good things, i.e. the dualism inherent in human speech is not *natural* (as shown in the examples from nature: well, fruits), but against the order of creation.[110] This might refer back to Matthean tradition, where the Q-tradition of the tree bearing fruit is taken up a second time (Matt 12:33–37) in the context of ethics concerning speech and with the focus on the impossibility of proper conduct: πῶς δύνασθε ἀγαθὰ λαλεῖν πονηροὶ ὄντες; While Matthew takes the possibility into consideration that good persons act accordingly (12:35), the author of James determines a negative metaphorical judgement over all humankind that is not to be counted either as τέλειος ἀνήρ or as wise, for the salty well cannot give sweet water.

Hence the central proposition of the entire passage presents an opposition between fallen and new creation, associating "unnatural" conduct in the language of creation metaphors with the fallen creation and "natural" conduct – as is promoted through the argumentation with reference to the recipients, who have gained the privileged status (1:18) – with the new creation. From a pragmatic point of view, the examples are explicitly referential and descriptive, but on the perlocutionary level they exert a directive impulse:[111] Again creation metaphors are to remind the recipients of the dualism between old and new creation and their responsibility for appropriate conduct according to their status (cf. Jas 1:18). The *ekphrasis* combines metaphors, miniature parables and figurative examples within an argumentative setting and gains persuasive power through the high quantity of figurative language used. The force of the illustrations arises from their simplicity and universal intelligibility as well as their vividness and coherence throughout the passage.

---

[110] Cf. Frankemölle, *Jakobus* (n. 19), II 520. The wise and perfect refers to the new status as ἀπαρχή τῶν κτισμάτων (Jas 1:18; 3:13–18), the argumentation is implicitly based on creation-theology and eschatology.

[111] Cf. Theodor Lewandowski, *Linguistisches Wörterbuch* (3 vols.; UTB; 5th ed.; Heidelberg: Quelle & Meier, 1990), III 788–789; cf. also John L. Austin, *Zur Theorie der Sprechakte* (2nd ed.; Stuttgart: Reclam, 1998), 116–133.

3. The Ethics Conveyed

As has become evident from the above analysis, the text focuses on protreptic ethics, i.e. it does not primarily focus on concrete moral actions but deals with an abstract, less material version of ethical character formation on a meta-level. Instructions like "don't be δίψυχος" (1:8) or "do not live your faith ἐν προσωπολημψία" (2:1) and the like are difficult to apply and are therefore in urgent need of having their subject concretized through illustration by concrete metaphors. This is implemented in the Letter of James through the use of creation metaphors, which carry the dual potential of being easily comprehensible but also being applicable to the theological concept of the new creation. Although abstract values like love, empathy or justice do occur in the argumentation, it is significant that the Letter of James does not base its discourse *primarily* on those values. The author's way of conveying ethical instruction becomes evident e.g. in Jas 1:14–15, where the implications of ἐπιθυμία – sin and death – are illustrated with the help of a transferral to the sphere of creation and grounded in an analogy to the process of giving birth. It is precisely the figurative rendering of instruction which promises the potential for a profound impact in protreptic ethical instruction.

Throughout the letter, however, the argumentation is corroborated by various standards in order to establish precepts of moral action. They are founded implicitly on certain moral concepts and ideas such as can be derived from the motivations and rationales employed. Standards of conduct or elements of ethics are described with their advantages and disadvantages, are evaluated, on the other hand they are discussed, recommended or discarded. Linguistically this often works without the use of explicit imperatives. In 1:27 e.g. we find the description and definition of the virtue of piety, in 2:14, 17, 20–26 of faith and works, in 3:15–18 of the virtue of wisdom. Jas 3:17 presents a catalogue of the characteristics of wisdom; Jas 1:3–4 a genealogy of virtues is presented in the case of endurance, faith and testing, in 1:15 a genealogy of vices in the case of lust, sin and death (cf. also 3:16; 4:1), Jas 1:13–18 conveys teaching on virtues and vices, with the consequences being explicitly demonstrated in 3:16 (consequences of resentment and controversies are disorder and bad behaviour), 3:18 (consequence of peace is justice/righteousness) as well as in 4:1 (from controversies arises lust).

Leading values mentioned in the Letter of James include perfection (1:4; 3:17–18) and blamelessness (1:4), steadfast faith (1:5–8), patience (1:2–3; 5:7–8), royal law/law of freedom/brotherly love (2:8; 2:12)[112], the correlation of faith and works (2:14–26), wisdom (3:15–18); among vices

---

[112] Cf. Niebuhr, "Ethik und Anthropologie" (n. 13), 340–341.

the author mentions being δίψυχος (1:6–8; 3:9–10), possessing riches (1:10–11; 5:1–6), the judgement of others (2:1–4; 4:1), withdrawal from works of faith/alms (2:14–26; 5:3–5), friendship with the world (4:4–5) and its consequences. An explicitly negative evaluation can be found in 4:16: πᾶσα καύχησις τοιαύτη πονηρά ἐστιν. Jas 3:15–18 present an extended discourse on norms, a "Belehrung über Verhaltensweisen und über das Verhältnis der Verhaltensweisen zueinander" and a description of the impact of a certain kind of conduct.[113] All of these values focus on character formation and hence rank among individual material-ethical goods in the sense that they are related to individual salvation. The focus is obviously not on formal-ethical principles in a deontological sense or with reference to the Jewish or Hellenistic traditions. Rather are all these values teleologically oriented in that the norms and maxims of action they are based on all centre in *perfection* in order to win the crown of life (1:12).

This perfection stands for correct moral conduct as expected from the ἀπαρχή τῶν κτισμάτων (1:18) – i.e. while the overall epistolary argumentation concerning protreptic ethics is based on these values, the individual arguments and admonitions are corroborated by creation metaphors, which function as a concretization of the abstract concept of the new creation, and the appeal for right Christian moral conduct. This means, the letter does not *explicitly* ground its dispositional ethics in abstract norms and standards but via the concretization of creation metaphors *implicitly* in the sum of all norms and values mentioned, which constitute the ideal of the perfect Christian existence.[114] The right disposition for perfect ethical conduct is therefore grounded in the affiliation to the new creation (cf. 1:18; in the sense of 2 Cor 5:17). Hence the corroborating images as well as the underlying maxims of James' ethical admonition primarily focus on the ingroup perspective and revolve around identity-formation within the early Christian community.[115]

---

[113] Berger, *Formen und Gattungen* (n. 12), 269; generally, loc. cit., § 68 for "Normendiskurs;" Hermann von Lips, *Weisheitliche Traditionen im Neuen Testament* (Neukirchen-Vluyn: Neukirchener Verlag, 1990), 437–438: a literary form, "[die] nicht der atl.-jüdischen Weisheitstradition, sondern (wahrscheinlich) der hellenistischen Popularphilosophie [entstammt];" cf. also Frankemölle, *Jakobus* (n. 19), II 557–558: closest parallels in Wis 7:22–8:1; cf. also 1 Cor 13:4–7; *T. Dan* 4.

[114] Cf. Wolter, "Ethos und Identität" (n. 18), 439: Paul's ethos is founded on πίστις. Cf. also Konradt, "Handlungsanweisungen" (n. 15), 311: "Verankerung des Lebenswandels im Konversionsgeschehen." For the close relations between Jesus tradition in Q and the teaching of the Letter of James cf. Patrick J. Hartin, *James and the Q sayings of Jesus* (JSNT.SS 47; Sheffield: JSOT Press, 1991), *passim*.

[115] Cf. Margaret MacDonald, *Pauline Churches: a socio-historical study of institutionalization in the Pauline and Deutero-Pauline writings* (SNTS.MS 60; Cambridge: Cambridge University Press, 1988), *passim* for early Christian ethical conventions as "markers" of Christian identity and culture and as community stabilizing and community pro-

The basic framework of conveying ethics in the epistle is an argumentative setting. The argumentation gains its persuasive power by opening up the affective dimension of character formation through the author's use of figurative examples in order to advance and illustrate the rather abstract argumentation, which remains on a meta-level throughout chapters 1–3, dealing with the correct spiritual disposition, i.e. with protreptic ethics, not with instructions for concrete actions. The author usually employs images to form inductive teaching situations, i.e. the figurative examples substantiate the argumentation just as the argumentation explains the metaphoric miniature or fragmentary allusions to tradition. Hence ethical teaching in the Letter of James is not restricted to cognitive transmission of imperative or implicitly directive instruction, but it is not exclusively characterised by the associative freedom of figurative language either. The combination of figurative and argumentative aspects and thus of the affective and aesthetic level with the cognitive level in the Letter of James presumes the recipients' involvement in interpreting the figurative passages and their being thus forced to discern and regenerate their own disposition. Images are employed as minute allusions which draw associations within the argumentation and thus touch the affective and mnemonic level in the recipient while all the same carrying on the argumentation. In this way, the use of figurative language comes close to Aristotle's rhetoric use of figurative language as examples for the rhetorical argumentation.[116]

Nature is employed as a mirror to reflect the fallen creation (cf. esp. Jas 3). In recurrence to ancient mirror theories, Jas 1:23–25 presents the man who looks into the mirror of the λόγος and – if this is done properly – is transformed into the new creation, which has already been sown into the addressees and will be allowed to grow if it is nurtured by a continued connection to the character-forming and thus life-giving word. In order to safeguard this connection to the word of the gospel, the author alludes to and thus reminds the recipients of a variety of traditional material. On the assumption that the Letter of James is addressed to Christians (1:18) it could be stated that through being reminded of familiar tradition, the recipients are made aware of the fact, that they do not live according to the word as they should according to their status as new creation (1:18, 21). The new law for this status is equivalent with the implanted word (1:21), with the νόμος τῆς ἐλευθερίας (1:25) and the νόμος τελεῖτε βασιλικός (2:8): it might even be labeled the "law of the new creation." Through the

---

tecting factor; cf. also Zimmermann, "Implicit Ethics" (n. 13), 402: "The values, such as virtues or the Torah, take their importance not from logic, but from their acceptance in a certain community."

[116] Aristotle subsumes the use of an "example" (παράδειγμα) under inductive argumentation. Cf. Zimmermann, "Jesus' Parables and Ancient Rhetoric" (n. 68), 243–247.

appeal of stooping into the law (1:22–25) the addressees are reminded of their conversion and first insight; they are enabled to evaluate their present conduct, recognize their "misconduct" – and then the intention to turn back may arise from within.

Thus the text intends to form and improve the recipients' character through insight into their present state and recurrence to their individual memory and experience.[117] The primary intent of the Letter of James is not to convey normative standards for Christian conduct through language of obligation; the author rather employs the recipients' mnemonic and imaginative forces to stimulate them to formulate their own normative admonition out of the letter's free-associative depiction: while the frame for associations is set by the traditional material used and by interpretation following the figurative miniatures, the recipients are only provided with hints and implicit imperatives. In that the spontaneous selection of associations is left to the individual, the impact of the letter will be different depending on the individual as well as on the specific situation according to the associations yielded to in the respective moment of reception. While the main *ductus* of the argumentation and the propositions of traditional material used are predetermined, the author leaves the impact of his teaching to the instructive potential of the individual recipient's connotative perception. Owing to the timelessness of images especially from everyday situations as well as from religious tradition, the validity and effectiveness of the argumentation are not restricted to the original rhetorical situation and the text may claim effective and universal influence.

4. Conclusions: The Conveyance of Ethics through Figurative Language

Summa summarum it has to be established that in the Letter of James ample application is made of figurative language:

– *Metaphors* serve to explain abstract or complex theological concepts through their correlation with specific and uncomplicated concepts and illustrating images from familiar contexts. They are used to convey familiar contents in an innovative-heuristic and therefore attractive and motivating way. The surplus value of metaphors in ethical argumentation lies in the potential of the semantic tension generated to intensify persuasive propositions through vivid images that assert an impact beyond cognitive

---

[117] Cf. Garleff, *Urchristliche Identität* (n. 42), 41–42: ethics is founded "in der Erinnerung zu vergegenwärtigenden Heilsgeschehens;" "der Verweis auf die Story der Bekehrung ([Jas] 1,13–15) dient wie gesehen ... der Begründung des Ethos" (306).

reasoning. Metaphors operate with respect to the affective aspect, arousing attention, irritation, reflection or fear.

– *Moral agents* draw on the tradition of the interpretative community and are thus based on and further generate group identity. In addition to their purpose of enabling the addressees' identification with the depicted character, whose conduct is presented as exemplary, the Old Testament role models reinforce the addressees' identification with their community and its moral rules. Succinct reference to the narrative personages initializes a polyvalent interpretation and latitude for associations concerning their stories, concerning ethical instruction, personal memories and theological concepts associated with the symbolic figure. This invitation for the interaction of the recipient induces more intense ethical stimulations than a verbose argumentation.

– *Macarisms* in the Letter of James are phrased in figurative language. They convey paradoxical propositions, which attract attention and require further argumentative reasoning on the side of the author as well as further enquiry and a reflection on moral values and value hierarchies on the side of the recipients. The positive phrasing is intended to persuade the recipients to comply with the proposed ideals, to adopt the aspired objectives as their own and act accordingly, motivated by the positive reinforcement.

– *Parables* are employed in order to add an affective component to the cognitive argumentation but their polyvalence and their ambiguity are limited. The use of parabolic examples in the Letter of James prevents a positively active participation of the recipient in the process of the construction of meaning in that the figurative miniature is usually presented at the beginning of the argument in order to achieve an inductive teaching situation, but is then specified by the syntactic or semantic context in order to ensure the clarity and unambiguity of the author's intended interpretation and pragmatics. This phenomenon can be ascribed to the communication situation of the epistolary genre.

– *Parables in situational adaptation* or "personalized parables" involve the recipients more explicitly and more existentially in the ethical argumentation than regular parables and appeal to their moral judgement. They are also followed by an interpretation in form of a diatribic passage which defines the authorial intention, gives moral impulses and ethical instruction.

– In *compilations* of traditional material, James takes up fragments of tradition, prompting the recipients to associate the missing sections and providing for a certain latitude concerning the individual's associations. However, these associations function as affective corroboration of the author's argumentation; his intention and the pragmatic impact of his propositions are always ensured through explicit interpretation.

– The *ekphrasis* combines metaphors, miniature parables and figurative examples within an argumentative setting and gains persuasive power through the high quantity of figurative language usage. The force of the illustrations arises from their simplicity and universal intelligibility as well as the vividness and coherence throughout the passage.

Concerning the constellation of images in the Letter of James it becomes obvious that more or less the whole range of textual images is derived from the field of nature – from faunal and botanical creation as well as from the human sphere and the elements of nature.[118] As *"Bildspender"* metaphors from the non-human creation are paralleled with the human sphere – creation imagery constitutes a "root metaphor" of early Christian religious language and the central figurative motif in the Letter of James.[119] Most pieces of figurative language are taken from tradition, especially from Old Testament wisdom texts (cf. Sir 24; 28),[120] but are compiled in an innovative way (e.g. Jas 1:9–11), set within a distinctive context that differs from the original, e.g. gospel context (e.g. Jas 3:12). In this way, traditional metaphors are reinterpreted in the light of the new creation and are reinstalled in Christian contexts. However, it seems to be the author's strategy to allude to multiple familiar traditions and thus lay the foundations for the recipients' connotative perception.

Epistolary literature had to develop new forms of self-determined, independent aspects in teaching which took into account the communication situation marked by the author's personal absence. The Letter of James demonstrates one possibility in particular: figurative language is regularly applied in very brief sketches, i.e. often merely sparse facets are mentioned and the recipients are invited to complement the depiction with their associations and memories. This form of open and active learning in the post-conversional state promises the potential for further character formation. It is clearly evident, that James' ethical teaching is characterised by a con-

---

[118] With reference to the elements of nature cf. e.g. Jas 3:6 (fire); 1:6; 3:11–12 (water); 1:6 (wind/air); 5:7 (earth).

[119] "Wurzelmetapher:" cf. Von Gemünden, *Vegetationsmetaphorik* (n. 32), 2 according to the terminology of Earl R. MacCormac, "Die semantische und syntaktische Bedeutung von religiösen Metaphern," in van Noppen, *Erinnern* (n. 40), 84–107, 94 and based on Stephen Pepper, *World Hypotheses and the Structure of Metapsychology* (Berkeley, Calif.: University of California Press, 1942).

[120] Cf. the correlation of Torah, wisdom and creation in Sirach; cf. e.g. Jessie F. Rogers, "Wisdom and creation in Sirach 24," *JNSL* 22 (1996): 141–156; Leo G. Perdue, *Wisdom and Creation: The Theology of Wisdom Literature* (Nashville, Tenn.: Abingdon Press, 1994), esp. 243–290 and Roland E. Murphy, "Wisdom and Creation," *JBL* 104 (1985): 3–11.

gruence of form, content and pragmatic purport: the argumentation proceeds on a meta-level and is corroborated by figurative language, which
both cooperates in advancing ethical instruction with a focus on character
formation and intends to prepare within the recipients the foundation, the
ethical grounding, for subsequent admonitions and instructions (cf. chapters 4 and 5). It is the formation of character which is aimed at – on the
figurative level as well as through the kind of ethics conveyed within the
entire argumentative text, for the main stress concerning ethical instruction
in the Letter of James is on protreptic ethics.

The "Ethics" of Badmouthing the Other:

Vilification as Persuasive Speech Act in First Clement

LAMBERT D. JACOBS

1. Introduction

In the process of getting your audience to follow your advice, it is not enough to merely advertise your own goods. You must also get rid of the competition. In ancient texts one way to do that was to show the opponents in a bad light. In a brief, but very informative study Andrie du Toit describes how vilification operated as pragmatic device in early Christian letters.[1] He remarks: "[v]ilifying your opponent, like praising your addressees, has through the centuries been a useful persuasive weapon from the arsenal of a skilled speaker or writer."[2] Sean Freyne, in another important study of vilification in early Christian texts, describes the goal of such strategies as "aimed at destroying the social and political *persona* of one's adversary."[3]

That the author of 1 Clement was exactly that – an extremely skilled writer – has been well and truly established. Vielhauer is one of many scholars who attest to the rhetorical skills of the author of 1 Clement, when he writes: "[d]iese rhetorisch-stilistischen Elemente sind in größere literarische Zusammenhänge eingefügt, in homiletische und paränetische Ausführungen."[4]

Welborn argues from the fact that the church in Rome did not have the right (yet) to intervene so drastically in the local matters of the church in Corinth.[5] Therefore more rhetorical skill was definitely required.[6] Welborn

---

[1] Andrie B. du Toit, "Vilification as a Pragmatic Device in Early Christian Epistolography," *Bib* 75 (1994): 403–412.

[2] Du Toit, "Vilification" (n. 1), 403.

[3] Sean Freyne, "Vilifying the Other and Defining the Self: Matthew's and John's Anti-Jewish Polemic in Focus," in *"To See Ourselves as Others See Us:" Christians, Jews, "Others" in Late Antiquity* (ed. Jacob Neusner and Ernest S. Frerichs; Chico, Calif.: Scholars Press, 1985), 117–143.

[4] Philipp Vielhauer, *Geschichte der urchristlichen Literatur: Einleitung in das Neue Testament, die Apokryphen und die Apostolischen Väter* (Berlin: de Gruyter, 1975), 534.

[5] Laurence L. Welborn, "Clement, First epistle of," *ABD* 1 (1992): 1055–1060, 1056. Cf. also Chrys C. Caragounis, "From obscurity to prominence: The development of

posits "[t]hat the author did not possess the authority he claims is evident from the rhetorical character of the letter: he must *persuade* by argument and *induce* by example; that is, it is not yet his to *command*."[7] That he then also employed the persuasive technique of vilifying the opponents in the community of Corinth, should be fairly obvious.

With reference to the categories of vilification identified by Du Toit,[8] I shall endeavour to show how the author of 1 Clement has in fact applied this group of speech acts very skilfully. We shall attempt to answer the questions: what was his intention in showing the offenders in a bad light and how did he achieve that? In this objective I fully agree with Luke Johnson when he sets about surveying the anti-Jewish vilification in the early Christian writings: "I do not worry about what to *do* with this language so much as about what the language was *doing*."[9]

One should keep in mind that the "historical" opponents in 1 Clement could in fact have had exactly the same characteristics (or not at all!).[10] That we cannot establish. What is however important, is to show how the offenders are portrayed in the text and against the rhetorical situation painted by the author.

2. Hypocrisy and falseness

To label someone as a hypocrite and a fraud or as pretending to be someone or something that he is not, was well known in early texts.[11] It is also listed prominently in the vice lists of the New Testament.[12]

Günther explains the use of the word group ὑποκρίνω in the epistolary literature as follows: "[e]s ist eine der aus der Sünde stammenden Verhal-

---

the Roman church between Romans and 1 Clement," in *Judaism and Christianity in First-century Rome* (ed. Karl P. Donfried and Peter Richardson; Grand Rapids, Mich.: Eerdmans, 1998), 245–279, 276.

[6]   Barbara E. Bowe, "Clement, Epistles of," *EDB* (2000): 263–264, 263, confirms: "[i]n keeping with acceptable *rhetorical strategy,* the author(s) provides only vague allusions to the exact nature of the dispute and its cause" (italics mine).

[7]   Welborn, "Clement, First" (n. 5), 1056 (italics mine).

[8]   Du Toit, "Vilification" (n. 1), 405–410.

[9]   Luke T. Johnson, "The New Testament's Anti-Jewish Slander and the Conventions of Ancient Polemic," *JBL* 108 (1989): 419–441, 419 (italics mine).

[10]   Cf. Du Toit, "Vilification" (n. 1), 411–412 under the heading: "The Relationship between the Encoded Adversaries and Their Real-life Counterparts."

[11]   Du Toit, "Vilification" (n. 1), 405, lists a number of occurrences in the New Testament and the Apostolic Fathers.

[12]   Cf. Rom 1:29; 3:13; 2 Cor 4:2; 1 Thess 2:3; 1 Pet 2:1; 3:10.

tensweisen gemeint, die die eigene Person auf Kosten der Wahrheit ins Licht setzt und so einen falschen Schein erweckt."[13]

An excellent example of such a warning against hypocrites can be found in 1 Clem 15:1, where the readers are exhorted:

Τοίνυν κολληθῶμεν τοῖς μετ᾽ εὐσεβείας εἰρηνεύουσιν καὶ μὴ τοῖς ὑποκρίσεως βουλομένοις εἰρήνην.

(Therefore let us unite with those who devoutly practice peace, and not with those who *hypocritically* wish for peace.)[14]

The next five verses in chapter 15 continue to show then how these deceitful people operate. The most important characteristic is that what is in their hearts and what comes from their lips are not the same.[15] To strengthen the warning, Scripture citations abound in the chapter, e.g. the citation of Ps 61:5 in 15:3:

καὶ πάλιν Τῷ στόματι αὐτῶν εὐλογοῦσιν τῇ δὲ καρδίᾳ αὐτῶν κατηρῶντο.

("... They blessed with their *mouth,* but they cursed with their *heart.*")

Then follows a citation of Ps 78:36–37 in 1 Clem 15:4:

Ἠγάπησαν αὐτὸν τῷ στόματι αὐτῶν καὶ τῇ γλώσσῃ αὐτῶν ἐψεύσαντο αὐτόν ἡ δὲ καρδία αὐτῶν οὐκ εὐθεῖα μετ᾽ αὐτοῦ οὐδὲ ἐπιστώθησαν ἐν τῇ διαθήκῃ αὐτοῦ.

("They loved him with their *mouth,* but with their *tongue* they lied to him; their *heart* was not right with him, nor were they faithful to his covenant.")

A very strong curse is launched against the opponents when two further Scripture citations follow in 1 Clem 15:5a. The first reference is to Ps 31:18:

διὰ τοῦτο ἄλαλα γενηθήτω τὰ χείλη τὰ δόλια τὰ λαλοῦντα κατὰ τοῦ δικαίου ἀνομίαν.

(Therefore, "let the deceitful *lips* that speak evil against the righteous be struck speechless.")

And then follows an even stronger death wish in 1 Clem 15:5b where Ps 12:3 is quoted:

---

[13] Walther Günther, "Lüge: ὑποκρίνω κτλ," *TBNT* II/1 (1969): 917–919, 922, 918. Cf. also Ulrich Wilckens, "ὑποκρίνομαι κτλ," *TWNT* 8 (1969): 558–571.

[14] I provide the English translation of citations from 1 Clement throughout to enhance the readability of the text and for this purpose the recently revised text of Michael W. Holmes, ed., *The Apostolic Fathers: Greek Texts and English Translations* (3rd ed.; Grand Rapids, Mich.: Baker, 2007) is used.

[15] Andreas Lindemann, *Die Apostolischen Väter 1: Die Clemensbriefe* (HNT 17; Tübingen: Mohr Siebeck, 1992), 58, speaks of "das Wesen der Heuchelei, indem sie vom Widerspruch zwischen 'Mund (bzw. Zunge)' und 'Herz' reden."

καὶ πάλιν Ἐξολεθρεύσαι κύριος πάντα τὰ χείλη τὰ δόλια γλῶσσαν μεγαλορήμονα τοὺς εἰπόντας Τὴν γλῶσσαν ἡμῶν μεγαλυνοῦμεν τὰ χείλη ἡμῶν παρ' ἡμῖν ἐστιν τίς ἡμῶν κύριός ἐστιν.

(And again: "May the Lord utterly destroy all the deceitful *lips*, the boastful *tongue*, and those who say, 'Let us praise our *tongue;* our *lips* are our own. Who is lord over us?'")[16]

Related to hypocrisy is also the accusation of falseness. Du Toit maintains that characteristics with the ψεύδ-prefix are employed very often when referring to the opposition.[17]

What is interesting to note is that the warning in 1 Clem 15 is not against hypocrisy as such, but against being hypocritical about peace. The two types of people played off against each other, are described as being earnest about peace versus saying that they are but not really meaning it.[18] The main concern, however, stays peace and harmony in the community of Corinth.

3. Belittling the opponents

When one can describe the opponents as only a few or as not very important, then the picture of them in the minds of the audience becomes "smaller." Eventually it is not really worthwhile to follow such an insignificant cause.

In 1 Clem 1:1 the cause of the problematic situation in the Corinthian community is described as:

τῆς τε ἀλλοτρίας καὶ ξένης τοῖς ἐκλεκτοῖς τοῦ θεοῦ μιαρᾶς καὶ ἀνοσίου στάσεως ἣν ὀλίγα πρόσωπα προπετῆ καὶ αὐθάδη ὑπάρχοντα εἰς τοσοῦτον ἀπονοίας ἐξέκαυσαν.

(... the detestable and unholy schism, so alien and strange to those chosen by God, which *a few* reckless and arrogant *persons*[19] have kindled to such a pitch of insanity.)

Again it must be stressed that there could actually have been only a few dissidents, but it is important for the author of 1 Clement to describe them thus. Later on we hear again that the trouble has been started by only a few, when 1 Clem 47:6 states:

---

[16] The translation of Lindemann, *Clemensbriefe* (n. 15), 57, is extremely strong: "*Ausrotten* möge der Herr alle trügerischen Lippen, die prahlerische Zunge ..." (italics mine).

[17] Du Toit, "Vilification" (n. 1), 405. Cf. also Ulrich Becker and Hans-Georg Link, "Lüge: ψεύδομαι κτλ," *TBNT* II/1 (1969): 919–922, 920.

[18] Wilckens, "ὑποκρίνομαι" (n. 13), 569.

[19] Lindemann, *Clemensbriefe* (n. 15), 26, also highlights that "einige wenige Personen" caused the trouble in Corinth.

αἰσχρά ἀγαπητοί καὶ λίαν αἰσχρά καὶ ἀνάξια τῆς ἐν Χριστῷ ἀγωγῆς ἀκούεσθαι τὴν βεβαιοτάτην καὶ ἀρχαίαν Κορινθίων ἐκκλησίαν δι᾽ ἓν ἢ δύο πρόσωπα στασιάζειν πρὸς τοὺς πρεσβυτέρους.

(It is disgraceful, dear friends, yes, utterly disgraceful and unworthy of your conduct in Christ, that it should be reported that the well-established and ancient church of the Corinthians, because of *one or two persons,* is rebelling against its presbyters.)

The troublemakers are also cut down to size as young, foolish and people of no real importance, when 1 Clem 3:3 describes the crisis as:

οὕτως ἐπηγέρθησαν οἱ ἄτιμοι ἐπὶ τοὺς ἐντίμους οἱ ἄδοξοι ἐπὶ τοὺς ἐνδόξους οἱ ἄφρονες ἐπὶ τοὺς φρονίμους οἱ νέοι ἐπὶ τοὺς πρεσβυτέρους.

(So people were stirred up: those *without honour* against the honoured, those of *no repute* against the highly reputed, the *foolish* against the wise, the *young* against the old.)

Du Toit explains how the subtle use of the indefinite pronoun τινές can work together towards "belittling" the strength and appearance of the opposition.[20]

4. Inflated self-esteem

Related to belittling your opponents is the charge that they think far too much of themselves. Du Toit describes this act of vilification as follows: "[o]pponents are often depicted as people with an inflated self-consciousness which manifests itself in arrogance, boasting and self-elevation."[21]

This is an accusation often levelled against the group causing the division in Corinth. Right at the outset of the letter we read in 1 Clem 1:1 that these people are:

πρόσωπα προπετῆ καὶ αὐθάδη ὑπάρχοντα.

(a few reckless and *arrogant* persons.)

Later on we find them in 1 Clem 14:1 to act:

τοῖς ἐν ἀλαζονείᾳ[22] καὶ ἀκαταστασίᾳ μυσεροῦ ζήλους ἀρχηγοῖς ἐξακολουθεῖν.

(those who in *arrogance* and *unruliness* have set themselves up as leaders in abominable jealousy.)

The implication in 1 Clem 16:1 is that they exalted themselves over the church in Corinth:

---

[20] Du Toit, "Vilification" (n. 1), 406.

[21] Du Toit, "Vilification" (n. 1), 407.

[22] It is so apt when Andreas Lindemann and Henning Paulsen, *Die Apostolischen Väter: Griechisch-deutsche Parallelausgabe* (Tübingen: Mohr Siebeck, 1992), 95, translate ἀλαζονεία here with "Prahlerei."

Ταπεινοφρονούντων γάρ ἐστιν ὁ Χριστός οὐκ ἐπαιρομένων ἐπὶ τὸ ποίμνιον αὐτοῦ.

(For Christ is with those who are humble, not with those who *exalt themselves over his flock.*)

Then they are contrasted in 1 Clem 16:2 with Jesus Christ:

τὸ σκῆπτρον τῆς μεγαλωσύνης τοῦ θεοῦ ὁ κύριος Ἰησοῦς Χριστός οὐκ ἦλθεν ἐν κόμπῳ ἀλαζονείας οὐδὲ ὑπερηφανίας[23] καίπερ δυνάμενος ἀλλὰ ταπεινοφρονῶν καθὼς τὸ πνεῦμα τὸ ἅγιον περὶ αὐτοῦ ἐλάλησεν.

(The majestic sceptre of God, our Lord Christ Jesus, did not come with the *pomp* of *arrogance* or *pride* [though he could have done so], but in humility, just as the Holy Spirit spoke concerning him.)

Another strong accusation is aimed at the offenders in Corinth in 1 Clem 21:5, when they are said to be:

μᾶλλον ἀνθρώποις ἄφροσι καὶ ἀνοήτοις καὶ ἐπαιρομένοις καὶ ἐγκαυχωμένοις[24] ἐν ἀλαζονείᾳ τοῦ λόγου αὐτῶν προσκόψωμεν ἢ τῷ θεῷ.

(foolish and senseless people, who *exalt* themselves and *boast* in the *arrogance* of their words, rather than God.)

In 1 Clem 30:1 a powerful list of character traits to be strongly avoided is given, listing also:

βδελυκτὴν ὑπερηφανίαν.

(detestable *pride.*)

Then a Scripture citation (linking Prov 3:34, Jas 4:6 and 1 Pet 5:5) is called upon in support in 1 Clem 30:2:

"Θεὸς γὰρ φησίν ὑπερηφάνοις ἀντιτάσσεται ταπεινοῖς δὲ δίδωσιν χάριν."

("For God," it says, "resists the *proud,* but gives grace to the humble.")

Another reference to pride and arrogance comes in 1 Clem 35:5 where the readers are exhorted to steer away from:

ὑπερηφανίαν τε καὶ ἀλαζονείαν κενοδοξίαν[25] τε καὶ ἀφιλοξενίαν.

(... *pride* and *arrogance, vanity* and inhospitality.)

---

[23] Here again the translation of Lindemann and Paulsen, *Apostolischen Väter* (n. 22), 97, is on target with "im Gepränge der *Prahlerei* und des *Übermuts*" (italics mine).

[24] Du Toit, "Vilification" (n. 1), 408, remarks: "The καύχησις-label was, of course, a quite popular *denigrating* device" (italics mine). Cf. also Rudolf Bultmann, "καυχάομαι, καύχημα, καύχησις κτλ," *TWNT* 3 (1938): 646–654, and Josef Zmijewski, "καυχάομαι κτλ," *EWNT* 2 (1981): 680–690.

[25] Lindemann and Paulsen, *Apostolischen Väter* (n. 22), 119, translate κενοδοξίαν with "leere Ruhmsucht."

The members of the congregation are admonished in 1 Clem 30:6 to avoid self-praise:

ὁ ἔπαινος ἡμῶν ἔστω ἐν θεῷ καὶ μὴ ἐξ αὐτῶν· αὐτεπαινέτους γὰρ μισεῖ ὁ θεός.

(Let our praise be with God, and not from ourselves, for God hates those who *praise themselves*.)

Bultmann highlights the warning against boasting that is found in 1 Clement: "[i]n der späteren Literatur wird die alttestamentlich-christliche *Warnung* vor dem Selbstruhm und die *Mahnung* zur Demut fortgeführt."[26]

In portraying the offenders as people who are arrogant and who deem themselves as far too important, the intended readers are influenced to keep away from them and to expose them for what they are, boastful and conceited. This provides a powerful persuasive tool in the hand of the author.

5. The charge of blasphemy

The utmost form of human arrogance is when a human being lifts his voice against the living God. That cannot be endured. If an author can lay the charge of blasphemy at the feet of his opponents, then his case is half won. Blasphemy also features prominently in the vice catalogues of the New Testament.[27]

In the text of 1 Clem there is no full blown case of blasphemy in the sense of "cursing or slandering the name of God,"[28] but the implication is levelled that the seditious party in the community created a situation where the name of God's elect, the church in Corinth, had been slandered.[29] We read right at the outset in 1 Clem 1:1:

Διὰ τὰς αἰφνιδίους καὶ ἐπαλλήλους γενομένας ἡμῖν συμφορὰς καὶ περιπτώσεις βράδιον νομίζομεν ἐπιστροφὴν πεποιῆσθαι περὶ τῶν ἐπιζητουμένων παρ' ὑμῖν πραγμάτων ἀγα- πητοί τῆς τε ἀλλοτρίας καὶ ξένης τοῖς ἐκλεκτοῖς τοῦ θεοῦ μιαρᾶς καὶ ἀνοσίου στάσεως ἣν ὀλίγα πρόσωπα προπετῆ καὶ αὐθάδη ὑπάρχοντα εἰς τοσοῦτον ἀπονοίας ἐξέκαυσαν ὥστε τὸ σεμνὸν καὶ περιβόητον καὶ πᾶσιν ἀνθρώποις ἀξιαγάπητον ὄνομα ὑμῶν μεγάλως βλασφημηθῆναι.

---

[26] Bultmann, "καυχάομαι" (n. 24), 653 (italics mine). Cf. also Zmijewski, "καυχάο- μαι" (n. 24), 688–690.

[27] Hermann W. Beyer, "βλασφημέω, βλασφημία, βλάσφημος," *TWNT* 1 (1933): 620– 624, 623.

[28] Henry L. Carrigan Jr., "Blasphemy," *EDB* (2000): 191.

[29] Carrigan, "Blasphemy" (n. 28), 191, defines blasphemy as such: "It is not only an act committed against God ... but also an act of slandering, abusing, or reviling other people or groups ..."

(Because of the sudden and repeated misfortunes and reverses that have happened to us, brothers, we acknowledge that we have been somewhat slow in giving attention to the matters in dispute among you, dear friends, especially the *detestable* and *unholy* schism, so alien and strange to those chosen by God, which a few reckless and arrogant persons have kindled to such a pitch of insanity that *your good name,* once so renowned and loved by all, *has been greatly reviled.*)

At a later stage in the letter, in 1 Clem 47:7, the blame is again placed on those who brought strife to the community, for the fact that other malevolent forces are blaspheming the name of the Lord:[30]

καὶ αὕτη ἡ ἀκοὴ οὐ μόνον εἰς ἡμᾶς ἐχώρησεν ἀλλὰ καὶ εἰς τοὺς ἑτεροκλινεῖς ὑπάρχοντας ἀφ' ἡμῶν ὥστε καὶ βλασφημίας ἐπιφέρεσθαι τῷ ὀνόματι κυρίου διὰ τὴν ὑμετέραν ἀφροσύνην ἑαυτοῖς δὲ κίνδυνον ἐπεξεργάζεσθαι.

(And this report has reached not only us but also those who differ from us, with the result that you heap *blasphemies upon the name of the Lord* because of your stupidity, and create *danger for yourselves* as well.)

Referring also to the above quoted text, Otfried Hofius explains how the accusation of blasphemy functioned in paraenetic expressions:

"Die Christen werden vor einem Verhalten gewarnt, das dazu Anlaß gibt, daß ihr Heilsstand (Röm 14, 16), ,der Name Gottes und die (christl.) Lehre' (1 Tim 6, 1) oder ,das Wort Gottes' (Tit 2, 5) unter den Nichtchristen *verlästert,* d.h. *in Verruf gebracht* und damit zum Gegenstand von Spott und Verachtung werden (vgl. Ign Trall 8, 2; 1 Klem 47, 7; 2 Klem 13)."[31]

The charge that the wrongdoing of the opposing party in Corinth caused the church to fall in dishonour with the surrounding churches, is supported by Chadwick:

"The action of the Corinthian community in deposing one group of clergy and replacing them by another cannot have failed to embarrass other churches in Greece and Asia Minor. The Corinthian church may have started by supposing that their clergy were their own private affair, and that they could set them up and put them down by some sort of democratic process. They must quickly have discovered that no church could live to itself alone ..."[32]

The fact that they have caused the church and God Himself to be "blasphemed" was a severe accusation, one that the readers could not take light-

---

[30] In his commentary on this text, Horacio E. Lona, *Der erste Clemensbrief: Übersetzt und erklärt* (KAV 2; Göttingen: Vandenhoeck & Ruprecht, 1998), 512, states the seriousness of the matter in no uncertain terms: "[d]ie erste Folge aus dem Bekanntwerden des Konflikts auch außerhalb der Gemeinde ist die Lästerung des Namens Gottes." And then he adds: "[w]eil die Gemeinde die Sache Gottes in der Welt repräsentiert, wirft die verlorene Eintracht Schatten auf den Namen Gottes selbst."

[31] Otfried Hofius, "βλασφημία κτλ," *EWNT* 1 (1980): 527–532, 529.

[32] Henry Chadwick, "Justification by Faith and Hospitality," in *Studia Patristica* (ed. Frank L. Cross; vol. 4/2; TU 79; Berlin: Akademie-Verlag, 1961), 281–285, 283.

ly, and one that would indeed go a long way towards influencing them against the offenders in Corinth.

6. Obscure, shadowy characters

A strong technique of vilification is to portray your opponents as dark, shadowy characters. Du Toit explains: "[t]o discredit antagonists they are occasionally depicted as stealthy characters who carry out their hidden agendas in the dark."[33]

Again the role of the indefinite pronoun τίνες can play a role here. Apart from showing the offenders as smaller in number and less important, τίνες "may also be aimed at a *deliberate blurring* of the faces of opponents in order to portray them as negative, shadowy characters."[34] Lindemann calls τίνες here a "typischer Topos antiketzerischer Polemik" and states that it refers to the "Aufrührer" and not in general to the Christians in Corinth.[35]

To indicate how this shadowy, obscure portrayal of people can be obtained, Du Toit cites 1 Clem 59:1 where the dissident few in Corinth are warned:[36]

Ἐὰν δέ τινες ἀπειθήσωσιν τοῖς ὑπ' αὐτοῦ δι' ἡμῶν εἰρημένοις γινωσκέτωσαν ὅτι παραπτώσει καὶ κινδύνῳ οὐ μικρῷ ἑαυτοὺς ἐνδήσουσιν.

(But if *certain people* should disobey what has been said by him through us, let them understand that *they* will entangle themselves in no small sin and danger.)

The pejorative, negative tone in this text is unmistakable.

7. Evil / witchery / sorcery

Related with the above is a technique of vilification whereby the opponents are shown to influence the congregation through evil or witchery or sorcery.[37] A hint of such an insinuation in the text of 1 Clement can be found in 1 Clem 57:5, where we read:

---

[33] Du Toit, "Vilification" (n. 1), 406.
[34] Du Toit, "Vilification" (n. 1), 406.
[35] Lindemann, *Clemensbriefe* (n. 15), 164.
[36] Du Toit, "Vilification" (n. 1), 407.
[37] Du Toit, "Vilification" (n. 1), 407.

ἔσται γὰρ ὅταν ἐπικαλέσησθέ με ἐγὼ δὲ οὐκ εἰσακούσομαι ὑμῶν ζητήσουσίν με κακοί[38] καὶ οὐχ εὑρήσουσιν ἐμίσησαν γὰρ σοφίαν τὸν δὲ φόβον τοῦ κυρίου οὐ
προείλαντο οὐδὲ ἤθελον ἐμαῖς προσέχειν βουλαῖς ἐμυκτήριζον δὲ ἐμοὺς ἐλέγχους.

(At that time, when you call upon me, I will not listen to you. *Evil ones* will seek me but
not find me, for they *hated wisdom* and did not choose the fear of the Lord, nor did they
desire to pay attention to my advice, but mocked my correction.)

Then the reason for this judgement is given in 1 Clem 57:6:

τοιγαροῦν ἔδονται τῆς ἑαυτῶν ὁδοῦ τοὺς καρποὺς καὶ τῆς ἑαυτῶν ἀσεβείας[39]
πλησθήσονται.

(Therefore they will eat the fruit of their own way and be filled with their own *ungodli-
ness.*)

Those that stay obedient to the Lord and steer clear of the evildoers, will
escape the judgement, as promised in 1 Clem 57:7:

ὁ δὲ ἐμοῦ ἀκούων κατασκηνώσει ἐπ᾽ ἐλπίδι πεποιθὼς καὶ ἡσυχάσει ἀφόβως ἀπὸ παντὸς
κακοῦ.

("But the one who hears me will dwell safely, trusting in hope, and will live quietly, free
from fear of all *evil.*")

People judged to have evil powers or do evil things, are definitely to be
avoided by the readers of this message.

8. Moral depravity

An extremely important device in digging a hole for the opposing party
was to show that they lacked moral integrity.[40] The misdeeds could be of a
sexual nature or could have some financial connotation or could simply
imply that someone ate or drank too much.

In 1 Clem 30:1 a long list of moral vices is given that the people of Corinth should steer clear of. They are admonished thus:

Ἁγίου οὖν μερὶς ὑπάρχοντες ποιήσωμεν τὰ τοῦ ἁγιασμοῦ πάντα φεύγοντες καταλαλιάς
μιαράς τε καὶ ἀνάγνους συμπλοκάς μέθας τε καὶ νεωτερισμοὺς καὶ βδελυκτὰς ἐπιθυμίας
μυσερὰν μοιχείαν βδελυκτὴν ὑπερηφανίαν.

---

[38] The translation of Lindemann and Paulsen, *Apostolischen Väter* (n. 22), 143, supports the notion of sorcery, when they read κακοί here as "Böse." Kirsopp Lake, *The
Apostolic Fathers, with an English Translation* (vol. 1; LCL; London: Heinemann, 1912),
107, also sees it as "evil."

[39] Lake, *Apostolic Fathers* (n. 38), 109, translates ἀσεβείας strongly with "wickedness."

[40] Cf. Du Toit, "Vilification" (n. 1), 408–409.

(Seeing then that we are the portion of the Holy One, let us do all the things that pertain to holiness, forsaking *slander*, disgusting and *impure embraces, drunkenness* and *rioting* and *detestable lusts,* abominable *adultery,* detestable *pride.*)

In 1 Clem 35:5 another vice list appears, including the accusations of pride and arrogance mentioned earlier:

πῶς δὲ ἔσται τοῦτο ἀγαπητοί ἐὰν ἐστηριγμένη ᾖ ἡ διάνοια ἡμῶν πιστῶς πρὸς τὸν θεόν ἐὰν ἐκζητῶμεν τὰ εὐάρεστα καὶ εὐπρόσδεκτα αὐτῷ ἐὰν ἐπιτελέσωμεν τὰ ἀνήκοντα τῇ ἀμώμῳ βουλήσει αὐτοῦ καὶ ἀκολουθήσωμεν τῇ ὁδῷ τῆς ἀληθείας ἀπορρίψαντες ἀφ' ἑαυτῶν πᾶσαν ἀδικίαν καὶ πονηρίαν πλεονεξίαν ἔρεις κακοηθείας τε καὶ δόλους ψιθυρισμούς τε καὶ καταλαλιάς θεοστυγίαν ὑπερηφανίαν τε καὶ ἀλαζο-νείαν κενοδοξίαν τε καὶ ἀφιλοξενίαν.

(But how shall this be, dear friends? – if our mind is fixed on God through faith; if we seek out those things that are well-pleasing and acceptable to him; if we accomplish those things that are in harmony with his faultless will, and follow the way of truth, casting off from ourselves all *unrighteousness* and *lawlessness, covetousness, strife, malice* and *deceit, gossip* and *slander, hatred of God, pride* and *arrogance, vanity* and *inhospitality.*)

These can of course be just normal moral exhortation, but the implication could very well be that these are the kind of acts that the offenders occupied themselves with.[41]

9. A perversive influence

Largely because of their moral depravity, the offending opponents are portrayed as leading the readers on the wrong path. Spreading their evil doings – the yeast metaphor is used often in the New Testament for this[42] – they have a bad influence on the community.

This is especially true in the text of 1 Clement. The people leading the revolt against the presbyters are portrayed as people who should not be followed. Du Toit remarks: "[i]n 1 Clem, due to the purpose of that document, the antagonists are the scapegoats causing all sedition, tumult and strife among the Corinthian Christians."[43]

In 1 Clem 21:5, a text already cited in the section on arrogance, the audience are urged rather to offend these arrogant people than to offend God. The text reads:

---

[41] Colin G. Kruse, "Virtues and Vices," in *Dictionary of Paul and His Letters* (ed. Gerald F. Hawthorne and Ralph P. Martin; Downers Grove, Ill.: Intervarsity, 1993), 962–963, 962, refers to the use of vice lists in the Pauline letters "to depict the depravity of unbelievers."

[42] Cf. Mark 8:15; Acts 15:24; Gal 5:9.

[43] Du Toit, "Vilification" (n. 1), 409.

μᾶλλον ἀνθρώποις ἄφροσι καὶ ἀνοήτοις καὶ ἐπαιρομένοις καὶ ἐγκαυχωμένοις ἐν ἀλαζονείᾳ τοῦ λόγου αὐτῶν προσκόψωμεν ἢ τῷ θεῷ.

(*Let us offend foolish and senseless people,* who exalt themselves and boast in the arrogance of their words, rather than God.)

The danger of the possible influence of the offenders is also evident in 1
Clem 30:1 when the readers are admonished to flee away from all their
evil doings. We read:

Ἁγίου οὖν μερὶς ὑπάρχοντες ποιήσωμεν τὰ τοῦ ἁγιασμοῦ πάντα φεύγοντες καταλαλιάς
μιαράς τε καὶ ἀνάγνους συμπλοκάς μέθας τε καὶ νεωτερισμοὺς καὶ βδελυκτὰς ἐπιθυμίας
μυσερὰν μοιχείαν βδελυκτὴν ὑπερηφανίαν.

(Seeing then that we are the portion of the Holy One, let us *do all the things* that pertain
to *holiness, forsaking slander,* disgusting and *impure embraces, drunkenness* and *rioting*
and *detestable lusts,* abominable *adultery,* detestable *pride.*)

The nature of the examples given from the Old Testament and the recent
history is also such that these people are characterised as trustworthy examples to be followed, but that the community should be on the lookout
for anyone with wrong intentions trying to lead them astray.

10. Associated with dubious historical characters

A strong vilifying technique is to associate the opposition with characters
from history of whom the mere mentioning of their names would immediately ring a negative bell. Du Toit mentions the negative association that
the names Balaam[44] (used in 2 Pet 2:15; Jude 11 and Rev 2:14)[45] and Jezebel (used in Rev 2:20–23)[46] carried.[47] In their respective articles on Bi-
leam/Balaam, Groß explains how the image of Bileam "verdunkelt sich"[48]
and Kuhn confirms how the name Bileam is used "als abschreckendes Beispiel."[49]

---

[44] Jo Ann Hackett, "Balaam," *ABD* 1 (1992): 569–572, 572, adds: "Rabbinic commentators generally saw in Balaam a representative of all that was bad in 'the nations.'"

[45] Christopher A. Rollston, "Balaam," *EDB* (2000): 144–145, 144, confirms: "Furthermore, the NT references to Balaam are all negative, viewing him as a prototype of
false teachers in the NT period."

[46] Karla G. Bohmbach, "Jezebel," *EDB* (2000): 713–714, 713, states: "Is Jezebel an
archetypal wicked woman? (Her name is used symbolically in Rev. 2:20–23 to refer to a
prophetess who is 'beguiling' the congregation at Thyatira 'to practice fornication and to
eat food sacrificed to idols.')."

[47] Du Toit, "Vilification" (n. 1), 410.

[48] Walter Groß, "Bileam," *NBL* 1 (1991): 300–301, 300.

[49] Karl Georg Kuhn, "Βαλαάμ," *TWNT* 1 (1933): 521–523, 523, states: "Man sieht
deutlich: Das Stichwort: 'Bileam' als abschreckendes Beispiel ist der christlichen Pole-

In 1 Clem the use of examples and non-examples abound (see below). It is important to note where these are used. Immediately after the problem in Corinth is attributed to jealousy and strife in 1 Clem 3, a series of Biblical characters with a bad track record on jealousy is listed in chapter 4, viz. Cain,[50] Jacob, Joseph's brothers, Moses' fellow Egyptian, Dathan and Abiram, etc.

The ring that this list has to it is something in the order of: don't even think of following these upstarts in Corinth, unless you want to be counted with such dubious characters as Cain and his colleagues. And as Lindemann stated in his commentary on this chapter: "[z]weifellos ist die Reihe in 1 Clem nicht einfach ad hoc zusammengestellt worden."[51] The names on the list were carefully selected to show the dangers of "Eifersucht" and "Neid" in the community.

11. Prone to judgement

The looming judgement day of the Lord is often used as a vilifying technique. The people following the wrong way are heading for the wrath of God. Du Toit shows how such an expression most often is not aimed at the opponents or the false teachers in the congregation, but is directed as a warning or admonition at the congregation themselves.[52]

In 1 Clem 9:1 death is used as a warning against those people who cause strife and jealousy among the congregation:

Διὸ ὑπακούσωμεν τῇ μεγαλοπρεπεῖ καὶ ἐνδόξῳ βουλήσει αὐτοῦ καὶ ἱκέται γενόμενοι τοῦ ἐλέους καὶ τῆς χρηστότητος αὐτοῦ προσπέσωμεν καὶ ἐπιστρέψωμεν ἐπὶ τοὺς οἰκτιρμοὺς αὐτοῦ ἀπολιπόντες τὴν ματαιοπονίαν τήν τε ἔριν καὶ τὸ εἰς θάνατον ἄγον ζῆλος.

(Therefore let us be obedient to his magnificent and glorious will, and presenting ourselves as suppliants of his mercy and goodness, let us fall down before him and return to his compassion, laying aside the fruitless toil and the strife and the jealousy that *leads to death*.)

The episode regarding Lot's wife is cited in 1 Clem 11:2 as warning against those who incur the judgement of God:

---

mik als stehender Vergleich vorgegeben und erfordert daher gar nicht mehr jedesmal die volle inhaltliche Erfüllung. Es genügt auch schon die Andeutung des Vergleichs."

[50] Don C. Benjamin, "Cain and Abel," *EDB* (2000): 208–209, 208, shows how for Josephus and many rabbis, "Abel represents the virtuous, Cain the *greedy* and *grasping*. Abel is an innocent victim, Cain a *murderer*" (italics mine).

[51] Lindemann, *Clemensbriefe* (n. 15), 36.

[52] Du Toit, "Vilification" (n. 1), 410.

συνεξελθούσης γὰρ αὐτῷ τῆς γυναικὸς ἑτερογνώμονος ὑπαρχούσης καὶ οὐκ ἐν ὁμονοίᾳ εἰς τοῦτο σημεῖον ἐτέθη ὥστε γενέσθαι αὐτὴν στήλην ἁλὸς ἕως τῆς ἡμέρας ταύτης εἰς τὸ γνωστὸν εἶναι πᾶσιν ὅτι οἱ δίψυχοι καὶ οἱ διστάζοντες περὶ τῆς τοῦ θεοῦ δυνάμεως εἰς κρίμα καὶ εἰς σημείωσιν πάσαις ταῖς γενεαῖς γίνονται.

(Of this his wife was destined to be a *sign*, for after leaving with him she changed her mind and was no longer in harmony, and as a result she became a pillar of salt to this day, that it might be known to all that those who are double-minded and those who question the power of God fall under *judgment* and become a *warning* to all generations.)

Those people who think about following the seditious leaders in the community are warned about the serious consequences of such a step in 1 Clem 14:2:

βλάβην γὰρ οὐ τὴν τυχοῦσαν μᾶλλον δὲ κίνδυνον ὑποίσομεν μέγαν ἐὰν ῥιψοκινδύνως ἐπιδῶμεν ἑαυτοὺς τοῖς θελήμασιν τῶν ἀνθρώπων οἵτινες ἐξακοντίζουσιν εἰς ἔριν καὶ στάσεις εἰς τὸ ἀπαλλοτριῶσαι ἡμᾶς τοῦ καλῶς ἔχοντος.

(For we shall bring upon ourselves no ordinary *harm*, but rather great *danger*, if we recklessly surrender ourselves to the purposes of people who launch out into strife and dissension in order to alienate us from what is right.)

By taking Prov 1:23–33 as vantage point, the gloomy future of the offenders is sketched in 1 Clem 57:4:

ἐπειδὴ ἐκάλουν καὶ οὐχ ὑπηκούσατε καὶ ἐξέτεινον λόγους καὶ οὐ προσείχετε ἀλλὰ ἀκύρους ἐποιεῖτε τὰς ἐμὰς βουλάς τοῖς δὲ ἐμοῖς ἐλέγχοις ἠπειθήσατε τοιγαροῦν κἀγὼ τῇ ὑμετέρᾳ ἀπωλείᾳ ἐπιγελάσομαι καταχαροῦμαι δὲ ἡνίκα ἂν ἔρχηται ὑμῖν ὄλεθρος καὶ ὡς ἂν ἀφίκηται ὑμῖν ἄφνω θόρυβος ἡ δὲ καταστροφὴ ὁμοία καταιγίδι παρῇ ἢ ὅταν ἔρχηται ὑμῖν θλῖψις καὶ πολιορκία.

(Because I called and you did not obey, and because I held out words and you paid no attention, but ignored my advice and disobeyed my correction, I therefore will laugh at your *destruction* and rejoice when *ruin* comes upon you, and when *confusion* suddenly overtakes you, and *catastrophe* arrives like a whirlwind, or when *tribulation* and *distress* come upon you.)

By portraying the opponents as highly likely candidates for the wrath and judgement of God, the readers are in a way "scared" out of following the ways of these people.[53]

12. Ludicrous characters

The opposing party can also be vilified by ridiculing themselves as person or their thinking or ideas. Du Toit explains: "[a]lthough characterised as

---

[53] Freyne, "Vilifying" (n. 3), 137.

being of a 'lighter nature,' a witty remark ridiculing the adversary could be devastating."[54]

Freyne describes how this technique is applied with great skill by the author of the Fourth Gospel: "John's dominant strategy in dealing with opponents is that of *irony* which flows over into *caricature* and *parody*. Thus Jesus' opponents appear limited (ch. 3), self-opinionated (ch. 7–8) and finally, *foolish* (ch. 9). There is a gradual deterioration in their character ..."[55] In 1 Clem 21:5 the offenders in the community are portrayed as:

ἀνθρώποις ἄφροσι καὶ ἀνοήτοις καὶ ἐπαιρομένοις καὶ ἐγκαυχωμένοις ἐν ἀλαζονείᾳ τοῦ λόγου αὐτῶν.

(*foolish* and *senseless* people, who exalt themselves and boast in the arrogance of their words.)

Those who doubt the promises of God in Scripture are addressed in 1 Clem 23:4 as:

ὦ ἀνόητοι.[56]

(You *fools*.)

Regarding this portrayal of the doubters, Maier remarks: "[t]he quotation from an unknown source which describes those who doubt that the prophesied events will occur may be interpreted as a purely *rhetorical caricature* of the rebels as doubters in God's promises."[57] By making the opponent a laughing stock in the eyes of the readers, they are discouraged to be associated with such people.

13. Conclusion

What has been shown convincingly is that the author of 1 Clement was a skilled artist, especially when the vilification of the opponents in Corinth was concerned. By constantly showing the offenders in a bad light, belittling them, typecasting them as dark, shadowy figures, calling them all kinds of names, the intended readership of this letter almost had no other option but to steer clear of such people. Following the opposition would

---

[54] Du Toit, "Vilification" (n. 1), 410.

[55] Freyne, "Vilifying" (n. 3), 131 (italics mine).

[56] Lake, *Apostolic Fathers* (n. 38), 51, did not hesitate to translate this address with "Oh, foolish men!"

[57] Harry O. Maier, *The Social Setting of the Ministry as Reflected in the Writings of Hermas, Clement, and Ignatius* (Dissertations SR 1; Waterloo, Ont.: Wilfrid Laurier, 1991), 137 (italics mine).

have been a sure recipe for major disaster. No decent church could risk being associated with them.

What can be noted from quite a few of the texts and vilifying techniques that were discussed, is the fact that in showing up the opponents for what they are the author is also directing the readers to the correct behaviour. Freyne has shown convincingly that this is also very much the case in Matthew and John. He states: "[o]ur examination of the ways in which Matthew and John have chosen to discredit their opponents has shown that each has directed their attacks at those points where they themselves are seeking to make *exclusive claims for their own communities*."[58] Freyne continues regarding vilifying language in these two Gospels with an assessment that can just as easily be applied to 1 Clement: "[y]et there is another aspect to this extreme language that calls for attention also and which helps to relate it to our authors' social concerns: it serves at once to *warn their own communities* and to sharply *define their tasks*."[59]

To obtain such results the author of 1 Clement applied a group of speech acts that can loosely be grouped under the strategy of vilification. Apparently – if we can believe the testimony of Eusebius[60] on this – something worked, because peace and order were apparently restored in the community of Corinth. Perhaps the consequences of the alternative were just so clearly described by the skilled rhetorician at work in 1 Clement that the Corinthians could hardly choose otherwise.

---

[58] Freyne, "Vilifying" (n. 3), 137 (italics mine).
[59] Freyne, "Vilifying" (n. 3), 137 (italics mine).
[60] *Hist. eccl.* 4.22.1; 23.11. Cf. Bowe, "Clement" (n. 6), 264.

V.   Hermeneutical Questions

Ethics and Genre:

The Narrative Setting of Moral Language in the New Testament

RICHARD A. BURRIDGE

1. Introduction

I am delighted to be able to participate in this conference on Moral Language in the New Testament here at the University of Pretoria for two main reasons:

Firstly, this is an area which I have been working on over the last ten years as I have sought to apply my previous work on the literary genre of the gospels[1] to the interpretation of the ethical material in the New Testament.

Secondly, I have been conducting this research not only against the background of the various debates about morality and ethics (such as on sexuality or women in leadership) going on in my own church and the Anglican Communion worldwide (as well as in many other denominations) – but also in the light of the debates about the use of the Bible here in South Africa, both to support apartheid and also to critique it.[2] Prof Jan van der Watt has been particularly helpful and supportive in hosting me for many visits over the last decade, and making library facilities available here, as well as sitting through various papers laying out earlier versions of my thinking, so I am very grateful to him for inviting me to share in this conference – and my thanks also to many others who have assisted my research here at Pretoria, such as Prof Andries van Aarde.[3]

In terms of the background outline of this conference with its three levels of investigation – intratextual, intertextual and extratextual – this is a second level paper. That is to say, I shall be looking at the textual and in-

---

[1] Richard A. Burridge, *What are the Gospels? A Comparison with Graeco-Roman Biography* (SNTSMS 70; Cambridge: Cambridge University Press, 1992; paperback 1995; revised 2nd ed. Grand Rapids, Mich.: Eerdmans, 2004).

[2] Richard A. Burridge, *Imitating Jesus: An Inclusive Approach to New Testament Ethics* (Grand Rapids, Mich.: Eerdmans, 2007), see especially chapter 8, 347–409.

[3] I wish to thank Prof Van Aarde for publishing an earlier version of some of the material in this lecture as "Being Biblical? Slavery, Sexuality and the Inclusive Community," *HTS* 64 (2008): 154–174.

tertextual level of New Testament interpretation. The background outline notes that "the nature of a certain text unit (on macro- and micro-level) influences its meaning and quality." It then goes on to talk about the "variety of genres in the New Testament" and how they convey ethics. I think this is very important: genre is an area which has been largely ignored in New Testament ethics, as I demonstrate in the opening chapter of *Imitating Jesus*.[4]

It is extraordinary to stop and consider this, when we take into account how Jesus is often perceived as one of the world's great moral teachers, and the New Testament is seen as containing some of the best ethics in existence. Yet in many ways, this is a genre mistake. None of the books in the New Testament are written in the genre of ethical treatise, and it is arguable that Jesus did not see himself as a moral teacher; to view him as such is to ignore the rest of his life, ministry, death and resurrection.

So can attention to genre help us with New Testament ethics? In this paper, I want to look at both the macro- and the micro-levels: that is to say, at both the overall genre of the New Testament books in their whole and finished form, as well as at the more micro-level of the types of ethical material within the New Testament. In both cases, we shall examine the texts against the backdrop of the use of the Bible under apartheid in South Africa.

2. Apartheid and Biblical Interpretation

However, apartheid is also another recent example of the debate about biblical interpretation which goes on between groups who claim to be biblical and those who want to be inclusive, similar to those over sexual morality or the role of women. Today, we are clear that apartheid was a terrible doctrine, unchristian, evil and repressive. We praise people like Archbishop Desmond Tutu who wanted to include blacks in society as those who properly read their Bibles. When Tutu was told to keep out of politics because it did not fit with the Bible, he wondered which Bible his opponents were reading!

However, hard though it may be for those outside South Africa to understand today, apartheid was a scriptural doctrine, taught by a reformed, Bible-reading church. Those who wanted blacks included were dismissed as dangerous liberals, radicals, or even Communists. They were accused of defending atheism and violence, and were subject to the whole rigours of the "total strategy" of an oppressive police state. Even Archbishop Des-

---

[4]   Burridge, *Imitating Jesus* (n. 2), 5–16.

mond Tutu as General Secretary of the South African Council of Churches had to undergo detailed legal scrutiny by the Eloff Commission in 1982.[5]

Now it is hard to credit that prayerful, faithful Christians believed that this evil system was "biblical." However, the fact is that it relied upon many biblical passages, some of which we shall examine shortly, all undergirded by an appeal to Romans 13:1–7 and Paul's insistence on a proper obedience for the laws of God and human beings, with the state as the agent of God. This has formed a focus for my own research over the last decade on how the New Testament is used in ethics. Being from a politically active family involved with anti-apartheid beliefs, I used to think that Afrikaners were all neo-Nazis, and not "real Christians" at all. I assumed that they were hypocrites pretending to "be biblical" as a fig leaf to cover their exploitation of the black community for their own advantage.

However, having spent the last decade working on this in South Africa, I have realised that this is an unfair picture. The Dutch Reformed Church was, and is, a reformed Protestant church, priding itself on being biblical. There has always been a concern for the centrality of scripture, backed up by excellent faculties of biblical studies and theology in major universities such as Pretoria or Stellenbosch. The theological basis for apartheid, or "separate development" as it is best translated, is a report of the Dutch Reformed Church, significantly entitled *Human Relations and the South African Scene in the Light of Scripture*, and formally approved by the General Synod of the DRC as recently as October 1974.[6] Now this is a problem: it is easy to dismiss the DRC and the Afrikaners as hypocrites hiding behind a biblical justification. It is much more difficult to face the fact that a biblically centred church, full of prayerful people, guided by the Spirit, could have come up with a biblical doctrine that we, only a few years later, find so abhorrent.[7] Furthermore, it is as challenging as it is uncomfortable: how can we be so sure that we are right when we claim to be biblical? Or will

---

[5] Archbishop Desmond Tutu, *The Rainbow People of God: South Africa's victory over apartheid*, (ed. John Allen; London: Doubleday, 1994), see pp. 53–78 for the full text of his submission to the Commission; also John Allen, *Rabble-Rouser for Peace: The Authorised Biography of Desmond Tutu* (London: Rider, 2006), 197–198 has further discussion of this investigation.

[6] *Human Relations and the South African Scene in the Light of Scripture*, Dutch Reformed Church, 1976. Afrikaans report entitled, *Ras, Volk en Nasie en Volkereverhoudinge in die lig van die Skrif*, approved and accepted by the General Synod of the Dutch Reformed Church in October 1974.

[7] It is significant that the Dutch Reformed Church itself continued to struggle with a biblical understanding of apartheid, producing another report only twelve years later: *Church and Society: A Testimony of the Dutch Reformed Church* (Pretoria, 1986). Once again, this is an attempt to be thoroughly grounded in the scriptures and to tackle the issues facing South African society of the time, including mixed marriages.

future generations think that we, or parts of our church today, are as misguided in what we think is biblical now as were those who supported slavery or apartheid?

Accordingly, I set out to analyse how the Bible was used both to support apartheid by the Dutch Reformed Church, and also the part it played in the struggle for liberation as a test case for how the New Testament is applied to ethics today. The result was published last year as *Imitating Jesus: An Inclusive Approach to New Testament Ethics*.[8]

3. Ethics and Genre at the Micro-level: Literary Forms

My approach draws heavily upon my previous work on literary genre as the key to interpret the New Testament, beginning with my doctoral work on comparing the gospels to Graeco-Roman biography.[9] In this new book, I analyse the use of the New Testament under apartheid through the four main literary genres or types of ethical material at the micro-level, namely rules, principles, paradigms or examples and overall world-view – a division which is used by many biblical ethicists, going back to Gustafson.[10] It's a large study, but let me try briefly to summarize the results.[11]

3.1 Rules

This treats the New Testament as moral handbook and looks for material in prescriptive form or the genre of commands: the idea is "for best results, follow the maker's instructions." Such a rule-based reading of the Bible fits into a deontological approach to ethics, to do with moral duty, as Kant, Bonhoeffer or Barth. It works well with direct instructions like the Ten Commandments or the Sermon on the Mount but runs into difficulties when deciding which commands are still binding today, particularly when contemporary moral dilemmas do not appear in the Bible. The DRC's Report on *Human Relations and the South African Scene in the Light of Scripture* interpreted God's command to "be fruitful and multiply" (Gen 1:28) to include the separate diversity of peoples, confirmed in Deut 32:8–

---

[8]   Burridge, *Imitating Jesus* (n. 2).
[9]   Burridge, *What are the Gospels?* (n. 1).
[10]   For such a four-fold approach to ethical material, see, for example, James M. Gustafson, "The Place of Scripture in Christian Ethics: A Methodological Study," *Interpretation* 24 (1970): 430–455, esp. 439–444; Richard B. Hays, *The Moral Vision of the New Testament: A Contemporary Introduction to New Testament Ethics* (San Francisco: Harper, 1996), 209.
[11]   Burridge, *Imitating Jesus* (n. 2), chapter 8, 347–409.

9 and Acts 17:26–27 with "the boundaries of their territories."[12] Similarly, commands forbidding the marriage of Israelites with other peoples were used to prohibit mixed marriages in South Africa under article 16 of the Immorality Act.[13] These instructions and other passages came together to form what Loubser calls "the Apartheid Bible."[14]

The Report's approaches to biblical commands were critiqued by Willem Vorster, Professor of New Testament at the University of South Africa, Pretoria, who argued that "the Bible simply becomes an "oracle book" of "proof texts" or "a book of norms;" furthermore "both apartheid and anti-apartheid theologians in the NGK [= DRC in Afrikaans] undoubtedly operate with exactly the same view of Scripture. The main difference is the (political) grid though which the Bible is read … In essence there is no difference in the use and appeal to the Bible between apartheid and anti-apartheid theologians."[15]

3.2 Principles

Secondly, we step back from specific commands to look for the principle underlying the texts, such as the love-principle in Situation Ethics, or the liberation principle in South America. The problems are which principle to apply and whether the principle really arises from the text or actually is imposed upon it by the interpreter. In Gen 1:28, differing exegeses of the same creation stories could lead to the contrasting "principles" of either "separate development" (God made us all different), as argued by the DRC Report,[16] or, on the other hand the principle of "unity" (God made us one in our diversity), as argued by Archbishop Tutu and the liberationists. Equally, the Report handling of the story of Pentecost in Acts 2:6–11 produced the principle of everyone hearing "God's great deeds in our own language" – and so they justified separate racial churches, according to language groups, an Afrikaans church, an English church, Xhosa, Zulu and so forth. On the other hand, Douglas Bax criticised the DRC Report's exe-

---

[12] *Human Relations and the South African Scene in the Light of Scripture* (n. 6); see 14–15 on Gen 1:28.

[13] *Human Relations and the South African Scene in the Light of Scripture* (n. 6), 93–99.

[14] Johannes A. Loubser, *The Apartheid Bible: A Critical Review of Racial Theology in South Africa* (Cape Town: Maskew, Miller, Longman, 1987), ix–x.

[15] Willem S. Vorster, "The use of Scripture and the NG Kerk: a shift of paradigm or of values?," in *New Faces of Africa* (*Essays in honour of Ben [Barend Jacobus] Marais*; ed. Jan W. Hofmeyr and Willem S. Vorster; Pretoria: University of South Africa Press, 1984), 204–219, quotations from pp. 210 and 212; see also the discussion by Dirk J. Smit, "The Ethics of Interpretation – and South Africa," *Scriptura* 33 (1990): 29–43.

[16] *Human Relations and the South African Scene in the Light of Scripture* (n. 6), 14–15.

gesis and produced the opposite principle of the Spirit at Pentecost "breaking down the barriers that separate humanity."[17] Thus we have the same hermeneutical, interpretative method of looking for a principle being applied to the same texts (Creation and Pentecost) – and yet producing two completely contrasting principles for the pro-apartheid government and for the liberation struggle. All of which poses the obvious question, which one is really "being biblical," really interpreting the ethical material in the text correctly?

3.3 Paradigms/examples

Bible narratives are the classic stand-by of the Thought for the Day speaker, or a Sunday morning preacher, recounting a scriptural story about travelling patriarchs and then saying: "isn't that just like you and me?" The immediate problem is the vast culture gap between the biblical world and our own day – but this did not stop it being used in South Africa. When the persecuted Huguenots like the De Villiers, or Du Plessis, or all the other French South African surnames escaped through Holland onto leaky boats which finally made it round the coast of Africa to the rich and fertile fields of the Frenchoek valley near Stellenbosch in the Cape, "flowing with milk and honey," it is no wonder that they opened their Bibles to the Israelites coming into the Promised Land, and thought "that's us! Thanks be to God!" However, this also led them to view the locals like the natives of Canaan as "hewers of wood and drawers of water," and to apply the material in Joshua and Judges to the Bantu; from such biblical narratives, they derived prohibitions against mixed marriages, and justified the oppression and slavery of the native peoples.[18] When the British authorities moved towards the abolition of slavery, then they were seen like the Egyptians, oppressing the chosen ones of God; so Boers moved inland where 500 of them defeated 20,000 Zulus at Blood River. This apparently miraculous victory led them to make their Covenant with God, which was ceremonially enacted every year on December 16th at the Vortrekker monument in Pretoria, modelled on that of the ancient Israelites.[19]

---

[17] Douglas Bax, "The Bible and apartheid 2," in *Apartheid is a heresy* (ed. John de Gruchy and C. Villa Vicencio; Cape Town: Philip, 1983), 112–143; see 128–130.

[18] See for example, John W. de Gruchy, *The Church Struggle in South Africa: Twenty-Fifth Anniversary Edition* (Minneapolis, Minn.: Eerdmans, 2005), 171–174, and Michael Battle, *Reconciliation: The Ubuntu Theology of Desmond Tutu* (Cleveland, Ohio: Pilgrim Press, 1997), 31–32.

[19] See Zolile Mbali, *The Churches and Racism: A Black South African Perspective* (London: SCM Press, 1987), 191–193; on a research visit to the University of Pretoria, I was moved by the way Prof. Jan van der Watt of its Theology Faculty was able to tell me the story of Blood River twice, once from the Afrikaner perspective, and again from the Zulus'.

This Exodus paradigm of God's people escaping from oppression to the Promised Land also of course influenced European settlers in North America, where it led to the decimation of the so-called "red Indians;" arguably it continues to fuel much of the rhetoric and self-belief of the Republican Right today. The irony, however, is that exactly the same Exodus paradigm lies at the heart of much liberation theology, in South Africa as in South America – and it led to the black theology which influenced Archbishop Tutu and Allan Boesak. Once again, we have the awkward situation that the same biblical story is being used with the same method of interpretation and application by both sides, with the Afrikaners as the victims in their own reading, but seen as the oppressors by the black churches. As a member of the "colonial remnant," Snyman links the hermeneutics of the Afrikaans churches with that of Liberation Theology: "[f]or the one, God is a God of deliverance. For the other, he is a conquering god. Same texts, two views, two experiences."[20]

3.4 World-view

Lastly, we draw even further back to the overall world-view of the Bible as whole, leading to a biblical theology, like the Barthian approach of ethicists like Oliver O'Donovan and Michael Banner. However, the Bible is not a single book, but a collection of many genres and languages and cultures over many centuries. Fusing it all into a single vision is difficult – and the Dutch Reformed Church viewed their understanding of "human relations in the light of scripture" as biblical, based upon the whole scheme of creation – fall – incarnation – redemption, while the liberationists argued exactly the same for their understanding.

Thus this brief study of the Bible in South Africa leads to a very disturbing conclusion. We must properly recognize that both sides believed in the Bible, based their view upon it and often used the same method of biblical interpretation (whether rules, principles, examples or world-view) upon the same biblical passages – yet they came to startlingly different conclusions. It is all very worrying for claims of "being biblical" in our current debates about ethics. More significantly for the purpose of this conference, attention to the genres or literary forms of ethical material at the micro-level does not appear to prevent misinterpretation of the text, but rather seems to have assisted interpretation on both sides of the debate.

---

[20] Gerrie Snyman, "Social Identity and South African Biblical Hermeneutics: A Struggle Against Prejudice?," *JTSA* 121 (2005): 34–55; quotation from p. 39.

4. Ethics and Genre at the Macro-level: a Biographical Approach to New Testament Ethics

To move towards an answer, I want to look at genre at the macro-level, namely the overall literary type or genre of the entire work in its final form. In my doctoral study, *What are the Gospels?*, I argued that classical literary theory and a comparison with Graeco-Roman biography leads to the conclusion that the gospels are the same genre as other lives of famous men in the ancient world.[21] Therefore, in order to be biblical, we have to interpret the gospels according to this genre, in the same way as other ancient lives were read. Graeco-Roman biography is very different from modern examples, with the post-Freudian concern for personality and contemporary interest in "celebrity." The ancients wanted to depict the subject's character with a portrait of them through combinations of their deeds and words, through anecdotes and stories as much as their sayings or speeches. Furthermore, both the deeds and the words lead up to the person's death, dealt with in some extended detail in ancient lives, as in the gospels; often it will also reveal something further about the person's life, or bring the author's major themes to a climax.

So to find the heart of Jesus' ethic, the overall genre requires that we must consider both his ethical teaching *and* his actual practice. As Luke puts it, "In the first book, I wrote about all that Jesus began to do and to teach" (Acts 1:1). Therefore, we have to look at Jesus' sayings and sermons, but also at his actions, in healing, miracles, and the events narrated, in order to grasp the evangelists' portraits if we are properly to understand how Jesus' ethics fit into this. Often those who claim to be biblical appeal to his words, like the Sermon on the Mount, which are indeed very demanding and rigorous. But to do that alone is to ignore the overall biographical genre of the gospels and treat them as just a collection of ethical teachings. It also violates the genre of the Sermon on the Mount, which is a speech within a biography, designed to display something about the speaker, Jesus, and which forms part of a carefully balanced sequence of five discourses in Matthew's gospel.

Meanwhile, on the other side, the desire to be inclusive can appeal to his deeds, to the narrative about his relationships with people – but again that is only half the story; it needs not to neglect his teachings. To be properly biblical requires a biographical approach to the gospels' portraits of Jesus through his deeds and words, his teachings and his ministry, and to follow this on through Paul's letters and the rest of the New Testament. This is what I have been engaged upon for the last decade. While the ex-

---

[21]   Burridge, *What are the Gospels?* (n. 1); see chapter 10.

ample of the use of the Bible under apartheid forms the test case for the last chapter of *Imitating Jesus*, most of this book is taken up with a biographical study of New Testament ethics through deeds and words, which I would now like to outline to see if it helps us with being biblical today.

4.1 Jesus' teaching[22]

If you ask most people about Jesus of Nazareth, we find what Goldsmith terms the "common assumption that Jesus was primarily, or most importantly, a teacher of morality."[23] Yet, amazingly, the gospels do not portray Jesus as just a teacher of morality. Furthermore, I am arguing that to read them as ethical treatises or for moral guidance is to make a genre mistake, for that is not what they are. They are biographical portraits of Jesus which do include some examples of his teaching. However, Jesus' ethical teaching is not a separate and discrete set of moral maxims, but part of his main proclamation of the kingdom of God as God's reign and sovereignty are recognized in the here and now. Such preaching is primarily intended to elicit a whole-hearted response from his hearers to live as disciples within the community of others who also respond and follow, more than to provide moral instructions to be obeyed. When he touched upon the major human moral experiences, such as money, sex, power, violence, and so forth, Jesus intensified the demands of the law with his rigorous ethic of renunciation and self-denial. However, at the same time his central stress on love and forgiveness opened the community to the very people who had moral difficulties in these areas. Therefore, as befits a biographical narrative, we must now turn from Jesus' teaching to confront this paradox in his activity and behaviour.

4.2 Jesus' example

Jesus' demanding ethical teaching on things like money, sex and power should require very high standards from those around him, with the result that ordinary fallible human beings would find him uncomfortable. However, when we turn from his words to the biographical narrative of his activity, the converse is true. It is religious leaders and guardians of morality who found him uncomfortable, while he keeps company with all sorts of sinners – precisely the people who are not keeping his demanding ethic. He is criticized as "a glutton and a drunkard, a friend of tax collectors and sinners" (Matt 11:19 // Luke 7:34). He accepts people just as they are and

---

[22] See Burridge, *Imitating Jesus* (n. 2), chapter 2, 33–80.

[23] Dale Goldsmith, *New Testament Ethics: An Introduction* (Elgin, Ill.: Brethren Press, 1988), Appendix 1, "Jesus the Teacher," 177–180; quotation from p. 177; see also Charles W. Carter and R. Duane Thompson, *The Biblical Ethic of Love* (American University Studies Series 7: Theology and Religion 79; New York, N.Y.: Lang, 1990), 128: "Jesus Christ was the world's greatest teacher of righteousness."

proclaims that they are forgiven without the need to go to the temple or offer sacrifice. His healing ministry is directed towards such people and the Eucharistic words at the Last Supper suggest that he saw his forthcoming death as being "for" them. A biographical approach means that it is not enough simply to look at Jesus' words and moral teachings; to be properly biblical involves facing the paradox that he delivers his ethical teaching in the company of sinners whom he accepts, loves and heals. Furthermore, a major purpose of ancient biography was *mimesis*, the practice of imitation, of following the subject's virtues. This is reinforced by the Jewish habit of *ma'aseh*, precedence, where the disciple is expected to observe and imitate his master as a way of imitating Torah and ultimately becoming holy as God is holy. Therefore, to imitate Jesus, it is not enough simply to extract his ethical teaching from the Sermon on the Mount; we must also imitate his loving acceptance of others, especially the marginalized, within an open and inclusive community.

4.3 Paul[24]

The Pauline letters occupy about a quarter of the New Testament, and contain a wide range of ethical material, dealing with many moral issues. Yet we can still discern the same basic outline as with Jesus. It is still supremely an ethic of response, even though Jesus' preaching of the kingdom has become proclaiming Jesus as king, so that Christology is central for Paul's theology and ethics. Paul's demand for a response to what God is doing is the same, with the same centrality of the love command, seen as fulfilling the law, to be lived out within a community of other disciples in corporate solidarity as the body of Christ. The particular ethical issues handled cover similar topics such the state, sex, marriage and divorce, money, property and poverty, and the various forms of human relationships. In all of these, Paul makes rigorous ethical demands, yet also refers to the mixed nature of his early communities. Throughout, he constantly appeals to his readers to "be imitators of me, as I am of Christ" (1 Cor 11:1; see also Gal 4:12; 1 Thess 1:6). Exactly what they are to imitate is made explicit in Rom 15:1–7, where he tells his early Christians to "bear with the failings of the weak" and not to please themselves "as Christ did not please himself." He appeals to them to welcome others "just as Christ has welcomed you."

Paul is often seen as uncomfortable reading for those wanting open debate in an inclusive community today. Yet our biographical approach suggests that this is precisely how we should read Paul – as following the creative complementarity of Jesus' rigorous and demanding ethics together

---

[24] See Burridge, *Imitating Jesus* (n. 2), chapter 3, 81–154.

with his acceptance of sinners within his community. As the biographical genre of the gospels means that we should take Jesus' deeds and example into account as much as his words, so the epistolary genre of Paul's letters directs us to set his ethical teaching within the contingent context of his early Christian communities. As Jesus' pastoral acceptance of "sinners" means that his demanding teaching cannot be applied in an exclusive manner, so too Paul's ethical teaching must always be balanced by his appeal to the imitation of Christ – and this entails accepting others as we have been accepted.

4.4 The four gospels

Space and time do not permit us to go through each of the gospels in turn as I do in the book.[25] However, this same combination of words and deeds can be found here also. Each evangelist has a particular ethical slant in his account of Jesus. Thus Mark stresses the ethic of discipleship in the context of eschatological suffering; Matthew demonstrates how Jesus is the truly righteous interpreter of the law; Luke depicts his universal concern especially for the marginalized, while John portrays Jesus as the divine love who brings truth into our world. These different emphases all reflect how Christology is central in their four portraits, but each of them also combines words and deeds, as Jesus' moral teaching takes place in the narrative context of his acceptance of people within an open and inclusive community. All of this is then set forth in their biographical narrative for us to emulate and imitate the example of Jesus' ethical concern and loving acceptance.

5. Biblical Understandings of Apartheid and the Inclusive Community

Biblical interpretation is never a private matter but needs to be validated by the community of believers. The problem is that the pro-apartheid account of "human relations in the light of scripture" came out of a bible-reading prayerful Christian community, the Dutch Reformed Church, supported by the best biblical scholars in their land. When I asked a professor at Stellenbosch University how the DRC got it so wrong, he explained that it was because the authorities would not listen to the voices of "outsiders" such as other world reformed churches, and also that they stifled the protests "inside" the church, including whites such as Beyers Naude and the pleas of the blacks. That same professor was involved in setting up the

---

[25] See Burridge, *Imitating Jesus* (n. 2), chapters 4, 5, 6, and 7.

Centre for Contextual Hermeneutics at Stellenbosch in 1991 and it was as biblical interpretation was related to its political and social context that things began to change. Subsequently, a very important development has been the work of Professor Gerald West with his *Institute for the Study of the Bible* at the University of Kwa-Zulu Natal in Pietermaritzburg. Here he has pioneered a method of enabling the voices of what he terms "ordinary readers" to be heard alongside those of biblical scholars and church authorities. Once again, therefore, we see the effect of admitting the excluded group, the ordinary black readers in their social context into the community of those interpreting the Bible and how this led to change. It was notable and exciting that Archbishop Rowan invited Professor West to coordinate the biblical aspects for the 2008 Lambeth Conference, both the preparatory material and the actual Bible studies.

It is also significant that after the first elections, President Mandela invited Archbishop Tutu to chair the Truth and Reconciliation Commission. Here too, there was an opportunity to listen to the experiences of all involved, from all sides, blacks, whites and coloured, oppressors and oppressed, victims and torturers alike, so that a full understanding could take place. The testimony of the representatives of various churches about their use of the Bible is interesting. I was able to visit the TRC in 1998, and I have analysed the transcripts of the Faith Communities hearings at East London, November 17–19, 1997.[26] Thus Dominee Freek Swanepoel from the Dutch Reformed Church admitted that "the church had erred seriously with the Biblical foundation of the forced segregation of people ... We have indeed taught our people wrongly with regard to apartheid as a Biblical instruction."[27] This is just one powerful example of many places where church representatives confessed that their previous claim to be biblical was wrong.[28] So what is significant is admitting the excluded group to the discussion about what the Bible really says.

Thus I want to argue that the biographical genre of the gospels requires us to imitate Jesus' deeds as well as keeping his words, which means that study of biblical ethics must be undertaken in an inclusive community

---

[26] See Burridge, *Imitating Jesus* (n. 2), 397–405.

[27] Taken from the Research Institute on Christianity in South Africa (RICSA) transcripts of the TRC hearings in East London, November 17–19, 1997, 246–265; see also, *Facing the Truth: South African Faith Communities and the Truth & Reconciliation Commission* (ed. James Cochrane, John de Gruchy and Stephen Martin; Cape Town: Philip, 1998), which contains details of the written submissions, oral testimony and witnesses, as well as a number of reflective essays; and Denise M. Ackermann, "Faith Communities Face the Truth," *JTSA* 103 (1999): 88–93.

[28] It is also significant that the later 1986 DRC Report, *Church and Society*, recognised that "the conviction has gradually grown that a forced separation and division of peoples cannot be considered a biblical imperative" (47, paragraph 305).

where the voices of those who have been marginalized need to be heard. Earlier I stressed the importance of combining words and deeds, holding scriptural teaching together with the example given in the rest of the narrative. The biblical teaching about the ethics of a topic like sexuality may not be immediately conclusive – but Jesus' example of his acceptance of those who were marginalized and excluded is clear. Equally, I argued that despite his strong moral demands in his letters, Paul also stressed the importance of maintaining an inclusive community with particular regard for weaker brothers and sisters who are to be accepted as we have been accepted. Paul's call to imitate Jesus is also reinforced by the biographical genre of the gospels with their concern for *mimesis*, or imitation of the example of their subject. This all means that those who want to be biblical must maintain an inclusive community of interpretation to discover God's will together through detailed study of what it means to be biblical.

6. Conclusion

In conclusion, I have argued that to be truly biblical, we have to imitate Jesus' teaching and his example, his deeds as well as his words. Jesus' demanding ethical teaching cannot be appreciated separately from his behaviour and activity. Both the biographical genre of the gospels on the one hand, and the ancient idea of imitation and Jewish rabbinic precedent on the other, suggest that Jesus' teaching must be earthed in his practical example, both of calling people to repentance and discipleship – but also his open acceptance of sinners, with whom he spent his life and for whom he died. Unfortunately, all too often those who do New Testament Ethics today end up doing one or the other: that is, teaching a rigorist ethic with extreme demands which seems condemnatory and alienates people – or having an open acceptance and being accused of having no ethics at all! Seeking to follow Jesus in becoming both "perfect" and "merciful" as God is perfect and merciful (compare Matt 5:48 with Luke 6:36) is not an easy balance to maintain, but one which is vital if we are to be properly biblical.

   To study the scriptures requires the context of an open and inclusive community of interpretation. To affect change in South Africa about apartheid as "human relations in the light of scripture" needed the "voices of protest," with blacks present in the Bible studies and their experiences being recounted. Only such an open and inclusive community which includes those who are being marginalized (whether that be black and coloured people, women, homosexuals or whoever) and really listens to their experience can really grapple with what the biblical teaching is.

This is how my biographical approach to Jesus and the gospels, indeed to the whole New Testament, applies to ethical debates. It requires attention to imitating Jesus' words and deeds, to hear the biblical teachings within the context of an open and inclusive community – and this applies to our current church debates as much as to apartheid. Such a debate within an inclusive community is the only way forward for us today if we truly want to maintain a claim to "being biblical."

The Familial Metaphorical Language of Inclusion in the New Testament and HIV/AIDS Destigmatization in Africa

1. Introduction

Anybody who reads about Africa will immediately be struck and dumfounded by the immense problems Africans are facing. It is shocking to realize that these problems are encountered in all spheres of life – social, cultural, economic, political, moral, etc. Indeed much of this continent has turned into a battleground of contending dooms such as overpopulation, poverty, starvation, illiteracy, corruption, social breakdown, vanishing resources, overcrowded cities, drought, xenophobia and homelessness of war refugees – including the most devastating effects of HIV/AIDS. Miriam Lyons concurs that HIV has found a wealth of opportunities to thrive among human conditions fuelled by poverty, abuse, violence, prejudice and ignorance. Social and economic circumstances contribute to vulnerability to HIV infection and intensify its impact.[1]

The worldwide epidemiology of HIV/AIDS has evoked resources from many national governments (particularly in the developing countries), the United Nations bodies and governmental organisations. AIDS is undoubtedly today the number one killer in Africa. An increasing number of people are falling sick suffering physically, emotionally, and spiritually – many in abandonment and desolation. Many women, young people, children and babies are severely socially and emotionally afflicted. Daily people die of AIDS in Africa. Daily children become orphaned when mothers and fathers leave them alone in a world that is not equipped to care for them. Daily infected people are discharged from hospitals that cannot give medical attention because they are too many.[2]

---

[1] Miriam Lyons, "The Impact of HIV and AIDS on Children, Families and Communities: Risks and Realities of Childhood during the HIV Epidemic" (www.undp.org/hiv/publications/issues/english/issue30e.html [2007], 3.4.2010).

[2] Elijah Mahlangu, "HIV/AIDS: The church's challenge," a paper presented at the workshop on Orphans and Vulnerable Children, Pretoria (2008, p. 2). See also Paulus J.

Time Magazine calls AIDS, "worse than a disaster because most disasters have a foreseeable end and there is no end to HIV/AIDS."[3] Maluleke maintains that the advent of AIDS ushered in a new era – the epidemic heralded a time of decision, testing and challenge after which nothing will be the same anymore.[4] In closing the XV International AIDS conference in 2004 in Bangkok, Peter Piot, the former CEO of UNAIDS said, "And finally, the world must accept the exceptionality of AIDS. There simply is no precedent in history for this crisis. And please let's not have an illusion that in a few years the world will return to what was, before AIDS! Friends, in short, AIDS has rewritten the rules. To prevail, we must rewrite the rules. The exceptional threat demands exceptional actions, be it on financing, development, trade rules, activist strategies, public survive delivery, or fiscal ceilings."[5]

Christoph Benn contends that more than any other disease in modern history, HIV/AIDS is threatening the health of nations and every fabric of societies by causing the death of millions of predominantly young people.[6] Commenting on the ravaging effects of the HIV/AIDS scourge to the African confinement, Vitolli says that indeed HIV/AIDS poses a profound challenge. AIDS is not only a medical condition but also a socio-economic, cultural and educational catastrophe. He laments that millions of Africans have been infected and affected, resulting in the devastating impact on societies: family networks are falling apart, the economy is being disrupted because the disease affects the most active and productive age group and tens and thousands of children are left orphaned.[7]

Despite the shattering magnitude of the AIDS pandemic, written theological reflections on HIV/AIDS had a slow start, there were no resources to turn to and theological thinking had to start from "scratch."[8] Maluleke used the words "theological impotency" in this respect, emphasizing that Western orientated theological education does not prepare African theolo-

---

de Bruin, "Vigs en menslike gedrag: 'n Teologiese-etiese beoordeling," *Koers* 55(3) (1990): 357.

[3] Peter Hawthorne, "AIDS in Africa: Fatal destiny," *TIME Magazine* 156/3 (2000): 30–35.

[4] Tinyiko Sam Maluleke, "Towards an HIV/AIDS-Sensitive Curriculum," in *HIV/AIDS and the Curriculum: Methods of Integrating HIV/AIDS in Theological Programmes* (ed. Musa W. Dube; Geneva: WCC Publications, 2003), 59–75.

[5] Peter Piot, Executive Director of UNAIDS since 1995 and retired in December 2008 when Michel Sidibé took over.

[6] Christoph Benn, "The influence of cultural and religious frameworks on the future course of the HIV/AIDS pandemic," *JTSA* 113 (2002): 3–18, 3.

[7] Robert J. Vitolli, "AIDS: A challenge to church and society," *African Ecclesial Review* 31/5 (1989): 298–312.

[8] Martha T. Fredericks, "HIV and AIDS: Mapping theological response in Africa," *Exchange* 37 (2008): 4–22.

gians for the day to day realities of the continent.[9] This article suggests a New Testament theological contribution in the reduction of the HIV/AIDS stigmatization scourge in Africa. The New Testament describes the church (God's people and new family) in familial metaphorical language. It will be demonstrated that the people living with HIV and AIDS are affirmed by the ethical and moral language encountered in the New Testament, thus addressing the stigma and discrimination they suffer as a result of being HIV+ or having AIDS. Familial language in five major perspectives in the New Testament (Mark, Luke-Acts, Matthew, John and Paul) will be investigated.

2. Stigma, Exclusion and Discrimination

Since the advent of HIV/AIDS, substantial research has been conducted in the area of AIDS and stigmatization. These investigations are not only conducted on the people living with the virus (or have AIDS) but on those affected (i.e. living with infected person or persons) including the wider community and health care personnel. In this direction a number of instruments have been developed to measure HIV/AIDS stigma. Stigma is often cited as one of the two giants confronting governments' and NGOs in their HIV/AIDS prevention work – funding and stigma. Campbell adds by saying that the stigmatization of people living with AIDS is a key obstacle to HIV prevention and AIDS care.[10]

People living with HIV/AIDS (PLWA) must deal not only with the disease symptoms but also with the associated stigma.[11] Stigma has been defined as an attribute that discredits or devalues individuals who are HIV+, but is increasingly interpreted as a socially constructed process based on the identification by society of certain personal characteristics or attributes as "different" and highly undesirable[12]. Because an HIV+ status is seen as highly undesirable, PLWA are labeled and set apart from the larger community. Holzemer and Uys have described a wide range of words and

---

[9]   Maluleke, "Towards an HIV/AIDS-Sensitive Curriculum" (n. 4), 59–75.

[10] Catherine Campbell et al., "I have an evil child at my house: stigma and HIV/AIDS management in South African Community," *American Journal of Public Health* 95/5 (2005): 808–815, 808.

[11] Priscilla S. Dlamini, Thecla W. Kohi et al., "Verbal and physical abuse and neglect as manifestations of HIV/AIDS stigma in five African Countries," *Public Health Nursing* 24/5 (2007), 389–399, 390.

[12] Peter Aggleton and Richard Parker, *A conceptual framework and basis for action: HIV/AIDS stigma and discrimination*, Geneva: UNAIDS, 2002 (http://pdf.dec.org/ pdf_docs/pnacq832.pdf#search=%22aggleton%20parker%20%HIV%20and%20AIDS-related%20stigma%20and%20discrimination%22%22, 25.9.2006).

phrases used in southern African communities to name the disease, most of which have negative implications.[13] In Tanzania, Nyblade et al.[14] report that PLWHA are called *maiti inayotembeyea* ("wailing corpse") and *mare-hemu mtarajiwa* ("expected to die"). The frequency of such negative labels supports the development of a rationale for devaluing, avoiding, rejecting, and excluding PLWA. As a result, PLWA are stigmatized and denied access to good things in life and suffer disproportionately from bad things, setting up a source of chronic stress that exerts negative effects on both mental and physical health.[15]

The fact that the word stigma has become very common, is not an understatement; lately so much has been said about the dangers of stigma in the fight against HIV/AIDS,[16] that one is inclined to agree with Japheth Ndlovu and others who have correctly found out that one of the most powerful impediments to the prevention of HIV transmission, and to effective treatment, is the stigmatization and discrimination, that is encountered by people living with HIV and AIDS.[17]

From the above discussion on stigmatization of the PLWA, stigma can be described as a social construction of deviation from an ideal or expectation, contributing to a powerful discrediting social label that reduces the way individuals see themselves and are viewed as persons. Therefore infected persons are generally perceived in negative social terms and margivelised as the carriers or hosts of a deadly disease.[18] Stigma can also be defined as:

---

[13] William L. Holzemer and Leana Uys, "Managing AIDS stigma," *Journal of Social Aspects of HIV/AIDS* 1/3 (2004): 166–174. Leana Uys, Maureen Chirwa, Priscilla Dlamini, Minrie Greef, Thecla Kohi, William Holzemer et al., "'Eating plastic,' 'Winning the Lotto,' 'Joining WWW' ... descriptions of HIV/AIDS in Africa," *Journal of the Association of Nurses in AIDS Care* 16/3 (2005): 11–21.

[14] Laura Nyblade, Rohini Pande, Sanyukta Mathur et al., *Disentangling HIV and AIDS: Stigma in Ethiopia, Tanzania and Zambia* (Washington DC: International Center for Research on Women, 2003; http://www.icrw.org/docs/stigmareport093003.pdf, 25.9.2006).

[15] Bruce G. Link and Jo C. Phelan, "Stigma and its public health implications," *Lancet* 367/9509 (2006): 528–529.

[16] Ezra Chitando & Masiiwa R Gunda, "HIV and AIDS, Stigma and Liberation in the Old Testament," *Exchange* 36 (2007): 184–197, 186.

[17] Japheth Ndlovu et al., "The Challenge of Stigma in Elizabeth Knox, in *One Body: North-South Reflections in the Face of HIV and AIDS* (vol. 1; ed. Elizabeth Knox-Seith; Copenhagen: The Nordic-FOCISSA Church Cooperation, 2005), 4–10.

[18] Richard Parker and Peter Aggleton, "HIV and AIDS-related stigma and discrimination: A conceptual framework and implications for action," *Social Science and Medicine* 57 (2003): 13–24. See also: Harriet Deacon, Inez Stephney, and Sandra Prosalendis, *Understanding HIV/AIDS stigma: A theoretical and methodological analysis* (Cape Town: Human Sciences Research Council, 2005).

- Making negative prejudiced judgements on the basis of perceived differences between individuals.
- The person is different in some way that calls into question deep-felt personal and community-held values, prejudices and taboos.
- Characterized by rejection denial, discrediting, disregarding of underrating and social distance

Self-stigmatization is as strong as being stigmatized by others and the community. Elements of a self-stigmatization include:

- The disabling feeling of shame, self-doubt, guilt, self-blame that a person living with HIV/AIDS may experience
- Intense feelings of lowered self-esteem, inferiority and utter helplessness
- "I am getting what I deserve"
- Fear and self-denial, etc.

3. HIV/AIDS Stigmatization: The Challenge to the New Testament Scholar and Exegete

Musa Dube has symbolically portrayed Africa as the bleeding woman in the Gospel of Mark 5:24–43, who is in search of healing. Dube laments:

"Mama Africa has been struck by a new disease: HIV/AIDS. She is now a nurse. She runs home-based care centers, for her dying children and people. She washes them, feeds them, holds them in her arms, and rocks them, singing a little song while she waits Her death. And when they finally die, she rises to close Her eyes, to wrap them and bury them. Mama Africa bears it in her own flesh, the wounds of their suffering. And they die in her loving arms ...[19]

The fight of HIV/AIDS and reduction of stigma and discrimination is not only a matter for health professionals. Its impact encompasses individuals, families, faith communities, entire nations and continents. In short, it is a global phenomenon. It has already been observed that HIV/AIDS has especially devastating socio-political and economic effects on Africa. This reality calls for all sectors in the community to work towards the prevention and care of those already infected. For an effective fight against the AIDS stigma, governments, NGOs and the church must make fighting HIV/AIDS their core business. All sectors everywhere must make it their responsibility to reduce the spread of HIV/AIDS as well as to minimize its

---

[19] Musa W. Dube, "Fifty Years of Bleeding, A storytelling feminist reading of Mark 5:24–43," in *Other Ways of Reading. African Woman and the Bible* (ed. Musa W. Dube; Geneva/Atlanta, Ga.: WCC, 2001), 50–60.

impact. Academic institutions and disciplines in Africa are also called upon to join in this "new struggle."[20]

Whilst New Testament biblical scholarship in Africa should remain true to its methodological practice in biblical interpretation and should remain true to scientific objectivity, the HIV/AIDS crisis and its effects cannot be ignored by the New Testament scholar and exegete. It has been sufficiently demonstrated in the foregone discussion that people living with HIV/AIDS are stigmatized, ostracized, discriminated, rejected, prejudiced and ex-cluded – from the family, families and community. The New Testament has familial language of inclusion that provides an interpretative grid and paradigm to destigmatize PLWHA including them as part of God's family.

4. Familial Language in the New Testament

Throughout the New Testament Jesus is the central figure and the authors concerned themselves with interpreting his utterances, actions and signi-ficance. The second important theme throughout the pages of the New Tes-tament is the idea of the church. This community understood and defined itself in a variety of ways. Schweizer maintains that one image which is not stated explicitly in the Bible and which does not seem to be in common use, but which has its roots in a variety of early Christian statements and which continues to have a clarifying and guiding force for us today, is the image of the church as the family of God.[21] Lassen maintains that in identi-fying and describing itself, the New Testament church employed family metaphors. She observes that the familial language played an important role in the formation of the early Christian church and its theology. God was commonly regarded and called Father, Jesus the Son and the believers the brethren.[22]

Judging from the large number of recent publications on the family and related matters in antiquity, it is clear that historians and biblical scholars nowadays share a renewed interest in the make-up, functions and general characteristics of families in the ancient Mediterranean world.[23] Study of

---

[20] See Musa W. Dube and Tinyiko Sam Maluleke, "HIV/AIDS as the new site of struggle: Theological and biblical and religious perspectives," *Missionalia* 29/2 (2001): 119–124, 119.

[21] Eduard Schweizer, *Church order in the New Testament* (London: SCM Press, 1961), 31.

[22] Eva Marie Lassen, "The Roman family: ideal and metaphor," in *Constructing Ear-ly Christian Families: Family as social reality and metaphor* (ed. Halvor Moxnes; Lon-don: Routledge, 1997), 103–119.

[23] Stephan Joubert and Jan W. van Henten, "Two a-typical Jewish families in Grae-co-Roman," *Neotest* 30 (1996): 121–140; see also Pieter W. van der Horst, *Ancient Jew-*

"the family" in modern and pre-modern societies continues to engage the interest of historians, demographers, sociologists, anthropologists, psychologists, and lawyers (amongst others). This is not only a recognition of the central role which the family has played in most societies but also a response to the complexity and variety of that role and indeed to the challenge of defining "the family."[24]

Spelling out the importance of family in biblical criticism, Van der Watt says: "The family imagery is the major way in which the relationship between God, Jesus and the believers are described ..."[25] Lassen contends that the family has played a significant role in the shaping of the Christian faith: "The family metaphors played an important role in the formation of early Christianity. The Christian theology was centred upon affiliation: God was the Father, Jesus the Son, the converts were the brothers and sisters of Christ and the true heirs of Abraham."[26] Garnsey and Saller maintain that: "(t)he family was a central institution of the Mediterranean society of the first century. Through the family, the wealth of the social status was transmitted in the family, the individual found support, solidarity and the protection ..."[27]

Malina, Joubert and Van der Watt maintain that the family was the nucleus of the ancient world. They say that as in other social structures in the Mediterranean world, everything and everyone within the family were viewed according to their gender roles.[28] Moxnes acknowledges the importance of family in the Bible particularly in the New Testament. He, however, observes that it is strange that, even if "family" is such an important topic in Christianity: "There have been few comprehensive studies of family in early Christianity, there has been interest in certain aspects in particular in ethical issues concerning marriage or the so-called household codes but much less on the social behaviour and forms of family as a social institution among early Christians."[29] Neyrey also indicates the need for further

---

ish epigraphs: Introductory survey of a millennium of Jewish epigraphy (300 BCE – 700 CE) (Kampen: Kok Pharos, 1991).

[24] Beryl Rawson (ed.), *Marriage, divorce and children in Ancient Rome* (New York, N.Y.: University Press, 1991), 7.

[25] Jan G. van der Watt, „Liefde in die familie van God: 'n Beskrywende uiteensetting van familie liefdesverhoudinge in die Johannesevangelie," *HTS* 53 (1997): 557–569.

[26] Lassen, "The Roman family" (n. 22).

[27] Peter Garnsey and Richard P. Saller (eds.), *El imperio romano. Economy, society and culture* (Barcelona: Critica, 1991), 151–152.

[28] Bruce J. Malina, Stephan J. Joubert and Jan G. van der Watt, *A time travel to the world of Jesus* (Johannesburg: Orion, 1996), 10.

[29] Halvor Moxnes, "Introduction," in idem, *Constructing* (n. 22), 1–9.

studies of fictive kinship, i.e. the ways in which the first Christians regarded and treated each other as "family."[30]

5. Familial Language in Mark

No fruitful discussion of Mark's Gospel can be conducted without due
consideration of what the Markan community was going through. Matera
correctly contends that any study of Mark's theology, requires a deep understanding of the experience of the community.[31] The starting point could
be the calling of Jesus' disciples (Mark 2:13–17). In the preceding pericope (2:1–12), in the healing of the paralytic, Jesus has undoubtedly made
himself unpopular with the Jewish leaders: "Why does this fellow talk like
that? He's blaspheming! Who can forgive sins but God" (2:7). The calling
of another disciple presents yet another family metaphor in the theology of
the Second Evangelist of the church. Levi is invited to the inner circle. In
the calling of a tax-collector to be one of his disciples, Jesus makes a
statement. Hurtado[32] maintains that tax-collectors were unpopular with the
Jews because they raised taxes for Herod and the Romans. In some instances they were accused of greed because they obtained their jobs by
bidding how much money they would raise, and their own reward was determined by their diligence in squeezing the utmost from the tax-paying
Jewish public. Cole[33] adds that the tax-collectors were often, if not always
rapacious and immoral, apart altogether from the nationalistic prejudice
against them, especially if they were directly working for the Romans, they
were classified as outcasts. The Gospels elsewhere couple them with sinners: "… a friend of tax-collectors and sinners" (Luke 7:34; see also Matt
18:17; 21:31).

Through the calling of Levi, the Markan Jesus makes his intentions and
acts even clearer. In Mark 1:16–20 Jesus called Simon, Andrew and John.
His calling detached them from their family and attached them to a new
fictive family. It was abnormal behaviour, if not traumatic in anticipation
for one to leave his own job, folks and father. In calling a controversial

---

[30] Jerome H. Neyrey, "Loss of wealth, loss of family and of honour," in *Modelling
Early Christianity: Social – Scientific Studies of New Testament in its context* (ed. Philip
F. Esler; London: Routledge, 1995), 139–158.

[31] Frank J. Matera, *What are they saying about Mark?* (New York, N.Y.: Paulist
Press, 1987), 53.

[32] Larry W. Hurtado, *Mark* (Good News Bible Commentary; Basingstoke: Pickering
& Inglis, 1983), 28.

[33] Robert A. Cole, *The Gospel According to St. Mark* (London: Columbia University
Microfilms International, 1973), 69.

person (2:14), the Evangelist indicates the new network of relationship, which Jesus came to establish – a new family.

Discipleship in Mark has strong familial language undertones. The setting of Mark 3:20–21, 31–35 is in a house. Malbon has done some research concerning the significance of the οἶκος as an architectural space in Mark's Gospel. It is one of a number of such spaces, which function symbolically in the narrative to convey the transformation and overturning of one order by another, which the ministry of Jesus represents.[34] "Jesus in a house expression" represents a new realm of Jesus' activities as against the Temple and the synagogue because he is no longer welcomed in these institutions. In the Gospel of Mark therefore the expression "house" has a specific significance. Taking into consideration that Paul's ministry was already impacting on communities at this time, there is a certain link between the frequent reference in Mark to house and house churches of the early Christianity (Rom 16:5; Col 4:15).[35] While in the house, Mark mentions two separate groups (the teachers of the law and Jesus' own family) who are both against him. The Jewish leaders lay charge against him (Βεελζεβοὺλ ἔχει), and his family came to take him for they were told that their relative (Jesus) was out of his mind. The response of Jesus, "whoever does the will of God is my brother and sister and mother" is significant. He clearly separates the disciples from his family and the crowd.[36]

Some concluding remarks on the church as a family in Mark will be appropriate. The author of the Second Gospel presents a reconstruction of how the Markan church envisaged itself. In the Graeco-Roman period belonging to a particular family was of great importance. Becoming a follower of Jesus resulted in the subordination of natural family ties. Thus, Mark's Gospel evinces a contra and counter-cultural ethos. Jesus called people to become his disciples. In their response, they left their families and occupations. It is granted that the church is nowhere identified in Mark's Gospel as the family of God, but the idea permeates the entire Gospel. Why should people forsake their family ties? Why should they be prepared to sacrifice belonging to a secured protection of their families? It is due to the fact that they have became members of a new family which according to its ethos and self-understanding is different from the previous

---

[34] Elizabeth Struthers Malbon, "Disciples/crowds/whoever: Markan characters and readers," *NovT* 28 (1986): 104–127, 113.

[35] Etienne Trocme, *The formation of the Gospel according to Mark* (Philadelphia: Westminster, 1975), 12.

[36] See Eduard Schweizer, *The Good News According to Mark* (Atlanta, Ga.: John Knox Press, 1975), 82–83; Ernest Best, *Following Jesus: Discipleship in the Gospel of Mark* (Sheffield: JSOT, 1981), 22–27.

one. They are a new people of God. They are the real family of God through Jesus and God is their Father.

People living with HIV/AIDS are stigmatized, discriminated against by their own family, communities and often their believing communities. These PLWHA in Africa maintain that more than the virus and the disease the most painful thing is the stark reality of stigmatization. Gideon Byamugisha (HIV+, Anglican priest from Uganda), once said "it is not the AIDS condition itself that hurts most but the stigmatization, rejection and discrimination." The stigmatization of the PLWA is indicative of the dysfunctional and stressed family in Africa. Elsewhere the author of this article shows that African traditional family ethics and values have striking similarities with God's family as portrayed in the New Testament.[37]

The most common manner of expressing the ethic of *Ubuntu* (personhood) is the South African proverb, "*umtu ngumuntu ngabantu*" (a person depends on others to be a person). In the Sotho languages, "*motho ke motho ka batho*" (you are a person through others). Besides family solidarity, which is the essence of the *Ubuntu* ethic, some family values are also enshrined in this concept. Respect of each other and the elderly, compassion of those who are suffering, commitment to the ideals of Africanism, self-sacrifice and love for your fellow man are part of *Ubuntu*. Some of the slogans in the New South Africa such as *Masakhane* (let us build) and *Simunye* (we are one) should be understood in the context of *Ubuntu*. Analogous ways of viewing reality are found in the New Testament. Therefore, the familial metaphor in Mark should provide a premise to the destigmatization of the PLWHA. The values and ethics found in this community are those of inclusiveness.

6. The Family of God in Matthew

Bornkamm maintains that there is no Gospel which is shaped by the consciousness of the existence of the church as Matthew's Gospel. Statements which depict the self-consciousness of the primitive church permeate the entire Gospel. It is for instance only in this Gospel where the word church is used (Matt 16:18). The disciples are the free sons of God (13:11), they

---

[37] Elijah Mahlangu, The family (reality and imagery) as a hermeneutical procedure for interpreting the gospels within the socio-cultural context of the ancient Mediterranean world: An African social-descriptive approach, (PhD Dissertation, University of Pretoria, 1999; cf. http://upetd.up.ac.za/thesis/submitted/etd-11132006-62036/unrestricted/00front. pdf, 5.4.2010).

are the salt of the earth and the light of the world, the city which is on the hill (5:13).[38]

In the parable of the wicked husbandman (21:41–46), Matthew portrays the church as God's new family. "Therefore I tell you that the kingdom of God will be taken away from you and be given to a people who will produce fruit" (v. 43). This verse is omitted from Mark and Luke, but this is not necessarily an indication that it is a later interpolation. Matthew was probably anxious to show his readers that Jesus was concerned with the problem of his rejection by the Jews and consequently the emergence of a new Israel.[39] Although Jesus in this parable addresses the Jewish leaders, the whole Jewish people share the responsibility for the rejection and the crucifixion of Jesus.[40] Commenting on the church as the new people, Kingsbury maintains that because Israel had repudiated Jesus, the Messiah, God has withdrawn his Kingdom from it and given it to the church. Therefore, the central thought of the Gospel is the community in which God in the person of Jesus chooses to dwell to the end to the age (1:23; 18:19–20; 28:20).[41]

The author of Matthew makes it clear in Matt 10:16–23 that family life will be disrupted and division within a family will occur within his community. Brother will hand over brother. The only situation which could cause normal family ties to be broken is to form alignments with other families. This means, therefore, that by virtue of their relationship with Jesus, the Matthean church members will forfeit former family relationships. At the same time members of this new community hear, "be on guard against men ..." (v. 17), "(they) will flog you in their synagogues" (v. 17), "all men will hate you" (v. 22), "when you are persecuted in one place flee to another ..." (v. 22). These statements indicate that the evangelist is not warning his community against faceless people. He is addressing them against unbelieving Jews in their surroundings. Matthew's church is to be separate from the Jews who are still to be converted; the latter belong to the lost sheep of Israel. They should be invited to come into the family – the Kingdom of God. The church is the result of those who have

---

[38] Günther Bornkamm, "End-expectation and Church in Matthew," in *Tradition and Interpretation in Matthew* (eds. Günther Bornkamm et al.; Philadelphia, Pa.: Westminster Press, 1963), 15–38.

[39] Randolph V.G. Tasker, *The Gospel according to Matthew* (Tyndale Bible Commentaries; London: Tyndale, 1961), 205.

[40] Rudolf Schnackenburg, *The church is the New Testament* (London: Burns & Oates, 1974), 70. See also Floyd V. Filson, *The Gospel according to St Matthew* (Black's New Testament Commentaries; London: Adam & Charles Black, 1960), 229.

[41] Jack D. Kingsbury, *Matthew* (Proclamation commentaries; Philadelphia, Pa.: Fortress, 1977), 78.

responded to the call of the coming king. It is a call to become the disciples of Jesus.

The familial language found in the First Evangelist contributes to the invitation of those who are ostracized, marginalized, stigmatized and discriminated against because of their HIV status. Gruesome stories of the treatment of the PLWHA emanate from Africa. An AIDS activist from Namibia said, "I so wish I could go out there, stand up and say I have HIV – but the problem is other people, HIV does not stigmatise or discriminate but people do." In Kwa-Zulu Natal, Gugu Dlamini[42] was beaten to death by her neighbours because she had spoken openly on radio about having HIV status. In Uganda, a man murdered his lover when she told him she was HIV+. In Kenya, a man pitch-forked his 15-year-old HIV+ nephew to death, while villagers stood by – because he disclosed that he was HIV+.[43]

In Matthew's Gospel the church is described as the real/new people, discipleship, and a manifestation of the Kingdom of God. The believers in Matthew's Gospel are seen as having entered the kingdom of God. The church is the result of those who have responded to the call of the coming King. It is a call to become the disciples of Jesus. In the Old Testament God (the Father) established a people for Himself through the patriarchs. The Matthean community, thus, regarded itself as the family which was distinct from the "old family," the unbelieving Jews. It is to this new family and community the PLWHA are invited to belong. In this community fear will be replaced with hope. It is a healing community – there is life after HIV, there is life with AIDS. It is a people who would assist those who are hurting to replace ignorance with knowledge. Notions of moral failing will be replaced with understanding. Blame will be replaced with respect. Every person has an inherent dignity and boundless value that nothing can take away. It is a community that will replace shame and denial with solidarity and openness – the members of this community are all in this together.

7. The Household of God in Luke-Acts

The portrayal of the church in Luke-Acts is different from what we have already observed in Mark and Matthew. Pelser maintains that it appears that the Lukan church is the result of salvation-history. The time of the church is the third phase in the process of salvation-history. The first is the

---

[42] Gugu Dlamini was an AIDS activist in Richmond, Kwa-Zulu Natal who was brutally murdered because she was open with her HIV+ status.

[43] Mahlangu, *Family* (n. 37), 7.

history of Israel, and the second the actions of John the Baptist and Jesus.[44] Conzelmann calls this the tripartite scheme.[45] Like in Mark, the word "churches" is not found in Luke. But the manner in which Luke presents Jesus' work presupposes that Jesus was establishing a community which would later form an eschatological community, referred to as the church.[46] Whereas the church is commonly thought as coming into existence after Easter, in Luke it comes into existence during the ministry of Jesus. Luke's (narrative) creation of his disciples is intended to set before his readers a model Christian community. They are meant neither to prefigure the church nor to represent the church in embryo: they are actually the church.

8. The Church (as Family) in John's Gospel

A number of Johannine scholars maintain that the Fourth Gospel is more concerned with the church than the synoptic gospels. Schnackenburg[47] says that on first sight John's Gospel does not seem to focus on the church as such. It rather seems as if the Fourth Gospel was considered as evidence of an individual, spiritualized, even "mystical" Christianity (cf. 3:16, 36; 4:23; 5:24; 6:56; 15:5; etc.). Kysar argues against individualism by stating the collective nature of the church. He maintains that the dismissal of the concept church in John's Gospel because the Evangelist does not mention the word "church" is premature. The Gospel articulates a view of the church without ever resorting to the use of the word.[48]

In the Fourth Gospel the church stands distinct from the Synagogue (3:1–8). The discourse between Jesus and Nicodemus is actually the church in conversation with the synagogue. Nicodemus appears not to have a personal agenda. He is made not to approach Jesus in his personal spiritual aggrandizement. The verb οἴδαμεν (3:2) may refer to the Pharisees or the *argontes* or both. It is possible that it is reference to the πολλοί of 2:23, because they saw the signs performed by Jesus. The discourse is therefore about the fact that Judaism cannot simply move forward over a level plain to achieve its goal in the Kingdom of God. This goal cannot be reached by

---

[44] Gert M. M. Pelser, "Die Kerk in die Nuwe Testament", *HTS* 51 (1995): 645–676.

[45] Hans Conzelmann, *Die Mitte der Zeit: Studien zur Theologie des Lukas* (Tübingen: Mohr Siebeck, 1977), 195. See also Kevin N. Giles, "The church in the Gospel of Luke," *SJTH* 34 (1981): 121–146.

[46] Izak du Plessis, "Discipleship according to Luke's Gospel," *Religion and Theology* 2 (1995): 58–71.

[47] Rudolf Schnackenburg, *The Gospel According to St John* (London: Burns & Oates, 1982), 102.

[48] Robert Kysar, *John the Marverick Gospel* (Louisville, Ky.: Westminster John Knox, 1993), 112.

either learned discussions between its distinguished teachers (such as Jesus and Nicodemus). Nicodemus comes with the question which Judaism must put to Jesus. It is the question of salvation. The Jews were proud that they were the descendants and children of Abraham by physical birth. To them to be a child of Abraham meant an exalted privilege and status. Jesus had to categorically state that to be a true son of Abraham is a spiritual matter and not a physical matter, but to be a son of God requires something more than that: "you must be born again" (3:3).

The Fourth Evangelist uses the family metaphor of birth to express a spiritual reality of faith. The word ἄνωθεν implies that another birth has already taken place. Van der Watt maintains that the family in the Mediterranean world was generally regarded as the basic social structure. Birth into a family therefore meant to become part of the family with everything that it involved especially on a social level.[49] Pursuant to this notion, Blasi says that in the first century Mediterranean world to be a child of someone meant to participate in an identity and in particular nexus of the parents' social networks. Just as one acquires family, friends, relatives, neighbours and a name from the parents, the Johannine church acquired these by being born in God's family. Birth was therefore an important way of determining one's identity. This birth metaphor suggests the social orientation of the Johannine community. The evangelist's discourse between Jesus and Nicodemus is meant to describe the separation of the Johannine Christians from the community of the local synagogue.[50]

Although the author of John is chiefly interested in Christology, the idea of the church as a new community is the impelling motive of the composition of the Fourth Gospel. For instance in the miracle of the healing of the man born blind (9:1–7), the plot gradually moves from the physical to spiritual blindness. After the healing the neighbours are divided. Others are almost sure that it was the man who was born blind, while the others saw close resemblance. The man puts an end to the speculation: ἐκεῖνος ἔλεγεν ὅτι ἐγώ εἰμι (9:9). He is interrogated by the Jews, and when he, with concealed humor, asked whether the Pharisees possibly wished to become his disciples, he is expelled from the synagogue. The man encounters Jesus, who reveals himself to him and he makes a full confession: ὁ δὲ ἔφη· πιστεύω, κύριε· καὶ προσεκύνησεν αὐτῷ (9:38).[51]

---

[49] Jan G. van der Watt, "Ethics in I John: A literary and social-scientific perspective," *CBC* 61/3: 491–511.

[50] Anthony J. Blasi, *A sociology of Johannine Christianity* (New York, N.Y.: Mellen Press, 1997), 257.

[51] Randolph V.G. Tasker, *The Gospel According to John* (London: Tyndale, 1960), 122–126.

HIV/AIDS has many implications to infected persons. Many of these people naturally go through a series of emotional reactions such as shock and denial, anger and fear, anxiety and grief, when they learn that they are HIV+. Other effects include fear of death, rejection and stigmatization. Such people need understanding, acceptance, care and love. The images of the family in Johannine ecclesiology (God as Father, Jesus as healer, born into God's family, love, image of the flock, etc.) are sufficient to provide an alternative community to the PLWHA. The stigmatization, discrimination and rejection experienced by these people may be likened to those experienced by the Johannine family in the hands of the synagogue and Jewish leaders.

9. Pauline Ecclesiology, an Inclusive *Laos*

In his letters Paul employs the family metaphor as an image of God's people. Roberts maintains that numerous metaphors in Paul's corpus are indicative of the importance of "ecclesiology" in his theology.[52] Pelser says that one of the main designations of the church in Paul's ecclesiology is the "people of God."[53] The word "*laos*" is consistently used to denote a particular people or group – whereas all other peoples or nations are designated by the term "*ethnos*". Therefore the word "*laos*" signifies what brings people together – God's election of them as his people (1 Cor 10:7; Rom 9:25–26). A title "people of God" suggests a dynamic vision of God's people, which is fundamentally on a historical pilgrimage.[54]

The family imagery by Paul is also found in Galatians 5:13–6:10. Here Paul spells out the identity of the Galatian believers. They experience God as their Father (1:1–3), through Jesus they have become the adopted sons of God (3:26), in their experience of baptism, they have "clothed" themselves with Christ (3:27). They are the sons of God (4:1–7). Paul uses the family term of adoption to explain the idea of belonging or becoming part of God's family. Lyall maintains that Paul is the only New Testament writer to use the metaphor of adoption. The term is used in three ways:

(1) In Rom 9:4, Israel the people of God are said to be adopted as sons. Their place as the chosen people is underlined.

(2) In Rom 8:15; Eph 1:5 and Gal 4:5 the apostle uses the term adoption in its legal sense. The metaphor points to the selection of the believers as

---

[52] John H Roberts. "Pauline ecclesiology," in *Guide to the New Testament* (ed. Andrie B. Du Toit; vol. 5; Pretoria: N.G. Boekhandel, 1985), 265–299.

[53] Pelser, "Die kerk" (n. 44).

[54] Schnackenburg, *Church in the New Testament* (n. 47), 77.

sons: their justification is their entry into sonship and from the point of conversion, they are members of God's family.

(3) Lastly adoption in Rom 8:23 has eschatological connotations. The believers are "eagerly waiting for adoption as sons, the redemption of our bodies ..." this refers to the final transformation at the parousia. They will have totally passed from their former state into something wholly new.

Thus, Paul employs the metaphor of adoption to describe the conversion of a person both Jew and Gentile, as God's new child into a new family who has responded to God's call. This therefore means that the natural family or kinship structure into which the person has been born and which previously defined relationships with the society are here changed by a new relationship.[55] The term ἀδελφός appears in Paul's letters. It is a favourite manner to refer to the members of the communities to whom he is writing. He also uses it with reference to those he perceived as colleagues in the work of the ministry (Gal 1:2; 1 Cor 16:20; 2 Cor 9:3; Col 1:2). Paul applies this familial language to the Christians to show that they are a new family, the people of God. They are the children of God, and also that of the apostle. They are brothers and sisters bound together in the relationship of love.[56]

10. Conclusion

HIV/AIDS and its effects such as stigmatization remain Africa's serious health and developmental catastrophe. This crisis and scourge is a threat to human life and existence in the African continent. The bible mentions synonymous conditions like λέπρα. People who had leprosy were ostracized, stigmatized and separated from family and community. Reading the New Testament, leprosy and other diseases were the object of Jesus' healing miracles. The church as the body of Christ ought to be a lotus of healing. Theologizing in the context of HIV/AIDS is fairly a recent development. However, theological reflections on HIV/AIDS did not become a factor until some seven years ago. Largely publications came from pastoral practitioners and counsellors. HIV/AIDS has indeed changed how the African church ministers and cares for its members and the wider community. The

---

[55] Wayne A. Meeks, *First Urban Christians: The social world of the Apostle Paul* (New Haven, Conn.: Yale University Press, 1983), 87.

[56] Helmut Koester, "1 Thessalonians – Experiment in Christian writing," in *Continuity and discontinuity in church history* (ed. George W. Williams; Leiden: Brill, 1979), 33–44.

New Testament theologian's and exegete's contribution in the fight against HIV/AIDS stigmatization is imperative.

It was indicated in this article that the familial metaphorical language of inclusion and accommodation is stark reality in the New Testament. These metaphors enshrine ethics and values of inclusion of the new people of God. The New Testament's message of God's grace, mercy, acceptance, love, inclusion, accommodation and sense of belonging is portrayed and communicated in kinship language. In Africa PLWHA are largely stigmatized by family and community. This familial language as found in the New Testament provides a model and grid to address issues around HIV/AIDS stigmatization in Africa. This new family of God as portrayed in the New Testament has no place for stigma, exclusion, isolation, alienation, estrangement and discrimination. It is in this community that the stigmatized victim of HIV/AIDS will receive a new identity and name. Names such as victims and sufferers, innocent victims, walking corpses, victims of circumstances, past tense, promiscuous, prostitutes, immoral, those with a ticket to hell, "them" and "us" will be replaced by son/daughter, brother and sister. It is in this community that their fear will be replaced by hope and the assurance that there is life after HIV/AIDS. It is in this community that their self-blame and condemnation will be replaced by inherent dignity and boundless value that nothing can take away.

Authors and Editors

Richard A. Burridge, Dr. theol., Professor of Biblical Interpretation, King's College, London, England.

Jörg Frey, Dr. theol., Professor of New Testament, Faculty of Theology, University of Zurich, Switzerland.

Sean Freyne, Dr. theol., Emeritus Professor of New Testament, School of Religions and Theology, Trinity College Dublin, University of Dublin, Ireland.

Friedrich Wilhelm Horn, Dr. theol., Professor of New Testament, Protestant Theological Faculty, Johannes Gutenberg-Universität Mainz, Germany.

Lambert D. Jacobs, M.A. M.Div., Research Associate in New Testament, University of Stellenbosch, South Africa.

Kobus Kok, Dr. theol., Senior Lecturer of New Testament, University of Pretoria, South Africa.

Matthias Konradt, Dr. theol., Professor of New Testament, Theological Faculty, Ruprecht-Karls-Universität Heidelberg, Germany.

Hermut Löhr, Dr. theol., Professor of New Testament, Protestant Theological Faculty, Westfälische Wilhelms-Universität Münster, Germany.

Susanne Luther, M.A. (Durham), Research Assistant in New Testament, Protestant Theological Faculty, Johannes Gutenberg-Universität Mainz, Germany.

Elijah Mahlangu, Dr. theol., Senior Lecturer, Bible and Religious Studies, University of Pretoria, South Africa.

François S. Malan, Dr. theol., Emeritus Professor of New Testament, University of the North, South Africa.

Karl-Wilhelm Niebuhr, Dr. theol., Professor of New Testament, Theological Faculty, Friedrich-Schiller-Universität Jena, Germany.

Jeremy Punt, Dr. theol., Professor of New Testament, University of Stellenbosch, South Africa.

Gert J. Steyn, Dr. theol., Professor of New Testament, University of Pretoria, South Africa.

Etienne de Villiers, Dr. theol., Professor of Dogmatics and Christian Ethics, University of Pretoria, South Africa.

Pieter G. R. de Villiers, Dr. theol., Honorary Professor of New Testament, University of the Free State, South Africa.

Jan G. van der Watt, Dr. theol., Professor of New Testament, Radboud University of Nijmegen, Netherlands.

Ruben Zimmermann, Dr. theol., Professor of New Testament, Protestant Theological Faculty, Johannes Gutenberg-Universität Mainz, Germany.

Index of References

Old Testament

New Testament

Judaica

Graeco-Roman Literature

Index of Modern Authors

Index of Subjects and Key Terms

Wissenschaftliche Untersuchungen zum Neuen Testament
Alphabetical Index of the First and Second Series

Bell, Richard H.: Deliver Us from Evil. 2007. *Vol. 216.*
– The Irrevocable Call of God. 2005. *Vol. 184.*
– No One Seeks for God. 1998. *Vol. 106.*
– Provoked to Jealousy. 1994. *Vol. II/63.*
Bennema, Cornelis: The Power of Saving Wisdom. 2002. *Vol. II/148.*
Bergman, Jan: see *Kieffer, René*
Bergmeier, Roland: Das Gesetz im Römerbrief und andere Studien zum Neuen Testament. 2000. *Vol. 121.*
Bernett, Monika: Der Kaiserkult in Judäa unter den Herodiern und Römern. 2007. *Vol. 203.*
Betz, Otto: Jesus, der Messias Israels. 1987. *Vol. 42.*
– Jesus, der Herr der Kirche. 1990. *Vol. 52.*
Beyschlag, Karlmann: Simon Magus und die christliche Gnosis. 1974. *Vol. 16.*
Bieringer, Reimund: see *Koester, Craig.*
Bittner, Wolfgang J.: Jesu Zeichen im Johannesevangelium. 1987. *Vol. II/26.*
Bjerkelund, Carl J.: Tauta Egeneto. 1987. *Vol. 40.*
Blackburn, Barry Lee: Theios Aner and the Markan Miracle Traditions. 1991. *Vol. II/40.*
Blanton IV, Thomas R.: Constructing a New Covenant. 2007. *Vol. II/233.*
Bock, Darrell L.: Blasphemy and Exaltation in Judaism and the Final Examination of Jesus. 1998. *Vol. II/106.*
– and *Robert L. Webb* (Ed.): Key Events in the Life of the Historical Jesus. 2009. *Vol. 247.*
Bockmuehl, Markus: The Remembered Peter. 2010. *Vol. 262.*
– Revelation and Mystery in Ancient Judaism and Pauline Christianity. 1990. *Vol. II/36.*
Bøe, Sverre: Cross-Bearing in Luke. 2010. *Vol. II/278.*
– Gog and Magog. 2001. *Vol. II/135.*
Böhlig, Alexander: Gnosis und Synkretismus. Vol. 1 1989. *Vol. 47* – Vol. 2 1989. *Vol. 48.*
Böhm, Martina: Samarien und die Samaritai bei Lukas. 1999. *Vol. II/111.*
Börstinghaus, Jens: Sturmfahrt und Schiffbruch. 2010. *Vol. II/274.*
Böttrich, Christfried: Weltweisheit – Menschheitsethik – Urkult. 1992. *Vol. II/50.*
– and *Herzer, Jens* (Ed.): Josephus und das Neue Testament. 2007. *Vol. 209.*
Bolyki, János: Jesu Tischgemeinschaften. 1997. *Vol. II/96.*
Bosman, Philip: Conscience in Philo and Paul. 2003. *Vol. II/166.*
Bovon, François: New Testament and Christian Apocrypha. 2009. *Vol. 237.*
– Studies in Early Christianity. 2003. *Vol. 161.*
Brändl, Martin: Der Agon bei Paulus. 2006. *Vol. II/222.*

Braun, Heike: Geschichte des Gottesvolkes und christliche Identität. 2010. *Vol. II/279.*
Breytenbach, Cilliers: see *Frey, Jörg.*
Broadhead, Edwin K.: Jewish Ways of Following Jesus Redrawing the Religious Map of Antiquity. 2010. *Vol. 266.*
Brocke, Christoph vom: Thessaloniki – Stadt des Kassander und Gemeinde des Paulus. 2001. *Vol. II/125.*
Brunson, Andrew: Psalm 118 in the Gospel of John. 2003. *Vol. II/158.*
Büchli, Jörg: Der Poimandres – ein paganisiertes Evangelium. 1987. *Vol. II/27.*
Bühner, Jan A.: Der Gesandte und sein Weg im 4. Evangelium. 1977. *Vol. II/2.*
Burchard, Christoph: Untersuchungen zu Joseph und Aseneth. 1965. *Vol. 8.*
– Studien zur Theologie, Sprache und Umwelt des Neuen Testaments. Ed. by D. Sänger. 1998. *Vol. 107.*
Burnett, Richard: Karl Barth's Theological Exegesis. 2001. *Vol. II/145.*
Byron, John: Slavery Metaphors in Early Judaism and Pauline Christianity. 2003. *Vol. II/162.*
Byrskog, Samuel: Story as History – History as Story. 2000. *Vol. 123.*
Cancik, Hubert (Ed.): Markus-Philologie. 1984. *Vol. 33.*
Capes, David B.: Old Testament Yaweh Texts in Paul's Christology. 1992. *Vol. II/47.*
Caragounis, Chrys C.: The Development of Greek and the New Testament. 2004. *Vol. 167.*
– The Son of Man. 1986. *Vol. 38.*
– see *Fridrichsen, Anton.*
Carleton Paget, James: The Epistle of Barnabas. 1994. *Vol. II/64.*
– Jews, Christians and Jewish Christians in Antiquity. 2010. *Vol. 251.*
Carson, D.A., O'Brien, Peter T. and *Mark Seifrid* (Ed.): Justification and Variegated Nomism.
Vol. 1: The Complexities of Second Temple Judaism. 2001. *Vol. II/140.*
Vol. 2: The Paradoxes of Paul. 2004. *Vol. II/181.*
Chae, Young Sam: Jesus as the Eschatological Davidic Shepherd. 2006. *Vol. II/216.*
Chapman, David W.: Ancient Jewish and Christian Perceptions of Crucifixion. 2008. *Vol. II/244.*
Chester, Andrew: Messiah and Exaltation. 2007. *Vol. 207.*
Chibici-Revneanu, Nicole: Die Herrlichkeit des Verherrlichten. 2007. *Vol. II/231.*

Ciampa, Roy E.: The Presence and Function of Scripture in Galatians 1 and 2. 1998. *Vol. II/102.*

Classen, Carl Joachim: Rhetorical Criticsm of the New Testament. 2000. *Vol. 128.*

Colpe, Carsten: Griechen – Byzantiner – Semiten – Muslime. 2008. *Vol. 221.*

– Iranier – Aramäer – Hebräer – Hellenen. 2003. *Vol. 154.*

Cook, John G.: Roman Attitudes Towards the Christians. 2010. *Vol. 261.*

Coote, Robert B. (Ed.): see *Weissenrieder, Annette.*

Coppins, Wayne: The Interpretation of Freedom in the Letters of Paul. 2009. *Vol. II/261.*

Crump, David: Jesus the Intercessor. 1992. *Vol. II/49.*

Dahl, Nils Alstrup: Studies in Ephesians. 2000. *Vol. 131.*

Daise, Michael A.: Feasts in John. 2007. *Vol. II/229.*

Deines, Roland: Die Gerechtigkeit der Tora im Reich des Messias. 2004. *Vol. 177.*

– Jüdische Steingefäße und pharisäische Frömmigkeit. 1993. *Vol. II/52.*

– Die Pharisäer. 1997. *Vol. 101.*

Deines, Roland and *Karl-Wilhelm Niebuhr* (Ed.): Philo und das Neue Testament. 2004. *Vol. 172.*

Dennis, John A.: Jesus' Death and the Gathering of True Israel. 2006. *Vol. 217.*

Dettwiler, Andreas and *Jean Zumstein* (Ed.): Kreuzestheologie im Neuen Testament. 2002. *Vol. 151.*

Dickson, John P.: Mission-Commitment in Ancient Judaism and in the Pauline Communities. 2003. *Vol. II/159.*

Dietzfelbinger, Christian: Der Abschied des Kommenden. 1997. *Vol. 95.*

Dimitrov, Ivan Z., James D.G. Dunn, Ulrich Luz and *Karl-Wilhelm Niebuhr* (Ed.): Das Alte Testament als christliche Bibel in orthodoxer und westlicher Sicht. 2004. *Vol. 174.*

Dobbeler, Axel von: Glaube als Teilhabe. 1987. *Vol. II/22.*

Docherty, Susan E.: The Use of the Old Testament in Hebrews. 2009. *Vol. II/260.*

Downs, David J.: The Offering of the Gentiles. 2008. *Vol. II/248.*

Dryden, J. de Waal: Theology and Ethics in 1 Peter. 2006. *Vol. II/209.*

Dübbers, Michael: Christologie und Existenz im Kolosserbrief. 2005. *Vol. II/191.*

Dunn, James D.G.: The New Perspective on Paul. 2005. *Vol. 185.*

Dunn , James D.G. (Ed.): Jews and Christians. 1992. *Vol. 66.*

– Paul and the Mosaic Law. 1996. *Vol. 89.*

– see *Dimitrov, Ivan Z.*

–, *Hans Klein, Ulrich Luz,* and *Vasile Mihoc* (Ed.): Auslegung der Bibel in orthodoxer und westlicher Perspektive. 2000. *Vol. 130.*

Ebel, Eva: Die Attraktivität früher christlicher Gemeinden. 2004. *Vol. II/178.*

Ebertz, Michael N.: Das Charisma des Gekreuzigten. 1987. *Vol. 45.*

Eckstein, Hans-Joachim: Der Begriff Syneidesis bei Paulus. 1983. *Vol. II/10.*

– Verheißung und Gesetz. 1996. *Vol. 86.*

Ego, Beate: Im Himmel wie auf Erden. 1989. *Vol. II/34.*

Ego, Beate, Armin Lange and *Peter Pilhofer* (Ed.): Gemeinde ohne Tempel – Community without Temple. 1999. *Vol. 118.*

– and *Helmut Merkel* (Ed.): Religiöses Lernen in der biblischen, frühjüdischen und frühchristlichen Überlieferung. 2005. *Vol. 180.*

Eisele, Wilfried: Welcher Thomas? 2010. *Vol. 259.*

Eisen, Ute E.: see *Paulsen, Henning.*

Elledge, C.D.: Life after Death in Early Judaism. 2006. *Vol. II/208.*

Ellis, E. Earle: Prophecy and Hermeneutic in Early Christianity. 1978. *Vol. 18.*

– The Old Testament in Early Christianity. 1991. *Vol. 54.*

Elmer, Ian J.: Paul, Jerusalem and the Judaisers. 2009. *Vol. II/258.*

Endo, Masanobu: Creation and Christology. 2002. *Vol. 149.*

Ennulat, Andreas: Die 'Minor Agreements'. 1994. *Vol. II/62.*

Ensor, Peter W.: Jesus and His 'Works'. 1996. *Vol. II/85.*

Eskola, Timo: Messiah and the Throne. 2001. *Vol. II/142.*

– Theodicy and Predestination in Pauline Soteriology. 1998. *Vol. II/100.*

Farelly, Nicolas: The Disciples in the Fourth Gospel. 2010. *Vol. II/290.*

Fatehi, Mehrdad: The Spirit's Relation to the Risen Lord in Paul. 2000. *Vol. II/128.*

Feldmeier, Reinhard: Die Krisis des Gottessohnes. 1987. *Vol. II/21.*

– Die Christen als Fremde. 1992. *Vol. 64.*

Feldmeier, Reinhard and *Ulrich Heckel* (Ed.): Die Heiden. 1994. *Vol. 70.*

Finnern, Sönke: Narratologie und biblische Exegese. 2010. *Vol. II/285.*

Fletcher-Louis, Crispin H.T.: Luke-Acts: Angels, Christology and Soteriology. 1997. *Vol. II/94.*

Förster, Niclas: Marcus Magus. 1999. *Vol. 114.*

Forbes, Christopher Brian: Prophecy and Inspired Speech in Early Christianity and its Hellenistic Environment. 1995. *Vol. II/75.*

Fornberg, Tord: see *Fridrichsen, Anton.*

Fossum, Jarl E.: The Name of God and the Angel of the Lord. 1985. *Vol. 36.*

Foster, Paul: Community, Law and Mission in Matthew's Gospel. *Vol. II/177.*

Fotopoulos, John: Food Offered to Idols in Roman Corinth. 2003. *Vol. II/151.*

Frank, Nicole: Der Kolosserbrief im Kontext des paulinischen Erbes. 2009. *Vol. II/271.*

Frenschkowski, Marco: Offenbarung und Epiphanie. Vol. 1 1995. *Vol. II/79* – Vol. 2 1997. *Vol. II/80.*

Frey, Jörg: Eugen Drewermann und die biblische Exegese. 1995. *Vol. II/71.*

– Die johanneische Eschatologie. Vol. I. 1997. *Vol. 96.* – Vol. II. 1998. *Vol. 110.* – Vol. III. 2000. *Vol. 117.*

Frey, Jörg and *Cilliers Breytenbach* (Ed.): Aufgabe und Durchführung einer Theologie des Neuen Testaments. 2007. *Vol. 205.*

– *Jens Herzer, Martina Janßen* and *Clare K. Rothschild* (Ed.): Pseudepigraphie und Verfasserfiktion in frühchristlichen Briefen. 2009. *Vol. 246.*

– *Stefan Krauter* and *Hermann Lichtenberger* (Ed.): Heil und Geschichte. 2009. *Vol. 248.*

– and *Udo Schnelle (Ed.):* Kontexte des Johannesevangeliums. 2004. *Vol. 175.*

– and *Jens Schröter* (Ed.): Deutungen des Todes Jesu im Neuen Testament. 2005. *Vol. 181.*

– Jesus in apokryphen Evangelienüberlieferungen. 2010. *Vol. 254.*

–, *Jan G. van der Watt,* and *Ruben Zimmermann* (Ed.): Imagery in the Gospel of John. 2006. *Vol. 200.*

Freyne, Sean: Galilee and Gospel. 2000. *Vol. 125.*

Fridrichsen, Anton: Exegetical Writings. Edited by C.C. Caragounis and T. Fornberg. 1994. *Vol. 76.*

Gadenz, Pablo T.: Called from the Jews and from the Gentiles. 2009. *Vol. II/267.*

Gäbel, Georg: Die Kulttheologie des Hebräerbriefes. 2006. *Vol. II/212.*

Gäckle, Volker: Die Starken und die Schwachen in Korinth und in Rom. 2005. *Vol. 200.*

Garlington, Don B.: 'The Obedience of Faith'. 1991. *Vol. II/38.*

– Faith, Obedience, and Perseverance. 1994. *Vol. 79.*

Garnet, Paul: Salvation and Atonement in the Qumran Scrolls. 1977. *Vol. II/3.*

Gemünden, Petra von (Ed.): see *Weissenrieder, Annette.*

Gese, Michael: Das Vermächtnis des Apostels. 1997. *Vol. II/99.*

Gheorghita, Radu: The Role of the Septuagint in Hebrews. 2003. *Vol. II/160.*

Gordley, Matthew E.: The Colossian Hymn in Context. 2007. *Vol. II/228.*

Gräbe, Petrus J.: The Power of God in Paul's Letters. 2000, ²2008. *Vol. II/123.*

Gräßer, Erich: Der Alte Bund im Neuen. 1985. *Vol. 35.*

– Forschungen zur Apostelgeschichte. 2001. *Vol. 137.*

Grappe, Christian (Ed.): Le Repas de Dieu / Das Mahl Gottes. 2004. *Vol. 169.*

Gray, Timothy C.: The Temple in the Gospel of Mark. 2008. *Vol. II/242.*

Green, Joel B.: The Death of Jesus. 1988. *Vol. II/33.*

Gregg, Brian Han: The Historical Jesus and the Final Judgment Sayings in Q. 2005. *Vol. II/207.*

Gregory, Andrew: The Reception of Luke and Acts in the Period before Irenaeus. 2003. *Vol. II/169.*

Grindheim, Sigurd: The Crux of Election. 2005. *Vol. II/202.*

Gundry, Robert H.: The Old is Better. 2005. *Vol. 178.*

Gundry Volf, Judith M.: Paul and Perseverance. 1990. *Vol. II/37.*

Häußer, Detlef: Christusbekenntnis und Jesusüberlieferung bei Paulus. 2006. *Vol. 210.*

Hafemann, Scott J.: Suffering and the Spirit. 1986. *Vol. II/19.*

– Paul, Moses, and the History of Israel. 1995. *Vol. 81.*

Hahn, Ferdinand: Studien zum Neuen Testament.
   Vol. I: Grundsatzfragen, Jesusforschung, Evangelien. 2006. *Vol. 191.*
   Vol. II: Bekenntnisbildung und Theologie in urchristlicher Zeit. 2006. *Vol. 192.*

Hahn, Johannes (Ed.): Zerstörungen des Jerusalemer Tempels. 2002. *Vol. 147.*

Hamid-Khani, Saeed: Relevation and Concealment of Christ. 2000. *Vol. II/120.*

Hannah, Darrel D.: Michael and Christ. 1999. *Vol. II/109.*

Hardin, Justin K.: Galatians and the Imperial Cult? 2007. *Vol. II /237.*

Harrison; James R.: Paul's Language of Grace in Its Graeco-Roman Context. 2003. *Vol. II/172.*

Hartman, Lars: Text-Centered New Testament Studies. Ed. von D. Hellholm. 1997. *Vol. 102.*

Hartog, Paul: Polycarp and the New Testament. 2001. *Vol. II/134.*

Hays, Christopher M.: Luke's Wealth Ethics. 2010. *Vol. 275.*

Heckel, Theo K.: Der Innere Mensch. 1993. *Vol. II/53.*
– Vom Evangelium des Markus zum viergestaltigen Evangelium. 1999. *Vol. 120.*
Heckel, Ulrich: Kraft in Schwachheit. 1993. *Vol. II/56.*
– Der Segen im Neuen Testament. 2002. *Vol. 150.*
– see *Feldmeier, Reinhard.*
– see *Hengel, Martin.*
Heemstra, Marius: The Fiscus Judaicus and the Parting of the Ways. 2010. *Vol. II/277.*
Heiligenthal, Roman: Werke als Zeichen. 1983. *Vol. II/9.*
Heininger, Bernhard: Die Inkulturation des Christentums. 2010. *Vol. 255.*
Heliso, Desta: Pistis and the Righteous One. 2007. *Vol. II/235.*
Hellholm, D.: see *Hartman, Lars.*
Hemer, Colin J.: The Book of Acts in the Setting of Hellenistic History. 1989. *Vol. 49.*
Hengel, Martin: Jesus und die Evangelien. Kleine Schriften V. 2007. *Vol. 211.*
– Die johanneische Frage. 1993. *Vol. 67.*
– Judaica et Hellenistica. Kleine Schriften I. 1996. *Vol. 90.*
– Judaica, Hellenistica et Christiana. Kleine Schriften II. 1999. *Vol. 109.*
– Judentum und Hellenismus. 1969, ³1988. *Vol. 10.*
– Paulus und Jakobus. Kleine Schriften III. 2002. *Vol. 141.*
– Studien zur Christologie. Kleine Schriften IV. 2006. *Vol. 201.*
– Studien zum Urchristentum. Kleine Schriften VI. 2008. *Vol. 234.*
– Theologische, historische und biographische Skizzen. Kleine Schriften VII. 2010. *Vol. 253.*
– and *Anna Maria Schwemer:* Paulus zwischen Damaskus und Antiochien. 1998. *Vol. 108.*
– Der messianische Anspruch Jesu und die Anfänge der Christologie. 2001. *Vol. 138.*
– Die vier Evangelien und das eine Evangelium von Jesus Christus. 2008. *Vol. 224.*
Hengel, Martin and *Ulrich Heckel* (Ed.): Paulus und das antike Judentum. 1991. *Vol. 58.*
– and *Hermut Löhr* (Ed.): Schriftauslegung im antiken Judentum und im Urchristentum. 1994. *Vol. 73.*
– and *Anna Maria Schwemer* (Ed.): Königsherrschaft Gottes und himmlischer Kult. 1991. *Vol. 55.*
– Die Septuaginta. 1994. *Vol. 72.*
–, *Siegfried Mittmann* and *Anna Maria Schwemer* (Ed.): La Cité de Dieu / Die Stadt Gottes. 2000. *Vol. 129.*

Hentschel, Anni: Diakonia im Neuen Testament. 2007. *Vol. 226.*
Hernández Jr., Juan: Scribal Habits and Theological Influence in the Apocalypse. 2006. *Vol. II/218.*
Herrenbrück, Fritz: Jesus und die Zöllner. 1990. *Vol. II/41.*
Herzer, Jens: Paulus oder Petrus? 1998. *Vol. 103.*
– see *Böttrich, Christfried.*
– see *Frey, Jörg.*
Hill, Charles E.: From the Lost Teaching of Polycarp. 2005. *Vol. 186.*
Hoegen-Rohls, Christina: Der nachösterliche Johannes. 1996. *Vol. II/84.*
Hoffmann, Matthias Reinhard: The Destroyer and the Lamb. 2005. *Vol. II/203.*
Hofius, Otfried: Katapausis. 1970. *Vol. 11.*
– Der Vorhang vor dem Thron Gottes. 1972. *Vol. 14.*
– Der Christushymnus Philipper 2,6–11. 1976, ²1991. *Vol. 17.*
– Paulusstudien. 1989, ²1994. *Vol. 51.*
– Neutestamentliche Studien. 2000. *Vol. 132.*
– Paulusstudien II. 2002. *Vol. 143.*
– Exegetische Studien. 2008. *Vol. 223.*
– and *Hans-Christian Kammler:* Johannesstudien. 1996. *Vol. 88.*
Holloway, Paul A.: Coping with Prejudice. 2009. *Vol. 244.*
– see *Ahearne-Kroll, Stephen P.*
Holmberg, Bengt (Ed.): Exploring Early Christian Identity. 2008. *Vol. 226.*
– and *Mikael Winninge* (Ed.): Identity Formation in the New Testament. 2008. *Vol. 227.*
Holtz, Traugott: Geschichte und Theologie des Urchristentums. 1991. *Vol. 57.*
Hommel, Hildebrecht: Sebasmata.
Vol. 1 1983. *Vol. 31.*
Vol. 2 1984. *Vol. 32.*
Horbury, William: Herodian Judaism and New Testament Study. 2006. *Vol. 193.*
Horn, Friedrich Wilhelm and *Ruben Zimmermann* (Ed.): Jenseits von Indikativ und Imperativ. Vol. 1. 2009. *Vol. 245.*
Horst, Pieter W. van der: Jews and Christians in Their Graeco-Roman Context. 2006. *Vol. 196.*
Hultgård, Anders and *Stig Norin* (Ed): Le Jour de Dieu / Der Tag Gottes. 2009. *Vol. 245.*
Hvalvik, Reidar: The Struggle for Scripture and Covenant. 1996. *Vol. II/82.*
Jackson, Ryan: New Creation in Paul's Letters. 2010. *Vol. II/272.*
Janßen, Martina: see *Frey, Jörg.*
Jauhiainen, Marko: The Use of Zechariah in Revelation. 2005. *Vol. II/199.*

Lambers-Petry, Doris: see *Tomson, Peter J.*

Lange, Armin: see *Ego, Beate.*

Lampe, Peter: Die stadtrömischen Christen in den ersten beiden Jahrhunderten. 1987, ²1989. *Vol. II/18.*

Landmesser, Christof: Wahrheit als Grundbegriff neutestamentlicher Wissenschaft. 1999. *Vol. 113.*

– Jüngerberufung und Zuwendung zu Gott. 2000. *Vol. 133.*

Lau, Andrew: Manifest in Flesh. 1996. *Vol. II/86.*

Lawrence, Louise: An Ethnography of the Gospel of Matthew. 2003. *Vol. II/165.*

Lee, Aquila H.I.: From Messiah to Preexistent Son. 2005. *Vol. II/192.*

Lee, Pilchan: The New Jerusalem in the Book of Relevation. 2000. *Vol. II/129.*

Lee, Sang M.: The Cosmic Drama of Salvation. 2010. *Vol. II/276.*

Lee, Simon S.: Jesus' Transfiguration and the Believers' Transformation. 2009. *Vol. II/265.*

Lichtenberger, Hermann: Das Ich Adams und das Ich der Menschheit. 2004. *Vol. 164.*

– see *Avemarie, Friedrich.*

– see *Frey, Jörg.*

Lierman, John: The New Testament Moses. 2004. *Vol. II/173.*

– (Ed.): Challenging Perspectives on the Gospel of John. 2006. *Vol. II/219.*

Lieu, Samuel N.C.: Manichaeism in the Later Roman Empire and Medieval China. ²1992. *Vol. 63.*

Lindemann, Andreas: Die Evangelien und die Apostelgeschichte. 2009. *Vol. 241.*

Lincicum, David: Paul and the Early Jewish Encounter with Deuteronomy. 2010. *Vol. II/284.*

Lindgård, Fredrik: Paul's Line of Thought in 2 Corinthians 4:16–5:10. 2004. *Vol. II/189.*

Livesey, Nina E.: Circumcision as a Malleable Symbol. 2010. *Vol. II/295.*

Loader, William R.G.: Jesus' Attitude Towards the Law. 1997. *Vol. II/97.*

Löhr, Gebhard: Verherrlichung Gottes durch Philosophie. 1997. *Vol. 97.*

Löhr, Hermut: Studien zum frühchristlichen und frühjüdischen Gebet. 2003. *Vol. 160.*

– see *Hengel, Martin.*

Löhr, Winrich Alfried: Basilides und seine Schule. 1995. *Vol. 83.*

Lorenzen, Stefanie: Das paulinische Eikon-Konzept. 2008. *Vol. II/250.*

Luomanen, Petri: Entering the Kingdom of Heaven. 1998. *Vol. II/101.*

Luz, Ulrich: see *Alexeev, Anatoly A.*

– see *Dunn, James D.G.*

Mackay, Ian D.: John's Raltionship with Mark. 2004. *Vol. II/182.*

Mackie, Scott D.: Eschatology and Exhortation in the Epistle to the Hebrews. 2006. *Vol. II/223.*

Magda, Ksenija: Paul's Territoriality and Mission Strategy. 2009. *Vol. II/266.*

Maier, Gerhard: Mensch und freier Wille. 1971. *Vol. 12.*

– Die Johannesoffenbarung und die Kirche. 1981. *Vol. 25.*

Markschies, Christoph: Valentinus Gnosticus? 1992. *Vol. 65.*

Marshall, Jonathan: Jesus, Patrons, and Benefactors. 2009. *Vol. II/259.*

Marshall, Peter: Enmity in Corinth: Social Conventions in Paul's Relations with the Corinthians. 1987. *Vol. II/23.*

Martin, Dale B.: see *Zangenberg, Jürgen.*

Mayer, Annemarie: Sprache der Einheit im Epheserbrief und in der Ökumene. 2002. *Vol. II/150.*

Mayordomo, Moisés: Argumentiert Paulus logisch? 2005. *Vol. 188.*

McDonough, Sean M.: YHWH at Patmos: Rev. 1:4 in its Hellenistic and Early Jewish Setting. 1999. *Vol. II/107.*

McDowell, Markus: Prayers of Jewish Women. 2006. *Vol. II/211.*

McGlynn, Moyna: Divine Judgement and Divine Benevolence in the Book of Wisdom. 2001. *Vol. II/139.*

Meade, David G.: Pseudonymity and Canon. 1986. *Vol. 39.*

Meadors, Edward P.: Jesus the Messianic Herald of Salvation. 1995. *Vol. II/72.*

Meißner, Stefan: Die Heimholung des Ketzers. 1996. *Vol. II/87.*

Mell, Ulrich: Die „anderen" Winzer. 1994. *Vol. 77.*

– see *Sänger, Dieter.*

Mengel, Berthold: Studien zum Philipperbrief. 1982. *Vol. II/8.*

Merkel, Helmut: Die Widersprüche zwischen den Evangelien. 1971. *Vol. 13.*

– see *Ego, Beate.*

Merklein, Helmut: Studien zu Jesus und Paulus. Vol. 1 1987. *Vol. 43. –* Vol. 2 1998. *Vol. 105.*

Merkt, Andreas: see *Nicklas, Tobias*

Metzdorf, Christina: Die Tempelaktion Jesu. 2003. *Vol. II/168.*

Metzler, Karin: Der griechische Begriff des Verzeihens. 1991. *Vol. II/44.*

Metzner, Rainer: Die Rezeption des Matthäusevangeliums im 1. Petrusbrief. 1995. *Vol. II/74.*

– Das Verständnis der Sünde im Johannesevangelium. 2000. *Vol. 122.*

Mihoc, Vasile: see *Dunn, James D.G.*
– see *Klein, Hans.*
Mineshige, Kiyoshi: Besitzverzicht und Almosen bei Lukas. 2003. *Vol. II/163.*
Mittmann, Siegfried: see *Hengel, Martin.*
Mittmann-Richert, Ulrike: Magnifikat und Benediktus. *1996. Vol. II/90.*
– Der Sühnetod des Gottesknechts. 2008. *Vol. 220.*
Miura, Yuzuru: David in Luke-Acts. 2007. *Vol. II/232.*
Moll, Sebastian: The Arch-Heretic Marcion. 2010. *Vol. 250.*
Morales, Rodrigo J.: The Spirit and the Restorat. 2010. *Vol. 282.*
Mournet, Terence C.: Oral Tradition and Literary Dependency. 2005. *Vol. II/195.*
Mußner, Franz: Jesus von Nazareth im Umfeld Israels und der Urkirche. Ed. von M. Theobald. 1998. *Vol. 111.*
Mutschler, Bernhard: Das Corpus Johanneum bei Irenäus von Lyon. 2005. *Vol. 189.*
– Glaube in den Pastoralbriefen. 2010. *Vol. 256.*
Myers, Susan E.: Spirit Epicleses in the Acts of Thomas. 2010. *Vol. 281.*
Nguyen, V. Henry T.: Christian Identity in Corinth. 2008. *Vol. II/243.*
Nicklas, Tobias, Andreas Merkt und *Joseph Verheyden* (Ed.): Gelitten – Gestorben – Auferstanden. 2010. *Vol. II/273.*
– see *Verheyden, Joseph*
Niebuhr, Karl-Wilhelm: Gesetz und Paränese. 1987. *Vol. II/28.*
– Heidenapostel aus Israel. 1992. *Vol. 62.*
– see *Deines, Roland.*
– see *Dimitrov, Ivan Z.*
– see *Klein, Hans.*
– see *Kraus, Wolfgang.*
Nielsen, Anders E.: "Until it is Fullfilled". 2000. *Vol. II/126.*
Nielsen, Jesper Tang: Die kognitive Dimension des Kreuzes. 2009. *Vol. II/263.*
Nissen, Andreas: Gott und der Nächste im antiken Judentum. 1974. *Vol. 15.*
Noack, Christian: Gottesbewußtsein. 2000. *Vol. II/116.*
Noormann, Rolf: Irenäus als Paulusinterpret. 1994. *Vol. II/66.*
Norin, Stig: see *Hultgård, Anders.*
Novakovic, Lidija: Messiah, the Healer of the Sick. 2003. *Vol. II/170.*
Obermann, Andreas: Die christologische Erfüllung der Schrift im Johannesevangelium. 1996. *Vol. II/83.*
Öhler, Markus: Barnabas. 2003. *Vol. 156.*
– see *Becker, Michael.*

Okure, Teresa: The Johannine Approach to Mission. 1988. *Vol. II/31.*
Onuki, Takashi: Heil und Erlösung. 2004. *Vol. 165.*
Oropeza, B. J.: Paul and Apostasy. 2000. *Vol. II/115.*
Ostmeyer, Karl-Heinrich: Kommunikation mit Gott und Christus. 2006. *Vol. 197.*
– Taufe und Typos. 2000. *Vol. II/118.*
Pao, David W.: Acts and the Isaianic New Exodus. 2000. *Vol. II/130.*
Park, Eung Chun: The Mission Discourse in Matthew's Interpretation. 1995. *Vol. II/81.*
Park, Joseph S.: Conceptions of Afterlife in Jewish Insriptions. 2000. *Vol. II/121.*
Parsenios, George L.: Rhetoric and Drama in the Johannine Lawsuit Motif. 2010. *Vol. 258.*
Pate, C. Marvin: The Reverse of the Curse. 2000. *Vol. II/114.*
Paulsen, Henning: Studien zur Literatur und Geschichte des frühen Christentums. Ed. von Ute E. Eisen. 1997. *Vol. 99.*
Pearce, Sarah J.K.: The Land of the Body. 2007. *Vol. 208.*
Peres, Imre: Griechische Grabinschriften und neutestamentliche Eschatologie. 2003. *Vol. 157.*
Perry, Peter S.: The Rhetoric of Digressions. 2009. *Vol. II/268.*
Philip, Finny: The Origins of Pauline Pneumatology. 2005. *Vol. II/194.*
Philonenko, Marc (Ed.): Le Trône de Dieu. 1993. *Vol. 69.*
Pilhofer, Peter: Presbyteron Kreitton. 1990. *Vol. II/39.*
– Philippi. Vol. 1 1995. *Vol. 87.* – Vol. 2 ²2009. *Vol. 119.*
– Die frühen Christen und ihre Welt. 2002. *Vol. 145.*
– see *Becker, Eve-Marie.*
– see *Ego, Beate.*
Pitre, Brant: Jesus, the Tribulation, and the End of the Exile. 2005. *Vol. II/204.*
Plümacher, Eckhard: Geschichte und Geschichten. 2004. *Vol. 170.*
Pöhlmann, Wolfgang: Der Verlorene Sohn und das Haus. 1993. *Vol. 68.*
Poirier, John C.: The Tongues of Angels. 2010. *Vol. II/287.*
Pokorný, Petr and *Josef B. Souček:* Bibelauslegung als Theologie. 1997. *Vol. 100.*
– and *Jan Roskovec* (Ed.): Philosophical Hermeneutics and Biblical Exegesis. 2002. *Vol. 153.*
Popkes, Enno Edzard: Das Menschenbild des Thomasevangeliums. 2007. *Vol. 206.*

– Die Theologie der Liebe Gottes in den johanneischen Schriften. 2005. *Vol. II/197.*

Porter, Stanley E.: The Paul of Acts. 1999. *Vol. 115.*

Prieur, Alexander: Die Verkündigung der Gottesherrschaft. 1996. *Vol. II/89.*

Probst, Hermann: Paulus und der Brief. 1991. *Vol. II/45.*

Puig i Tàrrech, Armand: Jesus: An Uncommon Journey. 2010. *Vol. II/288.*

Rabens, Volker: The Holy Spirit and Ethics in Paul. 2010. *Vol. II/283.*

Räisänen, Heikki: Paul and the Law. 1983, ²1987. *Vol. 29.*

Rehkopf, Friedrich: Die lukanische Sonderquelle. 1959. *Vol. 5.*

Rein, Matthias: Die Heilung des Blindgeborenen (Joh 9). 1995. *Vol. II/73.*

Reinmuth, Eckart: Pseudo-Philo und Lukas. 1994. *Vol. 74.*

Reiser, Marius: Bibelkritik und Auslegung der Heiligen Schrift. 2007. *Vol. 217.*

– Syntax und Stil des Markusevangeliums. 1984. *Vol. II/11.*

Reynolds, Benjamin E.: The Apocalyptic Son of Man in the Gospel of John. 2008. *Vol. II/249.*

Rhodes, James N.: The Epistle of Barnabas and the Deuteronomic Tradition. 2004. *Vol. II/188.*

Richards, E. Randolph: The Secretary in the Letters of Paul. 1991. *Vol. II/42.*

Riesner, Rainer: Jesus als Lehrer. 1981, ³1988. *Vol. II/7.*

– Die Frühzeit des Apostels Paulus. 1994. *Vol. 71.*

Rissi, Mathias: Die Theologie des Hebräerbriefs. 1987. *Vol. 41.*

Röcker, Fritz W.: Belial und Katechon. 2009. *Vol. II/262.*

Röhser, Günter: Metaphorik und Personifikation der Sünde. 1987. *Vol. II/25.*

Rose, Christian: Theologie als Erzählung im Markusevangelium. 2007. *Vol. II/236.*

– Die Wolke der Zeugen. 1994. *Vol. II/60.*

Roskovec, Jan: see *Pokorný, Petr.*

Rothschild, Clare K.: Baptist Traditions and Q. 2005. *Vol. 190.*

– Hebrews as Pseudepigraphon. 2009. *Vol. 235.*

– Luke Acts and the Rhetoric of History. 2004. *Vol. II/175.*

– see *Frey, Jörg.*

Rüegger, Hans-Ulrich: Verstehen, was Markus erzählt. 2002. *Vol. II/155.*

Rüger, Hans Peter: Die Weisheitsschrift aus der Kairoer Geniza. 1991. *Vol. 53.*

Sänger, Dieter: Antikes Judentum und die Mysterien. 1980. *Vol. II/5.*

– Die Verkündigung des Gekreuzigten und Israel. 1994. *Vol. 75.*

– see *Burchard, Christoph*

– and *Ulrich Mell* (Ed.): Paulus und Johannes. 2006. *Vol. 198.*

Salier, Willis Hedley: The Rhetorical Impact of the Semeia in the Gospel of John. 2004. *Vol. II/186.*

Salzmann, Jorg Christian: Lehren und Ermahnen. 1994. *Vol. II/59.*

Sandnes, Karl Olav: Paul – One of the Prophets? 1991. *Vol. II/43.*

Sato, Migaku: Q und Prophetie. 1988. *Vol. II/29.*

Schäfer, Ruth: Paulus bis zum Apostelkonzil. 2004. *Vol. II/179.*

Schaper, Joachim: Eschatology in the Greek Psalter. 1995. *Vol. II/76.*

Schimanowski, Gottfried: Die himmlische Liturgie in der Apokalypse des Johannes. 2002. *Vol. II/154.*

– Weisheit und Messias. 1985. *Vol. II/17.*

Schlichting, Günter: Ein jüdisches Leben Jesu. 1982. *Vol. 24.*

Schließer, Benjamin: Abraham's Faith in Romans 4. 2007. *Vol. II/224.*

Schnabel, Eckhard J.: Law and Wisdom from Ben Sira to Paul. 1985. *Vol. II/16.*

Schnelle, Udo: see *Frey, Jörg.*

Schröter, Jens: Von Jesus zum Neuen Testament. 2007. *Vol. 204.*

– see *Frey, Jörg.*

Schutter, William L.: Hermeneutic and Composition in I Peter. 1989. *Vol. II/30.*

Schwartz, Daniel R.: Studies in the Jewish Background of Christianity. 1992. *Vol. 60.*

Schwemer, Anna Maria: see *Hengel, Martin*

Scott, Ian W.: Implicit Epistemology in the Letters of Paul. 2005. *Vol. II/205.*

Scott, James M.: Adoption as Sons of God. 1992. *Vol. II/48.*

– Paul and the Nations. 1995. *Vol. 84.*

Shi, Wenhua: Paul's Message of the Cross as Body Language. 2008. *Vol. II/254.*

Shum, Shiu-Lun: Paul's Use of Isaiah in Romans. 2002. *Vol. II/156.*

Siegert, Folker: Drei hellenistisch-jüdische Predigten. Teil I 1980. *Vol. 20* – Teil II 1992. *Vol. 61.*

– Nag-Hammadi-Register. 1982. *Vol. 26.*

– Argumentation bei Paulus. 1985. *Vol. 34.*

– Philon von Alexandrien. 1988. *Vol. 46.*

Simon, Marcel: Le christianisme antique et son contexte religieux I/II. 1981. *Vol. 23.*

Smit, Peter-Ben: Fellowship and Food in the Kingdom. 2008. *Vol. II/234.*

Snodgrass, Klyne: The Parable of the Wicked Tenants. 1983. *Vol. 27.*

Söding, Thomas: Das Wort vom Kreuz. 1997.
   Vol. 93.
– see *Thüsing, Wilhelm.*
Sommer, Urs: Die Passionsgeschichte des
   Markusevangeliums. 1993. *Vol. II/58.*
Sorensen, Eric: Possession and Exorcism in the
   New Testament and Early Christianity. 2002.
   Vol. II/157.
Souček, Josef B.: see *Pokorný, Petr.*
Southall, David J.: Rediscovering Righteous-
   ness in Romans. 2008. *Vol. 240.*
Spangenberg, Volker: Herrlichkeit des Neuen
   Bundes. 1993. *Vol. II/55.*
Spanje, T.E. van: Inconsistency in Paul? 1999.
   Vol. II/110.
Speyer, Wolfgang: Frühes Christentum im anti-
   ken Strahlungsfeld. Vol. I: 1989. *Vol. 50.*
– Vol. II: 1999. *Vol. 116.*
– Vol. III: 2007. *Vol. 213.*
Spittler, Janet E.: Animals in the Apocryphal
   Acts of the Apostles. 2008. *Vol. II/247.*
Sprinkle, Preston: Law and Life. 2008.
   Vol. II/241.
Stadelmann, Helge: Ben Sira als Schriftgelehr-
   ter. 1980. *Vol. II/6.*
Stein, Hans Joachim: Frühchristliche Mahl-
   feiern. 2008. *Vol. II/255.*
Stenschke, Christoph W.: Luke's Portrait of
   Gentiles Prior to Their Coming to Faith.
   Vol. II/108.
Sterck-Degueldre, Jean-Pierre: Eine Frau na-
   mens Lydia. 2004. *Vol. II/176.*
Stettler, Christian: Der Kolosserhymnus. 2000.
   Vol. II/131.
Stettler, Hanna: Die Christologie der Pastoral-
   briefe. 1998. *Vol. II/105.*
Stökl Ben Ezra, Daniel: The Impact of Yom
   Kippur on Early Christianity. 2003. *Vol. 163.*
Strobel, August: Die Stunde der Wahrheit. 1980.
   Vol. 21.
Stroumsa, Guy G.: Barbarian Philosophy. 1999.
   Vol. 112.
Stuckenbruck, Loren T.: Angel Veneration and
   Christology. 1995. *Vol. II/70.*
–, *Stephen C. Barton* and *Benjamin G. Wold*
   (Ed.): Memory in the Bible and Antiquity.
   2007. *Vol. 212.*
Stuhlmacher, Peter (Ed.): Das Evangelium und
   die Evangelien. 1983. *Vol. 28.*
– Biblische Theologie und Evangelium. 2002.
   Vol. 146.
Sung, Chong-Hyon: Vergebung der Sünden.
   1993. *Vol. II/57.*
Svendsen, Stefan N.: Allegory Transformed.
   2009. *Vol. II/269.*
Tajra, Harry W.: The Trial of St. Paul. 1989.
   Vol. II/35.
– The Martyrdom of St.Paul. 1994. *Vol. II/67.*

Tellbe, Mikael: Christ-Believers in Ephesus.
   2009. *Vol. 242.*
Theißen, Gerd: Studien zur Soziologie des Ur-
   christentums. 1979, ³1989. *Vol. 19.*
Theobald, Michael: Studien zum Römerbrief.
   2001. *Vol. 136.*
Theobald, Michael: see *Mußner, Franz.*
Thornton, Claus-Jürgen: Der Zeuge des Zeu-
   gen. 1991. *Vol. 56.*
Thüsing, Wilhelm: Studien zur neutestament-
   lichen Theologie. Ed. von Thomas Söding.
   1995. *Vol. 82.*
Thurén, Lauri: Derhethorizing Paul. 2000.
   Vol. 124.
Thyen, Hartwig: Studien zum Corpus Iohan-
   neum. 2007. *Vol. 214.*
Tibbs, Clint: Religious Experience of the Pneu-
   ma. 2007. *Vol. II/230.*
Toit, David S. du: Theios Anthropos. 1997.
   Vol. II/91.
Tolmie, D. Francois: Persuading the Galatians.
   2005. *Vol. II/190.*
Tomson, Peter J. and *Doris Lambers-Petry*
   (Ed.): The Image of the Judaeo-Christians
   in Ancient Jewish and Christian Literature.
   2003. *Vol. 158.*
Toney, Carl N.: Paul's Inclusive Ethic. 2008.
   Vol. II/252.
Trebilco, Paul: The Early Christians in Ephesus
   from Paul to Ignatius. 2004. *Vol. 166.*
Treloar, Geoffrey R.: Lightfoot the Historian.
   1998. *Vol. II/103.*
Troftgruben, Troy M.: A Conclusion Unhinde-
   red. 2010. *Vol. II/280.*
Tso, Marcus K.M.: Ethics in the Qumran Com-
   munity. 2010. *Vol. II/292.*
Tsuji, Manabu: Glaube zwischen Vollkommen-
   heit und Verweltlichung. 1997. *Vol. II/93.*
Twelftree, Graham H.: Jesus the Exorcist. 1993.
   Vol. II/54.
Ulrichs, Karl Friedrich: Christusglaube. 2007.
   Vol. II/227.
Urban, Christina: Das Menschenbild nach dem
   Johannesevangelium. 2001. *Vol. II/137.*
Vahrenhorst, Martin: Kultische Sprache in den
   Paulusbriefen. 2008. *Vol. 230.*
Vegge, Ivar: 2 Corinthians – a Letter about
   Reconciliation. 2008. *Vol. II/239.*
Verheyden, Joseph, Korinna Zamfir and *Tobias
   Nicklas* (Ed.): Prophets and Prophecy in
   Jewish and Early Christian Literature. 2010.
   Vol. II/286.
– see *Nicklas, Tobias*
Visotzky, Burton L.: Fathers of the World. 1995.
   Vol. 80.
Vollenweider, Samuel: Horizonte neutestament-
   licher Christologie. 2002. *Vol. 144.*

Vos, Johan S.: Die Kunst der Argumentation bei Paulus. 2002. *Vol. 149.*

Waaler, Erik: The *Shema* and The First Commandment in First Corinthians. 2008. *Vol. II/253.*

Wagener, Ulrike: Die Ordnung des „Hauses Gottes". 1994. *Vol. II/65.*

Wagner, J. Ross: see *Wilk, Florian.*

Wahlen, Clinton: Jesus and the Impurity of Spirits in the Synoptic Gospels. 2004. *Vol. II/185.*

Walker, Donald D.: Paul's Offer of Leniency (2 Cor 10:1). 2002. *Vol. II/152.*

Walter, Nikolaus: Praeparatio Evangelica. Ed. von Wolfgang Kraus und Florian Wilk. 1997. *Vol. 98.*

Wander, Bernd: Gottesfürchtige und Sympathisanten. 1998. *Vol. 104.*

Wardle, Timothy: The Jerusalem Temple and Early Christian Identity. 2010. *Vol. II/291.*

Wasserman, Emma: The Death of the Soul in Romans 7. 2008. *Vol. 256.*

Waters, Guy: The End of Deuteronomy in the Epistles of Paul. 2006. *Vol. 221.*

Watt, Jan G. van der: see *Frey, Jörg*
– see *Zimmermann, Ruben*

Watts, Rikki: Isaiah's New Exodus and Mark. 1997. *Vol. II/88.*

Webb, Robert L.: see *Bock, Darrell L.*

Wedderburn, A.J.M.: Baptism and Resurrection. 1987. *Vol. 44.*

Wegner, Uwe: Der Hauptmann von Kafarnaum. 1985. *Vol. II/14.*

Weiß, Hans-Friedrich: Frühes Christentum und Gnosis. 2008. *Vol. 225.*

Weissenrieder, Annette: Images of Illness in the Gospel of Luke. 2003. Vol. II/164.

–, and *Robert B. Coote* (Ed.): The Interface of Orality and Writing. 2010. *Vol. 260.*

–, *Friederike Wendt* and *Petra von Gemünden* (Ed.): Picturing the New Testament. 2005. *Vol. II/193.*

Welck, Christian: Erzählte ‚Zeichen'. 1994. *Vol. II/69.*

Wendt, Friederike (Ed.): see *Weissenrieder, Annette.*

Wiarda, Timothy: Peter in the Gospels. 2000. *Vol. II/127.*

Wifstrand, Albert: Epochs and Styles. 2005. *Vol. 179.*

Wilk, Florian and *J. Ross Wagner* (Ed.): Between Gospel and Election. 2010. *Vol. 257.*
– see *Walter, Nikolaus.*

Williams, Catrin H.: I am He. 2000. *Vol. II/113.*

Wilson, Todd A.: The Curse of the Law and the Crisis in Galatia. 2007. *Vol. II/225.*

Wilson, Walter T.: Love without Pretense. 1991. *Vol. II/46.*

Winn, Adam: The Purpose of Mark's Gospel. 2008. *Vol. II/245.*

Winninge, Mikael: see *Holmberg, Bengt.*

Wischmeyer, Oda: Von Ben Sira zu Paulus. 2004. *Vol. 173.*

Wisdom, Jeffrey: Blessing for the Nations and the Curse of the Law. 2001. *Vol. II/133.*

Witmer, Stephen E.: Divine Instruction in Early Christianity. 2008. *Vol. II/246.*

Wold, Benjamin G.: Women, Men, and Angels. 2005. *Vol. II/2001.*

Wolter, Michael: Theologie und Ethos im frühen Christentum. 2009. *Vol. 236.*
– see *Stuckenbruck, Loren T.*

Wright, Archie T.: The Origin of Evil Spirits. 2005. *Vol. II/198.*

Wucherpfennig, Ansgar: Heracleon Philologus. 2002. *Vol. 142.*

Yates, John W.: The Spirit and Creation in Paul. 2008. *Vol. II/251.*

Yeung, Maureen: Faith in Jesus and Paul. 2002. *Vol. II/147.*

Zamfir, Corinna: see *Verheyden, Joseph*

Zangenberg, Jürgen, Harold W. Attridge and *Dale B. Martin* (Ed.): Religion, Ethnicity and Identity in Ancient Galilee. 2007. *Vol. 210.*

Zimmermann, Alfred E.: Die urchristlichen Lehrer. 1984. ²1988. *Vol. II/12.*

Zimmermann, Johannes: Messianische Texte aus Qumran. 1998. *Vol. II/104.*

Zimmermann, Ruben: Christologie der Bilder im Johannesevangelium. 2004. *Vol. 171.*
– Geschlechtermetaphorik und Gottesverhältnis. 2001. *Vol. II/122.*
– (Ed.): Hermeneutik der Gleichnisse Jesu. 2008. *Vol. 231.*
– and *Jan G. van der Watt* (Ed.): Moral Language in the New Testament. Vol. II. 2010. *Vol. II/296.*
– see *Frey, Jörg.*
– see *Horn, Friedrich Wilhelm.*

Zugmann, Michael: „Hellenisten" in der Apostelgeschichte. 2009. *Vol. II/264.*

Zumstein, Jean: see *Dettwiler, Andreas*

Zwiep, Arie W.: Christ, the Spirit and the Community of God. 2010. *Vol. II/293.*
– Judas and the Choice of Matthias. 2004. *Vol. II/187.*

For a complete catalogue please write to the publisher
Mohr Siebeck • P.O. Box 2030 • D–72010 Tübingen/Germany
Up-to-date information on the internet at www.mohr.de